CONFLICT, WAR, AND PEACE

CONFLICT, WAR, AND PEACE

An Introduction to Scientific Research

Sara McLaughlin Mitchell
University of Iowa

John A. Vasquez
University of Illinois at Urbana-Champaign

Editors

 |

Los Angeles | London | New Delhi
Singapore | Washington DC

Los Angeles | London | New Delhi
Singapore | Washington DC

FOR INFORMATION:

CQ Press
An Imprint of SAGE Publications, Inc.
2455 Teller Road
Thousand Oaks, California 91320
E-mail: order@sagepub.com

SAGE Publications Ltd.
1 Oliver's Yard
55 City Road
London EC1Y 1SP
United Kingdom

SAGE Publications India Pvt. Ltd.
B 1/I 1 Mohan Cooperative Industrial Area
Mathura Road, New Delhi 110 044
India

SAGE Publications Asia-Pacific Pte. Ltd.
3 Church Street
#10-04 Samsung Hub
Singapore 049483

Printed in the United States of America

Library of Congress Cataloging-in-Publication Data

Conflict, war, and peace : an introduction to scientific research / edited by Sara McLaughlin Mitchell, University of Iowa; John A. Vasquez, University of Illinois at Urbana-Champaign.

pages cm
Includes bibliographical references and index.

ISBN 978-1-4522-4449-5 (pbk. : alk. paper)

1. War—Mathematical models. 2. Peace—Mathematical models. I. Mitchell, Sara McLaughlin. II. Vasquez, John A., 1945-

U21.2.C654 2013
303.6—dc23   2013020249

This book is printed on acid-free paper.

Acquisitions Editor: Charisse Kiino
Editorial Assistant: Lauren Johnson
Production Editor: Laura Barrett
Copy Editor: Gillian Dickens
Typesetter: C&M Digitals (P) Ltd.
Proofreader: Stefanie Storholt
Cover Designer: Michael Dubowe
Marketing Manager: Erica DeLuca
Permissions Editor: Jennifer Barron

13 14 15 16 10 9 8 7 6 5 4 3 2 1

CONTENTS

METHODOLOGICAL CONTENTS

PREFACE

This book serves two purposes: (1) it introduces students to the scientific study of peace and war, and (2) it provides readers with an overview of current scientific knowledge about war. Both of us have taught courses concerned with questions of war and peace for some time. What amazes us is how little of the scholarly work on war and peace has found its way into undergraduate classrooms. Too many popular textbooks written while much of the scientific study of war was in its infancy continue to be used in subsequent editions without much attempt to incorporate recent scientific evidence or thinking about war. Too many students, in our view, are being educated about the causes of war with simplistic theories and insufficient regard for scientific evidence or the best scholarly thinking on the subject.

While the quantitative study of conflict has made significant progress in the past few decades, this approach and knowledge have not adequately found their way into undergraduate education. Many international conflict classes introduce students to risk factors prevalent in cases of war and peace, such as military alliances, arms races, power parity, territorial disputes, and democracy, but even textbooks that provide surveys of the theoretical and empirical findings in the literature rarely teach students about the process of conducting scientific research. Students are often exposed to these approaches in American politics classes, where they might carry out analyses of survey data, but it is much less common in international relations classes. More importantly, they are given little experience or training in how to read scholarly articles. From our point of view, political science majors should be able to read the major journals within their field upon graduation, and we have prepared this text reader to help them accomplish that goal.

There are several reasons for this paucity of scientific education. One is that so few scientific studies are available for undergraduate use. Most studies published in academic journals and books devoted to the subject are typically aimed at a scholarly audience. We hope to correct this situation by bringing together in a single volume the best and most important research on war and peace in the past twenty years. Like many other college instructors, we believe it is essential that students read actual research, not just summaries of it.

Nevertheless, scientific studies of war and peace can be difficult to read, and most undergraduates have not been taught how to read quantitative articles.

Indeed, one of the reasons scientific research on war has not been available for the classroom is the feeling that students cannot read or comprehend it. This was brought home to us quite some time ago when one of us went on leave for a semester and was replaced by a promising doctoral student, who proceeded to replace most of the quantitative studies in an upper-level course on the causes of war with simpler material. When asked why he did this, he replied "that quantitative material is too difficult for students to understand." This is often true, but what is so disappointing is that it never seemed to occur to him that one of the purposes of college courses is to teach students how to read and analyze material that they might not have been able to read before they took the course. That is precisely what we try to accomplish in this text reader.

One of our main objectives in this book is to teach students how to read scientific studies of peace and war or what is sometimes called peace science research. On the webpage for the book, we have provided a learning package designed to help students learn more about scientific research by conducting elementary data analyses. Our experience has been that much of the complexity of scientific research disappears as students actually attempt to go about conducting their own research. Faced with problems of marshaling data and making inferences, they find that abstract concepts and methodological concerns become more relevant and hence easier to understand.

The book reprints some of the most important research on war and peace. Each article is followed by a commentary highlighting and interpreting the main findings. The commentaries are divided into two sections: major contributions and methodological notes. The major contributions sections highlight the theoretical advances of each article and relate each study to the broader literature on the topic. The methodological notes sections carefully take readers through the methodological assumptions and techniques used in the analysis. Each reprinted article contains a variety of methodological issues that could be addressed, but in a collection, such exhaustive treatment would be cumbersome. Instead, we have chosen to treat a few issues in depth for each piece. For example, although statistical significance is important for all of the reprinted studies, it is treated in depth only in the commentary on Sample's article on arms races and war. In this way, each commentary focuses on one primary methodological lesson. The commentary also introduces readers to a number of terms (printed in **boldface**) that will aid students in their comprehension of the scientific study of war. Those who are very new to the scientific method may want to read the commentary first, while more advanced students can go right to the article that is reprinted. We hope that this book will help reduce scientific illiteracy among liberal arts majors and introduce them to the norms of scientific inquiry. All of the articles are reprinted in their original form, complete and unabridged.

Another reason that scientific studies on war and peace have not been used in the classroom or have had a wide readership has been the sentiment of many traditional scholars that such studies have not generated much knowledge. For some, this reflects a deeper philosophical position that politics, history, and war cannot be studied scientifically. This book seeks to address this question by furnishing an interim report on what we have learned. Although we are still far from a general scientific theory of war, we have a body of evidence, derived mostly from the 1816 through 2001 period, about some of the factors that appear to be associated with the onset of conflict and war in the modern era, as well as factors related to peace among states. The book is organized to highlight some of the key research studies on interstate conflict. In this way, students get an overview of the field. Of equal importance, this book is meant to provide general readers, particularly those unfamiliar with contemporary academic international relations inquiry, with an overview and guide to the scientific study of war. Many practicing scientists, medical doctors, and psychologists who have been concerned about nuclear weapons and the dangers of nuclear proliferation in today's world have felt the need for such an overview, and we hope this volume helps meet that need. We also think that many who are responsible for the diplomacy and military policy of their states will find this volume worthwhile, not because it provides specific advice, but because much of the research raises serious questions about the adequacy of popular beliefs about what causes war and how peace can be maintained.

This book can be used in two ways. For those interested primarily in knowledge about war and peace, the chapters can be read in order. We assume that in many international relations courses, the book will be used in this manner. For those interested primarily in methods and in quantitative analysis, we have classified the reprinted articles according to the main statistical techniques they employ and suggest that they be read according to the difficulty of the statistical analysis. To facilitate the use of the book in this manner, we have provided a methodological table of contents following the main table of contents. The online learning package will also be useful for those who lack an extensive background in social science data analysis.

Acknowledgments

We are grateful to Elise Frasier and Nancy Loh for their assistance at CQ Press. We are also grateful to Emily E. Barrett for her assistance in obtaining permissions for the reprinted articles. Several outside readers for CQ Press have provided invaluable advice. We would like to acknowledge Ivan Arreguin-Toth, Boston University; David Scott Bennett, Pennsylvania State University; Faten Ghosn, University of Arizona; Yinan He, Seton Hall University; Nathan Jensen, Washington University in St. Louis; Jason Lyall, Yale University; Laura Neack, Miami University; William Reed, University of Maryland; and Richard Stoll, Rice University for their suggestions. Although we have benefited from the advice and comments we have received, the final responsibility for the contents of this volume remains with us. In addition, we thank Marie T. Henehan, whose earlier book (Vasquez and Henehan 1992) has been an inspiration and model for us.

We dedicate this book to our respective daughters who bring great joy into our lives. Sara Mitchell dedicates the book to Vivian Mitchell and John Vasquez dedicates the book to Elyse Henehan Vasquez. We are also grateful to the undergraduate students we have worked with over the past few decades who have inspired us to write this material.

Chapter 1

Introduction

Sara McLaughlin Mitchell and John A. Vasquez

The Nature of Science

Through the ages, many have written about war, and a considerable amount of this effort has been devoted to understanding why people kill each other. Those of us committed to the scientific study of war believe that part of the reason so little progress has been made in understanding is that inquiry has not followed a sufficiently rigorous method. Philosophical analyses of the physical world, for example, even when conducted by such a brilliant thinker as Aristotle, did not produce a cumulative body of knowledge. A substantial advancement in our understanding came only with the development and application of the scientific method. Only through the use of controlled observation, the collection of evidence, careful inference, and the belief that hypotheses must always be tested before being accepted was progress made. This same kind of rigor and commitment to the truth—no matter which privileged theories are challenged—will be necessary before any real knowledge about war and peace is acquired.

Lewis F. Richardson, one of the first to study war scientifically, expressed these kinds of concerns when he decided to apply scientific methods to this problem. He felt there were many vehemently held opinions about war, its causes, and ways to prevent it but little attempt to subject those opinions to systematic testing to see if they were accurate. In communications with Quincy Wright, another pioneering scholar in the collection of data on war, Richardson (1960a, 1960b) discussed his search for a more reliable answer to the war puzzle based on historical facts rather than intuitive reasoning. He said many people who discuss politics seem more interested in persuading others of the rightness of their cause than in understanding and explaining the recurring patterns of behavior that we observe. As a result, few take the time to carefully study the world in an empirical fashion.

Richardson's argument should make it clear that science is primarily an empirical method of inquiry that can be used to study how the world works. The scientific method cannot tell us what is good or what values should be pursued. Once we have an understanding of how the world works, we may be in a position to make changes so that humans can do things—fly, for example—that they were unable to do before. Pure science can produce an applied science of engineering, and clearly many of the early peace researchers hoped that a scientific study of war would help control and prevent war.

In this way, the normative—what we value or the way we believe people ought to behave—informs the empirical. Normative factors determine the uses to which we might put knowledge, as well as shape what we study and how we define problems, but they should not blind us to the way the world actually works. Nor should our values and beliefs so shape our observations and the way we make inferences that evidence is ignored or consciously manipulated. Because normative issues play such a large role in shaping inquiry, it is important to remember that when we speak of scientific objectivity, we mean simply that scholars should not distort their evidence to fit their beliefs; that is, they should be honest and truthful. We do not mean that science is

1

neutral in terms of the values its research is used to support. Science has had a tremendous impact on how we live, what we believe, and how we think. All of these things have normative implications, but science itself is not a method for telling us whether these things are good or bad. For that, we must look to other discourses.

At the start, it is important to keep in mind the purpose of the scientific approach. Science aims to uncover general patterns, not the unique. It seeks to uncover the **nomothetic** (from the Greek, *nomos*, meaning "lawlike") rather than the **idiographic** ("the particular"), which falls within the domain of historical descriptions. A scientific study does not attempt to understand the particular causes of a specific war but rather analyzes a large number of wars to identify the conditions associated with war as a general social phenomenon. A scientific approach involves four basic processes: (1) identifying generalizations or empirical patterns, (2) constructing an explanation or theory of the observed generalizations, (3) deriving a testable hypothesis, and (4) testing the hypothesis against empirical evidence.

The earliest stages of a science are usually devoted to identifying generalizations. One way to identify these generalizations is to come up with a verbal statement that describes a general pattern—for example, "rivalry brings about war, not peace." Such a statement might be refined, qualified, and made more precise; with some reflection and study, it eventually becomes a working hypothesis about one of the factors associated with the onset of war. Such statements need not always be verbal; they can also be mathematical, with symbols representing concepts.

For example, the finding that no two fully democratic states have fought an interstate war against each other in history was uncovered by a scholar who paired data on wars with data on states' regime characteristics (Babst 1964).

The crucial point for the scientifically orientated, however, is that the hypothesis can be tested with empirical evidence before being accepted. Ransacking history for anecdotes that support an argument is no substitute for a systematic review of all the relevant evidence (Singer 1969). In this regard, those who take a scientific approach do not object to careful historical analyses of particular wars; indeed, they usually read a great number of them. Nor do they object to case studies or even theoretical history. Their objection is to attempting to establish generalizations through an overreliance on argumentation and armchair philosophizing, as was often done in the 1950s and 1960s. Science outlines a set of criteria for determining which statements will be accepted and rejected. It is a self-imposed system for determining beliefs and knowledge about the empirical world.

Science insists on shifting through the evidence, and this usually involves counting—if for no other purpose, at least to count those instances that support a generalization and compare them with those instances that do not. Much of the research in the early stages of a science, and hence in this book, is confined to just that: seeing how many cases support or fail to support a hypothesis. In the democratic peace literature, for example, scholars have compiled multiple data sets on interstate conflict and regime type to ensure that the early patterns observed by Babst (1964) hold across space and time and with a variety of different measures of these general concepts.

Counting, of course, involves statistics, and there is a popular prejudice against statistics. Some even argue that anything can be proved with statistics or that statistics lie. Of course, statistics do not lie; people lie, and they can use either statistics or words to do so. What separates the sophisticated from the statistically illiterate is that the former can read and tell when statistics are being misused and the latter cannot. Those who are illiterate tend to reject or accept blindly any statistical argument because they are unable to evaluate it or even understand others' evaluations. This book aims to give you the skills necessary to examine the evidence yourself. It progresses from the simple use of percentages to more complicated techniques, such as duration and selection models, teaching you how to read tables and interpret statistics so that you can evaluate an author's interpretations and conclusions.

Once some generalizations are established, the next step in scientific inquiry is to try to construct an explanation of these patterns. An explanation answers the question "why?" and often takes the form of a causal analysis. While explanation logically follows discovery of patterns, the two often go hand in hand with theoretical hunches suggesting patterns and empirical patterns reshaping theory (Popper 1962). Although the two go together, it is important to understand that the practices that lead to discovery and theory construction are analytically distinct from the philosophical justifications and rules used for accepting or rejecting a hypothesis. The logic of discovery is not the same as the logic of confirmation. Discovery may occur for a variety of reasons— because of a correct view of the world or by serendipity, for example. Confirmation, however, involves following specific procedures to test a hypothesis and assess its adequacy in light of the evidence.

The democratic peace literature provides a nice example of this back-and-forth process. A philosopher, Immanuel Kant, predicted the emergence of the democratic peace before many democracies existed in the world in his 1795 paper, *Perpetual Peace* (Kant 1970, 1991). Once Babst's study was published, other scholars began to confirm the empirical pattern using different data sources. This was followed by a healthy debate about the causal relationship between democracy and peace. Why don't democracies fight wars against other democracies? In this book, we describe a variety of theoretical answers that emerged focusing on institutions, norms, and information.

Once a new hypothesis is developed, it is then subjected to empirical testing. One argument about why democracies do not fight relates to Kant's idea that the citizens in democratic states do not want to pay the costs for fighting wars. This makes democratic leaders more cautious about initiating wars, especially if they want to keep their jobs and remain in office. This theoretical model predicts a new hypothesis that democracies will be more likely to win the wars they fight. They are likely to be more cautious initiators because their leaders will face more severe consequences for failed foreign policies. This hypothesis was subjected to empirical testing, and the analyses supported the claim, with democracies winning more than 80% of the interstate wars they have fought since 1816 (Lake 1992).

The scientific study proceeds in this way as scholars compile new empirical evidence, develop new theories, and test these novel hypotheses with additional data. It is important as well to control for other factors that might cause war, such as relative power or military alliances, to ensure that the key findings we have observed (e.g., the democratic peace) are robust. The best way to learn about the scientific research, in our view, is to actually do it. We hope that the articles presented in this book will serve as useful illustrations of the merits and promise of the scientific approach.

Factors Related to the Onset of War

What do we know about war? How much confidence do we have about our knowledge? These questions guide our inquiry throughout this book. The two questions go together because the scientific approach assumes that we can never be sure that what we think is true actually is true. Science is an open-ended process; it is a way of thinking about empirical truth and searching for it rather than an end or body of knowledge that, once established, is beyond refutation. What we establish today might have to be rejected tomorrow because of new tests or evidence. When we use the word *true*, we must always be tentative. What we really mean is that a hypothesis has passed empirical tests and has not been falsified by the evidence; it is consistent with the evidence. Because of this aspect of science, some scholars prefer not to use terms such as *true* and *false*, substituting *accurate* and *erroneous, adequate* and *inadequate*, or *accept* and *reject*. While these terms indicate the tentative nature of empirical truth, they tend to become functional equivalents of *true* and, as such, can be seen as intellectual euphemisms. For this reason, we will not always shy away from using *true* and *false,* but readers should be aware of the tentative way in which we employ these terms.

With these caveats in mind, it should be clear that appropriate questions are "What have we learned about war?" and "How accurate are our beliefs about war and peace in light of the evidence?" The past fifty years have seen the testing of a number of popular beliefs about the causes of war and raised serious questions about various explanations of war. Most of these tests, however, have been confined to mapping what J. David Singer (1979) has called the *correlates of war.* In other words, much research has not attempted to delineate the causes of war but simply to identify all factors that seem to correlate with war. Discovering which of these factors associated with war act as causes and which are simply correlates or epiphenomena is something that will require making difficult inferences and is best done once the mapping of correlates is more complete.

Nevertheless, the articles reprinted in this book represent the various empirical patterns and theoretical arguments that have characterized the modern scientific study of warfare. The book is organized around the concept of dangerous dyads and peaceful dyads. The dangerous dyads portion of the book focuses on several factors that Stuart Bremer (1992b) identified as increasing the risks of interstate conflict between pairs of states, including relative capabilities, arms races, alliances, contiguity/territorial disputes, and rivalry. The first part of the book reprints Bremer's "Dangerous Dyads" article and uses this as an organizing schema for the second part. Part II includes articles on territory (Chapter 3), alliances (Chapter 4), rivalry (Chapter 5), arms races (Chapter 6), the steps to war model (Chapter 7), and the diversionary theory of warfare (Chapter 8). Most of the articles adopt a dyadic approach (looking at the relations between a given pair of countries) like Bremer and focus on the factors that increase the risk of militarized conflict between the members of the dyad. The studies analyze violent conflicts such as wars that involve many battle deaths, as well as threats, displays, and uses of force

that end short of war, what we call militarized interstate disputes (or MIDs). In addition to showing which factors increase the risks for MIDs and wars, the reprinted articles also give us some sense of the overall size of these risk factors by showing how the probability of conflict changes as the independent variables change. For example, we can compare the probability of war for pairs of states that have ongoing territorial disputes over their shared land border to the probability of war for states that have no border disputes. Bremer's "Dangerous Dyads" model identifies multiple risk factors that make war more likely, and this book illustrates how these various factors interact to generate conflict. This is similar to medical research that might identify a series of risk factors for heart disease (family history, being overweight, poor diet, lack of exercise, smoking, etc.) and then analyze the effect of each variable on the chances for a person to get the disease.

The third part of the book examines the factors that explain why some dyads are able to maintain peace, with an emphasis on the Kantian peace. This research focuses on factors that explain why some pairs of states are more peaceful than others. This includes the three legs of the Kantian tripod for peace (Russett and Oneal 2001): democracy (Chapters 9 and 11), economic interdependence (Chapters 9 and 10), and international organizations (Chapter 9). We also include recent empirical work on nuclear weapons (Chapter 13) and power preponderance (Chapter 11) as a potential source of dyadic peace, and we discuss the role of territorial border agreements for promoting future peace between pairs of countries (Chapter 12). The last part of the book examines the consequences of war and identifies factors that promote the durability of peace. We focus on the consequences of war for leader survival (Chapter 15) and the factors that promote more durable peace settlements following war (Chapter 14). After completing the book, readers should have a good sense for factors that increase pairs of states' risks for war and possible solutions to these dangerous situations.

Chapter 2

Dangerous Dyads

Conditions Affecting the Likelihood of Interstate War, 1816–1965

Stuart A. Bremer

Clauswitz's assertion that war is "nothing but a duel on a large scale" reminds us that one of the core questions in the study of conflict is "who fights whom?" A good deal of theoretical speculation and some empirical evidence suggest that war is more likely to occur between states that are

geographically proximate,

roughly equal in power,

major powers,

allied,

undemocratic,

economically advanced, and/or

militarized

than between those that are not. Some of the component propensities in this summary statement are so widely assumed to be true that they have become "stylized facts" that, to some observers, need no further verification. But a closer scrutiny of the empirical evidence on which this confidence is based reveals one or more critical deficiencies in the relevant research. The most important of these follow.[1]

Inappropriate unit of analysis. In spite of the fact that interstate wars arise out of the interactions between states,[2] the overwhelming majority of empirical studies of war have been undertaken at the systemic or (less frequently) national level. If one is willing to make a number of critical and controversial assumptions, then some of these nondyadic studies will yield deductions that pertain to the question of who fights whom, yet the direct evidence they offer is, at best, inconclusive. My own assessment is less generous, because I view these studies as largely irrelevant to the dyadic question.

Limited spatial-temporal domain. In spite of the fact that wars are comparatively rare events, too many empirical studies to date have used narrow spatial and/or temporal domains. The spatial domain most frequently used is typically limited to the major powers, and the favored temporal domain is the post–World War II period. And there appears to be a fairly clear inverse relationship between the spatial and temporal domains used in previous studies, that is, the longer the time period studied, the fewer the states included. I do not dispute the fact that, within a given resource constraint, there is an inevitable tradeoff between the two domains; my point is rather that, given the comparative rarity of interstate war, narrow spatial and/or temporal domains provide us with a very weak basis for drawing conclusions about who fights whom.

Source: Stuart A. Bremer, "Dangerous Dyads: Conditions Affecting the Likelihood of Interstate War, 1816–1965," *Journal of Conflict Resolution* 36, no. 2 (June 1992): 309–41. © 1992 SAGE Publications, Inc.

Faulty case selection strategy. As Most and Starr (1989) point out, there has been a tendency in previous empirical work to use research designs that exclude a control group. That is, cases are selected for analysis based on the values of the dependent or independent variables, rather than some other factor not obviously related to either of these. For example, tests of the impact of some factor on war at the dyadic level are limited to dyads that experience war. Such practices logically lead to problems in assessing necessary and/or sufficient conditions and limit the value of conclusions drawn in ways that are not always readily apparent to the casual reader.

Bivariate analytical methods. Although less true now than earlier, empirical studies of war still tend to be bivariate in nature. This by itself is not indicative of negligence, for the number of potentially important factors that are excluded from any analysis must necessarily be very large in number, but the problem of spurious and masked associations in bivariate analyses is a serious one. However, the call for multivariate analyses of interstate war is especially difficult to respond to because the basic frequency of war is small and the statistical degrees of freedom can quickly be exhausted by the addition of independent variables. Recognizing this estimation problem does not, however, obviate the need for more multivariate analyses of who fights whom.

Questionable measures of war. Many years ago Duvall (1976) pointed out that the onset and amount of war are two conceptually different phenomena (an opinion shared at the time by others, including myself), yet too often the various standard measures of war are still treated as substitutable for one another. For theoretical and methodological reasons, it is important to distinguish between the occurrence of war and the manner in which it evolves thereafter. More important for the topic under discussion here is the fact that tests with different measures of war as the dependent variable do not, with few exceptions, add up to multiple tests of the same hypothesis. On the contrary, they usually entail the testing of implicitly different hypotheses. I believe this is one key reason why it has proved so difficult to integrate the findings of empirical studies of interstate war.

All of the factors indicated above contribute to a general lack of comparability between empirical studies of interstate war. Different levels of analysis, different spatial-temporal domains, different cases, different analytical methods, and different measures of war all make it very difficult to assess the relative importance of factors that purportedly contribute to the occurrence of war. While not claiming to avoid or solve all the problems outlined above, this study does aim to rectify the more serious errors found in previous research. To discover or verify the relative importance of the seven factors listed at the outset of this article, a broad spatial-temporal domain (i.e., all states, 1816–1965) is used here, and the interstate dyad is the unit of analysis. A uniform measure of war that clearly reflects the focus of this study—the onset of interstate war—is employed, and both bivariate and multivariate analyses are conducted. Given that the primary mission of this article is of a "fact finding" nature, no elaborate formal models will be presented, nor will I dwell at length on subtle theoretical issues. However, I think the results reported below do have important theoretical implications and suggest directions for future modeling work. Now, let us briefly review the theoretical arguments and empirical literature relevant to the seven predictors of war under consideration here.

Seven Predictors of War

Geographical Proximity and War

The proposition that war is more likely to occur between states that are geographically proximate than between those that are not is disputed by few, and even considered trivial by some, perhaps because of the strong geopolitical component that is inherent in the very act of war. Boxers, after all, cannot fight until they are physically able to reach one another. This analogy is somewhat misleading, however, since the proposition does not state that war is more likely if the armed forces of two states are within striking distance of one another. Rather it argues that war is more likely between states that share a common border zone, regardless of whether that border zone is a heavily fortified no-man's land or an almost forgotten boundary for which little physical evidence exists save its designation on maps.

A stronger and more interesting argument for why geographical proximity promotes war builds on the notion that proximity engenders serious conflicts of interest between states, a fraction of which are bound to lead to war. Shared access to a physical area can lead directly to interstate friction, even if the states involved agree as to where the border lies between them. A common example of this is where insurgents use the territory of an adjacent state as a basing area, and the state thus being used is unable or unwilling to suppress the insurgents' activities on its territory. A large variety of other examples of how proximity can introduce an unwelcome degree of interdependence between states can be cited. Because this enforced "common fate" breeds frustrations and rivalries between states, so the argument runs, interstate tension increases and, ceteris paribus, war is more likely.

The empirical evidence linking war and proximity is scattered but generally consistent.[3] Several studies have found an association between the number of borders states have and their foreign conflict behavior generally or war involvement specifically (Richardson 1960b; Rummel 1972; Starr and Most 1976, 1978; Terrell 1977). These studies do not enable us to conclude that sharing a common border increases the likelihood of conflict and war between a given pair of states because they do not demonstrate that the increased conflict involvement of states with many neighbors is directed toward those neighbors. Thus, the evidence that these studies present for the proposition must be considered indirect.

More direct evidence is to be found in studies by Gleditsch and Singer (1975), Garnham (1976), and Gochman (1990a).[4] Gleditsch and Singer found that the average intercapital distance between warring states was significantly less than the average such distance between all states over the period from 1816 to 1965. Garnham also employed an intercapital measure of distance to assess proximity, and found that the distance between warring pairs of states was significantly less than what would be expected by chance. This led him to conclude that "international war is more probable between more proximate pairs of nation-states" (p. 240). Gochman reported that about two-thirds of militarized interstate disputes occurring between 1816 and 1976 were between states that shared a common land border or were separated by 150 miles or less of water. Gochman also found that the proportion of disputes in which contiguity was present has tended to increase with the passage of time. Hence, if any trend is present in the effect of proximity on conflict, it would appear to be in the opposite direction from that commonly thought; that is, proximity may be more salient today than it was a century and a half ago.

Power Parity and War

Whether equality in power between states promotes war or peace has been hotly debated in the theoretical literature. Both sides make convincing arguments that appeal to common sense. One side argues that states that are radically different in power should not engage in war because the clearly weaker side would not be so foolish as to initiate or allow itself to be drawn into a war it cannot win. Hence, at the dyadic level, preponderance promotes peace. The other side of the debate argues that when two states are relatively equal in power, neither can be certain of victory, and they therefore deter one another from war. Ergo, power parity promotes peace between states. The first of these two views is found in more contemporary treatments of the question (e.g., Organski 1968; Blainey 1973; Gilpin 1981), whereas the second prevails in the older balance of power tradition (e.g., Claude 1962).

Although many empirical studies have examined the relationship between power and war, very few have looked specifically at the dyadic level. Garnham (1976) examined two-nation wars during the period from 1816 to 1965 and found that warring pairs of states were more equal with respect to several power-base measures (i.e., area, population, fuel consumption, iron and steel production) than would be expected by chance. This led him to conclude that power parity is more likely to lead to war than preponderance. Weede (1976) restricted his analysis to a smaller spatial-temporal domain (i.e., contiguous Asian dyads over the period from 1950 to 1969), but found essentially the same result, that is, that preponderance of power promotes peace. More recently, Gochman (1990b) found evidence to support the proposition that major powers are more likely to engage in war with other major powers when their capabilities are relatively equal. After reviewing the empirical literature on dyadic power and war, Sullivan concludes that "though the findings do not speak with one voice, a tendency seems to be, with some certain exceptions, that situations of preponderance are more likely associated with nonwar than the opposite" (1990, 129), an assessment with which I essentially agree.

Power Status and War

As with geographical proximity and war, there may be a tautological element in the proposition that major powers are more likely to engage in war than minor powers. It can be quite convincingly argued that major powers achieve and maintain their status as such because, in large measure, they pursue an active, interventionist, perhaps even aggressive, foreign policy that brings them more frequently into violent conflict with other states. The literature on war making and state making suggests that the two phenomena are intimately connected (Rasler and Thompson 1989). To the extent that this is true, it may be impossible to determine on balance whether states become major powers because they engage frequently in war or states engage frequently in war because they are major powers. A true test of the two propositions may come when and if Germany and Japan are readmitted to the major power club.

The nondyadic empirical evidence is quite clear (Bremer 1980b; Small and Singer 1982); major powers are much more likely to become involved in wars

than minor powers. Ceteris paribus, dyads that contain one or more major powers should be more war prone than those that do not.

Alliance and War

In the modern era, alliances tend to be seen as defining "security communities" among their members, and, as such, it is expected that they will reduce the likelihood of war between members. In truth, this expectation may be based largely on a few durable and institutionalized alliances like NATO in the post–World War II era rather than on alliances in general. Yet the assumption that allies are more likely to resolve disputes by means other than war and, therefore, are less likely to engage in war with one another seems deeply ingrained in conventional wisdom. The older, more traditional view of alliances sees them as growing out of expediency and reflecting nothing deeper than a temporary need of two or more states to coordinate their actions against one or more other states. In this second view, alliances are not seen as contracts but rather as bargains, wherein it is understood by all parties that each has the right to withdraw quickly should a better deal come along. Under this conception of alliances as limited, transient arrangements, war between allies should be neither more nor less frequent than between nonallied states. In theory, then, alliances may or may not reduce the chances of war between allies, but they should not increase the likelihood of war between allies.

Perhaps for this reason, Bueno de Mesquita's assertion that "war is much more likely between very close allies than between enemies" (1982, 30) was a counterintuitive, if not startling, deduction from his expected utility theory.[5] And the empirical evidence he offered (1981, 159–64) seemed to confirm this assertion. After a thoughtful review of Bueno de Mesquita's arguments and evidence, Ray concluded that "in light of the fact that it would be surprising to find that allies are even as conflict prone as unallied pairs of states, it is not unreasonable to conclude that allied dyads were disproportionately involved in international conflict with each other in the 1816–1974 time period" (Ray 1990, 86). Thus, contrary to most theoretical expectations, war appears to be more likely between allied states than between nonallied states, at least since the end of the Napoleonic era.

Democracy and War

At a time when democracy seems to be experiencing a resurgence, the argument that democracies are less war prone (at least vis-à-vis one another) gives some grounds for optimism about an otherwise turbulent future. The philosophical justifications for why democratic states should be less war prone than others will not be repeated here.[6] Instead, I will focus on the empirical debate that has been underway for some years.

Until recently, the prevailing appraisal of the empirical evidence regarding the linkage between democracy and war proneness supported the conclusion that democracies were neither more nor less war prone than other states. Studies by Wright (1965), Rummel (1968), Russett and Monsen (1975), and Small and Singer (1976) all reached this conclusion. Rummel (1983) challenged this conclusion and gave evidence that democracies were less war prone and especially so vis-à-vis one another. This prompted Weede (1984) to reexamine the question focusing on the period from 1960 to 1980, after which he concluded that democracies were neither more nor less likely to engage in war than other states. Chan (1984) considerably extended the analysis of Rummel's contention by examining the period from 1816 to 1980, and, although he did not dispute the proposition that democracies do not tend to fight one another, he did conclude that democracies were not less war prone in general than undemocratic states. Domke (1988) used Gurr's Polity (I) data set and failed to find any consistent association between the degree of democracy and likelihood of war. Dixon (1989) also failed to find much association between the degree of democracy and the frequency of war over a long span of time (1816–1971), but his study, like most others discussed here, was conducted at the national rather than dyadic level.

Maoz and Abdolali (1989) did include a dyadic analysis as part of their larger study of regime type and militarized interstate conflict. They found strong evidence that democracies tend not to go to war with one another, but little evidence that democracies tend to be less war prone overall.

Most of the studies surveyed above contain one or more serious design flaws, such as using a monadic level of analysis when a dyadic one is called for, failing to control for the number of democracies, or using an inappropriate measure of war. Nevertheless, the weight of evidence they yield clearly supports the proposition that democracies have a much lower likelihood of becoming involved in wars against other democracies than would be expected by chance. Russett has even gone so far as to assert that "this is one of the strongest nontrivial and nontautological generalizations that can be made about international relations" (1990, 123). The evidence as to whether or not democracies are less war prone overall is far less conclusive, but the absence of strong evidence to the contrary leads one to conclude that democracies have been neither more nor less war prone than nondemocracies.

Development and War

The rise of international political economy as a subfield has resensitized many to the importance of economic factors and international conflict. A central focus of much of the literature in this area is the way in which economically advanced states relate to each other and, more importantly, to states that are not economically advanced. Although war appears not to be a central concern of most of those engaged in research in this area, two propositions relating to war can be deduced from their work. The first derives from the Leninist thesis that states that are more economically advanced will tend to come into sharp conflict with one another as they compete for markets and resources in a largely zero-sum world. Of course, a critical caveat for the Leninist thesis is that these states be capitalistic in nature, and this is, no doubt, an important theoretical distinction. Unfortunately it is not a distinction that can be used meaningfully in empirical analyses because, with few exceptions over the last 2 centuries, all more advanced states have also been capitalistic. For this reason the proposition examined here is simply that more advanced states are more likely to start wars with one another than are other states.[7]

The second proposition that is suggested by this literature is that war is more likely between more advanced and less advanced states than between pairs of more or less advanced states. This would follow from an admittedly unsophisticated dependencia theory that states that the likelihood of war increases when a more advanced economy attempts to penetrate a less advanced economy, or when a less advanced economy attempts to shake off the yoke imposed by a more advanced economy. If this pattern of conflict were widespread, then one would expect to see a disproportionate amount of war between more and less advanced economies.

Efforts to uncover empirical studies that bear directly on these propositions were unsuccessful. Studies that include measures of development, as opposed to economic size, were not conducted at the dyadic level (e.g., Rummel 1968), whereas dyadic studies (e.g., Garnham 1976) used measures of economic size rather than development. And some (e.g., Bremer 1980a) that considered the linkage between economics and war were neither dyadic nor concerned with development. It would appear, then, that we are in virgin territory, empirically speaking, with respect to these propositions.[8]

Militarization and War

According to the old maxim, "states that seek peace should prepare for war." The questions that concern us here are whether states that devote a disproportionate share of their resources to military preparedness succeed in reducing their chances of war, as the maxim implies they should, or will such states exhibit a higher likelihood of war? I should emphasize that more militarized states are not necessarily those with the largest absolute military capability. Several countries in the Middle East, for example, maintain armed forces much larger than most other countries of comparable size and are more militarized, as I use the term here, even though their armed forces are small in a global sense.

The war-avoidance properties of militarization flow clearly from the logic of deterrence. If a state can persuade a potential attacker that the costs of war will be high relative to the expected gains, then the odds of being attacked will be lower. And this logic applies to small states as well as large since, although small states may not be able to avoid defeat in wars with large states, they can, by extensive military preparations, guarantee that victory will be costly to the large states and thereby deter attacks. According to deterrence theory, then, more militarization means less war.

As is usually the case, for each maxim there is an equally convincing counter-maxim. In this instance it would be that "those who live by the sword, die by the sword." For a variety of reasons, states that prepare for war may get exactly that for which they prepare. The construction of a "garrison state" may call forth leaders that are bellicose and unyielding rather than flexible and accommodating. The militarization of a society may cause leaders and followers alike to conclude that war is inevitable rather than merely possible. Justifying the sacrifices that high degrees of military preparedness require may strengthen enemy images and even lead to collective paranoia. And, of course, other states may not see the defensive motivation behind the heightened military posture, and perceive instead a substantial threat to their own security. On balance, I find the second argument more persuasive than the first so the exact proposition under examination is stated accordingly; that is, pairs of more militarized states are more likely to begin wars than other states.

The empirical evidence on this proposition is, at best, indirect. The most germane comes from the numerous but inconclusive studies on the relationship between arms races and war. On one side of this question we find Wallace (1979, 1981, 1982, 1990) who has presented evidence that arms races do increase the likelihood of war between racing states. On the other side, we find Diehl and others (Diehl

1983, 1985a; Weede 1980) who dispute this connection. To a great extent the outcome of this debate hinges on the definition of what constitutes an arms race.[9]

Even if it were shown conclusively that arms races increase the likelihood of war, this would not constitute direct confirming evidence for the proposition under consideration here for two reasons. First, the arms race thesis is dynamic while the militarization hypothesis is static. That is, continued increases in preparedness are central to the former, while high levels of preparedness are the concern of the latter. Second, the arms race thesis is not concerned with the relative defense effort of racing states, while the militarization hypothesis is. Two states could be involved in a low level arms race with neither reaching the stage of militarization referred to here, although continued, large increases in resources devoted to the military should eventually lead to that stage.

Definitions and Measurements

Given the way in which our seven key propositions are stated and the underlying theoretical arguments from which they derive, it seems obvious that the interstate dyad is the appropriate level of analysis. An interstate dyad is defined as any pair of states that are members of the interstate system, where system membership is defined by the standard Correlates of War rules.[10] Because I wish to test the veracity of the propositions over a long historical period (i.e., from 1816 to 1965) rather than at only one point in time, the basic observational unit must be time based, and I have selected the year as the time unit. Hence, the interstate dyad-year is the observational unit employed in the analyses that follow. Aggregating over time and space yields a population of 202,778 nondirectional[11] interstate dyad-years during the 1816 to 1965 span.

Defining War Occurrence

One of the key reasons that the findings derived from empirical studies of war do not add up in a cumulative fashion is the wide variation in operational definitions of war that have been employed. Thus, for example, two studies may, as this one does, accept the Correlates of War definition of what constitutes a war, yet adopt quite different measures of war participation (e.g., nation-months of war underway versus battle deaths begun), and, by doing so, make it virtually impossible to compare their findings in any direct way. Too often, I think, the measurement of war has been guided by statistical considerations[12] or by an eclecticism that sees the various war measures as more or less substitutable rather than by a deeper theoretical examination of the questions under review.

As stated above, the seven propositions under examination deal only with the likelihood of wars between states and say little directly about the length, severity, or ultimate size of those wars that do occur. Hence, measures of war that rest on the latter are inappropriate for this study. If wars did not have the analytically annoying and sometimes catastrophic tendency to change in composition (i.e., states enter and leave a war after its start or before its end, occasionally switching sides in the process), our definition of war onset would be straightforward at this point. But because wars do have this tendency, we must deal with the question of whether a distinction is to be made between the initial combatants (originators) in a war and those states that become involved after its start (joiners).

I share the growing view that war must be seen as a process rather than only an event,[13] and, according to this view, it is important to distinguish between the occurrence of a war and how it evolves thereafter. In other words, the question of why wars begin is fundamentally different from the questions of why wars grow in size, duration, or severity. Studies that fail to make this distinction are fundamentally flawed. If we turn back to the seven propositions under study, it seems clear that their focus is the likelihood that a war will begin between two states and not the likelihood that a state will join an ongoing war. Hence, I will examine only the original participants in a given war and disregard subsequent joiners in the analyses that follow.

If all wars began as one-on-one confrontations, then for each of the 56 interstate wars that began during the period under study there would be one dyad of original participants, but the historical record is not quite so simple.[14] In 13 of the 56 qualifying wars, two or more states became involved in war with one or more other states on the very first day of the war.[15] These may be instances of genuine collusion or very fast joining behavior (I favor the former interpretation), but unfortunately the available historical evidence does not allow us to distinguish reliably between the two. In view of this, we are left with little choice but to treat these simultaneous outbreaks of dyadic war as independent events even though we strongly suspect they are not.[16] Employing this assumption, one finds 93 cases of war onset at the dyadic level during the period from 1816 to 1965.[17] Because the year *prior* to the beginning of each war was used as the observation point for the seven independent variables rather than the year of the war itself, three of the 56 wars are not usable due to the fact that not all of the participants on one side were members of the interstate system in the year prior to the war. This reduces the number of war dyads by eight, leaving a total of 85.

Geographical Proximity

To ascertain whether any given pair of states are geographically proximate to one another, I turned to the Correlates of War contiguity data set.[18] In that data set, four types of direct state-to-state contiguity are distinguished: contiguous by land, or separated by 12, 24, or 150 miles or less of water. In this study I have chosen to disregard the tripartite water distance distinction and deal with only three types of contiguity. Thus, in a given year, a dyad is either land contiguous, sea contiguous (i.e., separated by 150 miles of water or less), or not contiguous. At this time, unfortunately, the contiguity data extend only from 1816 to 1965, and it is this limitation that essentially defines the temporal span of the whole study. Applying these criteria to the 202,778 interstate dyad-years yielded 10,542 cases of land contiguity, 3,019 cases of sea contiguity, and 189,217 cases of no contiguity.[19]

Relative Power

To assess the degree to which any pair of states is equal in power, I have used the Correlates of War material capabilities data set[20] that covers the period from 1816 to 1985 and records the military personnel, military expenditures, iron and steel production, energy consumption (after 1859), urban population, and total population for state system members. In the usual fashion, I first derived indexes of military, economic, and demographic capability by computing each state's average share of system-wide capability across the two variables within each of the three dimensions and then averaged these values to arrive at the Composite Index of National Capability (or CINC).[21]

Based on these CINC scores, I computed the larger-to-smaller capability ratios for all dyad-years and classified them into three groups. If the capability ratio was less than or equal to three, then the dyad was considered to constitute a case of small power difference. If the ratio was larger than 10, then the power difference was coded as large, whereas a ratio between 3 and 10 was coded as a medium power difference. If either of the CINC scores was missing (or equal to zero) for a ratio calculation, then the power difference score for that dyad was coded as missing also.

The 3-to-1 threshold was chosen because of its prominence in the folklore of military strategy while 10-to-1 threshold is quite arbitrary.[22] To my surprise, the use of these thresholds yielded roughly equal groups of dyad-years. That is, 74,620 of the 202,778 dyad-years were found to exhibit a large power difference, 56,432 were characterized by a medium power difference, and 62,055 by a small power difference. The 9,671 remaining cases (less than 5%) were missing.

Power Status

To investigate the effects of power status, each dyad-year was examined to determine whether both, one, or neither of the relevant states were or was a major power in that year. Accordingly, the dyad was coded as having a power status of major-major,

major-minor, or minor-minor. The identity and qualifying years for major powers were the same as those defined by Small and Singer (1982) and used by many other analysts. Applying these criteria across the entire spatial-temporal domain yielded the following breakdown: 2,267 major-major dyad-years, 36,907 major-minor dyad-years, and 163,604 minor-minor dyad-years.

Alliance

To distinguish those dyads that are allied from those that are not, I have used the Correlates of War formal alliance data set (Small and Singer 1969) as amended and modified by Alan Sabrosky.[23] In that data set formal alliances among nations are divided into three types: mutual defense pacts, neutrality agreements, and ententes. Using this data set, I was able to classify each dyad-year as falling into one of four groups: defense, neutrality, entente, and none. The total number of dyad-years this produced were 11,176; 647; 3,531; and 187,424, respectively.

Democracy

Defining and measuring democracy is difficult, and especially so when a dichotomous measure is desired. Therefore, in this study I will draw on two different efforts to classify political systems. The first is the dichotomous division of states done by Steve Chan[24] (Chan 1984) in which a state is classified as democratic if its chief executive is directly or indirectly elected in a popular fashion and its legislative branch is also elected and able to constrain the executive in an effective manner (see Chan 1984, 629–31 for further details). Using this data set, which covers the period from 1816 to 1980, I was able to assign each of the dyad-years to one of three groups: both states democratic (21,644), one democratic state (78,349), and both states undemocratic (99,580). In addition, data were missing for 3,205 dyad-years, and these were assigned to the missing group.

The second data collection I use to assess whether or not states are democratic is Ted Robert Gurr's Polity II data set (Gurr, Jaggers, and Moore 1989), which contains, among other things, a variable reflecting the degree of "institutionalized democracy" found in a state in a given year. Like Chan's measure, this index is based on the competitiveness of leader selection processes and constraints on executive authority. In its raw form, this index varies from 0 to 10 (undemocratic to democratic). I dichotomized the variable by classifying states as democratic that had a value of 5 or greater on Gurr's index and otherwise as undemocratic.[25] Using the Gurr-based index I found 22,859 dyad-years in which both states were democratic, 80,668 with one democratic state, and 80,801 with neither state democratic. This left 18,450 dyad-years coded as missing when values were missing for one or both states.

Development

Given the paucity of macroeconomic time-series data for years prior to World War II, any effort to differentiate more advanced economies from less advanced economies based on, for example, GNP or GDP per capita would suffer from serious design deficiencies.[26] Rather than abandoning the effort to consider the relationship between development and war, I derived an index based on the Correlates of War material capabilities data set that may capture some of the economic differentiation between states that is sought.

It will be recalled that in deriving the composite index of national capability, two component indexes assessing the economic and demographic dimensions were used. In a general sense, these component indexes reflect the share of system-wide economic and demographic capabilities that a state possesses in any given year. A more economically advanced state should be characterized by possessing a share of system-wide economic capability that is greater than its share of system-wide demographic capability. Hence, in years when this was found to be true, I classified a state as more advanced; otherwise, less advanced.[27] The next step involved examining each pair of states in each year and assigning it to one of three groups: both more advanced (7,160 dyad-years), one more advanced (61,823 dyad-years), and both less advanced (128,939 dyad-years). The remaining 4,856 dyad-years had to be assigned to the missing group because data were not available for one or both of the relevant states.

Militarization

As with measuring development, assessing whether states are more or less militarized over the century and a half under study is difficult, given the lack of historical data. Ideally, one would wish to measure what is sometimes referred to as defense effort (i.e., the ratio of defense expenditures to GNP), but this is not a viable measure for most states in most years over the century and a half under consideration due to the insufficiency of macroeconomic data. Instead, I relied on the material capabilities data set discussed above, and classified a state as more militarized if its share of system-wide military capabilities was greater than its share of system-wide demographic capabilities. I classified it less militarized if this was not true. The classification of each dyad-year was then based on whether both, one, or neither of the two states making up the dyad were more militarized in that year. This produced 29,366; 87,720; and 76,467 dyad-years, respectively, leaving 9,225 dyad-years as missing due to the absence of data for one or both sides.

Bivariate Results

To begin the assessment of the relative merit of the seven propositions stated in the introduction, I use a simple and straightforward method. I calculate and compare the conditional probabilities of war in a dyad-year given the presence of the conditions specified by each proposition. The degree to which the conditional probabilities relevant to a proposition vary from one another is then used as evidence for the proposition. The relevant information is found in Table 1. For each dyad type, the first column in this table shows the observed number of war onsets, together with the expected number of onsets (in parentheses) if the type distinctions are ignored. The latter are the products of the unconditional dyadic probability of war (85/202,778) and the number of dyad-years each dyad type was observed, which is given in the second column. The third column contains the conditional probability of war, pr(War), for each dyad type, which is the observed number of war onsets divided by the total dyad-years. These probabilities have been multiplied by 1,000 to facilitate reading. To help distinguish large and small effects, I include as well in the table standard normal (Z) values and their associated probabilities. These are derived from a difference of proportions test where each group is posited to be a random sample drawn from a known population. The Z and pr(Z) values reflect, then, the likelihood of obtaining a conditional probability of war this or more different from the unconditional probability of war if the distinction used to define the group was truly irrelevant to war propensity.[28]

Proximity and war. The top of Table 1 reveals the probabilities of war in a dyad-year when the 202,778 dyad-years are segregated by geographical proximity. It is obvious that the presence of land or sea contiguity significantly increases the probability of war occurring in a dyad, with land contiguous dyads being slightly more war prone than sea contiguous ones. Ignoring the latter distinction yields a probability of war per dyad-year, given either land or sea contiguity, of .0045. Because this value is 35 times greater than the probability of war when contiguity is absent, there can be little doubt that the effect of state-to-state contiguity on the occurrence of war is quite strong.[29] The large Z values and their small associated probabilities strongly reinforce this conclusion.

Power difference and war. The conditional probabilities of war onset given large, medium, or small power differences are the next shown in Table 1.

The first impression conveyed by these results is that, relatively speaking, the three probabilities do not differ all that much from one another. The Z values are all within the +1 to −1 range, suggesting that the power difference distinction is not much better than a random split. Together, these values lead to the conclusion that the effect of power difference

Table 1 Conditional Probabilities of War by Dyad Type, 1816–1965

Dyad Type	War Dyads	Total Dyads	pr(War)*	Z	pr(Z)
		Proximity and war			
Land contiguous	48 (4.4)	10,542	4.55	20.74	<.0001
Sea contiguous	13 (1.3)	3,019	4.31	10.43	<.0001
Not contiguous	24 (79.3)	189,217	0.13	−6.21	<.0001
		Power difference and war			
Large difference	27 (31.3)	74,620	0.36	−0.77	.22
Medium difference	28 (23.7)	56,432	0.50	0.89	.19
Small difference	29 (26.0)	62,055	0.47	0.59	.28
Missing	1	9,671			
		Power status and war			
Major-major	5 (1.0)	2,267	2.21	4.16	<.0001
Major-minor	42 (15.5)	36,907	1.14	6.75	<.0001
Minor-minor	38 (68.6)	163,604	0.23	−3.69	.0001
		Alliance and war			
Defense pact	20 (4.7)	11,176	1.79	7.08	<.0001
Neutrality treaty	2 (0.3)	647	3.09	3.32	.0004
Entente	1 (1.5)	3,531	0.28	−0.39	.35
No alliance	62 (78.6)	187,424	0.33	−1.87	.031
		Democracy and war (Chan)			
Both democratic	1 (9.1)	21,644	0.05	−2.68	.0043
One democratic	14 (32.8)	78,349	0.18	−3.29	.0005
Both not democratic	70 (41.7)	99,580	0.70	+4.37	<.0001
Missing	0	3,205			
		Democracy and war (Gurr)			
Both democratic	2 (9.6)	22,859	0.09	−2.45	.0071
One democratic	25 (33.8)	80,668	0.31	−1.52	.0643

(Continued)

Table 1   (Continued)

Dyad Type	War Dyads	Total Dyads	pr(War)*	Z	pr(Z)
Both not democratic	36 (33.9)	80,801	0.45	+0.37	.3557
Missing	22	18,450			
		Development and war			
Both advanced	6 (3.0)	7,160	0.84	+1.73	.0418
One advanced	25 (25.9)	61,823	0.40	−0.18	.4286
Both not advanced	54 (54.0)	128,939	0.42	−0.01	.496
Missing	0	4,856			
		Militarization and war			
Both more militarized	38 (12.3)	29,366	1.29	+7.32	<.0001
One more militarized	30 (36.8)	87,720	0.34	−1.12	.1314
Both less militarized	16 (32.1)	76,467	0.21	−2.84	.0023
Missing	1	9,225			

*To facilitate reading all probabilities have been multiplied by 1,000.

is, at best, small. The effect that is present, however, is in the direction postulated; that is, war is about one-third more likely in dyads characterized by small or medium power differences than in those with large power differences.

Power status and war. The next set of conditional probabilities in Table 1 are obtained when the whole set of dyad-years is divided into subsets based on the power status of the states involved. Major-major dyads have the highest probability of war, whereas minor-minor dyads have the lowest probability of war, and, because the probability of war in the former is about 10 times larger than the latter, the proposition that major-major dyads are more war prone seems to have considerable merit. In addition, because the probability of war in dyads that include one major power is about 5 times greater than those that contain no major power, it appears that the effect of power status may be additive rather than interactive.

The absolute Z values are all greater than three, which confirms the conclusion that the power status of a dyad has a major impact on its war propensity.

Alliance and war. The conditional probabilities of war onset when members of a dyad are linked by different types of formal alliance bonds are shown next in Table 1. Both the defense pact and neutrality treaty categories show significantly higher than expected war probabilities, whereas the opposite is true for ententes. However, due to the small number of war dyads in the neutrality and entente categories, a better estimate of the impact of alliance on war may be obtained by collapsing some of the categories. If the three types of alliance are merged, the conditional probability of war given any alliance is .0015 (Z = +6.53) versus .00033 when no alliance is present, a likelihood ratio of about 4.5 to 1. If instead, because of their low relative frequency of war, ententes are combined with the no alliance category, then the corresponding probabilities are .0019 (Z = +9.88) and .00033, yielding a likelihood ratio of 5.6 to 1. Hence, regardless of how ententes are coded, the likelihood of war in allied dyads is about 5 times greater than that in nonallied dyads. These results confirm the paradoxical proposition that alliances encourage war between members rather than inhibiting it.

Democracy and war. Proposition 5 stated that war between undemocratic dyads is more likely than between democratic dyads, and the results obtained using Chan's data shown in Table 1 support this assertion. The probability of war onset between democracies is much smaller than between states that are not democratic, or, stated in the direction specified by the proposition, war onset between pairs of undemocratic states is about 14 times as likely as between pairs of democratic states. Because war onset in undemocratic dyads is about 4 times as likely as between mixed (i.e., one democratic, one undemocratic) pairs of states, it appears that the contention of some that both states must be democratic before the war-inhibiting effect of democracy is felt is unsupported. If the latter were true, then the probabilities of war onset when one or neither state was undemocratic should both be about .00047 rather than .00018 and .00070 respectively. The large Z and small pr(Z) values indicate that the presence of a democracy in a dyad significantly reduces its war propensity. Shifting over to the Gurr-based index of democracy yields similar but not identical results. As shown in Table 1, the probability that two undemocratic states will begin a war is much greater than the probability that two democratic states will do so. But, unlike the Chan-based results, we do not find a significant difference in the probability of war between dyads containing one or no democratic states. In these results, then, we find evidence only for what has been called the "joint democracy" effect.

Due to the attention that the democracy and war question has received of late, a somewhat more extended discussion of the joint democracy effect may be in order. Some (e.g., Babst 1972) assert that democracies do not (ever) fight one another. Using the Chan data, we find one such war onset (the Franco-Thai war of 1940), whereas the Gurr data reveal two (the Spanish-American war of 1898 and the Second Kashmir war of 1965). The first of these poses a problem because the onset of this war (December 1, 1940) followed the establishment of the Vichy regime in France, which certainly was not a democracy. Because democracy (and the other six factors) are measured in the year *prior* to the war onset year, this change is not recorded. The same is true for the Second Kashmir war—according to Gurr's data Pakistan was moderately democratic (6) in 1964, but moderately undemocratic (4) in 1965. However, the date of measurement has no impact on the Spanish-American war case because Spain has a value of 7 on the Gurr index and the United States a value of 10 for both 1897 and 1898. A reanalysis using the year of the war onset rather than the year prior to war onset as the measuring point for democracy led, as expected, to the elimination of the Second Kashmir case but not the other two cases. It did not call for any change in the conclusions reached from the first analysis.

Those who contend that democracies *never* go to war with one another may wish to question whether Spain was really democratic in 1898 or insist on fine-grained temporal distinctions in order to "save" their proposition.

I have no basic quarrel with such efforts as long as they are done dispassionately and systematically,[30] but we should not forget that it is not possible to "prove" that the probability of any event is zero. Indeed, in the present analysis, if we assume no wars between democracies and substitute zeros for the observed war onsets during the 21,644 (Chan 1984) and 22,859 (Gurr et al. 1989) joint-democratic dyad-years, the resulting Z values are −3.01 and −3.10, respectively. The probabilities associated with these values are .0013 and .001, indicating that, although unlikely, it is far from impossible to observe zero wars during the period of observation if democratic dyads were truly not different from other dyads. The object of this discussion is not to denigrate the importance of our finding—the evidence is quite strong that democracies *very rarely* initiate war against one another—but rather to point out that it is fruitless to debate the question of whether democracies *never* or only *very rarely* fight one another.

Development and war. The sixth proposition stated that war was more likely to occur between states that are economically advanced than between those that are not, and the results shown in Table 1 lend support to it. Dyads containing two advanced states are twice as likely to begin wars as those that contain one or fewer advanced states, but the Z values indicate that this effect is quite weak.

Militarization and war. The last part of Table 1 reveals the conditional probabilities of war when dyads are grouped according to whether both, one, or neither of the states involved are more militarized. Pairs of more militarized states are about six times as likely to begin a war in a given year than pairs of less militarized states, and, based on the small size of the probability of war in mixed dyads, one might conclude that the effect of militarization is largely interactive. Naturally, the argument that this relationship between militarization and war is spurious, due to the tendency for states preparing for war to become more militarized in preparation for the coming war, cannot be refuted. However, regardless of whether the proposition is causal or merely descriptive in nature, the assertion that militarized pairs of states are more likely to begin wars finds support here.

All seven propositions set forth at the beginning of this article have found support in the simple bivariate analyses, but some of the relationships found are stronger than others. From strongest to weakest, I would rank the various effects as follows.

1. Proximity

2. Power status

3. Alliance

4. Militarization

5. Democracy

6. Development

7. Power difference

It is interesting that the factor that has received perhaps the greatest amount of theoretical attention, power difference, is found here to be the weakest predictor of war onset. If subsequent analyses bear out the weak effects of relative power, the potential implications for international relations theory may be truly profound. But such a judgment must await the results of more complex analyses such as those presented below.

Multivariate Results

There are a variety of reasons for suspecting that the bivariate analyses reported above do not provide a sound basis for identifying types of dyads that are particularly war prone. Chief among these is the suspicion that the seven factors dealt with here are not uncorrelated with one another. Under this condition, apparently strong relationships with war may be spurious and weak relationships with war may become strong when the effects of other factors are removed. And, of course, not only the strengths of association may be affected, but also their direction as well. For example, the bivariate results suggest that both contiguity and alliance increase the likelihood of war onset in a dyad, but an analysis of the joint effects of both factors reveals that the existence of an alliance between a pair of contiguous states *decreases* their likelihood of war, and the conclusion that alliances make war more likely is not fully warranted.

In order to assess the joint and individual effects of the seven factors under consideration on war onset, all dyad-years were recoded to reflect the most war prone conditions revealed by the bivariate analyses. For example, the contiguity variable was assigned a value of one if the dyad was contiguous by land or sea (as defined above) and zero if not. The classification rules for all factors are given in Table 2.

Because each of the seven variables in Table 2 is now binary in nature, they jointly define 2^7 or 128 possible dyad types. In the analyses to be reported below, a case is defined as one of these dyad types, and the dependent variable of interest then becomes the number of war onsets that that particular dyad type experienced. Because some of these dyad types have been more common in history than others, ceteris paribus, one would expect them to experience more war onsets than rarer dyad types. Therefore, the number of dyad-years for each dyad type is also recorded. Defining cases in this fashion and not counting those dyad-years in which data are missing for one or more variables yield 118 dyad types that collectively account for 193,106 dyad-years.

The question to be addressed here is the relative contribution of each of the seven factors under consideration to the likelihood of war beginning within dyads. Because the dependent variable, number of war onsets, is bounded (i.e., may not be less than zero) and discrete (i.e., only integer values are possible) the standard regression model is not appropriate (King 1989). However, the Poisson (or Exponential Poisson, as King refers to it) regression

model is, because it assumes that the dependent variable has precisely those characteristics mentioned above. The general functional form of this model is

$$E(Y_i) = \exp(X_i B)$$

When the number of observations varies from case to case, as they do here, the recommended modified functional form is

$$E(Y_i) = \exp(X_i B + \ln(N_i))$$

where N_i is the number of observations (i.e., dyad-years) for the ith case.[31] Estimating the parameters of this model requires the use of a maximum likelihood technique and involves numerical rather than analytical solutions. Although these methods are not yet widely used, King (1989) makes a persuasive argument that they should be, and in this particular case, the Poisson regression model would seem to be well suited to the problem at hand.

Estimating an exponential Poisson model with the 118 dyad types as cases yields the coefficients reported in Table 3. The log-likelihood value for the entire model is −97.438. Although a value of zero would indicate a perfect fit between the model and data, the log-likelihood value has no lower limit. Hence, to interpret this value an explicit alternative model must be stated and estimated. In this instance the alternative (or null) model is based on the assumption that the only factor that accounts for different numbers of wars is N, the dyad-years of observation. Estimating this model yields a log-likelihood value of −156.84. Because the log-likelihood value is the log of the probability that the particular set of observed values would have been generated if the assumed model were true, the probability of obtaining the observed values if the null model were true is $e^{-156.84}$, which is approximately 7×10^{-69}. Adding the seven independent variables to our equation raises this probability to $e^{-99.438}$, or approximately 5×10^{-43}. Both of these are incredibly small numbers, because the probability of obtaining any particular result in this instance is extremely

Table 2   Value Assignment Rules for More War-Prone Dyads

Variable	Assignment Rule
Contiguous	1 if land or sea contiguous, 0 otherwise.
No large power difference	1 if small or medium power difference, 0 otherwise.
At least one major	1 if major-major or major-minor, 0 otherwise.
Allied	1 if any alliance, 0 otherwise.
Both not democratic	1 if both not (Chan) democratic, 0 otherwise.
Both more advanced	1 if both more advanced, 0 otherwise.
Both militarized	1 if both more militarized, 0 otherwise.

low, but what interests us is the relative size of the probabilities. Because the probability that the full model (if true) would have generated our observed values is about 6×10^{25} times greater than the comparable probability for the null model, we may safely conclude that the full model is more credible. For those who wish to evaluate such results in more conventional terms, a test statistic, c, which is chi-square distributed with $k - 1$ degrees of freedom, can be computed (King 1989, 84–87) as follows

$$c = 2(LL_{Full} - LL_{Null})$$

where LL represents the log-likelihood values. The c value in this instance is approximately 118, far, far beyond the .001 level of significance.

An examination of the coefficients[32] in Table 3 reveals that the majority of our expectations stemming from the bivariate analyses are confirmed, but a few are not. Because the seven variables were coded in such a way that values of one were assigned to the more war-prone condition identified in the bivariate analyses, the naive expectation is that the signs of the seven coefficients will be positive. The strongest predictor of the seven is contiguity, and, as expected, its presence significantly increases the likelihood of war in a dyad. Second in importance is the absence of democracy in a dyad, which also increases a dyad's likelihood of war. The third most important factor, both more advanced, does not have the expected positive effect, however. The next two factors, which measure the presence of a major power and overwhelming preponderance in a dyad, both have a similar, positive impact on the likelihood of war. The existence of an alliance within a dyad slightly *decreases* the likelihood of war starting within that dyad. The final condition, both militarized, has a very weak positive effect and adds virtually nothing to the explanatory power of the equation. This lack of any significant relationship between militarization and war is surprising because readiness for war is seen by some as a dangerous condition in and of itself, and by others as an early warning indicator of war. Joint preparedness, as measured here, does not seem to constitute either of these.

The failure to find any significant effect of militarization on war led to some experimentation with the possible interaction of this factor with the six others.

Table 3 Multivariate Poisson Regression Analysis of Dyadic War Onset, 1816–1965

Variable	Coefficient	Standard Error	t Ratio	Significance
Intercept	−5.468	1.206	−4.53	.00001
Log (dyad-years)	0.471	0.130	3.62	.0003
Contiguous	1.780	0.362	4.91	<.00001
Both not democratic	1.285	0.295	4.35	.00001
Both more advanced	−1.275	0.507	−2.52	.01184
At least one major	0.658	0.263	2.50	.01239
No large power difference	0.619	0.243	2.54	.01098
Allied	−0.397	0.287	−1.38	.16641
Both militarized	0.098	0.240	0.41	.683

Only one combination proved noteworthy, and that was the condition of both militarized and allied. Substituting the product of these two variables in place of the militarization term yields the results shown in Table 4. The log-likelihood value increases to −92.555, suggesting a notable improvement in the model, and, more importantly, the contributions of the seven factors become clearer and stronger. In particular, the alliance coefficient now shows a strong, negative association between being allied and the likelihood of war, and the interaction term shows a strong positive association with war. Hence, by itself, the existence of an alliance reduces the chances of war in a dyad, but this effect is nullified if the parties to the dyad are both more militarized.

In order to understand better the relative importance of the seven factors, let us consider a hypothetical dyad and its expected number of war onsets over a 100-year period. To begin, I will assume that the dyad has the predicted characteristics of a least war-prone one; that is, it is composed of noncontiguous, allied minor powers, at least one of which is democratic and one of which is less militarized, and one state has overwhelming preponderance over the other.

The expected number of wars that would originate in such a dyad over 100 years is about 0.003, based on the coefficients of the revised model.

Table 5 summarizes how the stepwise alteration of each factor transforms the dyad from least war prone to most war prone. It is readily apparent that contiguity has the strongest impact, followed closely by economic status and alliance. The presence or absence of joint democracy is next in importance, with relative power and power status having significantly less of an impact. As expected, the interaction term makes only a small contribution to the expected number of wars because its main effect is reflected in the alliance term. The third column in Table 5 shows the proportionate increase in the expected number of wars that each factor makes; the reader can readily assess the relative importance of the seven factors.

Implications and Conclusions

In closing I will consider some implications for theory and research, beginning with the individual factors and concluding with the overall pattern they reveal.

Table 4 Revised Multivariate Poisson Regression Analysis of Dyadic War Onset, 1816–1965

Variable	Coefficient	Standard Error	t Ratio	Significance
Intercept	−4.950	1.077	−4.60	<.0001
Log (dyad-years)	0.425	0.118	3.61	.0003
Contiguous	1.683	0.342	4.92	<.0001
Both not democratic	1.273	0.294	4.33	<.0001
Both more advanced	−1.412	0.498	−2.83	.0046
At least one major	0.545	0.257	2.12	.0342
No large power difference	0.607	0.243	2.50	.0123
Allied	−1.464	0.539	−2.72	.0066
Both militarized and allied	1.541	0.557	2.77	.0056

Table 5 Expected War Onsets per Dyad in a Century

Action	Expected Wars	Proportionate Increase
Start with least war-prone dyad	0.003	
Add contiguity	0.015	5.4
Remove alliance	0.066	4.3
Make one or both less advanced	0.300	4.6
Make one or both not democratic	0.963	3.2
Remove overwhelming preponderance	1.767	1.8
Give one or both major power status	3.048	1.7
Add alliance and make both militarized	3.290	1.1
Result: most war-prone dyad	3.290	

The importance of contiguity in accounting for the onset of interstate war argues that it should be commonly included in almost all studies of war, if only as a control variable. Whether it is only a measure of opportunity for war, or whether it taps something deeper that reflects the willingness to engage in war as well, is unclear, but its importance is not, and the argument for its inclusion applies to all levels of analysis. These results suggest that Diehl's conclusion that "although geography may not be the most important factor in international relations, its significance justifies increased and more careful attention from scholars of international conflict" (1991, 24) is true, but understated, for in this competition between many purportedly important preconditions for war, contiguity finished first.

Alliances have been found to reduce significantly the likelihood of war between allies, except under the special condition where both are more militarized, in which case they have almost no impact. Thus our theoretical expectations are generally confirmed and the bivariate finding that alliances promote war between allies is shown to be essentially spurious. There is nothing in this finding inconsistent with the argument that alliances promote the spread of war, once it breaks out, however (Siverson and Starr 1990).

In the economic sphere, these results suggest that the likelihood of war starting between "have" states is considerably lower than between "have" and "have not" or between "have not" states. This could reflect a mutual recognition among advanced economies that war is, in Mueller's words, "abhorrent—repulsive, immoral, and uncivilized—and methodologically ineffective—futile" (1989, 217), or, less charitably, it may indicate the presence of cartel-like collusion among richer states to avoid war between themselves in order to maintain their exalted economic positions. More conclusively, the (neo)-Leninist notion that competition between advanced economies is a major determinant of war has found little support. However, more research is certainly needed on this factor before any definitive conclusions can be drawn.

Democracy has once again shown itself to be a war-reducing factor, and its effect is readily apparent even after the effects of many other factors have been removed. It would not appear that the bivariate relationship between democracy and war is spurious, as some have contended; on the contrary, democracy is once again shown to be a quite powerful inhibitor of war. More studies are needed like that of Morgan and Campbell (1991) and Morgan and Schwebach (1991) to ascertain more precisely what it is about democracy that serves to inhibit war.

The results obtained in these analyses clearly support the position that power preponderance is more conducive to peace in a dyad than the lack thereof. Although its effect is not as strong as others considered here, and certainly weaker than hard-core realists would have us believe, the existence of overwhelming preponderance is, ceteris paribus, a "pacifying condition." It should be noted that these are precisely the dyads where one side should perceive itself to have a high probability of winning any war, based on relative capabilities. According to expected utility theory (Bueno de Mesquita 1981), the decision for war is based on this probability times the utility of victory. If we can assume that the utility of victory is independent of the probability of victory across our 200,000 dyads, then, if this theory is true, we should observe that dyads with large power differences are the more war-prone ones, precisely the opposite of what has been found here. This suggests that some reexamination of a basic premise of expected utility theory may be in order. At the very least, the way in which the probability of victory is typically operationalized should be questioned.

I have long felt that the designation of some states as major powers was an overly subjective classification and somewhat ad hoc. With respect to war, there is also the distinct possibility that the well-established propensity for major powers to engage in war is tautological (i.e., states are considered major powers because they fight many wars). In view of this I would have preferred to find *no* significant association between power status and war after controlling for other factors like power difference. Yet, under this condition, the major power effect remains and is found to be about as influential as power preponderance. This suggests to me that there is another important characteristic, for which the major power designation serves as a proxy, that remains to be identified.

Perhaps the most important contribution of this study is that it provides, for the first time, a direct assessment of the relative importance of more than a few factors that are alleged to promote or inhibit the outbreak of war. In order of declining importance, the conditions that characterize a dangerous, war-prone dyad are:

1. presence of contiguity

2. absence of alliance

3. absence of more advanced economy

4. absence of democratic polity

5. absence of overwhelming preponderance

6. presence of major power.

The first four of these are each over twice as important as each of the last two. If the order of this list were compared to that of the implicit research priorities that have guided war and peace research, the correlation would not be positive. This leads to the rather sobering conclusion that our priorities may be seriously distorted.

Taken together these results give a stronger endorsement to the idealist prescription for peace than to the realist one. Core components of the Wilsonian recipe for a more peaceful world were: establish collective security alliances, spread democracy, promote economic progress, and reduce armament levels. All of these save the last have been found to reduce strongly the likelihood of war at the dyadic level, and even the last factor is not discredited given that nothing in these findings suggests that high levels of military preparedness reduce the likelihood of war. In contrast, some of the primary concerns of realists, that is, relative power and power status in this analysis, have been shown to be less important than the above. Moreover, realists generally dismiss domestic factors as unimportant, yet these results suggest that they have a greater impact on the likelihood of war than others which they consider far more important. Certainly the results reported here do not constitute a head-to-head test of idealism versus realism (perhaps such a test is not possible), but they do suggest that a deeper examination of the idealist position might bring us closer to understanding the conditions that foster peace. We now have neorealism; perhaps it's time to seriously entertain neoidealism.

Notes

1. In stating these criticisms, it is not useful to single out individuals who are guilty of particular "sins" of research. Indeed, all war (and peace) researchers (including the author) have committed one or the other of these sins in the past.

2. After assessing a variety of war data collections, Most and Starr conclude that all share the following definition: "A war is a particular type of outcome of the *interaction* of at least dyadic sets of specified varieties of actors in which at least one actor is willing and able to use some specified amount of military force for some specified period of time against some other resisting actor, and in which some specified minimal number of fatalities (greater than zero) occur" (1989, 73, italics in original).

3. See Diehl (1991) for a recent review of geography and war.

4. The work of Diehl and Goertz (e.g., Diehl and Goertz 1988; Goertz and Diehl 1990) which focuses upon territorial changes does not deal directly with the overall propensity for proximate states to engage in war, but the basic thrust of their work certainly supports the notion that geographical proximity is an important determinant of interstate conflict.

5. Of the 347 propositions about alliances that Holsti, Hopmann, and Sullivan (1985) gleaned from the traditional literature, not one posits that an alliance should increase the likelihood of war between member states. This may be a good indicator of just how counterintuitive Bueno de Mesquita's assertion is.

6. See Waltz (1959) and Doyle (1986).

7. This proposition is also broadly consistent with the lateral pressure theory (Choucri and North 1975) because it posits, ceteris paribus, that technologically advanced societies should exhibit high levels of conflict among themselves.

8. I should note that the distinction between more and less advanced states cuts across other distinctions made in this study. Among major powers, for example, England falls into the first category throughout the 19th century, whereas Russia does not, and Germany moves from less advanced to more advanced during that century. Similarly, economically advanced states need not possess large capabilities, as witnessed by the existence of Austria, the Netherlands, Belgium, and so on in the contemporary system. In short, distinguishing more advanced from less advanced states should provide us with a different perspective on the possible preconditions of war.

9. For a recent "recap" of this debate see Siverson and Diehl (1989).

10. Save a few modifications that have been made since the publication of Small and Singer's *Resort to Arms,* the states examined here and their qualifying years are the same as those given in Table 2.1 of that volume (Small and Singer 1982).

11. A nondirectional dyad is one in which no distinction is made between the U.S.-USSR and USSR-U.S. dyads, for example. In directional dyads this differentiation is, of course, retained.

12. For example, the distributions of many war measures are badly skewed, and transformations have been done to bring in outliers to which regression analysis is very sensitive.

13. Duvall (1976) is an early (in print) advocacy of this view, while Most and Starr (1989) contains a more recent endorsement of it. My own view is elaborated in Bremer (1991).

14. As implied above, I rely on the war data compiled by the Correlates of War project. More specifically, they were derived from Small and Singer (1982).

15. Seven wars began as two-to-one confrontations, two as three-to-one, one as four-to-one, and two as five-to-one. In one case, the Seven Weeks War, the initial confrontation was between two and five states.

16. Avoiding this assumption would require solving the rather formidable problem of identifying when and

under what conditions two or more states will undertake joint action against one or more other states. This is an important and interesting question but beyond the scope of this article.

17. The observant reader will note that I have not dealt with the question of war initiation. This is because the propositions under consideration are nondirectional in nature and have little to say about which of the two states involved in a war will be the first to undertake sustained combat.

18. The particular version of this data set that I used was supplied to me by Charles S. Gochman, to whom I here express my thanks. Those interested in learning more about this data set should consult Gochman (1991).

19. Relying only on direct state-to-state contiguity as a measure of geographical proximity may partially distort the results reported below, because indirect contiguities (e.g., state-to-dependency-to-state contiguities) will not be recorded. The United States and Great Britain are not directly contiguous at any time but obviously they shared a geographical proximity with one another via Canada until it achieved its independence. In general, I expect this absence of indirect contiguity to weaken the observed effect of geographical proximity. A test of this supposition will be possible in the near future with data recently provided to me by Randolph Siverson and Harvey Starr, because their contiguity data set does include colonial borders. These data are described in Siverson and Starr (1991).

20. The revised and expanded version of this data set was kindly provided to me by the Correlates of War project.

21. Although the version of the capability data set I employed has significantly less missing data than previous versions, some data (e.g., from 19th-century Latin American states) are still missing. After experimenting with several alternative methods of handling missing data, I adopted the following procedure. If both values within a dimension were missing, then the score on that dimension was recorded as missing. If only one of the two values was missing, then the score on that dimension was set equal to that of the value present. If, after this procedure, any one of the three

dimensional values was missing, then the CINC score was recorded as missing.

22. This is the same threshold value used by Weede (1976) to define what he called overwhelming preponderance.

23. These data were supplied to me by Alan Sabrosky, to whom I express my gratitude.

24. I would like to thank Steve Chan for supplying me with these data.

25. To assess the agreement between the Chan and Gurr classification of states, I compared the state-year dichotomous codings in those 6,675 cases where values were present in both collections. The Yule's Q coefficient of correlation between the two data sets was +0.93, suggesting that they are highly similar but not identical.

26. Under the most optimistic assumptions about data availability, I would estimate that the number of dyad-years for which the relevant data could be assembled would be less than 20% of the total dyad-years under consideration. A more realistic estimate might be as low as 10%. Clearly, our ability to test a generalization when 80% to 90% of the needed data are missing is very limited, and especially so in this case, because the missing data would be concentrated heavily in the pre–World War II era and less advanced states.

27. I believe this procedure for identifying economically advanced states errs more on the side of excluding "truly" more advanced states than of including "truly" less advanced states.

28. The exact formula used to derive the Z values was

$$Z = \frac{(P_c - P_u)}{\sqrt{P_u(1 - P_u)/N_c}}$$

where P_c and P_u are the conditional (group) and unconditional (population) probabilities of war and N_c is the number of dyad-years the relevant group is observed. See Blalock (1972, 193–97) or any other basic statistics text for more information.

29. The reader may wonder why there are as many as 24 cases of noncontiguous war dyads. A quick check of these cases reveals that many are characterized by

indirect contiguity, an effect that cannot be assessed with the available data. The problem, of course, is not assessing whether indirect contiguity was present in those 24 instances, but rather of determining which of the 189,193 observations of no war with no direct contiguity are really instances of no war with indirect contiguity.

30. By this I mean that the democratic measurement of *all* states is reviewed and not just of those cases that are seen as "deviant," and that *all* changes in democracy are measured with the same temporal precision, not just exceptional cases. A comprehensive analysis is required, of course, because recodings may generate another set of "deviant" cases.

31. Further information about this method may be found in King (1989, 121–26), Maddala (1983, 51–54), and Greene (1990, 707).

32. The intercept and log (Dyad Years) terms in this table have no substantive importance and will not, therefore, be discussed. It should be noted that, in theory, the coefficient of the latter term should be 1.0, but divergence from this value is harmless (King 1987, 381). I report in this and the following table the standard errors, *t* values, and associated significance levels of the coefficients because some readers may consider them important. Because the "sample" here encompasses 95% of the "population," my own judgement is that they are of marginal value.

EDITORS' COMMENTARY

Major Contributions: Dangerous Dyads

Bremer's study is a landmark article in the scientific study of peace and war. It had three major and lasting impacts. First, it fundamentally changed the way we study war. Bremer compares the militarized interstate disputes (MIDs) that go to war with those that do not and asks what separates the many MIDs that do not go to war from the few that do. A MID is the threat or use of militarized force, something similar to a crisis, but broader in that it includes less dangerous events. Bremer tries to understand why war occurs by examining why some dyads (pairs of states) have MIDs that escalate to deadly wars and others have either no MIDs or MIDs that do not go to war in any given year. Prior to his analysis, scholars had data only on the wars that occurred. This made analyses more limited because there were fewer than 100 wars, and having data only on wars and not on other forms of conflicts confined studies to only certain kinds of inquiries. For example, scholars would study things like which nation-states had wars and which did not. They would also look at whether many wars were correlated with certain factors, such as the number of alliances in the system or the distribution of capability. MIDs, although they do not capture decision-making processes, at least raise the question of why decision makers escalate or do not escalate disputes to war. More than two decades later, scholars are still analyzing MIDs and their escalation because this has been such a fruitful area of inquiry.

The second thing Bremer's article did was to introduce the concept of the dyad. Prior to Bremer, scholars would look at why some nation-states were more prone to war than others (a **monadic** approach) and why systems with certain characteristics had more wars than others (a **systemic** approach). A **dyad** is simply a pair of states (i.e., two states), as opposed to a **triad** (three states) or even a **monad** (looking at a single state such as the United States). Analyzing dyads does something that had not been done before quantitatively—it looks at the *relationship* between two states and sees why they are conflict prone or peaceful. Rather than excluding dyads that did not fight conflicts, Bremer includes all possible dyads in the system and then seeks to understand why conflicts were initiated in 85 of 202,778 dyads from 1816 to 1965.[1] Focusing on dyads assumes that the relationship between two countries is the key to understanding peace and war. In contrast, looking just at the single nation-state, as was prevalent in foreign policy studies, implies that it is something intrinsic about the country that makes it war prone or peace loving. A dyadic analysis (looking at relations between two states) implies that any given country can be at any one time both war prone and peace loving depending on the relationship it has with another country. Likewise, it assumes that the dyadic relationship is more important than any particular system characteristic, such as bipolarity. It turned out that looking at the dyad was tremendously successful and produced many more findings than previous empirical studies on war.

The third impact of Bremer's article was that he introduced a new method for analyzing data. This study shifted the field away from conducting correlations to calculating probabilities. In effect, the field gradually moved away from looking for the correlates of war to examining what factors increase or decrease the probability of war. Bremer's article was one of the first war studies to conduct a bivariate analysis, which examines the relationship between two variables (e.g., alliances and war), and a multivariate analysis, which examines the same relationship (e.g., alliances and war) while taking into account other factors (e.g., contiguity).

None of these impacts, of course, constitute the reason Bremer wrote his article. He did it to try to identify the dangerous dyads (i.e., what characteristics increase the probability that they will go to war). His most noteworthy finding is that two states that are contiguous, which share a land border or are fairly close by sea, have a higher probability of going to war than those that do not share a border.

Being contiguous is more dangerous than being far away. As Bremer was to later explain, this is not unlike the probability of getting into a traffic accident. It is more likely that you will have an accident within fifty miles from home than further away because that is where you do most of your driving. Of course, one would not, as one of our friends did, take off your seat belt because the probability of getting into an accident beyond fifty miles from home goes down!

Contiguous states may be more likely to go to war because this is where most of their interactions occur—some of these will be cooperative, some of them will also involve disagreements, and a small number of those may escalate to war. The further apart two states, the fewer the interactions and hence the disagreements. Of course, states far away may be unable to reach each other due to limited military capability (like lacking a navy) even if they have disagreements (Boulding 1962).

Bremer also found that other characteristics are important both for war and for peace. Two major states are more apt to fight each other, while two minor states are less likely to fight. Having an alliance with the other state in the dyad increases the likelihood of war, especially if the states are both increasing their militaries. If both sides in the dyad are democratic, this reduces the probability of war. Surprisingly, Bremer found that large, medium, or small differences in power are **statistically insignificant** (see methodological notes) in terms of their impact on the likelihood of war. Altogether, Bremer looks at seven predictors of war (geographical proximity, power parity, power status, alliances, democracy, development, and militarization) and the theoretical rationale for expecting that they either increase or reduce the probability of war between dyads. He concludes his analysis by looking at the combination of these variables to see what kinds of dyads have the highest likelihood of going to war (Table 5).

In a later article, Bremer (2000) extended this study by asking who fights whom, when, where, and why. This is an important set of questions because it provides a more in-depth way of conducting a dyadic analysis. It looks not just at dangerous dyads but also at who fights whom and, by implication, who does not fight whom. This is meant to identify an empirical pattern. Bremer then follows up by asking why this pattern occurs. Identification of empirical patterns coupled with subsequent explanation was a hallmark of the research approach of the Correlates of War project expounded by J. David Singer (1979, 163). Although less popular today because scholars like to have an ex ante theoretical rationale for patterns before they find them, at the time, this was Singer's reaction to much theoretical analysis without any attempt to even find empirical patterns, let alone test hypotheses (Singer 1969).

Bremer ends his review of who fights whom with his top four findings based on a review of the empirical literature: states that are geographically proximate are most apt to fight each other. Next are those that have a history of fighting (or multiple MIDs) with each other. Third, he finds that the strong tend to fight the strong. Last, he argues that ideologically similar states tend not to fight each other. Of course, the major finding in this area is that joint democracies do not fight each other (see Oneal and Russett 1999, Chapter 9, this volume).

Since Bremer published his article, the finding on contiguity has been heavily studied. Vasquez (1993, chap. 4; 1995) questions whether contiguity is the real factor making MIDs escalate to war. He argues that contiguous states fight wars primarily because they are disputing territory. Being contiguous is a constant, and since contiguous states are not always fighting wars, something must vary that makes them be at war sometimes and at peace at other times. Vasquez and Henehan (2001) show that territorial disputes are much more war prone than other types of MIDs. Hensel (2000) and Vasquez (2001) show that territorial disputes have an increased probability of going to war regardless of whether states are contiguous. In fact, Vasquez (2001) finds that noncontiguous states that have territorial disputes have a higher probability of going to war than contiguous states.

This does not mean that contiguous states are not prone to conflict. Senese (2005) has the most definitive analysis to date. He finds that contiguous states are more apt to have a MID of some sort, but when controlling for that fact (in a two-stage model), he finds that states that have a territorial MID are more likely to go to war. In other words, once states have a territorial dispute, they are more apt to go to war no matter if they are contiguous.

Methodological Notes: Percentages and Probabilities

The key to understanding this article is to concentrate on Table 1. There are four basic statistics that permit you to infer whether a given factor, such as contiguity, significantly increases or decreases the probability of a dyadic war. The easiest statistics to understand are the two numbers in column 2 under "War Dyads." In the row labeled *land contiguous,* the two numbers are 48 and (4.4). On the previous page, Bremer tells us that these two numbers represent the observed and expected number of wars. The value 48 reveals that land contiguous dyads have 48 wars, and the (4.4) value tells us the expected number of wars if the two variables were statistically independent. In other words, if wars were randomly distributed among 10,542 land contiguous dyads in the data (see column 3), one would "expect" that the land contiguous dyads would only have 4.4 wars. Since the land contiguous dyads have so many more wars than expected, we can infer at least initially using bivariate analysis that the hypothesis that land contiguity increases the probability of war can be accepted. Thus, whenever the number of observed wars is greater than the expected, we can see this as a factor increasing the probability of war, so long as the difference is considerable, as it is in this case.

Now look at the row labeled *not contiguous*. Look at the two numbers—24 observed and (79.3) expected. What do you think these two numbers tell us about the probability of war among dyads that are not contiguous? When the states in dyads are not contiguous, they experience 24 wars, but 79.3 are expected. This means that this kind of dyad has many *fewer* wars than expected. From this we can infer that when a dyad is noncontiguous, it experiences a reduction in the probability of war. If you turn to the fifth column where Z scores appear, you will see that the numbers there can be negative or positive. In this case of noncontiguous dyads, the number is –6.21. This means that being noncontiguous decreases the probability of war. This is exhibited by the negative (–) sign. Whenever the observed number of dyadic cases is less than the expected number of cases, there will be a reduction in the probability of war, and this is indicated by a negative Z score.

The fourth column, pr(War), contains the most interesting and detailed information. It reports the "conditional probability" of war. *Conditional probability* means the probability of war when dyads are in the "condition" reported in column 1. Thus, when states are in the condition of "land contiguous," Bremer reports that the probability of having a war is 4.55. This number, however, has been "adjusted" by Bremer to make it easier to read, as he reports in the page preceding the table. The actual probability is 0.0045, and he has multiplied it by 1,000 to make some of the smaller probabilities easier to read. This is a very small probability of war, but that is not too surprising because Bremer is looking at the probability of war in any specific dyad *in any given year* (the so-called dyad year).

But how do we interpret the conditional probability of war? It only makes sense if we know what the overall general probability of war is in a given data set. This is called the **base** probability or **unconditional** probability of war (i.e., the probability of war among all dyads). Bremer reports this as a fraction on the page preceding the table—85/202,778. If we divide 85 (the number of dyadic war cases) by the denominator 202,778 (the number of total dyad years), we get a probability of 0.000419. Since the probability of war for land contiguous dyads is 0.0045 and that is considerably higher than the unconditional probability of 0.000419, we can conclude that land contiguity increases the probability of war. By looking at the conditional probabilities in column 4 (pr(War)) and comparing each with the unconditional probability to see if it is higher or lower, one can see whether the "condition" increases or lowers the probability of war.

What is most important is whether this difference is statistically significant—in other words, whether the relationship between contiguity and war is random and due to chance or whether there is some sort of connection between the two variables. **Statistical significance** is used to accept or reject a null hypothesis being tested. In Table 1, Bremer is testing to see if each variable is statistically independent from the dependent variable of war onset. Under the null hypothesis of independence, we would expect a particular condition (e.g., contiguity) to have a similar probability of war in comparison to another condition (e.g., all dyads). Bremer calculates a Z score comparing the conditional (P_c) and unconditional (P_u) probabilities of war. If two variables were statistically independent, the Z score would be equal to zero because the likelihood of war would be the same for all dyads and those in the specific condition (e.g., contiguity), and thus the difference between P_c and P_u would be zero. As the Z score gets larger (either in a positive or negative direction), we are more likely to reject the null hypothesis of independence and conclude that the two variables are related to each other. Positive Z scores tell us that the conditional probability (P_c) is much larger than the unconditional probability (P_u), such as the case for comparing war in contiguous dyads to war in all dyads. Negative Z scores imply the opposite, that the chances for war are higher in the unconditional case (e.g., all dyads vs. jointly democratic dyads).

In footnote 28, Bremer presents the formula used to calculate the Z scores in Table 1:

$$Z = \frac{\left(P_c - P_u\right)}{\sqrt{P_u\left(1 - P_u\right)/N_c}}.$$

For the first row in Table 1 (land contiguity), this Z score is calculated as follows:

$$Z = \frac{(.00455 - .000419)}{\sqrt{(.000419)(.99958)/10,542}}.$$

$$Z = 20.74 \ (p < .0001).$$

The last column in Table 1, pr(Z), tells us the chances that the relationship as reported in the two probabilities is random or significant given the sample size. You can see that the chances that it is random are <0.0001, only 1 out of 10,000. In political science, by convention it is accepted that if the chances of a relationship being random are only 5 out of 100 ($p < 0.05$) or smaller, then we accept it as nonrandom or statistically significant. The basic idea is that if we were to conduct this test 100 times, 95 of the tests would conclude that the calculated Z score was significantly different from zero (e.g., that land contiguity and war are related to each other).

It should be clear that the probabilities Bremer calculates are just simple percentages. This can be seen in the unconditional probability of war, which is reported as a fraction (85/202,778). The numerator is derived by summing the number of observed wars in column 1 for each type of contiguity (land, sea, and noncontiguous: 48 + 13 + 24 = 85), and the denominator is derived by summing the three numbers in column 3, total dyads, which are the total number of dyads for which Bremer has data on contiguity. Likewise, the conditional probability of war for land contiguity (0.00455) is derived by the number of wars for land contiguous dyads that have the condition of being "land contiguous," or 48/10,542.

You may wonder where the "expected" value comes from. Remember the expected value is the number of wars a dyad in a certain condition can be expected to have *if the number of wars were distributed randomly*. To determine this, we multiply the base probability of 0.000419 times the number of (total) dyads that have a condition, in this case 10,542, which will produce the expected value of 4.4.

As noted earlier, Bremer also conducts multivariate analysis, which takes into account the correlations among the seven risk factors for war. This is important because there may be relationships among the variables that are not uncovered when looking at each risk factor's individual effect on dyadic war onset. For example, economic development and democracy might share a positive correlation if economically advanced states are also more likely to be democratic. In Table 3, Bremer estimates a Poisson regression model, which is designed to model the probability of a random variable that captures the number of times an event has occurred in a certain period (e.g., year). This model is appropriate because he measures the number of war onsets in a given year. Positive coefficients (e.g., 1.780 for contiguous dyads) imply that the number of war onsets is expected to be higher in that condition, while negative coefficients suggest that the number of war onsets would be lower under that condition (e.g., both more advanced, −1.275). Statistical significance tests in this table are conducted by calculating a *t*-ratio (column 4), which divides the estimated coefficient (column 2) by the estimated standard error (column 3). The final column provides the probability that the *t*-ratio would be this large under the null hypothesis (where the coefficient would be zero). We use the same approach and consider a variable to have a statistically significant effect if the probability (or **p-value**) is less than 0.05. We can see that most variables are statistically significant in predicting the number of war onsets, except allied and both militarized. There are some differences between the bivariate and multivariate results. Using a multivariate model, we would conclude that economically advanced states are less likely to fight wars, while the bivariate model would tell us that these dyads have a higher likelihood of war. The differences reflect the failure of the bivariate model to account for the correlations among the independent variables. We would have a high level of confidence in our findings if they showed similar patterns in the bivariate and multivariate models. For example, contiguity has a positive effect on the chances for war in the bivariate and multivariate models. This tells us that this risk factor for war has a strong effect no matter what other risk factors we take into consideration.

Note

1. Bremer includes only the initial pair of states in a large multilateral conflict, such as World War II (Germany-Poland). This has the advantage of capturing the triggering conditions for the start of the war, but it has the downside of losing a large number of conflict cases. Many studies after Bremer's piece included these "joiner dyads" in their analysis.

Questions

1. Under the Democracy and War (Chan) finding in Table 1:
   (a) What do the numbers of observed and expected wars tell us?
   (b) What does the Z score tell us? Is it statistically significant?

2. What factors in Table 1 are not significant? How do you know they are not significant?

3. Which of these risk factors could most easily be manipulated by the states involved? Could dangerous dyads figure out a way to engineer peace?

Further Reading

Bennett, D. S., and A. C. Stam III. 2004. *The behavioral origins of war.* Princeton, NJ: Princeton University Press.

Bremer, S. A. 2000. Who fights whom, when, where, and why? In *What do we know about war?* ed. J. A. Vasquez. Lanham, MD: Rowman & Littlefield.

Hensel, P. R. 2000. Territory: Theory and evidence on geography and conflict. In *What do we know about war?* ed. J. A. Vasquez. Lanham, MD: Rowman & Littlefield.

Senese, P. D. 2005. Territory, contiguity, and international conflict: Assessing a new joint explanation. *American Journal of Political Science* 49 (4): 769–79.

Vasquez, J. A., and M. T. Henehan. 2001. Territorial disputes and the probability of war, 1816–1992. *Journal of Peace Research* 38 (2): 123–38.

Chapter 3

Bones of Contention

Comparing Territorial, Maritime, and River Issues

Paul R. Hensel, Sara McLaughlin Mitchell, Thomas E. Sowers II, and Clayton L. Thyne

For several decades, scholars have called for an issues-based approach to world politics (Diehl 1992; Hensel 2001; Mansbach and Vasquez 1981; O'Leary 1976; Potter 1980; Vasquez 1993). This call has been met by research examining the issues involved in militarized conflict (Hensel 1996a; Holsti 1991; Mitchell and Prins 1999; Senese 2005; Vasquez and Henehan 2001), as well as studies that examine both militarized and peaceful interaction over territorial issues (Hensel 2001; Huth and Allee 2002; Mitchell 2002). The appearance of so many studies is a promising sign, but there is an important gap in this literature. Aside from work on militarized conflict, which has only been able to measure issue salience with broad issue categories, there has been no systematic comparison of how issues are managed. If an issues approach is to become a serious scholarly research program, much more needs to be done to investigate the similarities and differences in the management of different types of issues, and to determine the extent to which multiple types of issues can be explained by the same theories and aggregated in the same analyses.

This paper uses newly collected data to compare states' management of three distinct types of issues: disagreements over territory, maritime zones, and cross-border rivers. We examine states' decisions to use both militarized and peaceful foreign policy tools to manage or resolve disagreements over these issues, emphasizing the impact of issue salience and recent interactions over the issue. Our findings suggest a number of commonalities in the handling of these issues: states are more likely to employ both militarized action and peaceful techniques over issues that are seen as more salient, that have already led to armed conflict, and that have experienced unsuccessful peaceful settlement efforts. We conclude by discussing implications of these results, and by suggesting possible directions for additional research on contentious issues.

An Issues Approach to World Politics

Hensel (2001) outlines a systematic approach to the study of issues, drawing from work by such scholars as Randle (1987), Holsti (1991), Diehl (1992), and Vasquez (1993). The central element of an issue-based approach is that policy makers are concerned with achieving their goals over specific issues, rather than simply pursuing such vague notions as power or security. An issue can best be described as "a disputed point or question, the subject of a conflict or controversy" (Randle 1987, 1), or with respect to armed conflict, "what states choose to fight over, not the conditions that led to the choice of military force as the means" (Diehl 1992, 333). Issues in world politics are thus the subjects of disagreements between nation-states.

Source: Paul R. Hensel, Sara McLaughlin Mitchell, Thomas E. Sowers II, and Clayton L. Thyne, "Bones of Contention: Comparing Territorial, Maritime, and River Issues," *Journal of Conflict Resolution* 52, no. 1 (February 2008): 117–43. © 2008 SAGE Publications, Inc.

Issues can involve competing views over the disposition of concrete or tangible stakes, such as control over a particular territory, the removal of a leader, or the implementation or termination of a specific policy (e.g., trade or immigration). Issues may also involve competing views on intangible stakes, such as influence, prestige, or ideological or philosophical questions (Holsti 1991, 18–19; Diehl 1992; Randle 1987, 1–2). Whatever the stakes, policy makers are concerned with issues because of the "values" that the issues represent, such as physical survival, wealth, security, independence, or status. Because of these values, issues vary in salience, which can be defined as "the degree of importance attached to that issue by the actors involved" (Diehl 1992, 334) or "the extent to which (but principally, the intensity with which) peoples and their leaders value an issue and its subject matter" (Randle 1987, 2).

Finally, state leaders may choose among numerous cooperative or conflictual policy tools to pursue their goals over issues. Leaders may choose to negotiate over their differences, either bilaterally or with the nonbinding assistance of third parties. They may also agree to submit their disputes to binding third party judgments, or they may unilaterally threaten or use military force to achieve their goals. From an issue-based perspective, these policy tools are best seen as substitutable techniques that can be used to pursue the same end of achieving issue-related goals.[1] The purpose of this paper is to examine states' choices between these techniques for managing issues. We focus on issue salience in terms of both general differences in salience between different types of issues (territorial, maritime, river) and variation in salience within each issue type being studied (e.g., high salience territory vs. low salience territory).

Categorizing Issue Types

Bearing these general points in mind, the success of any issue-based approach depends on the conceptualization of issues. It is not enough to argue that numerous issue types exist or that "issues matter" without guidelines for how to identify, categorize, or measure issues and their salience. An early effort by Rosenau (1971) classifies issues by the tangibility or intangibility of the values to be allocated and the means employed to effect allocation. Yet a single issue type, such as territory, may be important for both tangible and intangible reasons. Additionally, a variety of means can be used to effect allocation of any issue, ranging from military force to negotiations or adjudication. It would be difficult and misleading to categorize any particular issue as involving either tangible or intangible means. The International Crisis Behavior (ICB) project categorizes issues into four categories based on the specific substantive area of contention, including military security, political-diplomatic, economic development, and cultural status (Brecher and Wilkenfeld 1997). However, these categories are not mutually exclusive. Territorial issues, for one, can be important for reasons related to any of these four categories. Holsti (1991) has provided the most comprehensive categorization by listing dozens of issues that have been at stake in war since 1648, but this list is meant as a description of the issues that have led to war rather than a comprehensive list of issues that might lead to war, and there is no comprehensive theoretical differentiation between the various issues.

We propose an alternative categorization that is based on the *tangible* and *intangible* values that issues hold for the contending states. The following list—adapted from Lasswell and Kaplan (1950), Maslow (1970), and Mansbach and Vasquez (1981, 58)—represents the values that we believe are most useful for the study of international conflict and cooperation, sorted alphabetically rather than in any order of presumed importance:

Tangible Values

Security: Safety from external danger (absence of threats or protection from threats)

Survival: Provision of basic human needs (food/water/shelter) Wealth: Accumulation of resources, goods, or money (beyond basic human needs)

Intangible Values

Culture/Identity: Related to one's cultural, religious, or ideological beliefs or identity

Equality/Justice: "Fairness" or impartiality in the distribution of other values Independence: Ability to formulate and implement one's own policies Status/Prestige/Influence: The degree of respect one is accorded by others

Several scholars have attempted to rank values in relative importance. Holsti (1991, 24) for example, suggests that "[c]ontests over strategic territory, for example, are more likely than disagreements over trade policy to generate contests of arms. Security is a more important value in most eras than is welfare." Similarly, Maslow produces a hierarchy of human needs, whereby higher needs become important only when more fundamental needs are met. Physiological needs, such as food and water, are most fundamental, followed by security needs, belongingness needs, self-esteem needs, and self-actualization needs. Yet Lasswell and Kaplan (1950, 56–57) explicitly rejected any effort to produce universal rankings: "While there may be similarities of 'motive, passion and desire' among various persons and cultures, there are differences as well, differences especially in the comparative importance attached to the various values. No generalizations can be made a priori concerning the scale of values of all groups and individuals. . . . In particular, it is impossible to assign a universally dominant role to some one value or other." We follow Lasswell and Kaplan in remaining agnostic over ranking the priority of values for nation-states, although (as will be seen) we attempt to rank issues by salience.

Different types of issues can be seen as varying along these two dimensions of tangible and intangible salience. Although individual examples of each issue type may vary in both tangible and intangible salience, general types of issues may be classified as being relatively high or low along each dimension. "Relatively high" values indicate that a typical issue generally has important value for the state's leadership or for a substantial portion of its population. "Relatively low" values indicate either that the issue does not involve any meaningful salience of this type, or that it only has such value for a small portion of the state's population. Table 1 offers examples of issues that typically take on high or low values along each dimension.

Territory, for example, is often described as quite important to states for both tangible and intangible reasons (Hensel 1996b; Hensel and Mitchell 2005; Vasquez 1993). Territorial claims often involve land that contains economic and/or strategic value, thus

Table 1   Variations in Issue Types Based on Tangibility and Salience

	Relatively Low Intangible Salience	Relatively High Intangible Salience
Relatively High Tangible Salience	River (Turkish dam projects on Euphrates River) Maritime (Cod Wars)	Territory (Golan Heights, Alsace-Lorraine) Regime survival (Castro)
Relatively Low Tangible Salience	Firms or industries (Airbus subsidies, shrimp imports) Treatment of individuals (caning of Michael Fay)	Identity (treatment of Germans in South Tyrol) Influence (Russia and elections in former Soviet republics)

relating to the tangible values of wealth and physical security. Beyond this tangible importance, many territories also take on enormous intangible significance, coming to be viewed as part of a state's national identity as well as being tied closely to the intangible values of independence and perhaps status/prestige. Although individual territorial claims may involve specific pieces of land with little tangible value or with little intangible significance for either participant, territorial issues in general may be seen as taking on relatively high values on both dimensions. Issues of regime survival also seem to take on high values of both tangible and intangible salience, at least for the members of the targeted regime (e.g., U.S. efforts to remove Fidel Castro and his regime from Cuba). Although the issue may be primarily intangible (involving influence or prestige) for the challenger seeking to remove the regime, the targeted regime and its supporters likely see the issue as one of both physical survival (tangible) and continued independence (intangible).

Many issues can take on relatively high values along either the tangible or intangible dimension, although they are lacking in the other dimension. Issues involving cross-border water resources can be quite salient, particularly in water-scarce areas such as the Middle East, as can maritime issues for coastal states that depend heavily on fishing (e.g., the "Cod Wars" between the United Kingdom and Iceland). Yet river and maritime issues rarely approach territorial issues in intangible value. Similarly, Russian efforts to support pro-Russian candidates and policies in former Soviet republics and U.S. efforts to support pro-American candidates and policies in Latin America have much more to do with the intangible value of influence than with any tangible value for Russia or the United States. Austria's post–World War II demands over the treatment of ethnic Germans in South Tyrol and Russia's demands over the treatment of ethnic Russians in the Baltic states are based primarily on intangible values like identity and have little tangible value (neither Austria nor Russia seeks to annex the areas where their kinsmen live).

Finally, issues with little tangible or intangible value include issues associated with individuals, firms, or industries. Disagreements such as U.S. complaints over European subsidies to Airbus (a competitor to American aerospace firms) or a number of recent WTO disputes over shrimp imports may be important to individual firms or industries. Likewise, concern for a state's national who is imprisoned abroad, such as the 1994 American attempt to prevent the caning of U.S. citizen Michael Fay for vandalism in Singapore, may be quite important for the individual whose livelihood or freedom is threatened. Yet there is little tangible or intangible value in such issues for most of the state's leaders or population.

Based on this categorization of issues as having relatively high or low values of both tangible and intangible salience, it is possible to offer some general expectations about the relative salience of different types of issues. We are not willing to offer a detailed ranking of, say, the dozens of issues identified by Holsti (1991). We do expect, though, that the most salient types of issues overall will be those that take on relatively high values of both tangible and intangible salience, such as claims to territory. Not only do these issues have tangible values at stake for the participants, but they also have the added complication of intangible values that are not easily negotiated or compromised. We classify issue types with relatively high values of either tangible or intangible salience (but not both) as having moderate salience overall. Examples include competing claims over maritime zones or cross-border rivers (tangible), as well as over the treatment of minorities or communal groups (intangible).[2] Finally, we consider issue types with relatively low values of both tangible and intangible salience as having low salience overall. Examples include issues related to specific individuals or corporations.

Salience within Issue Types

In addition to differences in salience between issues, the salience of specific issues *within* any general issue type can vary considerably. For example, some maritime areas may be highly salient to one or more states. The territorial sea around Iceland, for example, almost produced a war between Iceland and the United Kingdom in the 1970s because the fisheries in this area are extremely important to both claimants' economies. Other maritime areas are less salient to leaders. The United States contests Canada's claim of sovereignty over the Northwest Passage, for example, arguing that it is an international waterway. However, commercial navigation through the Passage is not currently practical, and neither side views the issue as justifying drastic measures. Similarly, the Golan Heights territory is highly salient to both Israel and Syria for its strategic position as well as for its control over scarce water resources. In contrast, some claimed territories, such as Navassa Island (claimed by Haiti from the United States), offer neither military nor economic benefits.

Variation in salience within issues might make a huge difference in understanding the linkage between issues and conflict. For example, Diehl (1992, 340) notes that "different issues may share some characteristic that make them equally likely to promote violence," and that "the same issue may prompt different behavior because of variation along one of the issue characteristic dimensions." Although a variety of empirical analyses have found territorial issues to be more conflictual than other issues overall, then, it seems likely that certain nonterritorial issues are also quite conflictual, and that certain territorial issues are much less conflictual than the overall patterns seem to indicate.

Hypotheses on Issue Management

As noted earlier, states may choose among numerous policy tools to pursue their goals with respect to contentious issues. They may threaten or use militarized force, or they may pursue peaceful settlement options, such as bilateral negotiations, negotiation with the nonbinding assistance of third parties (e.g., good offices, inquiry, conciliation, or mediation), or submission of the issue to the binding judgment of a third party (e.g., arbitration or adjudication). We are interested in identifying factors that make leaders more or less likely to select each of these foreign policy options.[3] The effectiveness of these different settlement techniques lies beyond the scope of the present paper, though, and will be left for future work.

Hypotheses on Issue Salience

We begin by considering the impact of issue salience, which is central to an issue-based conception of world politics. Most issue scholars argue that salience, or the value attached to an issue by the participants, affects the choices that the participants make over the management of the issue. For example, Randle (1987, 9, 17) describes the existence of a contentious issue as creating the basic conditions for competition and conflict between states, but argues that more salient issues are more likely to produce the commitment of high levels of resources and the willingness to bear significant costs: "The severity of the conflict depends upon how intensely the parties value the matter at issue." Similarly, Diehl (1992, 339) suggests that salience could be a "loose necessary condition" for conflict behavior: "When the stakes are high enough, states will be willing to use military force to achieve their goals."[4]

From this perspective, policy makers should be willing to pursue costlier or riskier options to achieve their goals over issues that are considered highly salient than over less important issues. The threat or use of military force is a particularly dangerous option because it cannot guarantee a satisfactory outcome but involves the risk of extensive human and economic costs. Low-salience issues are unlikely to be seen as justifying the costs and risks of military action, especially when more peaceful foreign policy techniques such as negotiations could be used instead. When a highly salient issue is at stake, though, leaders should be quite concerned with both gaining the benefits of winning on the issue and avoiding the costs of losing on the issue, which may outweigh the costs and risks of using force to achieve their goals.

As we have already discussed, issue salience can have several different meanings. We expect militarized conflict to be more likely to be used for managing issues that are generally considered highly salient—most notably territorial issues, which typically feature relatively high values of both tangible and intangible salience—than for generally less salient issues with relatively low values of tangible and/or intangible salience.[5] We also expect within-issue salience to have a similar effect, such that issues of any issue type that are more salient than other issues of the same type should be more likely to produce militarized conflict. In other words, the use of militarized force should be more likely when a claim is highly salient, regardless of the general type of claim involved (territory, maritime, or river). This is one of the first studies to allow testing of both meanings of salience. Hensel (2001), for example, finds that militarized conflict is more likely over more salient territorial issues than over less salient territories, but that study could not determine whether similar patterns also hold for other issue types or whether that result is unique to territory. We thus propose the following hypotheses:

Hypothesis 1a: States are more likely to threaten or use militarized force over issue types that are generally more salient than over issues that are generally less salient.

Hypothesis 1b: States are more likely to threaten or use militarized force when the specific issue under contention is more salient.

Although we hypothesize that armed conflict should be more likely over highly salient issues than over less salient issues, conflict is not the only way that such issues will be handled, nor is it necessarily the most frequent way. We expect that peaceful settlement activities should also be more likely over highly salient issues than over those that are less salient. The main reason for the higher likelihood of peaceful activities is the expected costs and risks from different policy options. If the state believes that it can achieve its desired outcome through either military force or peaceful negotiations, then the option with the lowest costs should be more likely to be chosen *(ceteris paribus)*. And when the issue is highly salient, it is reasonable to expect the costs of militarized conflict to be relatively high, as the opponent should be likely to oppose any military moves to settle the issue.

Although there may not be a high probability of diplomatic success from a given round of peaceful settlement attempts, we expect that these options will be employed much more often when issues are salient. We also expect that third parties will be more likely to become involved in seeking to manage or settle highly salient issues, either as active participants in nonbinding settlement techniques (e.g., good offices or mediation), or by pushing the claimants to resolve their issues peacefully before they escalate and threaten regional stability. Indeed, we expect that peaceful activities should be even more likely than militarized conflict at any given level of salience, although both militarized and peaceful activities should be more likely as the salience of the issue increases.

As with militarized conflict, we expect peaceful issue management to be influenced by both meanings of issue salience. We expect peaceful settlement techniques to be more likely to be used for the management of issues that are generally considered highly salient—most notably, territorial issues—than for managing generally less salient issues. We also expect within-issue salience variation to have a similar effect, such that issues of any issue type that are more salient than other issues of the same type should be more likely to produce peaceful settlement efforts. This expectation leads to the following hypotheses:

Hypothesis 2a: States are more likely to pursue peaceful settlement attempts over issue types that are generally more salient than over issues that are generally less salient.

Hypothesis 2b: States are more likely to pursue peaceful settlement attempts when the specific issue under contention is more salient.

Hypotheses on Past Issue Management

Beyond the impact of issue salience, we also expect interactions between states at one point in time to have important consequences for their relations in the future. For example, research on recurrent conflict and rivalry suggests that as states build up a longer history of militarized conflict, they view each other with much greater distrust and suspicion, leading them to see the other as a more serious threat in future relations. Furthermore, to the extent that earlier conflicts led to changes in the *status quo* (e.g., the seizure of disputed territory or the destruction of a river diversion project) or led to casualties, the history of conflict may harden both sides' positions and promote militarized conflict as a more appropriate policy option. Drawing from such arguments, research on the evolution of interstate rivalry (Diehl and Goertz 2000; Hensel 1999, 2001) and repeated crises (Colaresi and Thompson 2002; Leng 1983) has found substantial evidence that states become increasingly likely to become involved in future militarized conflict as they accumulate a longer history of conflict.

Hensel's (1999) evolutionary approach to rivalry suggests that past interactions between two states could lead them along either a more conflictual path toward rivalry or a more cooperative path toward better relations, depending on what the states do to each other and what outcome results. Most evolutionary research on rivalry has focused on militarized conflict as both the primary independent variable (the type of past behavior being studied) and the primary dependent variable (the type of future behavior being explained).[6] Yet the general evolutionary arguments that have been laid out could potentially be applied equally well to peaceful forms of interaction, in terms of both the past behavior being studied and the future behavior being explained. Indeed, Hensel (1999) explicitly calls for

extending this approach to nonmilitarized interactions, and Hensel (2001) examines evolution in both militarized and nonmilitarized dimensions of territorial claims in the Americas. The present study goes even further.

Past armed conflict is not the only form of interaction that can shape states' perceptions of the adversary, issue satisfaction, or expectations about the future. Armed conflict is only one of numerous tools that can be used to manage or settle contentious issues, and the occurrence and outcome of peaceful settlement techniques should have similar effects. Much like two states that have engaged in repeated armed conflict are likely to expect similar actions to continue in the future (Hensel 1999, 184–86; Hensel 2001, 88), two states that have repeatedly failed to settle their contentious issues peacefully are likely to expect their negotiating partner to be less interested in compromise or peaceful settlement. This situation should increase the likelihood of armed conflict, as peaceful techniques seem less promising. On the other hand, just like two states that have not previously engaged in armed conflict, two states that have not yet gone through failed negotiations may be more optimistic about the prospects for a peaceful settlement, with less expectation of failure or armed conflict in the future. Thus, peaceful options should be more appealing and militarized options less so.

Considering both militarized and peaceful past interactions leads us to suggest that future conflict should be more likely when states have longer histories of either conflict or failed peaceful efforts, either of which should produce the expectation (on both sides) that peaceful techniques are unlikely to settle the issue successfully. As with salience, the same factors that predict greater armed conflict may also predict greater efforts to settle issues peacefully. When an issue has been marked by repeated conflict or by the repeated failure of peaceful efforts, the adversaries may attempt negotiations in an effort to avoid the risk of future conflict, if not to settle the conflict permanently. Third parties should also be much more likely to promote peaceful settlement in such situations, whether by direct involvement or simply by promoting direct negotiations between the claimants. This discussion suggests the following hypotheses:

Hypothesis 3: States are more likely to threaten or use militarized force when they have a history of recent militarized conflict over the same issue and/or a history of recent failed attempts to settle the same issue peacefully.

Hypothesis 4: States are more likely to pursue peaceful settlements when they have a history of recent militarized conflict over the same issue and/or a history of recent failed attempts to settle the same issue peacefully.

It must be emphasized that issue characteristics alone will not explain all interstate behavior. We control for two other factors that we expect to have systematic effects: joint democracy and relative capabilities. Drawing from the vast literature on democratic peace, we expect militarized conflict to be less likely between two democratic adversaries than when one or both claimants are not democratic. Furthermore, because of the norms of peaceful conflict resolution that are said to characterize democracies' foreign policy, we expect peaceful conflict management to be more likely to be attempted between two democratic adversaries than when one or both claimants is not democratic (Dixon 1994; Russett and Oneal 2001).

The relative capabilities of the two claimants should also have an important effect. We expect militarized conflict to be most likely between evenly matched adversaries, and less likely in situations where one claimant is substantially stronger than its opponent (Kugler and Lemke 1996; Organski and Kugler 1980). We also expect peaceful conflict management to be less likely between uneven adversaries because the stronger state should have little urgency for settling its issues with a much weaker opponent. Peaceful settlement activities should be more likely between relatively even adversaries, which face a higher perceived risk of armed conflict and a greater risk of losing should they fail to settle their contentious issues (Hensel 2001).

Research Design

Testing the hypotheses presented above, like the development of the issues approach more generally, involves a number of specific data requirements. Multiple types of issues must be identified systematically, the salience of each issue must be measured in a way that allows comparison both within and across issue types, and both militarized and peaceful attempts to manage or settle each issue must also be identified. The Issue Correlates of War (ICOW) project has attempted to meet each of these requirements and has currently completed the coding of data on three types of issues: territorial claims (Western Hemisphere and Western Europe from 1816 to 2001), maritime claims (Western Hemisphere and Europe from 1900 to 2001), and river claims (Western Hemisphere, Western Europe, and the Middle East from 1900 to 2001).

Identifying Contentious Issues

The most important requirement for systematic data on issues is evidence of explicit contention by official representatives of two or more nation-states. For the three current ICOW issue types, this means evidence that official representatives of at least one state make explicit statements claiming sovereignty over a specific piece of territory that is claimed or administered by another state, or contesting the use or abuse of a specific international river or maritime zone. Requiring explicit statement of a claim by official government representatives helps avoid charges of tautology, which might otherwise weaken or discredit the endeavor (e.g., by arguing that all wars are about territory because the combatants seek to capture territory to win the war, or by assuming that any conflict between neighbors sharing a river must be over the river itself).

It is also important that the claim be stated by official government representatives, or individuals authorized to state official government policy, and that this statement is not disavowed by other official sources. Many potential claims are stated by private individuals, legislators, corporations, rebel groups, or other actors, typically for personal or financial motivations. Unless official governmental representatives support the claim, though, it does not qualify for inclusion in the data set. For example, although various individuals have pushed for the creation of a Greater Albania incorporating parts of Kosovo, Serbia's Presevo Valley, and Macedonia as well as Albania itself, we have seen no credible evidence that this is the official position of the Albanian government.

Finally, this definition does not require any specific form of contention or interaction over the claim, beyond the explicit statement of the claim itself. In particular, it does not require that one or both sides resort to militarized force over the claim, meaning that the data set includes a number of cases that never led to the threat or use of force by either claimant. Similarly, it does not require that the adversaries negotiate over the claim, submit it to third party arbitration or adjudication, or take any action whatsoever over the claim. Some cases may not lead to any action of any kind, instead being allowed to fade away gradually. Both peaceful and militarized actions over a claim are more properly the subject of systematic analysis using complete compilations of all issue claims, rather than tools to be used for case selection.

Based on these coding rules, the ICOW Project has identified a total of 244 claims to distinct territories, maritime zones, or rivers in the regions for which data collection is currently complete in version 1.10 of the ICOW data set, representing 416 dyadic claims. This total includes 122 territorial claims (representing 191 dyadic claims), 86 maritime claims (143 dyadic claims), and 36 river claims (82 dyadic claims), covering a total of 10,041 claim-dyad-years (the unit of analysis). The complete list of cases is available on the ICOW Web site at http://data.icow.org.

Dependent Variable: Issue Settlement Attempts

Each ICOW claims data set includes data on attempts to manage or settle the issues involved in a claim. In this paper we focus on two general dependent variables: militarized conflict and peaceful settlement attempts. Militarized attempts to settle issues are identified using version 3.02 of the Correlates of War Project's Militarized Interstate Dispute (MID) data set (Ghosn, Palmer, and Bremer 2004). Each militarized dispute that occurred between two adversaries involved in an ongoing territorial, river, or maritime claim was examined to determine whether the dispute involved an attempt to change the territorial, river, or maritime status quo with respect to that specific claim.[7] This determination was based on standard news sources and diplomatic histories, as well as on the chronologies of each ICOW claim. This definition yields 318 militarized attempts to settle contentious issues (205 territorial, 19 river, and 94 maritime).

Although militarized attempts to settle issues can be identified using readily available data sets, much more work is required to identify and code peaceful attempts to settle ICOW claims because this information is not available in any other social science data set. Four specific topics can be covered by these peaceful attempted settlements, including (1) negotiations meant to settle the entire claim; (2) negotiations over a smaller part of the claim; (3) negotiations over procedures for future settlement of the claim ("procedural" attempts, such as talks over submitting the claim to arbitration by a specific third party); and (4) negotiations over the use of the claimed territory, river, or maritime area without attempting to settle the question of ownership ("functional" attempts, such as talks over navigation along a disputed river border). All other negotiations, such as talks over a ceasefire to stop an ongoing crisis, are excluded.

The ICOW Project codes settlement attempts that involve bilateral negotiations, negotiations with nonbinding third party assistance (inquiry, conciliation, good offices, or mediation), or submission of a claim to binding arbitration or adjudication (Hensel 2001). It is important to include all of these different types of peaceful settlement attempts because each is meant to accomplish the same goal of issue management. For example, data sets used in past research on issues or in conflict management (e.g., the MID, ICB, and SHERFACS data sets) have focused on armed conflict and have considered only peaceful attempts to manage ongoing crises or wars. An exclusive focus on attempts to manage claims that have become militarized (Dixon 1993, 1994; Wilkenfeld and Brecher 1984) is likely to understate the effectiveness of peaceful means for dispute settlement, because it examines only the most intractable and conflictual issues and excludes cases that avoided militarized conflict entirely. Indeed, less than 9 percent of the peaceful settlement attempts in this paper's analyses (141 of 1687, or 8.4 percent) began during militarized disputes or wars, meaning that over 90 percent of these cases would have been left out of most research on conflict management.[8] Of the 1687 total peaceful settlement attempts, 1004 were for territorial claims, 190 for river, and 493 for maritime claims.

Independent Variables: Within-Issue Salience

Besides the differences between general issue types, which may be addressed easily with dummy variables to indicate whether a given observation is part of a territorial, maritime, or river claim, the ICOW project has collected an index of within-issue salience for each issue type. This index allows scholars to distinguish between claims of higher and lower salience for a given issue type. According to our previous theoretical discussion, these measures should help us explain how risk influences foreign policy decisions given that decision makers should be willing to pursue costlier or riskier options to settle disputes as issue salience increases. For each of the three current ICOW issue types, salience is measured through six different indicators, each addressing an aspect of the claimed issue that should increase its general value to claimant states. Each indicator is measured separately for each of the two states involved in a given dyadic claim, providing a possible range from zero (no valuable characteristics for either state) to twelve (all six characteristics are present for each state).

For territorial claims, the six indicators used to construct the general measure of territorial claim salience include: (1) territory that is claimed by the state as homeland territory, rather than as a colonial or dependent possession; (2) territory that has a permanent population rather than being uninhabited; (3) territory over which the state has exercised sovereignty within the previous two centuries; (4) territory that is believed to contain potentially valuable resources; (5) territory with a militarily or economically strategic location; and (6) the presence of an explicit ethnic, religious, or other identity basis for the claim.[9] The six indicators used to measure river claim salience are: (1) river location in the state's homeland territory rather than in colonial or dependent territory; (2) use of the river for navigation; (3) level of population served by the river; (4) the presence of a fishing or other resource extraction industry on the river; (5) use of the river for hydroelectric power generation; and (6) use of the river for irrigation. The six indicators for maritime claim salience are: (1) maritime borders extending from homeland rather than colonial or dependent territory; (2) a strategic location of the claimed maritime zone; (3) fishing resources within the maritime zone; (4) migratory fishing stocks crossing into and out of the maritime zone; (5) the known or suspected presence of oil resources within the maritime zone; and (6) relation of the maritime claim to an ongoing territorial claim (involving maritime areas extending beyond either claimed coastal territory or a claimed island).

Additional information on the coding of each variable is available in the codebooks for each respective data set, available on the ICOW project Web site at www.icow.org.

It must be emphasized that this salience index is meant as a measure of variation in salience within each specific issue type, to help scholars distinguish between the most and least salient issues. This salience measure alone should not be assumed to give an accurate measure of the relative salience of different types of issues. For example, a river claim with a salience score of seven out of twelve is not necessarily more salient overall than a territorial claim with a salience score of six. Comparisons of that type will require variables measuring both issue type and within-issue salience, both of which are used in our analyses.

Independent Variables: Recent Issue Management

Testing Hypotheses 3 and 4 requires data on past militarized conflict over the issue and past failed peaceful settlement attempts. Militarized conflict is measured for these purposes as any militarized dispute over the issue in question within the previous ten years before the observation. Failed peaceful attempts include all peaceful settlement attempts (whether bilateral or third party) within the previous ten years that failed to produce an agreement, or that produced an agreement that was not carried out by at least one of the sides. We measure each of these variables using a weighted score to indicate the number of events and how recently they occurred. Events in the most recent year before the observation contribute a value of 1.0 to the weighted score. Earlier events' weights decline by 10 percent each year (e.g., an event ten years earlier contributes a value of 0.1). The weighted values for all events in the past decade are added together, producing a range from 0 to 5.4 for recent militarized disputes, and from 0 to 10.3 for recent failed peaceful settlement attempts.

Control Variables

Joint democracy is measured as a dummy variable indicating whether both sides were considered political democracies during the year of observation. We use a threshold of six or higher on the Polity IV index of institutionalized democracy to define a state as a democracy. Relative capabilities are measured using the Correlates of War (COW) project's Composite Index of National Capabilities (CINC) score for each state, taking the proportion of the dyad's total capabilities held by the strongest side (Singer 1988). The lowest possible value of 0.5 indicates that the two sides are exactly even during the year in question, whereas the highest possible value of 1.0 indicates that the stronger side holds all of the dyad's capabilities.

Empirical Analyses

Our theory suggests that states are more likely to threaten or use military force over their contentious issues when the general issue type is more salient, when the specific issue at stake has greater within-issue salience, and when the adversaries have more experience with recent militarized conflict over the same issue and/or recent failed efforts to settle the same issue peacefully. We also hypothesize that states are more likely to attempt peaceful settlement of their contentious issues in similar circumstances— when the general issue type is more salient, there is greater within-issue salience, and greater experience with recent militarized conflict or failed peaceful efforts. Thus peaceful and militarized means for managing contentious issues are substitutable and driven by similar processes. We now test these hypotheses using logistic regression analysis, beginning with an aggregated analysis of all three issue types, and then separate analyses for each issue type.

Table 2 presents the results of a logistic regression analysis of both militarized conflict and peaceful settlement attempts over territorial, maritime, and river issues. All results are reported using one-tailed significance tests and robust standard errors. Table 3 supplements these analyses by presenting the marginal impact of each variable.

With respect to militarized conflict, there is a statistically significant difference between the three general issue types, but only when recent issue management is not considered (Model I). With territorial issues left out as the referent category, conflict is less likely over maritime issues ($p < .035$), whereas there is no significant difference for river issues ($p < .23$), but these results lose their significance once recent issue management is added (Model II). This suggests that territorial issues are more likely than maritime or river issues to produce militarized conflict overall, but that once the first confrontation has begun, there is little difference between these three issues in future conflict propensity. Within-issue salience significantly increases the likelihood of armed conflict in both analyses ($p < .001$). As Table 3 indicates, the probability of militarized conflict increases substantially with issue salience, regardless of the issue type, from a baseline probability around .01 (i.e., one militarized dispute per hundred eligible years) with a within-issue salience value of zero to approximately five times that probability, with the maximum possible salience value of twelve. This pattern holds for all three issue types, which indicates that the general issue-based theoretical approach gives us quite a bit of purchase for understanding the likelihood of militarized confrontation over contentious issues.

Other factors beyond salience also play an important role. Recent militarized conflict and failed peaceful efforts both significantly increase the likelihood of additional conflict ($p < .001$). As Table 3 indicates, a change from 0 to 1.0 in the weighted recent conflict measure—consistent with having a single militarized dispute in the previous year, or several disputes further back in the past decade—more than doubles the risk of conflict (from .021 to .050). The maximum value of 5.4 increases the probability of conflict to .751.[10] The failure of recent peaceful settlement attempts has a statistically significant effect, though the substantive effect is notably smaller. A change from 0 to 1.0 increases the probability of conflict by about 18 percent (from .022 to .026), and the maximum value increases this probability to .105.

Table 2   Likelihood of Militarized and Peaceful Settlement Attempts of Maritime, River, and Territorial Issues

	Militarized Conflict		Peaceful Techniques	
	Model I	Model II	Model III	Model IV
Issue salience				
Maritime claim	−0.24**	0.02	−0.52***	−0.31***
	(1.83)	(0.12)	(6.70)	(3.83)
River claim	−0.20	−0.13	0.46***	0.39***
	(0.80)	(0.50)	(4.63)	(3.59)
Within-issue salience	0.22***	0.13***	0.13***	0.08***
	(8.18)	(4.89)	(9.62)	(5.37)
Recent management				
Militarized disputes	—	0.92***	—	0.31***
	(12.08)		(5.24)	
Failed peaceful attempts	0.16***	—	—	0.47***
	(3.58)			(14.69)
Joint democracy	−0.20*	−0.32**	0.43***	0.29***
	(1.37)	(1.95)	(5.94)	(3.79)

	Militarized Conflict		Peaceful Techniques	
	Model I	Model II	Model III	Model IV
Capability imbalance	−2.07***	−1.53***	−1.42***	−0.95***
	(5.58)	(3.75)	(7.03)	(4.42)
Constant	−3.16***	−3.49***	−1.59***	−1.98***
	(8.01)	(8.32)	(7.50)	(8.84)
N	9940	9940	9940	9940
LL	−1295.47	−1186.60	−3728.55	−3522.21
χ^2	155.43	387.10	246.56	545.99
	$p < .001$	$p < .001$	$p < .001$	$p < .001$
	(5 d.f.)	(7 d.f.)	(5 d.f.)	(7 d.f.)

Note: Absolute values of robust Z statistics in parentheses:
*$p < .10$. **$p < .05$. ***$p < .01$ (one-tailed tests).

These results are consistent with our hypotheses, with greater within-issue salience and, to a lesser extent, more salient general issue types substantially increasing the probability of armed conflict. How the claimants have managed their issue in the past decade also has an important role, with both militarized conflict and failed peaceful efforts greatly increasing conflict. These results also hold after controlling for characteristics of the claimants themselves. Both control variables perform as expected, with conflict being significantly less likely between two democracies ($p < .03$) and between less evenly matched adversaries ($p < .001$).

Turning to peaceful issue management efforts, Models III and IV of Table 2 suggest that greater attention is devoted to more salient issues, as within-issue salience significantly increases the probability of peaceful settlement attempts ($p < .001$). However, the results are not as straightforward for differences between issue types. Maritime claims are significantly less likely ($p < .001$) than the referent group of territorial claims to see peaceful efforts, as expected, but river claims are significantly more

likely ($p < .001$, two-tailed test). This finding may reflect the influence of one or more factors beyond issue salience levels—perhaps higher perceived benefits from cooperation over shared river resources than from attempted cooperation over territorial or maritime issues, both of which involve stronger components of sovereignty over a specific piece of land or portion of the sea. For example, Prescott (1987, 131–33) suggests that "resource development disputes"—such as disagreements over shared rivers—are generally easier to resolve than "territorial disputes" because they may be settled through division or joint exploitation for mutual benefit, and their settlement does not require the transfer of territory. Peaceful settlement of river claims may also be more likely than peaceful settlement of territorial claims because parties rarely have an emotional attachment to rivers, and altering claims to rivers does not require the resettlement of people across national boundaries. In any case, Table 3 indicates that all three issue types show similar patterns of within-issue salience, with the most valuable issues (salience = 12) of each issue type being more than

Table 3   Marginal Effects

	Militarized Conflict Probability (Change)	Peaceful Techniques Probability (Change)
Territorial claim		
Salience = 0	.010	.074
Salience = 12	.049 (+.039)	.167 (+.093)
Maritime claim		
Salience = 0	.010	.055
Salience = 12	.050 (+.040)	.128 (+.073)
River claim		
Salience = 0	.009	.105
Salience = 12	.043 (+.034)	.228 (+.123)
Recent militarized disputes		
0 (min.)	.021	.110
1	.050 (+.029)	.145 (+.035)
5.4 (max.)	.751 (+.701)	.402 (+.257)
Failed peaceful attempts		
0 (min.)	.022	.096
1	.026 (+.004)	.146 (+.050)
10.3 (max.)	.105 (+.079)	.933 (+.787)
Joint democracy		
0 (no)	.023	.115
1 (yes)	.017 (−.006)	.147 (+.032)
Capability imbalance		
.50 (min.)	.039	.151
1.0 (max.)	.018 (−.021)	.100 (−.051)

Note: Calculations are based on Model II and Model IV from Table 2, with all other variables held at their mean or modal values. Estimates were generated using the MFX command in Stata 9.

twice as likely as the least valuable (salience = 0) to be the subject of peaceful settlement attempts in any given year.

Greater attention is also devoted to issues that have been handled in more threatening ways in the recent past, with peaceful management efforts being significantly more likely when there have been more recent militarized disputes ($p < .001$) and more failed peaceful settlement attempts ($p < .001$). Moving from 0 to 1.0 on the weighted scale of recent conflict increases the probability of peaceful efforts from .110 to .145 (an increase of approximately one-third). The same change in the weighted scale of recent failed peaceful efforts increases the probability even further, from .096 to .146 (an increase of roughly one-half). Finally, joint democracy increases the probability of peaceful conflict management ($p < .001$), whereas a greater capability imbalance reduces this probability ($p < .001$).

Table 3 also suggests some instructive comparisons between issue management techniques. As discussed above, the baseline probability of militarized conflict in any given year ranges from about .01 to .05 depending on issue type and within-issue salience. It is much more likely that peaceful techniques will be employed to manage an issue, with baseline probabilities ranging from .055 to .228 depending on issue type and within-issue salience. This finding is consistent with Hensel's (2001) finding that militarized conflict makes up a relatively small portion of attempts to settle territorial claims in the Western Hemisphere and indicates that focusing primarily on militarized conflict, as in most existing research on contentious issues, misses most attempts to manage or settle issues, even for the most salient issues.

The final table disaggregates the analyses from Table 2 into separate analyses for each issue type (territorial, maritime, river). Models I–III in Table 4 report a disaggregated analysis of militarized conflict. In general, the results from Table 2 hold across all three issue types, suggesting that these results reflect general patterns of issue management that are not unique to one type of issue. For example, all three issue types see a significantly increased risk of militarized conflict when there is greater within-issue salience and more recent militarized disputes over the issue, and both territorial and maritime issues see an increased risk when there have been more recent failed settlement attempts. For the control variables, two of the three individual issue types (territorial and river) show significant effects in the same direction as in the aggregated analysis; the effect for the third issue type (maritime) is in the same direction but misses conventional levels of statistical significance.

Table 4 Likelihood of Settlement Attempts of Territorial, River, and Maritime Issues: Disaggregated Analyses

Militarized Settlement Attempts	Model I Territorial Claims	Model II River Claims	Model III Maritime Claims	Peaceful Settlement Attempts	Model IV Territorial Claims	Model V River Claims	Model VI Maritime Claims
Within-issue salience	0.14***	0.11*	0.12***	Within-issue salience	0.11***	0.01	0.03
	(4.00)	(1.38)	(2.49)		(5.87)	(0.24)	(1.06)
Militarized disputes	0.84***	0.76***	1.08***	Militarized disputes	0.34***	−0.15	0.31**
	(9.10)	(2.85)	(7.16)		(4.76)	(0.44)	(2.21)
Failed peaceful attempts	0.21***	0.05	0.12*	Failed peaceful attempts	0.45***	0.30***	0.61***
	(3.33)	(0.23)	(1.60)		(11.00)	(4.36)	(8.06)
Joint democracy	−0.48**	−1.47*	−0.19	Joint democracy	0.41***	0.83***	−0.06
	(1.78)	(1.40)	(0.81)		(4.08)	(4.01)	(0.48)
Capability imbalance	−1.77***	−5.23***	−0.66	Capability imbalance	−1.12***	−0.37	−0.48
	(3.43)	(3.23)	(0.91)		(4.01)	(0.43)	(1.20)
Constant	−3.34***	−0.43	−4.14***	Constant	−2.06***	−1.60***	−2.25***
	(6.11)	(0.30)	(5.65)		(7.00)	(2.35)	(5.07)
N	6022	762	3156	N	6022	762	3156
LL	−734.65	−77.14	−369.28	LL	−2162.11	−358.26	−978.62
χ^2	270.26	34.62	104.80	χ^2	390.08	38.56	107.99

Note: Absolute values of robust Z statistics in parentheses:
*p < .10. **p < .05. ***p < .01 (one-tailed tests).

Finally, Models IV–VI in Table 4 report a disaggregated analysis of peaceful settlement attempts. As with the analysis of militarized conflict, the results are generally similar across issue type, although only one variable—a history of failed peaceful settlement attempts—is significant for all three issue types. For the other variables, the results are significant for either one or two issue types, and they are generally in the same direction for all three. There is no case where a variable that is significant in one direction for one issue type is anywhere close to significant in the opposite direction for another. For both militarized and peaceful settlement attempts, then, it appears reasonable to include multiple issue types in aggregated analyses. There are no major differences in the management of these three issues, at least for the regions that are currently covered by ICOW data collection.

Taken together, these analyses suggest that the salience of a contentious issue strongly influences the ways in which states try to settle their differences. States are more likely to use both militarized conflict and peaceful methods when the issue at stake is more salient, both when the general issue type is considered more salient and when the specific issue under contention is higher in within-issue salience. Recent issue management also plays an important role, as histories of both militarized conflict and failed peaceful settlements increase pressure to take further action to settle the issue. These patterns generally hold across all three issue types being studied, even after controlling for the impact of joint democracy and relative capabilities. Our analyses demonstrate the impact of variation in salience both within and across issue types, which produces the first systematic empirical examination of multiple issues.

To assess the robustness of our results, we examined several additional specifications of the independent variables.[11] First, rather than examining the effect of all militarized disputes on settlement attempts, we limited the measure to fatal militarized action within the previous five and ten years (dropping less severe instances of militarized action).[12] Results for each of these specifications remained

consistent with our original measure, which provides further evidence that any type of militarized dispute between the parties is significantly more likely to yield future militarized or peaceful settlement attempts, regardless of the issue type.

Second, it is possible that the effect of previous militarized disputes is dependent on their outcome, rather than simply their occurrence. For instance, a pattern of long-running stalemated militarized disputes may push the disputing parties to attempt to settle the issue peacefully (Zartman 1989). To test this idea, we included a variable indicating whether or not the parties' most recent militarized dispute ended in a stalemate. As expected, the claimants are significantly more likely to attempt both militarized and peaceful settlements following a stalemated militarized dispute. However, this effect matters only for territorial and river claims when considering militarized settlement attempts, and only for territorial claims when considering peaceful settlement attempts.

Third, although our theory considers only the effect of previous peaceful settlement attempts that ended in failure on the likelihood of future settlement attempts, it is possible that previous successful settlement attempts also affect future settlement attempts. For instance, we might expect success with previous peaceful settlements to lead to continued peaceful settlement attempts, and fewer militarized settlement attempts. To test this hypothesis, we include a variable counting the number of recent successful settlement attempts, using the same weighting scheme described earlier in this paper. As expected, successful peaceful settlement attempts are generally more likely to lead to future peaceful settlement attempts. Surprisingly, though, past successful settlement attempts do not significantly decrease the likelihood of future militarized settlement attempts. This finding concurs with similar findings in the rivalry literature, which suggest that past efforts to settle rivalries through mediation have an insignificant effect on the future incidence and escalation of militarized action between the rivals (Bercovitch and Diehl 1997).

Finally, our theory suggests that a variety of independent variables will simultaneously affect the likelihood of both militarized and peaceful settlement attempts, which is why we use logistic regression in our analyses. However, it is possible that states may purposefully choose one settlement type in lieu of the other. For instance, states may prefer to settle highly salient issues peacefully to avoid the risk of a severe conflict. One way to test for potential substitution between conflict management techniques is to run the analyses using multinomial logistic regression, which allows both dependent variables to be analyzed in the same model. The results in our online appendix demonstrate that the results remain consistent whether using the logistic or multinomial approach.[13] Ultimately, these alternative tests provide continued support for our primary theory and suggest several interesting avenues to explore in future research.

Conclusions and Implications

International relations scholars often assume that states' foreign policy interests are dominated by a single overarching goal, such as the maximization of power or survival in an anarchic environment. We believe that this vision of world politics is quite limited, and we argue that states contend over many issues—some of which are more salient or important than others. It is important to examine how different contentious issues are managed because foreign policy decisions vary based on the issue at stake and the salience of the issue at hand. We have argued that different types of issues vary along two general dimensions of salience: the tangible importance of an issue, such as economic or strategic value, and the intangible importance of an issue, such as prestige or identity value. Territorial issues are generally salient for both tangible and intangible reasons, whereas maritime and river issues generally lack the intangible dimension and are less salient overall. The salience of issues within each general issue type (territorial, river, and maritime claims) varies as well, with some cases of each type being much more important to leaders than others.

States can choose from a number of techniques to resolve disagreements over issues, ranging from militarized conflict to bilateral negotiations to submission to third parties. We contend that states should be more likely to employ militarized conflict over more salient issues, in terms of both issue types that are generally more salient (particularly territory) and cases with higher within-issue salience. We also argue that such issues should be more likely to produce peaceful settlement attempts than less salient issues, although we leave the effectiveness of these peaceful efforts for future research. We expect that peaceful efforts to resolve issues with greater salience—although more frequent than such efforts over less salient issues—are less likely to be successful. We further expect that past efforts to manage a given issue will have an important influence on subsequent efforts to manage the same issue, with both militarized conflict and peaceful settlement attempts being more common for issues with recent histories of armed conflict and/or failed peaceful efforts. Empirical analyses of territorial, river, and maritime claims provide support for each of these hypotheses.

These results suggest a number of implications for the future development of a systematic issues approach to world politics. First, although this study offers important clues about when states are most likely to choose various techniques for issue management, it does not address the effectiveness of these different techniques. Although this study suggests that both militarized and peaceful settlement attempts are most likely to be employed in similar situations—over issues that are more salient, when armed conflict has erupted recently, and when recent peaceful attempts have failed—characteristics of both the issues and the claimants are likely to have different effects on the success of these different techniques. Studies of the effectiveness of issue management can also contribute to the scholarly literature in important ways, because most research on this topic (Andersen et al. 2001; Dixon 1993, 1994; Greig 2001) has been limited to management of militarized crises or rivalries. Well under half of the issues in this study have produced even a single militarized dispute, and over 90 percent of the peaceful settlement attempts did not begin while a militarized dispute was ongoing between the claimants. This finding suggests that the conflict management literature has systematically excluded a large fraction of management efforts, and that this exclusion may have biased the results of this research by focusing only on the most difficult cases, thereby understating the ability of settlement techniques to resolve issues peacefully.

Collection of data on distinct issue types also allows empirical analysis of different efforts to construct international institutions. For example, Zacher (2001) has suggested that a norm of territorial integrity has emerged over the last century, although his evidence relies exclusively on international crises. The ICOW territorial claims data set includes two centuries of territorial issues, allowing systematic analysis of the extent to which this developing norm has led to the settlement of existing claims to territory, avoidance of militarized conflict over them, or avoidance of claims that might have emerged following decolonization. With respect to rivers, hundreds of international treaties have been signed over international rivers, and the ICOW river claims data set allows analysis of the extent to which these treaties (or the institutions that they created) have prevented or settled serious disagreements over the rivers in question (Hensel, Mitchell, and Sowers 2006). Finally, decades of effort culminated in the UN Convention on the Law of the Sea (UNCLOS), which in principle should promote the peaceful management of maritime resources. The ICOW maritime claims data set allows systematic analysis of whether this convention has had the intended effect (Nemeth et al. 2007). Beyond analysis of issue specific institutions, we can also learn more about the characteristics of institutions that may enhance the effectiveness of their conflict management efforts such as institutionalization, average democracy levels, or average member preference similarity (Hansen, Mitchell, and Nemeth 2008). Together, these issue areas have the potential for great increases in our

understanding of the promise or pitfalls of international institutions for the management of issues in world politics.

Finally, this study demonstrates that systematic data may be collected on both contentious issues and issue salience, overcoming a major obstacle to systematic issue-based research (Diehl 1992). The ICOW project has collected systematic data on three issues, creating appropriate measures of salience for each one, yet many other issue types could be collected in the future. The three issues that have been collected all feature prominent tangible components of salience, but future research could address issues with more intangible than tangible salience. For example, it may be worthwhile collecting data on interstate disagreements related to identity groups. When Austria has objected to Italian treatment of the ethnic Germans in South Tyrol since World War II, it has generally been concerned with intangible salience related to the Austrians' cultural ties with the affected community. Austria has had little tangible salience in this case, because it has not sought to annex the territory where the ethnic Germans live; Austria would receive little tangible benefit even if all of its demands were met. Collecting systematic data on issues such as this would allow comparison of an issue with generally high values of both tangible and intangible salience (territorial) with issues that generally have tangible salience (river and maritime claims) and issues that generally have intangible salience (identity-based or communal claims).[14]

Notes

Authors' Note: This research was supported by National Science Foundation grants #SES-0079421 and #SES-0214417. Doug Lemke, Will Moore, and Brandon Prins contributed valuable comments, but the authors bear full responsibility for all errors and interpretations. All ICOW data codebooks and publicly released data sets are freely available at http://www.icow.org. Files specifically for this article are at http://jcr.sagepub.com/supplemental.

1. Our definition of substitutability is consistent with Most and Starr's original conceptualization of the

term. Instead of attempting to identify mutually exclusive outcomes from a given set of independent variables, we suggest that a given factor (e.g., issue salience) could be expected to simultaneously "lead to, stimulate or 'cause' a variety of empirically distinct foreign policy acts, events or behaviors" (Most and Starr 1989, 106). In other words, states do not choose one foreign policy tool (e.g., militarized force) in lieu of another tool (e.g., bilateral talks), but treat the tools as complementary choices for resolving contentious issues.

2. For now, we do not differentiate between the general salience level of issue types that have primarily tangible salience and those that have primarily intangible salience. Some scholars have suggested that primarily intangible issues should be more difficult to resolve than primarily tangible issues (Vasquez 1993, 192). Yet the difficulty of dividing an issue or reaching a compromise solution is conceptually distinct from issue salience, and it is not clear that (ceteris paribus) states assign greater value to an issue that is difficult to divide than to one that is more easily divisible. For a more in-depth discussion of issue divisibility, see Hensel and Mitchell (2005).

3. An earlier paper (Hensel 2001) separated peaceful settlement attempts into three categories: bilateral negotiations, nonbinding third-party activities, and binding third-party activities. That distinction is impractical in the present paper, though, particularly with our focus on the management of each individual issue type as well as aggregated analyses. For example, there are too few binding third-party activities to run certain analyses.

4. Diehl (1992, 339) also emphasizes that this is not a sufficient condition: "States may find other ways short of war to achieve their goals (i.e., threats or compromise) or other necessary conditions may be absent," and notes that war may even occur on occasion when salience is relatively low as a result of low expected costs or other opportunity-related factors.

5. Even if a specific territorial issue has low within-issue salience, states could conceivably handle it as a salient issue because of the importance often attributed to territory in general. As Hensel (1996b) notes, territory seems likely to have reputational importance as an indicator of how a state might be expected to handle other issues in the future. Showing weakness over any territorial claim may lead other states to begin or escalate territorial claims against the state.

6. Besides the general expectation that more past conflict makes future conflict more likely, Hensel (1999) argues that the outcomes of previous confrontations also have an important impact, which might move the adversaries in either a more peaceful or more conflictual direction. This outcome-specific effect lies outside of the scope of the present paper, which focuses primarily on issue salience, but it would be worth investigating in future research on issue management.

7. Although the MID data set includes some information about issues—dispute participants may be coded as seeking to alter the territorial, policy, regime, or "other" status quo—we examine each militarized dispute to be sure. Not all disputes coded by COW as involving territorial issues meet our coding rules. For example, disputes over fishing rights or maritime zones with no mainland/island component involve maritime rather than territorial issues, and not all pairs of adversaries in multiparty disputes are contending over their own territorial issues. We have also identified several militarized disputes that did involve territorial issues but were not coded as such by COW, and we have added our own codings for river and maritime issues.

8. Raymond's (1994) data on international arbitration and mediation offer a partial exception, as they include numerous cases that began outside of the context of ongoing militarized conflict. Yet Raymond's data are limited to conflict management cases involving at least one major power and involving states that share a direct or indirect border, and his data set ends in 1965. Thus, only a small fraction of our cases would appear in Raymond's compilation.

9. See Hensel and Mitchell (2005) for more discussion of each indicator of territorial salience.

10. We should note, however, that such values are extremely rare. The mean value of this variable is 0.14, and fewer then 50 of the 9944 observations have values of 3.0 or higher. Extreme values on the variable measuring failed peaceful attempts are also rare; the mean is 0.43, and fewer then 50 observations have values of 6.0 or greater.

11. Results for alternative variable specifications are available in an online appendix.

12. Limiting the militarized dispute variable to fatal militarized disputes drops the number of nonzero observations from 1382 in the original models to 333 for militarized disputes within the previous 10 years, and 226 for militarized disputes within the previous 5 years.

13. The primary difference is that a handful of coefficients drop from significance in the multinomial models, but they never change signs. Overall, these results suggest that policy makers do not necessarily choose exclusively peaceful *or* militarized means to settle an issue claim, but often employ multiple foreign policy tools to pursue their issue-related goals.

14. It may also be worth comparing the management of these issues, all of which are generally considered to be salient for national leaders and/or for relatively large segments of their constituents, with recent work on the management of international trade disputes (Reinhardt 2001). Although trade disputes are quite salient for the firms or industries involved, they generally have little impact on most members of society and would thus be considered as having generally low salience along both the tangible and intangible dimensions.

EDITORS' COMMENTARY

Major Contributions: Territorial Conflict

Hensel et al. (2008) develop an **issue-based approach** to the study of interstate conflict, where issues are the subjects or disputed points in a conflict, the things that states are fighting over. In the Falkland Islands war between the United Kingdom and Argentina in 1982, for example, the primary thing at stake was claimed ownership of the islands by the United Kingdom, a point contested by Argentina. This was a territorial issue. Many schools of thought in international relations, such as realism, assume that states have general security goals such as maximizing power. Realist theories tend to ignore the potential for variation in foreign policy interactions across different types of issues, such as border disputes, trade wars, or environmental disagreements. States might be willing to incur greater military costs for some types of issues, such as control of a resource-rich piece of territory, while they may be reluctant to expend military resources for other goals, such as reducing trade barriers. Furthermore, we might see variation in interstate conflict for the same type of issue (e.g., a land border dispute) if one piece of territory contains more valuable resources than another. An issue-based approach recognizes that states interact over different types of issues in world politics and that these issues vary in their *salience* or importance. The type of issue at stake and the level of issue salience influence the foreign policy strategies that states will employ to pursue their issue-related goals.

A good example of a traditional approach to conflict that does not focus on issue variation is Kenneth Waltz's (1979) neorealist theory, which assumes that states seek to maximize security in an anarchic system without a central authority. Waltz argues that a bipolar system with two nuclear powers (e.g., the Cold War) is best positioned to preserve peace in the international system. In this theory, the specific issues over which countries have diplomatic disagreements do not influence the overall possibility for cooperation or conflict. Some realist theorists allow for the possibility of cooperation in one issue area to affect another area, but they believe that states' security goals have the highest priority. One example is the emphasis on relative gains (Grieco 1988), where states may not want to cooperate in one issue arena (e.g., trade) for fear that the gains accrued from such interactions could be converted to enhance power in another arena (e.g., military). The United States, for instance, might make itself more vulnerable to future military threats from China by engaging in extensive trade with the state, allowing China to experience sizable changes in economic growth per year and then use that profit to build its military capabilities. In addition to focusing on relative gains, realists also tend to classify military and security interactions as "high politics" and interactions in economic or other areas as "low politics," implicitly recognizing a hierarchy of foreign policy issues. Realists assume that the realm of high politics drives states' foreign policy decision-making processes.

Other perspectives in the conflict literature recognize that states may have varying levels of opportunity for conflict, an argument related to the issue-based approach, especially if the sources of variance in conflict opportunities stem from what is being contested. Stuart Bremer's (1992b) "Dangerous Dyads" article in this volume (Chapter 2) identifies factors that can increase or decrease the risks for pairs of states to engage in conflict, such as contiguity, power parity, alliances, major power status, and regime type. Bremer shows that dyads that are contiguous by land or sea have a much higher risk for militarized conflict, demonstrating that there is considerable variance in dyadic opportunities for conflict. The issue-based approach explains the linkage between contiguity and war by focusing on the nature of the stakes involved in a land border dispute. It is not merely the enhanced fighting capabilities close to home or increased interaction opportunities with neighboring states that spark war, but rather the specific territorial claims that states press against their neighbors that can lead states down the path to war (Vasquez 1995).

Another prominent explanation for conflict, the bargaining model of war (Fearon 1995), identifies three primary causes of war: incomplete information about states' capabilities or resolve, commitment problems, and issue indivisibility. The model envisions two states bargaining over an issue, such as a piece of territory, yet recognizes that some particularly important pieces of land may be **indivisible** such that there is no division that both sides would accept. While recognizing this possibility of issue indivisibility, a factor that relates to the issue-based approach emphasis on issue salience, rationalist scholars have tended to either minimize the frequency of its occurrence (Fearon 1995) or subsume it into the category of commitment problems (Powell 2006). Fearon and others define a commitment problem as a source of war because the states involved are reluctant to make a bargain or agreement to settle a dispute because there is no one to enforce it if the other side backs out.

Hensel and his colleagues (2008) build upon existing research on contentious issues to understand variation in foreign policy interactions (Rosenau 1966; Mansbach and Vasquez 1981; Diehl 1992; Hensel 2001). They expand upon this research in several ways. First, they assume that issues can involve tangible or intangible stakes. Tangible stakes involve things that are (in theory) divisible, such as control over a particular territory, the removal of a leader, or the implementation of a specific trade policy. Tangible stakes are visible (you can take a picture of it, as Rosenau [1966] says) and material. Issues involving intangible stakes generate disagreements over more psychological, symbolic, or philosophical questions, such as influence of one state over another or the belief that a piece of territory is important due to its religious significance and may be considered sacred. Often such land will have a building or some other construction to indicate that it is sacred; however, it is not the building but its indication that this is sacred land that is key. Some issues such as territorial disputes are high on both salience dimensions (tangible and intangible) as humans have strong psychological attachments to territory and because many resources that states depend on come from specific territories, such as oil or water. Thus, conflicts over land borders often involve more militarized conflicts and wars compared with other geopolitical issues such as cross-border rivers or maritime areas, which can achieve high tangible salience but tend to remain low on the intangible salience dimension. Some issues, such as the treatment of firms or industries, tend to be low on both salience dimensions and thus are unlikely to generate militarized conflict between countries.

Second, Hensel and his colleagues (2008) assume that states can use cooperative or conflictual foreign policy tools to achieve their issue goals. In their study of issues in world politics, Mansbach and Vasquez (1981) examined variation in foreign policy behavior across different issues. They found that U.S.–West German and U.S.-Soviet behavior during the Cold War varied significantly by issue area, with certain issue areas generating almost exclusively conflictual behavior and others generating almost exclusively cooperative behavior. U.S.–West German conflict centered on Nazi-related questions, while U.S.-Soviet conflict focused on arms control issues (Mansbach and Vasquez 1981, 23–26). Hensel et al. show that understanding variance in issue salience gives us purchase for understanding when states would prefer a particular type of foreign policy strategy. Issues that are highly salient for tangible and intangible reasons increase the chances for both peaceful and militarized attempts to settle the issues at stake.

This relates to another key finding in the article—namely, that territorial disputes are more conflict prone than other geopolitical issues. There is a large literature showing that contiguity (Bremer 1992b) and territorial disputes (Luard 1986; Holsti 1991; Vasquez 1993; Vasquez and Henehan 2001; Hensel 1996b, 2000; Huth 1996; Huth and Allee 2002; Senese and Vasquez 2008) are the leading sources of warfare in the past few centuries. The territorial studies, however, argue *contra* Bremer that it is not contiguity that causes conflict but the fact that neighbors fight over their borders. Hensel (2000) and Vasquez and Henehan (2001) find that states that have territorial disputes have a higher probability of going to war whether they are contiguous or not contiguous.

These previous studies, however, tend to identify historical cases of militarized disputes or wars and then determine in a post hoc manner what issue(s) were being contested. This is problematic because we are selecting a set of cases where bargaining failed because the parties ended up in a MID. The Issue Correlates of War (ICOW) project, developed by Hensel and Mitchell, seeks to overcome this problem by coding cases based on the issues at stake. Rather than ask how many wars involved disagreements over land borders, they identify all instances of diplomatic disagreements over land borders and then determine why some of those cases ended in MIDs and others were settled peacefully. In the study reprinted here, Hensel et al. show that less than half of all contested areas involving traditional land borders produced even a single militarized conflict. Yet the authors also find that territorial issues are much more likely to end in militarized conflict than issues involving maritime areas or cross-border rivers.

This leads to the key theoretical idea in the study—namely, that we can predict the likelihood of conflict by focusing on differences in issue salience both across and within issue types. **Across-issue salience** involves a comparison of different types of issues, such as territorial, maritime, and river conflicts. The authors find that territorial disputes are much more likely to end in violence than maritime or river issues, with conflict being least likely over rivers. This supports the theoretical idea that issues with high intangible salience are more contentious in general. The second comparison involves examining issues of the same type (e.g., territory) but of different salience levels, what the authors call **within-issue salience.** Some territorial disputes, such as the conflict between Israel and Syria over the Golan Heights, are important to both sides for many reasons (homeland territory, strategic location, valuable resources, ethnic groups living on territory, etc.). Other claimed territories lack military or economic benefits, such as Navassa Island (claimed by Haiti from the United States). Hensel et al. show that territorial issues such as the Golan Heights are much more likely to result in militarized conflicts and multiple diplomatic efforts to resolve the issue in comparison to territorial issues such as the Navassa Island case.

Hensel and his colleagues (2008) also demonstrate that the manner in which issues have been settled in the past influences the chances for militarized conflict in the future. This relates to the literature on crisis bargaining and rivalry, which shows that conflict begets conflict. Hensel et al. find that states that have attempted to settle a territorial, maritime, or river issue with militarized force in the recent past are more likely to use violent tactics in the future. Yet militarized conflict also draws the attention of outsider mediators, which enhances peaceful efforts to settle the contested issues. Pairs of states that use militarized force early in their dyadic interactions can lock themselves into a violent path, resulting in issue rivalry (Mitchell and Thies 2011) and putting states on the steps to war (Senese and Vasquez 2008).

Methodological Notes: Log Odds and Logistic Regression (Logit) Models

The authors analyze data collected by the ICOW project. This involves the identification of cases in which two or more countries have a diplomatic disagreement over the ownership or usage of a territory, maritime zone, or river that crosses or forms an international boundary. The ICOW project uses **content analysis** of documents (e.g., news stories) to collect its data. Content analysis involves reading statements and coding (or classifying) them into preexisting categories. For example, an examination of documents on issue claims is read to determine whether the disagreement involves a territory, a maritime zone, or a river. Precise rules are given to coders so that they can make these three distinctions. The ICOW project codes an **issue claim** only when official representatives from all governments involved make statements about their positions on the contested issues and the states disagree about each other's claims. The authors analyze three regions (Western Hemisphere, Europe, and the Middle East) with a total of 244 contested geographical areas and 416 dyadic claims. There are more dyadic claims than contested areas because some cases, such as the maritime claims to Antarctica, involve more than two countries. The authors then generate a **claim dyad-year,** which involves a case for each year two countries have diplomatic disagreement over a territory, maritime, or river issue. For example, Honduras and Nicaragua have a maritime claim over the area around San Andrés and Providencia. Nicaragua challenged Honduras' claim in December 1999 when the government ratified an earlier treaty with Columbia (affecting its claimed maritime space). Nicaragua took the case to the International Court of Justice and it was settled in October 2007. This case contributes nine years to the claim dyad-year data set, one case for each year from 1999 to 2007. There are a total of 9,944 claim dyad-year cases when all the cases in the three regions are combined.

The ICOW project codes the salience of each issue with specific indicators tailored to the particular issue at stake. For example, territorial issue salience is based on factors such as homeland versus colonial possession, strategic location, and the presence of valuable resources or ethnic groups in the territory. River issue salience is coded based on the level of population living along the river, hydroelectric power generated from the river, and the use of the river for navigation. Each issue is scored one point for each country in the dyad for each dimension of salience, resulting in a 0 to 12 scale that can be compared across issues.[1] This captures the within-issue salience concept described earlier. Across-issue salience is coded using dummy variables that turn on or off (1 or 0) for two of the three issues (maritime claim and river claim). The third category of territorial claim (the omitted category) is captured through the inclusion of a constant (or Y-intercept) in the model.[2]

Hensel and his colleagues (2008) are interested in militarized and peaceful interactions over issues, and thus they create two **dependent variables.** Militarized conflict is coded 1 in a given claim dyad-year if the two countries experienced one or more MIDs over the issue at stake. This information is taken from version 3 of the Correlates of War project's MID data set (Ghosn, Palmer, and Bremer 2004), yet includes only cases where the MID directly involved the specific issue in contention. Militarized conflict is quite rare, occurring in only 304 of the 9,944 dyad-years (3 percent). The authors also code all peaceful attempts to settle the issue at stake, including bilateral negotiations (direct talks between the two governments in the dispute) and negotiations with third-party assistance (inquiry, conciliation, good offices, mediation, multilateral negotiations, arbitration, or adjudication). The authors create a dummy variable that equals 1 in a claim dyad-year if the issue experienced one or more peaceful attempts that year and zero otherwise; peaceful attempts are more common than militarized ones, occurring in 1,303 of the 9,944 dyad-years (13 percent).

Log Odds

Both of the dependent variables are **dichotomous** (0/1) measures, which necessitates the use of a statistical model that accounts for the distributional nature of these discrete random variables. Hensel et al. (2008) use a logistic regression or **logit model.** Given that the dependent variable (y) can take on two possible values (e.g., 0 for no militarized conflict, 1 for militarized conflict), we can model the probability that $(y = 0)$ or $(y = 1)$ as a function of a series of independent variables (e.g., issue salience, previous militarized conflict). The model uses the concept of the **log odds,** or the natural logarithm of the odds ratio. To understand the idea of the log odds, see Table 3.1, which shows the cross-tabulation of car accidents in Florida in 1988, whether these accidents involved fatalities, and whether a seatbelt was worn (Lindsey 2004, 42).

We could determine the risk of a fatal injury for individuals wearing no seatbelt in comparison with those who wore a seatbelt to see if seatbelts lower the risk of fatal

Table 3.1   Illustration of Log Odds Ratio

Seatbelt	Fatal Injury	Nonfatal Injury	Total
No	1,601	162,527	164,128
Yes	510	412,368	412,878
Total	2,111	574,895	577,006

injuries. The odds of a fatal injury compared with a nonfatal injury for those not wearing seat belts (first row of table) would be calculated as follows (Lindsey 2004, 55–57): 1,601/162,527 = 0.0099. We could compare this to the odds of a fatal injury versus a nonfatal injury for people wearing seatbelts (second row of table): 510/412,368 = 0.0012. We can see that the odds of dying in a car accident in Florida in 1988, while small in general, were much higher for individuals not wearing seat belts. We can then construct the odds ratio for this example: [1,601/510]/[162,527/412,368] = 7.96. This would tell us that the odds of a fatal injury are close to eight times higher for individuals not wearing seat belts relative to those who wore them. The **log odds ratio** is then calculated as the natural logarithm of this odds ratio (ln 7.96).

Statistical Significance

To return to the model that Hensel et al. (2008) use, they are calculating the log odds of militarized conflict or peaceful settlement attempts and modeling these changing odds as a function of several independent variables. If an estimated coefficient in a logit model has a positive sign and is statistically different from zero, we can conclude that this independent variable increases the probability or log odds of the event being modeled (the dependent variable). Consider the coefficient for within-issue salience in Table 2, Model I, which equals 0.22 and is statistically significant at the 99 percent level. This positive coefficient tells us that as we increase issue salience from a low value (0) to a high value (12), the likelihood of militarized conflict is increasing. This provides support to the hypothesis by Hensel et al. that countries are more likely to use militarized foreign policy strategies to pursue issue-related goals if the contested issue is highly salient. A negative and statistically significant coefficient (e.g., the effect of joint democracy on militarized conflict in Table 2, Model I, which equals –0.20) tells us that the likelihood of the dependent variable is declining as we increase the value of the independent variable (e.g., jointly democratic dyads are less likely to experience militarized conflict than other dyads).

Substantive Significance

Given that the underlying model has a binary process, we can also calculate $p(y = 0)$ or $p(y = 1)$ when we set the independent variables at a given value. Scholars often refer to these calculations as the **substantive significance** for a model because they give us an idea about the overall size of the effects; in the logit model, they are calculated as **predicted probabilities**. In the seatbelt example, if the risk of fatalities was 0.0012 for those wearing seatbelts versus 0.0015 for those not wearing seatbelts, we might conclude that it is really not worth the effort to put on a seatbelt. Yet the data for Florida suggest that the risk of death is about eight times higher for those not wearing seatbelts, and thus we might conclude it is wise to buckle up. In international conflict models, the size of the effects of our independent variables is often quite small because militarized conflict is a rare event. Medical researchers use a benchmark of a log odds ratio of 2.0 or greater to denote sizable effects, yet few variables in international conflict studies achieve this level of substantive significance (Bennett and Stam 2004, 68). Bennett and Stam (2004) note that contiguity is one of the few variables that has a sizable effect, with a log odds ratio greater than 2 in most dyad-year models of conflict.

Hensel and his colleagues report the substantive significance (or marginal effects) for their models in Table 3. The probability for each dependent variable is calculated by changing the value of one independent variable and keeping the other variables set at their mean or mode. Consider the first variable of territorial claim as we change the within-issue salience from its minimum to its maximum (e.g., similar to the Golan Heights vs. Navassa Island illustration). For this calculation, maritime claim and river claim are set to zero; recent militarized disputes, failed peaceful attempts, and capability imbalance are set at their mean values; and joint democracy is set at its mode because it is a dichotomous variable. We then change the value of issue salience to see how the risk of militarized conflict or peaceful settlement attempts changes as salience levels increase. We can see that for territorial claims, the probability of militarized conflict equals 0.049 and the probability of peaceful attempts equals 0.167 for the most salient territories (or about a 1 in 20 chance for a MID in a given claim dyad-year), while the chance for a MID is 0.010 and the chance for a peaceful attempt is 0.074 for the least salient territorial claims (or a 1 in 100 chance for a MID). Hensel et al. report the change in probabilities in parentheses, which helps us see which variables have the largest effects overall. Recent militarized conflict, for example, increases the chances for another militarized dispute by 0.701 as we increase this measure from its minimum to its maximum. Thus, we would conclude that states with a history of militarized conflict over a territorial claim have a very high risk of future conflict. Scholars examine both statistical and substantive significance to determine which factors influence the likelihood of interstate conflict and cooperation.

Notes

1. For territorial claims, ICOW codes tangible and intangible salience separately (Hensel and Mitchell 2005). Three indicators are used for tangible salience (populated area, resource value, and strategic location) while three other indicators are used for intangible salience (homeland ties, identity ties, and historical possession). Since the other two types of issue claims (maritime and river) are primarily over tangible issues, ICOW does not code intangible indicators in these cases.

2. Thus, to see how changes in within-issue salience affect the chances for militarized conflict, we can vary the salience indicator from low (0) to high (12). To see how across-issue salience influences conflict or cooperation, we can turn one issue "on" while turning the other issues "off" (e.g., we could set the maritime claim variable equal to 1, the river claim variable equal to zero, and the territorial claim variable equal to zero and then calculate the probability of militarized conflict).

Questions

1. What three types of issue claims do Hensel et al. examine? How are they similar or different?

2. What is the difference between tangibility and intangibility? Do the authors find these two characteristics equally important for predicting conflict?

3. How does the probability of a militarized dispute change as *within*-issue salience increases from its minimum (0) to its maximum (12)?

4. Which variable(s) has the largest substantive effect in terms of increasing the chances either for militarized conflict or for peaceful settlement attempts? Which variable(s) has the smallest substantive effect?

5. Why do you think *within*-issue salience has a statistically significant effect on the chances for peaceful settlement attempts for territorial disputes but has no effect on the likelihood of peaceful settlement attempts for maritime or river issues?

Further Reading

Diehl, P. F. 1992. What are they fighting for? The importance of issues in international conflict research. *Journal of Peace Research* 29 (3): 333–44.

Hensel, P. R., and S. M. Mitchell. 2005. Issue indivisibility and territorial claims. *Geo Journal* 64 (4): 275–85.

Huth, P. K., and T. Allee. 2002. *The democratic peace and territorial conflict in the twentieth century.* Cambridge, UK: Cambridge University Press.

Mansbach, R., and J. Vasquez. 1981. *In search of theory: A new paradigm for global politics.* New York: Columbia University Press.

Senese, P. D., and J. Vasquez. 2008. *The steps-to-war: An empirical study.* Princeton, NJ: Princeton University Press.

Chapter 4

Alliances and the Expansion and Escalation of Militarized Interstate Disputes

Brett Ashley Leeds

Alliances and Militarized Conflict

Despite the fact that many theories of interstate conflict place military alliances in a privileged position, scholars of international relations have had a surprisingly difficult time describing, explaining, and predicting the influence of military alliances on the probability of war.[1] Alliances have been credited both with deterring military action and with spreading it. Allies have been known to restrain partners and enforce bargains, and also to reduce negotiating flexibility and make conflict-avoiding agreements more difficult to reach. In this chapter, I provide evidence that both views of alliances have a basis in fact. While alliances play an important role in influencing the initiation of military conflict and have a well-deserved place in a strategy of general deterrence, when general deterrence fails and conflict emerges among states with allies committed to assist them, the resulting disputes can be particularly severe.

The primary lesson of this study, for both researchers and policymakers, is that alliances can have multiple effects on the probabilities of war and peace. By exploring the influence of different types of alliances at different stages in the evolution of militarized disputes, we can learn more about their overall impact. Those who view alliances as problematic due to their potential to involve outsiders in disputes tangential to their direct interests and to

turn bilateral disputes into worldwide conflagrations (a story frequently told about World War I) must temper their indictment with a recognition of the deterrent properties of alliances. At the same time, those who champion clear alliance commitments as the route to peace must recognize that when deterrence fails, alliances may be associated with particularly intractable negotiating problems and serious military conflicts.

There are several ways in which this study represents a "new direction" in research on the relationship between alliances and international conflict. Theoretically, it builds on bargaining models of war and signaling models of alliances, both of which have been developed relatively recently (e.g., Fearon 1995; Wagner 2000; Filson and Werner, 2002; Morrow 1994; Smith 1995). Empirically, it takes advantage of analysis techniques that allow researchers to connect processes at different stages (e.g., Reed 2000). By starting with a directed dyadic research design and using modeling procedures that link dispute initiation and dispute evolution together, I am able to provide a better understanding of the complexities of the impact of alliances on conflict than has been available in the past. Finally, the study uses a relatively new dataset that provides rich information about the content of alliance agreements (Leeds, Ritter, Mitchell, and Long 2002). This allows

Source: Brett Ashley Leeds, "Alliances and the Expansion and Escalation of Militarized Interstate Disputes," in *New Directions for International Relations: Confronting the Method-of-Analysis Problem,* Alex Mintz and Bruce Russett, eds. (Lanham, MD: Lexington Books, 2005), 117–34.

me to match alliances explicitly to the potential conflicts where they would be relevant.

The chapter proceeds as follows. In the next section, I explain the theoretical perspective on the causes of militarized disputes and war and the role of alliances in foreign policy that underlies the argument in this chapter. I then develop specific hypotheses about the relationship between alliances and the expansion and escalation of disputes once conflict emerges. In section four, I describe the research design used to evaluate these hypotheses and the empirical evidence in support of them. Section five offers concluding observations about the influence of alliances on war and peace.

The Causes of War and the Role of Alliances

Under what conditions does militarized interstate conflict begin? A particularly compelling contemporary perspective views militarized conflict as emerging from bargaining failures (Blainey 1973; Fearon 1995). Because the shadow of force lies over all international interactions, force need rarely be used. Most of the time, the joint understanding of the likely outcome of any militarized conflict leads state leaders to agree on a distribution of benefits consistent with their ability to achieve gains through force without actually resorting to arms. Yet, due to uncertainty about the outcome of a conflict and the incentives to misrepresent one's power and interests to achieve a more favorable bargain, militarized disputes and war sometimes occur. They occur when the parties disagree about the bargain that is consistent with their ability to compel or resist change and believe that the benefits to be gained through the threat or use of military force exceed the costs involved in militarization.

Given this perspective, what role do alliances play in the emergence of militarized disputes?[2] Contemporary theorists have argued that alliances affect the initiation of militarized interstate disputes through the information they provide to potential challengers about the likelihood that they can gain a more favorable distribution of benefits through the overt

threat or use of force (Morrow 1994; Smith 1995, 1998; Fearon 1997). Specifically, alliances provide potential challengers with fairly reliable information about whether a dispute is likely to remain bilateral or to involve outside parties. When their potential targets have allies committed to assist them in conflict, challengers can expect that they are likely to face a multilateral force and are less likely to be successful at achieving their goals. On the other hand, when the potential challenger has allies of its own committed to join in the challenge or to remain neutral, challengers can feel more confident of their ability to gain in conflict (Leeds 2003a).

Leeds (2003a) provides evidence that alliances do affect the probability of dispute initiation in precisely this manner. Defensive alliances discourage attacks on potential targets, but offensive alliances and neutrality pacts embolden challengers and make the initiation of disputes more likely. Recent research has pointed out, however, that the initiation of military hostilities is not the end of the bargaining process, but merely a new stage in bargaining. The conflict ends once the two sides reach agreement on an acceptable division of benefits, and what they learn during the dispute influences the bargain they are willing to make. Escalation to war and longer and more costly wars are a result of particularly intractable bargaining problems (Wagner 2000; Filson and Werner 2002; Smith and Stam's contribution to this volume).

So what role should alliances play once a dispute begins? Alliances that were in place before the dispute began were already known, and the parties were willing to engage in conflict fully aware of their existence. The information provided by existing alliances about the prior commitments of outsiders should not be able to encourage a bargained solution after the conflict begins any more than it could before overt conflict emerged. As Fearon (1994a) has noted, because previously known alliances were accounted for in the calculus that led to the breakdown of general deterrence, they are unlikely to have much impact on the success of immediate deterrence; if challengers willing to initiate disputes are aware of alliances, they are unlikely to back down from escalating a dispute because of them (see also Huth and Russett 1984; Huth 1988).

Yet, some new information does become available to both the challenger and the target after the dispute begins. Just as the challenger and target are likely to learn more about the settlements that their adversaries would accept in lieu of war during the dispute process, both also learn more about what the ally views as an acceptable settlement and the actions the ally might be willing to take to encourage his or her preferred outcome.

When a leader's ally becomes involved in a dispute with an outside state, one can imagine that leader would have two competing interests. On the one hand, if the leader views involvement in war as undesirable, he or she would want to avoid allowing the dispute to escalate. If the leader were unsuccessful at moderating the demands of the adversary (which is likely if general deterrence has failed), then the leader might work to moderate the demands of the ally to avoid being drawn into an unwanted conflict. The French were unwilling to face Germany without British support in 1938, and thus encouraged their ally, Czechoslovakia, to give in to German demands for the Sudetenland rather than escalate the conflict. The Soviets and Americans similarly restrained their Arab and Israeli allies in 1973 in the interest of avoiding super-power confrontation. In this sense, allies might be able to use their influence, and particularly their power to deny assistance in the event of unmoderated demands, to resolve the crisis and avoid escalation to war. Along these lines, Gelpi (1999) has argued that allies are particularly effective mediators due to their means of influence over their partners.

Despite the fact that a leader might want to avoid involvement in war, it is not clear that leaders will always prefer to pressure their allies to give in, because allies also have an interest in the post-dispute distribution of benefits. Leaders prefer to see their allies resolve conflicts of interest peacefully and prefer not to engage in war if all else is equal, but they also have an interest in the distributional

outcome of the conflict, and are likely to prefer a distribution of benefits that favors their ally. This creates a countervailing pressure to the desire to avoid war. Thus, leaders of outside powers may under some circumstances compel their allies to moderate their bargaining positions and facilitate settlement as a result, and under other circumstances may allow or even encourage their allies to maintain a tough bargaining stance that makes settlement more difficult. Thus, while Gelpi claims that allies are in the best position to encourage compromise on behalf of their partners, Smith (1995) notes that having allies committed to assist them may tend to make states particularly intransigent in their bargaining positions and increase the risk of escalation to war.

To complicate matters, any action that encourages moderation on the part of an ally may correspondingly toughen the bargaining stance of the adversary, and vice versa. It is difficult, therefore, to claim a single systematic influence of allies on the bargaining positions of states in a militarized dispute. What is probably fair to claim, however, is that the existence of alliances is likely to result in more parties being involved in the bargaining process because more states have a direct interest in the outcome of the bargaining and escalatory processes. Thus, the main effect of alliances is to turn bilateral crises into multilateral crises, and bilateral bargaining problems into multilateral bargaining problems.

This in itself is significant because political bargains become more difficult to achieve as additional actors join the bargaining process. Raiffa (1982, 257) writes, "Significant conceptual complexities arise when even a single new party is added to a two-party negotiation." This is especially true in the absence of specific institutional rules.[3] International bargaining tends to take place under ad hoc rules established by the participants themselves, and few alliance treaties specify rules for determining a joint position of a crisis coalition. While the extent to which additional parties complicate bargaining depends on the possible outcomes and the distribution of preferences over outcomes, it is reasonable to assume that all else being equal, increasing the number of parties that must be satisfied by a bargain to avoid war makes the negotiation of a successful settlement less likely, and war correspondingly more likely. This would also be commensurate with the observation that multilateral wars tend to last longer than bilateral wars.[4] It is harder to resolve a conflict that involves more actors.

Expected Influences of Alliances on the Conflict Process

Alliances affect dispute initiation by influencing a potential challenger's beliefs about the probability that a conflict will remain bilateral. Challengers prefer to initiate disputes when they believe they can win in military conflict, and challengers are more likely to believe they can be successful when they expect that they will receive outside support and when they believe that their targets will not receive outside support (Leeds 2003a; see also, Gartner and Siverson 1996; Morrow 1994; Smith 1995, 1998). Recent theoretical and empirical research suggests that alliances are a fairly reliable signal of future intentions because most of the time leaders form alliances under which they are willing to fulfill their obligations (Morrow 1994; Smith 1995, 1998; Fearon 1997; Leeds, Long, and Mitchell 2000; Leeds 2003b). It follows, therefore, that when challengers with allies committed to their assistance initiate disputes, or when challengers choose to start a dispute with a target with one or more allies committed to assist the target in defense, these disputes are unlikely to remain bilateral.[5] When alliances that provide for active assistance fail to deter challenges, they will often be associated with disputes that become multilateral crises.[6] Specifically:

H1: When a conflict initiator has an offensive alliance in place when a dispute begins, it is more likely that more than one state will be involved in the dispute on the side of the initiator.

H2: When a conflict target has a defensive alliance in place when a dispute begins, it is more likely that more than one state will be involved in the dispute on the side of the target.

Some alliances, however, are not aimed at providing active support, but instead offer a commitment to remain neutral in an emerging conflict. Through neutrality pacts, potential challengers can receive promises from outsiders not to intervene to help the potential target, clearing a path for military success (Moul 1988; Werner 2000). Neutrality pacts should be associated with a higher probability of a dispute remaining bilateral, as they make it less likely that outsiders will intervene to help a target.

H3: When an initiator has a neutrality pact in place when a dispute begins, it is less likely that more than one state will be involved in the dispute on the side of the target.

Thus, alliances that are in place before conflict emerges should affect the probability that a militarized interstate dispute becomes a larger, multilateral affair. While alliances may sometimes deter the initiation of hostilities, disputes that emerge among states with allies may be particularly severe due to their likelihood of involving multiple participants. We can imagine circumstances under which a leader's desire to avoid escalation to war would cause him or her to impose moderation on an ally's claims. One can also imagine circumstances under which a leader will encourage increased toughness in an ally and make the ally's bargaining position more intransigent. These countervailing effects make it difficult to predict the impact of outside allies on a state's willingness to capitulate or to hold firm absent more information about the outside state's value for war and for the political settlement. It does seem reasonable to suggest, however, that regardless of the content of the preferences of outside states, adding additional states to the negotiating process who must be satisfied with a settlement for war to be avoided will make negotiated settlements harder to reach and war more likely. Thus:

H4: Multilateral conflicts are more likely to escalate to war than bilateral conflicts.

Research Design and Empirical Analysis

My empirical examination of the influence of alliances on the evolution of militarized disputes begins with a model of the initiation of disputes. As Reed (2000) has shown, many of the same factors that influence how disputes evolve also influence whether they emerge in the first place, and in order to achieve a proper understanding of the evolution of disputes, we must account for the emergence of the dispute in our empirical analysis. This methodological advance is an important new direction in international relations research. In this case, using a maximum likelihood probit estimation with selection allows me to analyze the impact of alliances on dispute expansion and dispute escalation conditional on dispute initiation. It also allows me to estimate the joint impact of alliances on the failure of general and immediate deterrence.

I assemble a dataset that includes all states in interactions with the states in their politically relevant international environments in each year from 1816 to 1944 (Maoz 1996). The unit of analysis is the directed dyad-year.[7] I employ a two-stage probit technique that accounts jointly for the probability that a dispute emerges and the likelihood that it expands and/or escalates.[8] The dependent variable in the first (selection) equation is the initiation of a militarized interstate dispute (MID), defined as an instance "in which the threat, display, or use of military force . . . by one . . . state is directed towards . . . another state" (Jones, Bremer, and Singer 1996).[9] The independent variables are drawn from Leeds (2003a). That study reveals that defensive alliances to a potential target are negatively related to the initiation of militarized disputes, and a potential challenger's offensive alliances and neutrality pacts are positively related to dispute initiation. Control variables have generally predictable effects. Stronger initiators are more likely to initiate disputes against weaker targets, contiguous states are more likely to engage in military conflict, and jointly democratic dyads and states with similar alliance portfolios (and we infer, more similar foreign policy interests) are less dispute prone.[10]

The uncensored cases in the second stage of analysis are all the dyad-years in which a new militarized interstate dispute is initiated by the challenger against the target. The unit of analysis is the militarized interstate dispute. For each MID, I create three different dependent variables, all of which are coded dichotomously based on the answers to the following questions: (1) Did more than one state participate in the dispute on the side of the initiator?; (2) Did more than one state participate in the dispute on the side of the target?; (3) Did the dispute escalate to war?

I begin by evaluating the influence of alliances on the likelihood that a dispute involves more than two states. Because I have argued that alliances influence the initiation of disputes by providing information to potential challengers regarding the probability that outsiders will intervene in any emergent conflict, it follows that some types of alliances, namely, those that obligate signatories to assist their partners in the event of hostilities, should be systematically associated with the expansion of military conflict. On the other hand, neutrality pacts specifically obligate states to refrain from intervention on the opposing side and should be associated with a lower probability of outside assistance to the opponent.

In the first model, the dependent variable is whether or not, if a dispute emerges, more than one state participates on the side of the initiator. In the second model, the dependent variable represents the active participation of more than one state on the side of the target. In both cases, the dependent variable is coded dichotomously, with disputes in which the initiator or target was the only state involved on his or her side of the dispute coded 0, and cases in which multiple states are involved coded 1.

The independent variables of primary interest are variables representing outside alliances to the initiator and the target. Using the Alliance Treaty Obligations and Provisions (ATOP) dataset (Leeds, Ritter, Mitchell, and Long 2002), I coded three variables. First, I developed a dichotomous variable representing whether the target in the dispute had any alliance commitments when the dispute began that would obligate any other state to come to its assistance in a conflict with the initiator. Second, I coded another dichotomous variable representing whether the initiator of the dispute had any alliance commitments when the dispute began that would obligate any other state to assist the initiator in a conflict that the state initiated against this target. Third, I coded a dichotomous variable that indicates whether the initiator had any existing agreements when the dispute began that would preclude outside states from intervening to help the target (that is, any relevant neutrality pacts).[11]

I also include two additional control variables that may influence whether additional states participate in disputes.[12] First, I include a variable representing how strong the initiator is in comparison to her target. A long debate has ensued in international relations scholarship over the incentives for outsiders to join ongoing disputes. Some have argued that states have an interest in balancing power and should work to protect weak targets from challengers, who once they succeed in defeating their target, may seek further aggrandizement at the expense of outside states. Others claim that states have an incentive to bandwagon. By joining stronger states, they may get a chance to share in the spoils of conflict.[13] Because the strength of the initiator in comparison to the target may influence state decisions to intervene, I include a measure of relative power. It is drawn from the Correlates of War capabilities index, and is calculated as the CINC score of the initiator divided by the sum of the scores of the initiator and target (Singer 1988). The result is bounded between zero and one with higher values indicating stronger initiators, and lower values indicating weaker initiators.

Second, I include in each equation a variable representing whether outsiders join the adversary. Because it may be the case that intervention on one side of a conflict begets intervention on the other side, I control for the influence that the addition of one outsider may have on the decisions of other states to join conflicts.

Table 1 presents the empirical results of this analysis. The results are entirely supportive of hypotheses 1 through 3. When an initiator begins a dispute with an offensive ally, it is more likely that the initiator will receive outside assistance. When a target has a defensive ally at the time the dispute begins, it is more likely that the target will receive assistance. When the initiator has a neutrality pact, however, the target is less likely to get outside help, all else being equal. At the same time, allies to the target seem to deter assistance to the initiator, and allies to the initiator seem to deter assistance to the target.

The control variables are statistically significant as well. The power relationship between the initiator and the target influences the likelihood that outsiders will join, and these results seem to suggest more support for bandwagoning than balancing. Stronger initiators tend to attract more assistance, and weaker targets attract less. When outsiders join one side of the dispute it becomes more likely that outsiders join the other side. Intervention does seem to beget intervention.

How much influence do alliance commitments have on the probability that a dispute expands? To answer this question, I perform two analyses, both of which are reported in Table 2.[14] First, I evaluate the impact of alliances on dispute expansion conditional on dispute initiation. If a dispute has been initiated, the average probability that outsiders help the initiator increases from 18.9 percent to 22.8 percent when the initiator has an offensive ally. If a dispute has been initiated, the average probability that outsiders help the target increases from 13.5 percent to 38.3 percent when the target has a defensive ally, and decreases from 20.6 percent to 12.4 percent when the initiator has a relevant neutrality pact.

In evaluating the effects of alliances on dispute expansion, we must keep in mind, however, that these alliances also have an effect on whether the dispute is initiated to begin with. Defensive alliances to targets decrease the probability of dispute initiation, and offensive alliances to initiators increase the probability of dispute initiation. Thus, I evaluate the impact of alliances on the probability of dispute expansion throughout the entire process. In other

Table 1 The Effects of Outside Allies on the Probability That Outsiders Help in Militarized Interstate Disputes, 1816–1944

	Outsiders Help Initiator, Coefficient (s.e.)	Outsiders Help Target, Coefficient (s.e.)
Power of Initiator in Relation to Target	0.447 (0.100)**	−0.352 (0.168)*
Target has Def. Ally When Dispute Begins	−0.449 (0.090)**	0.857 (0.131)**
Initiator has Off. Ally When Dispute Begins	0.229 (0.070)**	−0.466 (0.170)*
Initiator has Neut. Pact When Dispute Begins	—	−0.378 (0.172)*
Outsider Joins Target	0.331 (0.097)**	—
Outsider Joins Initiator	—	0.669 (.179)**
Constant	−3.067**	−0.822
Selection: Dispute Initiation		
Joint Democracy	−0.127 (0.053)*	−0.143 (0.059)*
Contiguity	0.530 (0.030)**	0.523 (0.031)**
Power of Challenger in Relation to Target	0.186 (0.038)**	0.185 (0.038)**
Similarity in Alliance Portfolios	−.0388 (0.038)**	−0.411 (0.40)**
Potential Target has Defensive Ally	−0.194 (0.034)**	−0.205 (0.034)**
Potential Challenger has Offensive Ally	0.189 (0.038)**	0.184 (0.038)**
Potential Challenger has Relevant Neut. Pact	0.209 (0.036)**	0.203 (0.039)**
Constant	−2.321**	−2.301**
Rho (Chi^2)	.949 (50.02)**	−0.005 (0.99)
N (total, uncensored)	69730,812	69730,812
Chi^2	69.22**	68.93**

$*p < 0.05; **p < 0.001$

words, I examine the full impact of these types of alliances on the probability that a dispute both emerges and expands.[15] Because the probability of dispute initiation in the sample is very low, these probabilities are small, but the differences between them are interesting. The combined probability of initiation and expansion on the initiator's side is 0.25 percent without an offensive ally and 0.49 percent with an offensive ally. The combined probability of initiation and expansion on the target's side is

Table 2   Changes in Population Risk Based on Analysis in Table 1

Dependent Variable/ Independent Variable	Risk of Dep. Var. in Sample	With Ind. Var. = 0	With Ind. Var. = 1	Percentage Change
Probability Conditional on Initiation				
Initiator Help/Offensive Ally	19.8	18.9	22.8	+21%
Target Help/Defensive Ally	19.1	13.5	38.3	+184%
Target Help/Neutrality Pact	19.1	20.6	12.4	−40%
Probability of Initiation and Expansion				
Initiator Help/Offensive Ally	0.31	0.25	0.49	+96%
Target Help/Defensive Ally	0.30	0.24	0.44	+83%
Target Help/Neutrality Pact	0.30	0.31	0.29	−6%

0.24 percent without a defensive ally and 0.44 percent with a defensive ally; 0.29 percent when the initiator has a neutrality pact and 0.31 percent when the initiator does not have a neutrality pact.

Thus, while offensive alliances have a relatively small impact on the probability of expansion once a dispute is initiated, they have a fairly large impact on the combined probability of dispute initiation and expansion, doubling the likelihood. Defensive alliances decrease the likelihood that a dispute will be initiated, but because they have a very large impact on the probability of dispute expansion if a dispute begins, they make larger disputes more likely on balance.

This empirical analysis provides support for the claim that alliances are good predictors of the probability that disputes will be multilateral crises; states with allies committed to assist them are more likely to receive outside help in disputes. Thus, defensive and offensive alliances do seem to be associated with the probability that disputes expand to involve additional actors. Those who have argued that alliances serve as a conduit for the expansion and diffusion of conflict will find support in this analysis (e.g., Siverson and Starr 1991).

Next I consider the influence of military alliances on the probability of particularly severe disputes—those that end in war. The dependent variable in this analysis is a dichotomous variable indicating whether the dispute is coded by the Correlates of War project as escalating to war (Small and Singer 1982; Sarkees 2000). I analyze both the direct and indirect effects of alliances on escalation. In one model, I include variables representing outside alliances to the initiator and target as independent variables. In the second, I include a variable representing whether more than two states were involved in the dispute before it escalated to war to capture dispute expansion.

I include two control variables as well. First, I include a dichotomous measure of joint democracy, coded 1 if both states score a six or higher on the POLITY democracy scale (Jaggers and Gurr 1996). While scholars tend to agree that democratic states are less likely to become involved in militarized disputes with one another (e.g., Russett and Oneal 2001), there is much less agreement on the relationship between joint democracy and the escalation of disputes to war (Dixon 1993; Senese 1997). Very few democratic disputes emerge, which makes it difficult to evaluate the phenomenon. While some argue that even once military hostilities have erupted, democratic states are better at bargaining to agreement short of war, others claim that democracies may be particularly prone to getting locked into an escalatory process and finding it difficult to back down from crises once they have begun (e.g., Fearon 1994b). Because a number of scholars have suggested, however, that jointly democratic dyads may exhibit unique tendencies, I include a control variable to isolate these effects.

Second, I include a measure of the difference in power between the initiator and the target. Many have argued that conflicts are most likely to escalate to war when both sides are uncertain who would win a war, and this is most likely when the two sides are relatively equal in power. Using the Correlates of War National Capability Index, I calculate the difference in power between the stronger state in the dyad and the weaker state. Smaller values mean that the states are relatively equal in power, whereas larger values indicate more difference in power between the two combatants.[16]

The results of this analysis are presented in Table 3. Once we account for the factors that cause disputes to emerge in the first place, alliances have little direct influence on the likelihood that the parties bargain to a settlement before reaching the threshold of war. Defensive alliances seem to have some restraining effect (the negative coefficient is significant at the 0.10 level), but alliances to the initiator do not have a discernible effect on the probability that disputes end in war. Bilateral disputes, however, are less likely to escalate to war. Since alliances do have a clear impact on the likelihood that a dispute expands, they may be indirectly related to escalation. While jointly democratic dyads are neither more nor less likely than other dyads to end up in war once they have begun a dispute, similarities in power are correlated with a greater probability of escalation.[17]

Table 3   The Effects of Outside Allies on the Probability That Militarized Interstate Disputes Escalate to War, 1816–1944

	Model 1, Coefficient (s.e.)	Model 2, Coefficient (s.e.)
Joint Democracy	−0.251 (0.342)	−0.160 (0.335)
Difference in Capabilities	−1.734 (0.956)	−2.023 (0.984)*
Target has Def. Ally When Dispute Begins	−0.300 (0.180)	—
Initiator has Off. Ally When Dispute Begins	0.066 (0.186)	—
Initiator has Neut. Pact When Dispute Begins	−0.071 (0.195)	—
Bilateral Dispute	—	−0.479 (0.134)**
Constant	1.567	−0.518
Selection: Dispute Initiation		
Joint Democracy	−0.143 (0.059)*	−0.143 (0.059)
Contiguity	0.523 (0.031)**	0.523 (0.031)**
Power of Challenger in Relation to Target	0.192 (0.038)**	0.192 (0.038)**

(Continued)

Table 3   (Continued)

	Model 1, Coefficient (s.e.)	Model 2, Coefficient (s.e.)
Similarity in Alliance Portfolios	−0.408 (0.040)**	−0.406 (0.40)**
Potential Target has Defensive Ally	−0.191 (0.033)**	−0.193 (0.033(**
Potential Challenger has Offensive Ally	0.185 (0.038)**	0.185 (0.038)**
Potential Challenger has Relevant Neut. Pact	0.202 (0.039)	0.202 (0.039)
Constant	−2.306**	−2.307**
Rho (Chi^2)	0.138 (0.19)	−0.179 (0.45)
N (total, uncensored)	69730,812	69730,812
Chi^2	6.97	15.77**

$*p < 0.05; **p < 0.001$

Turning once again to the substantive importance of the primary independent variables in influencing the escalation of disputes to war (reported in Table 4), we find that once a dispute emerges, the average probability of escalation to war is only 4.7 percent for a bilateral dispute, but 11.5 percent for a multilateral dispute similar in all other characteristics. It appears that bargains are more difficult to reach short of war when multiple parties are involved. Because alliances are so likely to be associated with dispute expansion, they may indirectly cause escalation as well.

While the direct effect of alliances on the probability of war once a dispute has emerged is relatively weak, there is a fairly clear impact of alliances on the combined probability that a dispute is initiated and

Table 4   Changes in Population Risk Based on Analysis in Table 3

Dependent Variable/Independent Variable	Risk of Dep. Var. in Sample	With Ind. Var. = 0	With Ind. Var. = 1	Percentage Change
Probability Conditional on Initiation				
War/Multilateral Dispute	7.5	4.7	11.5	+145%
Probability of Initiation and Escalation				
War/Offensive Ally	0.09	0.08	0.14	+75%
War/Defensive Ally	0.09	0.11	0.04	−64%
War/Neutrality Pact	0.09	0.08	0.11	+38%

escalates to war. The probability that a dispute will emerge and escalate to war in a given dyad averages .04 percent with a defensive ally to a target and 0.11 percent without—the risk of war is nearly tripled when a target does not have an ally. The average probability of initiating a dispute and escalating it to war is 0.08 percent for a potential challenger without an offensive ally and 0.14 percent for a potential challenger with an ally committed to assist her. Gaining a neutrality pact similarly changes the joint probability of initiation and escalation from 0.08 percent to 0.11 percent.

In the end, the data suggest that the strongest impact of alliances is on the probability that a dispute is initiated. Defensive alliances to a target make dispute initiate less likely, and offensive alliances to the initiator and neutrality pacts with the initiator make dispute initiation more likely. Once initiation occurs, however, alliances are associated with dispute expansion, and dispute expansion is in turn associated with a higher probability that a dispute escalates to war. There is reason to believe that even defensive alliances, when they fail to deter aggression, are associated with particularly severe conflicts. On balance, however, in the sample studied here, defensive alliances have made war less likely. Because they deter initiation, they reduce the overall risk of war, even if they raise the risks once a dispute begins.

Conclusion

International relations scholars have devoted tremendous energy to explaining the causes of war and developing effective deterrent strategies. Both in developing explanations and recommending policy, scholars have turned frequently to military alliances. Despite intense interest, however, scholars have been frustrated by their inability to discern clear systematic relationships linking alliances to deterrence success and to the probability of war. One of the primary reasons for this difficulty is that, until recently, statistical analyses of factors affecting general deterrence, and particularly those linking general and immediate deterrence, have been scarce.

As some researchers have suspected, similar policies can have different effects on the probable success of general deterrence and of immediate deterrence, and a full understanding of their impacts requires a linked analysis of both (e.g., Huth 1999).

Alliances are a case in point. Defensive alliances are an effective means of general deterrence. Promises to assist a potential target in the event of overt conflict do make a challenger less likely to attack. When general deterrence fails, however, alliance commitments can serve to expand conflicts and complicate the bargaining required for successful settlement. When alliances fail to deter the initiation of disputes, they are more likely to be associated with conflicts that expand, and in turn, that escalate to full-scale war.

Overall, the appropriate conclusion to reach seems to be that most of the influence of alliances on military conflict occurs before an overt military dispute emerges. Challengers do use the information they have about the probability that they or their targets will receive assistance in deciding whether to begin a dispute, and this information seems to be fairly reliable: alliances are good predictors of the likelihood that a dispute becomes a multilateral crisis. Multilateral crises are more difficult to resolve in a low-cost manner than are bilateral crises, and thus, alliances may be indirectly associated with a greater risk of war. The evidence provided here, however, suggests that the general deterrent impact of defensive alliances is strong enough to make their overall impact pacifying.

Notes

Author's Note: This research was supported by the National Science Foundation (grant # SES-0095983). I would like to thank Vesna Danilovic, Erik Gartzke, Håvard Hegre, Jack Levy, Sara Mitchell, Cliff Morgan, Bill Reed, Jeff Ritter, Holger Schmidt, Randy Stevenson, and Ric Stoll for helpful advice on this research. Replication data is available at www.ruf.rice.edu/~leeds.

1. For a review, see Vasquez (1993).
2. For the purpose of this study, alliances are defined as "written agreements, signed by official representatives

of at least two independent states, that include promises to aid a partner in the event of military conflict, to remain neutral in the event of conflict, to refrain from military conflict with one another, or to consult/co-operate in the event of international crises that create a potential for military conflict" (Leeds, Ritter, Mitchell, and Long 2002, 238).

3. For an application of this claim (based on social choice theory) to international relations, see Miers and Morgan 2002.

4. In the Correlates of War data, version 3.0 (Sarkees 2000), the mean length of multilateral wars is 552 days, while the mean length of bilateral wars is 358 days.

5. I refer to alliances that include promises of active military assistance in the event of attack on a member's sovereignty or territorial integrity as defensive alliances, and alliances that include promises of active military assistance in conflicts not precipitated by attack on a member's sovereignty or territorial integrity as offensive alliances. Some alliances, because they include promises of active assistance in both of these situations, are both defensive and offensive alliances. See Leeds et al. (2002, 241) for a discussion of this categorization, and Leeds (2003a, 432–33) for examples of treaty language characteristic of defensive alliances, offensive alliances, and defensive and offensive alliances.

6. Additional evidence in support of this claim is provided by Huth (1998), who shows that major powers are more likely to intervene in crises when they have alliance commitments to participants (see also Huth and Russett 1988), and Siverson and Starr (1991) who identify alliances as agents of conflict diffusion. An alternative argument, however, is offered by Smith (1995). Smith suggests that because reliable alliances deter conflict initiators, the observed cases in which challengers attack targets with allies should be biased toward targets who will not receive support. It is worth noting that the question addressed here—are disputes involving challengers and targets with allies more likely to expand?—is a slightly different question than that addressed in studies that demonstrate that allies are more likely to join conflicts than non-allies (e.g., Huth 1998; Werner and Lemke 1997).

7. I assembled this dataset using the EUGene computer program (Bennett and Stam 2000). The indicators for my dependent variables and most of my independent variables are not available for the pre-1816 era, and the data for my primary independent variables are only available through 1944, so my temporal domain is constrained to the years between 1815 and 1945. The directed dyadic research design allows one to distinguish factors leading to the initiation of a dispute from factors conducive to being the target of a dispute. Limiting the spatial domain to interactions among states who are plausible candidates for military conflict restricts the sample in a way that appears not to threaten proper inference (Lemke and Reed 2001a).

8. All analysis was performed using the *heckprob* command in STATA 7.0; this is a probit model with sample selection.

9. This study uses the dyadic version of the MID data (version 1.1) provided by Zeev Maoz. Only pairs of states that engage one another directly are included as disputing dyads, and only original initiators and original targets are included at this stage of analysis. Decisions to join ongoing disputes are studied separately. Original initiators are states that are coded as original participants on side A (the side to take the first militarized action), and original targets are those that are coded as original participants on side B. The data can be obtained at http//spirit.tau.ac.il/~zeevmaoz (January 29, 2001).

10. See Leeds (2003a) for discussion of the expected influence of these variables and their operationalization. There are two changes in the analysis presented as the first stage of the selection equation here from the analysis reported in Leeds (2003a). First, since the variable representing membership in a common alliance never reaches conventional levels of statistical significance in any of the models, I have eliminated it from the analysis. This has no effect on the interpretation of the other variables. Second, in the two-stage format, I am unable to adjust the analysis to account for temporal dynamics. Without accounting for the cross-sectional time series nature of the data, one inference does change. Joint democracy, which was negative but statistically insignificant in the original analysis (using a population-averaged panel data model), is negatively related to the initiation of disputes here.

11. Many alliance treaties state that the obligations arise only under clearly specified circumstances. I have been careful to include only alliances that would be applicable to conflicts arising in the dyad in question. I also checked the dates of alliance formation and of dispute initiation and only included alliances that were in effect on the date the dispute began. It is important to note that obligations were coded in the Alliance Treaty Obligations and Provisions (ATOP) dataset based solely on the texts of the written alliance agreements and independent of the behavior that followed them. Please see Leeds, Ritter, Mitchell, and Long (2002) for further discussion of the distinctions among different types of obligations in the ATOP dataset and the specific nature of alliance commitments.

12. In designing my statistical models, I have included different control variables in my models of different aspects of dispute evolution. While there are a number of variables that prior research has shown to have some empirical effect on disputes or war, our theories tell us that different variables affect different parts of the dispute process. For instance, while contiguity has a relatively strong effect on the probability that a dispute is initiated since contiguous states find it easier to fight one another and tend to interact on a great number of issues over which disputes might arise, we have no compelling theories that suggest that once a dispute has begun contiguous states are more or less likely to engage in multilateral disputes or to escalate their disputes to war. Contiguity, therefore, is included as a control variable in the model predicting dispute initiation, but not in models of dispute expansion or escalation. The fact that the control variables in my models of dispute initiation are different from the variables in my models of various aspects of dispute evolution has the additional benefit of identifying the joint probit models.

13. For a discussion of this debate, see Walt (1987).

14. What I report here is the change in the average risk for the population given changes only in the characteristics of interest. In other words, I reanalyze predicted probabilities retaining all the same characteristics of the observations except for their alliances. Thus, the figures represent the average risk for a population where targets do have defensive allies versus one in which targets do not have defensive allies.

15. In the case of assistance to the initiator, we see a clear statistical connection between the initiation and expansion stages. The rho (the correlation between the error terms of the selection and outcome models) is highly significant. In fact, most of the influence of offensive allies is on the decision to initiate. In the case of assistance to the target, however, the error terms of the initiation and expansion equations are not significantly correlated. Empirically, it may be possible to study the two stages independently, and an independent test of the expansion model leads to similar inferences. Because there is theoretical reason to believe that a joint estimation is warranted, however, I choose to report the two stage model.

16. Please note that this measure of dyadic power relations is different from the measure included in the models of dispute expansion. In the models of dispute expansion, I include control variables that measure whether the initiator is stronger than the target. Larger values indicate the initiator is strong and the target is weak in comparison, and smaller values indicate that the target is strong in comparison to the initiator. In this analysis, the measure of dyadic power relations does not indicate who is stronger, but rather how much difference there is between the power of the stronger and weaker actors. Large values indicate that one state is much stronger than the other (but not who is the stronger state) and smaller values indicate that the two states are fairly equal in power.

17. These models have extremely poor predictive ability—neither predicts any wars, and thus neither improves on a null model. Because the outcome models are so poor, it is not surprising that the rhos are insignificant—the error terms in the outcome equations surely include much more than the unobservable relationship to the initiation model.

EDITORS' COMMENTARY

Major Contributions: Alliances

Leeds's (2005) study seeks to understand the relationship between military alliances and interstate wars. She defines military alliances as written agreements between two or more states that include promises for **defense, offense,** or **neutrality** in the event of military conflict; promises to refrain from military conflict with allies (**nonaggression**); or promises to **consult** partners in international crisis situations. Leeds spearheaded the collection of information on these types of alliance treaties and provisions in a major data collection project from 1815 to 2003, called the Alliance Treaty Obligation and Provisions (ATOP) data set (Leeds et al. 2002).[1]

The ATOP project includes information on 648 military alliance treaties. This data set is useful for testing the relationship between alliances and war, an area of the conflict literature where there has been disagreement. On one side are scholars who argue that alliances can deter the onset of war by enhancing the credibility of potential intervention by third parties and thus raising the costs of war (e.g., Smith 1995; Leeds 2003a). On the other side are scholars asserting that alliances can increase the chances for war by generating counteralliances and arms races and raising the prospects that bilateral conflicts will spread to multilateral wars (e.g., Levy 1981; Vasquez 1993).

Some of the earliest work on interstate alliances and war was conducted by the Correlates of War (COW) project. J. David Singer collaborated with Melvin Small, a historian, to collect data on formal alliances from 1816 onward (Singer and Small 1966b; Small and Singer 1969). They were interested in examining whether alliances were related to war onset or peace. The COW alliance data set records the highest level of commitment in an agreement, ranging from an entente (or consultation pact), to a nonaggression/neutrality pact, to a defense pact. In one of their first published studies (Singer and Small 1966a), the authors found that states that rank high on having alliances also rank high on the amount of war they experience, while those that rank low on alliance membership also rank low on war participation (see also Vasquez 1993, 183–85). This relationship holds more strongly for the central system, which includes the strongest states and focuses on Europe. They subsequently tested a second hypothesis—the greater the number of alliance commitments in the system, the more war in the system. They found support for this hypothesis for the twentieth century (from 1900–1945) but not for the nineteenth century (Singer and Small 1968). A subsequent study looking at how alliance blocs affect the distribution of capability uncovered a similar intercentury difference (Singer, Bremer, and Stuckey 1972). In this case, when alliances in the system reflect a preponderance of power, wars tend to be frequent but not very severe (nineteenth century after 1815), but when alliance aggregation reflects parity, wars tend to be infrequent but quite severe, as in the two world wars. All of these studies focused on the systemic-level relationship between alliances and war.

Levy (1981) extended data on alliances back to 1495 and provided evidence that alliances, especially those involving Great Powers, were generally followed by war within five years, except for the entire nineteenth century, when they were associated with peace. While Levy showed that alliances were sometimes associated with war, he found that most wars were not preceded by alliances and thus were not necessary conditions for war. This means that when alliances are present (in most centuries), they can increase the chances for war, but many wars that have occurred since 1495 do not involve any alliances that preceded the war. Since these early studies, the COW data have been updated (Gibler and Sarkees 2004; Gibler 2009).

One of the criticisms of the COW data collection has been that the data examine whether an alliance commitment simply exists without going into detail about the nature of that commitment. This became an important theoretical issue because Sabrosky (1980) found that when alliances are put to the test when a war breaks out, alliance partners do not always follow through and enter a war in which their allies are involved. He found that states are reliable allies only about 25 percent of the time. Leeds et al. (2000) challenged this finding by arguing that Sabrosky (1980) did not look at the specific obligations states undertook in their formal commitments. Their ATOP data set codes information about all types of commitments in military alliances and also considers any situations where commitments may be limited to specific situations. For example, some alliance treaties have provisions for both defense and consultation. By using an ordinal scale of commitment, as the COW alliance data set does, this omits information about the multiple types of commitments that states might make in a treaty. Furthermore, alliances often specify that the provisions pertain only to certain targets or places. Many European alliances would be paired with wars outside the region in Sabrosky's (1980) study, even though the wars are unrelated to the alliances in question. For example, when European states are fighting in the Boxer Rebellion or the Franco-Mexican War, alliances signed for defensive purposes in the European continent are not relevant to these conflict situations. Their inclusion thus increases the number of cases that appear as unreliable alliances. Leeds et al. (2000) used the more precise data on alliance commitments to match those alliances that are potentially triggered by interstate wars (e.g., relevant to the war in question). They found that about 75 percent of allies are reliable in wartime and do as promised in their alliance treaties. By considering what states promise to do in military alliances, we get a better sense of their overall efficacy.

ATOP data have now become standard data on which to test hypotheses related to alliances. One of the major studies using the data is Leeds's (2003a) article, which asks whether alliances deter the onset of militarized conflict. Obviously, only certain kinds of alliances—namely, defensive alliances—would be expected to do this; other types, such as offensive alliances, would have the opposite effect. Leeds is interested in whether the presence of defensive alliances would deter challengers from using the threat or use of force, that is, restrain them from initiating militarized interstate disputes (MIDs; see also Bremer 1992b, Chapter 2, this volume). Sometimes this is referred to as **general deterrence** (Asal and Beardsley 2007, Chapter 13, this volume). Looking at the prenuclear 1815 to 1944 period, Leeds (2003a, 435–36) finds that states with defensive alliances are 28 percent less likely to have MIDs initiated against them compared with those potential target states without defensive alliances. Defensive alliances have a muting effect on MIDs—that is, they do not eliminate all MIDs being initiated, but they do reduce them in a statistically significant fashion.[2]

She also shows that other types of alliances increase the likelihood of attack, such as alliances with promises for offensive aid or neutrality. Potential challengers with an offensive alliance pact are 47 percent more likely to initiate a MID and 57 percent more likely to initiate a MID if they have a neutrality pact. Johnson and Leeds (2011) show that these results for MID initiation hold in a longer period (1816–2000).

Leeds's (2005) study in this volume addresses the question of war onset and relates it to her earlier (2003a) study. She still maintains that defensive alliances reduce the number of MIDs and thus indirectly have a negative impact on war, but she considers what happens if deterrence fails and MIDs are initiated in the presence of a defensive alliance. In this circumstance, she finds that allies are reliable, as shown in Leeds et al. (2000)—that is, they intervene in the MID in support of their allies. She then shows that multiparty MIDs are more prone to escalate to war, a finding consistent with other studies (Petersen et al. 2004). The reason multiparty disputes are more war prone is that they make bargaining more difficult and intractable, thereby preventing a peaceful or at least a nonviolent settlement.

Leeds (2005) thus untangles a very complex process involving defensive alliances and their impact on MID and war onset. These are two very different dependent variables, but by having a negative impact on the initiation of MIDs, defensive alliances have an indirect impact on war since, by definition, there cannot be a war without a preceding MID in this data set. Nonetheless, because they are reliable, defensive alliances help conflict spread once a MID is initiated. Deterrence failure then increases multiparty MIDs, and these have been found, as Leeds shows, to be more likely to escalate to war.

Leeds (2005) also helps to untangle the varying effects of alliances on war onset by looking at the different types of alliances—defensive, offensive, and neutrality pacts. She hypothesizes that when an initiator has an offensive alliance, it is more likely that a dispute will expand. This makes sense in that the initiator will be emboldened by the added support of an ally. She also hypothesizes that when the target has a defensive alliance, this alliance will be reliable and the dispute will expand on the target side. Finally, she takes neutrality pacts at their word and that allies will remain neutral when a conflict erupts. Each of these hypotheses is supported at the bottom of Table 3.

Leeds (2005) also has some interesting control variables. She finds that when outsiders join one side of a dispute, other states will join the other side. This clearly reflects contagion, and it is consistent with a finding of Yamamoto and Bremer (1980) that as one major state intervenes in a war, others are more likely to intervene. She also finds that when the initiator is stronger than the target, it is more apt to gain outside support, something that goes against **balance of power** expectations but supports **bandwagoning** (i.e., states join the stronger side rather than the weaker side). Under realist theory, states are believed to have an interest in balancing the strongest state in the system, often through alliances. Allying with the strongest state(s), on the other hand, is called bandwagoning. This is considered dangerous because if the strongest state wins a war, the weaker ally has nothing to protect it against the dominant power. Levy and Thompson (2005) show that bandwagoning is more common for sea powers such as the United Kingdom and United States, while balancing alliances form more often against rising land powers such as Germany and Russia.

Methodological Notes: Selection Bias and Two-Stage Models

Leeds (2005) is very concerned about possible **selection bias** in her analysis. Selection models account for the dynamic stages of the conflict process by considering the possibility that unobserved factors that influence the onset of a militarized dispute may be correlated with factors that predict whether the dispute will escalate to war (Reed 2000, Chapter 11, this volume). For example, factors that increase the chances for deterrence, such as power preponderance, may have the opposite effect on escalation to war. Leeds estimates two different selection models. In Table 1, the two stages are MID onset in stage 1 (the selection equation) and allied support to the target in stage 2 (the outcome equation). For stage 1, she collects information on 69,730 politically relevant directed dyads; cases only enter stage 2 if an ally came to the support of the target state in the MID (812 cases). In Table 3, the two stages of the selection model are MID onset in stage 1 and escalation to war in stage 2.

Consider the effect of the variables that predict MID onset on the potency of variables that seem to account for MID escalation to war. In Table 3, for example, the selection stage is given at the bottom of the table and the factors thought to affect escalation to war are at the top. It can be seen that most of the variables at the bottom of the table are significantly related to dispute initiation. For example, contiguity is positively related to MID onset (i.e., contiguous states are more apt to experience MIDs). This is also the case when the potential challenger has an offensive alliance. But note when the target has a defensive alliance, it is less likely to have a MID initiated against it (note the negative sign). This is similar to Leeds' (2003a) empirical findings. States with similar alliance portfolios (an indicator of similar interests) and jointly democratic dyads are also less likely to become involved in a MID.

Once we control for the selection process of dispute initiation, however, many of these variables have different effects on dispute escalation to war. Note that all of the alliance variables are statistically insignificant, as is joint democracy. This means that whatever is related to war onset has something to do with what produces MID onset in the first place. This is true despite the fact that the rho statistic is not significant. The rho statistic is a way of measuring whether there is an overall selection between the two samples by seeing if their error terms are correlated (Reed 2000). Nonetheless the selection variables wipe out the variables at the top.

Contrast Table 3 with Table 1, which examines whether outsiders aid an initiator or a target. This table looks at whether a MID expands to become a multiparty MID. It can be seen that many of the variables in the selection stage at the bottom of the table are significant, but the variables in the second stage that predict whether an outside state will help an initiator or target are also significant. The independent variables that predict MID onset do not wipe out the effects of variables that predict MID enlargement once we control for the relationship between the onset and enlargement of MIDs. Consider the effect of defensive alliances. In the first stage in Table 1, we can see that defensive alliances with potential targets reduce the chances for MID onset. In the second stage, if the target state has one or more defensive allies when the MID begins, the dispute is less likely to escalate to a multiparty MID.

Tables 2 and 4 examine how strong these relationships are by reporting the probability of a dispute expanding or escalating to war. In Table 2, column 3 reports the probability for initiation or expansion (top and bottom of the table) when the independent variable is zero (absent) and column 4 when the independent variable is 1 (present). It can be seen in row 4 that when the initiator does not have an offensive alliance, the probability of getting help is 0.25, but when it does have an offensive ally, the probability of third-party assistance goes up to 0.49. In other words, just about 50 percent of the time, a state gets help from an alliance partner in which the treaty specifies offensive obligations. The next row reports the probabilities of a target getting help when it does not have a defensive alliance and when it does. When it does not have an alliance with defensive provisions, the probability of getting help is 0.24, and when it does, it goes up to 0.44. This is consistent with the idea discussed earlier that alliance partners generally do as promised, often coming to the aid of their allies in conflict situations. This table gives us a much better understanding of how allies affect the probability of war once a MID has occurred and deterrence has failed.

Notes

1. These data and a description of the alliances can be found at http://atop.rice.edu/data.
2. Sometimes this finding is seen as contradictory to some of the findings that relate alliances positively to war onset. This is not entirely true since the dependent variable in Leeds' (2003a) study is MID onset and not war onset (Senese and Vasquez 2005, Chapter 7, this volume). Also, it must be kept in mind that several studies have shown that alliances in the nineteenth century tend to be followed by peace, and not by war, and Leeds has included the post-Napoleonic nineteenth century in her time period.

Questions

1. Go to Table 2. When a target has a neutrality pact, what is the probability it will get help? When it does not have a neutrality pact, what is the probability that it will get help? Do this for both the initiation of a MID (top part of the table) and the initiation and expansion of a MID (bottom part). Is this consistent with the theoretical expectations of hypothesis 3?

2. According to Leeds, do MIDs that expand have a higher probability of going to war than bilateral (or two-party) MIDs?

3. Once a MID occurs and a defensive alliance has failed to deter a MID, is the defensive alliance likely to prevent war onset?

Further Reading

Leeds, B. A. 2003a. Do alliances deter aggression? The influence of military alliances on the initiation of militarized interstate disputes. *American Journal of Political Science* 47 (3): 427–39.

Leeds, B. A., A. G. Long, and S. M. Mitchell. 2000. Re-evaluating alliance reliability: Specific threats, specific promises. *Journal of Conflict Resolution* 44 (5): 686–9.

Sabrosky, A. N. 1980. Interstate alliances: Their reliability and the expansion of war. In *The Correlates of War, II,* ed. J. D. Singer. New York: Free Press.

Smith, A. 1995. Alliance formation and war. *International Studies Quarterly* 39 (4): 405–25.

Chapter 5

The New Rivalry Dataset

Procedures and Patterns

James P. Klein, Gary Goertz, and Paul R. Diehl

Introduction

Less than two decades ago, the predominant research mode in international conflict research was cross-sectional, time-series analysis in which conflict events (disputes, crises, wars) were treated as independent observations. The 1990s saw the emergence of a new research agenda focused on enduring rivalries, longstanding competitions between the same pair of states. Rivalry research presumed that conflict events were related to one another over space and time. This had significant implications for how one modeled the initiation, dynamics, and termination of such conflicts. See Diehl & Goertz (2000) on the 'rivalry approach'. Early rivalry research used the phenomena simply as a case-selection device, especially when rivalries were suitable for testing propositions about deterrence or power transitions. Subsequently, however, rivalries became foci of research in their own right. Rivalries have now become an integral feature of international conflict research, with new books, articles, and conference papers appearing each year that deal with these relationships. See Goertz & Diehl (2000) for a summary of rivalry research.

If the concept of rivalries assumes that conflict is related over space and time, there must be some agreement on which conflicts are indeed related and which are independent. This involves finding the appropriate point on a continuum between endpoints in which all conflict events between dyads are related ('one large rivalry') and all conflict events are independent. There has been some excellent case study work on rivalries (Thompson, 1999), but large-N empirical research on rivalries requires systematic conceptualizations and operational definitions. There are only a handful of rivalry data collections (Bennett, 1997; Diehl & Goertz, 2000; Thompson, 2001). Moreover, there remains debate as to the appropriateness of each dataset. Yet, the most commonly used has been that developed by Goertz & Diehl (1993; Diehl & Goertz, 2000); a large number of studies produced by other scholars as well as those by the authors themselves have adopted the definitions used in their collection.

The original Diehl & Goertz dataset on international rivalries was based heavily on the Correlates of War (COW) Project Militarized Interstate Dispute (MID) Data Set (Jones, Bremer & Singer, 1996), which included only data through 1992. The COW Project has now extended that data through 2001 (Ghosn, Palmer & Bremer, 2004), and we have extended the rivalry data accordingly. Notably, we have adopted additional criteria beyond the time-density approach used to define the original population of rivalries. The net result is a new dataset (RIV5.01) on international rivalries that covers the

Source: James P. Klein, Gary Goertz, and Paul R. Diehl, "The New Rivalry Dataset: Procedures and Patterns," *Journal of Peace Research* 43, no. 3 (2006): 331–48. © 2006 *Journal of Peace Research*. Reprinted by permission of SAGE Publications, Inc.

1816–2001 period and is designed to replace the original Diehl & Goertz (2000) collection. Below, we begin with a discussion of some of the conceptual and operational bases on which the original rivalry collection was based, and we identify and discuss all the major changes made vis-à-vis the earlier rivalry collection. We then turn to empirical analyses that highlight the conceptual dimensions of our rivalry concept.

The Rivalry Conceptualization

Before reviewing the specific details of operationalization and data gathering, it is useful to review our conception of a rivalry. It is very easy to confuse the *concept* of a rivalry with how that concept is operationalized. In this section, we deal exclusively with the concept of rivalry and its four dimensions. In the next section, we outline how we have put this concept into practice. In addition, we suggest that there has been confusion in the literature dealing with the distinction between 'enduring rivalries' and the concept of 'rivalries' per se. Confusion may exist because many have focused on 'enduring rivalries' as their core concept; in contrast, we started with a concept of rivalries (Diehl & Goertz, 2000: Part I) and then looked at an important subset of rivalries, the enduring kind.

In our original conception (for a full discussion, see Diehl & Goertz, 2000), we regarded rivalries as possessing and varying across four constituent 'secondary-level' (Goertz, 2005) dimensions: (1) spatial consistency, (2) duration, (3) militarized competitiveness, and (4) linked conflict. Figure 1 provides an overview of our concept of a rivalry and its operationalization. For purposes of comparison, we have included Thompson's (1995, 2001) conceptualization and operationalization. Much confusion about conceptualization and operationalization can be avoided by tracking issues with regard to this figure.

Spatial Consistency

The first dimension of rivalries revolves around the character and number of actors.

In short, actors in rivalries consist of *states*, and rivalries are *dyadic*. Rivalries consist of the same pair of states competing with each other, and the expectation of a future conflict relationship is one that is specific as to whom the opponent will be. These two aspects of spatial consistency have gone virtually unchallenged and largely unaddressed in the literature. As no two rivalries are coterminous anyway, such a conceptualization allows scholars to ask questions about how related or 'linked' rivalries intersect and diverge. See Diehl & Goertz (2000: ch. 12).

Duration

A second dimension of rivalries is their duration. Historically, scholars focused on enduring rivalries because of their importance in understanding international conflict. We have always held that the concept of rivalry itself not be limited to 'enduring' rivalries. For a variety of methodological and theoretical reasons, it is crucial to allow for short-term rivalries (e.g. as a control group); in Diehl & Goertz (2000), we designated these shorter-term rivalries as 'proto-rivalries'. The key point then and now is that the rivalry concept should allow for both shorter and longer (enduring) rivalries. It is reasonable for various theoretical and methodological purposes to focus on some subset of rivalries (e.g. severe or long-term), but one should not build this into the concept of rivalry per se.

Although we always regarded rivalry as a continuous concept, we have sharpened the distinction between isolated conflict and rivalry. The new dataset is based on the notion that there are two broad categories of conflict: isolated conflict and rivalry. We no longer regard isolated conflicts as rivalries. In previous research, we and others often used this category of conflicts to signify rivalries that never evolved beyond their nascent stages. Yet, an examination of individual cases reveals that it was probably a mistake to consider these rivalries at all, as most lacked the essential components of rivalries. Isolated conflicts tended to be single instance military confrontations between two states embedded in multilateral wars and lesser disputes. Such states

Figure 1   The Rivalry Concept: A Three-Level View

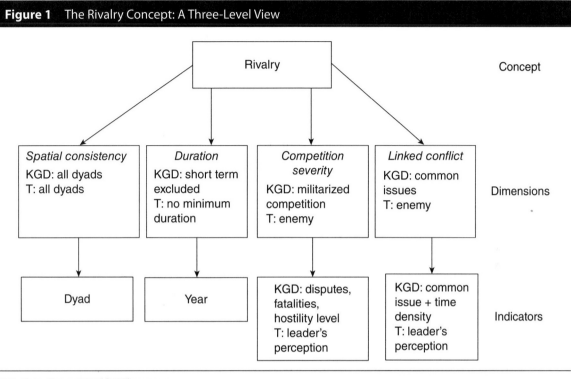

KGD: Klein, Goertz & Diehl; T: Thompson.

joined different sides in those conflicts but had limited contact with one another, and their decisions to join were not motivated by a desire to confront the state in question (e.g. Canada and Bulgaria in World War II).

With respect to Thompson's (2001) conceptualization, we fundamentally agree that the concept of rivalry should include long- and short-term conflicts. Nevertheless, Thompson sets no minimum duration criterion. In principle, a rivalry could last one month. In practice (i.e. in the data), a rivalry may be limited to the duration of a war. We exclude such short-term or transient conflict from the rivalry category. As we describe below, we do not consider one or two dispute confrontations, which are coterminous with short durations, to be rivalries. This ensures that conflict lasts long enough or repeats

itself with enough frequency that states regard themselves in a protracted competition.

Militarized Competition

As a third dimension, we saw 'rivalry relationships' as forming a particular subset of 'international relations'. We did not focus on 'relations' in general, but *militarized* and *conflictual* ones in particular. A rivalry relationship is one in which the military component of foreign policy is an important element: much of their foreign policy is conceived of and conducted in military terms. This dimension, not surprisingly, has been the one that has provoked the most debate in discussions of enduring rivalries.

When states are engaged in a rivalry, they have conflicting goals over the disposition of scarce goods. Having conflicting goals does not necessarily mean that the preferences of the competitors are irreconcilable or that the competition is entirely zero-sum (although this may be the case in some rivalries). These goods may be intangible, such as political influence (as in 'power politics' conceptions) or ideological/religious dominance. The competition may also be over more tangible goods, such as natural resources or territory. In practice, it is likely that individual rivalries reflect varying mixes of these sources of competition. As in conflict and war studies in general, we limit ourselves to competitions that take a military turn.

We have retained this conceptualization, but it still stands in marked contrast to other rivalry definitions. Thompson (1995, 2001) does not explicitly require overt military actions to qualify as a rivalry. His conceptualization is based largely on perception, rather than action; states must regard each other as 'enemies'. In a related fashion, there must be actual or latent threats that pose some possibility of becoming militarized, but these do not have to be manifest with any frequency. Another notable difference between our conceptualization and those of others is the level of severity required for a rivalry to exist. Thompson's (1995, 2001) use of the terms 'strategic' and 'principal' indicate that he regards only the most severe forms of competition as rivalries (and his list of cases is consistent with this). It is crucial, however, to allow for variation on the severity dimension. Although there are various questions that require a focus exclusively on the most severe rivalries, we think that truncating the rivalry concept this way unnecessarily limits the range of questions that can be considered, as well as posing some potential methodological difficulties (e.g. selection effects). As with the duration dimension, our concept allows rivalry to vary significantly on the military competition continuum, once the threshold of such competition is crossed.

Linked Conflict

A final dimension of rivalries is that the conflicts within them are 'linked', that is, they are related over space and time. Events in a rivalry are not independent of one another, but rather are interconnected by several elements (including the unresolved issues over which states dispute). There are two conceptual linkages between disputes. The first is the 'pull of the past'. Rivals have a joint history, and events in the rivalry (particularly past military confrontations) exercise an influence on present and future behaviors. The initial interactions in a rivalry often set the tone for future confrontations. Failure to resolve disputes over a given issue or set of issues can set the stage for future conflicts over the same. States also develop or 'lock-in' policies and strategies for the rivalry based on those initial confrontations. Rivals may also 'learn' from these confrontations, which can affect the strategies they pursue in the rivalry (Maoz & Mor, 2002). For example, it is clear that the 1967 Arab-Israeli War (and indeed previous wars as well) conditioned subsequent war and rivalry behavior in the Middle East.

The second linkage element is in the form of 'expectations of future conflict'. Rivals expect that mutual disputes, crises, and war are likely to continue into the future. These expectations condition current foreign policy choices, which then may have downstream consequences for the dynamics of rivalries and their potential for peaceful resolution. For example, decisions to build up one's military capabilities or join an alliance are made in anticipation of continuing threats into the future. With policy inertia and the inculcation of rivalry hostility into domestic political audiences, such expectations are mechanisms to keep the rivalry going and provide continuity between present and future conflicts. One might argue that India's intervention in the 1971 Bangladesh War was influenced not only by past wars with Pakistan, but also by the prospect that it would again confront Pakistan in the future over Kashmir.

Overall, we have largely maintained the four components of our rivalry concepts from our original formulation. The major changes concern the duration dimension, in which we now make a much cleaner distinction between isolated conflict and rivalry, as well as an explicit emphasis on the linked conflict dimension, only implicit in the original conceptualization. We stress that it is important to allow for variation on the duration and competition/ severity dimensions. We still maintain our concern for the long-term and severe conflicts as the major threats to international peace, but one should not build those concerns into the concept of a rivalry itself. As illustrated below in our descriptive analyses, we can only see important patterns and address interesting hypotheses by being able to compare rivalries of different durations and severities.

The Rivalry Operationalization

As illustrated in Figure 1, one must keep the various dimensions of the rivalry concept separate from how they are operationalized in terms of data creation and analysis. For example, there are various alternatives for operationalizing the competitiveness and severity of a rivalry. Even for duration, there are alternatives such as using the number of disputes instead of calendar time to indicate duration. Consistent with the changes in conceptualization, we made several changes to the measures used to identify rivalries. We also made several other alterations in order to improve the validity and utility of the collection.

Spatial Consistency

As a first step, we took all possible dyadic combinations of states involved in a given dispute on opposite sides (for example, the Cuban Missile Crisis is a part of both the US—Soviet Union rivalry and the US—Cuba rivalry). That is, we initially included all possible dyadic disputes in a multilateral dispute.[1] In our original data and in the new dataset, we stipulated that there must have been direct interaction or intent for interaction between the two sides. In the original data, we eliminated those dyads in which there was no clear contact between two states in a multilateral coalition (considerations of contiguity and the length of relative participation in the dispute, as well as consultation of historical narratives, assisted in these decisions). We also eliminated pairs of states that were involved on opposite

sides of the same dispute, but with no temporal overlap in participation (i.e. one disputant exits the dispute before the other enters). In the new data, we used the COW and Maoz (2005) lists of dyadic disputes to accomplish the same task (our original coding rules and Maoz's were almost identical).[2]

A related concern (N = 4) was what to do about states that entered, exited, and reentered a given dispute on the same side between the date it was first initiated and when it terminated (e.g. Syria in the Israeli—Lebanese war and Greece in some disputes between Cyprus and Turkey). We did not want to count these as multiple disputes. Accordingly, we counted these cases as only one instance of dyadic interaction and set the beginning date as the date of first entry and the end date as the date of last exit. When states switched sides during a war (N = 6, all during World War II), these were considered new disputes and potentially part of a new rivalry.

In addition, we identified a problem heretofore ignored in our previous formulation or indeed any previous rivalry conception: successor states. What happens to the ongoing rivalries when a state breaks apart (e.g. Soviet Union) or two states combine (e.g. Yemen)? We examined all cases of secession and unification, focusing on rivalries occurring before or after those events. In the overwhelming majority of cases, no coding issues arose. COW coding and international legal rules often made clear the identity of the successor state in secessions. For example, Turkey is the successor state for the Ottoman Empire. In other cases, militarized disputes did not occur for any of seceding states, rendering the need for coding decisions moot. In other instances, any disputes that occur following secession (e.g. involving the Koreas after World War II) were unrelated to previous rivalries. Unifications posed some different problems, but most of the coding was straightforward. For example, none of East Germany's rivalries continue after German unification. In other instances, however, disputed concerns continued after unification, and, therefore, these rivalries were combined, even as they involved somewhat different states on one side. For example, unified Yemen continued a border dispute with Saudi Arabia begun when Yemen was divided, and China's dispute with Vietnam over the Spratly Islands predates Vietnamese unification.

Duration, Militarized Competition, and Linked Conflict

The original rivalry dataset relied extensively on inductive logic to identify rivalries. The primary focus was on the militarized interstate disputes' (version 2.1 of the dataset—see Jones, Bremer & Singer, 1996). Specifically, we relied on the time density of militarized disputes to identify rivalries and distinguish between them. Conflict events closer in time were said to be connected (or part of the same rivalry), whereas those more distant in time were thought to be part of different competitions or rivalries. Disputes that occurred within 10–15 years of each other were considered part of the 'same rivalry'. A dispute was considered part of the same rivalry if it involves the same two states and occurred within 11 years of the first dispute of the sequence, 12 years after the second dispute, or up to 15 years after the fifth dispute.

As we moved to a starker distinction between rivalries and isolated conflict in the new dataset, we also had to decide operationally how to define those two categories. Although we drew upon the methods used in the previous version of the data, we made a number of important additions and modifications as well.

As in the previous version, we constructed a list of all disputes in which a pair of states (dyad) was involved. Our initial decision was to separate out all those instances in which only one or two disputes occurred between two states *over the whole 1816–2001 period*. All of these were automatically labeled as isolated conflicts, and no further tests were applied to this set of cases.[3] This coding decision was similar to that in the original collection. The vast majority of these cases were disputes in which the states were secondary participants in large multilateral disputes and wars (e.g. Liberia in the tanker war component of the broader Iran-Iraq war). Most of

them also lasted only a very short period. Both of these conditions indicate that there was little expectation of future confrontations by the two states, an essential component of a rivalry in our conception. Including them in any rivalry analyses would likely distort results, as we regard them as 'noise' in models of rivalry competition.

The remaining sets of cases included dyads with three or more militarized disputes over the period 1816–2001. These are potential rivalries. Our previous definition required some minimum passage of time (10 years for proto-rivalries and 20 for enduring rivalries). This is no longer the case. Now the interrelation of issues primarily determines whether disputes belong to the same rivalry. The time or duration component of rivalries is no longer a strict definitional characteristic but, rather, is simply one possible mechanism that helps determine which disputes are interconnected and, therefore, which disputes are part of the same (or different) rivalries. Our contention is that states regard other states as rivals primarily through experience, as indicated by repeated confrontations with that enemy. Yet, the establishment of a rivalry can happen quickly if states clash several times in a short period. A series of disputes becomes a coherent rivalry when the issues are sufficiently linked. Issues are sufficiently linked when the course or outcome of one MID concerning one issue has an impact on the course or outcome of MIDs on subsequent issues. The temporal element is not unimportant; such confrontations must be connected in order to be part of a rivalry, and proximity in time is one possible connector. Yet, unlike the last version of the dataset, it is not the only one. Disputes may also be connected by the presence of unresolved issues that persist over a broad period.

Using the narratives (see below) constructed for all dyads with three or more disputes, we identified the issues involved in each dispute. In a number of cases, disputes over the same issue were combined in the same rivalry even though they did not meet the temporal-proximity criterion in the original formulation (e.g. there is more than a 15-year gap in disputes).

Most cases in which we 'combined' disputes (which would have been separate rivalries under the old scheme) involved disputes that were 19–25 years apart and clearly involved the same issues (e.g. Burma/Myanmar v. Thailand and Turkey v. Iraq respectively). Thus, some rivalries are now coded as longer and involving more disputes than they would have under the old rivalry definition. Temporal proximity was not irrelevant as there were instances in which 40–50 years separated disputes, with periods of peace in between; in those cases, we chose to code them as separate rivalries, reflecting that a generation or more had passed since the last militarized conflict, state policies did not necessarily reflect rivalry concerns, and other changes in the two states suggested the rivalry had ended.

In other instances, we removed disputes from rivalries in which they were temporally proximate but wholly unrelated to the rivalry as a whole. This is not to say that rivalries must be about a single issue. States may fight over essentially the same issues during a rivalry (e.g. the Egyptian-Israeli conflict since 1948). Yet, it is also plausible to conceive of a rivalry in which there is some variance in the issues (e.g. Britain and France in the 19th century). States may compete over a series of goods, and the confrontations may vary according to which goods are in dispute at the time. For example, the rivalry between Turkey and Greece after World War II has gradually moved away from conflict over Cyprus to disputes over competing claims in the Aegean Sea. Major powers, in particular, are likely to fight over multiple issues. We looked for clear evidence to suggest that disputes over the different issues were unrelated to a rivalry competition. A purely issue-based conception, for example, would separate the 1971 Bangladesh War from the India-Pakistan rivalry, simply because it was not fought over Kashmir, clearly a coding result without validity. Those cases with such evidence often involved disputes before and after a major event (such as a World War) or a significant regime change in one or both of the rivals, such that its policy orientation was significantly changed—in addition to the subjects of the disputes being dramatically different. Thus, some three-dispute dyads that would qualify as rivalries under time-density criteria were placed in the isolated category, as the connection between two or more of those conflicts was tenuous. There were other modifications made to the above formulations. A number of three- or four-dispute dyads had *all* of their conflicts related to an ongoing war. We did not regard these as meeting our notion of rivalry, but they were best treated as ephemeral. Accordingly, we coded these in the isolated category. For example, the United States and Cambodia engaged in five MIDs from 1964 until 1975. Under the previous coding system, this series of disputes would be coded as a rivalry, given the number of disputes and the length of time involved. Because all of the disputes were associated with the Vietnam War, however, this string of disputes was moved to the isolated conflict category.

Strictly speaking, the rivalry dataset includes data on only the disputes that constitute a given rivalry. This means there are no precise beginning or termination dates for each rivalry. Consistent with our earlier work, we consider the beginning of the first dyadic dispute to be the first behavioral sign that a rivalry exists, and, similarly, the end of the last dyadic dispute is the last behavioral sign of the rivalry. In our previous work, we assumed that the rivalry began or ended 10–15 years before or after these behavioral signs. Yet, this is at odds with our new coding rules above, in which some rivalries continued even though they experienced periods of 15+ years without a dispute. Thus, in the next phase of our rivalry project, we intend to code more specific end dates for all of the rivalries (if indeed they have ended) based on a variety of indicators including issue resolution, treaties, and the like, as well as 'dispute-free' periods, and potentially beginning dates as well (Bennett, 1997). Therefore, at this stage in our data collection, we retain our previous coding of termination by maintaining that the end of the last MID is the last 'behavioral manifestation' of rivalry, and we consider the rivalry to have ended in the 10–15 years after this time.

In comparing Thompson's (2001) dataset with the one here (or its predecessor), most observers note that the major difference lies on the competition/severity dimension. His idea is that elite perception of the enemy status of rivals motivates the severity of the rivalry. As we have argued above, we think that the differences on the conceptual level are more important, but, as Figure 1 illustrates, these differ in operationalization as well. Because our approach is fundamentally linked to the COW militarized dispute dataset, severity is fundamentally defined by the COW militarized dispute criteria (Ghosn, Palmer & Bremer, 2004). The use of COW disputes to form rivalries results in a lower severity threshold than in Thompson's collection. Militarized disputes do not always involve 'enemies', and, therefore, some rivalries can exist over issues (e.g. fishing rights) that are not of principal importance to states.

In short, consistent with our conceptualization of rivalry, we have included a wide range of rivalries in terms of their severity and duration. We have gathered extensive information about rivalries with three or more disputes. Furthermore, we have examined all potential rivalries to see if they meet our issue criteria. As a result, some disputes have been split off into the isolated conflict category, while others have been merged into rivalries. We believe that the RIV5.0 dataset possesses greater face validity because it is now based on an examination of the dyadic histories of rivalries and not inferred from the temporal proximity of the disputes.

Other Changes

All dyads with three or more disputes that pass the tests above have narratives attached to them in the dataset. These narratives come in several forms. Most notable is our own collection of historical information about the dyad and individual militarized interstate disputes; this includes brief descriptions about the latter. Most of this was original data collection, and, to make these data more useful to students of rivalry and international conflict in general, we include an extensive bibliography of historical references. Brief summaries of the 1993–2001

disputes were taken from the COW website[4] and placed in appropriate dyad files. These narratives were supplemented by two additional sets of information. First, we include the narratives about conflict management and other third-party intervention attempts from William Dixon's project on that subject. Second, we include Bennett's narratives on enduring rivalries used in his research (Bennett, 1996, 1993). The narratives not only allow scholars to examine our coding decisions, but also provide important contextual information for understanding individual rivalries.

Not all scholars will agree with every one of the changes made (or even with the original formulations). Through documentation, we have made our decisions transparent, and scholars will be able to undo or reformulate the dataset to their own needs and preferences. For example, other scholars could easily identify enduring rivalries using the old time-density criteria from the dyadic files we compiled for each rivalry; thus, they could reproduce the categories of isolated, proto-, and enduring rivalries or create their own divisions of the rivalry continuum. They might also decide to divide rivalries that we combined for issue reasons.

Conceptual, Theoretical, and Empirical Issues

Based on the operational criteria noted above, we have identified 915 cases of isolated conflicts and 290 cases of rivalry over the 1816–2001 period; this is almost identical to the distribution of cases (isolated vs. proto-/enduring rivalries) in the previous version of the dataset; the spatial and temporal distributions are similar to that reported in Diehl & Goertz (2000). As we have argued in this article, the key distinction, both conceptually and in terms of data collection, is that between isolated conflict and rivalry. Consistent with our argument that rivalry is a continuous concept, our concept of rivalry allows for shorter and longer rivalries and rivalries with more and fewer disputes.[5]

Of the 290 cases of rivalry, 115 are enduring and 175 are proto-rivalries under our previous coding criteria. The cases of enduring rivalry experience a mean of 13 disputes and last an average of 36 years from the first until the last behavioral sign of the rivalry. The 175 cases of proto-rivalry experience a mean of four disputes and last an average of 11 years. We now turn to identifying rivalry patterns that highlight the dimensions of our rivalry concept, followed by a comparison of our data with Thompsons to identify the degree of overlap in the two primary rivalry datasets.

Power Symmetry and Rivalry

Some scholars have defined rivalries as those occurring between states of equal capability. Vasquez (1996a: 533) has most clearly stated this position, going so far as to argue that 'relative equality is a prerequisite of rivalries'. Thompson does not take a direct position that a measure of power symmetry should be included in the concept of rivalry. Nevertheless, he does state that 'other things being equal, symmetrical capabilities should be expected to make rivalry more likely and more enduring' (Thompson, 2001: 573). In his criticism of the dispute threshold approach, he implies that the absence of a measure of symmetry allows dubious cases into the data (Thompson, 1995: 197). Some of the more doubtful cases for him are highly asymmetric (e.g. US rivalries with Haiti, Mexico, and Spain). Asymmetrical states supposedly cannot compete because one side would be able to dominate the other. In Table 1, we examine the distribution of rivalry cases according to their power symmetry.

Here we code a rivalry as symmetric if the national material capabilities (Singer, Bremer & Stuckey, 1972) composite variable of the rivals exceeds a three-to-one ratio at any point in the history of the rivalry. This is a common measure of power preponderance (e.g. Mearsheimer, 1989). One concern might be that the symmetry measure would change during the life of the rivalry, especially during longer rivalries, but this occurs in only 9% of the rivalries.

In both categories—isolated and rivalry—the overwhelming majority of cases are asymmetric. In fact, in instances of rivalry, nearly 80% of the cases—229—take place between states with significant power disparity. One such example is that between the People's Republic of China and Vietnam. Relations between these two neighbors clearly indicate rivalry, even though China's capability dwarfs that of Vietnam by a factor of up to 17 to 1. The two countries have a consistent record of hostility for several decades into the mid-1990s. As in our previous dataset and related published research, we prefer to assess how these 'mixed' cases differ (if at all) empirically from symmetrical cases, rather than a priori define the former out of the dataset.

Another manner of examining the claim that rivalries take place between states of roughly equal size is to observe how individual disputes between rivals are distributed across the power configurations. Consistent with the logic that only those states of roughly equal capability are capable of maintaining a rivalry is the expectation that, as rivalries progress, the probability that an asymmetrical rivalry will continue should diminish because of the superior position of the stronger state in the relationship. Therefore, we should expect to see the number of disputes occurring between asymmetric rivals diminish over time; that is, the rivalries with the most disputes should be between states of relatively equal capability or in symmetric rivalries.

Table 1 Power Symmetry and Rivalry

	Rivalry Type (%)		
	Isolated	Rivalry	All
Symmetric	24	21	23
Asymmetric	76	79	77
Total	100	100	100
N (Rivalries)	915	290	1,205

Table 2   Power Symmetry over Time in Rivalry

	Dispute Sequence (%)				
	1–2	3–5	6–12	13+	All
Symmetric	30	36	40	58	36
Asymmetric	70	64	60	42	64
Total	100	100	100	100	100
N (Disputes)	1,718	676	495	413	3,302

Table 2 displays the sequence of disputes in a rivalry by our measure of symmetry. All disputes are included in the analysis, including isolated conflicts as well as rivalry disputes. When the analysis is performed in this manner, the results are slightly different from the aggregate rivalry analysis in Table 1. In the initial stages of rivalry, we find a large percentage (70%) of disputes occurring between asymmetric rivals. Nevertheless, the proportion of asymmetric disputes continues to represent a full 42% of the disputes at the 13+ dispute range. The results of Table 2 provide strong support for the argument that rivalries exist in dyads experiencing periods of power preponderance. The continued and significant presence of asymmetric disputes in mature rivalries suggests that rivalry can be sustained even between states of divergent capabilities. They account for a non-trivial number of the cases, even in situations in which the number of disputes between rivals is well above average. One example is the Russia/USSR—Japan rivalry. For most of the rivalry, Russia's power is four to five times that of Japan. Nevertheless, the two engage in a long series of disputes at regular intervals — it is one of the longest rivalries in our dataset at 140 years with the third most disputes (49). The rivalry is sustained even as the capabilities of the two sides remain asymmetrical for most of the rivalry.

There is also support in the data for the hypothesis that symmetry is an important consideration in rivalry dynamics. This is especially so in rivalries of greater than average length. When rivalries move into advanced stages, symmetric cases constitute nearly 60% of the rivalries. Although symmetry is a dynamic element clearly present in a non-trivial number of rivalries, important causal hypotheses should not be built into the definition precluding the possibility of testing.

Conflict Linkages

The most distinctive feature of the rivalry approach relative to the more traditional cross-sectional, time-series approach to conflict studies is that the rivalry disputes are linked to one another. In our discussion of the rivalry concept, we have emphasized that disputes in rivalry are linked over space and time by the pull of the past and the expectation of future conflict. Rivalry disputes are directly linked to one another when unresolved issues continue to motivate mutual hostility. It is useful to think about the various ways that this dimension of the rivalry concept is manifested. Below, we analyze this dimension by observing the occurrence and sequence of wars, along with dispute outcomes and waiting times.

War Sequence and Dispute Linkage. One mechanism by which disputes are linked in rivalry is through the pull of the past. Often, the initial interactions in rivalry set the tone for subsequent rivalry dynamics. Failure to resolve significant initial issues can lead states to lock in policies and strategies that motivate the rivalry. One way to examine this claim is to examine the occurrence of wars in the sequence of disputes within the rivalry.

A traditional claim in the cross-sectional, time-series approach to conflict is the volcano model of war occurrence (Diehl & Goertz, 2000). The idea is that a conflict of interest creates tension that builds over time in a dyad. The disputes increase in hostility, and as the pressure builds, it erupts into a war. The war then provides an opportunity for the dyad to resolve its conflict. This understanding of war suggests that wars are a means of resolving issues between countries. Under this framework, we should expect to see wars in the latter stages of rivalry.

Figure 2 displays the timing of wars in rivalry, indicated in terms of its occurrence in the rivalry dispute order. For example, if a war takes place in the first dispute of the rivalry, it is coded a 1, in the second dispute it is coded a 2, and so forth.[6] Quite surprisingly, the vast majority of wars take place at or near the beginning of rivalry. Nearly 50% occur by the third dispute, and about 90% happen by the sixth dispute. Equally apparent, wars do not occur later in the rivalry. Less then 10% of all the wars occur after the 11th dispute. Indeed, if one tracks the occurrence of the *first war* in a rivalry, the probability is dramatically greater at the outset of a rivalry, rather than in latter stages. This evidence undermines the volcano model of war dynamics. Instead, from the rivalry perspective, wars may set the stage for rivalry development. Disputed issues in the war may become firmly established in the rivalry because of the war. Wars may provide a 'pull of the past'

mechanism for motivating future disputes and a thread that links the disputes together.

The finding that rivalries experience wars early in their existence should not imply that wars do not occur in later stages or necessarily that the risk of dispute escalation is dramatically less at that time. Looking at disputes as the unit of analysis, rather than wars, the likelihood that a dispute will escalate to war is approximately 10% in the first phases of rivalry (the first six disputes in the rivalry sequence). That number drops, but not precipitously, to 6% for the 7th–54th disputes in the sequence. Thus, many rivalries experience war early in the competition, but the threat of severe militarized confrontations does not go away. Those whose competitions involve many disputes are still at significant risk for their second or third (or in a few cases even more) war later in the rivalry. There is no learning sufficient to head off future wars. The presence of wars at several junctures of the India-Pakistan and Egypt-Israel rivalries are illustrative of this.

Figure 2   War Timing in Rivalry

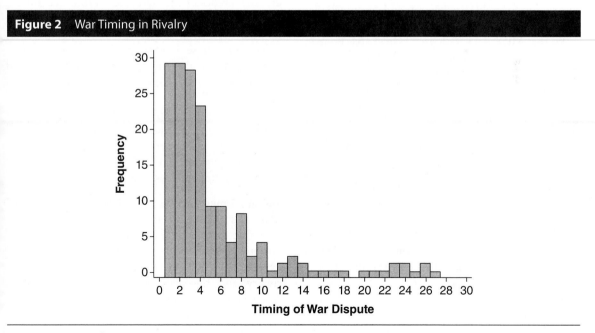

Note: Six wars occur after the 30th dispute.

Dispute Outcomes and Linkage. If wars precipitate a pull-of-the-past dynamic motivating future disputes in the rivalry, then what keeps a rivalry going? There has been scant research into this question that is fundamental to the concept of rivalry. What mechanism actually links one dispute to the next in rivalry? Gartzke & Simon (1999) presented the most direct challenge to the linkage assertion, arguing that rivalries are epiphenomenal and disputes are unrelated to one another. Several studies have subsequently discredited this study, finding strong dependency to exist between rivalry disputes (e.g. Colaresi & Thompson, 2002).

One such linkage mechanism is the manner in which the sources of conflict within individual disputes are resolved. A stalemate outcome to a dispute provides one linkage mechanism that connects a string of disputes in a rivalry. With indeterminate outcomes, neither party to the dispute comes away from the dispute satisfied with the outcome, and the issue that brought the rivals to militarized action remains unresolved (Maoz & Mor, 2002). Thus, the motivation for militarized action and continued disputes in the rivalry remains.

In the MID data (Ghosn, Palmer & Bremer, 2004), there are two related variables that measure the manner of dispute resolution: the outcome and settlement variables. Each of these variables has multiple categories that, for our purposes, measure the same concept. Therefore, we have collapsed these values into three categories, consistent with our previous work on this topic (Goertz, Jones & Diehl, 2005). The fundamental rule we follow in condensing these variables is to identify the number of parties satisfied with the outcome or settlement to the dispute. We are most interested in cases in which neither party is satisfied with the outcome or settlement of the dispute. For the outcome variable, this is 'stalemate', and for the settlement variable, this is the 'none/unclear' outcome.

We expect that rivalries will have a preponderance of indecisive outcomes as well as an increasing proportion of both stalemated outcomes and none/unclear settlements over time. In early stages of a rivalry, some conflicts may be resolved and a rivalry never develops. For those rivalries that do develop, unresolved conflict (indicated by stalemates and lack of settlements) is characteristic of early confrontations (Stinnett & Diehl, 2001). As rivalry processes become ingrained in policymaking and interactions, states will repeatedly confront one another, often over the same issues, and yet be unable to find a resolution to their conflicts. By the latter stages of rivalry, the two sides will be cooperating less as the rivalry hostility becomes self-reinforcing. According to the punctuated equilibrium model (Diehl & Goertz, 2000), this is, in part, why a political shock is necessary to break the logjam and disrupt existing patterns.

Table 3 displays the frequency of dispute outcomes as they occur over time in rivalry. Table 4 provides a similar picture of dispute settlements.[7] A brief examination of the distribution of various outcomes in these two tables indicates evidence to support our expectations. At all stages in the development of rivalry, stalemate and the none/unclear categories are the predominant outcomes. From the outset, stalemate constitutes around 60% of the dispute outcomes. As the rivalry locks in, cooperative outcomes and those indicating victories occur more infrequently. In the later stages of rivalry (defined here as >13 disputes), stalemates and no settlements constitute well over four-fifths of the cases. These results are further suggestive that disputes are not independent of one another and there is some temporal dependence in rivalries, here in the form of outcomes. Further evidence is found upon examination of the timing of disputes.

Waiting Times and Dispute Linkage. If stalemated outcomes provide one method of linking disputes in a rivalry, another is the duration or 'waiting time' until the next dispute appears. It seems reasonable to expect that if the underlying issues that motivate the rivalry and the disputes therein have not been resolved, then one might reasonably expect that the time from the end of one dispute to the beginning of the subsequent dispute should be rather short.

Figure 3 displays the waiting time between disputes measured in years. In this analysis, the waiting times are calculated from the end of one dispute to the beginning of the next in the rivalry sequence; these are generally rounded to the nearest year, except for the lowest end of the scale, where '1' indicates that the waiting time between disputes was somewhere between one day and one year. The mean wait time for rivalries in the dataset is 2.7 years with a median of 1.15.[8] About 65% of the disputes that occur in rivalry take place within two years of each other and 80% within three years. There are numerous disputes that start prior to the termination of the previous dispute. That is, some rivalries are so intense that the rivals clash simultaneously on different issues or in different locations.

Comparing Rivalry Datasets

Finally, we compare the two primary datasets available to researchers interested in the rivalry data (see also Hewitt, 2005). Thompson (2001) has produced a rivalry dataset using an alternative coding

Table 4   Frequency of Dispute Settlement over Time

MID Settlement	Dispute Sequence (%)				
	1–3	4–6	7–12	13+	All
Imposed	21	9	6	3	16
None/unclear	61	77	81	83	68
Negotiated	18	14	13	14	16
Total	100	100	100	100	100
N (Disputes)	2,247	492	390	423	3,552

None/unclear = no satisfied parties.

Imposed = one satisfied party.

Negotiated = two satisfied parties.

methodology. He delves into the diplomatic history of countries and identifies a rivalry based on the perceptions of leaders and decisionmakers. The key criterion for Thompson is that two states identify one another as rivals. Thompson's list includes 174 strategic rivalries from 1816 until 2001. Thompson's data and our own are the two leading collections in use in the rivalry research program. Given the existence of these two collections, researchers interested in using a rivalry dataset might reasonably wonder to what degree they overlap.

Comparing the two lists, there are 107 cases of general agreement. General agreement exists when there is spatial and temporal overlap of at least one year. In most cases, there is broad overlap; the number of cases with minimal overlap, such as one or two years, is relatively small. These 107 cases of spatial and temporal overlap constitute 61% of Thompson's cases and 37% of our rivalries. To examine the overlap, we measured the rivalry years of these 107 cases in both datasets (Thompson: 5,167; Klein, Goertz & Diehl: 3,077). We then measured the rivalry years that we agreed on in these

Table 3   Dispute Outcomes over Time in Rivalry

MID Outcome	Dispute Sequence (%)				
	1–2	3–5	6–12	13+	All
Victory	36	24	17	12	23
Stalemate	57	69	78	85	71
Compromise	7	7	5	3	6
Total	100	100	100	100	100
N	580	631	491	413	2,115

Stalemate = no satisfied parties; stalemate, released, unclear, and missing.

Victory = one satisfied party; victory A/B, yield A/B.

Compromise = two satisfied parties; compromise.

107 cases (2,511). These 2,511 constitute 49% of Thompson's rivalry years and 82% of our rivalry years in these 107 cases. Much of the difference is attributable to our treatment of beginning and ending dates for the rivalry. Thompson's mean duration is 48 years. In point of significant contrast, our rivalries last on average 28 years. We noted above that rivalries begin roughly in the ten years prior to the first behavioral indicator of the rivalry. Similarly, we have argued that the end of a rivalry occurs roughly in the ten years after the last behavioral indicator of a rivalry. Therefore, a difference of 20 years (10 years for the start and 10 years for the end) in mean duration is consistent with our previous arguments (28 + 20 = 48), and in fact, the two datasets are in much greater agreement than they first appear where they overlap.

We code 183 cases that Thompson does not identify as rivalries, and Thompson codes 67 cases that we do not. These cases of disagreement are considerable

and a non-trivial matter. The 67 Thompson rivalries that we do not identify comprise 39% of his cases, and the 183 rivalries in our data that he does not identify comprise 63% of our data. These cases of disagreement present a number of puzzles. These datasets purport to capture essentially the same phenomenon. One possible explanation is that 67 rivalry cases are picked up in our isolated conflict category, and indeed 56 (83%) are. That leaves only 11 cases (e.g. Ghana-Nigeria, 1960–66; UK-Burma, 1816–26) that appear in Thompson's collection but not our own. The excess cases that we code that Thompson does not are those of low-level severity that would elude Thompson's mutual enemy-identification criterion.

Conclusion

Datasets should be capable of serving different theoretical purposes and testing a variety of important questions. We have tried to construct the new

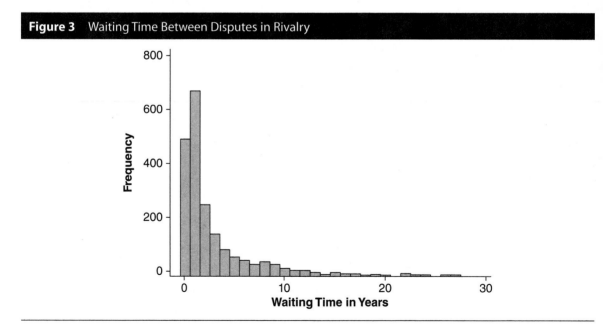

Figure 3 Waiting Time Between Disputes in Rivalry

Note: Zero years indicates a negative waiting time. There are two waiting times between 40 and 50 years.

rivalry dataset in this spirit. Rivalries began as a useful case-selection device, and, indeed, may still serve that function for a number of theoretical propositions that necessitate an examination of cases with a prior history of serious conflict. Yet, the rivalry dataset herein will be useful in addressing a whole range of questions about the origins, dynamics, and termination of interstate conflict. We have made our coding decisions transparent and all the data (including excluded cases) available. Thus, scholars may decide to focus only on a subset of rivalries (e.g. major powers, those experiencing war) for certain theoretical concerns. Scholars may also use our previous classification scheme (i.e. proto- and enduring rivalries), as we have included a variable in the data to capture this previous coding; we do not proclaim a monopoly on virtue with respect to data construction, and, indeed, robust findings with multiple datasets and definitions are the building blocks of scientific progress. We do, however, hope that scholars will adopt the rivalry perspective that conflicts are indeed connected over space and time and that such connections are critical for understanding how new conflicts arise and old conflicts are resolved (or not).

Notes

Authors' Note: Replication data for this article are available at http://www.prio.no/jpr/datasets. The complete new rivalry dataset, including all documentation, is available at ftp://128.196.23.212/rivalry/riv500web.zip. Authors' contact adress: ggoertz@u.arizona.edu.

1. For each dyad that experienced one or more disputes, we created a dyadic file that includes historical information about the conflicts and the MIDs between the dyad.
2. http://correlatesofwar.org. It should be noted that the raw data in the narrative files do include the dyadic disputes that were eliminated. Again, this allows scholars to examine the list of dyadic conflicts we have excluded (a file in the dataset distribution lists all excluded dyadic conflicts) and potentially to apply different coding procedures. Such coding decisions were made with reference to Maoz's (2005) dyadic data as well as COWs dyadic data files for one- or two-dispute cases, whereas we investigated all three-or-greater-dispute cases ourselves. Furthermore, some changes made in the MID3.02 dataset create inconsistencies with the Maoz dataset for the pre-1992 period. In other instances, Maoz (2005) includes several coding changes not reflected in the MID set for the 1993–2001 period. In these cases, we have followed the 3.02 dataset codings.
3. In two instances, two dispute rivalries lasted long enough (>10 years) for us to consider it a rivalry. Such length meant that leaders and bureaucracies had to adjust their policymaking to long-term threats, something characteristic of rivalries.
4. http://correlatesofwar.org
5. Some scholars have found the proto- and enduring-rivalry distinctions to be quite useful (e.g. Maoz & Mor, 2002). Thus, we have added a variable to the dataset indicating whether a rivalry is considered enduring or protounder our previous classification scheme.
6. Here we again use rivalry as the unit of analysis, and, thus, multilateral wars are counted more than once.
7. Only rivalry conflicts are included; isolated conflicts are excluded.
8. This average is calculated by recoding the negative waiting times (those where one dispute begins before its predecessor ends) to zero. Here we are interested in calculating the average length of time between disputes when there is an actual gap in time. By including the negative wait times, the average would be artificially reduced.

EDITORS' COMMENTARY

Major Contributions: Rivalry

Concepts are the lenses through which we see the world. Without concepts to label certain phenomena, it is sometimes even difficult to see or distinguish them. The Eskimo or Inuit of Alaska, for example, have up to fifteen words for snow—one for deep fallen snow, another for snow that has crust on it, another for snow that clings, and so forth.[1] In English, we have no word for snow that will not cling to itself, and therefore we cannot see it readily. We must pick it up and see if it will make a snowball. A word-label, which is all a concept is, highlights certain things in the world and obscures other things. The trick to a successful science is to have concepts that see and portray the world in a manner that highlights what is causally significant and obscures what is irrelevant or distorting.

Beginning with the release of the militarized interstate dispute (MID) data set, international relations scholars studied war in terms of whether an individual dyadic MID escalated to war or whether a MID in a dyad-year (see Bremer 1992b, Chapter 2, this volume) escalated to a war. This made statistical studies very atomistic in that they focused on the characteristics of individual dyadic MIDs without ever seeing how the MIDs might be connected to each other. One of the first scholars to do so was Russell Leng (1983), who looked at recurrent conflict. He found that when crises between two (evenly matched) states persist and repeat, it becomes increasingly difficult to avoid war. This was because as disputants move from one crisis to the next, their bargaining tends to increase in hostility. However, other than the phrase *recurrent conflict*, Leng had no conceptual label for connected crises.

In the early nineties, Goertz and Diehl (1992b, 1993) and Wayman and Jones (1991) put a label on recurrent conflict and conceptualized it as **rivalry**. Using different measures, they maintained that certain MIDs were connected, and this had great importance for understanding war. In 2000, Diehl and Goertz wrote a landmark book bringing together and extending their work on interstate rivalry. Their conceptualization of rivalry (Klein, Goertz, and Diehl 2006, 333) has several major components: (1) *spatial consistency* (the primary actors are states and the rivalries are dyadic), (2) *duration* (rivalry occurs over a reasonably long period of time), (3) *militarized competition* (rivals' foreign policies are conducted in military terms), and (4) *linked conflict* (rivals' conflicts are related in some way over time and space).

The concept of rivalry was a major contribution because it shifted the focus away from the characteristics of individual dyadic MIDs to what was producing those characteristics. For Diehl and Goertz (2000), what made some dyads go to war was the underlying *relationship* between the states. The nature of the relationship influenced whether the disputes recurred or not. The disputes were not independent but deeply connected, and to understand how and why they were connected would be a key to unlocking why states went to war. The promulgation of a new concept, rivalry, helped us see the world in a different way—a way that promised to make us see what was causally significant and push to the side what was of less importance.

As they began to research their ideas, they produced some important findings. The most significant is that the probability of an enduring rivalry having at least one war is 0.59 (Diehl and Goertz 2000, 62–63, 200). In other words, there are six out of ten chances that an enduring rivalry will go to war. In fact, enduring rivals account for about half (49.4 percent) of the interstate wars fought since 1815, with proto-rivalries accounting for another 32.9 percent (Diehl and Goertz 2000, 199). Subsequent research by others using different measures and data on rivalries has confirmed these patterns (Colaresi, Rasler, and Thompson 2007, 88–89, 130). The authors also show in Figure 2 that most wars occur fairly early in a rivalry, consistent with Leng's (1983) finding that wars usually occur by the third crisis in a dyad with repeated conflicts.

Diehl and Goertz (2000) **operationalize** (see methodological notes below) their concept of rivalry in terms of the number of MIDs that occur within a particular time frame. An **enduring rivalry** is one that has six or more MIDs within a twenty-year period, a **proto-rivalry** is a dyad that has three to five disputes within roughly ten years, and an **isolated rivalry** consists of a dyad that has only two or fewer disputes. More precisely, to be in a rivalry, a dispute must occur within eleven years of the first dispute, twelve years after the second, and up to fifteen years after the third MID (Klein et al. 2006, 337). Diehl and Goertz (2000, 145–46) then list all the enduring rivalries that their operational measure produces, with a total of sixty-three rivalries. The updated data set (Klein et al. 2006) expands this list of enduring rivalries to 115 cases.

One of the great advantages of their operationalization is that it is highly **reliable**—in other words, the rule for what is an enduring or proto-rivalry is so clear and precise that anyone could apply it to the raw data and get the same list of enduring rivalries. Contrast this with the main alternative list of rivalries by Thompson (2001), a data-coding approach that relies on perceptions of decision makers (and historians' reporting of those perceptions) to determine who are rivals (see also Thompson 1995). States are coded as rivals in this alternative data set if the leaders of each state in the dyad view the other state as a historical enemy. Thompson (1995) identifies 174 strategic rivalries from 1816 to 1999. He distinguishes **positional rivals** that are competing in a general strategic situation (e.g., the United States and U.S.S.R. in the Cold War) from **spatial rivals** who compete over specific border disputes (e.g., India and Pakistan over Kashmir). To **replicate** Thompson's list, one would have to do a great deal of reading (see Thompson and Dreyer 2011) and make an assessment. This is a large task that no one has yet undertaken, and assessments might vary depending on the observer's preexisting knowledge of a particular case. To replicate Diehl and Goertz's (2000) list, one simply looks at the MID data and counts the number of disputes between the two states.[2]

In the current article, Klein et al. (2006) seek to update their rivalry data through 2001. In doing so, they also make some changes in their operational measures and provide an illustration for students about some of the issues related to measurement. They then present some findings from the new data.

Klein et al. (2006) are attempting to make changes that respond to some of the criticisms that have been made of their earlier efforts, as well as their own thoughts. The first thing they do is to now treat dyads with two or fewer disputes as "isolated conflict" and not label it as a rivalry.

The more extensive change they make is to group proto and enduring rivalries into a single category, labeled *rivals*. They had discussed this earlier in their article of "taking the enduring out of enduring rivalries." They still have kept the distinction of proto and enduring rivalries in the actual data set, and they have published a new list of enduring rivalries (Diehl and Goertz 2012, 105–8), but basically now they are comparing all rivals with nonrivals.

Their major change, however, has been in the way they determine whether a given series of MIDs are linked. Before, it was just done by time between disputes (or duration between MIDs). As they admit, this was mostly an inductive procedure. This was quite evident in their rule for when a rivalry terminated—if there is no MID for ten years, then the rivalry is said to have ended. Bennett (1996, 1997) criticized this procedure and created a new data set that identified the ending of rivalries when the issue underlying the rivalry has been resolved. Klein et al. (2006) build on this issue approach both to determine when a rivalry ends and to identify the number of MIDs within a rivalry. MIDs that are over the same issue are included in the rivalry even if they are more than ten years apart. Before that would not be the case.

This issue approach is more theoretical and deductive. It also allows them to hypothesize one of the factors that make rivalries persist. They hypothesize that disputes recur because they are stalemated, and states cannot come up with a settlement over a specific issue, such as disagreement over ownership of a piece of territory. They probe this hypothesis empirically in Tables 3 and 4 and find some evidence consistent with the hypothesis. Rivalries with a higher number of militarized disputes have a higher percentage of MIDs with stalemated and unclear outcomes. Militarized disputes also recur because the issue is sufficiently salient that the parties will not drop their claims to it. Earlier work by Tir and Diehl (2002) provides some evidence on this point in that they find that a large number of rivalries are over territorial issues (see also Vasquez and Leskiw 2001). Mitchell and Thies (2011), developing a new measure of rivalry based on the frequency of territorial, maritime, and river disputes, show that dyads have a higher probability of MIDs if they have two or more geopolitical disputes (or an **issue rivalry**) ongoing at the same time. Thus, the presence of territorial disputes and multiple areas of contestation can increase the risks for recurrent conflict.[3]

To get at the issue content of rivalries, Klein et al. (2006) wrote issue narratives for each rivalry—a very labor-intensive procedure. These narratives are an important contribution to our information base. However, a side effect of this is to make the database similar to Thompson and Dreyer (2011) in that the rule for determining what is or is not a rivalry is no longer based on the clear and transparent rule of counting the MIDs that have occurred. Instead, one has to trace historically the issue(s) under contention. While this may increase the validity of the data, it comes at a cost of reducing the reliability of the data. One positive note, however, is that we have two historical reconstructions of events that occurred in major interstate rivalries that can now be compared.

The work on rivalry established that rivalry is an important factor in bringing about war. The rivalry process is really a war process. Rivalry has also been employed as a context for testing other conflict theories, such as deterrence (Huth and Russett 1993), power transition theory (Geller 1993), arms races (Gibler, Rider, and Hutchison 2005), and diversionary theory (Mitchell and Prins 2004, Chapter 8, this volume). Understanding why rivalry relationships emerge in the first place and how they evolve over time will help us unlock the factors that bring about war.

Methodological Notes: Research Design and Measurement

Klein et al. (2006) end their article by comparing their data and conceptualization of rivalry with that of Thompson (2001). When scholars have different concepts and measures of something, the question immediately arises as to which data set should be used or which is the more accurate data set. In science, such questions as they relate to data are dealt with in terms of measurement **reliability** and **validity**. A good measure should be both reliable and valid. A measure is reliable, as noted above, when the rules for collecting data are so precise and clear that scholars working independently of each other can get the same data (e.g., the same lists of rivals). One can test for reliability by having multiple persons try to collect the same data. If scholars agree 85 percent or more of the time, the measure is said to be reliable. Validity is a different question. A measure is valid if it measures what it is supposed to measure. In the example above, do repeating MIDs actually measure the presence of a rivalry between two states? Do perceptions of decision makers as to who are the primary enemies of a state (Thompson 1995) actually measure the existence of a rivalry between the two states? There are no definitive tests that can be conducted to answer such questions. Rather, an argument must be made that these things indicate the presence of the concept.

Measures are created through **operational definitions** that tell scholars what observable phenomena in the world indicate the presence of the concept. Observation is the key. In fact, the phrase *operational definition* or **operationalize** comes from physics, where scientists tried to develop operations in the lab that would indicate such abstract concepts as mass, force, and energy. For example, the concept of democracy may be operationalized by seeing if a state has periodic free elections, multiple competitive parties, a competitive process for selecting the chief executive, and so forth. These things indicate the presence of democracy and are often called **indicators**. These measures are often indirect because what is observed, especially behavior, may not capture the richness of a concept. Thus, a conceptual definition of democracy may be "rule by the people," whereas the operational definition tells us what observable practices and behavior are present when there is rule by the people. A valid measure must provide indicators that we think capture the presence of rule by the people even though they might be indirect. Scholars consider the **face validity** of the data produced, or whether the measures make sense "on the face of it." Klein et al.

(2006) note that Thompson (1995) questions one of their enduring rivalry cases, asking if the United States and Haiti can be rivals since the disparity of power between them is so great. What Thompson is saying is that on the face of it, it does not seem that weak states are able to compete and therefore they are not really rivals with major powers, since competition is an essential part of the definition of rivalry.

Measurement can become complicated when there are multiple measures of the same thing. These can be useful when they indicate different aspects of a concept, but when they produce competing concepts, one may be uncertain about which is the better measure. One way of resolving this dilemma is to see which produces the best findings or results, or **pragmatic validation**. Measures that produce statistically significant and strong findings and that correlate with other variables of interest in the ways we expect may be more useful for scientific research. Multiple indicators can also elucidate the different meanings of a concept. For example, Klein and his colleagues (2006) show that most rivals are asymmetric, which they operationalize as having an unequal power ratio. But when Vasquez (1996a) argues that only relative equals can be rivals, what he has in mind is power status—Major-Major and minor-minor dyads versus Major-minor dyads—not the power ratios that Klein et al. use. In the article by Susan Sample (2002, Chapter 6, this volume), she shows that Major-minor dyads behave differently from the relatively equal Major-Major and minor-minor dyads. By having different indicators of the same concept, sometimes the results vary and scholars can talk past each other.

The statistics used in the Klein et al. (2006) article to test their hypotheses in Tables 3 and 4 are very straightforward. They are simple percentages or frequencies. These tables show that one can learn a great deal from a careful comparison of frequencies. Table 3, for instance, shows that as states go from one to two disputes, to three to five, to six to twelve, and all the way up to thirteen or more disputes, the number of stalemates increases from 57, to 69, to 78, and to 85 percent, respectively. This is consistent with the expectation that if stalemated outcomes increase the chances for future disputes, then the number of stalemates should be higher as the number of dyadic disputes rises.

Notes

1. See Woodbury (1991).
2. However, most empirical studies using either major measure of rivalry (Diehl and Goertz 2000; Thompson 2001) reach similar conclusions about the effects of rivalry on conflict, especially the increased likelihood of recurrent conflict for interstate rivals. Mitchell and Thies (2011) develop an additional measure of rivalry based on the total number of ongoing diplomatic issues over borders, using data collected by the Issue Correlates of War project (discussed in Hensel et al. 2008, Chapter 3, this volume).
3. Dreyer (2010, 782) shows that rivalry can begin with a single issue early in a relationship and then evolve into a rivalry over multiple issues. The China-Vietnam rivalry, which began over regional positional issues in the 1970s, eventually included many contested issues, such as territorial claims over the Paracel and Spratly Islands and the treatment of Chinese workers in Vietnam.

Questions

1. Which measures of rivalry do you think are most *reliable*—the original Diehl and Goertz (2000), the new Klein et al. (2006), or the Thompson (1995; see also Thompson and Dreyer, 2011) measures? Why? Which measures are most *valid*? Why?

2. Why do you think militarized disputes recur?

3. Go to the new list of the enduring rivals in the appendix of Diehl and Goertz (2012). Compare the rivals between relative equals (Major-Major and minor-minor) with those between unequal states (Major-minor). A list of major powers is provided in the commentary of Sample's (2002) article. Do you think all the enduring rivals that are listed have face validity? If not, which do and which do not?

Further Reading

Colaresi, M. P., K. D. Rasler, and W. R. Thompson. 2007. *Strategic rivalries in world politics: Position, space, and conflict escalation*. Cambridge, UK: Cambridge University Press.

Diehl, P. F., and G. Goertz. 2000. *War and peace in international rivalry*. Ann Arbor: University of Michigan Press.

———. 2012. The rivalry process: How rivalries are sustained and terminated. In *What do we know about war?* ed. J. A. Vasquez, pp. 83–109. Lanham, MD: Rowman and Littlefield.

Thompson, W. R., and D. R. Dreyer. 2011. *Handbook of international rivalries, 1494–2010*. Washington, D.C.: CQ Press.

Chapter 6

The Outcomes of Military Buildups

Minor States vs. Major Powers

Susan G. Sample

Introduction

Do military buildups by states deter other states from acting aggressively against them, or do they only increase the chance that any conflict between countries is likely to be taken to the level of war? This ancient question has generated a substantial literature arguing both sides of the question through diplomatic history and, more recently, empirical analysis. The argument of deterrence goes back at least to the Latin: if we want peace, we must prepare for war. It was the devastation of World War I that gave popular credence to the opposite thesis that military buildups contributed to the occurrence of war. The academic dispute is politically dramatic because the opposing positions are so clearly and directly related to policy choice. They offer completely contradictory advice on how to obtain national security: either build up your military to deter others and thus avoid war, or avoid building up your military so that your conflicts cannot get out of hand. Empirical studies in the last several years have resolved some of the old questions and have suggested that a positive relationship between military buildups and dispute escalation may indeed exist. However, a number of vital questions have been left unaddressed by this literature that are almost exclusively focused on the major states of the international system.

Major states, whose conflicts have been central to the general wars that have led to the death of countless millions and defined and redefined the international system over time, are unquestionably worthy of intensive study. However, we must remember that a significant segment of the world's population lives in minor states, and wars between them destroy individual lives just as surely as any general war. Pakistan and India have fought several wars in the last fifty years, and even though they now possess nuclear capability, they are not considered major states. The lives of a fifth of the world's population are dependent on the nature of the relationship between these two countries. The longstanding conflict between Eritrea and Ethiopia (which, of course, began as a civil war) has killed thousands in battle and contributed to countless more deaths through the famine that it facilitated. All studies of the causes of war have at their most fundamental level a desire to prevent wars, or to resolve them. So we cannot assume that minor states and major states follow the same paths to war when we now have the data that allow us to test the assertion, and theoretical reason to do so. Perhaps minor states do follow similar courses to those of major states in their international disputes, but if they do not, we must know that. We have traditionally assumed, or acted as if we assumed, that the behavior of the major states

Source: Susan G. Sample, "The Outcomes of Military Buildups: Minor States vs. Major Powers," *Journal of Peace Research* 39, no. 6 (2002): 669–91. © 2002 *Journal of Peace Research*. Reprinted by permission of SAGE Publications, Inc.

reflects that of all states faced with similar challenges. But it remains an empirical question, and one that is not unimportant.

This study makes these tests. It analyzes the role of mutual military buildups in the escalation of minor state disputes. It does so in the context of comparing three basic classes of disputes: those among minor states (minor state disputes), those among major states (major state disputes), and those between major and minor states (mixed disputes). Theoretically, one might argue that the constraints of the anarchical international system should yield patterns of outcomes of disputes that are essentially similar in all categories, with differences traceable only to issues related clearly to relative power. Or it is conceivable that minor states and major states operate under sets of rules and norms whose differences are more than just the sum of the power differential.

The conclusions of these tests suggest that military buildups are positively associated with dispute escalation under specific circumstances, but the reality is more complex than such a simple statement implies. Different classes of disputes show many similarities in their escalation dynamics, but also a few differences that are traceable both to relative power differentials and to something else. Even given the similarities, we have been mistaken in simply assuming that major states represent the whole system. This outcome has implications for international relations theory, and the relative complexity of our theories themselves. To the extent that minor state disputes and mixed disputes show certain differences in their patterns of escalation beyond what can easily be explained by the power distribution itself, we must ask ourselves why. Is this the result of minor states reacting to the constraints put on them by the Great Powers? Or is it the fact that minor states react differently because they know that they can never be in contest for control of the international system? I argue that the differences and the similarities alike may be explained through integration of the insights of three theoretical approaches that are typically placed in opposition to one another: traditional realism, cognitive psychological approaches, and the insights derived from critical theory and constructivism in international relations theory. Evaluating the outcomes of different classes of disputes allows us access to the larger theoretical questions regarding both the validity of theories and the role of theory more generally.

Empirical and Theoretical Background

World War I and the Cold War were the two threads holding 20th-century studies of military buildups together.[1] The catastrophe of WWI precipitated the growth of a substantial academic enterprise trying to understand how the arms races on the eve of the war had contributed to the outbreak of the conflict. To a large extent, there was no real question of *whether* the arms buildups contributed to the war; the question was only *how* they had done so. We can see this characteristic in the classic formal modeling done by Lewis Richardson (1960a) and those who followed him. The arms race debate during the Cold War was more complex simply because it was a debate. The dominant strand of thought throughout the Cold War was that the military buildup was fundamentally necessary to the security of the United States and Soviet Union by deterring conflict through the threat of the use of nuclear weapons (Spanier, 1980; Huntington, 1958). Still, the intellectual legacy of WWI did not die, but was played out in a new environment that suggested that the cost of another arms race–driven war would be globally devastating.

It was not until the late 1970s that the debate was moved from historical/theoretical/political debate into the realm of empirical testing. While still highly charged politically, the issue of arms buildups and war causation was finally addressed in a systematic, scientific fashion. In a first, and eventually highly criticized test, Wallace (1979) found a strong connection between ongoing arms races and the escalation of militarized disputes to war. Further tests by others suggested that a positive relationship might exist, but if it did, this first study had probably overstated the relationship between arming and war (Altfeld, 1983; Weede, 1980; Wallace, 1980).

Diehl (1983, 1985a) found no significant relationship between arming and escalation. However, he failed to put the question to rest because of his use of both a different testing sample and a different means of determining when an unusually rapid military buildup was occurring. This made it impossible to tell which change led to his conclusions. This made the study a superior alternative to Wallace but did not build directly on it in a way that would allow direct comparison of results and a real theoretical discussion of why the results were, in fact, different. Many of the remaining questions regarding testing sets and proper measures of an arms buildup were addressed in Sample's work (1996, 1997, 1998a). Those tests were structured to build directly on both Wallace and Diehl in a way that would allow a direct comparison of the studies, and, in doing so, managed to resolve some of the debate inherent in the earlier studies. These tests found a positive relationship between arming and escalation, though not as strong as Wallace had originally asserted.

What all of those studies had in common, however, was the fact that the tests were only conducted using major state disputes. For the original studies, there were several practical reasons for limiting the domain to major states. Constructing a valid and reliable measure of an unusual military buildup has been more difficult than it might first appear (see the discussion in Sample, 1997). The use of military expenditure data to do so can itself be criticized. It is difficult to be certain of the data, and there may be no guarantee that it reflects real military capacity. The original data is in different currencies, meaning that the exchange rates may or may not translate the numbers to a really comparable base (Diehl & Crescenzi, 1998). Bolks & Stoll (2000) have shown that the use of capital naval ships is a good measure of major state military capability, but such a measure, while perhaps better than expenditures for major states, is not really generalize able to all states in the system. For a variety of reasons, the use of expenditure data still has a number of advantages over other possible data sources for this purpose (Sample, 1998b). There are still gaps in those data,

particularly regarding the minor states, but when the Correlates of War dataset was young, and the first studies conducted, those gaps were larger. This made a study looking at a few hundred major states disputes much more practicable than one attempting to look at a few thousand minor and mixed-state disputes as well. Now, however, it is possible to do the more inclusive test, including all disputes, which is preferable for theoretical reasons. By looking at both major states and minor states, we can ask whether they are essentially the same, rather than allowing the nature of our test to require us to assume that they are. Whether we find that the dispute sets are different or similar, the results are important.

These studies of the effect of arms buildups on dispute escalation come at the question of deterrence at a slightly odd angle because they are not a direct test of deterrence. The basic theoretical argument in the deterrence literature is straightforward and rational: a state's willingness to initiate conflict will be subject to its rational evaluation of the balance of capabilities and the balance of interests in a given situation. As can be seen in the measures used, and the control variables employed, the literature on arms buildups is trying to tap into something more than just the rational calculation implied in deterrence. While the arms buildup literature naturally has implications for deterrence, then, the juncture between the two has to be examined carefully.

Empirically, deterrence is difficult to test. It is naturally difficult to tell cases of successful deterrence from instances where no aggressive action was ever intended (Fearon, 1994a; Huth & Russett, 1993). After all, is it clear that the United States and the Soviet Union never engaged in war because they were able to deter each other? Or did they never engage in war because they never had any real intention of doing so? Because there was no use of nuclear weapons in war after World War II, to some extent deterrence was tested by considering whether state behavior conformed with the logic of the theory (Kugler, 1984).

By examining the historical record, we know that while possession of nuclear weapons would seem automatically to make challenging that state irrational, non-nuclear states often challenged nuclear states during the Cold War and got what they wanted (Organski & Kugler, 1980; Kugler, 1984). Huth & Russett (1984) also originally found that possession of nuclear weapons was not necessarily associated with instances of successful deterrence. Huth (1988) argued that this could occur because the threats of nuclear states against non-nuclear states were not credible for a combination of military, political, and ethical reasons. However, in a later revision of his model, Huth (1990) found that nuclear weapons were, in fact, related to successful deterrence, suggesting that when it came to a question of actual escalation, a non-nuclear state did not risk war with a clearly more powerful opponent.

A missing element of these deterrence studies could be the failure to distinguish between general deterrence and immediate deterrence. If one is considering the possible relevance of military buildups in the escalation equation, that distinction is critical because the very fact of the dispute implies the failure of general deterrence, but leaves the possibility of immediate deterrence open. General deterrence suggests that possession of overwhelming force (like nuclear weapons) should prevent disputes from occurring: if the balance of capabilities is not in your favor, it hardly seems rational to challenge someone who can pulverize you. Huth & Russett (1993) take a systematic comparative look at general deterrence in an attempt to uncover patterns in the circumstances when a dispute is initiated. Their findings are notable. While the theoretical frameworks are often discussed as mutually exclusive, particularly the rational theoretical and cognitive psychological approaches, Huth & Russett found some support for both models in their test.

Immediate deterrence, on the other hand, deals with the likelihood that a dispute will escalate to war. Separating the two in our tests is absolutely critical because the very policies that make one successful may make the other fail (Fearon, 1994a; Huth & Russett, 1993). Fearon argued that it is possible that arms buildups decrease the chance that disputes will occur between states, but increase the chance that two states in a dispute will escalate to war. In order to overcome the general deterrent effect of an arms buildup, a challenger has to be pretty determined about the issue, and probably willing to use force. This could be a built-in self-selection bias in cases where disputes have occurred, the very unit of analysis of the studies of the effects of arms buildups. In a preliminary test of this question, Sample (2000) found that ongoing military buildups were actually related to dispute initiation as well as dispute escalation. This suggested that the effects of military buildups were not changing from one stage to another due to that self-selection, but it remains important to maintain the distinction between general and immediate deterrence in a study that looks at the outcomes of disputes.

Methodology

A perennial problem in many of our social scientific inquiries is the fact that different tests are conducted in such a way as to make direct comparison, and thus a cumulation of scientific knowledge, profoundly difficult. In the literature on military buildups, different measures of the principal variable conflicted with different dispute sets, and the whole enterprise ground to a halt for a time over how to gain any knowledge in the face of these disagreements. Sample's (1997) study made a conscious effort to structure its tests in such a way as to make the outcomes directly comparable to the work of both Wallace and Diehl, while addressing several of the more significant criticisms of Wallace's work. This study follows the same general pattern—by building directly on the previous tests conducted by Sample (1998a), the goal is to make the results regarding minor and mixed disputes here a direct addition to those earlier studies. Thus, any variation in findings between major, minor, and mixed disputes can be attributed to real empirical patterns, rather than possibly being the artifact of unconscious methodological or testing differences.

The domain of this test is all militarized interstate disputes (using the Correlates of War Militarized

Interstate Dispute dataset) between 1816 and 1992.[2] Obviously, unlike previous studies of military buildups and dispute escalation, this study includes disputes involving minor states as well as major ones. Multilateral disputes are divided into bilateral dispute dyads.[3] While this was one of the criticisms of Wallace's original study, the reasons for doing so outweigh any real problems that might come of it. Primarily, it bypasses the problem of trying to determine whether to code a multilateral dispute as being characterized by a rapid military buildup when some of the states involved are building up rapidly and others are not. Despite the fact that one may legitimately argue that multilateral disputes are multilateral and should be treated that way, subsequent testing showed that dividing these disputes into dyads did not alter the statistical results in any significant way. Because the coding rules require both states to be engaging in a rapid military buildup for the dispute to be coded that way, some of the resulting bilateral disputes ended up coded as occurring during a military buildup, others did not. There is no statistical bias inherent in the choice (Sample, 1996, 1997).

Other than the mutual military buildup, this study includes those other variables that might have an intervening impact on the likelihood of escalation in the presence of a buildup. These include measures of relative and shifting capabilities, the defense burden of the two states, whether the dispute was over the issue of territory, whether the states were contiguous, and whether one or both states possessed nuclear weapons. With the exception of contiguity, the variables follow from those in Sample (1998a).

The rapid **mutual military buildup** is measured by whether there is an ongoing buildup in both states prior to the militarized disputes. The measure used here is based on that designed by Horn (1987). In the preceding ten years, a country must exhibit higher than average military growth rates for that period, which are increasing from the beginning of the decade to the end. Growth rates are compared to the country's own average in that period, 1816–1913 or 1914–93, a division which allows us to control for the inflationary trend of the 20th century. While previous studies suggested that military buildups did increase the likelihood of dispute escalation among major states, this test will allow us to see whether those findings were only applicable to major states, or whether minor states show similar reactions to the military buildups of others.

While the rapid military buildup is the central variable, I also take into account certain other variables likely to be related to escalation, military buildups, or both of these. I include level of militarization, the issue over which two states are in dispute, nuclear weapons, and specific power-related variables. Militarization, or the *defense burden* of the state, is a static measure of the proportion of its resources a country is spending on its military at a given time.[4] A dispute where one or both countries have a high defense burden might be more likely to escalate to war than a dispute where this is not the case. One plausible explanation for this is the window of opportunity problem: one state or both may doubt its long-term ability to sustain a high level of spending or preparation for conflict, and thus decide that prosecuting outstanding conflicts now, rather than later, is a sensible strategy.

This measure of the defense burden or high level of militarization is distinct from the dynamic measure of how fast a country's military expenditure is growing, or its rate of military buildup. A state could be dedicating a large proportion of its national resources to the military (thus having a high defense burden) without being engaged in a rapid military buildup, or vice versa. The variables are definitely distinct, but at the same time, because they are both measures of military preparation, there is enough concern that they will be related to one another to justify including the defense burden as a control variable in a study of the effect of military buildups.

The theoretical background for the arms race literature has been a little fuzzy historically. Is it that arms buildups affect the balance of capabilities, thus impacting the likelihood of conflict, or to explain their effect must we address literature that abandons the assumption of rationality in policymaking in favor of more cognitive or psychological approaches to interaction? Both approaches have been used in examinations of the effects of military buildups. For instance, Huth & Russett (1993) include a measure for arms buildups in their test of general deterrence, and it is intended to measure the changes in relative power, not to tap into any psychological process that might be involved in the cause and effect of military buildups. This makes sense within the rational model of policymaking. It also indicates the necessity to control carefully for the balance of capabilities and changes in that balance if one intends to address the second meaning of an arms buildup, tapping into patterns which do not necessarily follow from the assumption of rationality.

Traditionally, war has been thought of as the outcome of an unresolvable conflict over power. All states operate within the same anarchical system, thus the constraints upon all are essentially the same. This suggests that the overall patterns of dispute escalation should be essentially similar whether the states involved are major or minor ones because the outcome of disputes should follow patterns based on the relative power of the states involved, or changes in that power structure. For this reason, I include three power-based variables in the study: whether or not there has been a rapid closing of the power gap between the states in the preceding decade, or *rapid approach;* whether the two states are equal in power, or at *parity;* and whether they have experienced a *transition* in power in the preceding decade.

A rapid approach toward parity is a theoretically different creature from a mutual military buildup, although the latter may, in fact, affect the power balance between two states (Wayman, 1996). To the extent that arms buildups contribute independently to the likelihood of war, it must be the result of a more complex dynamic than simply the power balance or changes in it. A rapid approach toward power parity might convince the (perhaps temporarily) more powerful state that it is about to lose its ability to prevail in any future conflicts, violent or not, with the approaching state. Or the approaching state might feel that the rapidly changing balance of

power justifies its attempt to prosecute disputes that have lain in abeyance while it was weaker. The rapid approach is about power itself, unlike a mutual military buildup, which is about a dynamic relationship that includes the psychological perception of intention and threat, and is to that extent independent of the power balance between states at the time of their dispute.

The second power-related variable is the power balance itself—are the states at parity or not? This effectively tests one of the fundamental premises of traditional international relations thought, that a basically equal balance of power yields stability in the international system. That was the theoretical basis of the classical balance of power, and it was the theoretical basis behind Waltz's assertion that the Cold War bipolar system was stable. If each state had an equal chance of defeating the other in conflict, both would be highly reticent to risk war and the possibility of defeat.

Organski (1958) and Organski & Kugler (1980) challenged this empirically and theoretically. Empirically, Organski pointed out that the classical multipolar balance of power was characterized by nearly continuous war until the 19th century when Britain's preponderant power was able to overwhelm any European alliance of which it was not a part. If one really looked at the occurrence of war in the system, it seemed that it was preponderance that yielded the stability of the 19th-century European system in contrast to earlier years, not equality. Theoretically, it seemed just as plausible that when two states or alliances were equal, then each was equally capable of winning the war—there was no obvious reason why they should avoid war in that circumstance rather than seek it. In the case of preponderance, only one state has a real chance of winning a violent conflict, and a disproportionately powerful state can probably exert its power over a weaker state in more efficient ways than by warfare.

It has also been indicated that a transition in power increases the chance of war between states (Organski, 1958; Organski & Kugler, 1980). Originally an argument regarding the cause of general or world wars, the basic logic rests on the notion that when two states experience a transition, the rising state suddenly finds itself in the position to overturn the standing norms that define its relationship with the state it is passing. As a theory of major war, this can be overturning the order of the entire international system to support the challenger's interests. However, the logic of the power transition would seem to apply to small states as well. Minor states may be in contest over control of a regional subsystem (Lemke, 1993, 1996; Lemke & Werner 1996). Or it is conceivable that a bilateral relationship has been characterized by certain rules or norms or patterns that the previously weaker state no longer finds acceptable when it has the choice to change them, regardless of whether those norms also define any larger regional or global system. For instance, a long-term border conflict, which has been on the back burner, may suddenly boil over when a weaker state finds itself with the power to give it a plausible chance of victory.

In order to measure power, the study makes use of the Correlates of War capabilities data, weighting each of the six indicators of national power equally and comparing countries on the basis of their average holdings. If the less powerful country in a pair has at least 80% of the holdings of the other, they are considered to be at parity. The dispute is coded as taking place in the context of a rapid approach if the gap itself between the two countries has closed by 40% and the overall distribution of power between them has shifted by at least 5%. This last is in order to distinguish between countries that were originally quite close together and those that were not, since 40% of a small gap would not necessarily be read by the participants in the same way as 40% of a large gap. A transition is said to have occurred if one country passed the other in power holdings in the preceding ten years.

In addition to these power-related variables, the study also takes into account the specific *issue* at stake in the dispute and its likely impact on escalation. More specifically, disputes are coded as to whether they are over territory or over some other issue (that data is taken from the Militarized Interstate

Dispute data). The very idea that the nature of the specific issue is important to the likelihood of escalation actually stands in contrast to traditional realist thought, which focused on the power distribution as the real source of conflict between states (Vasquez, 1993, 1995). The shift towards studying the character and salience of issues also necessitates a more general shift toward the decision-making level of analysis in our studies of war. A reluctance to make that shift and the paucity of good data on issues meant that there was not much attention paid to issues for a long time (Diehl, 1992).

If the real source of conflict were to be found in the distribution of power, then the issue in contention would essentially be a symptom or reflection of an underlying struggle for power, and wars would occur over all issues, showing no clear pattern. The findings of studies looking at issues generally, and territory specifically, indicate just how important these questions are. Gochman & Leng (1983) found that the probability of dispute escalation was strongly associated with the character of the issue in contention in the first place. Empirically, the distribution of issues associated with war is not random. More wars have been fought over territorial issues than other types of issues, and disputes over territorial issues are more likely to escalate than other disputes (Holsti, 1991; Diehl, 1992). The general literature has grown, including Huth's work, which examines territorial disputes from beginning to end while attempting to bring the decision-making level of analysis into our understanding of these disputes through his integration of domestic political variables and the traditional power-based realist framework (Huth, 1996). Thus, it is clearly important to include territorial issues in this study.

I include contiguity between the disputants as well because it has long been recognized that a correlation exists between geographical contiguity and the occurrence of war between states. Lewis Richardson (1960) found that the war propensity of a country was directly related to its number of borders. Gleditsch & Singer (1975) found that the number of wars between states was related to the distance between their capitals. In his analysis of 'dangerous dyads', Bremer (1992b) found that contiguous dyads had a much higher probability of war in any given year than non-contiguous dyads. And Diehl (1985b) found that contiguity to the site of the dispute by at least one disputant was present in 12 of 13 wars in his study of enduring rivalries. In other words, neighbors fight, and they certainly fight more often than non-neighbors do.

I include *contiguity* because of both its acknowledged relationship to escalation and its possible relationship to territory as an issue. Without controlling for contiguity, the relationship between territorial disputes specifically could easily be confounded with the general effects of geographical proximity. If we describe the dynamics of politics as the interaction between the elements of opportunity and willingness (Siverson & Starr, 1990), then contiguity directly affects the opportunity for states to go to war through simple proximity. Territory more directly taps into the dimension of willingness, and suggests that states fight over territory itself, not just on territory because it is proximate or creates the chance of increased interactions. Thus, the inclusion of the issue and a measure of contiguity allows us to see how both impact escalation independently, and to separate out their respective effects.

The one remaining variable included in the study is the possession of *nuclear weapons* by one or both disputants. Nuclear deterrence theory suggests that, despite rapid buildups, the chance of war should decline precipitously once states possess nuclear capability (Brodie, 1946). This is really only a slight twist on the basic deterrence argument. The destructive capacity of nuclear weapons being what it is, the costs of a war where they are used must be infinitely higher than any possible benefits. As a consequence, disputes where the use of nuclear weapons can plausibly be threatened should not escalate. Nearly all disputes between major states and involving major states after 1945 are characterized by the possession of nuclear weapons. Because of their overwhelming threat, it could be that a nuclear arms race is qualitatively different from military buildups in the pre-nuclear era,

and that the post-nuclear world is just fundamentally different from the pre-nuclear world.

The test conducted here is structured as logistic regression analysis, with escalation to war as the dichotomous dependent variable. The other variables are also coded dichotomously. The dispute set consists of a total of 2,304 dyads included in the analysis: 267 are between major states, 1,196 are between minor states, and 841 are between a major and a minor state. After looking at all the disputes together, the set will be disaggregated to compare the three different classes of disputes in order to discover if they follow similar paths of escalation or not.

Findings

The results of this study are complex. There are clear patterns in escalation, and military buildups do increase the chance of dispute escalation, but it is not an entirely consistent finding, nor a simple story. The dynamics of dispute escalation between different classes of disputes show many commonalities, but also some differences. Both the similarities and the differences indicate that we need to revisit our assumptions about the structure of the international

Table 1 Independent Variables Included in the Analysis

1. Mutual military buildups

2. Rapid approach toward parity in the preceding decade

3. Power equality

4. Transition of power in the preceding decade

5. Defense burden

6. Territorial issue

7. Possession of nuclear weapons by one or both parties to the dispute

8. States are contiguous

system and the behavior of states within it: we should not automatically apply the same security policy strategies to all states and all disputes.

In order to compare fully the escalation patterns of different classes of disputes, the tests have been conducted on different sets of disputes, beginning with the entire set of 2,304 bilateral disputes.

In our analysis here of all interstate disputes, we find that rapid military buildups are indeed significantly related to the escalation of militarized disputes. Over the period from 1816 to 1992, disputes between states engaged in mutual military buildups were $100[\text{Exp } (B) - 1)] = 232\%$ more likely to escalate than disputes where the states were not engaging in such a buildup. This is in accord with earlier findings regarding the impact of military buildups on major state disputes (Sample, 1998a, 2000).

There are other important patterns of escalation to be found as well in this first test of all disputes. We find that a dispute is much more likely to escalate when the issue in contention is territorial, and

when the states are contiguous. This suggests that proximity is important to the escalation of disputes, and that territorial disputes are theoretically more than just contiguous conflicts. Disputes are also more likely to escalate when one or both countries have a high defense burden.

The one other variable that is significant in this first test is the presence of nuclear weapons, which appear significantly to decrease the likelihood of escalation. In doing this test, we realize that in many ways looking at all of the disputes together may lead to false impressions of the escalation dynamics because of the possible difference in different classes of disputes. However, it may be the best way to evaluate the impact of nuclear weapons. Because the vast majority of disputes involving a major country after World War II involve at least one nuclear state, the variable simply does not vary much in studies of major states only. In addition, the only war involving a major state on both sides of the conflict after World War II is the Korean War, so the dependent

Table 2   Logit Model: Escalation to War, 1816–1993—All Disputes, 1816–1993

Variable	B	S.E.	Wald	Sig.	Exp(B)
Mutual military buildup	1.2	.216	31.01	.000	3.32
Rapid approach	.002	.095	.000	.984	1.00
Equality	−.010	.254	.002	.969	.99
Transition	.467	.342	1.87	.172	1.60
Defense burden	.674	.136	24.61	.000	1.96
Nuclear	−.813	.275	8.71	.003	.444
Territorial issue	1.38	.154	80.98	.000	3.99
Contiguity	1.50	.27	30.59	.000	4.46
Constant	−4.35	.282	239.06	.000	.013
Model log-likelihood	1271.99		N = 2,304		
Model chi-square	293.39		d.f. 8	Significance <.001	

variable varies a little, but not a lot. So including minor state and mixed disputes allows the variables actually to vary in a way that may give us a better idea of what is going on. The significant relationship between the presence of nuclear weapons and the diminished chance of escalation here shows just how important it is to consider the post–World War II period separately in order to assess the claims that the world has just fundamentally changed since that conflict (Sample, 2000). To that end, the reported findings in the following tables are shown by era.

It is worth noting at the outset that the probability of a dispute escalating is different depending on whether the dispute is between two major states, a major state and a minor state, or two minor states. Quincy Wright (1965) found that major states were just more likely to fight than minor states, and that

is supported here. Of 268 total dyadic disputes between two major states, 14.9% (40) escalated. Disputes involving only one major state were slightly less likely to escalate (139 out of 1,017 escalated, or 13.7%). And minor state disputes were considerably less likely to escalate overall. Of 1,433 disputes between two minor states, 136, or 9.5%, escalated.

When we break the dispute set down by these classes of disputes, we find both similarities and differences in escalation patterns among classes of disputes. Regarding military buildups, major and minor state disputes show a similar pattern in the era before World War II, but mixed disputes are different. Both major state disputes and minor state disputes are significantly more likely to escalate if both states are engaged in a mutual military buildup before the war, though clearly not after.[5]

Table 3 Logit Model: Major State Dispute Escalation to War, 1816–1993

Variable	B	S.E.	Wald	Sig.	Exp(B)
Mutual military buildups					
All years	1.75	.58	9.07	.003	5.76
1816–1944	2.02	.66	9.38	.002	7.56
1945–93	9.24	55.00	.028	.867	10,320
Rapid approach					
All years	−.827	.707	1.37	.242	.437
1816–1944	−1.86	1.0	3.45	.063	.156
1945–93	.485	1.17	.171	.68	1.62
Equality					
All years	.613	.556	1.21	.271	1.85
1816–1944	1.74	.731	5.63	.018	5.67
1945–93	−1.34	1.18	1.29	.255	.263
Transition					
All years	.643	.816	.622	.430	1.90
1816–1944	.353	1.04	.116	.733	1.42
1945–93	.216	1.56	.019	.890	1.24

Variable	B	S.E.	Wald	Sig.	Exp(B)
Defense burden					
All years	.536	.440	1.48	.224	1.71
1816–1944	.589	.526	1.25	.263	1.80
1945–93	.561	.957	.343	.558	1.75
Nuclear					
All years	−1.17	.50	5.54	.019	.312
1816–1944	—	—	—	—	—
1945–93	−6.79	453.09	.000	.988	.001
Territorial issue					
All years	1.25	.443	7.99	.005	3.50
1816–1944	1.72	.55	9.73	.002	5.56
1945–93	−1.08	.96	.013	.911	.898
Contiguity					
All years	3.16	1.06	8.90	.003	23.64
1816–1944	3.13	1.10	8.14	.004	22.83
1945–93	16.32	76.99	.045	.832	1,226,969
Constant					
All years	−5.15	1.11	21.50	.000	.006
1816–1944	−5.43	1.20	20.56	.000	.004
1945–93	−11.91	446.51	.001	.979	.000
Model log-likelihood	All years	156.37		N = 267	
	1816–1944	106.81		N = 142	
	1945–93	39.79		N = 125	
Model chi-square	65.68	d.f. 8		Significance	<.001
	44.73	d.f. 7			<.001
	14.17	d.f. 8			= .078

As one can see in Tables 3 and 4, the relationship between military buildups and escalation is stronger for major state disputes than minor state disputes. For major states, the chance of escalation is $100(7.56 − 1) = 656\%$ more likely given a mutual military buildup. For minor states, the increase is about 232%. In either case, the increased chance of escalation is considerable for these disputes, while those between a major state and a minor state have no such relationship.

These results clearly indicate the importance of breaking the data at 1945. We see profoundly different results after the war. For both major state disputes and minor state disputes, the relationship vanishes altogether In fact, for major state disputes in that era, no variable is significant, suggesting the real difference in the postwar major state system. Statistically, this may be partially an artifact of the limited variability of the dependent variable, but theoretically, the fact that disputes between the major states were less likely to escalate under any circumstances is the point.

Before addressing the issue of an explanation for this set of findings—similarity between major and minor states, the fact that the mixed disputes are different, and the post–World War II era changes—it is necessary to look at the other relationships uncovered in this study. There are two highly notable similarities in the dispute escalation patterns of all disputes: the impact of territory disputes on the likelihood of escalation and the presence of nuclear weapons in the dispute dynamic.

The relationship between territory and escalation is perhaps the most robust relationship. While that relationship, like all others, fails among major states after World War II, it is highly significant and extremely strong in all other classes of disputes, before and after the war.[6] Disputes over territory are several times more likely to escalate than should be the case if the issue did not matter.

The powerful results support the assertion that territory is important to people and to states in ways that other issues simply are not. Vasquez (1993, 1995) suggests that human beings are inherently 'soft-wired' to treat territorial issues as critical, and are prone to fight over them in the absence of clear alternative norms or rules for their resolution. This would be something more than states just fighting over the resources that territory represents: countries fight for territory that seems to have primarily symbolic value. The war between Britain and Argentina in 1982 was one which neither country at the time could easily afford, and the Falklands/Malvinas, while granting that they have fishing stocks in their Exclusive Economic Zone, are hardly strategically valuable or resource rich, but the war still went forward.

The possession of nuclear weapons by one or both parties to the dispute seems to decrease the chance of dispute escalation considerably. If one evaluates all disputes (1816–1992), the variable for nuclear weapons possession is highly significant for both major state disputes and mixed disputes (no minor states were declared nuclear powers, so the variable is constant for those disputes). This finding is essentially in line with the empirical findings of Huth (1990) and seems to support the general argument that nuclear deterrence works. As I alluded to earlier, in the case of major state disputes it makes more sense to look at the whole Correlates of War period to ensure variability in both the dependent and independent variables. One can see that the statistical outcomes after World War II for the major states are completely insignificant: there is no pattern of escalation to war because, with the exception of Korea, there is no war between major states. After the war, the significance of the finding is not high for mixed state disputes either, but $p = .08$ and the direction of the relationship is certainly the same.

What these findings suggest is that the world did change after World War II, and that nuclear weapons may, in fact, decrease the likelihood of escalation in any disputes where they are part of the dynamic. The Cold War era is fundamentally different from the world before it. This fact may be more than just the result of nuclear weapons possession. Other explanations for the 'long peace' among major states have been offered, including war weariness, learned recognition of the terrible costs of major wars for nearly all the participants, and so on, but the findings here for both major state disputes and mixed disputes suggest that the nuclear factor cannot be ignored (Gaddis, 1987; Singer, 1991).

The relationships between the other factors and dispute escalation show more variability across categories of disputes as well as time periods. High levels of militarization, or high defense burdens, increase the propensity to escalate for both minor state disputes and mixed disputes before World War II. The impact of a high defense burden is much stronger on mixed disputes than it is on minor state disputes (a 504% increase compared to a 90% increase), but it is definitely significant in both instances.

Table 4 Logit Model: Minor State Dispute Escalation to War, 1816–1993

Variable	B	S.E	Wald	Sig.	Exp(B)
Mutual military buildups					
All years	.963	.333	8.38	.004	2.62
1816–1944	1.20	.569	4.44	.035	3.32
1945–93	.018	.760	.001	.981	1.02
Rapid approach					
All years	.016	.113	.021	.885	1.02
1816–1944	.090	.605	.022	.882	1.09
1945–93	−.022	.118	.034	.854	.978
Equality					
All years	−.058	.353	.027	.869	.943
1816–1944	−.085	.609	.019	.889	.919
1945–93	−.323	.547	.347	.556	.724
Transition					
All years	.854	.462	3.41	.065	2.35
1816–1944	.504	.895	.317	.574	1.66
1945–93	1.29	.632	4.17	.041	3.64
Defense burden					
All years	.434	.134	10.57	.001	1.54
1816–1944	.642	.248	6.68	.010	1.90
1945–93	−.610	.413	2.19	.139	.543
Nuclear					
All years	—	—	—	—	—
1816–1944	—	—	—	—	—
1945–93	—	—	—	—	—
Territorial issue					
All years	1.82	.259	49.16	.000	6.15
1816–1944	1.33	.375	12.55	.000	3.78
1945–93	1.85	.397	21.74	.000	6.38

(Continued)

Table 4 (Continued)

Variable	B	S.E	Wald	Sig.	Exp(B)
Contiguity					
All years	.616	.402	2.34	.126	1.85
1816–1944	1.99	.723	7.61	.006	7.34
1945–93	−.18	.525	.118	.731	.835
Constant					
All years	−4.22	.402	110.58	.000	.015
1816–1944	−4.05	.738	30.15	.000	.017
1945–93	−3.84	.517	55.23	.000	.021
Model log-likelihood	All years	607.16	N = 1,196		
	1816–1945	211.05	N = 238		
	1945–93	307.95	N = 958		
Model chi-square	99.53	d.f. 7	Significance	<.001	
	61.97	d.f. 7		<.001	
	36.87	d.f. 7		<.001	

Table 5   Logit Model: Mixed (Major-Minor) Dispute Escalation to War, 1816–1993

Variable	B	S.E.	Wald	Sig.	Exp(B)
Mutual military buildups					
All years	.322	.405	.631	.427	1.38
1816–1944	.000	.424	.000	1.00	1.00
1945–93	2.53	1.93	1.72	.189	12.56
Rapid approach					
All years	−7.41	9.85	.565	.452	.001
1816–1944	−9.15	16.40	.311	.577	.000
1945–93	−2.49	25.64	.009	.923	.083
Equality					
All years	1.66	1.03	2.59	.107	5.28
1816–1944	2.13	1.11	3.67	.055	8.38

Variable	B	S.E.	Wald	Sig.	Exp(B)
1945–93	—	—	—	—	—
Transition					
All years	−.102	1.47	.005	.945	.903
1816–1944	.115	1.49	.006	.938	1.12
1945–93	−1.47	44.73	.001	.974	.229
Defense burden					
All years	1.41	.277	26.10	.000	4.11
1816–1944	1.80	.361	24.76	.000	6.036
1945–93	−.167	.689	.059	.808	.846
Nuclear					
All years	−1.96	.381	26.32	.000	.141
1816–1944	—	—	—	—	—
1945–93	−.906	.521	3.02	.082	.404
Territorial issue					
All years	1.47	.260	32.00	.000	4.36
1816–1944	1.32	.319	17.11	.000	3.73
1945–93	2.32	.568	16.71	.000	10.21
Contiguity					
All years	2.33	.448	27.14	.000	10.29
1816–1944	2.97	.622	22.85	.000	19.52
1945–93	.93	.664	1.96	.162	2.53
Constant					
All years	−4.54	.474	91.57	.000	.011
1816–1944	−5.18	.669	60.03	.000	.006
1945–93	−4.17	.762	29.89	.000	.015
Model log-likelihood	All years	400.44	N = 841		
	1816–1944	255.82	N = 379		
	1945–93	127.53	N = 462		
Model chi-square	224.97	d.f. 8	Significance	<.001	
	140.05	d.f. 7		<.001	
	43.33	d.f. 7		<.001	

One explanation for this might be the fact that minor states do not have deep pockets. If a minor state is going to prosecute its cause in a dispute by raising it to the level of war, it may be or feel under a time constraint that requires it to act before it is no longer capable of sustaining its current level of military readiness. Major states, on the other hand, are unlikely to be in the same circumstance because they have more multidimensional power on which to draw (or they would not be major states). In a dispute involving two major states, a high defense burden on the part of one or both may not, in fact, be unsustainable, decreasing the chance that a given dispute will be seen as a 'now or never' proposition.

This does not explain, however, why we would see a different pattern after World War II. The structure of power, whether or not minor states have 'deep pockets', would not logically change after the war. For mixed disputes, the only variable that remains significant at the .05 level after World War II is territorial disputes, which strongly increase the likelihood of escalation. Minor state disputes show the same relationship with territory and escalation. The overarching history of the latter half of the 20th century may account for the change in the effects of defense burdens, while territorial disputes remain so clearly conflictual. The defense burden itself and the lack of 'deep pockets' may cease to have so much relevance when the territorial disputes are regarding critical border delineations in the post-colonial period.

The effects of contiguity are consistent across classes of disputes, but not across the 1945 divide. Before World War II, contiguity was significantly related to escalation of disputes, whether those disputes were between major states, between minor states, or were mixed. After the war, contiguity ceases to be relevant once we have controlled for disputes specifically over the issue of territory. If post-colonial border delineations make up a large portion of the conflicts between contiguous states, they would necessarily be about the issue of territory. In addition, as technology advances, it is possible that contiguity loses its dominance as a factor related to escalation. Gochman (1990a) found that the proportion of disputes between contiguous states had actually increased after 1870 (suggesting technology was not overcoming the problem of distance in force projection), but that increase may have primarily been before World War II, not after it, accounting for both findings.

The power-related variables—the rapid approach, power parity, and power transition—all showed curiously mixed, but quite interesting, results. Power parity is related to the escalation of mixed disputes before World War II ($p = .055$), and of major states as well ($p = .018$).[7] If the states are equal in power, the chance of a dispute escalating into war rises precipitously in both cases. This would conform to the argument regarding parity made by Organski (1958) and Organski & Kugler (1980), and most certainly does not support the classical balance of power arguments.

In the same period, a rapid approach toward parity seems to have a *negative* effect on the likelihood of major state dispute escalation (though, in this case, the p-value is .06—not highly significant, but worth noting).

The rapid approach has no impact on the minor state disputes in this period, nor on mixed disputes. After World War II, these relationships too vanish.

Before World War II, a power transition is not related to escalation of any class of disputes, but after the war, it is positively related to the escalation of minor state disputes. A minor state dispute, characterized by a transition in power in the preceding ten years, is 264% more likely to escalate to war than disputes where no transition has occurred. The most interesting thing about this finding is that it applies to minor states, but not major ones, when the power transition thesis itself was originally part of a theory of general war among major states. The explanation for this might be similar to that offered for the prewar importance of high defense burdens: the heightened sensitivity of minor states to windows of opportunity—in this case represented by the power transition.

Returning to the original question, how are we to explain the role of military buildups in dispute escalation, given the implication of these findings that the impact is complex? Before World War II, military buildups significantly increase the chance of escalation for both minor and major states, but not mixed state disputes. The key to understanding the impact of military buildups, before and after the war, is recognizing the interplay between three factors: the objective threats facing states created by specific power distributions, the effects of human cognitive perception, and the insights offered to us by more critical approaches that point to the impact of a security culture dominated over time by realpolitik (Sample, 1998a).

Recognition that psychological and constructivist approaches have something to offer our understanding of international politics is not meant to imply that the distribution of power between states is irrelevant to the likelihood of conflict; the findings of this study would not support such a contention.

Equality between major state disputes, or between mixed disputes, prior to World War II increases the likelihood of dispute escalation. Transitions in power increase the chance of escalation between minor states. These represent the real impact of the power distributions even in the context of analyzing the contribution of cognitive psychology and social constructivism.

Evidence from research in cognitive psychology has clear implications for understanding decision-making dynamics. It tells us that humans are prone to misperception, and that misperception often follows predictable patterns. For instance, humans tend to see themselves as the center of the plans of others, whether it is true or not. And they assume that their intentions are clear to others, whether it is true or not (Jervis, 1976). What is even more interesting is that this possibility, even probability, of misperception, does not explain why disputes would be prone to end in conflict. Why should it not be random, misperception sometimes leading to a fight, sometimes leading away from one?

That question may be answered by examining the impact of realism as a strategic culture as well as a theory, accepting some of the insight of constructivist and critical thought. Social reality can be affected by our beliefs about it. In the case of realism, the theory tells us that conflict is endemic in the system, and there is no overarching authority to guarantee state security. In such an environment, it is better to be safe than sorry; it is better to overestimate the risk presented by another state than to underestimate it and risk destruction. A number of policy prescriptions derive from this, including the promotion of military buildups as a means of acquiring security. Perhaps just as importantly, realism argues that states, in order not to appear weak, thus inviting aggression, must show resolve, or a willingness to fight or go to the brink in order to deter another state from believing that it can be bullied or easily defeated.

These elements, taken together with natural human patterns of misperception, mean that national leaders will, in the event that both countries have been building up their militaries, tend to assume that observed behavior is the result of deliberate and conscious threat. National leaders will be prone to seeing their country as the center of the long-term aggressive intentions of others when they find themselves in a militarized dispute in the context of a mutual military buildup. Not only are they faced with immediate conflict, whether initiated by themselves or the other state, but it seems, whether true or not, that the animosity is truly deep-seated and goes back at least over the several years of the military buildup. The proper response to this must be to show no fear—indeed, to show a willingness to take this to war if that is necessary to make the opponent back down.

The logic of this argument seems entirely applicable to the findings for both minor and major state disputes, and also explains why mixed disputes are different. Even once we control for the distribution of power between the states and recent changes in that distribution, military buildups still increase the chance that a dispute will lead to war if both are minor states or major states. That is a psychological and cultural impact, not that of objective threat reflected by the power balance. A dispute between one major state and one minor state is different, because when the positions of two states are so distinct, not only does the power distribution change, but the *meaning* of the situation does as well. A militarized dispute between a major and minor state, even in the context of a mutual military buildup, does not have the same symbolic or real meaning as between two states more similar in status. The minor state knows that it is not playing in the big leagues; the military buildup of a major state, while obviously threatening in an objective sense, is unlikely to be interpreted as part of a policy of animosity toward that small state. Likewise, the major state will be focused on the intentions of other major states, rather than on the intentions of any one minor state, so even if the minor state has been building up its military, it will not likely be perceived as a serious threat.

In the case of both minor state and major state disputes, there is more likely to be perception of long-term aggressive intent that is merged into the assumptions of conflict inherent in realism, and there is also likely to be more real threat going both ways. The combination of these things heightens the chance that one or both states will believe that force is the only way to resolve the dispute. With mixed disputes, however, the objective threat is more one-sided, and while there may be long-term aggression between two states (the United States and Cuba, for instance) there is no reason to assume that their arms buildups would be driving it. Therefore, there is no particular reason that we *should* find a positive relationship between military buildups and escalation in these cases.

We must also account for the changed relationship in the post World War II era. Military buildups have no impact on the likelihood of disputes escalating to war after World War II. This holds for both major and minor state disputes. Independently of the impact of the power distribution, mutual military buildups increased the chance of war for these

disputes before World War II, and did not do so afterwards. For major states with nuclear weapons, one can appeal to the overwhelming threat afforded by those weapons to explain why disputes would not escalate, but to understand minor state disputes as well, it requires the integration of the different elements of the preceding explanation.

Constructivism shifts the meaning of theories of international politics. Rather than simply being seen as competing explanations for the reality of things, the argument is that theories themselves take on a meaning and reality in the international system beyond their objective validity. To the extent that states believe that the assumptions of realpolitik explain the way the system works, they choose policies based on those assumptions, and create certain outcomes that are not necessarily intended or predicted by realism. In other words, theory itself affects real outcomes.

In this case, in order to explain both classes of disputes, and the change in the dynamic after World War II, we must understand that the use of nuclear weapons at that critical juncture gave the diffuse concept of deterrence new life. Previously, deterrence was seen as the natural outcome of the balance of power, but deterrence as theory, as strategy, became a far more dominant element of realism after World War II than it was before. What a military buildup *meant* changed meanings in the face of the nuclear threat. Leaders after the war *believed* that military buildups would decrease the likelihood of their going to war more decidedly than they had ever done, and this meant something to leaders of minor states as well as major ones.

The nuclear arms race, especially after the Cuban Missile Crisis, shifted the psychological dynamic and thus the outcome of militarized interstate disputes in the post–World War II era. Because deterrence as strategy was so dominant in the international system, the default assumption in the face of a mutual military buildup became that the intention of such buildups was defensive, not offensive. As before, that assumption could be in error in a given dispute. While the massive shift in objective threat really only applies to the major states that had nuclear weapons, the effects of the strategic cultural shift are more general. The dynamics of disputes generally were not then escalatory, as they were in earlier eras when deterrence was only considered as a consequence of the balance of power, not a dominant security strategy in itself.

Conclusion

The complexity of escalation and the role of mutual military buildups in escalation have only partially been unveiled by studies focusing on major states. The tests contained herein indicate that the international system is more complex than earlier scholars have allowed for. Outcomes of disputes between minor states, and between a major and a minor state, are not always directly reflected by the dynamics of major state escalation.

Dividing the disputes by class and era shows us both the similarities and the differences in escalation dynamics. One difference can be seen in the apparent importance for minor states of carefully judging timing of disputes: if an issue is deemed as critical, a minor state appears to be more sensitive to windows of opportunity during which it is possible to prosecute disputes (reflected in one instance by the significance of high defense burdens and in another by that of power transitions). The similarities that we see are just as significant: disputes over territory are significantly more likely to escalate than other types of issues. This is true of all circumstances except when the disputants are both major states in the post–World War II era. We also see that the possession of nuclear weapons diminishes the likelihood of escalation for both major state disputes and mixed disputes. Whether this is strictly because of nuclear weapons or a more complex alteration in the relationships of major states in the international system after the war this study cannot specify, but it is clear that postwar dynamics involving major states have changed.

Both the similarities and the differences point to the need to look carefully at the dynamics of different classes of disputes. Once we understand them,

our theoretical frameworks can explain the differences, but the problem previously was that most studies, by focusing on major states, did not necessarily recognize that they existed to be addressed in the first place. Previous tests seemed to have a built-in assumption that major and minor states would not differ greatly, or else any differences in the minor states were not terribly material to our comprehension of international politics.

In order to understand the differences as well as the similarities, it is necessary to accept a theoretical complexity that brings to bear elements from frameworks that have usually been considered only in opposition. The real interplay between the rational framework, that of cognitive psychology, and acceptance of the development of strategic cultures through constructivism means that we have to confront complexity.

After World War II, the profound changes in the escalation of disputes cannot simply be explained by reference to changes in the power structure. Disputes between two minor states or between a minor and a major state still escalated, only the circumstances under which they did so altered. In order to explain those changes, not only for major state disputes where we might find our solution in the structure of nuclear deterrence, but for all states, we must look to theory itself. Theory has an overarching role in creating the environment in which states act and determine what is proper action in the international system.

It is necessary, then, to look at the profound impact that theory had as strategy in the post–World War II world. While realism has largely dominated the thinking of inter-national leaders from the time of the Treaty of Westphalia, the focus on deterrence as the central aspect of realism is really a postwar shift. Before World War II, or more properly, before nuclear weapons were used in that war, deterrence was the logical theoretical outcome of the balance of power, though, empirically, that outcome was highly contestable. In any event, classical realism considered that statesmen sought to maintain the balance of power as their fundamental strategy to guarantee security.

After the war, deterrence itself became the strategy; balance might be the outcome of *that*, but it was deterrence that was the key. Deterrence theory told us that if one had sufficient power to make the other actor truly *pay* for any attempt at aggression then states would not take the risk. Not a new lesson, by any means, but a newly reified one. The patterns of escalation after the war seem to support the contention that deterrence theory altered the way national leaders viewed their options in the international system, thereby changing the way mutual military buildups affected dispute outcomes. While we might just look to the objective threat of nuclear weapons themselves to explain the changed relationship among major states, this argument explains the changed dynamics of minor state disputes as well.

The effect of an ongoing mutual military buildup before the war has more to do with perception and psychology in the context of an international strategic culture of realism than it has to do with objective calculation. That can be seen by the fact that the relationship is significant even when we control for changes in the power distribution. The offered evaluation of the altered role of deterrence after the war is entirely consistent with that explanation. The strategic culture of realism itself goes through a change that has an impact then on the entire system, including the way mutual military buildups are seen, and including disputes between minor states in which nuclear weapons were not directly involved.

As scholars, it seems that if we are to understand war in the world, particularly after World War II, we are obligated to embrace complexity. We cannot allow ourselves to become so enamoured of a single theoretical framework, no matter what that framework is, that we ignore patterns and dynamics of escalation that indicate the importance of developing new means of dealing with disputing states. It is clear from this study that if we seek security, it is important to work on developing new norms for resolving territorial disputes. If we want to move our academic debates into the policy realm in a realistic way, we must recognize that minor states are not simple reflections of the major states, but that the interplay of the dynamics in international politics creates differences in these disputes as well as similarities. Without recognizing both, our hopes of creating good policy are diminished. Small states are not Great Powers; while they exhibit many similarities, their paths to war are sometimes different, and if we want the path to peace to be broader, we must respect that difference.

Notes

Author's Note: The dataset used in this test may be found at http://www.prio.no/jpr/datasets.asp.

1. Actually, most studies have looked at 'arms races'. However, that term, as has been addressed elsewhere, is a misnomer; it suggests a pattern of action—reaction and a spiraling of conflict that does not necessarily reflect empirical reality (Sample, 1998a).

2. It would be more correct to say almost all disputes. I have eliminated most intrawar dyads, including some between parties who were actually at war at the time of their dispute (either the new dispute included a third party, or the dispute was over a separate issue). However, many intrawar disputes remain because of the staggered entry of states into multilateral wars, such as the US entry into both world wars. Late entries into a war do not necessarily meet the criteria of a rapid military buildup, and the statistical implications of these choices are not as great as has been supposed. A complete discussion of the controversy and the statistical and theoretical implications can be found in Sample (1997).

3. After dividing multilateral disputes into bilateral dyads, and removing those disputes discussed in note 2 above, I was left with a total of 2,718 dyads. There were 1,433 dyads involving minor states, 237 of which were dropped from analysis because of missing data, leaving 1,196 in the analysis. There were 1,017 total bilateral disputes between a major and a minor state, or 841 dyads included in the analysis due to those eliminated by missing data. And there were a total of 268 disputes among major states; 267 of those were included in the analysis. This yields a total of 2,304 usable dyads.

4. This measure is adapted from Diehl (1985a). Due to the variability of data availability, the COW time

period is divided into four periods: 1816–60; 1861–1914; 1919–39; 1945–93. Before 1860, total number of military personnel was regressed on total population. The actual military personnel figures were then fed back into the resulting equation to determine the level of the defense burden for that particular year. In cases where the result was more than one standard deviation from the mean for that country, it was coded as having a high defense burden in that year. The three later periods were done similarly; however, each country's annual military expenditures were regressed separately on their coal/steel production and their energy consumption. The resulting two ratios of actual to predicted expenditures were then averaged. Once again, if the result was more than one standard deviation above the mean, the country was considered to have a high defense burden in that year.

5. Major states are defined here by the Correlates of War definition. They are Great Britain (1816–present), France (1816–1940; 1945–present), Russia/USSR (1816–1917; 1922–present); Prussia/Germany (1816–1918, 1925–45; 1990–present); Austria-Hungary (1816–1917); Italy (1860–1943); China (1950–present); Japan (1895–1945); and the United States (1899–present).

6. This finding is essentially in line with that of Vasquez & Henehan's (2001) study of territorial disputes and war probability.

7. It would seem that mixed disputes should be categorically different on these variables. By definition, there will be few, if any, disputes between a major and minor state that are power equals, and it is also improbable that the two states would have experienced a recent power transition, or even a rapid approach toward parity. Equality drops out altogether after 1945. That is not terribly surprising, since we would not expect minor states to be equal to major ones. Those 'minor' states, like Germany and Japan, which do equal or surpass in power some major states, like Britain and France, are allies with those states in this period, so there are no relevant disputes. So why do we see them before 1945? Largely because the United States and Japan are rising states in the latter part of the 19th and early 20th centuries, and they do get into some militarized disputes with major states before they are coded as such (from 1898 and 1894, respectively).

EDITORS' COMMENTARY

Major Contributions: Arms Races

Modern scholarly interest in arms races goes back to at least the First World War, where the preceding Anglo-German naval race was seen as a factor bringing the war about. After the war, Lewis F. Richardson (1960a), a Quaker, physicist, and founder of **peace science**, was the first to use mathematical models to study arms racing. Richardson used a system of differential equations to predict changes in two states' military expenditures in a dyad such as the United States and Soviet Union. The model incorporated the idea of **reciprocity**, whereby one state increases its arms expenditures in response to an increase in arms by the other state, and **routine**, where states consider what they spent last year on the military when making new allocation decisions. Richardson identified the conditions under which runaway arms races could occur—namely, when the size of the effect for reciprocity was larger than the effect for routine. He did not include a variable for war in his mathematical model directly; rather, he assumed that runaway arms races would be associated with an increased chance of war.

Many scholars agreed with Richardson and thought of arms races as a factor bringing about war, what is often called the **armaments-tension spiral hypothesis**. The idea of this perspective is that increasing arms levels by two rival states raise the chances of war by generating uncertainty about the outcome of a military engagement and by creating a security dilemma where one side's attempt to make itself more secure reduces the security of the other side. Other scholars disagreed vehemently with this argument, especially during the Cold War, for which it was argued that having a strong military would deter war. This is the so-called peace through strength or **para bellum hypothesis**, drawn from the Roman general Vegetius ("Who would desire peace should be prepared for war"). Michael D. Wallace (1979, 1982) was one of the first to collect data on the relationship between arms racing and the escalation of disputes to war to help adjudicate between these two schools of thought empirically. Using a precursor to the militarized interstate dispute (MID) data focused on serious disputes involving great powers, he found that when a serious dispute occurred in the context of an ongoing arms race, it was highly likely to escalate to war. In fact, he found that of the twenty-eight dyadic disputes in which there was an arms race, twenty-three escalated to war. Conversely, of the seventy-one disputes in which there were no arms races, only three escalated to war.

Wallace's (1979) findings were challenged on several grounds by Paul Diehl (1983) in terms of the unreliability of Wallace's measure of arms races and the breaking up of a single dispute, such as the Second World War, into a large number of dyadic disputes, which Diehl argued inflated the number of cases supporting the hypothesis that arms races are related to war. Diehl used a more straightforward measure of mutual military buildups, looking only at single disputes (rather than breaking them up into dyadic disputes) and updating the data by extending them five years to 1970.

He also ensured that the military buildups in the dyads were mutual or that both sides were increasing their military expenditures significantly. By doing these three things, Diehl eliminated the strong relationship Wallace found, reducing Wallace's Yule's Q of .98 to a statistically insignificant .36.[1] Diehl reported escalation to war in only three of twelve dyads in comparison with ten of the seventy-four non–arms racing dyads experiencing war. While the risk of war was higher in the presence of mutual military buildups, the relationship was much weaker than Wallace had found. Diehl also showed that Wallace's findings were primarily a function of the two world wars and not a general pattern.

Diehl's (1983) article and the several changes he made in the research design led to an extensive debate in the field of conflict studies. In addition to contested findings linking arms races and escalation of MIDs to war, other empirical studies failed to uncover a general pattern of reciprocity when examining the relationship between military expenditures in several dyads such as U.S.-U.S.S.R., Greece-Turkey, and Israel-Egypt (e.g., Cusack & Ward 1981; Majeski 1983; Georgiou et al 1996). This was surprising because these are exactly the kinds of rival dyads in which we would expect to see action-reaction in states' military expenditure levels. Susan Sample (1997) helped to resolve the debate and untangle the conflicting findings by examining the cases of mutual military buildups that did not result in war. When she did this, she found something very interesting—most of the cases that did not go to war were of two kinds: those in the 1930s that would eventually go to war within five years and those in the post-1945 nuclear era that tended not to go to war. Once she introduced a five-year window and a **control** for historical era, she found that the relationship between mutually military buildups and escalation to war held in the prenuclear era, but not afterward. She concluded that arming was dangerous and increased the likelihood of war, but this danger was pacified by the presence of nuclear weapons. This is consistent with the neorealist view that nuclear weapons can have a pacifying effect, especially in a bipolar world (Waltz 1981).

In the current article, Sample (2002) extends her analysis in two important directions. First, all of the previous analyses had been based on data confined to the major states or **major powers**, as they are commonly called. This group includes only a handful of states: Britain, France, Russia, Germany, Austria-Hungary, the United States, Japan, and China after 1949 (Singer et al. 1972, 22). Susan Sample was the first to collect arms race data on the large number of minor power states. This is an important contribution not only because of the immensity of the task but because it greatly extends the domain of countries on which the hypothesis can be tested.

Sample (2002) finds five major things. First, she reconfirms Wallace's (1979) original findings that mutual military buildups increase the probability that a MID will escalate to war within five years for both major and minor states. However, she finds that this relationship does not hold in the post-1945 nuclear era. Thus, in most of modern history (i.e., 1816–1945), arms races have been dangerous. Second, she finds important differences depending on whether the dyad consists of Major-Major (MM) states, minor-minor (mm) states, or Major-minor (Mm) states (see Tables 3 and 4). In the pre-1945 era, mutual military buildups are statistically and significantly related to dispute escalation to war for Major-Major dyads and for minor-minor dyads, but not for Major-minor dyads (Table 5). This means that states that are relatively equal have a different relationship with each other compared with states that are unequal or asymmetric. This finding is relevant to the debate in the rivalry literature (see the reading by Klein et al. 2006, Chapter 5, this volume) over whether rivalry can be a competitive relationship only between relative equals or whether it can include nonequals. Some have argued that this is an empirical question. Sample's finding empirically addresses that question and suggests that Major-minor dyads behave differently than relative equals.

Third, Sample (2002) also finds that dyads that have territorial disputes are apt to go to war regardless of whether they have mutual military buildups or the type of dyad (MM, mm, and Mm). This means that territorial disputes are such a strong factor associated with war that military buildups do not affect the relationship between territorial disputes and war, a finding consistent with bivariate research on territorial disputes (Hensel 1996a; Vasquez and Henehan 2001; Senese and Vasquez 2005, Chapter 7, this volume). The one exception to this is Major-Major dyads in the post-1945 era; here territorial disputes are unrelated to escalation to war, something that is consistent with seeing the Cold War as a "long peace" between the United States and U.S.S.R.

Fourth, Sample (2002) finds evidence consistent with Bremer (1992b, Chapter 2, this volume) that contiguous states are more apt to go to war than noncontiguous states. The relationship holds for all three types of dyads (MM, mm, and Mm) for the pre-1946 era. This suggests that the typical war is between neighbors, and these conflicts, as Vasquez and Valeriano (2010) show, are often over territory. Last, she looks at several capability variables. Some of these findings are contrary to what one would expect from existing theory. For example, power transitions have no impact on war between major states where theoretically it should occur.[2] It does, however, have an impact on minor-minor dyads in the post-1945 period. Contrary to realist theory, minor-minor dyads and Major-minor dyads are not affected by a rapid approach in power or by relative equality, but Major-Major dyads are as anticipated. Why this relationship is not more consistent is a puzzle worth pursuing in future research.

Sample's (2002) analysis elucidates several things. She shows that mutual military buildups are related to war. She also shows that nuclear weapons have a major impact on this relationship. From a scientific point of view, her analysis shows the importance of controlling for historical era and for the type of dyad. Major-Major, minor-minor, and Major-minor dyads behave differently, with the biggest difference being between the relatively equal and the unequal dyads. She also confirms that territorial disputes and contiguity are associated with escalation to war. Other studies (Gibler et al. 2005) show that arms races are particularly dangerous in the context of rivalry, as two states that have built up a history of militarized disputes with each other are five times more likely to end up in an interstate war if they engage in arms races.

Methodological Notes: Statistical Significance

Sample (2002) uses logistic regression or a **logit model** to test her hypotheses. In Tables 3 to 5, Sample reports the statistical significance level of each of the variables in column 5 (*Sig.*). Social scientists typically employ a 95 percent confidence interval for their hypothesis tests, which means that if we drew 100 random samples from a population, 95 of the samples would contain the population parameter being estimated. Any number or **p-value** below 0.05 indicates that the estimated (logit) coefficient is **statistically significant** (i.e., that the variable is significantly related to the chances for dyadic escalation to war). For example, in Table 3, Sample reports the results for Major-Major dyads (e.g., the United States and U.S.S.R.). It can be seen in the first three rows for Mutual Military Buildups (All Years, 1816–1944, 1945–1993) that the relationship is significant at the 0.003 level for 1816 to 1944, significant at the 0.002 level for 1945 to 1993, and not significant (0.867) for 1945 to 1993. The estimated β for the All Years sample is equal to 1.75, and the standard error (*SE*) around that estimate is equal to 0.58. The "Wald" column provides the calculated *t*-statistic, which divides the estimated β by the estimated standard error; for the All Years sample, this value is 9.07 (or 1.75/0.58). The *p*-value is reported in the next column (*Sig.*), and this tells us the probability that the estimated *t*-statistic is larger than this score (Prob [$t > 9.07$] = 0.003). For a 95 percent confidence level and a two-tailed hypothesis test, the (critical) *t*-statistic would be equal to 1.96 (in large samples). We can use a general rule of thumb that any *t*-statistic (β/SE) greater than 2 (and thus corresponding to a *p*-value less than 0.05) implies that the relationship between two variables is statistically significant.

The chances that we would observe a β value this large in this sample if the true β were zero (e.g., mutual military buildups had no effect on escalation to war) is only 3 chances out of a 1,000. Therefore, we reject the null hypothesis that the effect of mutual military buildups on war is equal to zero (or $\beta = 0$). Conversely, for 1945 to 1993, the estimated β is equal to 9.24, and the *SE* is quite large (55), producing a *t*-statistic of 0.028 (9.24/55) with a *p*-value of 0.867. This tells us that the likelihood that β equals zero is quite high, so we accept the null hypothesis that the effect of mutual military buildups on war in the Cold War era is zero. The last column in Tables 3 to 5 (Exp (*B*)) provides a measure of how strong the relationship is by showing us the predicted probability of war or the **substantive significance**. The probability of war for major states (MM) when they have mutual military buildups from 1816 to 1944 (row 2) is calculated as 100*(7.56 – 1), or 656 percent. This tells us that the probability of escalation to war is 656 percent higher when major states have a mutual military buildup than when they do not. By comparing the numbers in this column, one can get an idea of the relative potency or strength of each significant variable. Thus, the 7.56 value is much larger than the 0.156 value for Rapid Approach, which is statistically significant at the 0.063 level (see row 4).

One of the contributions of Sample's (2002) article is that she does not conduct just a bivariate analysis that looks only at mutual military buildups and war; she also introduces several control variables. A **control variable** is one that is posited to change the nature of a relationship in a certain condition. Typical control variables are historical era, such as pre- and post-1945, or the status of actors, such as Major-Major, minor-minor, and Major-minor. Sample employs both of these and shows that whether mutual military buildups affect the probability of a MID escalating to war varies by these conditions or control variables. The other variables Sample includes in the analysis could be seen as competing independent variables; these include the power variables of power transition, equality of power, and rapid approach. Defense burden, which is another way of conceptualizing militarization, is also an independent variable, as is territorial disputes. By including them in the logit model, Sample is seeing if inclusion of these other factors that influence the chances for war wipe out the relationship between mutual military buildups and war. In this way, she compares the relative potency of the various independent variables. As we discussed previously, a multivariate model captures the relationship between two variables (e.g., arms races and war) while also taking into account the correlations among the independent variables in the model. Sample treats contiguity as an independent variable and shows that it has an independent effect on the probability of war, since it is often significant in the presence of mutual military buildups.

There are two ways of controlling for factors other than the particular variable of interest (e.g., arms races). First, one can do this by drawing separate subsamples of each value of a control variable and seeing if variables have a different impact in each sample. This is what Sample (2002) does in the three separate analyses of the Major-Major, minor-minor, and Major-minor dyads in Tables 3 to 5. By comparing subsamples based on the power status of the actors, she is able to see if something like territorial disputes has a varying effect on war. For example, in the 1945 to 1993 sample (Table 3) territorial disputes do not have a significant impact on war, whereas territorial disputes increase the chances for war from 1945 to 1993 in minor-minor and Major-minor dyads (Tables 4 and 5). The second way to control for other variables is to simply include additional variables in the logit model. Sample does this when she first looks at the "All Years" sample and then estimates separate subsamples for 1816 to 1944 and 1945 to 1993.

Common control variables in the study of interstate war are joint democracy, relative capability, and economic development because it is assumed that joint democracies behave differently than non–joint democracies, that states that are relatively equal (or unequal) behave distinctly, or that states that are economically industrialized will behave differently than those that are not. However, Achen (1986) argues that there is a limit to how many control variables one can introduce before an analysis becomes statistically meaningless. He and James Lee Ray argue for a "rule of three"— that is, the inclusion of no more than three control variables (Ray 2003b; for a contrary view, see Oneal and Russett 2005).

Notes

1. Yule's Q is a measure of association that ranges from -1 to $+1$. A Yule's Q equal to 1 would signify a perfect positive relationship between two variables (e.g., all cases of serious disputes with arms races would escalate to war). If the Yule's Q measure is zero, this indicates the two variables are statistically independent.

2. The power transition theory (Organski and Kugler 1980) expects war to be most likely when two states are in parity or near the point of a power transition and when the state

whose power is increasing (the challenger) is dissatisfied with the status quo established by the global or regional hegemonic state.

Questions

1. How does Susan Sample resolve the debate between Wallace and Diehl? What does she find about Diehl's suggestion that mutual military buildups do not escalate to war?

2. What new data does Sample collect and how does this make new analyses of the relationship between arms races and war possible?

3. What are the major control variables that Sample finds of importance? How do they influence the chances for war?

4. In Tables 3 to 5, when is the relationship between defense burden and escalation to war statistically significant? When is the relationship not significant? What column provides this information?

Further Reading

Diehl, P. F. 1983. Arms races and escalation: A closer look. *Journal of Peace Research* 20 (3): 205–12.

Gibler, D. M., T. J. Rider, and M. L. Hutchison. 2005. Taking arms against a sea of troubles: Conventional arms races during periods of rivalry. *Journal of Peace Research* 42 (2): 131–47.

Sample, S. G. 1997. Arms races and dispute escalation: Resolving the debate. *Journal of Peace Research* 34 (1): 7–22.

_____. 2000. Military buildups: Arming and war. In *What do we know about war?* ed. J. A. Vasquez. Lanham, MD: Rowman & Littlefield.

Senese, P. D., and J. A. Vasquez. 2005. Assessing the steps to war. *British Journal of Political Science* 35:607–33.

Wallace, M. D. 1979. Arms races and escalation: Some new evidence. *Journal of Conflict Resolution* 23 (1): 3–16.

_____. 1982. Armaments and escalation: Two competing hypotheses. *International Studies Quarterly* 26 (1): 37–56.

Chapter 7

Assessing the Steps to War

Paul D. Senese and John A. Vasquez

What causes war? While there has been no shortage of theorizing and empirical research on this question,[1] its primacy remains at the forefront of debate in both academic and policy circles. The reasons for this attention are numerous, including, of course, the immense human carnage that has been suffered over time. Quantitative analysis approaches, for their part, have moved from an emphasis on the correlates of war[2] to a focus on what factors increase the probability that a militarized dispute or crisis might escalate to war.[3] This is a research tack that has often been successful in other fields, especially epidemiology. In international relations most of the new studies on war have examined only the impact of one or two core variables (and perhaps a few control variables) that might increase (or decrease) the probability of war. This study, by contrast, presents and tests an explanation of how several key variables might combine in an additive fashion to affect substantially the probability that a militarized dispute escalates to war.

The Steps to War Explanation

The original steps-to-war explanation of conflict maintains that territorial disputes generally have a higher probability of escalating to war than expected by chance and in comparison to other types of dispute, such as disputes over general foreign policy or the character of a state's regime.[4] It also maintains that if these disputes are handled in a power politics fashion, the probability of escalation to war will increase markedly. Realist diplomatic culture, which has dominated international relations in the West since 1648, provides a variety of foreign policy practices for decision makers. Key within this discourse is the idea that as security issues arise, states should increase their power by making alliances and/or building up their military forces. The steps-to-war model, though, maintains that such actions often increase the probability of war because they produce a security dilemma that leads each state to feel more threatened and more hostile towards the other side and to take actions against its opponent.[5] As a result, alliances lead to counter alliances and military buildups lead to arms races. Furthermore, adopting one or more of these practices can be expected to lead to a repetition of disputes and an increased level of escalation across disputes.[6]

This analysis will empirically examine the impact of alliance formation, recurrent disputes and arms races on the probability of war breaking out between states that have territorial disputes with one another. It is posited that states disputing territory have a higher probability of going to war with each other than states that have other kinds of disputes. It is further posited that if a state with a territorial dispute makes an alliance with an outside party that can be used to aid it in its territorial dispute, this will increase the probability of war. If, in addition, states become mired in the repeated use of military force

Source: Paul D. Senese and John A. Vasquez, "Assessing the Steps to War," *British Journal of Political Science* 35 (2005): 607–33. Copyright © 2005 Cambridge University Press. Reprinted with the permission of Cambridge University Press.

(or the threat to do so), then this can be seen as further increasing the probability of war. Lastly, if states engage in this syndrome of behaviour and also build up their military forces to the extent of being engaged in an arms race, then the probability of war goes up yet again. In this sense, having a territorial dispute can be considered a first step to war, and engaging in other power politics practices can be seen as additional steps to war. Not too much emphasis should be placed on the order of these steps, however. The key claim is that each practice increases threat perception and therefore the probability of war. As these threatening practices accumulate, they make it more likely that eventually a crisis or militarized dispute will occur that escalates to war. This is true for any issue, whether territorial or not.

Why should this be the case? The reason that decision makers adopt these practices is that certain kinds of leaders (and their followers) follow the precepts of realist folklore, which maintain that when highly salient security issues arise, they should be prepared to use force to defend themselves or threaten force if other forms of politics fail. Realpolitik tactics and strategies of resolve within the larger context of coercion are seen as the hallmarks of getting what you want. In the face of contested issues, where each side is reluctant to give in, this approach often leads states into a series of recurring militarized confrontations or disputes. While this is true of all security issues, it is especially the case with territorial disputes, either because of the intrinsic value placed on the stake and/or the domestic political constituencies that develop around the issue. If the threat or use of force makes states insecure, realist folklore posits that they should increase their power. The conventional realist practices by which this is done are either through making alliances with those who will support the position or by building up military forces. Realism, then, provides a way of identifying and even predicting what leaders will do in situations of high security threat.

The steps-to-war explanation deviates from realism in that it sees such practices as producing a security dilemma in which alliances lead to counter alliances, and military build-ups lead to arms races, and escalation to a hostile spiral.[7] The end result is that the adoption of realist prescriptions becomes a series of steps that increase the probability of war. The vicious cycle generated by the security dilemma is reinforced both by the interactions of states and by the indirect effect these interactions have on the domestic political environment of each nation-state. Threatening interactions tend to produce at least reciprocal responses, so a state can compensate for the advantages a particular action gave the first state. Thus, an alliance made by actor A will leave actor B vulnerable unless it can match whatever advantage the alliance provided to actor A. Of course actor B may, if it can, seek a greater advantage (by having more powerful allies) and therefore can be seen as escalating and not just reciprocating. Domestically, such interaction tends to reinforce the positions of hard liners that the opponent is indeed a threat and such a threat must be met by taking a hard line. Escalatory interactions tend to increase both the number and influence of hard liners and push decision makers towards more realpolitik strategies.

Our analysis will test certain key aspects of this broad explanation of the onset of war. In doing so, it will focus on a set of propositions that link territorial disputes and the use of power politics practices to an elevated likelihood of war. Thus, a territorial dispute between two states where one or both sides have an outside ally that will support them is more likely to go to war than a dispute where neither side has an outside alliance. Likewise, a territorial dispute where outside alliances are present and the two states have also had a series of recurring militarized confrontations is more likely to escalate to war than one where an outside alliance is present but the states have not had many previous disputes. Lastly, territorial disputes where both sides have outside alliances, a history of prior conflict and an ongoing arms race are more likely to go to war than those that have all these conditions but are not engaged in an arms race.

This overview of the explanation should make it clear that the dependent variable in our analysis is the probability of war arising out of a militarized dispute. The independent variables can be seen as a set of risk factors for war that operate in a dynamic and non-linear fashion.[8] In this study, we are interested in seeing whether the mere presence of varied combinations of these risk factors at the beginning of a dyadic dispute will increase state tendencies towards war. In this sense, our tests are static rather than dynamic, even though our explanation has clear dynamic aspects. The reason for this is that the data we have available permit only this sort of test. Nevertheless, this is a meaningful test in that the 'static' conditions are presumed to be an outcome of the steps-to-war dynamic, and if they do not produce the predicted increase in the probability of war, then the explanation is incorrect and could be considered falsified depending on how inconsistent it is with the evidence. Conversely, if the evidence is consistent with the predictions, all that can be inferred is that the static variables are associated with an increase in the probability of war and that, while presumed dynamic aspects might also be operating in the manner we outline, a different sort of test would be needed to demonstrate that.[9]

We thus focus our attention on the following four propositions derived from the steps-to-war explanation:

PROPOSITION 1. Dyadic territorial disputes have a higher probability of escalating to war than general foreign policy disputes or disputes over the nature of one side's regime.

PROPOSITION 2. Dyadic territorial disputes where both sides have outside politically relevant alliances have a higher probability of escalating to war than dyadic territorial disputes where neither side has alliances.

PROPOSITION 3a. Dyadic territorial disputes where both sides have outside politically relevant alliances and have had a series of recurring disputes have a greater probability of escalating to war than dyadic territorial disputes where both sides have such alliances but have not had a history of militarized disputes.

PROPOSITION 3b. The effect of prior disputes is curvilinear. Initially, more prior conflicts steadily increase the probability of war for current disputes, but eventually this relationship reverses as a very high number of prior conflicts will actually engender a ritualization of relations whereby pairs stop their current disputes short of war.

PROPOSITION 4. Dyadic territorial disputes, where both sides have outside politically relevant alliances, have had repeated militarized disputes and have an ongoing arms race, have a higher probability of going to war than those that have these three conditions but do not have an ongoing arms race.

It is important to note that while previous research has been conducted on some of the factors listed in these propositions, almost all of this work has looked at the factors individually or at most at how two factors might combine or interact. One of the main things we do know from this prior work is that territorial disputes are highly war prone compared to non-territorial disputes. This has been established by a number of studies employing different research designs and databases, so that the finding seems to be robust.[10] Taken together, these studies imply that there is something about territory that makes it particularly intractable; and this observation is not limited merely to interstate conflict, as research focusing on civil wars has reached a similar conclusion.[11]

What is it about territory, which is a divisible stake, that makes it so intractable? The literature on interstate war suggests two things: first, territorial disputes tend to recur;[12] and secondly, the territorial disputes that are most war prone, such as those involving ethnic disputes, generate domestic constituencies that pressure leaders to pursue hard-line policies.[13] Simmons, in her analysis of Latin American territorial disagreements, goes so far as to argue that leaders may be so hemmed in by domestic hardliners that they may turn over territorial disputes on which they want to compromise to an arbitration board in order to avoid taking political heat.[14] However, she finds that if the territorial dispute is highly salient and the arbitration board sides against the country, then that country will not abide by the agreement and/or its leader will be overthrown. As stated in Proposition 1, we expect territorial disputes to exhibit a higher probability of war compared to non-territorial engagements. Nevertheless, we also expect that the accumulation of varied power politics practices (as stated in Propositions 2–4) will tend to increase the chances of non-territorial disputes going to war, similar to their effects on territorial ones.

With regard to alliances, the empirical research reveals evidence consistent with the claim in Proposition 2 that there is some association between making an alliance and both the onset[15] and expansion[16] of war. This work on alliances, however, is very complicated, showing that some periods associate alliances with peace and others with war. Gibler tries to explain why alliances in some periods are associated with peace, but others are associated with war by developing a typology of alliances which distinguishes those that go to war from those that do not.[17]

In Propositions 2–4 we emphasize politically relevant alliances and not alliances in general because not every alliance is relevant to every dispute or war in which an ally might be involved. If a state has an alliance with another state that commits it to fight only in a circumscribed set of conditions, these conditions may not be relevant to a situation that arises in another region or issue area.[18] For example, the United States during the Cold War had an alliance with Taiwan, and this alliance is relevant to US relations with China and other Asian states, but having Taiwan as an alliance partner is not relevant to disputes the United States might have with countries in sub-Saharan Africa or Latin America. Thus one of the problems of simply counting formal alliances is that active countries, like Britain and the United States, would be classified as having an ally for many

of the years since 1816, even though many of these alliance commitments would not be relevant to the dispute at hand.

The research that we propose and carry out is designed, in part, to separate out the impacts of various types of alliance scenarios by focusing on their relevance to the present dispute. The causal logic of realism stipulates that states make alliances in order to increase their power and help balance the power of opponents, which under some versions of realism should lead to a reduction in the probability of war by increasing the risk that an attacker will lose the war. The expectations of the steps-to-war explanation differ on this point. It argues, instead, that when one side makes an outside alliance, this increases threat perception and, in the presence of a subsequent militarized interstate dispute, this increases the probability of war, because it gives the side with an outside ally a potential advantage and in doing so makes it less risk averse. While some targets will back down in the face of a militarized interstate dispute (MID), we postulate that territorial disputes are of such salience that states will tend not to give in, but, rather, either allow the current dispute to stalemate (only to be repeated later) or go to war.[19] If the dispute stalemates, it is anticipated that the side without outside allies would try to get allies and/or build up its military forces before the next MID. If both sides have an outside alliance, then this is seen as having a higher probability of war since both sides have now engaged in and reciprocated some highly threatening actions. In addition, they are further along a realist strategy of coercion and now have fewer options to take before they decide that going to war is the best way of handling the situation they face. For this reason we expect the alliance configuration where both sides have outside alliances to be the most war prone and have focused on this in our propositions. However, we also anticipate that a dyad having even one outside alliance will be more war prone than a dyad with none at all.

Propositions 3 and 4 also place importance on the repetition of militarized confrontations. The original construction of the steps-to-war explanation derives this idea from the twin notion that crises between relatively equal states tend to stalemate and repeat and repeated crises tend to escalate to war.[20] As they repeat, one or both sides can be expected to escalate their use of force in order to coerce or intimidate the other side into agreeing to its issue position. Such bargaining tends to give rise to hard liners in each side, which makes the issue more intractable, reduces the prospects of compromise and encourages more escalation. As both sides climb this ladder of escalation the external bargaining situation and internal political climate increase the chance that a crisis will emerge that ends in war.

Since the original publication of the steps-to-war explanation, work on interstate rivalry has come to the forefront. This literature assumes that a pair of states that has a history of repeated MIDs is engaged in a rivalry. An enduring rivalry is conventionally operationalized as six disputes within a twenty-year period and is normally seen as an attribute of a dyad and not a dispute.[21] If rivalry and the repetition of disputes increase the probability of war, it is important in looking at dyadic conflict to have an idea of whether the current dispute is the first, second or nth dispute between the same pair of states. We therefore look at how the number of prior dyadic disputes affects the current dispute (Proposition 3a).

The literature on rivalry, regardless of the particular definition of rivalry employed, basically assumes that once a threshold of repeated disputes or level of hostility is crossed, the probability of war increases.[22] A key conclusion of this literature is that most wars that have been fought since 1816 have rivals in them. Put another way, war tends to increase in probability as disputes between the same states recur. All of this suggests that rivalry and recurring disputes are a step to war, but little empirical work has been done examining the effect of prior conflict on the probability of war in the light of the other steps to war.

However, all enduring rivalries may not be the same. We believe that pairs that have a very high number of previous disputes come to learn how to manage their relations and even to a certain extent

ritualize their MIDs so that they are not as dangerous as those they had earlier. In effect, at a certain stage interactions become patterned and generate between the two contenders a set of expectations about how to interact that take on a ritualized character. Such a depiction is nicely in line with an earlier assertion by Mansbach and Vasquez that a ritualized stage of relations 'involves the continuation of competition and repetitive probing, but within mutually understood limits, and governed by tacit rules in accordance with standard operating procedures that actors develop to prevent surprise and uncertainties... Hostile moves are undertaken by adversaries, but such moves are expected and so can be parried.[23] The Cold War relations of the United States and the Soviet Union provide an illustration of this process. A ritualization process implies that there should be a diminution in the probability of war for dyads that have experienced a very large number of prior MIDs. Put another way, the relationship between recurring disputes and war may not be linear but curvilinear (Proposition 3b), something which the idea of crossing a 'rivalry' threshold would miss.

Finally, Proposition 4 adds the condition of arms racing. The steps-to-war explanation sees arms racing as a way of preparing for war and not avoiding it.[24] The rationale for this is that building up military forces produces a security dilemma, in which one side's build-up increases the insecurity of the state that is the target of the build-up. This target state reciprocates by building up its military forces as a way of maintaining and even increasing its own power. This in turn can lead to a full-blown arms race, which in turn increases threat perception and hostility on each side. A militarized dispute that emerges in this atmosphere is more apt to escalate to war than one that occurs in the absence of arms racing.

In addition to these propositions, we will also take note of evidence applying to slight variations on Propositions 2–4, namely looking at the effects of outside alliances, recurring disputes and arms races on the likelihood of war for non-territorial disputes. Our basic expectation here is that the use of power politics practices will also increase the chances of war among non-territorial disputes; namely, that non-territorial disputes characterized by two or three of these practices are more apt to go to war than those that have only one, just as we expect with territorial disputes. However, while the probabilities of war should increase with the use of power politics practices, regardless of dispute type, we expect the chances of war for territorial cases to be higher than for non-territorial ones.

Research Design

To test the claim that the above steps actually do increase the chances of war among states, we will first look at the probability of war occurring when states have territorial disputes as opposed to other types of disputes (Proposition 1). This test serves as a base model for purposes of comparing whether and how much the probability of war increases with the presence of additional risk factors. Then we see whether the addition of each of the variables specified in Propositions 2–4 increases the probability of war. We examine whether dyads that are contending over territorial disputes in the presence of both sides having politically relevant outside alliances have a higher probability of war than dyads (contending over territorial disputes) that do not have any alliances (Proposition 2). Next, we compare these cases with those that are also involved in repeated disputes (Proposition 3), and lastly we examine those dyads that have all four conditions present—territorial disputes, both sides having outside alliances, repeated disputes and an ongoing arms race (Proposition 4).

Whenever a verbal theory is tested it must be transformed into a testable model. In doing so it is found that a single verbal theory often embodies a family of theories in which the variables can be linked in various ways. This introduces a certain ambiguity in the technical sense of that term in that a series of models can be derived from the same set of variables, even before control variables are introduced. In this analysis we emphasize the additive effects of each of the variables, as opposed to an

alternative that would treat them as a set of statistical interaction terms. We do briefly examine the role of statistical interaction below, as it relates to the interactions of territory with our other independent variables. Our prior explorations of such an alternative approach, with reference to the interaction of territorial disputes and outside alliances, suggest that the increased complexity does not add much to a more straightforward additive mode.[25]

Some might think that a proper theory should only give rise to a single model, yet this rarely occurs, even in the physical sciences. The philosophy of science approaches we adopt are those of Popper and of Lakatos, which assume that a theory will produce not one model but a research programme that tests various iterations of a theory.[26] Popper's approach of conjectures and refutations, where testing leads to a refining of a theory and then further testing, provides the basic justification for the research programme we follow. Now that previous research conducted by a number of scholars shows an increase in the probability of war when one or two of the 'steps' are present in militarized disputes, the next logical step is to assess the effects when all are present. In the past, this has not been done, in part due to the absence of data. The model we test here, which combines all the steps, is the one most closely tied to the logic of the theory. We want to take this more deductive approach rather than just inductively testing the various permutations that could be derived from the steps-to-war explanation.[27] Likewise, we limit control variables (although the effects of some are explored), because our purpose is to test the performance of the model we have derived and not to maximize the amount of variance (or uncertainty) we can account for. If we find that the evidence is consistent with the model's expectations, then controls, as well as testing the steps explanation against competing theories, can be a focus of future research.

The sample for the analysis will be all dyadic militarized interstate disputes in the MID2.1 dataset from the Correlates of War project. This sample is derived by taking the 2,034 MIDs in the set for the entire period of 1816–1992 and breaking them down into each pair of states in the dispute. This increases the number of cases to 3,045 dyadic disputes (reduced to 2,576 because of missing data on type of dispute). Such dyadic analysis is justifiable since each state involved in a dispute must decide for itself whether to escalate its involvement to the war stage and therefore should be treated individually. The most pronounced effect of this procedure is to place more weight on multiparty disputes, particularly those related to the two world wars. This procedure, however, probably increases the validity of our analysis because otherwise the onset of each of these wars would carry the same weight as a simple tuna-boat chase.[28]

In addition to examining the full time-span, we control for historical era by breaking down the full sample into two periods—the classic international power politics era of 1816–1945 and the Cold War 1946–92 nuclear era. We do this since numerous scholars have argued that nuclear weapons, beginning as early as 1946, ushered in a new era that fundamentally changed the way diplomacy was conducted so as to lower the probability of war between nuclear states. Now that we have lived through over fifty years of the nuclear era we can see that nuclear weapons have in fact raised the provocation threshold for total war. This conservatism on the part of nuclear states may have also led them to restrain their minor allies. In addition, the East-West alliance system may, because of the danger of escalation to the nuclear level, have actually limited mutual superpower intervention into ongoing wars, such as in Vietnam and Afghanistan, rather than encouraged the expansion of war as alliances had in the past.[29] Given this line of reasoning, we think that the post-1945 Cold War era is fundamentally different in an important aspect of international relations from the more classic and longer 1816–1945 power politics era. In a sense, the power politics aspect (as opposed to the territorial aspect) of the steps-to-war explanation may find its more natural domain in the pre-nuclear era. Thus, examining just the full span may produce misleading results and mask interesting differences across the sub-periods. This is especially the case since many arms races in the post-1945 period involve either states with nuclear weapons or states allied to them. Breaking down the full time-span results in 1,362 dyadic dispute cases (reduced to 1,131 because of missing data) from 1816 to 1945, and 1,683 dyadic disputes (reduced to 1,445 because of missing data) for the 1946–92 period.

Our dependent variable will be whether the current MID under contention or any other between the same two parties escalates to war within five years. While most studies utilizing MID data examine whether the dispute under question goes to war or not, the steps-to-war model sees the outbreak of war as a process, with the probability of war increasing as disputes recur. Specifically, it is hypothesized that as crises recur or accumulate the dyad or system is more apt to be plunged into war.[30] Because this is the case, it could be misleading to count disputes that do not immediately go to war but do eventuate in war within a reasonable time frame as evidence against the hypothesis.[31] For this analysis, then, the dependent variable will be whether the current dispute between the parties, or any one within the next five years, escalates to war. While this conception of the dependent variable differs from the typical study using MID data, the use of a five-year window (or sometimes longer) has a long history in the field.[32] The war data of the Correlates of War project, as opposed to the war codes in the MID data, are used in the analysis. The main difference between these two options is that the MID set has slightly more war cases.

The four major independent variables in our tests will be the type of dispute, the type of politically relevant alliance, the number of disputes that have occurred up to and including the current dispute, and whether there is an ongoing arms race. For the first of these, we will employ the revision type indicator in the MID set. This variable classifies actors involved in militarized disputes in terms of revisionist and non-revisionist states. The revision the former are trying to bring about by their resort to force is then classified in terms of whether it is over territory (territorial MID), a general foreign policy question (policy MID), the regime of its opponent (regime MID), or some 'other' miscellaneous question (other MID).[33]

The second independent variable we will examine is whether the disputants have politically relevant outside alliances. This new measure eliminates outside alliances of the disputants if they are not deemed relevant to the opposing state involved in the MID. Simply put, an alliance with a major state is always relevant because it is assumed that a major state is able to project its capability beyond its own region. An alliance with a minor state, however, is seen as only relevant if the alliance partner is in the same region as the MID target, because it is assumed that it cannot easily project its capability beyond that region even when otherwise inclined to do so.

A hypothetical example may make this rule clearer: on the one hand, if the United States and Brazil are in a dispute and the United States has an alliance with Argentina, then that alliance is relevant. On the other hand, if Brazil has an alliance with Portugal, this is not relevant, but if it had an alliance with the Soviet Union, the latter would be relevant because the Soviet Union is a major state. In a dyadic dispute, first, side B is treated as the target and the relevant alliances for it are computed, and then side A is treated as the target and its relevant alliances are computed. Regions are determined by the state membership list of the Correlates of War project with a couple of emendations to include some states in more than one region.[34] The formal alliance data of the Correlates of War project are used to generate the politically relevant alliance measures (No Alliance, only Allied to Each other, one Side Has outside Alliance, Both Sides Have outside Alliances, Allied to Each other and outside Alliances).[35]

Our third independent variable captures the extent to which a pair of states has been engaged in prior conflicts. We hypothesize (in Proposition 3a) that the more disputes a dyad has had before its current one, the greater the likelihood of war,

ceteris paribus. To measure this we determine how many disputes have occurred previously between the same pair of states. We call this variable 'Number of Prior MIDs' and use it in our analyses across all three time periods. This approach is quite straightforward for the full and pre-1946 spans. For the post-1945 period, however, it assumes that MIDs that occurred prior to 1946 will affect relations after 1945. This assumption has considerable face validity—there is substantial anecdotal evidence suggesting that states have long memories. For instance, most scholars believe that events like the two world wars have had profound effects on the behaviour of states since 1945.[36] Similarly, the memory of allied intervention in the Soviet Union in 1918 helped shape Soviet attitudes towards the West after the Second World War.[37]

The idea that repeated disputes encourage the emergence of a dispute that will escalate to war is at the heart of the idea of rivalry. In that sense our measure of prior disputes can be seen as an indicator of the degree of rivalry, although we are not directly measuring rivalry in its conventional form here. For example, Diehl and Goertz treat rivalry as a categorical variable by using the cut-off points of roughly 1–2 for isolated conflict, 3–5 for proto-rivalry, and 6+ for enduring rivalry, depending on the time frame in which these disputes occur.[38] Instead, we have chosen to treat repeated disputes (and indirectly rivalry) as an integer variable.

Treating it as an integer rather than a categorical variable assumes that crossing a particular threshold (especially six disputes and above) is not crucial and does not make for a marked change in a relationship at that specific number of disputes, but that rivalry emerges in a continuous pattern across disputes as hostility increases from one engagement to the next. An integer variable (and the concept of repeated disputes) sees each dispute as increasing the probability of war even after a particular threshold has been passed. For example, the eighth dyadic dispute is seen as more likely to go to war than the third, but less likely to go to war than the seventeenth.[39] Nevertheless, to assess the importance of various thresholds we will isolate three in our tests of Proposition 3a—the probability of war when two states are engaged in their first, sixth (a threshold relevant to Diehl and Goertz's measure of enduring rivalry) and fifteenth dispute (the mean number of disputes among enduring rivals for 1816–1992). This last scenario allows us to pinpoint the probability of war for the 'average enduring rivalry'.

Our proposition that as disputes increase, the probability of war also increases, has a *ceteris paribus* caveat. We think that this relationship is linear for most dyads, but we also expect that pairs having an extremely large number of recurrent disputes at a certain point become engaged in a kind of ritualized behaviour (Proposition 3b). This pattern makes their militarized confrontations less intense in terms of threat perception. They have somehow learned to manage their militarized confrontations in a way that takes on game-like ritualized characteristics, so these disputes are not at as great a risk of going to war. Their relationship is one of threatening and maybe using limited force, but one where taking the ultimate step is not anticipated. This implies that states which can get through a substantial number of MIDs are at less risk than those which just cross the six-MID threshold. Anecdotal evidence that something like this might be present in history can be seen by looking at East-West relations in the Cold War. The United States, Britain and France have a very large number of MIDs with the Soviet Union, but none escalate to war. The same holds for China and the United States after the Korean War.

To test this notion of ritualization, we introduce a quadratic specification to see if the relationship between the number of prior disputes and the probability of war is curvilinear and, more specifically, whether it approximates an inverted U shape. We do this by squaring the Number of Prior MIDs and introducing this new variable (Number of Prior MIDs Squared) into the model. We also graph the relationship to see if the kind of ritualization we hypothesize takes place. This examination of the quadratic specification is then compared to one that simply assesses the impact of Number of Prior MIDs

on its own. Such a progression allows us to test Proposition 3 to see if the relationship is better depicted as linear or curvilinear.

Our fourth, and final, independent variable is the presence of an arms race. Here, we use new data collected by Susan Sample for both major and minor states.[40] These data record arms races for each dyad in a MID based on the measure used by Horn,[41] which essentially examines the increase in military expenditure of two states over time. We employ Sample's categorical data to determine whether there is an ongoing arms race for each dyadic dispute.

One of the advantages of utilizing dyadic disputes as the unit of analysis, as opposed to comparing the long-term relations of a pair of states (the dyad) or rivals with each other,[42] is that we can pinpoint when the independent variables occur in relation to the dependent variable. This permits us to have a clear idea of the timing of our variables to make sure that each of the independent variables occurs before the dependent variable.[43] Thus, we know from the MID coding that a territorial revision claim has preceded the threat or use of force. We also have measured our alliance variables so that the formal alliance must be operating before the first day of the MID. Measuring the number of previous disputes permits us to know when a case crosses what might be considered various thresholds of rivalry. Lastly, an arms race must be ongoing in the year the MID occurs.

With these measures in hand, we utilize logistic regression to conduct two key tests of our four propositions. The first is to see if each of our four variables—territory, politically relevant alliances, number of previous disputes and arms races—has a positive and significant impact on the probability of a dispute escalating to war within five years. By using multivariate logistic regression, we have chosen to conduct a very rigorous test of the steps-to-war model; for each step to be seen as a significant factor, it must have a sufficient enough impact so that controlling for the other variables in the explanation does not wipe out the relationship. An easier and alternative test would be to treat the second, third and fourth independent variables (i.e., outside alliances, repeated disputes and arms races) as intervening variables. We have not done that here, since we want to have some sense of the relative potency of each variable, and controlling for each gives us some idea of that.

In presenting the findings for this first test, we rely on odds ratios instead of the parameter estimates from which they are derived; odds ratios are predominantly viewed as the easiest and most useful way of interpreting logit models. An odds ratio greater than one indicates an increased chance of war occurring, and an odds ratio less than one indicates a decreased chance of war occurring. The interpretation of these odds ratios is directly pegged to the presence of the particular risk factor associated with each independent variable.[44]

The second test focuses on the extent to which each of the steps actually affects the substantive probability of war. We are particularly interested in seeing if the various combinations of the variables specified in the four propositions produce a progressive (and meaningful) increase in the likelihood of war. To determine the relative probability of war, predicted probabilities are calculated using *CLARIFY* software.[45]

Finally, we do not test for selection effects in this analysis, primarily because we have done so in a previous study, focusing closely on the effects of territory.[46] In this prior work, we find that states that have a territorial claim have an increased likelihood of having a MID, but that controlling for this does not eliminate the relationship between having a territorial MID and having an increased probability of going to war. These findings imply that the greatest risk for war occurs once states are in a militarized dispute and a territorial claim is handled by the threat or use of force; the likelihood of war is not pre-determined by a mere territorial disagreement. Further, it was found that the estimate for error correlation across the two stages is not statistically significant. Other recent studies have also found no evidence of any sampling bias that would undermine

the use of the kind of research design and data we employ here.[47] In this study, we look solely at the effects of our risk factors on the characteristics of disputes that are already under way.

The Findings

The Full Period, 1816–1992

Table 1 reports logistic regression results for three models over the full 1816 to 1992 time period. We start by looking solely at the effect of revision type (i.e., territory, regime and other, compared to the reference category of policy) on the chances that disputes will eventuate in war (Model I). In Model II and Model III three variables are added: politically relevant alliances, prior disputes and arms races. These models allow us to assess the effects of each of our risk factors, including the precise nature of the relationship between recurring disputes and escalation to war as either linear (Number of Prior MIDs alone) or curvilinear (adding Number of Prior MIDs Squared).

It can be seen in Table 1 that territorial disputes have a significant impact. Their odds of escalating to war are at least 3.2 times higher than for policy disputes, depending on which other variables are included in the model, providing evidence consistent with Proposition 1. In addition, a separate model (not shown) estimated with regime disputes as the reference category found the odds of territorial disputes eventuating in war to be 5.4 times higher than for regime disputes. Models II and III do not support the expectations for outside alliances as spelled out in Proposition 2. This is due primarily to including the Arms Race variable (which results in a meaningful reduction of cases because of missing data); if that variable is dropped (not shown) then One or Both Sides Having an Outside Alliance significantly increases the likelihood of escalation to war. The test results for the two models provide evidence much more strongly in line with Propositions 3 and 4. Arms races have a significant positive impact on the probability of war; in fact, the odds for disputing states that are in an arms race to have a war are 5.2 times

Table 1 Odds Ratios for Escalation of the Current or Any MID within Five Years to War, 1816–1992

Variables in Model	Model I	Model II	Model III
Territorial MID†	4.22** (0.45)	3.29** (0.44)	3.24** (0.44)
Regime MID†	0.78 (0.18)	0.96 (0.27)	0.91 (0.26)
Other MID†	3.15** (1.01)	4.08** (1.58)	4.33** (1.68)
Only Allied to Each Other‡	—	Perfect Predictor§	Perfect Predictor§
One Side Has Outside Alliance‡	—	1.18 (0.22)	1.19 (0.22)
Both Sides Have Outside Alliances‡	—	1.14 (0.24)	1.17 (0.24)
Allied to Each Other & Outside Alliance‡	—	0.97 (0.24)	0.98 (0.24)
Number of Prior MIDs	—	1.02* (0.01)	1.09** (0.02)
Number of Prior MIDs Squared	—		0.998** (0.00)
Arms Race	—	5.37** (1.20)	5.24** (1.18)
Likelihood Ratio χ^2 (df = 3, 8, 9)	223.2**	164.0**	178.3**
Pseudo R^2	0.083	0.092	0.100
Number of cases	2,576	1,940	1,940

Note: Estimations were performed in Stata 8 (logistic). Main entries are odds ratio estimates, with standard errors in parentheses.

† As compared to the reference category of Policy MID.

‡ As compared to the reference category of No Alliances.

§ Only allied to each other is a perfect predictor of no war.

*p < 0.05; **p < 0.01.

higher than for disputants not engaged in an arms race. Finally, the significant estimates for the Number of Prior MIDs and Number of Prior MIDs Squared variables in Model III indicate the presence of a curvilinear relationship (in the form of an inverted U curve) between the number of previous disputes and the likelihood of war. This finding supports our notion (Proposition 3b) that as two states have a very large number of MIDs the probability of war actually begins to decrease.

Taken together, these results fail to falsify Propositions 1, 3 and 4. Thus, the explanation as a whole, while not perfect, is given some support by

the tests in Table 1. Next, we consider the performance of the steps-to-war model within the 1816–1945 and 1946–92 sub-periods to see if the explanation fits one historical era better than the other. We expect that this might be the case due to the advent of nuclear weapons and since an earlier study of just the type of dispute and alliance variables[48] showed that the full period masked important differences regarding the effect of alliances.[49]

The 1816–1945 Period

Table 2 reports the logistic regression results for 1816–1945. The test results for Model I show, as in the full period, that territorial disputes are significantly more likely to escalate to war than the modal type of dispute (policy MIDs). Specifically, the odds of war escalation are 3.25 times higher for territorial disputes than for policy disputes and 7.7 times higher (not shown) than for regime disputes. The magnitudes of these differences are reduced somewhat for the full steps-to-war specifications shown in Models II and III, but, nonetheless, remain highly significant.

In contrast to the findings for the full period, we see several statistically significant estimates for the impact of politically relevant alliances on the odds of escalation to war (Models II and III). Of primary theoretical interest is the finding that the odds of war for a dyadic dispute where both sides have an outside alliance are more than four times greater than for a dyadic dispute where there are no alliances. This finding is clearly supportive of Proposition 2. Also of interest is the finding that disputing states that are allied only to each other and have no simultaneous alliance with an outside party have no instances of war escalation for the current MID or any MID within five years. States that are 'Only Allied to Each Other' is a perfect prediction of peace. This provides evidence contrary to the 'friends as foes' hypothesis,[50] which maintains that states that are allied to each other are more likely to go to war with each other than states that are not allied. Our analysis demonstrates that 'friends as foes' holds only when the two states that are allied to each other also have an outside alliance with a third party. This is clearly shown in Model II as the odds of disputes between allies that also have outside alliances going to war are 4.3 times higher than for disputes among states with no allies at all. This also supports our general theoretical expectation in that the presence of outside alliances increases the chances of war, presumably by increasing threat perception and hostility. Making a separate alliance can be seen as a way of hedging one's bet, presumably because there is some underlying tension. When states in a dispute do not have any outside politically relevant allies, their alliance definitely has a pacifying effect.

Models II and III also allow us to assess if recurrent conflict has an effect on dispute escalation to war and, if so, the precise nature of that effect. Here we find clear support for the more linear expectation specified in Proposition 3a, compared to the curvilinear notion of Proposition 3b. So, for the 1816–1945 period, repeated disputes (as measured by Number of Prior MIDs alone in Model II) significantly increase the likelihood of war in a consistent manner, with no hint of significant ritualization. Besides clarifying the influence of recurring disputes, Models II and III provide evidence consistent with Proposition 4—the odds of war for disputants in an arms race are almost six times higher than the odds for those not engaged in such an arms build-up. Taken together then, all of the risk factors spelled out in our propositions (territorial disputes, both sides have outside alliances, repeated disputes and arms races) have the impact expected by the steps-to-war explanation, indicating that the odds of dispute escalation to war are highest during the 1816–1945 period when states have all four steps present.

We also tested the four propositions using a series of interaction terms (results not shown), beginning with a replication of our earlier study that looked at the interactions of Territory with One or Both Sides Having an Outside Alliance.[51] The replication produced the same results—namely, the interaction of Territory with One Outside Alliance is greater than 1 and significant, while Territory with Both Sides Having Outside Alliances is insignificant. When we added the Arms Race variable (which resulted in a reduction of cases from 1,115 to 736), the relationship between the two interaction terms and the dependent variable flipped; i.e., Territory and One Outside Alliance became insignificant and Territory and Both with an Outside Alliance became significant and less than 1. We also ran separate models including the interactions of Territory with the Number of Prior MIDs and with Arms Races.[52] The interaction of Territory and Prior MIDs is insignificant when looking at the 1,115 sample (i.e., without controlling for Arms Races), but becomes significant

Table 2 Odds Ratios for Escalation of the Current or Any MID within Five Years to War, 1816–1945

Variables in Model	Model I	Model II	Model III
Territorial MID†	3.25** (0.44)	2.14** (0.41)	2.10** (0.41)
Regime MID†	0.42* (0.16)	0.70 (0.39)	0.62 (0.36)
Other MID†	2.28* (0.84)	3.77** (1.72)	3.70** (1.69)
Only Allied to Each Other‡	—	Perfect Predictor§	Perfect Predictor§
One Side Has Outside Alliance‡	—	1.37 (0.32)	1.36 (0.32)
Both Sides Have Outside Alliances‡	—	4.33** (1.15)	4.35** (1.16)
Allied to Each Other & Outside Alliance‡	—	4.26** (1.47)	4.35** (1.51)
Number of Prior MIDs	—	1.05** (0.02)	0.99 (0.05)
Number of Prior MIDs Squared	—	—	1.00 (0.00)
Arms Race	—	5.76** (1.86)	5.81** (1.88)
Likelihood Ratio χ^2 (df = 3, 8, 9)	99.9**	127.4**	129.1**
Pseudo R^2	0.068	0.142	0.144
Number of cases	1,131	736	736

Note: Estimations were performed in Stata 8 (logistic). Main entries are odds ratio estimates, with standard errors in parentheses.

† As compared to the reference category of Policy MID.

‡ As compared to the reference category of No Alliances.

§ Only allied to each other is a perfect predictor of no war.

*$p < 0.05$; **$p < 0.01$.

and increases the likelihood of war when Arms Races are added to the model (and using the resultant restricted sample). These unstable results for the interaction terms lead us to conclude that, on the whole, the relationships between our risk factors and the likelihood of war are best modelled in an additive rather than multiplicative fashion. The additive model is also considerably less complex and hence more parsimonious.[53]

Table 3 presents predicted probabilities for the pre-1946 period as they relate to the four propositions under study. The estimates in Table 3 can be thought of as the probability of war that is predicted by the logistic regression model in the presence of certain risk factors, such as territorial disputes between states with outside alliances, a history of MIDs and arms races. Table 3 reports, first, that when policy or regime disputes are under contention and none of the four steps are present (i.e., they do not have territorial disputes nor alliances, recurring disputes or an ongoing arms race), the probability of war is 0.108 and 0.087,

Table 3   Probabilities for Escalation of the Current or Any MID Within Five Years to War, 1816–1945

Conditions	Territorial MID	Policy MID	Regime MID
No alliances	0.204	0.108	0.087
	(0.151–0.265)	(0.074–0.147)	(0.031–0.172)
Both Sides with Outside Allies	0.522	0.340	0.279
	(0.420–0.625)	(0.265–0.422)	(0.119–0.469)
Both Sides with Outside Allies & Sixth MID	0.580	0.395	0.326
	(0.486–0.674)	(0.320–0.472)	(0.147–0.525)
Both Sides with Outside Allies & Fifteenth MID	0.679	0.500	0.421
	(0.578–0.768)	(0.403–0.595)	(0.218–0.638)
Both Sides with Outside Allies, Fifteenth MID & Arms Race	0.920	0.846	0.787
	(0.864–0.961)	(0.754–0.916)	(0.597–0.921)

Note: Main entries are predicted probabilities, with 90 per cent confidence intervals in parentheses (both derived from Model II in Table 2). The base probability of war is 0.298.

respectively. These can be taken as benchmarks for purposes of comparison. In order for the evidence in Table 3 to be consistent with Propositions 1–4, each additional risk factor must result in increasingly higher probabilities of war; i.e., the probability of war for Proposition 2 should be higher than it is for Proposition 1, the probability of war for Proposition 3 should be higher than it is for Proposition 2, and the probability of war for Proposition 4 should be the highest of all.

Each of these expectations is borne out. Table 3 shows that the probability of territorial disputes going to war is 0.204. In order for Proposition 1 to pass testing, this probability must be higher than those for policy and regime disputes, which it is. The probabilities of war for 'other' disputes (not shown) mirror those for territorial MIDs. This is not an accident as each of these wars has been found to have important territorial elements.[54] To assure that these cases would not alter our findings, we conducted sensitivity analyses grouping policy, regime and 'other' disputes into a single category, and found

that the probability of war for these combined non-territorial cases is only 0.12, still well below that for territorial disputes.

Adding a second step (both states have politically relevant outside allies before the dispute arose), makes the probability of a dispute escalating to war rise to 0.522. This large jump (from 0.204) clearly supports Proposition 2. If we add a third step, a history of prior militarized disputes, then the chances of war increase still further. For instance, the likelihood of war for territorial disputes between states that both have outside alliances and are in their sixth dispute is 0.580.[55] If we isolate instead the fifteenth dispute, which is the average number of MIDs among those pairs that have at least six disputes, then the probability of war goes up even higher to 0.679. We take these as sufficient jumps to warrant support for Proposition 3,[56] suggesting that disputes between states that have a long history of repeated confrontations, in conjunction with both sides having outside allies, are more war prone than just having both sides with outside alliances.

Our test of Proposition 4 looks at the effect of all four factors being present. As predicted by the steps-to-war explanation, this condition is indeed the most war prone. It has the highest probability of going to war (0.920) in the table and in all the analyses we conducted for this study, clearly illustrating the extreme riskiness of bringing all four steps to war together.

Table 3 also reports the effects of taking these steps with policy and regime disputes. While it is clear that policy and regime disputes always have a lower probability of going to war than territorial disputes, it can be seen that handling them in a power politics fashion has the same progressive effect as handling territorial disputes in this manner. Thus, policy and regime disputes are more likely to go to war as dyads make outside alliances, have repeated confrontations and engage in arms races, with the highest probabilities being reached when all four steps have been taken (0.846 for policy and 0.787 for regime).

On the basis of these probability estimates for the 1816–1945 period, a number of conclusions can be stated. First, territorial MIDs are more war prone than policy or regime disputes. Secondly, as more of the hypothesized risk factors ('steps') are present, the probability of war goes up. Thus, just having outside allies is not as dangerous as having them when also involved in recurring disputes, and having allies while involved in recurring disputes is most dangerous if the dyad is also involved in an ongoing arms race. Thirdly, when both sides have an outside politically relevant alliance, dyadic disputes are always more war prone than disputes with no alliances. When both parties are allied only to each other, this is always associated with the absence of war. Fourthly, any issue (territorial or not), if handled in a power politics fashion, will become substantially more war prone. Each of these conclusions is highly consistent with the steps-to-war explanation.

The results in Tables 2 and 3 take us a long way in identifying key risk factors associated with pairs of states having their disputes escalate to war. These tables present important evidence that nation-states in dyadic territorial disputes, where both have politically relevant alliances with outside parties, have engaged in a history of repeated confrontations and have an ongoing arms race are increasingly likely to go to war, compared to when any of these steps are absent. This same overall pattern is present when the practices of power politics are employed with policy and regime disputes. Even though territorial disputes are always more war prone when each additional step is present, policy and regime disputes, for their part, also become more war prone as states have politically relevant alliances, have been involved in prior MIDs and/or have ongoing arms races.

The 1946–92 Period

The steps-to-war model fits the 1816–1945 period with all of its expectations being fulfilled. The analysis of the Cold War 1946–92 period, by contrast, reveals some disparate patterns, although important parts of the explanation are sustained. The results presented in Table 4 show this later period differing from the earlier one in two main respects. First, the estimated effects for some alliance configurations are reversed. Both sides having outside alliances, which was a distinct step to war for the early time span, is now a step in the opposite direction. The same is true for dyads that are allied to each other and also have an outside alliance—the odds ratio shifts to below one, although this estimate is not statistically significant. Dyads with one outside alliance remain positively related to war, but not significantly so for the models in Table 4.[57] On the whole, then, outside alliances are not having the same impact in the 1946–92 period.

The second major difference from 1816–1945 is that the effect of arms races is statistically insignificant in the Cold War 1946–92 period (Models II and III). In part, this may be due to the low number of cases (46) with arms races during these years. While these two differences are contrary to what is expected by the steps-to-war explanation, they are consistent with what we know about the Cold War period; namely, that the US-Soviet alliance structure

Table 4 Odds Ratios for Escalation of the Current or Any MID Within Five Years to War, 1946–92

Variables in Model	Model I	Model II	Model III
Territorial MID†	10.45** (2.51)	8.65** (2.27)	8.26** (2.18)
Regime MID†	3.28** (1.10)	3.57** (1.41)	3.36** (1.33)
Other MID†	2.18 (2.30)	Perfect Predictor§	Perfect Predictor§
Only Allied to Each Other	—	Perfect Predictor§	Perfect Predictor§
One Side Has Outside Alliance‡	—	1.47 (0.57)	1.33 (0.52)
Both Sides Have Outside Alliances‡	—	0.40* (0.18)	0.39* (0.18)
Allied to Each Other & Outside Alliance‡	—	0.55 (0.28)	0.51 (0.26)
Number of Prior MIDs	—	1.04** (0.01)	1.12** (0.03)
Number of Prior MIDs^2	—	—	0.998* (0.00)
Arms Race	—	1.27 (0.67)	1.20 (0.63)
Likelihood Ratio χ^2 (df = 3, 7, 8)	137.6**	147.7**	154.7**
Pseudo R^2	0.136	0.193	0.202
Number of cases	1,445	1,193	1,193

Note: Estimations were performed in Stata 8 (logistic). Main entries are odds ratio estimates, with standard errors in parentheses.

† As compared to the reference category of Policy MID.

‡ As compared to the reference category of No Alliances.

§ Only Allied to Each Other and Other MID are perfect predictors of no war.

*p < 0.05; **p < 0.01.

and nuclear arms competition did not result in a war between the major states in the system.[58]

The other results in Table 4 are similar to the earlier period. First, states allied only to each other never go to war. Secondly, territorial disputes are significantly likely to escalate to war. This effect is even more pronounced for the comparison between territorial and policy MIDs during this later period, with the odds of war for territorial cases at least eight times higher (compared to a threefold difference in the earlier period). The comparison of territorial

and regime MIDs, though, shows no increase—in fact there is a decline—but the odds of territorial disputes eventuating in war are still greater (at least by 2.5 times) than for regime disputes (not shown). While still a significant difference ($p < 0.01$), it is not nearly as large as the 7.7 times disparity discussed earlier for the pre–Cold War years. Although territory is clearly the most war prone type of dispute in both eras, regime and policy disputes are ranked differently across the periods, with regime cases exhibiting the lowest propensity for war prior to

1946 and policy engagements assuming that position after the Second World War. Thirdly, dyads tend to be more likely to have their disputes go to war within five years if they are involved in repeated encounters (Model II). Thus, territory and recurring disputes are more consistently potent (and, certainly, less time-bound) risk factors than alliances and arms races.

The exact nature of the recurrent conflict influence during the period after the Second World War, however, warrants a closer look. Specifically, the results for Model III in Table 4 suggest the presence of an inverted U-shaped relationship between repeated disputes and war. Figure 1 is a visual representation of the marginal impact that recurring disputes have on the chances of war. The likelihood of war within five years is shown over the full zero to fifty-five range on the Number of Prior MIDs measure.[59] As Figure 1 reveals, the twenty-eighth dispute between a pair is the most likely to eventuate in war.[60] Increasing numbers of prior disputes between zero and twenty-seven positively affect the probability of war, while previous engagements numbering beyond twenty-seven are negatively associated with

war.[61] Interstate wars occur less frequently when the number of prior disputes is both low and very high, with a higher level of war proneness prevalent when the number of previous disputes is intermediate (neither very high nor low). This middle range where disputants have already gone through a significant number of engagements, but have not yet learned to ritualize their entanglements in a way that limits escalation to war, is clearly the most dangerous during the Cold War period.

Such a finding supports Proposition 3b, that dyads with a very large number of disputes have a tendency to ritualize and manage their disputes after a period of time, so that the probability of any one of them escalating to war goes down. This result suggests an important nuance to the prevailing literature on rivalry;[62] namely, that while more previous disputes generally lead to higher chances of war, there appears to be a point above which subsequent disputes are actually pegged to a lower, not higher, probability of war. This curvilinear effect for the 1946–92 era, of course, differs from the more linear impact during the 1816–1945 span, implying that ritualization may be a Cold War phenomenon associated with nuclear

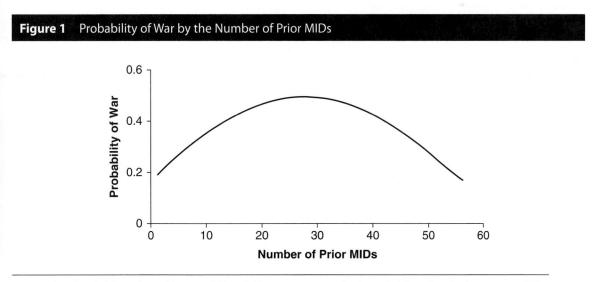

Figure 1   Probability of War by the Number of Prior MIDs

Note: Predicted probabilities derived from Model III in Table 4. Maxima point for the probability of war (0.5) is at 27 prior MIDs.

weapons. The danger of nuclear war may motivate actors to manage their disputes more carefully, but in doing so may also inadvertently increase the frequency of repeated disputes.[63]

Given these findings for the two sub-periods, what can be concluded about the steps-to-war explanation? First, the steps-to-war model fits the classic international power politics 1816–1945 era quite well. This period can be seen as its natural domain. Secondly, the model fits the shorter Cold War 1946–92 period less well, but even here some of its core propositions receive substantial support. Thirdly, the insignificance of arms races in the Cold War period may have something to do with attempts to manage arms races among nuclear states and their allies, which can reasonably be assumed to reduce the probability of war between major states during the era. If this is true, it may be the case that future non-nuclear arms races in the absence of the kinds of restraints constructed by the United States and Soviet Union may prove once again to be related to war. In this sense, the results for the full 1816–1992 period, which show that arms races are positively related to war, may be more accurate than the analyses of the breakdown of the two periods. This is especially the case since there are so few arms races in the second time period.

Fourthly, the Cold War alliance structure was successful in stripping alliances of their belligerent effects—although it did not make them universally a mechanism that prevented war (since only the Both Sides with Outside Alliances variable is statistically significant in Table 4). What it is about this alliance structure that brings about this effect deserves further exploration—two obvious candidates are nuclear weapons and bipolarity. Whether these Cold War effects will continue or whether arms races and alliances will revert to their earlier bellicose impacts only the future will tell. However, of the two variables—bipolar alliance structure and nuclear weapons—the former is already gone.

Further insights about the chances of war in the 1946–92 period can be gained by examining the predicted probabilities reported in Table 5. This table reports the highest probability for the various combinations. Before discussing these probabilities, though, an important caveat needs to be mentioned: it must be remembered that while the estimates for the dispute type and Prior MIDs variables are statistically significant, those for the One Side Has Outside Alliances and Arms Race indicators are not (Table 4, Model III). Nevertheless, we think looking at the probabilities for the various combinations of the independent variables can give us some clues about the risks they pose for dyads going to war and thereby provide a way of further evaluating the adequacy of the steps-to-war explanation for the Cold War era.

What is most noticeable about Table 5 compared to Table 3 is that the probability of war for the more recent period (ranging from 0.022 to 0.465) is considerably lower than it is for the 1816–1945 span (ranging from 0.087 to 0.920). This general result supports the notion that the Cold War was indeed a 'long peace', albeit one between major states and not necessarily including relations between major and minor states, which had several wars.[64] It is also clear that territorial disputes are the most war prone, as in the earlier period, with the war probability estimates for both policy (0.022) and regime (0.071) disputes falling comfortably below the lower bound of the 90 per cent confidence interval (0.085 to 0.244) for territorial disputes.

The major anomaly to note about the post-1945 period is that both sides having an outside ally does not produce the highest probability of a dispute going to war and hence does not even appear in Table 5. In fact, with one minor exception, this condition produces the lowest probabilities of going to war. This finding for the 1946–92 span is contrary to Proposition 2. An examination of the specific cases that have these conditions and do not go to war reveals precisely those that one would expect—members of the East and West blocs (United States–Soviet Union, United States–Czechoslovakia, United States–German Democratic Republic, United States–North Korea after 1953, Iran–Soviet Union, Turkey–Soviet Union, etc.). This implies that the East-West

Table 5   Probabilities for Escalation of the Current or Any MID within Five Years to War, 1946–92

Conditions	Territorial MID	Policy MID	Regime MID
No alliances	0.154	0.022	0.071
	(0.085–0.244)	(0.010–0.041)	(0.032–0.131)
One Side with Outside Ally	0.189	0.028	0.089
	(0.139–0.249)	(0.018–0.042)	(0.050–0.143)
One Side with Outside Ally, & Sixth MID	0.274	0.044	0.136
	(0.220–0.330)	(0.030–0.064)	(0.082–0.204)
One Side with Outside Ally, & Fifteenth MID	0.414	0.081	0.228
	(0.335–0.493)	(0.051–0.119)	(0.140–0.336)
One Side with Outside Ally, Fifteenth MID & Arms Race	0.465	0.105	0.273
	(0.263–0.655)	(0.037–0.205)	(0.114–0.465)

Note: Main entries are predicted probabilities, with 90 per cent confidence intervals in parentheses (both derived from Model III in Table 4). The base probability of war is 0.098.

alliance systems made states very cautious about initiating a war against a state that was a member of the opposing alliance. Although neither the 'Both Sides' variable nor the 'One Side' having an outside alliance are significant, the odds ratio estimate for the latter is in the correct direction and shows a slight increase in the predicted probability of war (see Table 5).

As with the earlier period, when disputes recur the probability of war increases—with it being 0.189 at the first dispute, 0.274 at the sixth, and 0.414 at the fifteenth. We also see that as more steps are taken the probability of war goes up accordingly with the highest probability of war (0.465) occurring when all four steps are present—territorial disputes, one side with an outside ally, recurring disputes,[65] and an ongoing arms race. Further, Table 5 makes it clear that it is not that territorial disputes are inherently war prone, but how they are handled that is the key, even though they are generally more war prone than non-territorial disputes. The predicted probabilities for policy and regime disputes also show that handling

them in a power politics fashion increases the probability of war, as was the case in the early period, albeit at much lower levels. A difference with the 1816–1945 period is that regime disputes are more war prone than policy disputes in the Cold War years, something which makes sense given the highly ideological nature of that era.

The progression in probabilities in Table 5 follows the pattern suggested by the steps-to-war explanation. For example, arms races, even though they do not have a statistically significant impact, do impart the increase in probability expected by Proposition 4. The main deficiency seems to lie in predicting the specific alliance configuration that would increase the probability of war. Only when one side has an outside ally is there a positive relationship to war (and even this estimate is not statistically significant). A look at these cases is interesting. They include several Cold War dyads where one side does not have an outside relevant alliance—such as United States–North Korea, United States/Britain/France–China in 1950. This category also includes a number of famous minor-minor rivalries that go to war where only one side has an outside ally—Egypt-Britain in 1956, Egypt/Syria/Jordan-Israel, Iraq-Israel, Iran-Iraq, Tanzania-Uganda. These cases, while they deviate from the theoretical expectations in Proposition 2, are not so anomalous that they cannot be explained by the logic of the steps-to-war explanation.[66]

Finally, one of the main differences with the earlier period is that in the Cold War era, having no alliances or having only one outside ally are the most war prone configurations, while a case of both sides with outside alliances is the least likely to go to war. In the 1816–1945 period the most war prone alliance configurations are both sides with outside alliances and allied to each other plus an outside alliance, with no alliances the least likely to be associated with war. Again this suggests that it is something about the alliance system of the Cold War era and its relationship to nuclear weapons that is the key to explaining the anomaly, while at the same time suggesting that certain fundamentals remain constant across the two time periods.

Conclusion

This study has provided evidence that the steps-to-war explanation can deepen our understanding of the process by which war occurs. First, it has tested and provided evidence consistent with four major propositions derived from the steps-to-war model for the 1816–1945 period. It has been shown that the probability of war breaking out between two states is higher for states disputing territory than for those disputing policy or regime questions (Proposition 1). More importantly, if states dispute territory and both have politically relevant outside allies this greatly increases the probability of war (Proposition 2). If, in addition, these territorial disputants who have outside allies have recurring disputes, then the probability of war is even higher still (Proposition 3a). Finally, if the dyads having all these factors present also are engaged in an ongoing arms race (Proposition 4), then their probability of war approaches such high levels (0.900 range) that war is almost certain within five years.

Secondly, for the Cold War 1946–92 period, territory and a history of prior disputes still have positive and significant impacts on the probability of war, but having outside alliances generally does not, nor do arms races. These latter two (statistically insignificant) factors do, however, under certain circumstances—for example, territorial with one side having an outside alliance—increase the probability of war in a manner consistent with the predictions of the explanation. Why these two factors do not behave more clearly in ways anticipated by the explanation needs further analysis, but it may well have something to do with the Cold War alliance structure and nuclear weapons.

Thirdly, this study has shown that the various foreign policy practices states use in pursuing their territorial disputes help distinguish those territorial disputes that go to war from those that do not. This holds for both the 1816–1945 and 1946–92 periods. States that resort to the threat or use of force to contest territory are on a path to war, but so long as they avoid recurrent disputes, making politically relevant alliances with outside parties or arms racing they can keep the probability of war fairly low. When dyads dispute territory and engage in even one of these steps, then the probability of war goes up. Of these three steps, the most dangerous in the 1816–1945 period is arms racing, followed by both sides having an outside ally, followed by a history of recurring disputes. In the less war prone nuclear Cold War period, the most dangerous is having a territorial dispute or any dispute that festers and recurs. However, it is also clear that states that have a large number of MIDs in the Cold War period learn to manage them, so that at a certain point they become less likely to go to war than those that preceded them. This finding makes a novel contribution to the rivalry literature by showing that when rivals reach a very large number of disputes they behave differently.

Fourthly, the analysis has shown that resorting to the use of power politics to handle disputes increases the probability of war. The only exception to this is with some of the alliance configurations in the post–Cold War era, but even here having one side with an outside alliance moves the probability of war in the expected direction. These findings, especially for the earlier period, support the claim that the use of power politics is a separate path to war, and inherently dangerous even in the absence of territorial disputes.

Generally, however, the most dangerous condition, as shown in our test of Proposition 4 in both periods (Tables 3 and 5) is when all four factors are present. While we have examined only the presence or absence of these conditions, the underlying theoretical rationale of the steps-to-war explanation suggests that these factors are interrelated and that they can form a syndrome of behaviour where one thing leads to another. Thus, as steps are added, it may become increasingly difficult to avoid taking additional steps.

In many ways these findings constitute an empirical breakthrough in the scientific study of the probability of war. They provide evidence, for the long 1816–1945 period, on a specific combination of factors that progressively increase the probability of war. They also provide evidence on how the most recent period of international history has changed in some regards, while remaining the same in others, compared to the previous era. Now that the core propositions have passed a rigorous set of tests, a research programme on the steps to war should begin to address how this explanation might compare with other explanations of war and what kinds of new data need to be collected to test the steps-to-war explanation further. The democratic peace and realist emphases on the role of capability are two obvious alternative explanations and theoretical approaches with which to begin. Important parts of each could be incorporated within the steps research programme. Such an approach might be more fruitful both from a theoretical and empirical perspective than simply trying to see which of the three is the best. In terms of the democratic peace, the steps-to-war explanation would predict that one of the reasons democratic dyads do not fight each other is that they may not have territorial disputes, and such disputes as they do have are not likely to be handled in a power politics fashion. An interesting line of future research would be to examine democracies and the steps to war. Mitchell and Prins have provided some evidence that democratic dyads do not contest territorial issues very much, which lends credence to the above proposition.[67] It would also be interesting to see whether they avoid having arms races with each other, making alliances against each other and having repeated disputes. In terms of the role of capability, the current explanation already posits that the process leading to war is apt to differ depending on whether the contending parties are equal. So, the key unanswered questions involve just how the probability of war differs for actors having disparate capabilities and at what stage (i.e., after what steps have been taken) strategic thinking about relative capability has its greatest impact on the probability of a dispute escalating to war.

Lastly, although this study has gone far in measuring the timing of various steps, more refined data need to be collected to get at the dynamics embodied within the theoretical explanation. Once this is done the temporal relationship between the various steps, and whether they are really steps, and how their sequential order might change given the nature of the contending actors can be more fully tested. Likewise, if there are different processes that lead to war and war is multicausal, then a pressing task for future research is to identify the main paths to war in the international system and ultimately measure the precise probability of war associated with each path.[68] These suggestions show that there is much to be done, but at the same time they show that the steps-to-war explanation can provide a rich and potentially highly progressive research programme.

Lewis Richardson, one of the founders of the scientific study of war, hoped that by the careful examination of statistical evidence we could begin to identify the factors responsible for interstate war.[69] This statistical analysis has identified several and measured the extent to which their presence or absence, singularly or in combination, affects the probability of a dispute occurring that will escalate to war within five years. Given these results, we think the steps-to-war explanation deserves further attention and that its research programme provides a highly promising avenue for furthering our knowledge about the onset of war.

Notes

Authors' Note: The research reported in this article has been generously supported by the National Science Foundation (U.S.) Grant #SES-9818557. The authors' special thanks go to Chris Leskiw for aid in constructing the politically relevant alliance indices, and to Amber Papasergio for technical assistance. They would also like to thank Claudio Cioffi-Revilla, Paul Hensel, Tracy Jarvis, Manus Midlarsky and the anonymous referees for valuable suggestions. The sole responsibility for the analysis remains theirs alone.

1. See, for example, Bruce Bueno de Mesquita and David Lalman, *War and Reason: Domestic and International Imperatives* (New Haven, Conn.: Yale University Press, 1992); Jacek Kugler and Douglas Lemke, eds, *Parity and War: Evaluations and Extensions of The War Ledger* (Ann Arbor: University of Michigan Press, 1996); Jack Levy, 'The Causes of War: A Review of Theories and Evidence', in Philip E. Tetlock et al., eds, *Behavior, Society, and Nuclear War* (New York: Oxford University Press, 1989); Hidemi Suganami, *On the Causes of War* (Oxford: Clarendon Press, 1996); Hidemi Suganami, 'Explaining War: Some Critical Observations', *International Relations*, 16 (2002), 307–36; William Thompson, *On Global War* (Columbia: University of South Carolina Press, 1988); Stephen Van Evera, *The Causes of War* (Ithaca, N.Y.: Cornell University Press, 1999); Paul F. Diehl and Gary Goertz, *War and Peace in International Rivalry* (Ann Arbor: University of Michigan Press, 2000).

2. J. David Singer, *The Correlates of War I* (New York: Free Press, 1979).

3. See Stuart Bremer and Thomas Cusack, eds, *The Process of War* (Amsterdam: Gordon and Breach, 1995); Michael Brecher and Jonathan Wilkenfeld, *A Study of Crisis* (Ann Arbor: University of Michigan Press, 1997); Claudio Cioffi-Revilla, *Politics and Uncertainty: Theory, Models and Applications* (Cambridge: Cambridge University Press, 1998).

4. John Vasquez, *The War Puzzle* (Cambridge: Cambridge University Press, 1993), chap. 4.

5. Suganami, 'Explaining War', pp. 313–14.

6. For evidence supporting this proposition, see Russell Leng, 'When Will They Ever Learn? Coercive Bargaining in Recurrent Crises', *Journal of Conflict Resolution*, 27 (1983), 379–419; Vasquez, *The War Puzzle*, chap. 5; Brecher and Wilkenfeld, *A Study of Crisis*, pp. 826–8, 837–8.

7. On the concept of the security dilemma, see John Herz, 'Idealist Internationalism and the Security Dilemma', *World Politics*, 2 (1950), 157–80. Realists also recognize how a security dilemma arises out of realist prescriptions; see, for example, Robert Jervis, 'Co-operation under the Security Dilemma', *World Politics*, 30 (1978), 167–214; and Van Evera, *The Causes of War*, p. 117n, but on the whole they are more sanguine about the pacifying effects of power and resolve.

8. For an analysis of how probabilistic causality can be used to formalize conflict and war when they are used as dependent variables, see Cioffi-Revilla, *Politics and Uncertainty*, pp. 31–4.

9. Likewise, the language of 'steps' implies a sequence of actions or transitions across phases (on sequences and war, see Cioffi-Revilla, *Politics and Uncertainty*, pp. 140–50, 158–63). The various risk factors for war—territorial disputes, relevant alliances, and so forth—may increase the probability of war, however, without necessarily having worked through sequences. To see whether the actual steps take place in the sequence we imply would require a more case-focused test, which would make most sense after the present sort of analysis has been conducted.

10. See, for example, Vasquez, *The War Puzzle*, pp. 129–30, 133–6; Paul R. Hensel, 'Charting a Course to Conflict: Territorial Issues and Interstate Conflict, 1816–1992', *Conflict Management and Peace Science*, 15 (1996), 43–73; Paul R. Hensel, 'Territory: Theory and Evidence on Geography and Conflict', in John Vasquez, ed., *What Do We Know About War?* (Lanham, Md.: Rowman & Littlefield, 2000); Paul Senese, 'Geographic Proximity and Issue Salience: Their Effects on the Escalation of Militarized Interstate Conflict', *Conflict Management and Peace Science*, 15 (1996), 133–61; John Vasquez and Marie T. Henehan, 'Territorial Disputes and the Probability of War,

1816–1992', *Journal of Peace Research,* 38 (2001), 123–38; Hemda Ben-Yehuda, 'Territoriality, Crisis and War in the Arab-Israel Conflict, 1947–94', *Journal of Conflict Studies,* 21 (2001), 78–108; Marie Henehan, 'The Effect of Territory on Dispute Escalation among Initiators: A Research Note' (presented at the Hong Kong Meeting of the International Studies Association, 2001); Paul Senese and John Vasquez, 'A Unified Explanation of Territorial Conflict: Testing the Impact of Sampling Bias, 1919–1992', *International Studies Quarterly,* 47 (2003), 275–98.

11. See Barbara Walter, 'Explaining the Intractability of Territorial Conflict', *International Studies Review,* 5 (2003), 137–53; Monica Duffy Toft, *The Geography of Ethnic Violence* (Princeton, N.J.: Princeton University Press, 2003).

12. Paul R. Hensel, 'One Thing Leads to Another: Recurrent Militarized Disputes in Latin America, 1816–1990', *Journal of Peace Research,* 31 (1994), 281–98.

13. See Paul Huth, *Standing Your Ground: Territorial Disputes and International Conflict* (Ann Arbor: University of Michigan Press, 1996); Bikash A. Roy, 'Intervention Across Bisecting Borders', *Journal of Peace Research,* 34 (1997), 3–14; see also Paul K. Huth and Todd L. Allee, *The Democratic Peace and Territorial Conflict in the Twentieth Century* (Cambridge: Cambridge University Press, 2002).

14. Beth A. Simmons, 'See You in Court? The Appeal to Quasi-Judicial Legal Processes in the Settlement of Territorial Disputes', in Paul Diehl, ed., *A Road Map to War: Territorial Dimensions of International Conflict* (Nashville, Tenn.: Vanderbilt University Press, 1999), pp. 205–37; Beth A. Simmons, 'Capacity, Commitment, and Compliance: International Institutions and Territorial Disputes', *Journal of Conflict Resolution,* 46 (2002), 829–56, pp. 835, 843.

15. See J. David Singer and Melvin Small, 'National Alliance Commitments and War Involvement, 1815–1945', *Peace Research Society (International) Papers,* 5 (1966), 109–40; Jack Levy, 'Alliance Formation and War Behavior: An Analysis of the Great Powers, 1495–1975', *Journal of Conflict Resolution,* 25 (1981), 581–613; see also T. Clifton Morgan and Glenn Palmer, 'A Model of Foreign Policy Substitutability: Selecting the Right Tools for the Job(s)', *Journal of Conflict Resolution,* 44 (2002), 11–32.

16. Randolph J. Siverson and Joel King, 'Alliances and the Expansion of War', in J. David Singer and Michael D. Wallace, eds, *To Auger Well: Early Warning Indicators in World Politics* (Beverly Hills, Calif.: Sage, 1979), pp. 37–49.

17. Douglas Gibler, 'Alliances: Why Some Cause War and Why Others Cause Peace', in Vasquez, ed., *What Do We Know About War?,* pp. 145–64. For a review of recent research on alliances, see Glenn Palmer and T. Clifton Morgan, *A Matter of Choice: A Two-Good Theory of Substitution in Foreign Policy* (forthcoming), chap. 7.

18. See Brett Ashley Leeds, Andrew Long and Sara McLaughlin Mitchell, 'Reevaluating Alliance Reliability: Specific Threats, Specific Promises', *Journal of Conflict Resolution,* 44 (2000), 686–99.

19. See Hensel, 'One Thing Leads to Another'.

20. Vasquez, *The War Puzzle,* pp. 184–90, 316–18. On repeating crises, see: Peter Wallersteen, 'Incompatibility, Confrontation, and War: Four Models and Three Historical Systems, 1816–1976', *Journal of Peace Research,* 18 (1981), 57–90; Stuart Bremer, 'Who Fights Whom, When, Where, and Why?', in Vasquez, ed., *What Do We Know About War?,* pp. 23–36, at p. 25; Leng, 'When Will They Ever Learn?'

21. Diehl and Goertz, *War and Peace in International Rivalry,* p. 45.

22. Diehl and Goertz, *War and Peace in International Rivalry;* Frank W. Wayman, 'Power Shifts and the Onset of War', in Jacek Kugler and Douglas Lemke, eds, *Parity and War* (Ann Arbor: University of Michigan Press, 1996), pp. 145–62; Frank W. Wayman, 'Rivalries: Recurrent Disputes and Explaining War', in Vasquez, ed., *What Do We Know About War?* pp. 219–34; William Thompson, 'Principal Rivalries', *Journal of Conflict Resolution,* 39 (1995), 195–223; William Thompson, 'Identifying Rivalries in World Politics', *International Studies Quarterly,* 45 (2001), 557–86.

23. Richard Mansbach and John Vasquez, *In Search of Theory: A New Paradigm for Global Politics* (New York: Columbia University Press, 1981), p. 117. For additional discussion on how dyadic interaction becomes patterned, see Edward Azar, 'Conflict Escalation and Conflict Reduction in an International Crisis: Suez, 1956', *Journal of Conflict Studies,* 16

(1972), 183–201. Azar recognizes a similar process in his normal relations range, where he maintains that it is not so much the level of hostility that makes for a crisis between two states, but how much that level deviates from the average or typical level of hostility. Thus, a typical negative act between the United States and the Soviet Union would not have as much impact as the same act would if it transpired between the United States and Britain. Azar's concept implies that states in long-term rivalries learn to manage their crises so as to make them less dangerous.

24. See J. David Singer, 'Threat-Perception and the Armament-Tension Dilemma', *Journal of Conflict Resolution,* 2 (1958), 91–123; Lewis F. Richardson, *Arms and Insecurity* (Pacific Grove, Calif.: Boxwood Press, 1960); Nazli Choucri and Robert North, *Nations in Conflict* (San Francisco: W. H. Freeman, 1975); Susan Sample, 'Arms Races and Dispute Escalation: Resolving the Debate', *Journal of Peace Research,* 34 (1997), 7–22.

25. Paul D. Senese and John A. Vasquez, 'Alliances, Territorial Disputes, and the Probability of War: Testing for Interactions', in Paul F. Diehl, ed., *The Scourge of War* (Ann Arbor: University of Michigan Press, 2004), pp. 189–221.

26. See Karl Popper, *Conjectures and Refutations* (New York: Basic Books, 1962); Imre Lakatos, 'Falsification and the Methodology of Scientific Research Programmes', in I. Lakatos and A. Musgrave, eds, *Criticism and the Growth of Knowledge* (Cambridge: Cambridge University Press, 1970), pp. 91–196.

27. On the dangers of the latter, see Bear Braumoeller and Anne Sartori, 'The Promise and Perils of Statistics in International Relations', in Detlef Sprinz and Yael Wolinsky-Nahmias, eds, *Models, Numbers, and Cases: Methods for Studying International Relations* (Ann Arbor: University of Michigan Press, 2004), pp. 129–51, at pp. 133–4.

28. For a comparison of using just the disputes without breaking them into dyadic disputes, see Vasquez and Henehan, 'Territorial Disputes and the Probability of War, 1816–1992', pp. 127–31, who find that with either sample the claims of what is Proposition 1 in our study are strongly supported. As a check on the robustness of the findings presented below, we also conduct supplemental analyses excluding the First World War and Second World War years.

29. On alliances and war expansion, see Siverson and King, 'Alliances and the Expansion of War'; Randolph J. Siverson and Harvey Starr, 'Opportunity, Willingness, and the Diffusion of War', *American Political Science Review,* 84 (1990), 47–67.

30. See Leng, 'When Will They Ever Learn?'; Manus Midlarsky, 'Preventing Systemic War', *Journal of Conflict Resolution,* 28 (1984), 563–84; Michael Colaresi and William Thompson, 'Hot Spots or Hot Hands? Serial Crisis Behavior, Escalating Risks, and Rivalry', *Journal of Politics,* 64 (2002), 1175–98.

31. Of the full 3,045 dyadic dispute cases in the data, 473 MIDs escalate to war, whereas our measure of going to war within five years has 596 escalating to war. This is an additional 123 cases out of 3,045 that go to war. However, if this were not done all these cases would count against the propositions even though the dyads involved in them go to war in a relatively short period of time. This being said, in previous work we have used dependent variables with and without the five-year window, and the results show no important differences; see, for example, Senese and Vasquez, 'A Unified Explanation of Territorial Conflict', Appendix, pp. 295–6.

32. See A. F. K. Organski and Jacek Kugler, *The War Ledger* (Chicago: University of Chicago Press, 1980); Levy, 'Alliance Formation and War Behavior'; Wallensteen, 'Incompatibility, Confrontation, and War'; Sample, 'Arms Races and Dispute Escalation'; Gibler, 'Alliances'; Douglas Lemke, *Regions of War and Peace* (Cambridge: Cambridge University Press, 2002).

33. See Daniel Jones, Stuart Bremer and J. David Singer, 'Militarized Interstate Disputes, 1816–1992: Rationale, Coding Rules, and Empirical Patterns', *Conflict Management and Peace Science,* 15 (1996), 163–213, p. 178. Non-revisionist states on opposing sides of a MID by definition do not have any revision type and hence their revision type is coded as 'non-applicable'. In our data when two non-revisionist states are coupled with each other in a dyadic dispute, that MID is dropped from the analysis. This is done because they are not contesting any substantive issue with each other. often such states are neutrals or third parties that are caught up in a dispute in which they are not a direct party. Examples of dyads with

non-applicable codes in 1914 include Switzerland-Germany, Switzerland-Austria/Hungary, Italy-Germany and Germany-Norway; examples in 1939 include Switzerland-Germany, Germany–United States, Germany-Latvia, Germany-Argentina and Britain-Uruguay. Of the 3,045 dyadic disputes in our data, 469 are coded as non-applicable; of these only three go to war within five years. Excluding them, rather than treating them as non-territorial disputes, makes it more difficult for Proposition 1 to be supported.

34. See Senese and Vasquez, 'Alliances, Territorial Disputes and the Probability of War', pp. 203–5 for elaboration.

35. Douglas Gibler and Meredith Sarkees, 'Measuring Alliances: The Correlates of War Formal Interstate Alliance Data Set, 1816–2000', *Journal of Peace Research*, 41 (2004), 211–22.

36. See, for example, John Mueller, *Retreat from Doomsday: The Obsolescence of Major War* (New York: Basic Books, 1989).

37. For an alternative measure discounting the influence of early disputes, see Mark Crescenzi and Andrew Enterline, 'Time Remembered: A Dynamic Model of Interstate Interaction', *International Studies Quarterly*, 45 (2001), 409–31.

38. Diehl and Goertz, *War and Peace in International Rivalry*, p. 45.

39. For this reason, we do not start counting the number of prior disputes only at the beginning of a specific enduring rivalry, as defined by Diehl and Goertz, *War and Peace in International Rivalry*, p. 45.

40. See Susan Sample, 'The Outcomes of Military Buildups: Minor States vs. Major Powers', *Journal of Peace Research*, 39 (2002), 669–92. For a historical approach to collecting data on arms races, see David Stevenson, *Armaments and the Coming of War: Europe 1904–1914* (Oxford: Clarendon Press, 1996), pp. 1–14.

41. Michael Horn, 'Arms Races and the International System' (doctoral dissertation: University of Rochester, 1987).

42. See John Vasquez, 'The Probability of War, 1816–1992', Presidential Address to the International Studies Association, *International Studies Quarterly*, 48 (2004), 1–27.

43. When the dyad or rivalry (e.g., Britain-Germany) is the unit of analysis, one would compare whether the

rivals (over the course of their history) that have territorial disputes, politically relevant outside alliances and arms races are more apt to have a war than those that have one or more of these factors absent. However, with such data one does not know for sure if the alliances, arms races and so forth precede the MID that escalates to war.

44. For a discussion of odds ratios and their advantages, see Tim Futing Liao, *Interpreting Probability Models: Logit, Probit, and other Generalized Linear Models* (Thousand Oaks, Calif.: Sage University Paper series on Quantitative Applications in the Social Sciences, Sage Publications, 1994), pp. 13–16.

45. Michael Tomz, Jason Wittenberg and Gary King, *CLARIFY: Software for Interpreting and Presenting Statistical Results, Version 2.1* (Cambridge: Harvard University, 5 January 2003), http://GKing.Harvard.Edu.

46. See Senese and Vasquez, 'A Unified Explanation of Territorial Conflict'.

47. Karen Rasler and William Thompson, 'Territorial Disputes and Strategic Rivalry' (presented at the Annual Meeting of the American Political Science Association, Philadelphia, 2003); Alex Braithwaite and Glenn Palmer, 'The Escalation, Geography, and Evolution of Militarized Disputes' (presented at the Annual Meeting of the Peace Science Society: International, Ann Arbor, 2003). Most studies in international relations looking at sampling bias use a censored probit approach. On the use of these types of techniques and their potential problems, see Charles Manski, 'Anatomy of the Selection Problem', *Journal of Human Resources*, 24 (1989), 343–60; Charles Manski, *Identification Problems in Econometrics* (Cambridge, Mass.: Harvard University Press, 1995).

48. See Senese and Vasquez, 'Alliances, Territorial Disputes, and the Probability of War', pp. 211–13.

49. All of the models reported here were also estimated with consideration of joint democracy and relative capability (results not shown). As expected, joint democracy was a prefect predictor of no war and was, therefore, dropped from the models. Also as expected, increasing levels of power preponderance significantly decreased the likelihood of war. Most important for our purposes here, however, is that the results reported in Tables 1–5 changed very little in

the presence of these additional factors. Further, to make sure that the results were not being driven by joining states, we also performed analyses excluding all pairs that were not party to the dispute on the first day. The results for this sub-sample of initiating dyads were almost identical to those for both initiators and joiners.

50. See Bruce Bueno de Mesquita, *The War Trap* (New Haven, Conn.: Yale University Press, 1981), pp. 73–83, 159–64; James Ray, 'Friends as Foes: International Conflict and Wars between Formal Allies', in Charles Gochman and Alan Sabrosky, eds, *Prisoners of War? Nation-States in the Modern Era* (Lexington, Mass.: Lexington Books, 1990), pp. 73–91.

51. Senese and Vasquez, 'Alliances, Territorial Disputes, and the Probability of War'. This earlier study did not control for the number of prior disputes or arms races and used a slightly different dependent variable—whether or not the current dispute involved a war.

52. These models were run first with just the one interaction term and then with the others also included.

53. Nevertheless, for certain time periods, sub-samples and model specifications, some significant interactions may be found. Because some of these sub-sample results are divergent, we can conclude that the relationship is at least additive. We find that the interaction of territory and both sides having outside alliances best fits a sub-sample with the years associated with the two world wars dropped (1914–18; 1939–45), along with the five-year window for war onset. This finding provides even stronger support for the steps-to-war explanation and suggests that something about the world war cases is making the relationship more additive than multiplicative.

54. 'Other' disputes and the four wars that arise out of them are discussed at length in Vasquez and Henehan, 'Territorial Disputes and the Probability of War, 1816–1992', p. 129, n. 9. For example, the Franco-Prussian War, which began with a crisis over the succession to the Spanish throne, was manipulated by Bismarck to help bring about German unification. The Spanish-Peruvian/Chilean War of 1865 began ostensibly as an attempt by Spain to protect its rights in Peru, but in actuality was a Spanish attempt to regain control over its former colony (see George C. Kohn,

Dictionary of Wars (New York: Doubleday, 1986), p. 443). The Lopez War is related to intervention in the Civil War in Uruguay, but also reflects Lopez's (and that of his father, the former president) territorial claims against Argentina and Brazil (see William Langer, *An Encyclopedia of World History*, 5th edn (Boston, Mass.: Houghton Mifflin, 1980), p. 848). Finally, the Football War, which starts over a football match, breaks out in the context of a long-term border dispute (see Paul K. Huth, *Standing Your Ground* (Ann Arbor: University of Michigan Press, 1996), p. 201). All but one of the fifteen dyadic 'other' MIDs that escalate are accounted for by these wars (out of a total of forty-nine 'other' MIDs). The remaining 'other' dispute that escalates is a 1900 MID between Russia and Japan, which is associated with the 1904 Russo-Japanese War that arises out of a territorial MID.

55. As stated earlier, distinct from Diehl and Goertz, *War and Peace in International Rivalry*, we do not place any temporal clustering restrictions on the occurrence of these disputes.

56. The 0.580 war probability for the sixth dispute falls below the upper bound of the 90 per cent confidence interval (0.420–0.625) for the first dispute. The 0.679 war likelihood for the fifteenth dispute, however, falls well above this upper bound.

57. These null findings are congruent with those found by Frank W. Wayman, 'Alliances and War: A Time-Series Analysis', in Charles Gochman and Alan Sabrosky, eds, *Prisoners of War?* (Lexington, Mass.: Lexington Books, 1990), pp. 93–113.

58. Interaction estimates for territory and the two outside alliance categories, as well as territory and arms races, are insignificant for the period after the Second World War.

59. Figure 1 depicts the probability of a territorial dispute eventuating in war based on the Number of Prior MIDs, with the other risk factors set to their modal values (i.e., no arms race and one side has an outside politically relevant alliance).

60. This point represents the maxima where the slope of the line is equal to 0.

61. Only eleven dyads have more than 27 MIDs from 1816 on: United States–Soviet Union (56), Russia-China (50), Britain–Soviet Union (40), Russia-Japan

(45), Israel-Syria (45), India-Pakistan (40), Israel-Egypt (36), Japan-China (35), Greece-Turkey (33), United States–China (29), and Argentina-Chile (28), for a total of 140 dyadic disputes preceded by 27 or more MIDs.

62. See, for example, Diehl and Goertz, *War and Peace in International Rivalry.*

63. A model including the interaction of Territory and the Number of Prior MIDs reveals an insignificant parameter estimate for the period after the Second World War.

64. See respectively, John Gaddis, 'The Long Peace: Elements of Stability in the Postwar International System', *International Security,* 10 (1986), 99–142; and J. David Singer, 'Peace in the Global System: Displacement, Interregnum, or Transformation?' in Charles Kegley Jr, ed., *The Long Postwar Peace* (New York: Harper Collins, 1991), pp. 56–84; Michael Brecher and Jonathan Wilkenfeld, 'International Crises and Global Instability: The Myth of the "Long Peace"', in Kegley, ed., *The Long Postwar Peace,* pp. 85–104.

65. Of course, as shown in Figure 1, when the number of prior disputes is greater than twenty-seven, the probability of war actually begins to decrease. We present the war likelihoods for the sixth and fifteenth dispute in Table 5 to retain consistency with the estimates for the 1816–1945 period shown in Table 3.

66. In the steps-to-war model any outside alliance is seen as increasing threat perception and hence the probability of war, so the fact that dyadic disputes with one outside alliance will go to war is not anomalous. What is anomalous is that they go to war more frequently than disputes where both sides have outside alliances.

67. Sara McLaughlin Mitchell and Brandon Prins, 'Beyond Territorial Contiguity: Issues at Stake in Democratic Militarized Interstate Disputes', *International Studies Quarterly,* 43 (1999), 169–83.

68. See Levy, 'The Causes of War', pp. 277, 279, 281; Vasquez, *The War Puzzle,* pp. 48–50; Suganami, 'Explaining War', p. 321.

69. Richardson, *Arms and Insecurity.*

EDITORS' COMMENTARY

Major Contributions: The Steps to War

Up until this point in the book, we have looked primarily at how individual factors have affected the probability of war occurring. We have seen that territory, alliances, rivalry, and arms races are all related to war in one way or another. Senese and Vasquez (2005) examine all of these factors together to see if a steps-to-war explanation is empirically accurate.

The steps-to-war explanation argues that as security issues arise, leaders try to increase their power just as realists tell us they should do. There are two ways of doing this—a quick fix by getting one or more allies or by building one's own military capabilities. Ironically, however, this leads to insecurity instead of security because one's opponent does the same thing. Such an outcome is known as the **security dilemma**, whereby actions taken by one state to increase its security are reciprocated by another state, increasing the mutual insecurity of both states. Vasquez (1993; see also 2009) originally outlined this explanation of war by tracing out how each of the realist steps that states take to enhance their security are in fact a series of steps toward war. This contradicts many realist explanations that hold that peace through strength will ensure peace. We saw these competing ideas in the discussion of Sample's (2002, Chapter 6, this volume) article, where realists see arms buildups as factors promoting peace, while other theorists recognize the dangers of two rival states arming against each other. Vasquez (1987) constructed the steps-to-war explanation in an attempt to make sense of about twenty-five years of statistical findings produced mostly by the Correlates of War project. Senese and Vasquez systematically test the expectations from the theory.

According to the logic of the steps-to-war model, two states are apt to go to war when they are contending over a highly salient issue. Of all the issues states can disagree on, territorial issues are seen as the most prone to war. This claim, which is embodied in the territorial explanation of war (Vasquez 1993, chap. 4; see also Vasquez and Henehan 2011), forms a subset of the steps-to-war explanation. The territorial explanation maintains that grievances over territory are most likely to give rise to security issues worth fighting and dying for (on the latter, see Senese 1996). This is not to say that other issues cannot give rise to war. Territorial issues are not a **necessary condition** of war (i.e., no war can be fought without them being present). Territorial disputes are only more likely to result in war in comparison to other issues. In fact, most territorial issues do not go to war (Hensel et al. 2008, Chapter 3, this volume), but they are most apt to produce war when they are handled through the use of power politics (i.e., the foreign policy practices of realism). The same is true of non-territorial issues; they are most likely to go to war when they are handled by the use of power politics. According to the steps-to-war approach, war is brought about by two processes—certain salient issues and by the use of power politics.

The steps to war is a dynamic process in which states try one thing, but when this fails to resolve the issue because of the way the other state reciprocates, another thing is tried that typically is more escalatory (i.e., a more coercive use of threat or force), and then that fails, and so on, until a militarized interstate dispute (MID) emerges that escalates to war (see also Vasquez 1993, 155; 2009, 169). The strategies and practices states implement to get the other side to agree to its issue position are more or less outlined in the dominant diplomatic culture of the time (which, from 1648 on, is realism or power politics). So in the presence of a territorial issue that has failed to be resolved by purely diplomatic means, states will resort to the threat or use of force. Repeated uses of force that fail to resolve the issue will make states insecure, and they will try to increase their power by making an alliance or building up their military. Forming an alliance leads the other side to make a counteralliance, and building up one's military leads to arms races. Each of these realist practices—alliances and military buildups—is seen as steps to war in that as these actions are taken, they increase threat perception and escalate the level of hostility between states in terms of both psychological attitudes and behavior. Meanwhile, the use of force through the initiation of MIDs continues, and as these repeat, a sense of rivalry develops that further increases hostility. A vicious circle ensues across the MIDs that resembles a kind of hostile spiral; this eventually produces a MID with characteristics that make it ripe to escalate to war. Although the steps are assumed to often follow a certain order—rise of a territorial dispute, formation of alliances, arms races, and repetition of MIDs— what is important, according to Senese and Vasquez (2005), is not so much the order as that the steps are mutually reinforcing.

The analysis by Senese and Vasquez (2005) is **multivariate** in that they look at how the presence of four factors increases the probability of a MID escalating to war. The statistical technique they use also permits them to not only examine the impact of one variable, say territorial disputes, but also to control for all other variables in the model simultaneously to see if that specific variable still has a statistically significant effect in the presence of the control variables. They begin by testing their propositions on the entire 1816–1992 period and then divide that into the 1816–1945 period and the Cold War nuclear era of 1946–1992 (Sample 2002). The steps-to-war explanation holds more or less for the overall period and fully for 1816–1945, but only partially for 1946–1992.

We begin by looking at the full period and then examine the deviations in the two subperiods. Senese and Vasquez (2005) start by comparing the relative effect of territorial disputes versus other types of disputes—namely, general foreign **policy** MIDs and **regime** MIDs. Policy MIDs involve attempts by one state to change the foreign policy behavior of another state, while regime MIDs are situations in which one state is trying to remove the governing regime in another state (Jones et al. 1996). Table 1, Model I examines only the issue variables by themselves in the full period of 1816–1992. The dependent variable is a dichotomous measure that equals 1 if a (current or future) MID was followed by war between the same pair of states within five years and zero otherwise. Their analysis shows that territorial disputes are positively and significantly related to a MID escalating to war within five years compared to regime or policy disputes.[1] Table 1, Model II introduces the three other variables—alliances, the number of prior MIDs (as an indicator of rivalry), and arms races. Alliances are not statistically significant, but rivalry and arms race are significant and positive predictors of war. Thus, of the four key factors in the steps-to-war model, only one (alliances) does not hold in the full sample.

When we turn to the 1816–1945 period in Table 2, Senese and Vasquez (2005) find that all four factors are significantly related to a MID escalating to war within five years. Now having an outside alliance is significantly related to war onset—specifically when both sides have outside alliances, war is more likely when both sides are allied to each other and also have an outside alliance.[2] It is also found, as can be seen in both Models II and III, that when controlling for the other steps to war, each step remains significant (i.e., one step does not wipe out the significance of the other steps). For example, alliances are significant, as are prior MIDs and arms races, even in the presence of the other variables.

The Cold War period is different and does not fit the steps-to-war explanation as well. Territorial disputes still predict escalation to war, as does rivalry, but both sides having outside alliances is not significant and neither is having an arms race. The latter is similar to what Sample (2002) finds, and Senese and Vasquez (2005) also attribute this deviation in part to the impact of nuclear weapons and the specific nature of the East-West alliance structure. Later they examine this Cold War deviation in more detail (Senese and Vasquez 2008, 231–44; see also Vasquez and Kang 2013).

Senese and Vasquez (2005) are interested not only in statistical significance but also whether the steps increase the probability of war in a stepwise fashion. In their propositions, they predict that taking additional steps will increase the probability of war. Hence, they expect that situations in which only two steps are present (e.g., territorial disputes and outside alliances) will have a lower probability of war than when three or four steps are present. Since the steps-to-war explanation only fully holds for the 1816–1945 period, it makes sense to report the substantive effects for this period, which they do in Table 3. It can be seen that when a territorial MID is present (column 2) and there are no alliances, the probability of a MID escalating to war within five years is 0.204. When both sides have an alliance, the probability increases to 0.522, and if the two sides are in a rivalry (i.e., have had six or more MIDs), the probability is 0.580. If, in addition, they have had 15 MIDs, the probability of war increases to 0.679, and when all four steps have been taken with both sides now also having an ongoing arms race, the probability of war is 0.920 (almost inevitable). This is a very difficult test for the steps-to-war explanation to pass, and the findings are quite consistent with the logic of the theory. There is in fact a stepwise increase in the probability of war.

Last, Senese and Vasquez (2005) test one other claim with regard to rivalry. Some have argued that when states are rivals and have many MIDs, as the United States and U.S.S.R. did in the Cold War, they learn how to manage their disputes, and their interactions take on a *ritualized* character. Senese and Vasquez predict that in these circumstances, states with very few or very many MIDs will be unlikely to experience war, but those with a moderate amount will have the highest likelihood of war. This relationship, as reported in Figure 1, is found to hold for the Cold War period.

What can be concluded about the steps-to-war explanation given the different results for the two subperiods? Clearly, the Cold War period is different, but does that mean that the nuclear era is the beginning of a new trend that has inaugurated a fundamental change in what brings about war? Or does it mean that something about the Cold War made things different, and now that it is over, the more fundamental forces exhibited for the much longer 1816–1945 period will return? Senese and Vasquez (2008) update their data through 2001 and thus have a few years of the post–Cold War era to test these two claims. Since these are only a few years, no definitive claims can be made, but they do present some evidence that outside alliances are now significantly related to war and that the post–Cold War period is more like the 1816–1945 period than the Cold War. Because of lack of data, they cannot test the effect of arms races. If their findings hold, then this would mean that the Cold War was different and not the start of a new trend. One of the beauties of science is that as more data are collected, we will have a better answer to this question.

Methodological Notes: Substantive Significance and Predicted Probabilities

This article provides a good example of how to use the **scientific method** to investigate international relations. The first step is to derive a proposition from a theory that must be true if the theory is true. A **proposition** is a statement that purports to explain behavior or some phenomena—in this case, why war occurs. If the derived proposition must be true if the theory is true, then finding that it is false (i.e., contradicted by the empirical evidence) must mean that the theory is false, at least as it is presently constituted. Karl Popper (1959), an important philosopher of natural science, places great emphasis on falsification. For him, progress in science in terms of accumulating knowledge is attained by rejecting inaccurate theories and concepts. Since we can never "prove" a theory because it is always logically possible that a future test will be inconsistent with a proposition, falsification is the only thing that is logically possible. Once a proposition is derived, the second step is to convert the abstract concepts so they can be observed. This is done by **operationalizing** the concepts (Klein et al. 2006, Chapter 5, this volume). A proposition that is fully operationalized replaces the concepts with observable variables. For example, Senese and Vasquez (2005) observe rivalry by looking at the number of prior MIDs. Once the concepts are operationalized, it is necessary to assemble data to test the hypotheses (the third step). Without high-quality data, tests are not very useful. Collection of data can take a long time. The original MID data, for instance, took several people more than a decade to collect. The fourth step is to design a test that will specify in advance what evidence will falsify a particular hypothesis and lead it to be rejected. This is done by making a **prediction** about what the evidence will look like in the data. Since the data in international relations are typically about the past, technically this is not a prediction about the future but a **retrodiction** about the past. Senese and Vasquez, for example, predict that when both sides have outside allies to support them, that will increase the probability of war occurring within five years.

The fifth step is to decide what statistics are most appropriate given the measures and the propositions for testing the hypotheses. Senese and Vasquez (2005) opt for **logistic regression** (Hensel et al. 2008) because their dependent variable, escalation to war, is a **dichotomy**; in other words, it is measured as either yes (present) or no (absent)—the MID either escalates to war or it does not. Dichotomous variables have special characteristics and logistic regression is an appropriate technique for analyzing these sorts of data. Steps three through five are typically discussed in the **research design** of a paper, which is what Senese and Vasquez do. Basically, the research design tells the reader how the hypothesis is being tested and justifies the decisions made regarding the procedures used. The research design should be sufficiently detailed so that other scholars can repeat the study (**replicate** it) as one would replicate an experiment in chemistry. After the research design is constructed, then the findings or results are presented and interpreted. The conclusion accepts or rejects the various hypotheses and sometimes offers suggestions for future research. In a complicated or potentially controversial piece of research, authors may discuss whether they think their findings are a function of "reality" or the peculiarities of the research design they have employed. In research papers you might write, you will want to keep in mind these various steps of applying the scientific method.

The measures that Senese and Vasquez (2005) employ are listed in Table 1, and their data sources are discussed in the research design. An important set of data are those for the issues under contention, particularly whether there are territorial disputes. The absence of data on territorial questions initially prevented the territorial explanation of war from being tested. The release of the MID data solved this problem. Unbeknownst to most people at the time, the MID data set included information on territorial disputes. The data set coded whether participants in a MID were either revisionist or status quo states and, if revisionist, what type of revision they were trying to bring about: one on territory, general foreign policy, a regime question, or "other" (Jones et al. 1996, 178). Later updates even referred to the revision-type variable as the issue over which the MID was being fought.

Senese and Vasquez (2005) use the "revisionist type" variable to see if territorial MIDs have a more significant likelihood of going to war than policy or regime disputes, as can be seen in Model I in Tables 1, 2, and 4. To get at this information, "revisionist type," which is a **nominal** or **categorical** variable consisting of four categories (territory, policy, regime, and other), is broken down into four separate variables (territorial vs. nonterritorial, policy vs. nonpolicy, etc.). These dichotomous variables are referred to as **dummy variables** since they are so simple. Nonetheless, they capture just what we want to know. In logistic regression, when a categorical variable is broken up into a series of dummy variables, it is necessary to run the models with a **reference group** (i.e., it is necessary to specify one of the four categories as a comparison group). In this case, policy disputes, because they are the most frequent, are selected as the reference group.[3] What this means is that all that is being tested is whether the variables in the model are more likely to go to war than the revision type specified in the reference group. Hence, Table 1 tells us that territorial disputes are significantly more likely to escalate to war than policy disputes, but regime disputes are not. To see if territorial disputes are more likely to go to war than regime disputes, a different logistic model has to be run, and Senese and Vasquez do that and report the results in the text.

We know that territorial disputes are more likely to go to war because in the tables, territorial MID has one or more asterisks by it, but regime does not, and the estimated coefficient is positive. As explained in the footnotes, one asterisk means that there are only 5 out of 100 chances that the relationship is random, and two asterisks mean there is only 1 out of 100 chances that it is random, so we accept the relationship as nonrandom or statistically significant. Senese and Vasquez (2005) also report the **odds ratio** for each variable, and it can be seen in Table 1 that territorial MIDs are four times more likely (4.22) to escalate to war within five years than policy disputes (the MIDs in the reference category). Senese and Vasquez report that territorial MIDs are five times (5.4) more likely to escalate to war than regime disputes. Note, like the study by Susan Sample (2002), that Senese and Vasquez test their hypotheses by seeing if the current MID or any MID involving the same two parties that occurs goes to war within five years.

A question that is important for the territorial explanation of war is why territorial disputes are more prone to escalating to war. Other research has provided some answers. It is known that disputes that recur are apt to go to war, and territorial disputes are more apt to recur than other types of disputes (Hensel 1994). Recurrence of disputes between the same parties leads to a sense of rivalry (Diehl and Goertz 2000). What is even more theoretically interesting is that territorial enduring rivalries have more severe MIDs than other enduring rivalries (Tir and Diehl 2002, 275–76). In addition, states that have territorial disputes tend to have more fatal MIDs (in which one or more military personnel are killed) than states that contend over policy or regime disputes (Senese 1996; Hensel 2000).

It should be noted that sometimes an odds ratio cannot be calculated because the logit model will exclude a variable if it is a **perfect predictor**. This happens in Tables 1, 2, and 4 for the variable "allied only to each other." A prefect predictor is when each case in the variable is always a case of peace or a case of war, (i.e., it is universally valid and there is no variation). In this example, states that are allied only to each other never have a war and are always at peace.

Besides calculating odds ratios, Senese and Vasquez (2005) calculate **predicted probabilities** in Table 3. Predicted probabilities are not conditional probabilities (like those in Bremer's [1992b] Table 1, Chapter 2, this volume) but probabilities that we would expect to see if we began with some baseline model and then changed the values of one or more variables to see how the probability of war would change (see Oneal and Russett 1999c, Chapter 9, this volume). The predicted probabilities in Table 3 are used to test Propositions 1 to 4 that as more steps to war are taken, the probability of war should increase. It can be seen as one reads down each column that the probabilities do increase. One question that arises is whether the differences in the predicted probabilities are statistically significant. For example, is the 0.204 for no alliances significantly lower than the

0.522 for both sides with outside alliances? To determine this, one needs to look at the **confidence levels** in parentheses below each probability.

The authors use a program called CLARIFY (Tomz et al. 2003) to generate confidence levels for the predicted probabilities. The program draws values of a parameter from a hypothetical **sampling distribution** (usually the normal or bell-shaped distribution), treating the estimated parameter value as the mean of this constructed sampling distribution (e.g., the value of 3.25 for a territorial MID in Table 2, Model I). It then draws at least 1,000 values and forms an empirical distribution. We can then construct a confidence interval around the estimated parameter by using a certain confidence level, such as 90 percent. We would determine the values of the predicted probabilities around the mean that contained 90 percent of the total area under the sampling distribution curve. For example, consider the effect of a territorial MID on the chances for war in Table 3. The mean value is 0.204, and the upper and lower values for the 90 percent confidence intervals are 0.151 and 0.265. This tells us that that the true population effect, or what we could observe if we analyzed all conflicts in all years of history, would fall somewhere between 0.151 and 0.265 in 90 percent of the constructed intervals. For 0.204 and 0.522 to be significantly different, the 0.204 value (territorial MID) must fall outside the confidence levels reported for 0.522 (territorial MID and both sides have outside alliances). We can see in this case that the two confidence intervals of (0.151, 0.265) and (0.420, 0.625) do not overlap, and so having alliances increases the chances for war.

Last, Senese and Vasquez (2005) test for a **curvilinear** relationship between the number of prior MIDs and the probability of war. The results are portrayed graphically in Figure 1. A **linear** relationship would suggest that as the number of MIDs increased, the probability of war would increase at a constant rate. This rate is represented as the slope of the line and tells us the value by which Y (dependent variable) changes given a one-unit change in X (independent variable).

A curvilinear relationship, on the other hand, allows for the slope to vary depending on the value of X. Consider the relationship in Figure 1. For dyads that have twenty or fewer prior MIDs, the slope of the curve is positive, telling us that each additional MID increases the chances for war. For dyads that have twenty to forty MIDs, the slope of the line is flat (near zero), telling us that experiencing additional MIDs does not really affect the probability of war. After forty MIDs, the probability of war is actually decreasing as we can see that the slope of the curve is now negative. To test for a curvilinear relationship, one creates another variable as Senese and Vasquez (2005) do in Model III of Tables 1, 2, and 4 that is not linear. So, the number of prior MIDs (X) variable posits a linear relationship, but if this variable is squared—number of prior MIDs squared (X^2) and added to the model—then this will capture a curvilinear relationship. If the squared term is statistically significant, as in Tables 1 and 4, Model III, then we know the relationship is in fact curvilinear. If it is not significant, as in Table 2, Model III, but the number of prior MIDs by itself is significant as in Table 2, Model II, then we would conclude that the relationship is linear. Thus, in the 1816–1945 period, each additional militarized dispute between dyads linearly increases the chances for war.

Notes

1. Note that they dismiss the small "other" category; see their discussion in footnote 54 for the reasons why.
2. Outside alliances include military alliances that involve major powers or alliances with minor powers in the same region as the militarized dispute.
3. See the footnotes to the three tables; "no alliances" is specified as the reference group for the alliance dummy variables.

Questions

1. Do arms races significantly increase the probability of war in 1816–1945? If so, what is the odds ratio and what does that mean?

2. In Table 3, which predicted probabilities for policy MIDs are not significantly different from each other due to overlapping confidence intervals? What does that imply?

3. Why do you think that the steps-to-war explanation does not fully hold for the 1946–1992 period?

Further Reading

Colaresi, M. P., and W. R. Thompson. 2005. Alliances, arms buildups and recurrent conflict: Testing a steps-to-war model. *Journal of Politics* 67 (2): 345–64.

Senese, P. D., and J. Vasquez. 2008. *The steps-to-war: An empirical study*. Princeton, NJ: Princeton University Press.

Vasquez, J. A. 2009. *The war puzzle revisited*. New York: Cambridge University Press.

Chapter 8

Rivalry and Diversionary Uses of Force

Sara McLaughlin Mitchell and Brandon C. Prins

The terrorist attacks on the World Trade Center and the Pentagon in 2001 revealed the extent to which the public rallies around its leader in times of crisis. George Bush's approval ratings increased to more than 80% following the attack, and a large majority of Americans supported the use of militarized force for retaliation.[1] An interesting question is whether a rally around the flag effect creates incentives for leaders to use force in general. Some scholars have argued that diversionary uses of force are attractive to leaders because they can increase a leader's public support and potentially his or her tenure in office.

We contend that diversionary behavior is conditional on the strategic and historical relationship among states. We expect the use of force to be more strongly tied to domestic political conditions in certain types of environments. Some states have very few opportunities for diversionary uses of force, even if domestic conditions worsen, whereas others operate in opportunity-rich environments. To date, many studies have concentrated on uses of force by the United States, a state that may have ample opportunities to use force. When we generalize diversionary arguments to a cross-national context, however, we must take into account the environment in which decision makers operate. We believe that states involved in enduring rivalries can more easily justify the use of force when domestic turmoil is high.[2] Our study thus helps to account for a puzzle

in the diversionary literature; many studies focusing on the United States and Great Britain find clear evidence of an increased likelihood in the use of force when domestic turmoil is high, whereas most cross-national studies find little or no evidence linking domestic economic and political conditions to the use of force. We believe that the latter sample contains many states with little or no opportunity to use force and that controlling for rivalry is one useful way to capture the variance in states' security environments.

We develop a model of diversionary uses of force that takes this broader environment into account. We also argue, consistent with recent formal models on diversion, that democratic states have the greatest incentives to use diversionary force but are faced with the fewest opportunities to do so (e.g., Smith 1996a). Potential adversaries hold strong beliefs about democratic states' willingness to stand firm in crises when domestic turmoil is high; the transparency of democratic regimes reduces the number of opportunities for diversionary force, even in highly competitive environments, such as enduring rivalry. On the other hand, we argue that nondemocratic states' use of force against their rivals is well timed; they take advantage of opportunities when domestic conditions are poor to improve their standing at home. Paradoxically, then, the initiation of diversionary force by nondemocratic regimes fits the pattern that we have expected traditionally from democratic states.

Source: Sara McLaughlin Mitchell and Brandon C. Prins, "Rivalry and Diversionary Uses of Force," *Journal of Conflict Resolution* 48, no. 6 (2004): 937–61. © 2004 SAGE Publications, Inc.

The study is organized as follows. First, we summarize the primary theoretical arguments in the diversionary use of force literature. Second, we argue that opportunity-rich environments, such as rivalry, offer a more appropriate environmental setting from which to test diversionary theory predictions. Our primary hypothesis is that domestic turmoil will be more likely to result in the use of militarized force by states in opportunity-rich environments of rivalry. Analysis of directed-dyadic, militarized dispute data provides support for our hypothesis, demonstrating that rivals are more likely to initiate the use of force when the inflation rate is high, but states uninvolved in enduring rivalries are actually less likely to use force when economic conditions worsen. But we demonstrate that this effect is driven largely by the diversionary behavior of nondemocratic regimes; democracies are no more or less likely to initiate force against their rivals when inflation levels rise. Our results illustrate why we must consider the international environment in which states operate when evaluating diversionary theories of conflict in cross-national settings and that regime type plays an important conditioning role in diversionary uses of force.

Diversionary Uses of Force

State leaders have a strong desire to remain in office, and their chances of doing so depend on their ability to manage domestic and foreign policies.[3] The notion of using force to divert attention away from domestic problems stems from the sociological literature on in-groups and out-groups (e.g., Coser 1956). When faced with a threat from an external source, individual members of a group tend to become more cohesive and supportive of their leader. A plethora of empirical studies find evidence of a rally around the flag effect (e.g., Mueller 1973), or an increase in a leader's popularity during an international crisis.[4] Because leaders know that the public is more likely to rally around them when faced with an external threat, they have incentives to draw attention to their enemies, perhaps through the use of militarized force.

Given the rally effect, leaders who face domestic discontent may engage in international conflict to generate events that obscure problems being experienced at home (Ward and Widmaier 1982). Such manipulation is also designed, particularly in democratic states, to demonstrate leadership skills and competency in governing.[5] Indeed, risky foreign policy moves may be used by politically threatened governments to boost their flagging poll ratings by solidifying public support prior to an election (Ward and Widmaier 1982; Stoll 1984; Levy 1989a). Furthermore, belligerent foreign policies may offer elites a way to rationalize their control over the levers of the state (see Schumpeter 1939; Levy 1989a).

Although early research (e.g., Rummel 1963) that focused on the relationship between internal conflict (such as protests, riots, civil wars, etc.) and external conflict (interstate war) found very little support for diversionary behavior, more recent empirical evidence does tend to suggest at least some externalization by political elites (see, e.g., Ward and Widmaier 1982; Stoll 1984; Ostrom and Job 1986; James and Oneal 1991; Morgan and Bickers 1992; DeRouen 1995; Enterline and Gleditsch 2000).[6] These more recent studies focus less on domestic violence and more on political and economic weakness, such as high inflation and unemployment, slow economic growth, and low (general or partisan) approval ratings. This newer research also focuses heavily on electoral periods. Evidence uncovered by Lebow (1981), for example, shows crisis initiation and escalation to be related to domestic discontent. Stoll (1984) concluded that in the United States at least, presidential uses of force were targeted toward the electoral calendar. Other studies have found some indication of a partisan effect. Morgan and Bickers (1992) and James and Hristoulas (1994) both discovered that political opposition was associated with diversionary behavior.

Theoretical models of foreign policy decision making also appear to establish electoral incentives for using force abroad (see, e.g., Smith 1996a; Richards et al. 1993; Blainey 1973). According to Downs and

Rocke (1995, 138), preference divergence between political elites and the electorate, coupled with the asymmetrical level of information that often exists when it comes to international affairs, naturally creates incentives for leaders to manipulate foreign policy events.[7] Smith (1996a) reaches a similar conclusion. In his model, electoral incentives rarely cause a head of state to behave tentatively.[8] Smith argues that

> if foreign policy evaluation is likely to be important at the next election then the range of international conditions under which intervention occurs increases... when the voters' evaluation of the government's foreign policy performance affects the outcome of an election, the model shows that suboptimal foreign policy decisions are made. Since the government cares, not only about taking the best course of action for the nation, but also about getting reelected, it is biased towards violent behavior. (p. 147)

As we discuss below, democratic leaders may have strong incentives to engage in violent behavior to enhance electoral fortunes, but their enemies know this as well, which ironically creates fewer opportunities for democratic leaders to engage in diversion.

The diversionary literature identifies a variety of domestic factors that increase the likelihood that a leader will use militarized force. These factors include a leader's public approval, elections, domestic economic conditions, partisan approval, and internal conflict. Most of the studies focusing on these variables reach the same general conclusion—that a leader is more likely to use force when the state is experiencing domestic turmoil. Such domestic turmoil includes declining levels of general or partisan approval, worsening economic conditions, and increasing levels of domestic violence. One limitation of this monadic view of diversionary behavior is that it does not really capture the international strategic environment well. In the next section, we elaborate on factors that increase or decrease opportunities to use diversionary force, focusing on rivalry and regime type.

Opportunity for Diversionary Uses of Force

It is not difficult to find historical anecdotes of diversionary behavior, such as the Crimean War, the Russo-Japanese War, and World War I (Levy 1989a). However, cross-national statistical analysis of the relationship between internal and external conflict has produced very little cumulative knowledge (Levy 1989a). Although more recent studies focusing on domestic factors, such as the state of the economy and elections, provide more support for diversionary arguments, these results are not fully consistent even in the U.S. case. For instance, Hess and Orphanides (1995) observed that U.S. conflict behavior increased dramatically as a result of elections and economic downturns (see also Russett 1989, 1990). Yet, Gaubatz (1991) reported that democratic states rarely engage in war around election time. Stoll's (1984) research, interestingly, can account for both observations if a state of war is controlled for. That is, Stoll found that uses of force declined prior to an election during peacetime, but they slightly increased during wartime.[9] When one broadens the spatial domain beyond uses of force by the United States, evidence for diversionary behavior may be even more questionable (see Leeds and Davis 1997).

Several explanations have been posited to help explain the inconsistencies in the empirical diversionary literature. Some scholars have argued that externalization is only one option leaders may choose in the face of domestic turmoil; other options include repression[10] (Enterline and Gleditsch 2000; Gelpi 1997b) and resolving international disagreements to free up resources for domestic purposes (Bennett and Nordstrom 2000). Other scholars focus on the differences in diversionary behavior across various regime types (Gelpi 1997b; Miller 1995; Russett 1989) or on the influence of the military on a state leader's decision to use force abroad (Dassel and Reinhardt 1999).

Smith (1996a) provides another perspective, contending that selection effects may help to account for the inconsistencies in the empirical relationship between domestic turmoil and the use of militarized force. Leaders, especially democratic ones, have incentives to engage in more adventurous foreign policies when they are experiencing domestic problems. However, their potential adversaries realize this and, as such, are less likely to target them at precisely the time when diversionary tactics would be most beneficial.

> Just when a democratic leader most needs opportunities to demonstrate his competence, foreign states that might provide a democrat with a tempting diversionary target have incentives to make themselves unavailable for conflict by avoiding controversial policies that might make them appropriate targets. (Clark 2003, 1017)

Leeds and Davis (1997) find empirical support for this argument.[11] An analysis of 18 industrialized democracies reveals no significant relationship between deteriorating economic conditions, electoral cycles, and the use of militarized force. They do find, however, that democracies are more likely to be targeted when their economy is strong, implying that leaders are careful not to target democratic states at the times when they would be most likely to respond. The conclusion is that democratic leaders have incentives to use diversionary tactics, but they are faced with few opportunities to do so.[12]

Selection effects and opportunity represent two sides of the same coin. To date, most research on diversionary behavior has assumed the probability of military action to be invariant across space and time. Meernik and Waterman (1996, 575) write,

> We have no way to evaluate presidential decision making when a use of force was considered, but not utilized. We are forced to assume that presidential decision making in a quarter when no use of force took place is analogous to decision making in a crisis where no force was used.

Focusing on the United States, Meernik (1994) tries to identify instances when a president has incentives to use force but chooses not to. This includes

situations in which there is a perceived threat to the territorial security of the United States or its allies, a threat to diplomatic personnel or U.S. citizens abroad, or a threat posed by ideological opponents of the United States (i.e., communists), among others. Meernik identifies 458 opportunities for the United States to use force between 1948 and 1988. His analysis reveals that international factors best predict when a president will use force, given an opportunity to do so. Contrary to Ostrom and Job (1986), he finds that domestic factors, such as the misery index and presidential popularity, have no discernable effect on whether the president will use force.

Meernik's (1994) study of opportunities is limited to the United States, which makes it difficult to generalize more broadly to other states. "With its status as a superpower and global range of interests, external opportunities for crisis activity always exist for the United States" (James and Hristoulas 1994, 339).[13] Other studies that do broaden the spatial domain (Leeds and Davis 1997) include countries with very different external opportunities. Some of the democratic states in Leeds and Davis's (1997) sample, for example, operate in an opportunity-rich environment (Israel), whereas others do not (the Netherlands). If the strategic and historical context of state interaction conditions foreign policy behavior, then the impact of domestic political and economic conditions on elite decision making may only be felt in enduring rivalry settings. Therefore, it is precisely in these types of hostile situations that we should look for evidence of externalization.

However, many formal models of diversionary behavior (especially Smith 1996a) suggest that diversionary motives operate differently for democratic and nondemocratic states, which implies that rivalry environments may have differential effects, depending on the regime type of the rival states. Although democratic leaders have the greatest incentives to use diversionary force, they may be faced with the fewest opportunities to do so. The transparency of democratic regimes sends a clear signal to their adversaries about the willingness of such states to stand firm in crises when domestic turmoil is high.

One implication of this is that democracies involved in rivalries may find themselves with fewer opportunities to use force against their rival when they have the strongest diversionary pressures to do so. In other words, the findings that democracies are more likely to be targeted in good economic times (Leeds and Davis 1997) may carry over to enduring rivalries that involve democratic states. We turn now to a more elaborate discussion about the context of rivalry and its impact on diversionary uses of force.

The Context of Rivalry

Historical context cannot be overlooked when evaluating the foreign policy decision making of state leaders. Indeed, the perceptions, misperceptions, and decisions of political elites reflect, in part, the enmity, mutual suspicion, and competitiveness of relations, both at the government and individual levels. The concept of rivalry has emerged, in part, to explain the divergent foreign policy behavior of states with extended adversarial relationships. Hensel (1998, 163) states that we can think of enduring rivals as

> actors whose relations are characterized by disagreement or competition over some stakes that are viewed as important, where each perceives that the other poses a significant security threat, and where this competition and threat perception last for substantial periods of time.

What distinguishes rivalry and nonrivalry environments is the presence of competition in rivalry, which increases the chances for militarized conflict.

> Rivalry means that the threat is immediate, serious, and may involve military force. Thus, competition in a rivalry . . . has a hostility dimension involving the significant likelihood of the use of military force. (Diehl and Goertz 2000, 24)

Furthermore, we can think of rivalry along a continuum, with isolated rivals at one end, enduring rivals at the other end, and proto rivals in between (Diehl and Goertz 2000; Hensel 1998, 1999).

The empirical record appears to demonstrate quite convincingly that enduring rivals behave very differently than most other states in the international system. According to Goertz and Diehl (1993, 148),

> 45 percent of militarized disputes take place in the context of enduring rivalries. Enduring rivalries are also the setting for over half of the interstate wars since 1816; the most serious enduring rivalries are almost eight times more likely to experience a war than pairs of states in isolated conflict.[14]

Evidence also suggests that crisis bargaining between rival states involves, among other things, a higher level of violence, an inability to resolve the fundamental issues at stake, and an unwillingness to accept outside assistance in settling existing quarrels (Brecher and James 1988; Brecher 1993; Hensel 1998). As such, crises between rival states are more likely to escalate to the level of full-scale war. Goertz (1994, 210) writes, "A rivalry sets the stage for escalating tensions in a dispute to culminate in war. Disputes without a violent past are more likely to be resolved peacefully, or at least without resort to all out force." Given the small number of enduring rivalries relative to all other dyadic relationships, we see that a large amount of the violent conflict in the international system is accounted for by these hostile and highly competitive relationships.

Enduring rivalries represent a specific type of strategic relationship. Indeed, similar to interstate crises, enduring rivalries present a set of conditions that facilitate foreign policy decision making. According to Snyder (1994, 316), for example,

> An international crisis is international politics in a microcosm. That is to say, a crisis tends to highlight or force to the surface a wide range of factors and processes which are central to international politics in general.

Rivalries, we think, present an analogous set of cases. Not only do settings of rivalry challenge assumptions that stipulate event independence, but such relationships also enable scholars to acquire more nuanced insights into the factors that contribute to foreign policy decision making as well as the outbreak of war.[15] Hensel (1998, 165) insists that specifying rivalry situations "allows us to generate and test more refined theories, and offers the possibility of more meaningful results than more general studies that do not distinguish between different types of contexts." Consequently, without controlling for this environment, our theoretical models risk misinterpreting the foreign policy decision making of political elites.

To date, rivalry contexts have been used to test theoretical conjectures from a variety of conflict models (Diehl and Goertz 2000; Goertz 1994; Hensel 1998). For example, the theoretical logic behind power transition depends in part on dissatisfaction. A rising power will typically only issue a challenge if the dominant state is perceived as a competitor and adversary. Arms races and deterrence models also require an environment of fear and insecurity. That is, without an opponent, such military buildups and dissuasion attempts make little sense. Vasquez (1996a) maintains that rivalries involving territorial disputes are more likely to experience war than rivalries over other issues.[16] Therefore, in all of these conflict models, historical context is expected to have an important conditioning effect on foreign policy decision making. But as Goertz (1994) points out, we need to go beyond the use of rivalry as a case selection mechanism and consider the causal impact of the rivalry environment more carefully:

> Given that rivalries have been used to study power transitions, arms races, and deterrence it is perhaps not surprising that so much international conflict occurs within this context. What these studies fail to capture, with their use of the concept as only a case selection tool, is that the rivalry context may play a *causal* role in determining which arms race, power transition, etc., escalate to war. . . . That past conflicts condition current ones and future expectations, that leaders learn realpolitik lessons, and that peoples learn to hate each other all mean that theories of enduring rivalries are historical theories. (p. 213)

Diversionary theories may also be more accurately assessed in adversarial contexts. Indeed, given the deep mistrust and animosity between rival states, political elites can more easily manipulate foreign affairs to satisfy their own personal and/or political objectives. That is, using military force for domestic political purposes in an opportunity-rich environment of rivalry does not present the same difficulties for decision makers. The mutual anticipation of violent coercion provides the pretext and justification for military actions that may have little strategic value. Moreover, political leaders in rivalry situations can effectively blame domestic turmoil (such as economic weakness) on foreign enemies, further concealing and diverting attention away from domestic political problems. A rivalry context, then, conditions the relationship between domestic weakness and externalization, facilitating and legitimating the use of military force to conceal political insecurity.

We believe that the rivalry context can increase the probability of diversionary conflict in both direct and indirect ways. Rivalry has a *direct* effect on the propensity for leaders to divert because they can identify a clear target against which to divert. In this sense, we would expect leaders to get involved in militarized disputes against their rivals when they are faced with increased domestic turmoil.

> When circumstances make a confrontation with one's real opponent too dangerous and costly, but at the same time the domestic political and international benefits of pursuing a rivalry are attractive (e.g., domestic political integration, personal or party politics, distraction from other problems), one is tempted to look for a rival with whom one can safely and plausibly quarrel.[17] (Schroeder 1999, 78)

It is also easier to exaggerate a threat against a rival state (as opposed to a nonrival state) in times of domestic turmoil.

Crises of legitimacy, calls to "rally 'round the flag," and the general constraints of the public are other domestic factors that may at times be critical to rivalry dynamics. These same factors may also tend to encourage politicians to exaggerate the threats associated with rival policies. (Thompson 1999, 22)

Enterline and Gleditsch (2000, 28) make a similar argument about diversionary uses of force being more plausible in highly threatening environments:

Diversion through foreign conflict involvement is likely to reduce popular dissent only when leaders can capitalize on a hostile interstate environment where the relevant target public may be persuaded to consider alleged threats plausible.... Some states have a large supply of long-standing rivals or plausible enemies that leaders may resort to in times of domestic pressures ... the impact of domestic pressure on the probability of a leader resorting to force abroad is likely to be mediated by leaders' *opportunities* to invoke credible threats to externalize through conflict abroad.

In addition to the direct effect of rivalry discussed above, we also believe that the rivalry context can have an *indirect* effect on the propensity for a leader to use force in times of domestic weakness. Some rivalries, such as the cold war rivalry between the United States and Soviet Union, involve the use of force in regional areas that are related to the overall strategic rivalry. In this regard, even if a state does not get involved in a militarized dispute directly against its rival, a regional dispute may be viewed as having importance for the rivalry in general (Mitchell and Moore 2002).[18] The indirect effect implies that being involved in an enduring rivalry will influence a leader's decision to become involved in a militarized dispute or crisis, even if the state faces nonrival opponents.

Our notion of rivalry as environment is similar to Most and Starr's (1989) concept of opportunity.[19] Drawing from the work of Harold and Margaret Sprout (1965), Most and Starr identify the ecological triad, which consists of an entity, its environment, and the relationship between the entity and its environment. The environment affects "the probability of certain outcomes. The environment not only presents the decision maker with what is possible, but what course of action is more (or less) likely under those particular circumstances" (Most and Starr 1989, 27–28). A leader's decision to use force to divert attention away from domestic problems depends on the strategic environment in which he or she is operating. States involved in enduring rivalries understand that their environment offers greater opportunities for using diversionary force. Leaders of states without rivals will find it more difficult to identify an external enemy and justify the use of force abroad to their constituents. This leads us to our primary hypothesis:

Hypothesis 1: Domestic turmoil will be more likely to result in the initiation of militarized force by states in opportunity-rich environments of rivalry.

We assert that the environment of rivalry modifies the relationship between domestic turmoil and the use of force. Because many diversionary scholars have focused their analyses on uses of force by the United States, they have selected cases in which the opportunity to use force is generally high, particularly during the cold war rivalry. When we generalize diversionary arguments to a broader set of states, however, we must consider the strategic environment in which these states operate. An environment of rivalry produces greater opportunities for diversionary uses of force.[20]

As noted above, however, the influence of rivalry environments may have differential impacts on the probability of force initiation, depending on a state's regime type. The transparency of democratic regimes makes it more difficult for democratic leaders to seize opportunities to divert public attention away from domestic turmoil. A strategic model of diversion implies that we would not find a strong relationship between domestic turmoil and rivalry for democratic states; nondemocratic states would avoid tangling with their democratic rivals when their economies are weak, elections are approaching, and so forth. On the other hand, nondemocratic states may have the ability to initiate force against rivals when domestic turmoil is high.

Hypothesis 2: Increasing domestic turmoil will have little or no effect on the initiation of militarized force by democratic states in opportunity-rich environments of rivalry.

Hypothesis 3: Increasing domestic turmoil will be more likely to result in the initiation of militarized force by nondemocratic states in opportunity-rich environments of rivalry.

Research Design and Data

Our theoretical hypotheses focus on the conditions that make diversionary uses of force by a given state more or less likely. We are interested in examining the relationship between domestic turmoil and the use of force, taking the potential environment of rivalry into account.[21] To test the relationship between domestic turmoil and the use of militarized force in rival and nonrival environments, we use the militarized interstate dispute (MID) (Jones, Bremer, and Singer 1996) data set, coupled with the world development indicators provided by the World Bank (1997). Using EUGene, a basic directed-dyadic data set is constructed for the years from 1960 to 2001.[22] The World Bank data have been merged with the conflict, polity, and capability data provided by EUGene. This data set allows us to examine the direct effect of rivalry on diversionary uses of force for all COW system members during the years 1960 to 2001 and to model effectively who does what to whom (Ray 2001). Not only does this data set enable one of the first empirical examinations of diversionary uses of force in a cross-national context, it also provides a dyadic framework with appropriate temporal and cross-sectional controls, which have been largely absent from most empirical studies on diversionary theory.

Measuring Rivalry

The concept of rivalry is clearly a dyadic phenomenon; hostility, tension, and militarized conflict between states can create a rivalry between them. Numerous scholars have identified criteria that can be used to identify the pairs of states in the international system that are rivals. Many of these criteria involve a certain number of militarized disputes in a given time period.[23] In this study, we adopt Diehl and Goertz's (2000) conceptualization of rivalry, which emphasizes spatial consistency, time, and militarized competitiveness. They define an enduring rivalry as a pair of states that have fought a minimum of six militarized disputes over a time period of 20 or more years. Diehl and Goertz (2000) code an enduring rivalry as ending when the states involved have experienced no militarized disputes for 10 years.[24]

Directed-Dyadic Data Set

The unit of analysis is the politically relevant directed dyad-year. Thus, we sample from all possible dyadic pairings of states by selecting those dyads that contain contiguous states (via a direct land border) or at least one major power.[25] Directed dyads are coded in both directions. For example, relations between the United States and Cuba in 1960 would be captured in two cases: the United States—Cuba and Cuba—United States. We have a total of 91,665 politically relevant directed-dyadic cases from 1960 to 2001. This design makes it possible to model the decision by one state to threaten, display, or use force against another state while capturing the effects of domestic turmoil for one side only. We create a dichotomous enduring rivalry measure that equals 1 if the two states in the dyad are enduring rivals based on Diehl and Goertz's (2000) criteria.[26] We then create an interaction term that combines our measure of rivalry with our measure of domestic turmoil. The interaction term shows how the environment of rivalry affects a state's decision to become involved in a militarized dispute, based on the amount of domestic turmoil the state is experiencing.

We measure domestic turmoil using data provided by the World Bank. The 2001 World Development Survey provides information on 207 nation-states from 1960 to 1999. Included in the survey are numerous series measuring different elements of economic, social, and political development. With 207 nations and 40 years, this theoretically would provide 8,280 country-year observations. However, missing data for many years and many countries limit the available observations to slightly more than 4,000. Of the many data series provided by the World Bank, we selected the consumer price index (CPI) as a measure of domestic turmoil. As is customary in economics, we measure inflation as the percentage change in the consumer price index (first-differenced CPI).[27]

The misery index (combination of unemployment and inflation figures) represents the most common measure of domestic unrest in the diversionary literature (see, e.g., Ostrom and Job 1986; James and Oneal 1991; DeRouen 1995; Meernik and Waterman 1996). Our measure of differenced CPI is meant to be an analogous measure of the domestic environment. Although there are ample data for both inflation and unemployment in the U.S. case, the situation becomes more difficult when we move to a cross-national sample. Due to a serious missing data problem for unemployment cross-nationally in the World Bank data set, we chose CPI to preserve the larger set of observations. We believe this decision is justified. Fordham (1998) includes separate measures of inflation and unemployment and maintains that they have similar effects on diversionary uses of force.

The data on conflict initiation come from the Correlates of War (COW) MID data set.[28] The 3.01 version of the MID data set contains 2,323 disputes for the period from 1816 to 2001 (Ghosn and Palmer 2003). Militarized disputes, according to Jones, Bremer, and Singer (1996, 166), are "confrontations that [lead] politicians to invest energy, attention, resources, and credibility in an effort to thwart, resist, intimidate, discredit, or damage those representing the other side." Given both their public nature and level of militarization, then, militarized disputes (MIDs) are suitable events for testing a diversionary hypothesis.[29] We code an MID participant as the initiator of a new militarized dispute if it is on side A and originated the dispute (i.e., fought on the first day). Although diversionary uses of force could plausibly occur when states are targeted (by responding to threats, displays, or uses of force by other states), we believe the clearest manifestations of diversionary behavior are decisions to initiate militarized disputes.[30]

Finally, we include four control variables in our empirical models: relative capabilities, peace years, geographical distance, and joint democracy. Capabilities are measured using the COW national capabilities data, in which each state's capability score is calculated as its percentage share of the total system capabilities.[31] This is based on all three COW capability dimensions (military, economic, and demographic). A relative power measure is created and captures the ratio of state A's COW capabilities (CINC) score to combined capabilities of state A and state B (A/A + B). We anticipate the effect of this variable to be positive because stronger states will attack when the probability of success is high and they have a clear power advantage (Leeds 2003a; Bennett and Stam 2000). We also include a measure of peace years that indicates the number of years since the states in the dyad last fought a militarized dispute, and as this measure increases, the probability of a militarized dispute in the dyad should diminish (e.g., Raknerud and Hegre 1997; Beck 1999; Reed 2000; Beck, Katz, and Tucker 1998).

Distance is measured using the great circle distance formula. Basically, this measures the distance in miles between capital cities, controlling for the curvature of the earth. Countries contiguous by land have a distance score of zero. Because the analysis below only considers politically relevant dyads, the distance measure is, by definition, restricted to those country pairings with a major power on one side. This operationalization makes theoretical sense because major powers alone typically possess the capabilities to project military power away from their borders. However, even for the major powers in the international system, distance should decrease militarized dispute involvement.[32]

A control for joint democracy is included in the statistical model. Dyadically, the evidence for a democratic peace remains robust. Democratic states not only appear to avoid militarized conflict with one another, but conflicts of interest that do arise are also more likely to be settled through third-party mediation and juridical arbitration (e.g., Russett and Oneal 2001). We use Polity IV to categorize states' regime types. Dyads in which both states reach a minimum of 6 on the democracy score are considered jointly democratic. In subsequent models, we separate democratic initiators from nondemocratic initiators and employ the same criteria for democracy (6 or higher on the Polity IV scale). Descriptive statistics for all variables are reported in the appendix.[33]

Empirical Analysis

To assess the relationship between domestic turmoil and conflict initiation, we use a pooled time-series estimator. With the use of pooled data, most likely the standard regression assumptions of constant variance and no autoregression are violated (Sayrs 1989). Indeed, nonindependence of observations may be a result of temporal, spatial, or both temporal and spatial contamination. It is easy to imagine different temporal observations correlated within a cross-sectional unit, different spatial observations correlated within a temporal unit, or perhaps even different temporal observations correlated across different cross-sectional units. Without controlling for this variation, we risk misspecifying the relationship between domestic turmoil and conflict involvement.

To control for the potential cross-unit and cross-time correlations, we employ a general estimating equation (GEE). The quasi-likelihood GEE model uses a population-averaged approach to estimation and is therefore well designed for pooled time-series data. In particular, the GEE approach allows for the specification of a within-group correlation structure. Such an error structure specification may help control temporal dependence within panels and thus reduce inefficiency and coefficient bias. According to Zorn (2001, 475), population-averaged models are "valuable for making comparisons across groups or subpopulations." With directed-dyadic data, this model specification seems particularly appropriate. In each of the estimated GEE models, we control for temporal dependence, using a peace-years count variable and three cubic splines (Beck, Katz, and Tucker 1998).

We begin by estimating a model for all potential initiators in politically relevant dyads. This analysis is designed to test hypothesis 1, which predicts diversionary uses of force to be more likely in environments of enduring rivalry. In Table 1, we present the estimation results from a GEE model, with annual MID initiation as the dependent variable and differenced CPI (natural log), relative capabilities, peace years, distance (natural log), and joint democracy as the independent variables, plus the cubic splines for temporal nonindependence (not shown). We also include our measure of rivalry and the interaction between rivalry and domestic turmoil (differenced CPI). We expect increases in inflation in an environment of rivalry to militarize the foreign policy process, although it may have no effect or even decrease the chances for conflict initiation in nonrivalry environments.

The results in Table 1 confirm our theoretical expectations. The rivalry variable is in the predicted positive direction and highly significant ($p = .000$); a state involved in an enduring rivalry is more likely to initiate militarized disputes in any given year.[34] This is to be expected given the measure of rivalry that we employ. More important, however, are the results relating to domestic conditions. We find domestic turmoil to be negatively and significantly related to conflict initiation in nonrival environments (the parameter for ln-differenced CPI). In other words, in opportunity-poor international environments, domestic turmoil tends to discourage dispute initiation. If this relationship is confirmed in future studies, it would indicate that domestic weakness typically tends to push political elites away from militarized conflict. For states not involved in enduring rivalries, militarized conflict initiation may occur during times of more prosperous domestic economic conditions.

Although nonrival states may avoid conflict during domestic turmoil, the exact opposite relationship holds for states involved in enduring rivalries. The positive sign for the interaction coefficient indicates that there is an added effect of domestic turmoil on the conflict propensity of rival states ($p = .002$).[35] This indicates that domestic economic weakness is particularly dangerous for rival states. As the inflation rate increases, rival states are more likely to use military force, which supports our primary theoretical conjecture. It appears that the foreign policy

decision making of rival leaders may differ fundamentally from the leaders of nonrival states. Thus, the evidence here supports our contention that rivalry conditions the relationship between domestic turmoil and conflict initiation. Models that purport to test diversionary theories without controlling for rivalry appear to be underspecified. Indeed, these results suggest that diversionary theory may apply best to states involved in relationships of rivalry.

We can see the conditional impact of domestic turmoil when we examine the predicted probabilities for militarized dispute initiation in Table 2. A one standard deviation decrease in inflation in nonrivalry environments drops the probability of MID initiation from .0062 to .0047. The absolute change is small, but the relative decrease is around 25%. Across the entire range of the inflation measure, the probability of MID initiation drops by 75% in nonrival dyads as we move from the minimum to the maximum value. In rivalry environments, domestic economic weakness increases the probability of conflict initiation from .034 to .044. Again, the absolute change may not appear all that large, but relatively speaking, this increase does reflect a 30% increase in the probability of MID initiation. Across the entire range of the inflation measure, the probability of MID initiation increases by 250% in enduring rivalry dyads as we move from the minimum to the maximum value.[36] These substantive effects are plotted in Figure 1 as well.[37] These results suggest that rival nations both have more opportunities to use force and are more likely to take advantage of diversionary incentives when domestic turmoil increases.

The control variables in the full models perform as expected, and all are highly significant. Consistent with the democratic peace literature, we find that joint democracy strongly reduces MID initiation ($p = .000$). We find a negative and significant relationship between years at peace and annual MID initiation. The longer a state has been involved in a militarized dispute with a specific country (or the greater the peace years with that country), the less likely its chances for future conflict initiation against that country ($p = .002$). Distance between capitals

Table 1   Full GEE Model Results for Directed-Dyadic MID Initiation, Politically Relevant Dyads, and Cubic Splines as Temporal Control

Variable	Unstandardized Beta	Standard Error
Enduring rival dyad	2.005***	.151
ln-differenced CPI	−0.040***	.015
Rivalry-differenced CPI interaction	0.078***	.025
Relative capabilities	0.533***	.176
Peace years	−0.020***	.007
ln distance	−0.379***	.047
Joint democracy	−0.626***	.167
Constant	−0.884**	.359

Note: $n = 37,589$; GEE = general estimating equation; MID = militarized interstate dispute; CPI = consumer price index. Wald $\chi^2(10) = 810.55$ ($p = .0000$). Dependent variable is directed-dyadic MID initiation. Spline coefficients not shown.

**$p < .05$. ***$p < .01$.

Table 2   Predicted Probabilities for Directed-Dyadic MID Initiation (All Cases)

Variable	Predicted Probability
No rivalry, 1 SD below mean of differenced CPI	.0062
No rivalry, 1 SD above mean of differenced CPI	.0047
Rivalry, 1 SD below mean of differenced CPI	.034
Rivalry, 1 SD above mean of differenced CPI	.044

Note: MID = militarized interstate dispute; CPI = consumer price index.

also tends to decrease conflict propensities, even for major powers ($p = .000$). Projecting force abroad remains costly and thus tends to discourage the threat, show, or use of military force to settle contentious issues. Finally, the positive sign on relative capabilities implies that challengers initiate the use of force when they have a distinct capability advantage and hence a high probability of success ($p = .000$).[38]

These results demonstrate the importance of rivalry as a source of opportunity for diversionary behavior, but we also argued above that the effect may be contingent on a state's regime type. Hypotheses 2 and 3 suggest that democracies may find it difficult to use force in times of turmoil due to the transparency of their regimes, whereas nondemocracies will find it easier to use force against rivals in bad economic times.

Tables 3 and 4 present empirical results and predicted probabilities from a GEE model of MID initiation for democratic initiators only, whereas Tables 5 and 6 present results for nondemocratic initiators.

Figure 1   Probability of Militarized Interstate Dispute (MID) Initiation for Rival States and Nonrival States

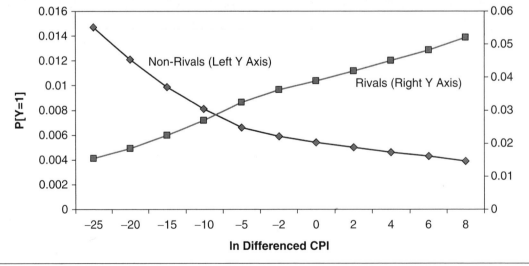

Note: CPI = consumer price index.

It appears that democratic initiators do not seize on domestic turmoil to divert attention to foreign affairs. Neither the variable for inflation nor the interaction term is statistically significant in Table 3. Table 4 shows also that the predicted probabilities for MID initiation by democratic states do not change, based on increases or decreases in the inflation rate. We infer from these results that democratic initiators typically shy away from the use of military force, due to institutional constraints and norms of political compromise, and that changes in domestic economic conditions appear to have little impact on democratic MID initiation decisions. Furthermore, even those democratic states in rivalry fail to initiate during periods of domestic weakness. We believe this indicates strategic behavior on the part of opponents. The transparency of democratic regimes enables potential targets to avoid foreign policy actions that might be seized on by democratic leaders for political effect.[39]

Nondemocratic initiators, however, fail to signal efficiently domestic conditions that heighten the probability of dispute initiation. In opportunity-rich environments, nondemocratic states initiate militarized disputes as economic conditions deteriorate. In Table 5, we can see that the parameter for the rivalry-inflation interaction is positive and highly significant. Indeed, as our measure of inflation increases by one standard deviation, the probability of MID initiation increases by nearly 25% (see Table 6). Diversionary moves by nondemocratic initiators are specifically directed at rival states. This suggests not only that rivals offer a politically acceptable target but also that targets fail to observe the domestic conditions that compel diversion. This regime-type distinction is also displayed in Figures 2 and 3. Figure 3, in particular, shows that the likelihood of conflict initiation increases as domestic turmoil increases, but only for nondemocratic initiators. We see that domestic turmoil tends to push rival states into violent foreign policy action but also that the transparency of democratic institutions diminishes opportunities for such diversionary moves by democratic states.[40]

It is clear that these empirical results support our conjecture that domestic turmoil increases the use of military force in opportunity-rich environments. Domestic turmoil tends to have an opposite impact, depending on whether states exist in opportunity-rich (rivalry) or opportunity-poor (nonrivalry) environments. But the effect of the rivalry context is dependent on regime type; unlike democratic leaders, autocrats are able to capitalize on domestic weaknesses when targeting their rival states. In short, both rivalry and regime type have profound effects on opportunities for diversionary uses of force.

Table 3 GEE Model Results for Directed-Dyadic MID Initiation, Politically Relevant Dyads, and Cubic Splines as Temporal Control (Democratic Initiators Only)

Variable	Unstandardized Beta	Standard Error
Enduring rival dyad	2.123***	.206
ln-differenced CPI	−0.00008	.036
Rivalry-differenced CPI interaction	0.0007	.053
Relative capabilities	0.748***	.239
Peace years	−0.027***	.011
ln distance	−0.0474***	.066
Democracy level of target	−0.053***	.020
Constant	−0.325	.501

Note: $n = 24,611$; GEE = general estimating equation; MID = militarized interstate dispute; CPI = consumer price index. Wald $\chi^2(10) = 500.55$ ($p = .0000$). Dependent variable is directed-dyadic MID initiation.

***$p < .01$.

Table 4 Predicted Probabilities for Directed-Dyadic MID Initiation (Democratic Initiators Only)

Variable	Predicted Probability
No rivalry, 1 SD below mean of differenced CPI	.0047
No rivalry, 1 SD above mean of differenced CPI	.0047
Rivalry, 1 SD below mean of differenced CPI	.038
Rivalry, 1 SD above mean of differenced CPI	.038

Note: MID = militarized interstate dispute; CPI = consumer price index.

Table 6 Predicted Probabilities for Directed-Dyadic MID Initiation (Nondemocratic Initiators Only)

Variable	Predicted Probability
No rivalry, 1 SD below mean of differenced CPI	.0050
No rivalry, 1 SD above mean of differenced CPI	.0042
Rivalry, 1 SD below mean of differenced CPI	.029
Rivalry, 1 SD above mean of differenced CPI	.036

Note: MID = militarized interstate dispute; CPI = consumer price index.

Table 5 GEE Model Results for Directed-Dyadic MID Initiation, Politically Relevant Dyads, and Cubic Splines as Temporal Control (Nondemocratic Initiators Only)

Variable	Unstandardized Beta	Standard Error
Enduring rival dyad	2.099***	.219
ln-differenced CPI	−0.041**	.016
Rivalry-differenced CPI interaction	0.089***	.029
Relative capabilities	1.028***	.302
Peace years	−0.017*	.009
ln distance	−0.310***	.077
Democracy level of target	0.090***	.022
Constant	−1.938***	.590

Note: n = 12,978; GEE = general estimating equation; MID = militarized interstate dispute; CPI = consumer price index. Wald $\chi^2(10)$ = 365.99 (p = .0000). Dependent variable is directed-dyadic MID initiation.

*$p < .10$. **$p < .05$. ***$p < .01$.

Conclusion

A diversionary theory of war has ample anecdotal support. From World War I, to the Falkland Islands, to Grenada and Panama, scholars continue to insist that military action often stems from political and economic problems at home. In fact, nearly 30 years ago, Rosecrance (1963) went so far as to suggest that elite insecurities take nations to war. Despite such an assertion, however, aggregate studies that attempt to tie domestic turmoil to the use of military force have uncovered mixed empirical evidence to date. Indeed, even studies on U.S. foreign policy behavior during the cold war cannot completely eliminate alternative explanations for the use of military force. As we move away from the U.S. case or attempt to generalize to a larger set of countries, confidence in the hypothesized relationship between domestic turmoil and externalization declines dramatically.

We agree with Meernik (1994) and Smith (1996a) that selection effects pose a very real problem for studies of diversionary behavior. Scholars cannot continue to assume that opportunities for using military force remain constant over time or that the decision to avoid militarizing an opportunity is the same as an opportunity never having presented itself

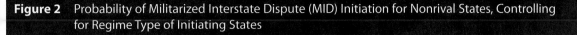

Figure 2   Probability of Militarized Interstate Dispute (MID) Initiation for Nonrival States, Controlling for Regime Type of Initiating States

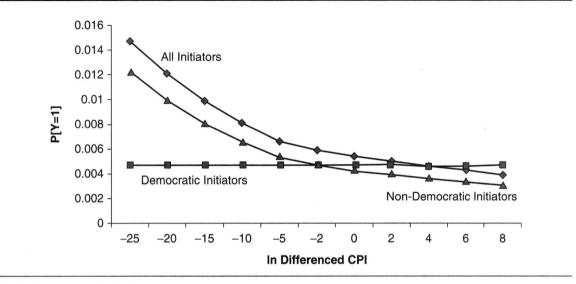

Note: CPI = consumer price index.

Figure 3   Probability of Militarized Interstate Dispute (MID) Initiation for Rival States, Controlling for Regime Type of Initiating States

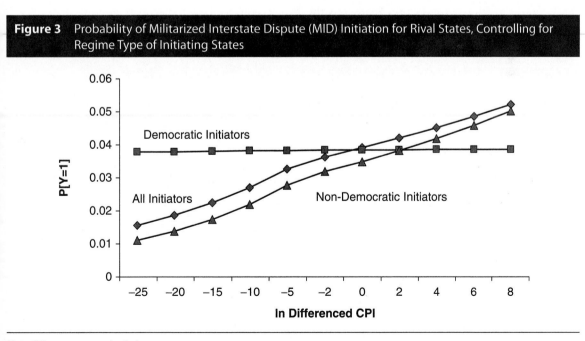

Note: CPI = consumer price index.

in the first place. We think that the external environment presents certain prospects for state leaders. That is, we contend that foreign policy decision making will be different in opportunity-rich environments compared with opportunity-poor environments. We consider the context of rivalry to be an important conditioning factor in diversionary uses of force. States involved in enduring rivalries presumably can more easily defend diversionary moves when economic conditions deteriorate, given the presence of such a hostile adversary. However, democratic and nondemocratic states are faced with different international environments. Because potential adversaries hold strong beliefs about democratic states' willingness to stand firm in crises when domestic turmoil is high, the transparency of democratic regimes reduces the number of opportunities for diversionary force, even in highly competitive environments, such as enduring rivalry.

We present empirical evidence that supports the conditioning impact of rivalry contexts. Using a directed-dyadic data set, we observe that domestic turmoil tends to increase the probability of military action in rivalry settings but actually has the opposite effect in nonrivalry settings. In other words, economic weakness tends to increase the likelihood of a state using military force if it is involved in an enduring rivalry. We also show that the results are driven largely by the behavior of nondemocratic regimes. Strategic interaction makes it difficult for democratic states to target their rivals in bad economic times. We think these results provide at least a partial explanation for the inconsistent findings on diversionary behavior. Opportunity-rich environments appear to provide leaders with the necessary conditions to use diversionary tactics, although only nondemocratic leaders are able to seize on these opportunities fully.

One interesting avenue for future work would be to examine negotiations between democratic and nondemocratic states over contentious issues, such as territory. If strategic avoidance is occurring, then we should observe nondemocratic states being willing to concede more to democracies in negotiations over such issues when domestic turmoil is high. In other words, domestic economic and political conditions may influence both decisions to use force and decisions for how to negotiate in peacetime.

Appendix Summary Statistics of Variables

Variable	Mean	Standard Deviation	Minimum	Maximum
MID initiation	0.012	0.109	0.0	1.0
Enduring rival dyad	0.023	0.150	0.0	1.0
ln-differenced CPI	−0.288	3.679	−25.4	7.483
Rivalry-CPI interaction	−0.442	.867	−25.4	3.293
Relative capabilities	0.501	0.418	0.0	1.0
Peace years	29.03	28.67	0	178
ln distance	7.789	1.158	1.609	3.392
Joint democracy	0.316	0.465	0.0	1.0

Note: MID = militarized interstate dispute; CPI = consumer price index.

Notes

Authors' Note: A previous version of this article was presented at the annual meeting of the Peace Science Society (International), Atlanta, Georgia, October 26–28, 2001. We are grateful to Fred Boehmke for his assistance. Replication data are available at http://www.yale.edu/unsy/jcr/jcrdata.htm.

1. In fact, the increase in President Bush's approval rating represents the largest rally effect in Gallup poll history [Gallup Organization Web site, (www.gallup.com), September 19, 2001]. We are certainly not suggesting that the Bush administration created this attack to increase public approval; rather, we are offering this as an example of how strong the rally 'round the flag effect can be.

2. Scholars have identified a wide variety of factors that make the diversionary use of force more attractive, including a poorly performing economy, a high level of internal conflict, and electoral periods.

3. This is especially true in democratic states, where leaders depend on mass support for reelection.

4. However, this finding is the subject of debate. For example, Lian and Oneal (1993) find no evidence of an empirical rally following the use of force by U.S. presidents. However, even though some rally effects are small, they must be judged against what would have happened to presidential approval in the absence of the external conflict, something very difficult to judge empirically.

5. The manipulation of macroeconomic policy follows a similar logic (Lewis-Beck 1990; Tufte 1978).

6. See Levy (1989a) for a nice discussion of the differences between the externalization of internal conflict and the internationalization of external conflict.

7. Such uncertainty, according to Downs and Rocke (1995), has a tremendous influence not only on what candidate will eventually be selected by the electorate but also on the decision making about the issues and candidates on the ballot. Indeed, not only are voters uncertain whether a leader they elect actually shares their policy preferences (and therefore will act in their interest), but they also may be uncertain about the quality of the information they possess regarding a leader's proposed policy prescriptions. In foreign affairs, then, as Downs and Rocke insist, voters must monitor both executive decisions and the information a leader chooses to divulge regarding international events. In regards to the former, the electorate must determine whether involvement is, in fact, the desired response to systemic conditions. In regards to the latter, the asymmetrical level of information between political elites and the public forces the public to remain skeptical of executive justifications.

8. Richards et al. (1993) also demonstrated that attitudes toward risk can have a serious impact on foreign policy decision making as well.

9. Some scholars have even concluded that the decision to use military force abroad has little if anything to do with the domestic political conditions of a country (see Meernik and Waterman 1996). Ward and Widmaier (1982), for instance, found little evidence that sustained an externalization argument, and they insisted that the circumstances that would enable a political leader to moderate conflict domestically by using military force abroad are nearly nonexistent.

10. We consider only international options for responding to domestic turmoil. Although such an approach is not uncommon in the diversionary literature, some recent studies have examined both domestic and international policy making in a unified framework. Enterline and Gleditsch (2000, 22), for example, combine arguments from the diversionary and repression literatures, treating diversion and repression as interchangeable policies that can be used in response to domestic problems. They find, however, that "repression and external conflict involvement appear to be largely independent and driven by different challenges. While there is some evidence that domestic conflict increases the likelihood of disputes and that external threat may promote repression, there is little support for the idea of direct substitution in kind since leaders frequently combine both dispute involvement and repression." This evidence for independence between decisions to repress and divert increases our confidence in examining only the diversionary side.

11. Clark (2003) also finds empirical support for the strategic model using a zero-inflated Poisson (ZIP) model. The ZIP model can account for opportunities that arise endogenously (such as a poorly performing economy) and those that arise exogenously (such as threats by a rival state).

12. Rousseau et al. (1996) observe that democratic states are unlikely to be initiators in general and far less likely to initiate violence once involved in a crisis-bargaining situation against other democracies.

13. Enterline and Gleditsch (2000, 27) make a similar point: "A number of recent studies consist of single country time-series analyses of the United States. . . . The generalizability of such studies to other states is questionable, since large actors, such as the United States, with greater involvement and influence over international affairs are likely to have considerably greater opportunities to manipulate foreign policy for domestic purposes than are smaller states."

14. See also Goertz and Diehl (1992b) and Diehl and Goertz (2000).

15. In a replication of Ostrom and Job (1986), Mitchell and Moore (2002) demonstrate that the failure to take the larger strategic rivalry context into consideration changes the inferences one would draw. When uses of force occur in the context of rivalry, then the probability of using force in one instance is not independent of the use of force in another instance. This subsequently affects the choice of an appropriate statistical model.

16. Vasquez (1993) argues that wars of rivalry are distinct from other types of wars and that there are multiple causal paths to war. Wars of rivalry are wars between equals; they are wars of "rivalry" because they are usually preceded by longstanding mutual hostility and conflict.

17. Schroeder (1999) argues that domestic considerations played a significant role in the Franco-Austrian dispute over Italy after 1815.

18. The United States, for example, is an actor in 32 crises between 1918 and 1994 (Brecher and Wilkenfeld 1997) that are not against a direct enduring rival, but an examination of these cases reveals that most of them (such as Vietnam and Korea) are related to the rivalry with the Soviet Union.

19. It is also similar to Goertz's (1994) conceptualization of rivalry as a context.

20. We look at the initiation of a militarized dispute and thus distinguish between targets and initiators.

21. We believe that the environment of rivalry has both direct effects, where states may choose to use force directly against an enduring rival, and indirect effects, where states may use force against nonrival states, but such uses of force are influenced by the rivalry environment. A state has multiple options in a given year, including (1) use no militarized force, (2) use militarized force against a rival state only, (3) use militarized force against a nonrival state only, (4) use militarized force against a rival state and a nonrival state, (5) use militarized force against more than one nonrival state, and (6) use militarized force against more than one rival state. We feel that a multinomial logit model, which could capture all of these choices, is more complex than the directed-dyadic design employed below. In this study, we assess only the direct effect of rivalry on diversionary conflict. We leave for later a study of the indirect effect of rivalry.

22. We created the data set using EUGene, version 2.40 (Bennett and Stam 2000, 2002).

23. For a good summary of these various approaches to measuring rivalry, see Diehl and Goertz (2000).

24. A list of enduring rivalries based on these criteria can be found in Diehl and Goertz (2000, 145–46).

25. One reviewer commented on the double selection criteria for opportunity: political relevancy and rivalry. We consider political relevancy to control for interaction opportunity, whereas rivalry controls for diversion opportunity. An earlier version of the study analyzed all dyads, and our results were very similar to those presented below. See also Lemke and Reed (2001a).

26. Because the Diehl and Goertz (2000) measure of rivalry is based on the number of disputes in a given time period, some scholars find it unsettling to use such a measure on the right-hand side of a model predicting the likelihood of militarized conflict. Although we recognize these issues, we do not employ other measures of rivalry (such as Thompson's [2001] data set on strategic rivalry). Our observation is that most of the recent studies employing either measure of rivalry produce similar findings, and thus we feel that our findings are robust to the particular operationalization of rivalry employed.

27. The first difference also avoids the potential problem of endogeneity, where conflict involvement could change inflation levels in a country. Due to extreme values and high variance, we take the natural log of the differenced consumer price index (CPI) series.

28. Fordham and Sarver (2001) argue that the militarized interstate dispute (MID) data set is not ideal for evaluating diversionary hypotheses because it excludes several important incidents related to diversion (such as the use of force against nonstate actors) and includes other incidents not so relevant (such as fishing disputes). Although we sympathize with this position, we use the MID data because we are interested in evaluating diversionary theory in a cross-national setting, and the MID data set is one of the few data sets that covers such a long time span and records militarized conflict involvement for such a large number of countries.

29. In the creation of the directed-dyadic data, we select the following options in EUGene: *Dispute Initiators* (code side A as initiator, as well as originators and joiners on the initiating side as initiators), *MID Exclusions* (include ongoing dispute dyad of new MID, keep target vs. initiator directed dyads if no new MID, and include all joiner dyads).

30. In previous versions of the study, we conducted analyses using militarized dispute involvement as the dependent variable. The results are very similar to those presented here for dispute initiation, with increasing inflation enhancing the likelihood of dispute involvement for rival states and decreasing the chances for nonrival states.

31. "EUGene calculates the COW composite national capabilities index as developed by Singer, Bremer and Stuckey (1972). This is an index of a state's proportion of total system capabilities in 6 areas: the country's iron/steel production, the country's urban population, the country's total population, the country's total military expenditures, the country's total military personnel and the country's total amount of energy production" (Bennett and Stam 2002, 13).

32. Given the asymmetrical distribution of this variable, we take the natural log to reduce its range and variability.

33. In the calculation of predicted probabilities, we use descriptive statistics based on the reduced sample size (due to listwise deletion of missing cases).

34. This is similar to the findings of Enterline and Gleditsch (2000) that increases in local threat make

repression and militarized dispute involvement more likely. They employ a different measure of rivalry than we do, one developed by Crescenzi and Enterline (2001). This finding is a bit tautological, given the coding rules for enduring rivalries. Thus, we focus below on the substantive effects for changes in inflation.

35. We tested for the joint significance of the component terms (rivalry, inflation) and the interaction. Wald tests reveal that the enduring rivalry and interaction variables are jointly and significantly different from zero for values of logged CPI between −15.5 and 8.5. On the other hand, the inflation and interaction variables are jointly and significantly different from zero for both rival and nonrival dyads. More detailed results are available from the authors upon request.

36. As one reviewer pointed out, these effects are even larger if you consider states that are involved in multiple enduring rivalries at the same time, such as the United States.

37. To include both plots in a single graph, it is necessary to create two Y-scales (on the left and right) because the baseline probability of dispute initiation is higher for states involved in rivalries.

38. A similar finding is found in Leeds's (2003a) study of alliances and MID initiation. Her research design is nearly identical to our own, with a directed-dyadic unit of analysis and a general estimating equation (GEE) statistical model.

39. Our results are consistent with the null results for domestic turmoil and its influence on dispute initiation in Leeds and Davis (1997). As they note, however, democracies were initiators in only 30% of their directed-dyad cases in a sample of 18 industrialized democracies. If we were to analyze dispute targeting, we would expect to find a negative and significant relationship between inflation and the likelihood of being a target of a dispute for democratic states.

40. The effects for the two submodels (democratic initiators and nondemocratic initiators) do not add up to the effect for the full model (all initiators) because we are estimating separate GEE models. Also, we include only the monadic variable for the target in the submodels.

EDITORS' COMMENTARY

Major Contributions: Diversionary Theory

Many theories of interstate conflict treat the state as a unitary actor, ignoring the ways in which domestic politics and economic conditions can influence leaders' decisions to use force. Mitchell and Prins' (2004) study seeks to understand how poor domestic conditions such as high inflation levels[1] influence the likelihood of a country initiating an interstate conflict, especially given an opportunity to target an enemy or rival of the state. Their study builds upon the **diversionary theory of war**, which stems from literature in the field of sociology. This research suggests that groups tend to become more cohesive when faced with external threats (Coser 1956). State leaders can take advantage of this process, often called the **rally 'round the flag** effect, by using force for political gain. The literature on the diversionary theory of war suggests that there are situations in which leaders behave exactly in this manner, an idea depicted in dramatic form in the movie *Wag the Dog*.

Charles Ostrom and Brian Job published an important article in 1986 examining the relationship between domestic politics and international conflict. Ostrom and Job sought to understand how domestic political factors influence U.S. presidents' decisions to use military force while also controlling for international factors, such as the existing distribution of power in the Cold War rivalry. Analyzing quarterly uses of force from 1946 to 1976, the authors find that U.S. presidents are more likely to employ military force when economic conditions in the country are poor (which they measure with the **misery index** by adding inflation and unemployment levels) and when the president has a high overall approval level. The basic idea is that the president can shift attention away from the poor domestic economy by demonstrating competence in the foreign policy arena but that the president will be strategic and choose situations where he has an approval buffer or when he could afford to lose some support as a result of engaging in international conflict.

James Meernik (1994) built upon this research by coding situations in which the United States had lower or higher **opportunities to use force**. Meernik identified situations that involved territorial threats to the United States or its allies, threats to U.S. military or diplomatic personnel, or situations that could lead to losses in regional influence or ideological goals for the United States. Meernik found that once opportunities to use force were controlled for, the effects of economic variables (misery index) and presidential approval on U.S. uses of force were no longer statistically significant. Other studies (e.g., James and Oneal 1991) raised similar questions about the diversionary findings in the U.S. case. However, several analyses provide support for the original Ostrom and Job (1986) findings linking domestic political and economic conditions to U.S. (Stoll 1984; Morgan and Bickers 1992; Hess and Orphanides 1995), British (Morgan and Anderson 1999), and Israeli (Sprecher and DeRouen 2002) uses of force.

While many studies of the diversionary theory of war focused on the United States and United Kingdom given the availability of leader approval and economic data and these states' global strategic interests, scholars were interested in testing the relationship in a broader sample of states. This was motivated by a consideration of (1) whether major powers were the most likely to engage in diversion given their global interests and whether diversionary conflict behavior generalizes to other states and (2) whether diversionary behavior was a threat to the findings of the democratic peace literature. If democratic leaders used military force for political gain, could this undermine peaceful relations between democratic states or the pacific stance of democratic states overall?

Mitchell and Prins (2004) address both of these questions in their article. They first deal with the puzzling set of empirical findings when comparing single-country analyses (e.g., United States, United Kingdom) with multicountry analyses. For example, when expanding tests of the diversionary hypothesis to 18 industrialized democracies, Leeds and Davis (1997) find no statistically significant relationship between worsening economic conditions, electoral cycles, and the use of force. This of course raises questions about whether the earlier findings for states such as the United States and the United Kingdom extend to other countries. One possibility is that major powers simply have more opportunities to use force and thus that diversionary behavior will not be observed as frequently for regional or minor powers. Meernik's (1994) study shows that even for a single major power such as the United States, variance in external opportunities to use force correlates positively with actual uses of military force.

Mitchell and Prins (2004) agree that not all states have equal opportunities to engage their militaries abroad in times of domestic turmoil. They focus on a set of states that are particularly conflict prone in the international system, those countries involved in enduring rivalries (see Klein et al. 2006, Chapter 5, this volume). Some pairs of states such as India and Pakistan, Ecuador and Peru, and Israel and Egypt have repeated military conflicts over time, often involving disagreements about their contiguous land borders. Mitchell and Prins argue that diversionary behavior is most likely to occur among the set of states that have high opportunities for the use of force. This includes major powers, which by definition have global strategic interests, and minor powers, which are involved in enduring rivalries. Countries that have peaceful relations with their neighbors and with other major powers (e.g., Norway) will not have the same opportunities to employ the military to rally the public in bad economic or political times. Mitchell and Prins' empirical analysis from 1960 to 2001 provides support for their theory, showing that states are more likely to initiate force against enduring rivals when inflation is high, while states that have no rivals to target are less likely to initiate military force when the economy gets worse. Thus, the puzzling findings of no apparent relationship between domestic conditions and use of force in some cross-national studies can be explained in part by the failure to control for states' varying opportunities to use military force.

The second question, whether the pattern of diversionary behavior varies across democratic and nondemocratic states, is also addressed in Mitchell and Prins' (2004) study. As noted above, Leeds and Davis (1997) found no relationship between economic/political conditions and uses of force in a sample of eighteen democratic states. They explain these results using a game-theoretic model of diversionary logic (Smith 1996a), which suggests that when democracies have opportunities to use force for domestic political gain, their international opponents recognize this opportunity and become more likely to give into their bargaining demands. When we consider strategic interaction, it is possible for situations where diversionary behavior might occur to be avoided due to the ability of the potential target states to alter their bargaining positions.

Mitchell and Prins (2004) build upon this idea and argue that if the strategic model of diversion is operating, then we will observe a stronger relationship between poor economic conditions and uses of force by autocratic governments. When democratic leaders are faced with rich opportunities for diversionary uses of force, the states being targeted will be more likely to accede to their bargaining demands, and thus we will observe fewer instances of military force in these scenarios. Mitchell and Prins split their empirical sample into two groups: democracies and nondemocracies. If democracies can signal resolve more easily in crisis bargaining, then strategic conflict avoidance should be most likely for these states; this would render the relationship between economic/political factors and uses of force insignificant. The results in Tables 3 and 5 and Figures 2 and 3 provide support for this hypothesis. The diversionary behavior that is observed in the entire sample is driven by the behavior of nondemocratic states. Inflation levels have almost no effect on democratic states' decisions to initiate the use of force. This demonstrates the importance of testing diversionary behavior in a dyadic framework because we need to control for the strategic incentives facing both states in a bargaining situation.

Methodological Notes: General Estimating Equation (GEE) Models and Autoregressive (AR) Processes

Mitchell and Prins' (2004) primary hypothesis is that the initiation of military force is more likely when a state has a high level of inflation domestically *and* the state has an external rival to target. Because this hypothesis requires matching the domestic conditions of one state to its decision to initiate the use of force, the authors use the **directed dyad-year** as their unit of analysis. Recall in Bremer's (1992b, Chapter 2, this volume) "Dangerous Dyads" piece that he paired all possible countries together for each year the states are independent, creating the **dyad-year** unit of analysis. Mitchell and Prins expand upon this by coding each dyad in two directions: from A to B and from B to A. Suppose we were coding the United States and Canada from 1920 to 2012. A dyad-year approach would create one case for the United States–Canada in 1920, another case for the United States–Canada in 1921, and continue up through 2012, creating a total of 93 dyad-year cases. A directed dyad-year approach codes one case for the United States–Canada in 1920, with the United States as the potential initiator, and a second case for Canada–United States in 1920, with Canada as the potential initiator. Each potential initiator's domestic conditions (e.g., the inflation rate in 1920) are then matched up with side A in the directed dyad observation. This doubles the number of cases to 186 for the U.S.–Canada dyad. This creates potential problems for assuming statistical **independence** across cases because a militarized conflict between the two states in a dyad gets counted twice in the data set; thus, we need to employ statistical models that can account for this dependence in the data. The advantage of the directed dyad approach is that it allows the analyst to track more closely "who does what to whom" (Bremer 2000; Ray 2001), and it allows for the inclusion of monadic variables in the analysis more easily.[2] Mitchell and Prins do not look at all possible directed dyad-years (like Bremer) but rather limit their analyses to **politically relevant dyads**. This includes only those cases in which states share a land or water border or the dyad involves one or more major powers. This kind of strategy is often used in conflict models to limit analysis to a set of cases where the general opportunity to use force is reasonably high.

Mitchell and Prins' (2004) theory links two variables, inflation and the initiation of force, through a third conditioning variable, enduring rivalry. The idea is that when rivalry is present (e.g., Greece-Turkey), high inflation in one state (e.g., Turkey) will increase the chances for that country to initiate force against the other state in the dyad (e.g., Greece). Such a scenario played out when Turkey initiated force against Greece in 2000 over competing claims in the Aegean Sea at a time when Turkey's inflation rate was more than 30 percent. This kind of theoretical argument requires one of two approaches for testing. As noted in the discussion of Susan Sample's (2002, Chapter 6, this volume) work on arms races, one strategy involves the splitting of the data into two subsamples and then testing for the effects of other variables on conflict onset. In Sample's work, for example, she divided dyads into different types (Major-Major, Major-minor, and minor-minor) and then estimated separate logit models linking the presence of mutual military buildups and escalation to war. If Mitchell and Prins use this strategy, this would have involved splitting the directed dyad year data set into two samples, one with rival dyads and one with nonrival dyads. The expectation would be that inflation would have a positive and statistically significant effect in the rival dyad sample but have no effect in the nonrival dyads. The authors employ this method to address their secondary question about how regime type influences diversionary behavior with models for democratic initiators (Table 3) and nondemocratic initiators (Table 5) estimated separately.

To test for the primary relationship between inflation, rivalry, and the use of force, Mitchell and Prins (2004) employ a second strategy, the use of an **interaction term**. This involves multiplying one variable (e.g., enduring rivalry) with another variable (e.g., inflation) and estimating the effects of these factors on conflict initiation in all politically relevant directed dyad-years. Because rivalry is a dichotomous variable (0/1), it is straightforward to estimate the effects in these models. The authors include rivalry (*Enduring Rival Dyad*), inflation (*ln-Differenced CPI*), and the interaction term (*Rivalry-differenced CPI Interaction*) in the same model (Table 1). The coefficient for the rivalry variable by itself (2.005) represents the effect of rivalry on the likelihood of conflict initiation for countries whose inflation rate is zero. We would conclude that rival dyads are more likely to experience militarized conflict even if they face no economic troubles at home. The coefficient for the inflation variable by itself (−0.04) represents the effect of inflation on conflict initiation for states *not* involved in enduring rivalries. We can see that this coefficient is negative and significant, such that states without the external opportunity of rivalry are actually less likely to initiate interstate conflicts when domestic economic conditions worsen. The interaction coefficient (0.078) shows the effect when both factors are present (enduring rivalry and an inflation rate different from zero). The positive and significant coefficient tells us that states are more likely to initiate force against their rivals when inflation is rising. We can set these variables at various levels and then calculate how the probability of conflict initiation changes. Mitchell and Prins show how the probability of conflict changes across various levels of inflation in Figure 1 while varying the opportunity conditions of rivalry and nonrivalry. The *Y*-axis on the left shows the probability of militarized interstate dispute initiation for nonrival dyads (which is small in general); we can see the chances for conflict initiation in this group decrease as inflation rises. The *Y*-axis on the right of the figure shows the probability of conflict initiation for rival dyads. Here we see that the baseline probability of conflict is much higher and that rising levels of inflation increase the chances for conflict initiation.

Using this kind of interactive model is important if different subgroups behave differently given changes in our key independent variables. The results in previous studies that found no statistically significant relationship between economic turmoil and conflict behavior can be explained in part by the failure to account for variance in external opportunities to use force. If some groups (rivals) are more likely to engage in diversion and other groups (nonrivals) are less likely to engage in diversion as inflation increases, aggregating these groups into a single model can produce the apparent result that there is no relationship between the variables of interest. Other studies have shown the same types of patterns that Mitchell and Prins (2004) present. Foster (2006) demonstrates that rivalry has a stronger effect on the diversionary behavior of minor powers, whereas major powers are less sensitive to domestic economic conditions given their global strategic interests. Mitchell and Thyne (2010) examine another form of opportunities to use force: diplomatic disputes over land or water borders. They find a similar result to the Mitchell and Prins study, whereby states that have ongoing border disputes have a higher chance of using force to pursue their diplomatic interests when inflation is high, while states without territorial disputes are less likely to initiate force when inflation is high. These studies show that domestic factors are useful for helping us understand the timing of the use of force in contexts where states have high opportunities for conflict involvement.

As noted earlier, the use of directed dyad-years as cases violates the assumption that many statistical models employ regarding the independence of cases. The logit model, for example, assumes that we can multiply the probability of individual events together, which is problematic when we have dependence of our cases by virtue of the way we constructed the data set. Cases could be related to each other across time, whereby the use of force in one dyad-year increases or decreases the chances for future uses of force (which we know is likely in enduring rivalries). Cases could also be related to each other across space, as fighting in one dyad (e.g., Israel-Syria) could spread to fighting in another dyad (e.g., Israel-Lebanon). Mitchell and Prins (2004) use a statistical model that captures this type of dependence in the data, the **GEE (general estimating equation) model**. To capture temporal dependence, the authors include a measure for **peace years**, which counts the number of years in each dyad since the last militarized dispute (Beck et al. 1998). The expectation is that as the number of peace years increases, conflict initiation is less likely.[3] Mitchell and Prins also capture temporal dependence by assuming that the **residuals** or errors in their statistical model follow an **autoregressive (AR)** process. In this case, large errors in the previous period correlate positively with errors in the current period. GEE models are similar to another strategy often employed in political science research, the use of **robust standard errors**. Both modeling approaches involve corrections in the variance-covariance matrix after the model is estimated. The idea is to correct for temporal or spatial relationships in the data through estimation strategies. We can also model the dynamics in the variables we are studying; for example, we could include a **lagged dependent variable** to indicate whether a dyad experienced conflict in the previous year. We can use this same kind of strategy by employing **spatial lags**, which captures the values of the dependent variable (e.g., militarized conflict) for other dyads close in geographic space (e.g., the effect of U.S.-Mexico interactions on U.S.-Canada interactions).

Notes

1. Inflation is an economic concept that captures price levels in an economy. It is typically measured with the Consumer Price Index (CPI), which measures the prices that urban residents pay for a typical basket of goods and services. Mitchell and Prins use the percentage change in CPI in their statistical models. Positive values indicate rising price levels in a country and negative values represent lower price levels. Citizens are worse off under situations of rising inflation because they are able to purchase fewer goods with the same amount of money.

2. By monadic, we mean a variable that pertains to a single state, such as military spending or the inflation rate. See the commentary on Bremer (1992b).

3. The authors also use **cubic splines** to capture the potential nonlinearities in the temporal dynamics of peace years. This can be captured more simply through the inclusion of cubic polynomials in the estimated model, such as time, $time^2$, and $time^3$ (Carter and Signorino 2010).

Questions

1. In Table 2, how does the probability of conflict initiation change when inflation increases from one standard deviation below its mean to one standard deviation above its mean? How do these probabilities vary across the contexts of rivalry and nonrivalry?

2. If the change in the inflation rate was at its maximum (8 percent) in Figure 1, what is the probability of conflict initiation for a state in a nonrival dyad? In a rival dyad? Are these predicted values quite different?

3. Looking at Figure 1, can you estimate the level of inflation for which an enduring rivalry dyad would have a similar probability of conflict initiation to a nonrivalry dyad? Hint: find the probability of conflict initiation around 0.15 for both groups and check the inflation levels.

Further Reading

Leeds, B. A., and D. R. Davis. 1997. Domestic political vulnerability and international disputes. *Journal of Conflict Resolution* 41 (6): 814–34.

Ostrom, C. W., and B. Job. 1986. The president and the political use of force. *American Political Science Review* 80 (2): 541–66.

Chapter 9

The Kantian Peace

The Pacific Benefits of Democracy, Interdependence, and International Organizations, 1885–1992

John R. Oneal and Bruce Russett

Just over two hundred years ago Immanuel Kant suggested that "republican constitutions," a "commercial spirit" of international trade, and a federation of interdependent republics would provide the basis for perpetual peace. The alternative, even starker in the nuclear era than in 1795, would be peace of a different sort: "a vast grave where all the horrors of violence and those responsible for them would be buried."[1] Consequently, Kant declared, we have a duty to work for peaceful international relations. Though he emphasized the absolute character of this moral imperative, he was no idealist; rather, he believed that natural processes based on self-interest impelled individuals to act in ways that would eventually produce a lasting and just peace. Kant was also realistic. He acknowledged that war was inherent in the anarchic international system and therefore cautioned that nations must act prudently until the federation of interdependent republics was established. But he also knew that the mechanisms of power politics produce only temporary respite from conflict, not lasting solutions.

Over the past half century much of the world has been at peace. Understanding that phenomenon, its causes and trajectory, is the fundamental challenge for international relations scholars today. We seek to show that Kant's realistic statement of liberal theory provides useful guidance for this task. Most political scientists now agree that the contemporary peacefulness can be traced in part to the so-called democratic peace, wherein established democratic states have fought no international wars with one another and the use or threat of force among them, even at low levels, has been rare.[2] This view is incomplete, however, because it fails to recognize the pacific benefits of the other liberal elements of Kant's program for peace. Moreover, the term hides the vigorous theoretical controversy about the processes underlying this separate peace—over whether democracy is really even its cause and over the degree to which the empirical phenomenon existed in other eras.

These theoretical and empirical concerns are linked. If, for example, peaceful relations among democracies during the cold war era were simply a consequence of their shared security interests vis-à-vis the opposing alliance system in a bipolar world, then their peacefulness would be spuriously related to the character of their regimes. The same conclusion would result if the democratic peace could be attributed to the hegemonic power of the United States to suppress conflict among its allies or to East-West differences in preferences unrelated to

Source: John R. Oneal and Bruce Russett, "The Kantian Peace: The Pacific Benefits of Democracy, Interdependence, and International Organizations, 1885–1992," *World Politics* 52, no. 1 (October 1999): 1–37. Copyright © 2012 Trustees of Princeton University. Reprinted with the permission of Cambridge University Press.

underlying differences in regimes.[3] One would not then expect to find a separate peace among democratic states in other periods evincing different patterns of interstate relations. We address these questions by reporting analyses covering 1885–1992, to show that peaceful relations among democracies existed throughout the twentieth century.[4] Extending the historical domain also allows us to assess the effect of the changing character of the international system on interstate relations.[5]

In keeping with the Kantian perspective, we expand our analysis beyond the democratic peace, incorporating the influence of economically important trade and joint memberships in international organizations. The classical liberals of the eighteenth and nineteenth centuries expected interdependence as well as popular control of government to have important pacific benefits. Commercial relations draw states into a web of mutual self-interest that constrains them from using force against one another. Thus interdependence and democracy contribute to what we have called the "Uberai peace." Kant emphasized, in addition, the benefits of international law and organization. Our previous analyses of the cold war era indicate that, during those years at least, trade and networks of intergovernmental organizations did reduce the number of militarized interstate disputes; these effects were on top of the benefits of democracy.[6] We show here that they also operated in earlier and later years.

Our Objectives and Method

Although the liberal and realist perspectives are often considered antithetical, in keeping with Kant's philosophical analysis we conduct our tests of the Kantian peace while taking into account important realist influences. We believe, as Kant did, that both perspectives matter, as both consider conflict and the threat of violence to be inherent in an anarchic world of sovereign states. The Hobbesian element of this understanding is central to realist theory, but it is also deeply embedded in the liberal tradition. Kant accepted Hobbes's description of a state of war among nations and believed that a balance of power

could prevent war; but history has shown all too clearly, as most realists acknowledge, that this "peace" is tenuous. Kant, however, was convinced that a genuine, positive peace could be developed within a "federation" of liberal republics that rested more on the three Kantian supports—democracy, interdependence, and international law and organizations—than on power politics. The pacific federation envisioned by Kant is not a world state but a federation whose members remain sovereign, linked only by confederational or collective security arrangements. Liberalism, that is, sees democratic governance, economic interdependence, and international law as the means by which to supersede the security dilemma rooted in the anarchy of the international system. For states not much linked by these ties, however, the threat of violence remains. In addition, liberal states must fear those illiberal states that remain outside the Kantian confederation.[7]

Thus we begin by assuming that the international system is anarchic and power is important. Yet despite the inherent possibility of violence, states do not fight all others or at all times even where realist principles dominate. Rather, they are constrained by power, alliances, and distance. States must be concerned with the balance of power and the coincidence of national interests expressed in alliances. Many states, moreover, are irrelevant to these calculations: in general, the farther apart two states are, the fewer are the issues over which to fight and the less the threat they pose to one another. Ultimately therefore realists are concerned only with states that have the opportunity and incentive to engage in conflict.[8] Accordingly because these constraints provide a baseline against which to assess the additional impact of the Kantian influences, we incorporate them as central features of our theoretical model. To the realist variables we add measures for the three Kantian constraints, hypothesizing that (1) democracies will use force less frequently, especially against other democracies; (2) economically important trade creates incentives for the maintenance of peaceful relations; and (3) international organizations constrain decision makers by promoting peace in a variety of ways. Since the modern international system is far from a pacific federation of democratic states, we expect both realist and Kantian factors to affect interstate relations. We explicitly consider how realist and liberal influences at both the dyadic and the systemic level have altered the functioning of the international system, addressing the role of the leading state and the influence of the changing Kantian variables over time.

Evidence for the pacific benefits of economic interdependence and membership in intergovernmental organizations (IGOs) is less widely accepted than is that for the democratic peace, and it has been subjected to less extensive critical scrutiny. We alone have assessed the effect of IGOs on conflict at the dyadic level of analysis. Moreover, theoretical expectations regarding the impact of trade and IGOs are more diverse than those concerning democracy. No one hypothesizes that democracies are *more* likely to fight each other than are other polities; but the liberal view of the pacific effects of trade is contradicted by those who expect conflict over the division of the gains from trade and by the dependency school and its intellectual predecessors and descendants, who expect conflict between large and small states.[9] As for IGOs, a plausible view might be that states form or join international organizations to manage—albeit often without success—disputes with their adversaries, the UN being an example. More commonly, realists regard international institutions as nearly irrelevant to the security issues at the heart of high politics, with no effect independent of existing power relations.[10] Even among those who hold that trade or IGOs play a positive role in promoting peace, the reasons advanced vary. Rational choice theorists emphasize political actors' complementary economic interests in maintaining peaceful interstate relations—interests that are reflected in the decisions of national leaders. Fearful of the domestic political consequences of losing the benefits of trade, policymakers avoid the use of force against states with which they engage in economically important trade. But one can also devise constructivist explanations about

how the communication associated with trade builds cross-national sentiments of shared identity.[11]

Even realists acknowledge that international institutions like NATO help to preserve peace among their members by supplementing the deterrent effect of sheer military power. Liberals emphasize the potential of institutions for communicating information and facilitating bargaining,[12] while constructivists see institutions as instruments for expanding people's conceptions of identity, relatedness, and self-interest. Because IGOs vary widely in their functions and capabilities, any or all of these explanations may be correct in a particular instance.[13] As with the consequences of democratic institutions, we do not attempt to resolve these theoretical debates here. Instead we seek to offer an empirical assessment of the effect of the Kantian influences on interstate relations.

In expanding the historical domain of the Kantian peace, one encounters hurdles (and opportunities) that arise from marked changes in the nature of political regimes, the importance of international trade, and the role of international organizations. As measured by the standard data on political regimes, Polity III,[14] the average level of democracy in the international system has risen since the early 1800s, in a pattern that is sporadic and wavelike.[15] Similarly, the mean level of economic interdependence as measured by the ratio of bilateral trade to gross domestic product fell after World War I but rose again in subsequent years. Most clear is the growth in the number of IGOs, though those associated with the creation and sustenance of a truly global economy largely emerge only after World War II. These trends for the 1885–1992 period are shown in Figure 1.[16] Higher levels of democracy, interdependence, and IGO membership should, of course, reduce conflict for the pairs of countries affected; but we also expect that as the number of democracies increases, trade grows, and IGOs proliferate, there will be important systemic influences on other pairs of states as well. The effect of the Kantian influences should, we hypothesize, be apparent over time as well as cross-nationally.

Figure 1   Kantian Variables

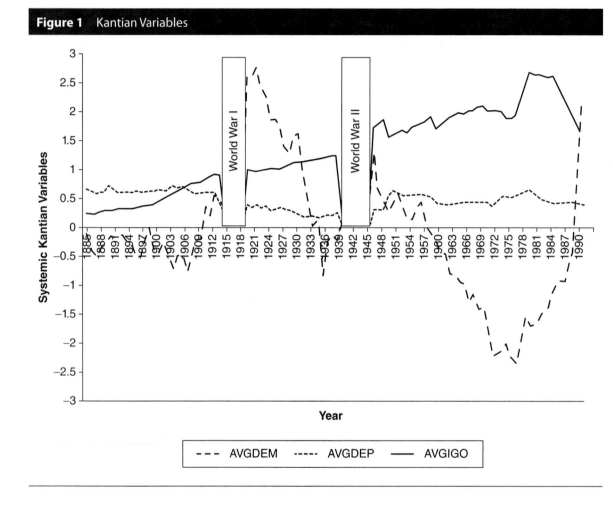

Our statistical method—pooled cross-sectional time-series regression analysis of data regarding pairs of states (dyads) observed annually —is well suited to the purposes at hand. It considers variance in states' involvement in militarized disputes across dyads in each year and in dyadic relations through time. Consequently we can determine the likelihood of conflict as a function of differences across thousands of pairs of states annually and of changes in dyadic relations or in the international system from year to year over a period of more than one hundred years. By measuring change in the Kantian variables through time, we can begin to disentangle their systemic effects from their strictly dyadic influences.

Changes over time in the average level of democracy, interdependence, and IGO involvement capture important elements of the norms and institutions of the international system. Wendt, for instance, contends that world politics has slowly evolved from Hobbesian anarchy to a Lockean system wherein the security dilemma is ameliorated by norms recognizing the right of sovereign states to exist; these, in turn effectively limit the use of force.[17] Thus, states are no longer subject to elimination: whereas twenty-two internationally recognized states were forcibly occupied or absorbed during the first half of the twentieth century, no state has lost its formal sovereignty through conquest since World War II.[18] The emergence of a Kantian subsystem of states, within which the unprovoked use of force is illegitimate, may have contributed directly to this evolutionary development and affected the probability that force will be used primarily by states that are not particularly democratic, interdependent, or involved in international organizations.

If democracies are more likely than are autocracies to win their wars, then the latter will have to be concerned about the security implications of weakening themselves in war, whether with democracies or other autocracies, especially as the number of democracies in the international system grows.[19] If most great powers are democratic, their peaceful relations should reduce the incentive for war for all states across their spheres of influence. If globalization increases and stimulates economic growth among interdependent states, nonliberal states will have to be concerned lest they be punished by global markets and trading states for instigating international violence that disrupts trade and investment; even antagonistic dyads with little mutual trade may find it prudent to avoid conflict.[20] If international norms and institutions for resolving disputes grow, even nonliberal states may be impelled to use regional or international organizations to help settle their disputes rather than accept the political, military, and economic costs imposed by the liberal community as penalties for using military force. Thus increases in the Kantian influences at the system level may have beneficial effects on the behavior of dyads that are not particularly democratic, economically interdependent, or involved in international organizations.

This is not an ecological fallacy.[21] We do not make inferences about dyadic conflict from information about conflict at the systemic level. In all our analyses we address the incidence of militarized disputes among pairs of states. We investigate the consequences of purely dyadic characteristics for dyadic behavior, but we also do consider the effects of evolutionary changes in the international system. To capture the effects of such systemic changes, we use the annual mean scores of democracy, bilateral trade as a proportion of gross domestic product (GDP), and joint memberships in IGOs graphed in Figure 1. They effectively gauge the pervasiveness of changes in international norms and institutions and document the example of the success of liberal states in the competition among nations. We also consider the influence of the leading state, the hegemon, on interstate relations. We investigate this aspect of leading realist theories with measures of the relative power of the hegemon, states' satisfaction with the status quo, and the hegemon's sense of its own security.

Historical Domain, Key Variables, and Sources of Data

As our analysis spans the years 1885 to 1992, it enables us to examine the effects of democracy, economic interdependence, and international organizations over a long period before the cold war and for a few years after. Realists often contrast the dynamics of bipolar and multipolar systems, though there is disagreement over their consequences for interstate relations. By Waltz's criteria, the international system was multipolar for the centuries preceding 1945 but bipolar during the cold war.[22] And the current, post-Soviet world is neither bipolar nor multipolar but perhaps is best understood as unipolar, at least as measured by the relative power of the United States (in its capabilities if not in its will to control or shape events). These theoretically based distinctions require us to consider the effects of the Kantian variables within different international structures, though evaluation of the post–cold war era necessarily remains tentative.

We omit from our analyses all but the first year of both World War I and World War II, because bilateral trade data for those years are fragmentary, as they are for the immediate postwar years, 1919–20 and 1946–49. Omitting all but the first year of the world wars, which consisted of conflicts between democracies and autocracies or between two autocracies, biases our results against finding evidence of the democratic peace, but it also provides assurance that our results are not determined by these dramatic but atypical events.[23] Most of our variables and data are discussed in previous publications. Here we concentrate on what is new.

Dependent Variable: Involvement in Militarized Disputes

We use the Correlates of War (COW) data on interstate disputes (MIDs). We code each year that a dyad was involved in a dispute in which one or both states threatened to use force, made a demonstration of force, or actually used military force against the other. The variable DISPUTE equals 1 if a dispute was ongoing and 0 if not. Some researchers urge that only the initial year of a dispute be noted since a dispute in one year increases the chances that the dyad will experience a dispute in subsequent years.[24] This procedure eases some problems but raises others. If leaders are rational, as all our theories assume, they will frequently reevaluate their positions, whether to escalate, deescalate, or maintain the existing strategy. We agree with Blainey: "The beginning of wars, the prolonging of wars and the prolonging or shortening of periods of peace all share the same causal framework. The same explanatory framework and the same factors are vital in understanding each state in the sequel of war and peace."[25] Moreover, we investigated 166 multiyear disputes during the post–World War II era and found that more than half involved a change in the level of force employed over the course of the dispute or that a new dispute arose as the first was concluding. Thus we report analyses of states' involvement in disputes rather than of just their onset; but as in earlier studies of the cold war era,[26] we reestimated key analyses using only the first year of disputes without finding material differences from those reported below.

Dyadic Independent Variables

We lag all independent variables by one year to ensure that they were not affected by a dispute to be explained. For some explanatory variables this precaution is clearly important; for example, conflict may limit trade just as trade may constrain conflict. A similar reciprocal relationship can be imagined for international organizations and conflict, as many IGOs—though hardly all—are formed among states that maintain peaceful relations. For other variables such considerations are irrelevant. Geographically proximate countries are prone to conflict, but the frequency of their disputes does not affect their proximity. To be consistent, however, we lag all the independent variables. This precaution does not put to rest all questions about the direction of causality, but it is a reasonable step at this time.[27] All the variables are listed by their acronyms in the appendix.

Democracy

We use the Polity III data to compute a summary measure of the political character of regimes, subtracting every country's score on the autocracy scale from its score on the democracy scale. The resulting variable (DEM_i) ranges from −10 for an extreme autocracy to +10 for the most democratic states. Because a dispute can result from the actions of a single state, the likelihood of conflict is primarily a function of the degree of constraint experienced by the less constrained state in each dyad. As that state is the weak link in the chain of peaceful relations,[28] we expect that the less democratic state (DEM_L) in a dyad is the stronger determinant of interstate violence. Conversely, the more democratic that state, the more constrained it will be from engaging in a dispute and the more peaceful the dyad. In previous analyses we found, as Kant had expected, that the *difference* between states' political regimes also affects the likelihood of conflict. Democratic-autocratic dyads were the most conflict-prone in the cold war era; two autocracies were less likely to fight, and two democracies were the most peaceful. We reconsider these findings below.

The Polity III regime scores exhibit some problems of comparability over time. Until 1918 about 40 percent of British males (disproportionately working class) were disfranchised by residence requirements; female suffrage was granted partially in 1918 and fully only in 1928.[29] In the United States women obtained the vote only in 1920, and blacks were systematically excluded until the 1960s. Swiss women achieved the franchise only in 1971. Some of these changes are reflected in the Polity data and hence in rising levels of democracy in the international system. For example, the United Kingdom goes from 6 to 7 on the democracy scale in 1880, to 8 in 1902, and jumps to 10 only in 1922. But Switzerland is coded at 10 from 1848, as is the United States from 1871. The consequences of these restrictions on political participation for foreign policy may not be trivial. In the contemporary United States, for example, women are significantly more averse to the use of military force than are men and vote in part on this basis.[30] Thus the exclusion of women from the franchise in earlier periods could have profoundly reduced the tendency of even the most "democratic" states to avoid conflict.

Economic Interdependence

For most of the post–World War II era the measurement of this Kantian variable is straightforward, because the International Monetary Fund reports statistics regarding bilateral trade. Since trade is expected to influence dyadic relations only if it is economically important, we divide the sum of a country's exports and imports with its partner by its GDP, as reported in the standard references for the years after 1950.[31] As with the influence of democratic institutions, we expect the likelihood of a dispute to be primarily a function of the freedom of the less constrained state to use force, that is, the bilateral trade-to-GDP measure of the state less dependent economically on trade with its dyadic partner ($DEPEND_L$). We also report tests for a positive effect of asymmetric dependence on conflict, as proposed by dependency theorists.

When we move back to the years before World War II, however, national economic data become more problematic. During the years 1920–38 the League of Nations compiled contemporary data on bilateral trade in current values, along with exchange rates.[32] While the accuracy and the comparability of

these data are undoubtedly less than in the later IMF reports, they are the best available. There are no institutional compilations of trade data for the years of the two world wars, nor for the period before 1914. Before World War I the annual editions of *The Statesman's Yearbook*[33] offer the closest approximations, but these data are less standardized, the appropriate exchange rates for converting the data to a common unit are less certain, and more data are missing.[34]

Because of these difficulties we collected alternative estimates for bilateral trade in the 1885–1949 period, compared them with the data from *The Statesman's Yearbook* and the League of Nations, and adjusted the data from our principal sources as appropriate.[35]

Information on dyadic trade, the numerator of the dependence measure, is only half of the problem for the pre-1950 era, however. To calculate the economic importance of trade we need estimates of nations' gross domestic products. No comprehensive collection of GDP data exists, but Maddison provides estimates in constant dollars for fifty-six countries in all regions of the world for 1870–1992.[36] We used these in a two-step procedure to estimate the GDPs in current dollars for a large number of countries. First, we regressed Maddison's constant dollar GDP estimates on states' total annual energy consumption, the region where they were located, the year, and various interactive terms. Annual energy consumption, collected by the Correlates of War (cow) project, is a good correlate of the size of national economies, as Morgenstern, Knorr, and Heiss noted twenty-five years ago.[37] More than 93 percent of the variance in Maddison's GDPs was explained. Based on the coefficients in this analysis, we were able to estimate the constant dollar GDPs for a large number of other countries. Second, we converted these constant dollar estimates to current dollars, using Maddison's U.S. dollar GDP deflator.

Joint IGO Memberships. The influence of international organizations on interstate conflict, the last Kantian variable, is assessed by the number of IGOs in which both states in a dyad share membership, as reported by the *Yearbook of International Organizations.*[38] Simply counting joint memberships (ranging from 0 to over 130 for some dyads in recent years) is far from an ideal measure of the importance and effectiveness of international organizations. It includes organizations that are weak and strong, regional and global, functional and multipurpose. Ideally the total should be broken down and some organizations given special weight, but this is hard to do as a practical matter and there is little theory to guide the attempt. For now we use the simple count of joint memberships in intergovernmental organizations; this variable is labeled IGO.

Capability Ratio. The first of the realist constraints on states' use of military force is relative power, specifically the balance of power within a dyad. The idea that an equal balance of power may deter conflict has deep historical roots, as does the idea that a preponderance of capabilities is more likely to preserve the peace by reducing uncertainty as to which side would win a contest of arms. Recent empirical work suggests, however, that it is preponderance that deters military action.[39] Our index of relative power (CAPRATIO) is the natural logarithm of the ratio of the stronger state's military capability index to that of the weaker member in each dyad. We make these calculations using the COW data on population, industry, and military forces.[40]

Alliance. Allies are generally thought to fight each other less than other states because they share common security interests. They often share other political and economic interests as well. We control for this influence using a variable (ALLIES) that equals 1 if the members of a dyad were linked by a mutual defense treaty, neutrality pact, or entente; it equals 0 otherwise.[41]

Contiguity and Distance. The potential for interstate violence exists when at least one member of a dyad can reach the other with effective military force. For most states the ability to do so is determined foremost by geographic proximity, especially as one goes farther back in history. Furthermore, neighbors are likely to have the most reasons to fight—over territorial boundaries, natural resources, the grievances of cross-border ethnic groups, and so on. Thus the constraint of distance reduces the capability to fight and most of the incentives to do so as well; this finding is extremely strong in previous research.

Accordingly, we include two different terms in our regression analyses to capture this effect as fully as possible. DISTANCE is the natural logarithm of the great circle distance in miles between the capitals of the two states (or between the major ports for the largest countries); using the logarithm acknowledges a declining marginal effect. Additionally we include NONCONTIG, a measure that equals 1 if two states are not directly or indirectly contiguous (via colonies or other dependencies). It equals 0 if they share a land boundary or are separated by less than 150 miles of water. Because of the widespread nature of colonial empires, these two measures are not highly correlated ($r^2 = 0.21$), especially up to World War II. The effect of distance in constraining conflict, however, is less for the great powers: those with the land, sea, or (in the last half-century) air capability to deliver substantial forces or destructive power globally. The COW project has identified these major powers on the basis of a consensus of historians. To give full consideration to realists' concerns, we add a third variable, MINORPWRS, coded 1 if a dyad is composed of minor powers and 0 for those that include at least one great power. (To be consistent with our view that conflict is endemic but subject to constraints, we reverse the terminology and coding of the last two variables from those in previous research reports where we used CONTIG and MAJOR. This has no effect on our statistical analyses, other than to reverse the sign of the coefficients. Note that some contiguous dyads also include one or two major powers.)

In most of the analyses below, we include all possible pairs of states for which information is available, using COW data regarding membership in the international system to generate these cases. Thus we do not limit our study to the politically relevant dyads, identified as contiguous states and dyads containing at least one major power. We continue to believe that such a restriction makes good theoretical sense, however. These dyads are much more likely to engage in military disputes. Politically relevant dyads constitute just 22 percent of all the dyads for which we have data; nevertheless they account for 87 percent of all the disputes. In other words, the politically relevant dyads are twenty-four times more likely to experience a militarized dispute than are those we have deemed to be "irrelevant." And some disputes among these other dyads are contagion effects of being drawn into conflicts through alliance commitments. We include all dyads in most of the analyses reported below to be sure we are not ignoring the causes of these other disputes,[42] but we also explore the consequences of including the non-relevant pairs.

Systemic Independent Variables

Kantian Systemic and Relative Dyadic Measures. To clarify the influence of the international system on the likelihood of dyadic conflict, we create three system-level Kantian variables and three realist variables, the latter designed to capture the hegemon's effect on interstate relations. The three Kantian variables are straightforward derivations of our basic measures: we simply computed the means of DEM, DEPEND, and IGO for each year. These are the measures (omitting the years of the world wars) graphed in Figure 1. In the analyses below, they are identified as AVGDEM, AVGDEPEND, and AVGIGO. We hypothesize that the greater these systemic measures, the more the global system will reflect the normative and institutional constraints associated with democracy, interdependence, and the rule of law. It is also possible to assess the standing of each dyad in each year relative to our three annual Kantian averages. Thus we calculated three relative dyadic measures: $RELDEM_L = (DEM_L - AVGDEM)/$the standard deviation of DEM; $RELDEPEND_L = (DEPEND_L - AVGDEPEND)/$the standard deviation of DEPEND; and $RELIGO = (IGO - AVGIGO)/$the standard deviation of IGO. These measures identify the dyads that were most democratic, interdependent, and involved in intergovernmental organizations at each point in time. By dividing by the standard deviations, we can directly compare these estimated coefficients. Combining systemic and relative measures in a single equation allows us to compare the effect of changing values of the Kantian variables through time versus the standing of dyads cross-sectionally relative to the annual means. We expect the systemic and relative variables to make independent contributions to the frequency of dyadic disputes.

Realist Systemic Measures. Hegemony. We also create three systemic variables associated with prominent realist theories regarding the hegemon's influence on international relations. Hegemonic-stability theory postulates that the most powerful state in the system, the hegemon, has the ability to constrain weaker states from resorting to violence.[43] This power to keep the peace might be manifested as dominance within the hegemon's sphere of influence and the ability to deter adversaries from using military force in a way detrimental to its interests. A crude but reasonable measure of the power of the leading state is its share of all the major powers' capabilities in each year. As before, we use COW data to make this calculation.

Identification of the hegemon is not obvious in all cases. Through much of recent history it is not clear whether any state was truly hegemonic.[44] It is generally agreed that in the thirty years before World War I the United Kingdom was closer than any other country to being hegemonic, although its power relative to both Germany and the United States was declining. During the interwar era the United States clearly had greater economic strength and military potential than the United Kingdom; but its actual military power was only about equal. Moreover, its geographic position and isolationist policy limited its involvement in the Central European system. Consequently, we accept Organski and Kugler's judgment that Britain was the hegemon in the interwar period as well.[45] In the post–World War II years, if any state can be said to have been hegemonic, it is the United States. Hence we use the proportion of capabilities held by the United Kingdom as the measure of the hegemon's power in the first sixty years analyzed and that of the U.S. after 1945. Our systemic indicator (HEGPOWER) has reasonable face validity, declining from 33 percent in 1885 to 14 percent in 1913, and dropping under 11 percent by 1938. America's hegemony is manifest immediately following World War II, when it controlled 52 percent of the major powers' capabilities. This declined to 26 percent by the early 1980s but rose to 29 percent with the collapse of the Soviet Union.

Satisfaction with the status quo. The power-transition theory originally advanced by Organski consists of propositions not only about the constraining influence of an imbalance of power but also about the role played by states' satisfaction with the status quo. States rising in power will challenge a hegemon only if they are dissatisfied with the international system it dominates. Lemke and Reed extend this rationale in an effort to subsume the democratic peace within power-transition theory.[46] They contend that democracies have fought less historically because the hegemon has been democratic since the end of the Napoleonic Wars. First Britain and then the United States, it is argued, used its power to construct an international system that provided benefits to itself and its mostly democratic allies. Thus democracies' satisfaction with the status quo created by the most powerful democratic state and reinforced by its system of alliances accounts for the peace among democratic dyads. Like Lemke and Reed, we assess this view by computing a measure of each state's satisfaction with the status quo based on the correspondence between its portfolio of alliances and that of the hegemon, as indicated by the tau-b measure of statistical association. Then we multiply the scores of the two states in a dyad to create a measure of joint satisfaction (SATISFIED).[47] This measure indicates the degree to which each dyad is content with the distribution of benefits achieved under the leadership of the dominant state.

Hegemonic tensions. Both hegemonic-stability theory and power-transition theory hold that the international system will be more peaceful when the hegemon is strong relative to its principal rivals. The hegemon may also affect the system by transmitting concerns for its own security to other states. International tensions involving the hegemonic power are likely to have consequences for its allies, its rivals, its rivals' allies, and even neutral states. "When elephants fight, the grass gets trampled," as the adage goes. It is also possible, to extend the metaphor, that when small animals fight, big ones will be drawn in. Large states may intervene in ongoing conflicts because they see an opportunity to achieve gains or avoid losses. Either way, international tensions may be contagious. To assess this view, we created a measure of the hegemon's sense of its own security, calculating its defense spending as a share of its GDP (HEGDEF).[48] We hypothesize that the global system will experience more numerous disputes when the hegemon is committing more of its resources to the military. In such times, the hegemon presumably perceives greater threats to its interests. To assess the scope of contagion, we consider whether involvement in disputes rises mostly for the hegemon itself, for the hegemon and its allies, or for unallied states.

Results

We evaluate the Kantian peace, 1885–1992, employing logistic regression analysis. First we assess the effects of democracy, interdependence, and IGOs using a simple dyadic specification. In this view the likelihood of conflict is primarily determined by the state less constrained economically or politically. We also consider the degree to which the political and economic characteristics of the other member of a dyad affect the likelihood of a militarized dispute. Next we disentangle the systemic and cross-sectional influences of the Kantian variables on dyadic conflict. We consider the effects of trends in the underlying variables and each dyad's degree of democracy, interdependence, and involvement in IGOs relative to these annual systemic averages. Finally we investigate central realist tenets regarding the role of the leading state in the international system.

We examine the involvement in militarized interstate disputes of nearly 6,000 pairs of states observed annually, for a total of almost 150,000 observations. Because of the lagged variables the analysis begins with disputes in the year 1886 that are explained by reference to conditions in 1885. As noted earlier, we do not consider the two world wars after the first year of conflict or the immediate postwar years; that is, we exclude disputes for 1915–20 and 1940–46.

Unless otherwise indicated, we estimate the coefficients in our regression equations using the general estimating equation (GEE) method. We adjust for first-order autoregression (AR1) and estimate statistical significance using robust standard errors that take into account the clustering of our data by dyads. Thus we respond to the concerns raised by Beck, Katz, and Tucker. We rely on GEE rather than on their recommended solution for temporal dependence because of doubts about its appropriateness, especially given the strong, theoretically specified relation between trade and the time elapsed since a dyad's last dispute.[49] We have, however, reestimated our key equations using their method as a check on our findings. Because our hypotheses are directional and we have corrected for these violations in the assumptions underlying regression analysis, we report one-tailed tests of statistical significance.

Evaluating the Kantian Peace Using the Weak-Link Specification

Our first test is the simplest. We expect the likelihood of conflict to be primarily a function of the degree to which the less constrained state along each of several dimensions is free to use military force. This is the weak-link assumption that this state is more likely to precipitate a break in the peace: the less the political or economic constraints on that state's use of force, the greater the likelihood of violence. Consequently we include the lower democracy score and the lower bilateral trade-to-GDP ratio. The number of joint memberships in international organizations is inherently a dyadic measure; it

completes the Kantian specification. We include in the regression equation a measure of the dyadic balance of power and an indicator of whether the members of a dyad are allied. We also control for the distance separating the two states, whether or not they are contiguous, and whether both are minor powers.[50] Our first equation then takes the form:

$$\text{DISPUTE} = \text{DEM}_L + \text{DEPEND}_L + \text{IGO}$$
$$\text{ALLIES} + \text{CAPRATIO} +$$
$$\text{NONCONTIG} + \text{DISTANCE} +$$
$$\text{MINORPWRS (1)}$$

The results of estimating equation 1, found in the first column of Table 1, provide strong support for the pacifying influence of democracy and trade: the more democratic the less democratic state in a dyad and the more economically important is trade, the greater is the likelihood of peace. The lower democracy and dependence measures are both significant at the .001 level. The number of joint memberships in IGOs, however, does not have a statistically significant effect on conflict in this specification (p < .40). This is a consequence of two things: the inclusion of all possible dyads in the analysis (not just those thought to be politically relevant) and the rapid growth in the number of international organizations over time. The realist variables perform generally as expected, though the indicator of alliance is only significant at the .07 level: (1) a preponderance of power rather than a balance deters conflict; (2) contiguous states are prone to fight, as are those whose homelands are geographically proximate; and (3) major powers are involved in disputes more than are smaller states. All these variables are significant at the .001 level.[51] Using the onset (or first year only) of a dispute as the dependent variable produced nearly identical results.

Column 2 of Table 1 shows the results of estimating equation 1 using Beck et al.'s correction for temporal dependence in the time series. The coefficients and significance levels are usually similar. The most notable exception involves the variable IGO. Its coefficient is now not only positive but nearly four times its standard error.[52]

Table 1   Models of the Kantian Peace, 1886–1992: Predicting Involvement in Militarized Disputes

Variable	1. 1886–1992 Simplest, All Dyads	2. 1886–1992 Peaceyears Correction	3. 1886–1939 All Dyads	4. 1886–1992, Politically Relevant Dyads
Lower democracy	−0.0658***	−0.0628***	−0.0568***	−0.0595***
(DEM$_L$)	(0.0106)	(0.0093)	(0.0106)	(0.0106)
Trade/GDP	−57.8650***	−31.0726**	−43.2490**	−35.2394**
(DEPEND$_L$)	(15.4901)	(10.6036)	(16.2861)	(12.3044)
International organizations	−0.0010	0.0160*	0.0068	−0.0068*
(IGO)	(0.0379)	(0.0042)	(0.0068)	(0.0039)
Capability ratio	−0.2337***	−0.1913***	−0.3638***	−0.2747***
(CAPRATIO)	(0.0502)	(0.0401)	(0.0664)	(0.0516)
Alliances	−0.2511	−0.3691**	−0.1727	−0.2822*
(ALLIANCES)	(0.1659)	(0.1574)	(0.1905)	(0.1677)
Noncontiguity	−2.0038***	−1.5864***	−1.3357***	−1.118***
(NONCONTIG)	(0.1836)	(0.1532)	(0.1844)	(0.1724)
Log distance	−0.4647***	−0.3615***	−0.3536***	−0.2610***
(DISTANCE)	(0.0571)	(0.0498)	(0.0620)	(0.0605)
Only minor powers	−1.8392***	−1.7208***	−1.8342***	−0.6754***
(MINORPWRS)	(0.1706)	(0.1351)	(0.1904)	(0.2082)
Constant	−1.9349***	−1.6174***	−2.2235***	−1.5765***
	(0.4731)	(0.4060)	(0.5316)	(0.4992)
Chi^2	1354.80	1920.45	494.98	193.43
P of Chi^2	0.0000	0.0000	0.0000	0.0000
Log Likelihood		−5732.4260		
Pseudo R^2		0.284		
N	149,373	149,404	33,346	33,334

*p < .05; **p < .01; ***p < .001, one-tailed tests; *p .001, one-tailed test but wrong sign

To see if the pacific benefits of the Kantian variables are limited to the cold war era, we first reestimated equation 1 for just the early years, 1886–1914 and 1921–39 using GEE. The results appear in column 3. Comparing them with column 1 shows much the same pattern as the analysis for all years. Both the lower democracy score (p < .001) and the smaller bilateral trade-to-GDP ratio (p < .004) are highly significant.

Democracy and interdependence had strong peace-inducing effects during the multipolar period after 1885 and before the cold war. The benefits of democracy are strongest in the interwar years, but, as Gowa[53] also reports, by the decade leading to World War I democracies had become less likely to engage in militarized disputes with each other—an important shift that is obscured by using the years 1886–1914 as the period of analysis. In light of this evidence, the absence of democratic peace in the nineteenth century—not its presence in the cold war era—becomes the anomaly to be explained. The answer may lie more in the lower inclusiveness of democratic politics in that century than in characteristics of the international system.

Our measure of joint memberships in IGOs is insignificant for the period 1885–1939. The other coefficients in equation 1 are reasonably similar for the early years and the entire period. The effect of alliances before 1940 is even weaker (p < .19) than when all years are considered.

We also estimated equation 1 after creating an indicator for the 1989–92 post–cold war years and forming interactive terms with each of the three Kantian variables. The results indicate that the influence of democracy has not changed in this short span of time and the benefits of interdependence have been reduced, but IGOs are more important constraints on the threat or use of force.

In the past we limited our analyses to the politically relevant states, in the belief that the relations of most other dyads are not importantly influenced by the political and economic influences we have modeled. To see how including all possible pairs of states affects our results, we reestimate equation 1 using just the contiguous pairs of states and those that contain at least one major power—the politically relevant dyads—for all years, 1885–1992. This excludes dyads that in the great majority of cases had no reasonable opportunity to engage in armed conflict because the states were too far apart and had few issues over which to fight.

The last column of Table 1 provides strong support for the pacific benefits of all three elements of the Kantian peace. For the dyads most prone to conflict, joint membership in international organizations does reduce the likelihood of conflict (p < .04). The benefits of democracy (p < .001) and interdependence (p < .002) remain apparent. These results for the extended period, 1886–1992, are consistent with those in Russett, Oneal, and Davis, where only the years 1950–85 were considered; and they are more significant statistically.[54]

Our tests with all possible pairs understate the pacific benefits of IGOs because most of these dyads do not have significant political-military relations. The probability that a nonrelevant dyad will become involved in a dispute is only 1/18 that of a major-power pair; it is 1/44 that of a contiguous dyad. Democracy, interdependence, and involvement in IGOs constrain states from using force; but if there is no realistic possibility of two states engaging in conflict, then the absence of these constraints will not increase the incidence of violence. With all dyads included a large number of false negatives obscures the hypothesized relationship. The theoretically interesting variables in equation 1 are simply irrelevant in explaining the state of relations, such as they are, between Burma and Ecuador, for example. Including numerous irrelevant dyads can bias the results, as we have recently shown with regard to trade.[55]

With logistic regression, the easiest way to show the substantive effects of the variables is to estimate the probability of a militarized dispute for various illustrative dyads. The same procedure is often used in epidemiological studies. For example, epidemiologists report the effect of various risk factors on the probability that an individual will contract lung cancer. As in our analyses, some of their independent variables are not subject to intervention (for example, age, heredity, gender; and for us distance and contiguity), while others are amenable to some degree of "policy" control (for example, diet, exercise, smoking; and for us alliances, democracy, interdependence, and IGOs). By statistical inference they, and we, can estimate the reduction in the probability of an event occurring if any one risk factor for a typical individual were different by a given amount.

For this, we calculated a baseline probability against which to make comparisons. We assumed the dyad is contiguous, because these states are particularly prone to conflict. Then we set each continuous variable at its mean value for the contiguous dyads, except that the lower dependence score was made equal to its median value, which is more representative. We postulated that the pair of states is not allied and does not include a major power. We then estimated the annual probability that this "typical" dyad would be involved in a militarized dispute using the coefficients reported in columns 1 and 4 in Table 1. Next we changed the theoretically interesting variables in succession by adding a standard deviation to the continuous measures or by making the dyad allied.

The first two columns of Table 2 give the percentage increase or decrease in the annual risk of a dyad being involved in a dispute under these various conditions. Column 1 is based on the coefficients estimated using all dyads, and column 2 is produced with the coefficients for just the politically relevant subset of cases.[56] Looking at the results in column 1, it is apparent that democracy and interdependence dramatically reduce the likelihood of conflict. Compared with the typical dyad, the risk that the more democratic dyad will become engaged in a dispute is reduced by 36 percent. If the dyad is more autocratic, the danger of conflict is increased by 56 percent. A higher dyadic trade-to-GDP ratio cuts the incidence of conflict by 49 percent. A larger number of joint memberships in IGOs has little effect on a dyad's likelihood of conflict if all pairs of states are used in the estimation process. When analysis is limited to the politically relevant dyads,

however, the benefit of joint memberships in IGOs is clear. If the number of common memberships is fifty-three rather than thirty-two, the likelihood of conflict is reduced by 13 percent. And when the analysis is limited to politically relevant pairs, the effects of democracy and economic interdependence are somewhat less than when all dyads are considered.

The substantive importance of the Kantian variables is confirmed if their effects are compared with the results of changing the realist variables. Consider again the second column of Table 2. If a state's preponderance of power is a standard deviation higher, that reduces the probability of a dispute by 31 percent, but that result would require a fourfold increase in the capabilities of the stronger state. An alliance lowers the incidence of interstate violence by 24 percent. This is substantially less than when the dyad is more democratic or with a standard deviation higher level of bilateral trade.

We have argued that the characteristics of the less constrained state largely account for the likelihood of dyadic conflict, but the potential for violence may be significantly affected by the nature of the other dyadic member.[57] Democracies are more peaceful than autocracies at the national (or monadic) level as well as dyadically; but in our previous research we found, as Kant expected, that democracies and autocracies are particularly prone to fight one another because of the political distance separating them. Other analysts think that asymmetric interdependence may lead to conflict.[58] To evaluate these hypotheses we considered the influence of the higher democracy score and trade-to-GDP ratio, adding these variables to equation 1 both individually and as interactive terms with the lower democracy score or trade-to-GDP ratio.[59]

The results, not reported in a table but available from the authors, indicated that the conflict-prone character of mixed pairs—one democracy and one autocracy—was limited to the post–World War II era. Plausibly the special institutional and ideological animosities between democrats and communists, solidified by the cold war, account for that. In the multipolar period, 1885–1939, dyads consisting

Table 2 Percentage of Change in Risk for Annual Involvement in a Militarized Dispute for Contiguous Dyads[a] (1886–1992)

	Based on		
	1. Equation 1 (All Dyads)	2. Equation 1 (Politically Relevant Dyads)	3. Equation 2 (All Dyads)
DEM_L increased by 1 std. dev.	−36	−33	
DEM_L decreased by 1 std. dev.	+56	+48	
$DEPEND_L$ increased by 1 std. dev.	−49	−33	
IGO increased by 1 std. dev.	−2	−13	
CAPRATIO increased by 1 std. dev.	−27	−31	−33
ALLIES equals 1	−22	−24	−22
$RELDEM_L$ increased by 1 std. dev.			−30
$RELDEPEND_L$ increased by 1 std. dev.			−36
RELIGO increased by 1 std. dev.			−18
$AVGDEM_L$ increased by 1 std. dev.			−26
$AVGDEPEND_L$ increased by 1 std. dev.			−33
AVGIGO increased by 1 std. dev.			+3

[a]In each case other variables are held at baseline values.

of two democracies were the most peaceful after about 1900. Autocratic pairs and mixed dyads had similar rates of conflict. We found no evidence that asymmetric interdependence raised the likelihood of a militarized dispute. Increasing trade had significant pacific benefits whatever the relative size of the states involved. We did find a declining marginal utility for high levels of economic interdependence.[60]

Disentangling the Systemic and Cross-National Influences of the Kantian Measures

Estimating equation 1 indicates that the likelihood of a dispute among all dyads is a function of the lower democracy score and the lower trade-to-GDP ratio in a dyad but not of states' joint memberships in international organizations. We suggested that the failure of the IGO variable to perform as expected results partly from including large numbers of irrelevant pairs of states that have no significant political relations and lack a realistic possibility of becoming engaged in a dispute. By contrast, limiting the analysis to contiguous dyads and those containing a major power highlights the benefits of international organizations. We also noted that our measure of joint IGO membership increases rather steadily over time. This may obscure the contribution of international organizations to peaceful interstate relations by making comparisons across time less meaningful, as with nominal GDPs in periods of inflation.

The influence of IGO membership can be reconsidered by distinguishing between the frequency of states' participation in international organizations through time and the standing of individual dyads relative to this annual measure at each point in time. We decompose each Kantian variable—the lower democracy score, the lower trade-to-GDP ratio, and the number of joint IGO memberships—into a systemic measure, the average value of states' democracy score, level of interdependence, or joint membership in IGOs (Figure 1), and a cross-sectional measure that ranks dyads relative to this annual average. The annual average of the number of joint IGO memberships (AVGIGO), for example, captures the prominence through time of international organizations, while the degree of involvement of individual dyads relative to this average (RELIGO) identifies those states that are more (or less) linked through the network of IGOs in each year.

To distinguish between the systemic and cross-sectional Kantian influences, we substitute in equation 1 AVGDEM and $RELDEM_L$ for DEM_L, AVGDEPEND and $RELDEPEND_L$ for $DEPEND_L$, and AVGIGO and RELIGO for IGO. Our second equation becomes:

$$DISPUTE = RELDEM_L + RELDEPEND_L + \\ RELIGO + AVGDEM + AVGDEPEND + \\ AVGIGO + ALLIED + CAPRATIO + \\ NONCONTIG + DISTANCE + \\ MINORPWRS \ (2)$$

Column 1 of Table 3 reports the results of estimating equation 2 using all pairs of states. All the relative and systemic Kantian variables except the annual average of states' involvement in IGOs have a negative sign, indicating that increasing values reduce the likelihood of a militarized dispute; all but AVGIGO are very significant statistically. As explained in the last section, we standardized the three relative measures to permit direct comparison

of their estimated coefficients. These indicate that economically important trade has the greatest conflict-reducing benefits, followed by democracy and joint memberships in international organizations. Two of the three Kantian systemic variables also affect the incidence of dyadic disputes: the likelihood of conflict drops when there are more democracies in the system and trade is more important economically; with both variables significant at the .001 level.[61] The influences of the other variables in the equation are relatively unchanged. Preponderant power reduces the likelihood of a dispute, as do distance, an alliance, or the absence of a major power in the dyad. Using the onset of a dispute as the dependent variable produced nearly identical results.

The results of estimating equation 2 are important for three reasons. First, they show that dyads relatively more involved in international organizations at any point in time tend to be more peaceful, supporting the Kantian hypothesis regarding IGOs. Second, the results indicate that the statistical significance of democracy and the trade-to-GDP ratio in equation 1 is the consequence of temporal as well as cross-sectional variation. This is valuable assurance of the robustness of the pacific benefits of these Kantian influences. We now have explicit justification for believing that states can modify their circumstances by policies that increase democracy, interdependence, and, given the significance of the relative IGO measure, participation in international organizations. Third, it supports the view that there are systemic consequences of increasing democracy and trade for all pairs of states, not just for the liberal dyads.

The estimated coefficients for equation 2 allow us to compare the substantive importance of the relative and cross-sectional measures. We again calculate the probabilities of conflict for various hypothetical dyads. In calculating the baseline risk, we assume as before that the dyad is contiguous and set each continuous variable at its mean (or median for the trade ratio) for this subset of cases. We make the dyad un-allied and assume it does not include a major power. We estimate the annual probability that this

Table 3 Models of the Kantian Peace, 1886–1992: Predicting Involvement in Militarized Disputes (Dyadic and Systemic Influences, All Dyads)

Variable	1. Only Kantian Systemic Variables	2. Systemic Kantian, Heg. Power, Satisfaction	3. Systemic Kantian, Heg. Defense Burden
Relative lower democ.	−0.3688***	−0.3576***	−0.4102***
(RELDEM$_L$)	(0.0680)	(0.0677)	(0.0703)
Relative trade/GDP	−0.7270***	−0.7045**	−0.5149**
(RELDEPEND$_L$)	(0.2333)	(0.2412)	(0.2132)
Relative IGO	−0.1304**	−0.1060*	−0.1602***
(RELIGO)	(0.0500)	(0.0512)	(0.0502)
Average democracy	−0.2383***	−0.2485***	−0.2702***
(AVGDEM)	(0.0412)	(0.0412)	(0.0423)
Average dependence	−292.4397***	−260.3094***	−355.5549***
(AVGDEPEND)	(36.4178)	(48.7066)	(39.7875)
Average IGOs	0.0043	0.0102	−0.0440***
(AVGIGO)	(0.0109)	(0.0115)	(0.0136)
Capability ratio	−0.2897***	−0.2787***	−0.3125***
(CAPRATIO)	0.0518	(0.0521)	(0.0135)
Alliances	−0.2554	−0.2186	−0.3330*
(ALLIES)	(0.1625)	(0.1665)	(0.1636)
Noncontiguity	−2.0080***	−2.0423***	−1.9225***
(NONCONTIG)	(0.1803)	(0.1828)	(0.1802)
Log distance	−0.4915***	−0.4637***	−0.5202***
(DISTANCE)	(0.0567)	(0.0597)	(0.0569)
Only minor powers	−2.0230***	−2.0073***	−2.0694***
(MINORPWRS)	(0.1893)	(0.1941)	(0.1911)
Hegemonic power		−1.5339	
(HEGPOWER)		(0.9502)	
Joint satisfaction		−0.0893	
(SATISFIED)		(0.1057)	

(Continued)

Table 3 (Continued)

Variable	1. Only Kantian Systemic Variables	2. Systemic Kantian, Heg. Power, Satisfaction	3. Systemic Kantian, Heg. Defense Burden
Heg. defense burden			17.9704***
(HEGDEF)			(1.9906)
Constant	−0.7345	−0.7113	−0.3735
	(0.4850)	(0.5075)	(0.4975)
Chi^2	1559.82	1530.24	1529.38
P of Chi^2	0.0000	0.0000	0.0000
N	149,372	147,963	149,372

*$p < .05$; **$p < .01$; ***$p < .001$, one-tailed tests

representative dyad would be involved in a dispute using the coefficients in column 1 of Table 3. Then one at a time we change each continuous variable by a standard deviation; finally we make the dyad allied.

Column 3 of Table 2 gives the annual probabilities of a dyad being involved in a dispute under these conditions. The effects of the cross-sectional Kantian variables, which rank dyads according to their position relative to the annual systemic averages, are again substantial. For dyads with a higher relative democracy score the risk of conflict is 30 percent below the baseline rate; a standard-deviation increase in relative dependence means a 36 percent lower probability of conflict; and when states' participation in IGOs is higher the likelihood of conflict is reduced by 18 percent. The substantive significance of the Kantian variables for interstate relations again emerges by comparing these effects with those that result from changing the realist variables.

A higher capability ratio means lowering the danger of violence by a third, and when two states are allied the probability of conflict is lower by 22 percent. Note also the effects of the Kantian systemic variables. The risk of a dispute drops by 26 percent if the systemic average of the democracy score

increases by a standard deviation (from −0.47 to +1.26); it falls 33 percent if the systemic average of the trade-to-GDP ratio rises by a standard deviation (about 30 percent to .006). There is effectively no change if the systemic average for states' participation in IGOs grows. Thus, two of the Kantian systemic variables have powerful effects throughout the international system. By normative or institutional means, an increase in the number of liberal states constrains the use of force even by dyads that are not democratic or interdependent.[62] The effect of IGOs is limited, however, to those states that participate jointly in more of these international forums relative to other pairs.

Assessing the Hegemon's Influence on Dyadic Conflict

In our last analyses we investigate the role of the hegemon. We first evaluate a central claim of the theory of hegemonic stability and power-preponderance theory.[63] Both of these realist theories predict that conflict becomes more likely as the power of the leading state declines relative to its principal rivals. At the same time, we also address the argument that it has been the power of the (democratic) hegemon to reward its allies that accounts for the democratic peace. In a final test we consider whether the hegemon's sense of its own insecurity, as indicated by the ratio of its military expenditures to its gross domestic product, is associated with a heightened danger of conflict globally.

We assess the importance of the hegemon's relative power and states' satisfaction with the status quo by adding two terms to equation 2: HEGPOWER, the proportion of the major powers' capabilities held by Britain (through 1939) and the U.S. (after 1945); and SATISFIED, our measure of joint satisfaction, based on the similarity of each dyadic member's portfolio of allies to that of the leading power. It is appropriate theoretically to include both in the same equation. If the hegemon is able to regulate the level of conflict in the international system, then its influence should be greatest with those states with which it is most closely allied. At the same time the advantages for a state of aligning itself closely with the hegemon should be greatest when the power of the leading state is relatively large vis-à-vis its principal rivals; the hegemon in that situation should be most able to confer benefits upon its supporters.

Column 2 of Table 3 suggests that the strength of the leading state relative to its principal rivals does matter. The measure of hegemonic power is nearly significant (p < .06). Strong hegemony seems to reduce violence in the international system. This apparent effect stems, however, from the inability of a weakened hegemon (Britain) to prevent the outbreak of systemwide wars. In an analysis not reported in the table, the coefficient of our measure of hegmonic power reversed signs when the first year of each of the world wars was dropped: hegemony was then positively related to the incidence of disputes in the system (p < .003). Apparently the pacific benefits of hegemonic strength do not apply during normal periods of international relations. By contrast, we found no evidence in these analyses that states' satisfaction with the status quo accounts for the democratic peace. The measure of joint satisfaction in column 2 of Table 3 is far from statistical significance, while the significance of relative and systemic democracy is little changed.[64]

Finally we consider whether the hegemon's sense of its own security, as indicated by the proportion of GDP it devotes to military expenditures (HEGDEF), is related to the likelihood of dyadic conflict. We add our measure of the hegemon's defense burden to equation 2. The results of this test are reported in column 3. As seen there, the defense burden of the leading state is positively associated (p < .001) with the likelihood of dyadic disputes. There are wide-ranging consequences when the hegemon feels endangered. Nor is the heightened danger of conflict limited to the world wars, as with hegemonic power, or significant only for the hegemon or its allies. In a separate analysis not reported in the table, we confirmed that other states, too, experience more disputes when the hegemon has increased the proportion of its resources committed to the military. Our systemic and relative Kantian variables nonetheless remain important. Even the systemic measure of states' participation in international organizations is now significant at the .001 level. The effectiveness of IGOs may depend in part upon the major powers not feeling a need to develop, and presumably use, independent military means for protecting and promoting their interests.

A Kantian System? Past and Future

Our analyses for the years 1885–1992 indicate that Kant was substantially correct: democracy, economic interdependence, and involvement in international organizations reduce the incidence of militarized interstate disputes. The pacific benefits of the Kantian influences, especially of democracy and trade, were not confined to the cold war era but extend both forward from that era and back many decades. Moreover, these benefits are substantial. When the democracy score of the less democratic state in a dyad is higher by a standard deviation, the likelihood of conflict is more than one-third below the baseline rate among all dyads in the system; a higher bilateral trade-to-GDP ratio means that the risk of conflict is lower by half. The pacific benefits of democracy in the twentieth century are clear, and the change from the nineteenth century is consistent with an evolutionary view: democratic institutions matured, and the suffrage was extended. In addition, as Kant believed, states may learn from the success and failure of their policies.

The benefits of joint membership in intergovernmental organizations are more modest but nevertheless significant for the politically relevant dyads—contiguous states and dyads containing at least one major power. For these particularly dangerous dyads, the probability of a dispute drops by 13 percent when the number of joint memberships in IGOs is greater by a standard deviation. The pacific benefits of international organizations are also apparent when the trend in this variable is eliminated: among all dyads, pairs of states more involved by a standard deviation in IGOs relative to the annual systemic average are 18 percent less likely to become embroiled in interstate violence.

By distinguishing the influences of the Kantian systemic averages from the standings of each dyad relative to the annual means, we also showed benefits of democracy and trade over time as well as cross-sectionally. The effects of the systemic Kantian influences on dyadic conflict are important. The international system is more peaceful when there are more democracies and when trade is greater. *All* dyads—even those not democratic or interdependent—become less dispute-prone when those systemic Kantian variables increase. The constraining effect of norms and institutions that emerge when there are more democracies and when trade is economically important for many states holds even for those that participate to only a limited degree in the Kantian subsystem.[65]

Over the period 1885–1992 states' participation in IGOs rose steadily, but there is little evidence of a trend toward increased democracy or economic interdependence over the complete span of time. A long trend toward greater interdependence may be masked by two aspects of our data. First, the sample changes over time. Less developed and more peripheral states are probably underrepresented before World War I. Only with the establishment of the IMF and UN agencies does information on states'

wealth and dyadic trade become reasonably complete. Thus, the average level of bilateral interdependence may be overstated in the early years. Second, decolonization in the late 1950s and the 1960s created dozens of new states that were less democratic and less integrated into the global economy than the states already in the system, lowering the average scores for democracy and interdependence. And as noted, the codings of democracy that we use overstate the democratic character of states in much of the nineteenth century before suffrage was extended to women and those without property.

Both democracy and interdependence do show a marked jump after World War II. The number of democracies has grown steadily since the late 1970s, especially after the cold war ended. Trade grew rapidly in the 1970s. Since 1987 these phenomena have been followed by a precipitous drop in the number of interstate wars, despite the entry of many new states into the system.[66] Our results for the early post–cold war years cover only 1989–92, but they indicate that the beneficial effects of democracy, interdependence, and IGOs continued past the end of the cold war. Moreover, our analyses of the 1885–1992 period suggest that the relative peace of the past decade owes less to the systemic effects of power and hegemony than to growing Kantian influences.

As for the realist influences, some of the dyadic characteristics—chiefly distance, power preponderance, and minor power status—also reduce the likelihood of disputes. This is not surprising, though the lack of a robust effect for alliances is. The Kantian influences have not abolished power politics. Realist variables at the systemic level also make a difference in the incidence of dyadic conflict. Both world wars occurred when Britain, the hegemonic state, was weak. Yet hegemony does not always work as hypothesized. During more normal periods of international relations, there were more militarized disputes when the hegemon was powerful than when it was weak; and when the hegemon felt threatened (as evidenced by higher military spending relative to its gross domestic product), the likelihood of disputes rose throughout the system.

Democracies fought two world wars side by side, along with some autocracies that shared their strategic interests. Was the democracies' common alignment purely a result of strategic interests? It is more likely that shared interests in democracy and economic freedom played an important role. By contrast, alliances had no systematic dispute-inhibiting influence prior to the cold war. For the post-1945 era, when a reasonably strong effect of alliances is evident, it strains belief to attribute that effect primarily to strategic interests. Of course the cold war was substantially about national security as understood by realists. But it was also about a clash of two fundamentally different political and economic systems. The governments, dominant classes, and peoples of the free-market democracies felt not only that their physical security and national independence were threatened but also that their prosperity and especially their political and economic liberties were at stake. Hence they allied with one another to preserve their common way of life.[67]

The post–cold war era is full of affirmations about the importance of democracy, freedom, and prosperity built on interdependent markets. Some may be just rhetoric, but sophisticated global economic actors understand the role that interdependence plays in their prosperity. In 1999 NATO fought a war against Serbia in the name of democracy and human rights in Europe, against a dictatorial government that did not constitute a strategic threat. In time we shall see whether peace will hold among democracies and interdependent states, but

to call the democratic peace "a byproduct of a now extinct period in world politics"[68] sounds very like a premature report of its death.

Analytically, we are progressing toward a synthesis of Kantian and realist influences and of dyadic and systemic perspectives. Kant argued that three naturally occurring tendencies operate to produce a more peaceful world. Individuals desire to be free and prosperous, so democracy and trade will expand, which leads to the growth of international law and organizations to facilitate these processes. Peace, therefore, does not depend upon a moral transformation of humanity as long as even devils are self-interested and can calculate.[69] For Kant, a child of the Enlightenment, this was evidence of an ordered universe and, perhaps, of providential design. Yet he did not think that the process was mechanical or the outcome certain: reason would not always prevail, and states and individuals would not always act in conformity with their enlightened interests. Human agents must learn from experience, including that of war, and change behavior.

The current unipolar character—inevitably transitory—of our world, with no other state close to the power of the United States, provides an opportunity to build a peace based not only on military force but also on Kantian principles. Hegemony does not last forever. Consequently, democracy should be extended and deepened, the "cosmopolitan law" of commerce expanded, and international law and respect for human rights institutionalized. Kant would say this is a moral imperative.

Appendix: Variables

ALLIES: 1 if dyad members linked by defense treaty, neutrality pact, or entente

AVGDEM: average democracy score for all states in a year

AVGDEPEND: average dyadic trade to GDP ratio for all states in a year

AVGIGO: average number of dyadic shared IGO memberships

CAPRATIO: logarithm of ratio of higher to lower power capability in a dyad

DEM_H: higher democracy score in a dyad

(Continued)

(Continued)

DEM_L: lower democracy score in a dyad

$DEPEND_H$: higher dyadic trade-to-GDP ratio in a dyad

$DEPEND_L$: lower dyadic trade-to-GDP ratio in a dyad

DISPUTE: involvement in dyadic dispute

DISTANCE: logarithm of dyadic distance in miles between capitals or major ports

HEGDEF: ratio of leading state's military spending to its

GDP HEGPOWER: leading state's proportion of the capabilities of all major powers

IGO: number of international organization memberships shared by a dyad

MINORPWRS: 1 if dyad does not include a major power

NONCONTIG: 1 if dyad is not contiguous by land border or less than 150 miles of water

$RELDEM_L$: DEM_L – AVGDEM/standard deviation of

DEM $RELDEPEND_L$: $DEPEND_L$ – AVGDEPEND/standard deviation of

$DEPEND_L$ RELIGO: IGO – AVGIGO/standard deviation of IGO

SATISFIED: tau-b measure of similarity of dyad members' alliance portfolios to that of the leading state

---

Notes

Authors' Note: We thank the Carnegie Corporation of New York, the Ford Foundation, and the National Science Foundation for financial support; Zeev Maoz for comments; and Jennifer Beam, Margit Bussmann, Soo Yeon Kim, Yury Omelchenko, Brian Radigan, and Jacob Sullivan for data collection and management.

1. Kant, *Perpetual Peace: A Philosophical Sketch,* in *Kant's Political Writings,* ed. Hans Reiss (Cambridge: Cambridge University Press, 1970), 105. See also James Bohman and Matthias Lutz-Bachmann, eds., *Perpetual Peace: Essays on Kant's Cosmopolitan Ideal* (Cambridge: MIT Press, 1997).

2. By convention in the social science literature, war is defined as a conflict between two recognized sovereign members of the international system that results in at least one thousand battle deaths. The most complete data on militarized international disputes (MIDs), compiled by Stuart Bremer and his colleagues, are available at http://pss.la.psu.edu/MID_DATA.HTM. The democracy data we employ were compiled by Keith Jaggers and Ted Robert Gurr, "Tracking Democracy's Third Wave with the Polity III *Data.,*" *Journal of Peace Research* 32, no. 4 (1995), available at http://isere.colorado.edu-/pub/datasets/polity3/politymay96.data. Both data sets are produced independently from the democratic peace research program, and the initial codings, from the 1980s, precede it. Reviews of the program include Steve Chan, "In Search of Democratic Peace: Problems and Promise," *Mershon International Studies Review* 41, no. 1 (1997); James Lee Ray, "Does Democracy Cause Peace?" *Annual Review of Political Science* 1 (1997); and Bruce Russett and Harvey Starr, "From Democratic Peace to Kantian Peace: Democracy and Conflict in the International System," in Manus Midlarsky, ed., *Handbook of War Studies,* 2d ed. (Ann Arbor: University of Michigan Press, forthcoming).

3. Henry Farber and Joanne Gowa, "Common Interests or Common Politics?" *Journal of Politics* 57, no. 2 (1997); Gowa, *Ballots and Bullets: The Elusive Democratic Peace* (Princeton: Princeton University Press, 1999); Douglas Lemke and William Reed, "Regime Types and Status Quo Evaluations," *International Interactions* 22, no. 2 (1996); Erik Gartzke, "Kant We All Just Get Along? Opportunity,

Willingness and the Origins of the Democratic Peace," *American Journal of Political Science* 42, no. 1 (1998).

4. The MIDs data (fn. 2) are unavailable after 1992, and data on dyadic trade are sparse and unreliable before 1885. In any event the further back one goes into the nineteenth century, the rarer are instances of democracy, intergovernmental organizations, and high levels of economic interdependence. The MIDs data include only disputes between recognized states and not, for example, extrasystemic (i.e., colonial) actions, covert operations, or domestic military interventions in support of a recognized government.

5. We will not here offer a new theory on why democracy produces peaceful relations. A recent statement is Bruce Bueno de Mesquita et al., "An Institutional Explanation of the Democratic Peace," *American Political Science Review* 93, no. 4 (1999).

6. John R. Oneal and Bruce Russett, "The Classical Liberals Were Right: Democracy, Interdependence, and Conflict, 1950–1985," *International Studies Quarterly* 40, no. 2 (1997); Russett, Oneal, and David R. Davis, "The Third Leg of the Kantian Tripod: International Organizations and Militarized Disputes, 1950–85," *International Organization* 52, no. 3 (1998); Oneal and Russett, "Assessing the Liberal Peace with Alternative Specifications: Trade Still Reduces Conflict," *Journal of Peace Research* 36, no. 4 (1999). Here we extend this line of research in three ways: (1) providing a conceptual synthesis of Kantian and realist theories that treats conflict as inherent but subject to important constraints; (2) extending the temporal domain for trade and IGOs into the nineteenth century; and (3) assessing realist theories regarding the role of the hegemon and Kantian theories about systemic influences in a way that addresses, among others, constructivist and evolutionary perspectives on the international system. Note that the Kantian influences may be mutually reinforcing in a dynamic system of feedback loops, as suggested by Wade Huntley, "Kant's Third Image: Systemic Sources of the Liberal Peace," *International Studies Quarterly* 40, no. 4 (1996); and Russett, "A Neo-Kantian Perspective: Democracy, Interdependence, and International Organizations in Building Security Communities," in Emanuel Adler and Michael Barnett,

eds., *Security Communities in Comparative Perspective* (New York Cambridge University Press, 1998).

We and others have begun to address some of these links, such as greater trade between democracies, the possibility that trade is diminished between conflicting states, the effect of democracy, trade, and peace in increasing membership in international organizations, and the effect of conflict on democracy. On the first, see Harry Bliss and Russett, "Democratic Trading Partners: The Liberal Connection," *Journal of Politics* 58, no. 4 (1998), and James Morrow, Randolph Siverson, and Tessa Tabares, "The Political Determinants of International Trade: The Major Powers, 1907–90," *American Political Science Review* 92, no. 3 (1998); on the second, see Soo Yeon Kim, "Ties That Bind: The Role of Trade in International Conflict Processes" (Ph.D. diss., Yale University, 1998); on the third, see Russett, Oneal, and Davis (this fn.); and on the last, see Oneal and Russett, "Why An Identified Systemic Model of the Democratic Peace Nexus' Does Not Persuade," *Defence and Peace Economics* 11, no. 2 (2000).

7. Michael W. Doyle, *Ways of War and Peace* (New York: W. W. Norton, 1997), chap. 8; David Lake, "Powerful Pacifists: Democratic States and War," *American Political Science Review* 86, no. 4 (1992).

8. Birger Heidt, "Inherency, Contingency, and Theories of Conflict and Peace" (Manuscript, Yale University, 1998); Benjamin Most and Harvey Starr, *Inquiry, Logic, and International Politics* (Columbia: University of South Carolina Press, 1989), chap. 2.

9. A useful review is Susan McMillan, "Interdependence and Conflict," *Mershon International Studies Review* 41, no. 1 (1997).

10. John Mearsheimer, "The False Promise of International Institutions," *International Security* 19 (Winter 1994–95).

11. Emanuel Adler and Michael Barnett, "Security Communities in Theoretical Perspective," in Adler and Barnett (fh. 6); Alexander Wendt, *Social Theory of International Politics* (New York: Cambridge University Press, 1998). For microlevel evidence that trading contacts expand elites' views of their self-interest, see Daniel Lerner, "French Business Leaders Look at EDC," *Public Opinion Quarterly* 24, no. 1 (1956); and Bruce Russett, *Community and Contention:*

Britain and America in the Twentieth Century (Cambridge: MIT Press, 1963), chap. 9.

12. Robert O. Keohane and Lisa Martin, "The Promise of Institutionalist Theory," *International Security* 20, no. 1 (1995); Lisa Martin and Beth Simmons, "Theories and Empirical Studies of International Institutions," *International Organization* 52, no. 4 (1998).

13. For a review of some relevant hypotheses and findings, see Russett, Oneal, and Davis (fn. 6).

14. Jaggers and Gurr (fn. 2).

15. Samuel P. Huntington, *The Third Wave: Democratization in the Late Twentieth Century* (Norman: University of Oklahoma Press, 1991).

16. For graphing purposes the scale for bilateral trade/ GDP has been increased by two orders of magnitude and that for IGO membership has been reduced by one order of magnitude.

17. Wendt (fn. 11). On some systemic effects of a high proportion of democracies, see Huntley (fn. 6); Nils Petter Gleditsch and Havard Hegre, "Peace and Democracy: Three Levels of Analysis," *Journal of Conflict Resolution* 41, no. 2 (1997); Sara McLaughlin Mitchell, Scott Gates, and Havard Hegre, "Evolution in Democracy-War Dynamics," *Journal of Conflict Resolution* 43, no. 6 (1999); and Lars-Erik Cederman, "Back to Kant: Reinterpreting the Democratic Peace as a Collective Learning Process" (Manuscript, Political Science Department, University of California at Los Angeles, December 1998).

18. For dates of independence, see Bruce Russett, J. David Singer, and Melvin Small, "National Political Units in the Twentieth Century: A Standardized List," *American Political Science Review* 62, no. 3 (1968). Germany and Japan temporarily lost sovereignty after World War II, but soon regained it (Germany as two states). Kuwait was briefly occupied in 1990—91; but a large, diverse coalition of states under the aegis of the United Nations forced Iraq to withdraw in order to protect the sovereignty of established states. South Vietnam is an exception to this generalization if one regards its unification with North Vietnam in 1976 as the result of external conquest rather than of an international-ized civil war. Whereas state extinction as a conse-quence of international war has become rare, the ideology of ethnic self-determination has led to the breakup of many states and empires.

19. A counterhypothesis would be that as democracies become more numerous and more confident in their individual and collective strength, they may become emboldened to pursue coercive relationships with those autocracies that remain. For evidence that democracies do win most of their wars, see Bruce Bueno de Mesquita, Randolph Siverson, and Gary Woller, "War and the Fate of Regimes: A Comparative Analysis," *American Political Science Review* 86, no. 3 (1992); Lake (fn. 7); and Allan C. Stam III, *Win Lose or Draw* (Ann Arbor: University of Michigan Press, 1996).

20. Thomas L. Friedman, *The Lexus and the Olive Tree* (New York: Farrar, Straus, and Giroux, 1999); and Stephen G. Brooks, "The Globalization of Production and International Security" (Ph.D. diss., Yale University, forthcoming).

21. Identified by W. S. Robinson, "Ecological Correlations and the Behavior of Individuals," *American Sociological Review* 15, no. 3 (1950). On how some inferences can be made, see Gary King, *A Solution to the Ecological Inference Problem* (Princeton: Princeton University Press, 1997).

22. Kenneth Waltz says that it is the power of the units (states) themselves that defines polarity and not the number or power of the alliances they lead; see Waltz, *Theory of International Politics* (Reading, Mass.: Addison-Wesley, 1979), 98–99. Thus the for-mation of two opposing alliance systems prior to World War I did not change the structure of the multipolar system. Waltz's emphasis on the systemic effects of nuclear weapons would also imply a break between 1945 and all previous years of modern his-tory. Dating the end of the bipolar cold war system is more problematic. Waltz's definition would argue for a break at the end of 1991, when the Soviet Union was dissolved. But William Dixon and Stephen Gaarder show a decisive shift in the pattern of Soviet-American conflict in 1988; see Dixon and Gaarder, "Presidential Succession and the Cold War: An Analysis of Soviet-American Relations, 1948–1992," *Journal of Politics* 54, no. 1 (1992).

23. Färber and Gowa (fn. 3) express this concern.

24. Stuart A. Bremer, "Dangerous Dyads: Conditions Affecting the Likelihood of Interstate War," *Journal of Conflict Resolution* 36, no. 1 (1992); Katherine

Barbieri, "International Trade and Conflict: The Debatable Relationship" (Paper presented at the annual meeting of the International Studies Association, Minneapolis, Minn., February 1998); Nathaniel Beck, Jonathan Katz, and Richard Tucker, "Taking Time Seriously in Binary Time-Series-Cross-Section Analysis," *American Journal of Political Science* 42, no. 4 (1998). See, however, our comment in fn. 49 below.

25. Geoffrey Blarney, *The Causes of War,* 3d ed. (New York: Free Press, 1988).

26. Oneal and Russett (fn. 6, 1999).

27. Kim (fn. 6), using a simultaneous equation model, finds that the effect of trade on conflict is much stronger than the reciprocal one. Russett, Oneal, and Davis (fn. 6) construct a model for predicting IGO membership that includes, among other factors, the absence of conflict. There is an effect, but it is weaker than the influence of IGOs on conflict.

28. William J. Dixon, "Democracy and the Peaceful Settlement of International Conflict," *American Political Science Review* 88, no. 1 (1994).

29. Trevor Wilson, *The Myriad Faces of War: Britain and the Great War, 1914–1918* (Cambridge, England: Polity Press, 1986), 660–61; Kenneth MacKenzie, *The English Parliament* (Harmondsworth: Penguin, 1980), 106.

30. Carole Kennedy Chaney, R. Michael Alvarez, and Jonathan Nagler, "Explaining the Gender Gap in U.S. Presidential Elections," *Political Research Quarterly* 51, no. 2 (1998). To take such changes into account, Zeev Maoz uses an adjusted threshold of democracy for all countries that shifts upward in 1870 (for general male suffrage) and 1920 (female suffrage); see Maoz, *Domestic Sources of Global Change* (Ann Arbor: University of Michigan Press, 1996), 54. Our use of unadjusted democracy scores thus leans against our hypothesis of democratic peace before World War I. Kristian Gleditsch and Michael Ward note that our continuous measure, Democracy minus Autocracy score, has the virtues of being symmetric and transitive; but the relative importance of its components is unstable over time; see Gleditsch and Ward, "Double Take: A Re-examination of Democracy and Autocracy in Modern Polities," *Journal of Conflict Resolution* 41, no. 3 (1997). For the period 1880–1969 this

aggregated measure is largely influenced by the degree of competition for executive recruitment; subsequently constraints on the executive are the main determinant. Fortunately the relatively stable earlier period covers all the pre–cold war years we add here. As no analysis of the democratic peace after World War II has yet addressed the 1969 break, we too leave that for later investigation.

31. International Monetary Fund, *Direction of Trade (ICPSR 7623)* (Washington, D.C.: IMF, 1993; distributed by Ann Arbor, Mich.: Inter-University Consortium for Political and Social Research). Robert Summers et al., *The Penn World Table (Mark 5.6a)* (Cambridge, Mass.: National Bureau of Economic Research, 1995). Due to missing data for trade and/or GDP, the great majority of dyads involved in the Korean and Vietnam Wars are omitted, as are most Arab-Israeli dyads. Since most of those are conflicting democratic-autocratic dyads with no trade, our analysis is likely to be biased against the liberal hypotheses. Because these conflicts spanned several years, excluding these cases mitigates the problem of temporal dependence in the time series, as does omitting all but the first year of the world wars. Also omitted are roughly 2,500 communist dyad-years: non-IMF members. These states traded among themselves but did not report it to the IMF and generally had little conflict. Had we been able to include them, the post-1950 sample would have been increased by only about 2 percent.

32. League of Nations, *International Trade Statistics* (Geneva: League of Nations, annual volumes).

33. Martin Epstein, ed., *The Statesman's Yearbook, 1913* (London: Macmillan, 1913), and earlier annual editions by other editors.

34. We took several steps to minimize missing trade data in this period. We used information regarding one state's exports to another to infer its partner's imports; we interpolated between known values of trade and used the average value of a dyad's trade to extrapolate; and we assumed, for those states for which we had data, that there was no trade between any two if neither reported any exports or imports with the other. As a result we have trade data for 61 percent of the dyads 1885–1913 and 1920–38. We conducted several tests to see if these methods might have biased our results. First we dropped all zero values of trade,

and then we dropped all interpolations and extrapolations. Analyses with the remaining "real" data, 1885–1940, revealed little change in the results. We also determined that the sample of dyads for which we have trade data is unlikely to be biased. To do this, we created a variable (MISSING) that equaled 1 if $DEPEND_L$ was missing and 0 otherwise and then changed all missing values of $DEPEND^{\wedge}$ to zero. We then estimated equation 1 below with the variable MISSING added. It was not statistically significant, indicating that the incidence of disputes among the dyads for which trade (or GDP) data are missing does not differ from that for the dyads for which data are available.

35. These include volumes by Brian R. Mitchell for each region of the world and for the United Kingdom (Cambridge: Cambridge University Press, various years); U.S. Department of Commerce, *Historical Statistics of the United States: Colonial Times to 1970* (New York: Basic Books, 1976); and Katherine Barbieria data posted at http://pss.la.psu.edu/TRD_DATA.htm. Exchange rates come from U.S. Federal Reserve Bank sources, *The Statesman's Yearbook*, and Global Financial Data Company, www:global fmdata.com.

36. Angus Maddison, *Monitoring the World Economy, 1820–1992* (Paris: Organization for Economic Cooperation and Development, 1995). His U.S. dollar GDP deflator is found in Maddison, "A Long Run Perspective on Saving" (Manuscript, Institute of Economic Research, University of Groningen, October 1991).

37. Oskar Morgenstern, Klaus Knorr, and Klaus P. Heiss, *Long Term Projections of Power: Political, Economic, and Military Forecasting* (Cambridge, Mass.: Ballinger, 1973); and also John R. Oneal, "Measuring the Material Base of the Contemporary East-West Balance of Power, *International Interactions* 15, no. 2 (1989).

38. We extended the data from the sources in Russett, Oneal, and Davis (fn. 6).

39. Bremer (fn. 24); Jacek Kugler and Douglas Lemke, eds., *Parity and War: Evaluations and Extensions of the War Ledger* (Ann Arbor: University of Michigan Press, 1996). Waltz (fn. 22), 117–23, reviews the balance of power literature and states his own version.

40. Data are from J. David Singer and Melvin Small, *National Military Capabilities Data* (Ann Arbor: University of Michigan, Correlates of War Project, 1995); the date of final modification of the data was December 28, 1994.

41. We updated J. David Singer, *Alliances, 1816–1984* (Ann Arbor: University of Michigan, Correlates of War Project, 1995), with material from N. J. Rengger, with John Campbell, *Treaties and Alliances of the World*, 6th ed. (New York: Stockton, 1995).

42. As recommended by William Reed, "The Relevance of Politically Relevant Dyads" (Paper presented at the annual meeting of the Peace Science Society [International], New Brunswick, N.J., October 1998).

43. Robert Gilpin, *War and Change in World Politics* (Cambridge: Cambridge University Press, 1981).

44. Bruce Russett, "The Mysterious Decline of American Hegemony, or, Is Mark Twain Really Dead?" *International Organization* 32, no. 2 (1985).

45. A. F. K. Organski and Jacek Kugler, *The War Ledger* (Chicago: University of Chicago Press, 1980). On measurement, see David Sacko, "Measures of Hegemony" (Paper presented at the annual meeting of the Peace Science Society [International], New Brunswick, N.J., October 1998).

46. Lemke and Reed (fn. 3).

47. We added 1 to each state's tau-b score to make it positive. The tau-b index of the similarity of alliance portfolios was introduced by Bruce Bueno de Mesquita, "Measuring Systemic Polarity," *Journal of Conflict Resolution* 19, no. 2 (1975). It was adapted as a dyadic measure of satisfaction by Woosang Kim, "Alliance Transitions and Great Power War, *"American Journal of Political Science* 35 (1991), and subsequently used by Lemke and Reed (fn. 3).

48. Military expenditure is a component of the COW index of militarily relevant capabilities. On the validity of our measure, see John R. Oneal and Hugh Carter Whadey, "The Effect of Alliance Membership on National Defense Burdens, 1953–88," *International Interactions* 22, no. 2 (1996). Changes in this index for the hegemon's military burden correlate highly with changes in the average military burden for all the major powers.

49. On GEE, see Peter J. Diggle, Kung-Yee Liang, and Scott L. Zeger, *Analysis of Longitudinal Data*

(Oxford: Clarendon Press, 1994). We used the computing algorithms in StataCorp, *Stata Statistical Software*, Release 5.0 (College Station, Tex.: Stata Corporation, 1997). For Beck, Katz, and Tucker's methods, see fn. 24. We express our doubts that the effects of the theoretical variables and of time are separable, as Beck, Katz, and Tucker's method requires, in Oneal and Russett (fn. 6, 1999). GEE allows for temporal dependence in the time series but gives the theoretical variables primacy in accounting for interstate disputes. Beck, Katz, and Tucker introduce the PEACEYRS variables into the estimation process as coequals of the theoretical variables. See also D. Scott Bennett, "Parametric Methods, Duration Dependence, and Time-Varying Data Revisited," *American Journal of Political Science* 43, no. 1 (1999).

50. Our recent specifications are found in Oneal and Russett (1997); and Russett, Oneal, and Davis (fn. 6). The controls, from Oneal and Russett (fn. 6, 1999), draw on Barbieri (fn. 24).

51. To test the robustness of these results, we estimated separate regressions for each theoretically interesting variable with just the controls for distance, contiguity, and major-power status. The signs and significance levels were consistent with those in the multivariate regressions, with one exception. Joint IGO memberships significantly ($p < .001$) reduced conflict in the restricted analysis. We also reestimated equation 1 after dropping the measure of economic interdependence because this variable has the most missing values. The pacific benefits of democracy remained strong ($p < .001$). Joint membership in IGOs, too, was significantly associated with a reduction in conflict ($p < .02$) when $DEPEND_L$ was omitted. Not surprisingly, interdependent states share memberships in international organizations.

52. We suppress coefficients for the four spline segments to save space. All are significant ($p < .001$). In this equation, and others presented subsequently, the coefficients for IGOs are the only ones not robust to the different methods for adjusting for temporal dependence. As our results suggest, joint membership in IGOs is most correlated of the three Kantian variables with the years of peace since a dyad's last dispute. Our methodological preference for GEE preceded our

work on IGOs. We also estimated equation 1 using conditional or fixed effects logistic regression. Greater democracy ($p < .001$) and interdependence ($p < .05$) continued to be associated with peaceful dyadic relations, as was the existence of an alliance. Joint membership in IGOs and a greater capability ratio increased the prospects of conflict. These results are based on the 20,289 observations for dyads that experienced at least one dispute; 129,092 cases were dropped because the dependent variable always equaled zero.

53. Gowa (fn. 3), 98–100.

54. Oneal, Russett, and Davis (fn. 6). Färber and Gowa (fn. 3), 409, analyze lower-level MIDs for 1816–1976 and find that democracy significantly affects the likelihood of conflict only after 1919. However, using interactive terms for years, we find evidence of democratic peace by 1900. Earlier than that even the most democratic states were not democratic by contemporary standards. As democracy developed, the common interests of democracies and their antagonisms with authoritarian states may have become more substantial. Support for the benefits of democracy in Färber and Gowa's analyses is weakened by their decision to exclude consideration of all years of the world wars. Due to possible simultaneity problems, they do not control for alliances. Since alliances show little impact in our analyses, this may not matter. For results for trade that agree with ours, see Christopher Way, "Manchester Revisited: A Theoretical and Empirical Evaluation of Commercial Liberalism" (Ph.D. diss., Stanford University, 1997). For results that differ from ours, see Barbieri (fn. 24); and idem, "Economic Interdependence: A Path to Peace or a Source of Interstate Conflict?" *Journal of Peace Research* 33, no. 1 (1996). Our analyses to date indicate that this is primarily due to our different measures of interdependence: Barbieri does not weight trade by its contribution to GDP. The results reported in Oneal and Russett (fn. 6, 1999) show that the pacific benefits of trade, 1950–92, are robust to several alternative specifications, samples, and estimation procedures.

55. Oneal and Russett (fn. 6, 1999).

56. This baseline probability is .031 among all dyads and .055 for the politically relevant pairs.

57. Maoz (fn. 30); Oneal and Russett (fn. 6, 1997); Oneal and James Lee Ray, "New Tests of the Democratic Peace Controlling for Economic Interdependence, 1950–1985," *Political Research Quarterly* 50, no. 4 (1997).

58. Robert O. Keohane and Joseph S. Nye, *Power and Interdependence: World Politics in Transition* (Boston: Little Brown, 1997); John A. Kroll, "The Complexity of Interdependence," *International Studies Quarterly* 37 (September 1993); Immanuel Wallerstein, "The Rise and Future Demise of the World Capitalist System," *Comparative Studies in Society and History* 16, no. 4 (1974); Barbieri (fnn. 24 and 54).

59.   If the effect of one variable (DEM_L, $DEPEND_j$ is thought to depend on the value of another (DEM_H, $DEPEND_h$), the test should include their interactive terms ($DEM_L * DEM_h$ and $DEPEND_L * DEPEND_H$). See Robert J. Friedrich, "In Defense of Multiplicative Terms in Multiple Regression Equations," *American Journal of Political Science* 26, no. 4 (1982).

60. Analyses in which we modeled the effect of interdependence as a hyperbola suggest that the benefits of trade increase rapidly and then approach a limit asymptotically. See Mark Gasiorowski and Solomon Polachek, "East-West Trade Linkages in the Era of Detente," *Journal of Conflict Resolution* 26, no. 4 (1982).

61. There is a mild downward trend in the likelihood of a dispute over the period 1885–1992. To insure that the systemic Kantian variables were not simply collinear with this secular trend toward decreasing rates of disputes, we included in each of the equations reported in Table 3 an indicator of time, which equals the year minus 1884. The coefficients of the Kantian variables changed very little, and the average democracy score and trade-to-GDP ratio remained significant at the .001 level; the measure of time was never significant at the .05 level in these tests. If equation 2 is estimated for just the 1885–1939 period, the coefficient of the average level of interdependence becomes statistically insignificant, primarily because the level of trade at the outset of World War I was higher than it was during the interwar years; the average level of democracy remained significant at the .001 level.

62. To insure that the effects of the annual averages of the democracy score and trade ratio were truly systemic and not confined to only those dyads that were relatively democratic or interdependent, we added three interactive terms ($AVGDEM *RELDEM_L$, $AVGDEPEND*RELDEPEND_L$, and $AVGIGO*RELIGO$) to equation 2. The results indicated that the effects of the systemic Kantian variables are not confined to just those dyads that rank high relative to the annual averages.

63. A. F. K. Organski, *World Politics* (New York Knopf, 1968); George Modelski, ed., *Exploring Long Cycles* (Boulder, Colo.: Lynne Rienner, 1987); Gilpin (fn. 43); Kugler and Lemke (fn. 39); K. Edward Spiezio, "British Hegemony and Major Power War, 1815–1939: An Empirical Test of Gilpin's Model of Hegemonic Governance," *International Studies Quarterly* 34, no. 2 (1990).

64. We tested alternative specifications in evaluating the role played by states' satisfaction with the status quo. We adopted the weak-link assumption, adding the smaller of the tau-b measures of satisfaction to equation 2, and investigated whether two dissatisfied states might also be peaceful; but these terms were not statistically significant.

65. See the references in fnn. 17 and 19 and the textual discussion accompanying them.

66. Monty G. Marshall, *Third World War* (Lanham, Md.: Rowman, Littlefield, 1999).

67. By controlling for states' interests, we have tried to show that the democratic peace is not an artifact of the cold war; see Oneal and Russett, "Is the Liberal Peace Just an Artifact of Cold War Interests? Assessing Recent Critiques," *International Interactions* 25, no. 3 (1999).

68. Gowa (fn. 3), 114.

69. Kant (fn. 1), 112.

EDITORS' COMMENTARY

Major Contributions: Democratic Peace

Oneal and Russett (1999c) describe the benefits of democracy, economic interdependence (e.g., trade), and international organizations for promoting peace in the international system. This study is part of the authors' broader research program of articles (e.g., Maoz and Russett 1993; Oneal and Russett 1997; Russett et al. 1998) and books (Russett 1993; Russett and Oneal 2001) that develop the theoretical linkages between Kantian factors and then subjects these hypotheses to rigorous empirical tests with data from 1885–1992. The **democratic peace** refers to the lack of wars between fully democratic states and the reduced chances for any type of militarized conflict between democracies. The democratic peace has been described as "the closest thing we have to an empirical law in international relations" (Levy 1988, 662). If it were an empirical law, it would mean that just as you can depend on gravity to pull down a pencil to the ground when you let it go, you can depend on democratic countries to remain peaceful in their interactions with other democracies.

The democratic peace has been analyzed at different levels of analysis. The most common claim is that **joint democracies** do not fight each other. This is a **dyadic** relationship and much of the empirical literature is based on finding that democracies do not fight each other. This is different from the position that democracies are inherently peaceful and do not fight wars unless attacked. This is the position known as the **monadic democratic peace**, often associated with President Woodrow Wilson's advice to "make the world safe for democracy." Wilson thought that democratic states were inherently peaceful, while monarchies and dictatorships were inherently war prone. The empirical evidence for this monadic proposition is mixed, with some studies finding no effect (Small and Singer 1976; Quackenbush and Rudy 2009) and others showing that democracies are more peaceful in general (Rummel 1997; Ray 2000; Boehmer 2008).

While **Immanuel Kant** (1724–1804) foreshadowed the modern democratic peace in his 1795 philosophical writings on *Perpetual Peace,* it was not until the twentieth century that researchers began to uncover a strong empirical correlation between democracy and peace (Babst 1964). In the past few decades, hundreds of studies have confirmed the empirical connection between dyadic democracy and peace. The theoretical models explaining this pattern of behavior, on the other hand, have been contested. The democratic peace is not only an influential scholarly model for understanding international conflict; the virtues of spreading democracy globally have been espoused by multiple U.S. presidents, from Woodrow Wilson (long before the scholarly work on the democratic peace was conducted) to Bill Clinton to George W. Bush.

Oneal and Russett (1999c) describe the three legs of the **Kantian tripod for peace** (Russett and Oneal 2001): (1) joint democracy, (2) economic interdependence, and (3) international organizations (IGOs). These correspond (roughly) to Kant's (1970,

99–105) three conditions for perpetual peace: (1) "The Civil Constitution of Every State shall be Republican," (2) "The Right of Nations Shall be based on a Federation of Free States," and (3) "Cosmopolitan Right shall be limited to Conditions of Universal Hospitality."[1] By republican governments, Kant was referring to what we conceive of as representative democracies today, those regimes with regular, fair, and free elections where multiple parties and candidates compete for office. Kant reasoned that when two democracies had an international dispute, they would be more inclined to settle the issue peacefully because the citizens in each state would not want to pay the costs of war. Kant's second condition describes a "federation of free states" or what Oneal and Russett view as the international organizations that have arisen in the system over time, such as the United Nations. In the post–World War II era, democracies have been more likely to create and join international organizations, and these institutions help to preserve the peace by managing conflicts between member states and by promoting a convergence of foreign policy interests (Russett and Oneal 2001, 163–166). The third condition of universal hospitality allows for travel of individuals between states and ensures that a "spirit of commerce" and free trade can take hold. Oneal and Russett focus on the extent to which countries depend on other states for trade. The authors view these three legs of the Kantian tripod as interconnected; "virtuous circles" arise as democracies trade more and join more IGOs, trade helps to promote IGO connections and democracy, and membership in IGOs promotes democratization and trade among members. Thus, in addition to each tripod factor lowering the risks for dyadic militarized conflict, they also reinforce each other and generate additional incentives for peace.

While most scholars accept the empirical regularity known as the democratic peace, there are disagreements about the causal process that most likely generates this observed correlation. Oneal and Russett (1999c) build upon several of the major theoretical models in the literature, including the structural model, the normative (or constructivist) model, the informational model, and the hegemonic model. The **structural model**, best articulated by Russett (1993) and Bueno de Mesquita et al. (2005), focuses on accountability in democratic states where leaders can be punished by the domestic audience for implementing foreign policies that result in unsuccessful wars. Close to 90 percent of democratic leaders lose office within one year after losing an interstate war, while more than 50 percent of nondemocratic leaders stay in power after a war loss (Goemans 2000, 58). This fits with Kant's view that nondemocratic leaders are more likely to engage in war because they have less to lose personally if things do not go well. If democratic leaders know that they can lose office, they are more selective in choosing wars to initiate such that they will try to pick wars they can win. This last idea stems from the **selectorate theory** (Bueno de Mesquita et al. 2005) and predicts that democracies are more likely to win the wars they fight. Lake (1992, 31) provides evidence to support this claim; democratic states have been victorious in 81 percent of the wars they have fought. The structural model views electoral and legislative institutions as constraining leaders and slowing the decision-making time to war. When democracies face other democracies, the constraints that operate in both states prevent escalation of diplomatic issues to war.

The **normative model**, developed initially by Dixon (1993, 1994) and Maoz and Russett (1993), has been extended in more recent constructivist work on the democratic peace (Peceny 1997; Wendt 1999; Mitchell 2002; Harrison 2004). The basic idea of this model is that democracies have norms of peaceful conflict resolution inside the state and that these norms carry over into foreign policy interactions. When two neighbors have a dispute over their property, they have legal or political channels that they can use to settle their differences. When democratic countries have disagreements with other democratic states, they expect the other side to operate with norms of compromise and nonviolence. Dixon and Senese (2002) provide evidence for this idea; as the lowest democracy score in a dyad increases, the probability of a negotiated settlement in a militarized dispute increases significantly. For instance, if two democracies (e.g., United States and Japan) had a dispute, they would be more likely to reach a settlement through peaceful negotiations than a dispute involving two nondemocracies (e.g., Saudi Arabia and Iran). This approach also expects democratic states to be more amenable to third-party conflict management (Dixon 1993; Raymond 1994; Mitchell 2002), such as working out differences with the help of a mediator or international court. Maoz and Russett (1993) argue that democratic norms operate more strongly in democratic regimes that have been in existence for a long time, such as the United States (see also Huth and Allee 2002). Maoz and Russett (1993) find empirically that older, democratic regimes are less likely to engage in militarized conflicts with other established democratic regimes. Thus, it is not simply the presence of certain types of institutions (e.g., elections, courts) that promotes peace; the longer the institutions are embedded in society, the more strongly the norms of peaceful conflict management take hold. Wendt (1999) provides a theoretical account of this broader dynamic describing the evolution of the international system from a Hobbesian-like arena where states do not trust each other to a more Kantian system where countries view other states' security as important to their own security.

Another theoretical perspective, the **informational model**, focuses on how states communicate with each other in crisis situations (Leeds 1999; Schultz 1999). This builds upon the **bargaining model of war**, which views lack of information about the enemy's capabilities or resolve as one potential source of war. Democracies can overcome informational problems more easily than autocracies because their political systems are more transparent, it is harder to mobilize forces in secret (e.g., the media are watching), and leaders' statements are more credible given the potential costs (e.g., losing office) they can face for misleading the public. Schultz (1999) finds that when democracies initiate militarized disputes against other states, the targeted states are more likely to back down. When two democracies face each other, the transparency of both regimes makes any kind of preemptive war difficult.[2]

A final theoretical perspective focuses on democracies as a set of countries generally satisfied with the status quo in the system. In the post-Napoleonic era, the hegemonic or most powerful states in the international system have been democratic states, such as the United Kingdom and the United States. These countries establish free trading regimes and international organizations to benefit their interests, but in doing so, they create a system that benefits other democratic regimes as well

(Ikenberry 2001). As Oneal and Russett (1999c) point out, some realist scholars have been skeptical of the democratic peace phenomenon because they think it is merely a function of coincidental interests in the Cold War (Farber and Gowa 1995). Many European democratic states in the Cold War had reasons to fear attack by the Soviet Union and thus formed cooperative ties with the United States. While some of Russett and Oneal's earlier studies had focused on the Cold War period, in the article in this volume, they extend their data back to 1885 to show that the democratic peace relationship is not merely a function of shared security interests during a particular historical period (although there are few democratic states prior to 1914). Analyzing dyadic data from 1886–1939 (Table 1, Model 3), they show that dyads are less likely to experience MIDs as the lower democracy score in the dyad increases. Trade also has a pacifying influence on dyads in this period. Recall that Bremer (1992b, Chapter 2, this volume) also found joint democracy to have a negative and statistically significant influence on the onset of war when examining a longer historical period (1816–1965).

There have been numerous critics of the Kantian tripod for peace, and we have reprinted three of them in this book—Barbieri (1996, Chapter 10), who challenges the findings on trade; Reed (2000, Chapter 11), who shows selection bias when estimating the effect of joint democracy on war; and Gibler (2007, Chapter 12), who argues that peace is due to stable borders and that neighbors with stable borders will be at peace whether they are democratic or not. Two other critics are Henderson (2002) and Mousseau (2002), both of whom have eliminated the statistical significance of joint democracy in empirical models. Henderson (2002) finds that cultural similarity wipes out the significance of joint democracy. Mousseau (2002, 2003, 2012) argues that capitalist countries with a contract-intensive economy and culture are the ones that do not fight each other (see also Gartzke 2007).

Methodological Notes: Levels of Analysis

Oneal and Russett (1999c) use **dyad-years** as their unit of analysis, creating at most 149,404 pairs of states for analysis in Table 1 (Model 2). Some of their earlier articles (e.g., Oneal and Russett 1997) had examined **politically relevant dyad-years** in which they limited cases for analysis to those pairs of states that shared a land or water border or contained one or more major powers. They find fairly similar results across these two samples. Theoretically, though, they expand their independent variables to include both dyadic- and systemic-level factors. The democratic peace has been studied at all major **levels of analysis** in international relations, including the monadic, dyadic, and systemic levels. The **monadic** level of analysis focuses on the nation-year and asks whether democratic countries are more peaceful than nondemocratic countries. The **dyadic** level of analysis examines pairs of countries and considers whether pairs of democratic countries (i.e., joint democracies) are more peaceful than other pairs (e.g., democracy and nondemocracy). The **systemic** level of analysis focuses on the system year as the unit of analysis and ponders whether peace in the system is more likely when there are many democratic countries in the world (Mitchell 2002).

One of the methodological problems of using the dyad-year is that it greatly increases the number of cases. While larger samples are generally better because they reduce the size of the standard errors around our estimates, having really large samples can increase the chances that any null hypothesis will be rejected. Having a sample size of 149,000+ (Oneal and Russett 1999c) or 193,000+ (Bremer 1992b) makes it more likely that there will be many statistically significant relationships as compared to say an analysis of 3,000 or so dyadic militarized interstate disputes (MIDs). For this reason, some scholars argue that if something is significant, a dyad-year analysis will turn it up, but on the whole, inflating the number of cases in this manner does not make for a very conservative or difficult test. Note that very few variables are statistically insignificant in Oneal and Russett's Table 1. In this case, we might use a higher threshold for significance (e.g., 99 percent), or we could place more emphasis on interpreting predictive probabilities that describe the substantive strength of each variable. Oneal and Russett present the substantive effects of the variables in their model to provide the reader with these kinds of probability comparisons so that we can assess which variables have the largest effect on the chances for dyadic militarized disputes.

Oneal and Russett (1999c) include dyadic measures for democracy (DEM_L), trade ($DEPEND_L$), and international organizations (IGO); these capture the ties or similarities between a particular pair of countries. They use a concept called the **weakest link**, which Dixon (1993) developed, which records the score of the least democratic or least trade-dependent state in a dyad. If one country had a Polity democracy score of -8 and the other state had a score of $+4$, the weakest link approach would give the dyad a score of -8. The idea is that the least democratic state is the one whose norms of compromise and nonviolence will dominate in dyadic interactions. The same approach is applied to trade dependence, where they record the country with the lowest trade dependence in a dyad. The IGO measure is a count of the total number of international organizations that the two states in a dyad jointly belong to, ranging from 0 to over 130. The authors also include systemic-level measures of democracy ($AVGDEM_L$), trade ($AVGDEPEND_L$), and IGOs (AVGIGO). This is designed to provide a snapshot for any given year of how democratic, trade dependent, or IGO filled the international system may be. As the average democracy score increases, for example, this tells us that the international system has many more countries that are democratic. To code average democracy, you would take every country's democracy score in a given year (e.g., 1950) and then take the **mean** by summing all country's democracy scores and then dividing by the number of countries. Oneal and Russett include these measures to capture the theoretical arguments of the normative model that focus on increasing peace in a democratic system due to norms of peaceful conflict management (Mitchell 2002). They also create relative scores that subtract the dyadic score from the systemic average to represent how similar a particular dyad is to the system at a given moment in time (e.g., $RELDEM_L = (DEM_L - AVGDEM_L)$). Early in the 1800s, most states were autocratic and thus nondemocratic dyads were pretty similar to the systemic average regime scores. In more recent periods, the system is populated by close to 50 percent democratic states, and thus dyads with higher democracy scores are closer to the systemic average.

The empirical analyses use a methodological approach very similar to Mitchell and Prins (2004, Chapter 8, this volume). They use a **GEE model** where they assume that the residuals follow an **autoregressive (AR)** process. This captures any dependence among dyadic cases over time (e.g., conflict in the Israel-Egypt dyad in 1967 could increase chances for future conflict) or across space (e.g., conflict in the Israel-Egypt dyad in 1967 could increase chances for conflict in the Israel-Lebanon or Israel-Syria dyads). They also estimate **subsamples** of the data (e.g., 1886–1939) to show how relationships might vary across different historical eras. They also include a variety of **control variables** to capture other factors that could increase the risks of dyadic conflict, such as the capability ratio, shared military alliances, distance between capital cities, minor power status, and noncontiguity. At the systemic level, they also include controls for the hegemonic state's power such as the hegemon's defense spending (HEGDEF) and its share of all capabilities held by major powers (HEGPOWER). This is designed to capture realist claims about the democratic peace being a function of the status quo established and maintained by the most powerful state in the world.

The empirical results provide support for dyadic- and systemic-level effects for the Kantian peace variables. Table 1 begins with a focus on dyadic-level factors. For all years in their sample (1886–1992) and for the pre–Cold War era (1886–1939), they find that dyadic militarized conflict is less likely in pairs of jointly democratic states and dyads with higher levels of trade dependence. Shared IGO memberships have no statistically significant effect on dyadic MIDs. Consistent with Bremer (1992b), they find that dyadic conflict is less likely in power preponderant dyads (where one state is much more powerful), in dyads with greater distances between them, or in dyads containing minor powers. Table 2 shows the **predicted probabilities** relative to a baseline model, which is a contiguous dyad that is not allied and contains no major powers; they set the other variables at their mean values. We can see in column 1 that as the least democratic score in a dyad increases by one standard deviation from its mean, the probability of a dyadic MID decreases by 36 percent. As the lowest value of trade dependence increases one standard deviation above its average value, the chances for a dyadic MID drop by 49 percent. These effects are larger than the predicted probabilities for other realist variables such as the capability ratio, which reduces the chances for MID by 27 percent when increased by one standard deviation above the mean.[3]

Table 3 shows the results for the systemic Kantian variables, while the predicted probabilities are presented in Table 2, column 3. We can see that dyads that are more democratic than the systemic average (RELDEM$_L$) have a much lower likelihood of dyadic conflict; similar effects are observed for trade and IGOs. While the number of shared IGOs does not have a significant effect in the dyadic measure, they do find that dyads whose shared IGO memberships are much higher than the systemic average are more peaceful (e.g., RELIGO is large and positive). The systemic levels for each Kantian variable matter as well; as the average democracy and average trade dependence levels in the global system increase, any given pair of states is less likely to experience a MID. This can help to explain the overall declining numbers of interstate wars in the modern era (Goldstein 2011). One interesting thing to note is that these systemic effects influence all countries, whether they have democratic institutions or not. Thus, the growth of a global Kantian system influences all countries, not just those states that are "particularly democratic, economically interdependent, or involved in international organizations" (Oneal and Russett 1999c, 9; see also Mitchell 2002).

Notes

1. "Nature also unites nations which the concept of cosmopolitan right would not have protected from violence and war, and does so by their mutual self-interest. For the *spirit of commerce* sooner or later takes hold of every people, and it cannot exist side by side with war" (Kant 1970, 114).
2. By preemptive war, we are referring to a situation where one side attacks the other because it sees that the other is taking actions to attack it. When two sides have active mobilization of their forces, either side could benefit from being the first to attack. Consider Israel's devastating attack on the Egyptian air force in its preemptive attack in the Six Day War in 1967.
3. While these are substantial effects, a critic would argue that Oneal and Russett should have reported the actual predicted probabilities, which, as we know from their other studies, are quite small. This is another downside from using the dyad-year—since the probability of war is so small, it is difficult to know for sure whether slight increases or decreases in the yearly probability of war or MIDs are substantively important.

Questions

1. Looking at Figure 1, in approximately what year did the international system experience the highest average democracy score? The highest average IGO score?

2. As described on page **200**, the authors "lag all independent variables by one year." What does this mean? Why are they doing this?

3. On page **196**, Oneal and Russett point out some problems of comparing regimes in different time periods. How might we address these issues?

4. On page **201**, they note that they remove some of the world war years (1915–1920, 1940–1946) due to missing trade data. What effects might this have on their analyses?

5. Oneal and Russett argue that some independent variables are not really subject to intervention (like hereditary factors for lung cancer) while other variables can be manipulated (e.g., whether a person smokes). Which variables in this study could be changed? Which ones would be the most "cost-effective" for promoting peace?

Further Reading

Maoz, Z., and B. Russett. 1993. Normative and structural causes of democratic peace, 1946–1986. *American Political Science Review* 87 (3): 624–38.

Mitchell, S. M. 2002. A Kantian system? Democracy and third party conflict resolution. *American Journal of Political Science* 46 (4): 749–59.

Mitchell, S. M., S. Gates, and H. Hegre. 1999. Evolution in democracy-war dynamics. *Journal of Conflict Resolution* 43 (6): 771–92.

Russett, B. 1993. *Grasping the democratic peace: Principles for a post–Cold War world.* Princeton, NJ: Princeton University Press.

Russett, B., and J. R. Oneal. 2001. *Triangulating peace: Democracy, interdependence, and international organizations.* New York: W. W. Norton.

Wendt, A. 1999. *Social theory of international politics.* New York: Cambridge University Press.

Chapter 10

Economic Interdependence

A Path to Peace or a Source of Interstate Conflict?

Katherine Barbieri

1. The Virtues and Vices of Trade

Throughout history, people have debated the virtues and vices of foreign trade. For many, trade represents a path toward peace and prosperity among nations.[1] For others, trade is viewed as a contributing factor in the impoverishment of some nations and tensions between other nations. Still others view trade as largely irrelevant to leaders' decisions to engage in, or refrain from, intense forms of interstate conflict. The trade-conflict debate has long focused on whether the benefits derived through trade outweigh the costs associated with economic dependence. Those viewing trade as a mutually beneficial relationship maintain that economic ties create a disincentive to conflict. Conversely, those who focus on the negative consequences of trading relationships find the 'trade promotes peace' proposition less convincing. Despite the prevalence of trade-conflict propositions in international relations literature, there are few empirical studies investigating related propositions.

The question of the impact of trade on interstate relations is not only theoretically interesting, but has important policy implications. For centuries nations have clung to the hope that trade and interstate ties will cement the bonds of friendship that make the resort to arms unfathomable. Yet, little evidence has been provided to substantiate such claims. In light of recent trends toward regional integration, and increasing efforts to expand trade linkages among previously hostile nations, it is important to consider the potential impact of such relations.

Part of an ongoing investigation designed to enlarge our understanding about the impact of interdependence on interstate relations during the 19th and 20th centuries (Barbieri 1992, 1994a,b, 1995), this article begins by examining the pre-WWII period, an era that so far has received little attention. First, I consider what may be termed the unconditional liberal hypothesis—that trade promotes peace regardless of the nature and context of economic linkages. Next, I consider a proposition frequently argued by critics of commercial liberalism—that the ability of trade to promote peace is contingent upon the nature and context of economic linkages. In particular, symmetrical trading relations may foster peace, while asymmetrical dependence creates tensions that may eventually manifest themselves in conflictual interactions. Thus, both the importance (salience) and the balance (symmetry) of the trading relationship must be considered in assessing whether or not economic interdependence will inhibit interstate conflict. The study also considers alternative factors believed to alter the conflict propensity of dyadic relationships, to control for the potential confounding

Source: Katherine Barbieri, "Economic Interdependence: A Path to Peace or a Source of Interstate Conflict?" *Journal of Peace Research* 33, no. 1 (1996): 29–49. © *Journal of Peace Research.* Reprinted by permission of SAGE Publications, Inc.

influence of contiguity, joint democracy, alliance commitments, and relative capabilities.

With few exceptions, economic linkages have been largely ignored in the literature devoted to the scientific study of conflict.[2] Broad historical studies of the impact of interdependence on international relations focus primarily on the system-level of analysis, with the exception of Domke's (1988) monadic level study. To date, systemic studies have failed to reach a consensus. While Domke (1988), Rosecrance (1986), and Mansfield (1994) maintain that the expansion of trade over time has resulted in a general reduction of intensive forms of interstate conflict, Waltz (1979) argues that the decrease in interdependence during the post-WWII period is one of a set of factors contributing to peace in that era. Apart from the lack of consensus at the system level, these studies tell us little about the dynamics operating within specific interstate relations. Just as global interdependence is believed to vary across historical periods, with differing consequences for interstate relations, it also varies in degree and character across pairs of states.

However, dyadic studies are largely confined to the post–World War II era. With the exception of Wallensteen (1973),[3] research in this area finds empirical evidence of a negative relationship between dyadic trade and conflict (Gasiorowski & Polachek, 1982; Gasiorowski, 1986a,b; Oneal et al., 1996; Polachek, 1980; Polachek & McDonald, 1992; and Sayrs, 1990)[4] Wallensteen's study spans a wider period (1920–68) and is also distinct in its identification of circumstances in which economic dependence may increase conflict (i.e., between topdogs and underdogs). In addition, Barbieri (1995) finds no evidence of an inverse relationship between trade and conflict in the post-WWII period.

Whether or not one accepts the argument that the post-WWII period is unique, it is important to determine empirically whether the trade-conflict relationship in this period is generalizable across the history of the interstate system, because the characteristics that define the post–Cold War era and relations within the evolving interstate system may be more reminiscent of earlier periods. Thus, to understand what the future may hold for interdependent relations, it is useful to begin with an examination of the past, because the notion that trade promotes peace is thought to transcend time, space, and level of analysis.

2. Theories of Trade and Conflict

Four propositions about the trade-conflict relationship are easily identified among a broad group of theorists: (1) the liberal argument that trade promotes peace; (2) the argument, advanced by neo-Marxists and others, that symmetrical ties may promote peace, while asymmetrical trade leads to conflict; (3) the suggestion that trade increases conflict; and (4) the belief that trade is irrelevant to conflict.

2.1 Trade Promotes Peace

Liberals, functionalists, and neo-functionalists argue that the expansion of interstate linkages in one area stimulates further cooperation in other areas (see Dougherty & Pfaltzgraff, 1990, ch. 10; Haas, 1958, 1964; Mitrany, 1964). Interstate linkages are thought to improve communication, reduce misunderstanding, and foster cultural and institutional mechanisms capable of mediating conflicts of interest that do arise. Ultimately, the recognition of mutual benefits through cooperation serves to foster peace, as national interests converge. A related economic argument attributes the inverse relationship between trade and conflict to states' recognition that trade is an increasingly more efficient means for acquiring products and markets than military conquest (Rosecrance, 1986). Finally, the argument receiving the most attention in related literature suggests that states are deterred from initiating conflict against a trading partner for fear of losing the welfare gains associated with trade (Polachek, 1980). Polachek's expected utility model of trade and conflict provides the basis for understanding both the arguments of advocates and critics of the proposition that trade promotes peace.

For Polachek and other liberals, trade patterns emerge naturally as a result of given heterogeneous factor endowments among nations. These trade patterns and the accruing benefits associated with trade affect rational leaders' foreign policy behavior, as they attempt to maximize social welfare. In a leader's expected utility calculus, the cost of conflict equals the lost welfare gains associated with potential trade losses (Polachek, 1980, 1992). Even if conflict does not lead to the cessation of trade, it will lead to inferior terms of trade, resulting in welfare losses (Polachek & McDonald, 1992). Leaders are deterred from initiating conflict against important trading partners for fear of losing welfare gains associated with trade. An extended liberal argument suggests that it is not merely the volume of trade, but the type of trade that exists between partners that affects utility calculations for conflict. Polachek & McDonald provide evidence that the more inelastic a country's import and export demand and supply to a target country, the smaller the amount of actor-to-target conflict.

While liberals recognize that gains from trade and the potential costs accompanying interdependence are not always equal, they argue that trade ties imply net positive benefits for both states. Thus, a clear link is established between expanded trade and peace within the liberal tradition. The link is tenuous for those who maintain that trade might entail net costs or for those who view states' concerns about absolute gains as subordinate to concerns about relative gains (Mastanduno, 1993; Snidal, 1993; Waltz, 1979). In addition, dependency theorists reject the notion of universal voluntary exchange, arguing that developing nations, as a result of historical-structural relationships, are not free actors and are therefore unable to make the same calculations proposed by the expected utility models (Abel & Tetreault, 1986). Thus, the existence of trade ties need not imply mutual benefits, but may reflect a lack of freedom to break free from undesirable trade relations.

2.2 Symmetrical Trade May Promote Peace

The notion that trade provides net benefits, which in turn reduces the likelihood of interstate conflict,

has not gone unchallenged. Theoretical critiques have focused on several aspects of the unconditional liberal claim, with an eclectic group of theorists highlighting the negative consequences of economic dependence (Balogh, 1963; Cooper, 1968; Emmanuel, 1972; Gasiorowski, 1986a, b; Hirschman, [1945] 1980; Wallensteen, 1973). Although critics of liberalism seldom explicitly address the trade-conflict, relationship, their commentary about the negative consequences of economic dependence is relevant to my study. For it is essentially the beneficial aspects of trading relationships that liberals assume foster peace. If costs outweigh benefits, as argued by critics of liberalism, the link of trade to peace appears less convincing. Moreover, this literature has argued that trading relations may even be a source of tension, particularly when relations are asymmetrical.

The negative consequences of dependence are believed to be greater in asymmetrical relations. The dependency school of thought and neo-Marxists have provided the most comprehensive treatment of the negative consequences of asymmetrical dependence. They argue that trade does not always entail net benefits, and may instead entail net costs. Rather than increasing the prosperity of trading partners, trade often results in the impoverishment of less powerful nations. A broad list of counter-claims has been advanced by dependency theorists in response to liberal claims of trade's universal benefits. These include the argument that: the gains from trade are enjoyed exclusively by developed states; trading relations between developed and developing nations retard the development process of the latter; trade destroys traditional political, economic, and social institutions; trade exacerbates inequalities in the wealth of nations; and trade relegates powerless states to a position of dependence.[5]

Moreover, dependent states may face negative political consequences when they become subject to the manipulation or coercion of the more powerful (i.e., less dependent) state in the trading relationship (Hirschman [1945] 1980). The power that arises from asymmetrical dependence may be used to gain concessions in either the political or economic domain (Hirschman; Keohane & Nye, 1977). Particularly when structural linkages exist, dependent states are less able to alter their trade patterns and may become subject to manipulation. Thus, such states will be unable to enjoy the benefits of trade without being vulnerable to coercion. When extensive economic dependence threatens national autonomy and poses problems for domestic foreign policymakers, tensions may arise among trade partners. The negative consequences of dependence are assumed to be more pronounced in asymmetrical relationships; however, all economic relationships entail costly aspects (Cooper, 1968).

Although most would agree that asymmetrical dependence serves as a source of leverage in a number of policy areas, it is unclear that the use of power arising from trading relationships is sufficient to create tensions that will manifest themselves in violent conflicts. Relations that fail to provide mutual benefits or impose disproportionate costs on one actor may be viewed as hostile relations. Yet, a hostile climate need not entail hostile acts. Hostilities might be suppressed when relations of subservience and dominance exist or when states perceive some aspect of the relationship as beneficial, and thus seek to preserve a sense of harmony. Still, it would appear plausible to argue that the existence and abuse of unequal power within asymmetrical relations creates a predisposition for conflict that is greater than that found in symmetrical trade relations. The absence of net benefits in a trading relationship neutralizes the pacifying influence of trade, assumed to exist by liberals. In fact, relations of unequal exchange may heighten tensions in interstate relations, making conflict more likely in such relationships.

Even in a climate of absolute gains for trading partners, tensions may arise over the distribution of the gains from trade. Neo-realists argue that states are preoccupied with concerns over relative, rather than absolute, gains (Mastanduno, 1993; Snidal, 1993; Waltz, 1979). States may view the gain to their partner as a potential loss to themselves and will be reluctant to grant other states the benefits associated with trade. Greater wealth and productive efficiency for a trading partner may eventually be translated into military power, meaning trade creates a negative security externality (Gowa, 1994). For this reason, states may be unwilling to subordinate national interests to supranational objectives associated with trade.

2.3 Trade Increases Conflict

A third group of theorists, arising primarily from Marxist-Leninist, resource scarcity (Choucri & North, 1975, 1989), and neorealist thought (Waltz, 1979), envisions conflict accompanying expanded global trade. Critics also reject the notion advanced by liberals that trade will always be a desirable substitute to military options for acquiring resources and markets (Rosecrance, 1986). The history of colonialism and imperialism illustrates how military force may be used in conjunction with trading strategies to establish and maintain inequitable economic relationships (Cohen, 1973). Thus, the expansion of trade may not promote peace, but may involve increased interstate conflict, as powerful states vie with one another for control over finite resources and markets (Lenin [1939] 1990), and use force to subjugate developing states to a position of dependence. Although interesting, these studies are focused at the system level of analysis and are less relevant to the study.

2.4 Trade is Irrelevant to Conflict

Finally, realist theorists have traditionally relegated economic relations to low politics, arguing that the influence of trade is subordinate to other considerations in determining the incidence of international conflict (Blainey, 1973; Blanchard & Ripsman, 1994; Buzan, 1984; Levy, 1989b). Instead, traditional security concerns and military factors dominate leaders' calculations of the utility of conflict (Bueno de Mesquita, 1981). In addition, realists recognize that economic instruments may be an important tool in the pursuit of the national interest (Morgenthau, 1964). In such instances, trade does not represent a path toward interstate peace, but a means for securing power. Trade relations represent transitory arrangements for pursuing the national interest; when demands change, trade ties can easily be broken. In no way does trade preclude the use of alternative strategies to further the national interest, including the use of force.

One way to reconcile the differences in the propositions advanced between different theoretical traditions is to consider the linkages among the arguments presented within each school of thought. The basis of trade's pacifying effect is presumed to arise from the benefits derived from economic linkages. When such ties are believed to contribute to poverty, domestic disequilibria, or discontent over the distribution of gains from trade, the pacifying influence of trade may be neutralized. In fact, the dynamic may be reversed, where increased trade leads to increased conflict. I now turn to a way in which we might envisage the separate relationships described among the theoretical approaches in an effort to develop a set of plausible hypotheses concerning the trade-conflict relationship.

2.5 Visualizing Interdependence

From theories critical of liberalism, it becomes clear that not all trading relations are equal. Some trading relations may contain the necessary conditions to foster peace, while others instill hostilities or exacerbate pre-existing tensions. To understand how such variations may obtain, it is necessary to consider the nature and context of economic linkages between states. Several theorists offer clues about the types of trading relations that are most likely to produce mutual benefits and therefore possess the greatest potential for fostering peace. Theorists also provide clues about the conditions most likely to breed contempt in economic relationships, suggesting which states are less likely to enjoy the pacifying influence of trade.

One of the most important distinctions arises in the different types of relationships entailed by interdependence and dependence. Interdependence generally implies relations of mutual need and, by extension, mutual vulnerability between actors, while dependence denotes asymmetrical relations. A further distinction is made, by Keohane & Nye (1977, pp. 8–9), between interdependence and interconnectedness. Interconnectedness merely represents weak linkages among states incapable of having a significant influence on interstate relations; while interdependence entails a vulnerability and sensitivity not found in less extensive linkages.[6]

Figure 1 is helpful in identifying the conditions believed to provide the most benefits and costs of trade, simplifying the relationship between interdependent, dependent, and independent relations. Rather than thinking about the presence or absence of interdependence and dependence, as a strict dichotomy, I conceptualize trade relations along a continuum, where characteristics of different types of relationships may coexist. Figure 1 represents a dyadic relationship, where each axis measures the trade share each state has of its partner's total trade.

Quadrants I and IV represent scenarios where one state is disproportionately dependent upon the other partner. Relations of dependence are generally considered by the literature to be the most conflictual. Quadrants II and III represent conditions of mutual (symmetrical) dependence, yet in the latter case dependence is minimal. Thus, dyads falling within Quadrant III have symmetrical, but not salient (i.e., important) economic relations. To distinguish between the balance and the extent of dependence, imagine a line dissecting the origin at a 45 degree angle and extending out to the point where each state has all of its trade with one partner. The closer dyads fall to the diagonal line, the more balanced the relationship. For some theorists, symmetry is the most important factor for fostering peace in a relationship regardless of the extent of such ties.[7] For others, relations falling within lower ranges of the line (i.e., in Quadrant III) lack the bonds sufficient to inhibit conflict. Generally, trading relationships that have both extensive and balanced dependence are believed to offer the greatest likelihood for peace (i.e., those falling within Quadrant II).

Figure 1   Dependence and Interdependence Continuum

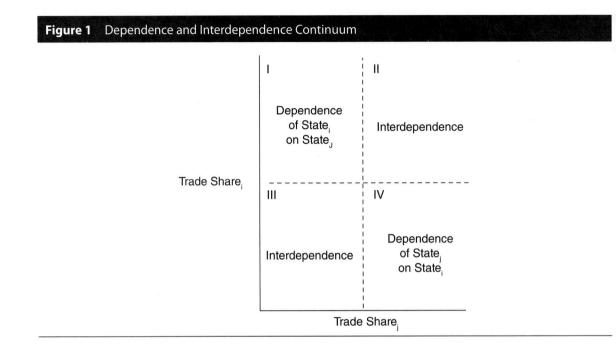

I now turn to an investigation of the competing propositions about the effects of economic interdependence on interstate relations. After discussing the nuances of different conceptions of interdependence, I introduce a set of measures that capture different dimensions of economic interdependence. Finally, I turn to an initial empirical investigation of the relationship between distinctive dimensions of interdependence and interstate conflict.

3. Hypotheses

Before turning to the empirical tests of the trade-conflict relationship, let me consolidate the alternative propositions articulated thus far in the form of hypotheses. Liberals suggest that trade promotes peace, regardless of the nature and context of interstate linkages. The greater the trade ties, the greater the deterrent to conflict. Support for the liberal hypotheses would therefore require empirical evidence that dyads composed of states with extensive economic linkages are less likely than others to engage in interstate conflict. Thus, we have the first hypothesis:

H1. Dyads composed of states with salient economic relationships are less likely than other dyads to engage in militarized conflicts.

Conversely, support for propositions advanced by critics of liberal thought would require evidence that relations characterized by symmetrical trade relations are more peaceful than asymmetrical ties. That is, symmetrical relations should promote interstate peace, while asymmetrical ties promote interstate conflict. From this, a second hypothesis emerges:

H2. Dyads composed of states with symmetrical dependence are less likely than others to engage in militarized conflicts.

From the conditions outlined in both liberal and radical schools of thought, I expect states with both mutual and extensive economic dependence to exhibit the least likelihood of interstate conflict. Such relations are assumed to provide mutual benefits, while remaining free from the conflictual elements believed to be endemic in relations of unequal exchange. From this I formulate the third hypothesis to be tested:

H3. The presence of both extensive and mutual dependence—interdependence—reduces the likelihood that dyads will engage in militarized conflict.

Finally, while the individual dimensions of interdependence may have a significant influence on the conflict propensity of dyadic relations, salience and symmetry may have both an additive and interactive effect on conflict. The final hypothesis tests the individual and combined effects of interdependence on the occurrence of interstate conflict.

H4. The interactive and additive effects of the two dimensions of interdependence—salience and symmetry—reduce the likelihood that dyads engage in interstate conflict.

4. Research Design

Peace by no means requires a natural harmony of interests between states, but should at a minimum entail a commitment to seek non-military means of resolving conflicts of interest that do arise. In relation to the topic at hand, I expect interdependence to condition relationships in a manner that constrains the types of conflict behavior exhibited in interstate relations. Presumably the benefits of interdependence should make conflicts of interest less likely to arise in such relations. However, when conflicts do arise, the presence of interdependence should make military actions non-options when states choose strategies for conflict resolution.

Previous empirical studies of trade and conflict have investigated the impact of increased economic ties on a myriad of interstate relations. In this study, I focus exclusively on conflictual events, assuming that the absence of intense conflict, rather than the presence of cooperation, is more consistent with the notion of peace. Sayrs (1990) highlights the shortcomings of viewing interstate relations on a continuum ranging from cooperative to conflictual; because in the closest relationships cooperation and conflict may coexist (Coser, 1956; de Vries, 1990). Thus, to investigate whether economic linkages create a sufficient bond to deter states from resorting to threats or uses of force, I confine my analysis to the conflict propensity of dyadic relations.

4.1 Sample and Unit of Analysis

The unit of analysis is the dyad year, where values are recorded for the dependent variable in a given year and for the explanatory variables in the preceding year. The study is limited to sovereign states, as defined by the Correlates of War Project (Small & Singer, 1982), provided data for all variables are available for each state in the dyad. The final sample includes a total of 14,341 dyad years, for the period 1870–1938, constituting 20% of the period's population of 70,293 dyad years (excluding WWI).

Data availability poses limitations to the selection of dyads. As one would expect, information concerning interstate trade is more readily available for developed states, leading to an inherent bias toward the exclusion of developing states, and the overrepresentation of major powers in the earlier years of the study. Every effort was made to minimize this bias. There is also a bias in favor of more salient trading relationships; for when states have a small volume of trade with another state, transactions are usually recorded in an aggregated category of minor trading partners. Thus, it is impossible to distinguish between the absence of trade in a given relationship and minimal flows of trade.

4.2 Operationalizing Variables

4.2.1 The Dependent Variables. The newly revised Militarized Interstate Dispute data set is used to measure various forms of intense interstate conflict, including the occurrence of disputes and wars. Militarized Interstate Disputes (MIDs) are defined as 'a set of interactions between or among states involving threats to use military force, displays of military force, or actual uses of military force' (Gochman & Maoz, 1984, p. 586), used here as a dichotomous variable, where states composing a dyad are coded as one when they engage on opposite sides of a dispute, and zero otherwise.[8] Disputes are coded for the first year in which they occur; that is, multiple year disputes are coded only once for a particular dyad. I also investigate whether interdependent dyads are less likely to engage in the most extreme form of militarized conflict—wars, using the standard Correlates of War definition (Small & Singer, 1982, p. 55). The sample includes 270 militarized interstate disputes and 14 wars.[9]

4.2.2 Interdependence. The primary difficulty in operationalizing interdependence arises from the absence of a clear consensus about what the phenomenon entails and how it should be measured. Hirsch (1986, p. 117) identifies more than sixteen operationalizations of trade dependence in his review of two decades of dependency research. Similarly, Hughes (1971) demonstrates the impact that different conceptions and operationalizations of economic integration have on empirical findings. As such, inconsistencies in empirical research on the trade-conflict relationship may be attributed in part to these differences in operationalization.

Even among theorists who have similar conceptions of interdependence, differences exist about the preferred method of operationalizing the construct. Within the trade-conflict literature, convincing arguments have been made for employing a number of measures, including measures that: assess the importance of a dyadic flow relative to a national income or product (Oneal et al., 1996); consider the elasticity of supply and demand for commodities traded (Polachek & McDonald 1992); consider the strategic importance of commodities traded (Blanchard & Ripsman, 1994); use the value of dyadic trade to measure interdependence (Polachek, 1980); and, analyses that incorporate measures derived from both total trade and GDP (Gasiorowski, 1986a, b; Soroos, 1977). Elsewhere, I provide a comprehensive treatment of the debates over appropriate operationalizations of dependence, but here I simply employ the most desirable measures, given the data limitations for the period analyzed (Barbieri, 1995, ch. 3).

The data used to measure interdependence were obtained from a trade database constructed by the author for the pre-WWII period (see Barbieri, 1995, appendix B). Only those states for whom data were available for imports, exports, and total trade were included.[10] I measure two dimensions of dyadic interdependence, the salience and the symmetry of dependence. By salience, I mean the importance or size of the trading relationship. Low levels of salience, however equal, are not assumed to provide the necessary bonds to deter conflict between states. By symmetry, I mean the equality of dependence between partners. I argue that the interactions of these two factors, salience and symmetry, comprise what is often termed interdependence.

The indicators used to capture dependence are based upon, but are not identical to, Hirschman's ([1945] 1980, p. 85) concentration of trade index.[11] I begin by calculating the share of trade each state maintains with each partner in order to assess the relative importance of any given relationship compared to others. Trade share measures the proportion of dyadic trade over total trade, both import and export flows, for each state with its trading partners. For example, for dyad$_{ij}$, composed of the States i and j, i's trade share is calculated as follows:

$$(1)\, Trade\, Share_i = \frac{Dyadic\, Trade_{ij}}{Total\, Trade_i}$$

The trade shares are then used to calculate dyadic measures of salience, symmetry, and interdependence, which conform to a uniform scale that ranges from 0 to 1. Dyadic salience, calculated in Equation 2, measures the extent to which trade partners are dependent upon a given trading relationship, where high salience exists when the relationship is important for each partner.[12]

$$(2)\, Salience_{ij} = \sqrt{Trade\, Share_i * Trade\, Share_j}$$

Symmetry, calculated in Equation 3, is measured by one minus the absolute value of the difference in trade shares composing the dyad, with higher scores indicating greater equality of dependence.

$$(3)\, Symmetry_{ij} = 1 - |\, Trade\, Share_i - Trade\, Share_j\, |$$

Finally, a measure of interdependence is created, consisting of the interaction of two dimensions of economic linkages often associated with the phenomenon—salience and symmetry. Here we are trying to assign a value that is high when both the extent and balance of dependence are high. Salience, symmetry, and interdependence have a range of values between zero and one, with mean values of 0.03, 0.9, and 0.03 respectively.[13]

$$(4)\, Interdependence_{ij} = Salience_{ij} * Symmetry_{ij}$$

4.3 Introducing Control Variables

Preliminary bivariate analysis identified statistically significant relationships between some of the dimensions of interdependence and interstate conflict (Barbieri, 1995, ch. 3). To assess whether these relationships might be confounded by factors affecting both trade and conflict, I control for factors consistently identified in the literature as altering the conflict propensity of dyadic relations. These factors, contiguity, joint democracy, relative capabilities, and alliance ties, are all theoretically interesting in their own right. Many of the arguments made about the control variables parallel, or are linked to, notions of interdependence. By fleshing out the separate effects of interstate bonds, I can begin to consider whether and why different types of intensive contacts may be more or less conflictual. However, in the interests of space, I focus my attention primarily on the economic linkages. For a more comprehensive evaluation of the relative impact of the control variables, see Bremer (1992b).

4.4.1 Contiguity and Geographic Proximity. Empirical tests have consistently revealed that contiguous dyads have both higher levels of trade (Aitken, 1973, p. 882; Arad & Hirsch, 1981) and higher levels of conflict (Bremer, 1992b; Goertz & Diehl, 1992a; Gochman,

1991) than other types of dyads. Gochman (1991, p. 96) suggests that 'the interaction opportunity and potential threat to extended interests is present not only with direct, but also indirect contiguity or proximity by way of dependencies'. Thus, it is important to control for both direct and indirect contiguity. The COW contiguity data set, as revised in 1993 by Philip Schafer, was used. Preliminary analysis (Barbieri, 1994a) indicated that there were no significant differences between different categories of contiguity; therefore, I chose to employ a dichotomous measure of contiguity, including indirect contiguity (by land and by sea up to 150 miles).

4.4.2 Joint Democracy. Whether or not one accepts the notion that democracies are inherently more peaceful than other states, the empirical evidence that democracies rarely go to war with each other is overwhelming (see Bremer, 1992a, b, 1993; Dixon, 1994; Maoz & Abdolali, 1989; Maoz & Russett, 1993; Morgan & Campbell, 1991; Morgan & Schwebach, 1992; Raymond, 1994; Russett, 1993). Although the causes of war and other types of militarized conflict are theoretically distinct, Bremer (1992b, 1993) provides evidence of the pacifying effect of joint democracy in less intense forms of militarized conflict.

Controlling for the influence of joint democracy is particularly important, since a high correlation is often assumed between economic (free market) and political freedom (democracy).[14] Dixon's (1994) illustration of the difficulty in disentangling the various normative and structural factors believed responsible for the joint democracy findings is compounded when we introduce trade into the analysis. Several linkages may be identified between regime type, political orientation, cultural linkages, and trade patterns, creating difficulties in separating the influence of these highly correlated variables.[15] Still, while the concepts of commercial and republican liberalism are linked, the notion that trade promotes peace is by no means contingent upon certain institutional, cultural, or political orientations. Trade is believed to offer a means through which states can transcend domestic political differences and achieve peace.

Data from Polity II (Gurr et al., 1989) are used to measure the level of democracy of each state in a dyad.[16] States with scores of five or greater on the democracy index are coded as democratic and below five as non-democratic. A dichotomous measure of joint democracy is employed, where dyads with two democracies are coded as one and those with one or no democracies as zero.

4.4.3 Alliances. Extensive economic linkages are regarded as a form of implicit (economic) alliance; yet, I must control for the presence of formal (security) alliances, which are also believed to affect the conflict propensity of dyadic relationships. This is particularly important since Gowa (1994) has shown that there is a high correlation between alliances and trade partners.

A version of the COW formal alliance data set (Small & Singer, 1969), revised by Alan Sabrosky, is used to measure alliances. Three types of formal alliances are reported in the data set: (1) mutual defense pacts, (2) neutrality agreements, and (3) ententes. I employ a dichotomous measure of alliance commitment, where the presence of any of the three types of formal alliances is coded as one and the absence of an alliance is coded as zero.[17]

4.4.4 Relative Power. The impact of relative power on interstate relations has received considerable attention in conflict studies, with theorists differing over whether power preponderance (Organski & Kugler, 1980) or power parity (Morgenthau, 1964) is most conducive to promoting peace. Empirical studies at the dyadic level support the power preponderance proposition (Bremer, 1993; Geller, 1993). The balance of power proposition is related, but not analogous to debates about the symmetrical nature of dependence. Although asymmetrical dependence is thought to confer disproportionate power on the less dependent state, this is not the only source of power. In addition, while relative power affects the conflict propensity of dyadic relationships, it may also affect the nature of economic dependence.

Relative power is operationalized as the relative capabilities available to each state in a given dyad.

The COW Composite Index of National Capabilities (CINC) scores are used to measure each state's share of the interstate system's total military, industrial, and demographic resources (Bremer, 1980a). A ratio of the larger to smaller state's capabilities is used to measure relative power.[18] The log of the relative capabilities is used in the logit regression analyses below to control for the large variations in CINC scores among states within the system. In addition, the log value has theoretical meaning, since it implies a decreasing marginal utility of increasing power differences. It makes little difference whether a state has 100 or 1,000 times more power than its opponent, since the preponderance of power should produce similar effects when power differences are great.

5. Analyses

In order to examine whether the presence and character of economic linkages significantly affects the conflict propensity of dyadic relations four separate logistic regression analyses are estimated for the analysis of the two dependent variables, MIDs and wars.[19] The four alternative logit models assess the impact of: (1) salience, (2) symmetry, (3) interdependence, and (4) both the additive and interactive effects of salience and symmetry—in a multidimensional model of interdependence.

5.1 The Null Model

Due to the rarity of the events under study—disputes and wars—any influence associated with their occurrence appears minimal. We must therefore consider not only the absolute, but the relative, effect of each variable on the probability that a dyad engage in militarized conflict. To underscore this point, I begin my analysis by estimating the null model for the samples and populations of the historical period analyzed. The null model includes only the intercept term (i.e. all β's for the explanatory variables are zero), and this allows me to calculate the mean probability that any dyad engages in a MID or war in a given year.

The mean probability that any dyad in the sample engages in a MID in a given year is approximately 0.019. That is, statistically significantly higher than the population mean probability of 0.007 per year for the pre-WWII period. The probability of war for the sample is 0.0009, also statistically significantly higher than the population mean of 0.0005. Thus, the conflict propensity of dyads in the sample is significantly higher than those found in the population.[20] This should be expected, since the sample is limited to dyads which have some minimal level of interaction, while the population contains both non-interacting and interacting dyads.[21]

Table 1   Effect of Interdependence on Militarized Disputes, 1870–1938

	Dispute Occurrence$_t$			
Independent variables	Model 1 Salience	Model 2 Symmetry	Model 3 Interdependence	Model 4 Full Model
Salience $_{t-1}$	3.11**	—	—	−22.64**
	(0.15)			(6.69)
Symmetry $_{t-1}$	—	−2.02**	—	−4.46**
		(0.43)		(0.80)
Interdependence $_{t-1}$	—	—	3.50**	26.60**
			(1.25)	(7.28)
Contiguity $_{t-1}$	1.67**	1.66**	1.68**	1.58**
	(0.14)	(0.14)	(0.14)	(0.14)
Joint democracy $_{t-1}$	−0.94**	−0.89**	−0.93**	−0.89**
	(0.19)	(0.19)	(0.19)	(0.19)
Alliance $_{t-1}$	−0.90	−0.09	−0.09	−0.09
	(0.21)	(0.21)	(0.21)	(0.21)
Relative capabilities $_{t-1}$	−0.19**	−0.29**	−0.18**	−0.32**
	(0.05)	(0.05)	(0.05)	(0.06)
Constant	−4.33**	−2.19**	−4.35**	0.15
	(0.15)	(0.43)	(0.15)	(0.82)
Likelihood ratio statistic (df)	273.1**(5)	284.4**(5)	272.1**(5)	301.4**(7)
Unrestricted log-likelihood[a]	−1203.5	−1197.8	−1204.0	−1189.3

Note: Standard errors appear in parentheses.

[a]Restricted log-likelihood = −1340.0 The restricted log-likelihood measure corresponds to the null model, while the unrestricted log-likelihood measures refer to models containing the explanatory variables.

*p ≤ 0.05; **p ≤ 0.01; N = 14341.

6. Results

6.1 Interdependence and Militarized Interstate Disputes, 1870–1938

Table 1 exhibits the results of the first set of analyses of the impact of various dimensions of interdependence on militarized interstate disputes. In Model 1, the Salience model, I explore the question of whether important trading relationships are less conflict-prone than insignificant trading relations. Evidence in support of the liberal hypotheses would require salience to have a negative influence on the probability that dyads engage in militarized disputes. The results from Model 1 reveal that, rather than inhibiting conflict, salient trading relationships are more conflict-prone than other types of relationships, contradicting the liberal argument. Thus, the expansion of trade linkages alone seems insufficient to promote peace and may promote increased tensions in interstate relations.

Using the estimated logit model, I calculate the probability of dispute occurrence associated with various levels of economic salience, holding the control variables constant at their mean values. The probability of a dispute occurring at the minimum level of salience is 0.023, compared to 0.029 at the maximum level of salience. Thus, economically important trading partners are 1.4 times as likely to engage in a dispute than are those dyads with limited economic importance. While these findings must be interpreted with caution, since most dyads are clustered around the lower ranges of salience, this exercise permits me to consider the directional influence of expanded economic ties on dyadic conflict.

In Model 2, the Symmetry Model, I address the question of whether symmetrical ties inhibit conflict. Supporting evidence is revealed in Table 1, as indicated by the statistically significant and negative coefficient for symmetry ($\beta = -2.017$). This supports the notion that the balance of dependence is more important for fostering peace than the extent of trade ties. States with a similar degree of dependence are less likely to engage in disputes. Using the logit estimates, I find that the probability of a dispute

when symmetry is at its minimum is 0.06, compared to 0.009 when states are equally dependent.[22] Dyads are more than seven times as likely to engage in a MID at the lowest level of symmetry than at the highest level. Thus, symmetry in exchange relations is seen to reduce the probability of militarized disputes, whereas symmetry in other forms of interstate relations (e.g., relative capabilities) is found to increase the probability of conflict.

To consider whether it is the combined effect of extensive and mutual dependence that leads to reductions in the conflict propensity of dyadic relationships, I turn to Model 3, the Interdependence Model. Surprisingly, the results from this model reveal that, rather than inhibiting conflict, high levels of interdependence increase the likelihood that dyads engage in militarized disputes. The statistically significant positive coefficient ($\beta = 3.5$) allows me to conclude with confidence that there is little evidence that those relations believed to be the most peaceful are foremost empirically. Not only does interdependence lack the strength to limit the probability of conflict, but from the findings I conclude that interdependence actually increases the likelihood of conflict. When interdependence is at its maximum, dyads are almost 25 times as likely to engage in a MID than when interdependence is at its minimum. Although these results should be interpreted cautiously, since few dyads have high values of interdependence, I can be fairly certain about the upward sloping relationship between interdependence and conflict.

Finally, the Full Interdependence Model examines the effects of the separate dimensions of interdependence and their interactive effect. Here I assume that each dimension—salience and symmetry—may independently affect conflict, but that there is also an interaction effect. By this, I mean that the growth of each condition, or the absence of either condition, may result in different effects on conflict than that which would exist if only one dimension were present. Model 4 provides evidence of the importance of considering both the additive and interactive effects of separate dimensions of interdependence. The coefficient for salience ($\beta = -22.644$) reverses its sign, from that observed in Model 1, while that for symmetry ($\beta = -4.457$) remains negative. The positive coefficient for interdependence ($\beta = 26.602$) reveals that the overall effect of the model produces a higher probability of conflict when interdependence rises. Although the salience and symmetry of the relationship initially inhibit conflict, as either dimension increases, the interaction effect reveals that the potential for conflict also increases. Thus, whether the relationship is symmetrical or asymmetrical, the extension of trade linkages will inevitably lead to an increased probability that dyads engage in militarized disputes.

To understand how the various dimensions of interdependence influence dyadic conflict, Figure 2 illustrates the overall impact of interdependence on dyadic conflict. The horizontal axis represents the trade share each state has with its partner, while the vertical axis represents the probability of a dispute occurring. The surface plane reflects the probabilities corresponding to various configurations of trade partner concentration. Overall, extensive economic linkages increase the probability of a dispute. Low levels of interdependence appear to have an insignificant effect on conflict; yet, as dyads become more dependent, the likelihood of conflict increases.

States within extreme ranges of either highly unequal or highly equal relations have the highest probability of engaging in a militarized dispute. This is encouraging in the sense that most of the dyads fall within the low to moderate levels of interdependence. Still, the findings suggest a cautionary note to those who view peace through integration as an indisputable outcome for the future. We might instead consider whether a hurdle effect is present in interdependent relations, whereby the benefits of such relations promote peace up to a certain point, after which the intensity of interstate relations, be they through economic or other bonds, might intensify conflict.

At most ranges, interdependence has little effect on conflict. The most adverse effect occurs among asymmetrical partners, where the probability of a dispute is 0.4. Yet, even among those with symmetrical ties, when interdependence is extensive, the

probability of a dispute exceeds 0.3. Again, caution is required in interpreting the results, since the values in the middle peak are rarely observed. The relationship is extrapolated from values corresponding to dyads falling within lower ranges of symmetrical but moderately extensive ties. Still, we can imagine that the directional influence is similar, and might exist if the trend toward greater interdependence occurs in the empirical world.

6.1.1 Control Variables. The findings from the control variables uncover few surprises for those familiar with empirical studies of dyadic conflict. Contiguous dyads are more likely to engage in militarized disputes and democratic states are less likely to engage in militarized conflict with other democratic states. Dyads composed of states with highly unequal power are less likely to engage in conflict. Although asymmetrical dependence increases the likelihood of conflict, power derived from other forms of inequalities appears to deter conflict. Finally, alliance commitment has no statistically significant effect on the probability that dyads engage in conflict. The results of the control variables should be interpreted with caution, since the sample does not reflect a random selection process, but they are consistent with previous findings for larger samples (e.g., Bremer, 1992b).

We can consider the goodness of fit for each alternative model in comparison to the null model (i.e., where the βs for all explanatory variables equal zero) by using the likelihood ratio test.[23] The likelihood ratio test assesses whether the inclusion of the explanatory variables provides a significant improvement over the null model for explaining MID occurrence. In Table 1 we see that the likelihood ratio statistic is statistically significant for each model, revealing the importance of considering economic interdependence and the control variables when seeking to uncover missing links in the conflict puzzle.

6.2 Interdependence and War

How does interdependence affect war, the most intense form of conflict? Table 2 gives the empirical results. The rarity of wars makes any analysis of

Figure 2 The Impact of Multidimensional Interdependence on MID Occurrence, 1870–1938

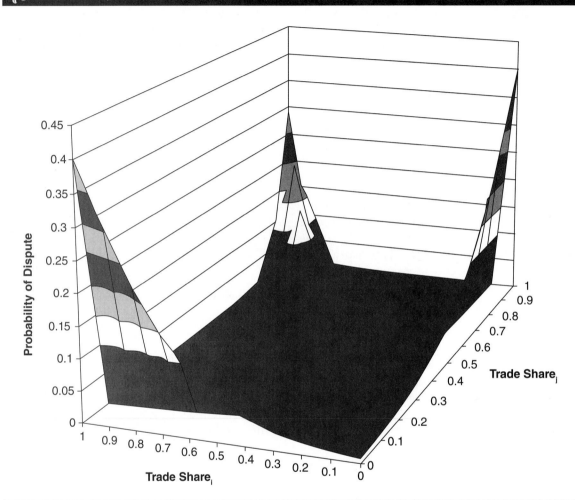

their causes quite difficult, for variations in interdependence will seldom result in the occurrence of war. As in the case of MIDs, the log-likelihood ratio tests for each model suggest that the inclusion of the various measures of interdependence and the control variables improves our understanding of the factors affecting the occurrence of war over that obtained from the null model. However, the individual interdependence variables, alone, are not statistically significant. This is not the case with contiguity and relative capabilities, which are both statistically significant. Again, we see that contiguous dyads are more conflict-prone and that dyads composed of states with unequal power are more pacific than those with highly equal power. Surprisingly, no evidence is provided to support the commonly held proposition that democratic states are less likely to engage in wars with other democratic states.

The evidence from the pre-WWII period provides support for those arguing that economic factors have little, if any, influence on affecting leaders' decisions to engage in war, but many of the control variables are also statistically insignificant. These results should be interpreted with caution, since the sample does not contain a sufficient number of wars to allow us to capture great variations across different types of relationships. Many observations of war are excluded from the sample by virtue of not having the corresponding explanatory measures. A variable would have to have an extremely strong influence on conflict—as does contiguity—to find significant results.

7. Conclusions

This study provides little empirical support for the liberal proposition that trade provides a path to interstate peace. Even after controlling for the influence of contiguity, joint democracy, alliance ties, and relative capabilities, the evidence suggests that in most instances trade fails to deter conflict. Instead, extensive economic interdependence increases the likelihood that dyads engage in militarized dispute; however, it appears to have little influence on the incidence of war. The greatest hope for peace appears to arise from symmetrical trading relationships. However, the dampening effect of symmetry is offset by the expansion of interstate linkages. That is, extensive economic linkages, be they symmetrical or asymmetrical, appear to pose the greatest hindrance to peace through trade.

Although this article focuses exclusively on the pre-WWII period, elsewhere I provide evidence that the relationships revealed here are also observed in the post-WWII period and more extended period, 1870–1985 (Barbieri, 1995). Why do the findings differ from those presented in related studies of the trade-conflict relationship, which reveal an inverse relationship between trade and conflict? Several explanations, other than the temporal domain, can be offered. First, researchers differ in the phenomena they seek to explain, with many studies incorporating both conflictual and cooperative interstate behavior (e.g., Gasiorowski, 1986a, b; Gasiorowski & Polachek, 1982; Polachek, 1980, 1992; Polachek & McDonald, 1992). Studies that focus exclusively on extreme forms of conflict behavior, including disputes and wars, differ in their spatial and temporal domains, their level of analysis, and their measurement of central constructs. Preliminary tests reveal that the composition of dyads in a given sample may have a more dramatic impact on the empirical findings than variations in measurement. For example, the decision to focus exclusively on 'politically relevant dyads' may be one source of difference (Oneal et al., 1996).

Perhaps the primary component missing from this and related research is the inclusion of a more adequate assessment of the costs and benefits derived from interdependence. I have repeatedly argued that the conflictual or pacific elements of interdependence are directly related to perceptions about trade's costs and benefits. Yet, a more comprehensive evaluation of these costs and benefits is needed to see whether a link truly exists between the benefits enjoyed in a given trading relationship and the inhibition of conflict in that relationship, or conversely, the presence of net costs for at least one trading partner and the presence of conflict in that relationship. For example, are trading relationships that contain two partners believed to benefit from trade less conflict-prone than those containing at least one partner perceived to be worse off from trade? I have merely outlined the types of relationships believed to confer the greatest benefits, but such benefits and costs require a more rigorous investigation.

In addition, while liberals generally assume benefits increase with the expansion of trade, benefits may actually conform to the law of diminishing returns. Costs, on the other hand, may grow exponentially, as interdependence grows. Thus, if we evaluate the net benefits of interdependence, costs may outweigh benefits as interdependence increases. Again, further exploration is needed to evaluate the functional form that conforms to the rise and/or decline of costs and benefits in interdependent relations. Of course, assessing the political costs of

Table 2 Effect of Interdependence on Wars, 1870–1938

Independent Variables	War Occurrence$_t$			
	Model 1 Salience	Model 2 Symmetry	Model 3 Interdependence	Model 4 Full Model
Salience $_{t-1}$	−0.97	—	—	−43.87
	(5.25)			(55.20)
Symmetry $_{t-1}$	—	0.70	—	−3.52
		(2.94)		(5.19)
Interdependence $_{t-1}$	—	—	−0.19	46.80
			(6.13)	(58.13)
Contiguity $_{t-1}$	2.60**	2.60**	2.57**	2.54**
	(0.79)	(0.78)	(0.79)	(0.79)
Joint democracy $_{t-1}$	−1.33	−1.36	−1.36	−1.34
	(1.05)	(1.04)	(1.05)	(1.06)
Alliance $_{t-1}$	0.03	0.02	0.02	0.05
	(0.78)	(0.78)	(0.78)	(0.78)
Relative capabilities $_{t-1}$	−0.61*	−0.59*	−0.61*	−0.64*
	(0.28)	(0.29)	(0.28)	(0.30)
Constant	−7.23**	−7.95**	−7.25**	−3.82
	(0.81)	(3.04)	(0.81)	(5.21)
Likelihood ratio statistic (df)	30.5**(5)	30.5**(5)	30.4**(5)	31.3**(7)
Unrestricted log-likelihood[a]	−95.8	−95.8	−95.8	−95.4

Note: Standard errors appear in parentheses.

[a]Restricted log-likelihood = −111.04. The restricted log-likelihood measure corresponds to the null model, while the unrestricted log-likelihood measures refer to models containing the explanatory variables.

*$p \leq 0.05$; **$p \leq 0.01$; $N = 14341$.

interdependence may be more difficult than assessing economic benefits. For example, it is easier to evaluate the variations in national growth corresponding to greater participation in trade than to assess the political impact of interdependence, such as losses in national autonomy.

Another area that requires further consideration concerns the interactive effects of several types of interdependencies for fostering interstate peace. One of the primary components of liberal theory focuses on the convergence of interests and transmission of commonalties that arise through economic and noneconomic linkages. These norms are believed to facilitate the emergence of formal and informal mechanisms to mediate conflict, when conflicts of interest do arise. This issue has been the subject of attention in the democratic peace literature, but remains unexplored in studies of economic interdependence. Yet, one could easily argue that an interactive effect might be present in the expansion of different types of interstate linkages for facilitating mechanisms conducive to conflict resolution. For example, the presumed norms of conflict mediation present in jointly democratic dyads might facilitate the resolution of conflict, when economic incentives create the impetus for such mediation. In other words, even if actors have an economic incentive to seek non-violent strategies to resolve conflicts of interest, the absence of sufficient mechanisms to offset conflict may make conflict more likely to arise. The issue of an interactive process between different types of interdependencies leads to another area of research that requires future exploration, the countervailing influences of different forms of interstate interdependencies.

What is clear from related empirical research is that commonalities and various types of interdependencies have different effects on interstate conflict. Contiguity is consistently found to increase the likelihood of conflict, while joint democracy is found to inhibit conflict. When tracing the rationale for these findings, theorists often use the concept of interstate ties to drive their explanation. Moreover, some theorists argue that extensive linkages found among contiguous states is a contributing factor to their high conflict propensity, while at the same time suggesting that linkages and commonalities found

among jointly democratic dyads contributes to their pacific relationships. One might therefore conclude that extensive linkages foster both peace and conflict. How do we determine the conditions under which one of these effects is more likely to arise in a given interdependent relationship? Clearly, there must be some underlying factors that influence the tendency for some forms of interdependence to inhibit conflict, while others increase conflict. That is, it is not interdependence itself that determines the impact on interstate relations, but some characteristic of the type of interdependence present in the relationship.

While I sought to answer several questions about the trade-conflict relationship, at the very least it should be clear that interdependence is a more complex relationship than generally depicted by theorists. It is also clear that economic ties have a significant influence on conflict. Although interdependence's impact on conflict is not that envisioned by liberals, the tendency for conflict studies to exclude this important relationship can no longer be accepted. Economic interdependence affects interstate relations. While it may not promote interstate peace, it is essential to understanding the puzzle of interstate conflict. Clearly, the time has come to elevate economic relationships from their traditional secondary status to center stage in the study of international relations.

Appendix A Descriptive Statistics, 1870–1938

Variable	Mean	SD	Min	Max	N[a]
Year	1916.6	18.929	1871	1938	14341
Dyadic trade[b]	35.414	90.107	0.0001	2872	14341
Total trade$_i$[c]	1703.3	3412.5	0.1049	150800	14341
Total trade$_j$	1031.1	1902.6	0.4985	58960	14341
CINC$_i$[d]	5.3158	7.2063	0.006	29.05	14341
CINC$_j$	3.3776	4.5669	0.006	23.72	14341
Democracy$_i$[e]	5.6619	3.7105	0	10	14341
Democracy$_j$	4.6851	3.7952	0	10	14341
Joint democracy[f]	0.2564	0.4367	0	1	14341

(Continued)

(Continued)

Variable	Mean	SD	Min	Max	N[a]
Contiguity[g]	0.268	0.443	0	1	14341
Alliance[i]	0.0561	0.2301	0	1	14341
HiAct[i]	0.2257	1.8822	−9	22	14341
Mid[k]	0.0188	0.1359	0	1	14341
War[k]	0.001	0.0312	0	1	14341
Capabilities ratio[l]	46.676	164.93	1	4501	14341
Log (LS ratio)[m]	2.2996	1.5913	0.0001	8.412	14341
Trade Share$_i$[n]	0.041	0.079	0.0000	0.993	14341
Trade Share$_j$	0.07	0.122	0.0000	0.983	14341
Salience[o]	0.0331	0.0428	0.0001	0.9685	14341
Symmetry[p]	0.9198	0.1219	0.0374	1	14341
Interdependence[q]	0.0278	0.0338	0.0001	0.9569	14341

Note: Subscripts i and j correspond to State$_i$ and State$_j$, respectively.

The variables corresponding to State$_i$, explained below, are similarly converted for State$_j$.

Pre-WWII trade data are derived from database created by the author (see Barbieri, 1995).

Conflict measures are from the new Militarized Interstate Dispute (MID) data set.

Alliance, contiguity, and CINC scores are from the COW Project.

[a]Refers to sample after introducing lag variables and excluding cases with missing values.

[b]Dyadic trade, excluding zero trade flow values.

[c]Imports plus Exports for State$_i$.

[d]Composite Index of National Capabilities (CINC) scores, COW Project.

[e]Democracy score for State$_i$, from *Polity II* (Gurr et al., 1989).

[f]Joint Democracy = 1 when Democracy$_i$ and Democracy$_j$ > = 5, and zero otherwise.

[g]Contiguity = 1 when direct or indirect contiguity is present and zero otherwise.

[h]Alliance = 1 when any type of alliance is present, zero otherwise.

[i]Highest level of force in a dispute, coded 1–22 (−9 indicates missing data).

[j]Mid = 1 when dyads engage on opposite sides of a dispute, and zero otherwise.

[k]War = 1 when dyads engage on opposite sides of a war, and zero otherwise.

[l]Larger to smaller CINC score ratio.

[m]Log of the Capabilities Ratio.

[n]TS_i = Dyadic Trade/Total Trade$_i$.

[o]Salience = SQR $(TS_i \times TS_j)$.

[p]Symmetry = 1 − ABS $(TS_i − TS_j)$.

[q]Interdependence = Salience$_{ij}$ × Symmetry$_{ij}$.

Notes

Author's Note: Special thanks to Stuart Bremer for his assistance, valuable comments, and provision of the Correlates of War data sets used here, including the alliance, contiguity, national capabilities, and new Militarized Interstate Dispute (MID) Data set. The new MID Data were collected by the Correlates of War Project at the University of Michigan in cooperation with the Department of Political Science at Binghamton University and the Peace Science Society (International). Thanks to Andrew J. Enterline, John Camobreco, Nils Petter Gleditsch, Håvard Hegre, Jack Levy, Michael McDonald, John Oneal, Glenn Palmer, Solomon Polachek, James Lee Ray, Gregory Raymond, and Bruce Russett for their helpful comments on this research. Thanks to Brian Pollins, Philip Schafer, and J. David Singer for their assistance on the trade database project.

1. For a comprehensive history of this and related economic thought, see Spiegel (1991); see de Wilde (1991) for a history of the interdependence tradition in political science.

2. For comprehensive reviews of the scientific study of conflict, see Bremer (1992b), Bremer & Cusack (1993), and Vasquez (1993).

3. Focusing on the post-WWII period, Russett (1967) also provides evidence that increased trade leads to increased conflict, but his study is concerned with intra-regional trade and conflict.

4. Other scholars provide evidence of an inverse relationship between trade and political climate and/ or orientation at the dyadic level, but view causation as flowing from politics to trade patterns (Dixon & Moon, 1993; Pollins, 1989a, b). The potential for simultaneity here is obvious, but will be analyzed at a later date. Polachek (1992) provides evidence that the effect of trade on conflict is greater than that of conflict on trade. To reduce the confounding influence that intense warfare has on trade patterns, my study excludes the WWI period.

5. For a comprehensive review of the dependency school of thought, see Blomström & Hettne (1984).

6. Sensitivity refers to the openness of a country to changes in other countries that are transmitted by a mutual interaction, vulnerability refers to the effects of changes in rules or policies (quote from Gasiorowski, 1986a, p. 24; see Keohane & Nye 1977, pp. 12–13).

7. Advocates of South-South economic unions may view less significant, but equal, economic linkages as a greater force for peace than extensive relations under the guise of unequal exchange. According to this view, the linkages among developing states would eventually expand, providing increasing benefits (economic and political) in the long run and breaking the cycle of dependence on developed states.

8. Since the dependent variable, MID occurrence, is really an event count, a case could be made that an event count model should be used in this analysis. I chose to dichotomize the occurrence of at least one event, since the probability that any dyad would experience a MID more than once is extremely rare (e.g., only 11 cases were identified in the sample), and the occurrence of at least one MID is sufficient to violate the conditions of peace.

9. Wars are a subset of MIDs and are included in the MID analysis.

10. For a comprehensive discussion of the trade database and a complete listing of sources, see Barbieri (1995, Appendix B). Sources of trade data include League of Nations (1910–40); *Statesmen's Yearbook;* and Mitchell (1982, 1983). Data were collected in local currency and converted to US dollars using exchange rates from Bidwell (1970); Gurr et al. (1989); *Statesman's Yearbook (1870–1940);* and the US Department of Commerce.

11. Hirschman notes that 'Examining the conditions under which country A will experience most difficulties in shifting its trade from one country B to other countries, we found that the fraction which B holds in A's total trade is an important element in evaluating the situation. This fraction depends on the size of its numerator, the trade of B with A, and on the size of its denominator, A's total trade' ([1945], 1980, p. 85; see also pp. 30–31).

12. The geometric, rather than arithmetic mean, is used, since the former assigns higher values to dyads where each state has high trade shares and lower values, than those derived from the arithmetic mean, when trade shares are highly unequal.

13. Although the dimensions of interdependence appear to be related, they are considered distinct phenomenon. Correlation tests reveal that salience and symmetry are only moderately correlated ($r = 0.55$).

However, a high correlation exists between salience and the interaction term, interdependence ($r = 0.90$). Despite the high correlation, I include interdependence as a separate variable, since preliminary tests reveal that it is statistically significant and it is assumed to be theoretically distinct from salience. See Friedrich (1982) for a useful discussion of the guidelines for including interactive variables. No other variables used in the study were found to be collinear. For correlation tests among the control variables, and between the control variables and the interdependence measures, see Barbieri (1995, Appendix A).

14. Rummell (1983, 1985) classifies states as libertarian only when domestic economic freedoms exist. We may assume that states with domestic economic freedoms are more likely to promote free trade policies, which leads to difficulties in separating the precepts of commercial and republican liberalism.

15. Surprisingly, correlation tests reveal no problem with multicollinearity among the control variables and the interdependence measures.

16. A state is classified as democratic if its chief executive is directly or indirectly elected in a popular fashion and its legislative branch is also elected and able to constrain the executive in an effective manner (Bremer, 1992b, p. 9).

17. Bremer (1993, p. 237) suggests that a dichotomous measure of alliance ties is sufficient to capture the effect of alliances on conflict, although variations exist on the effect of different alliance types.

18. A measure of overwhelming preponderance (Weede, 1976) was also employed in preliminary tests, with no significant differences observed in the results.

19. For information about logit regression analysis and interpretation of results from tests conducted, see Aldrich & Nelson (1984) and King (1989).

20. For a discussion of the tests used to compare the sample and population means, see Hayslett (1968, p. 86).

21. Hâvard Hegre (letter, 25 April 1995) suggests that the high conflict propensity found in the sample may be explained, in part, by the overrepresentation of major powers, which tend to be more conflict-prone than other states. The bias arises not only from the greater availability of data for major powers, but also from their tendency to conduct trade with more partners than do minor powers. Thus, they will be represented in more dyadic relationships.

22. The estimated logit models are used to calculate the dispute probabilities, while holding the control variables constant at their mean values.

23. Comparing the restricted and the unrestricted models (i.e., the null model versus the model incorporating the explanatory variables) allows us to evaluate whether the inclusion of the explanatory variables improves our understanding of conflict over that provided by the null model. When the likelihood ratio is significant, we may conclude that the unrestricted model provides a better explanation of conflict than that found in the null model. The likelihood ratio test statistic is computed as follows: $R = [2(\ln L_{unrestricted}^{*} - L_{Restricted})]$, where 91 is chi-squared distributed with degrees of freedom equal to the number of parameters of the null model (see King, 1989, pp. 84–87). In Tables 1 and 2, a significant likelihood ratio statistic, 91, means that the unrestricted model improves upon the explanatory power of the null model. LIMDEP Version 5.1 is used for this and other estimations performed here.

EDITORS' COMMENTARY

Major Contributions: Economic Interdependence

In addition to the pacifying effects of democracy and international organizations, the Kantian tripod for peace (Oneal and Russett 1999c, Chapter 9, this volume) identifies economic interdependence or trade as one of the key factors reducing the chances for dyadic militarized conflict. The idea that economic interdependence promotes cooperation in world politics is a longstanding yet contested idea. Neoliberal scholars such as Keohane and Nye (1977) discuss the benefits of interdependence, while scholars influenced by the Marxist tradition, such as Wallerstein (1974), warn of the conflict that can occur if economic interdependence creates inequities between developed and developing countries. Barbieri's (1996) article summarizes the various sides of this debate. She argues that the relationship between economic interdependence and interstate conflict is a *contingent* one, as some types of interdependence promote peace, while other types of interdependence promote conflict. Her empirical results show that this contingent effect depends on the overall salience (or importance) of trading relationships to both sides and the symmetry (or mutual dependence) in trade. Pairs of states that have a high dependence and an asymmetric trading relationship are more likely to engage in militarized disputes than states that have independent trading partners or dependent but symmetric trading ties.

In her thorough review of the literature on trade and interstate conflict, Barbieri (1996) notes that four basic relationships are possible: (1) trade promotes peace, (2) symmetrical trade promotes peace, (3) trade increases conflict, and (4) trade is irrelevant to conflict. The "trade promotes peace" thesis is the classic liberal or Kantian view and is discussed by Oneal and Russett (1999c). Trade is thought to reduce the likelihood of conflict by improving communication and transnational ties, by increasing the costs of war to each side (loss of gains from trade), by providing a more efficient strategy for obtaining resources than territorial conquest or imperialism, and by fostering the growth of preferential trade agreements and international organizations that can provide dispute resolution mechanisms to member states. Empirical evidence supporting this position can be found in several studies (Polachek 1980; Oneal and Russett 1999c; Russett and Oneal 2001). Recall that Oneal and Russett (1999c) found that a one standard deviation increase in trade dependence in a dyad reduces the likelihood of militarized disputes by 49 percent.

The second school of thought suggests that trade only promotes peace if it occurs between relative equals or symmetrical partners. Dependency theorists and neo-Marxists identify the costs that can occur in trading relationships, especially if one side reaps much fewer benefits from trade. Barbieri (1996) notes several possibilities, including the slowing of economic development in the weaker state, the destruction of social, economic, and political institutions, and increasing levels of wealth inequalities that can foster grievances in society. She also points to the neorealist argument about relative gains, where states could use profits from trade to develop their military capabilities.

The idea of symmetry relates to the third school of thought, which identifies the conditions that can make trading states more conflict prone. Strategies of colonialism and imperialism are prime examples of how military force can be used in conjunction with trading strategies to promote states' interests. Scarcity of resources inside a state can also lead to external competition (Choucri and North 1975). Barbieri (1996) argues that contiguous states are more likely to have trade with each other, and we know that contiguous states are much more likely to fight wars. Therefore, it is important to control for proximity when testing the trade-conflict relationship. The final theoretical argument is a realist one that trade is essentially irrelevant to states' decisions for war, as economic relationships constitute low politics (Hensel et al. 2008, Chapter 3, this volume). Barbieri's explanation focuses on the nature of trading relationships much like earlier research on complex interdependence.

Keohane and Nye (1977) emphasize two aspects of complex interdependence: (1) **sensitivity** or the extent to which one country is affected by the actions of another and (2) **vulnerability** or the extent to which a country can insulate itself from the costly effects of events that occur elsewhere. Interdependence is a situation in which countries are both highly sensitive and vulnerable to each other. As Barbieri (1996) notes, what this means for trading relationships is that two states are dependent on each other for trade (sensitivity) and their trading partnership is fairly symmetric (vulnerability).

She illustrates this logic in Figure 1. On the X-axis is **Trade Share$_j$**, which captures the percentage of state j's total trade that is conducted with state i. For example, this value is calculated as follows: Trade Share$_j$ = Dyadic Trade$_{ij}$/Total Trade$_j$. You can calculate a similar value for the Y-axis denoting the percentage of state i's total trade that is conducted with state j. If two states traded only with each other and had no trade with other countries, the trade share would take on a value of 1 for each state (upper right quadrant of interdependence, II). If neither state has any trade with the other state in the dyad, then the value would be equal to zero (lower left quadrant of independence, III).

Barbieri (1996) then calculates the **Salience** of the dyadic trading relationship, which involves multiplying Trade Share$_j$ with Trade Share$_i$ and then taking the square root of that number. This captures the degree of mutual dependence in a trading relationship. If the two states traded only with each other and no other states, the value for Salience would be equal to 1. If the two states had 50 percent of their total trade with each other, the Salience score would equal 0.5 or the square root of 0.25*0.25. Hypothesis 1 expects dyads with more salient trading partnerships to have fewer militarized conflicts.

Barbieri's next hypothesis captures the degree of symmetry in a trading relationship. If state i has 75 percent of its total trade with state j but state j has only 25 percent of its total trade with state i, then state i is more vulnerable to potential trade losses in this dyad (upper left quadrant I, Dependence of State$_i$ on State$_j$). Barbieri captures this type of scenario with a **Symmetry** measure, which equals 1 minus the absolute value of the difference between Trade Share$_i$ and Trade Share$_j$. If two sides have the same percentage of total trade with each other (e.g., 50 percent), the difference becomes zero and the Symmetry score takes on a value of 1. In the situation above where one trade share is 75 percent and the other is 25 percent, the Symmetry score is equal to 0.50. Lower values on the scale indicate a higher level of asymmetry in the trading relationship. Hypothesis 2 predicts that militarized conflict will be less likely in dyads with more symmetrical trade (quadrants II and III in Figure 1 should have less conflict than quadrants I and IV).

The final two hypotheses deal with the concept of **Interdependence**, linking the salience and symmetry of the dyadic trading partnership (Interdependence = Salience$_{ij}$ * Symmetry$_{ij}$). Barbieri (1996) predicts that the interactive effects of these two factors decrease the likelihood of militarized interstate disputes (MIDs). Thus, in the upper right quadrant (II) in Figure 1, one would expect countries that have both high salience and high symmetry to have more peaceful foreign policy relations. This is different from Oneal and Russett's (1999c) measure of trade, which employs a weakest link assumption, recording the less trade-dependent state's trade value (DEPEND$_L$). Oneal and Russett's analyses suggest that conflict becomes less likely as we increase along one dimension (e.g., the X-axis if state$_j$ has the smaller value for Trade Share) in Barbieri's Figure 1. Yet her analysis shows that this effect depends on the relative levels of salience and symmetry in the dyad. Small values of Trade Share for one state can predict peaceful interactions if the other side's Trade Share value is also small. If one state is much more dependent on the other side for trade, this can result in militarized conflict, even in cases where the overall level of trade salience is reasonably high.

In Table 1, Barbieri (1996) examines the onset of dyadic militarized disputes. When looking at Salience alone (Model 1), she finds, contrary to Hypothesis 1, that higher levels of Salience actually increase the chances for MIDs (although most dyads have low values on the Salience measure). In Model 2, she finds support for Hypothesis 2, showing that dyads with more symmetric trading relationships are less likely to have MIDs. In Model 3, she shows that highly interdependent dyads with high salience and highly symmetric trade are 25 times *more* likely to engage in a MID, which contradicts the liberal expectation for peaceful interactions in quadrant II of Figure 1. When she estimates all variables together (Model 4), she finds that conflict is most likely between dyads that have very unequal or very equal trade relationships. We can see this graphically in Figure 2, where she plots the predicted probabilities from Model 4. The peaks to the left and right of the graph correspond with the prediction that asymmetric trade dependence increases the risk of conflict (quadrants I and IV in Figure 1). However, the peak in the back of the graph shows an increased risk of war for interdependent dyads (quadrant II). Barbieri notes, however, that most dyads have low values for Salience; thus, the number of real-world cases that occur in the back region of Figure 2 is pretty small.

Finally, she looks at the effect of economic interdependence on war in Table 2. She finds that none of her theoretical measures (Salience, Symmetry, and Interdependence) has a statistically significant effect on the onset of wars. The MID and war models also produce an interesting difference for one of the control variables, Joint Democracy. While pairs of democratic states are significantly less likely to experience a militarized dispute in comparison with nondemocratic dyads (Table 1), they are no more or no less war prone (Table 2). This is similar to Reed's (2000, Chapter 11, this volume) finding that the pacifying effect of joint democracy is seen most strongly in the first stage of a potential militarized dispute and has little effect on the chances for escalation to war once a dispute is under way.

This article was the first of several by Barbieri. Her major study is *The Liberal Illusion* (2002), a full book-length treatment of the subject with several empirical studies. These analyses extend and deepen her critique of the liberal peace claim that trade and economic interdependence enhance the prospects for peace. Levy and Barbieri (2004) examine the question of trading with the enemy during wartime. One of the main liberal arguments for why trade encourages peace is that war will end the benefits of trade between states, and thus states will seek to avoid war if they are significant trading partners. Levy and Barbieri undercut that assumption by showing through numerous case examples that trading with the enemy during wartime has not been that unusual throughout history.

Methodological Notes: Missing Data

Barbieri (1996) tests her hypotheses using dyad-year data on 14,341 dyads for the 1870–1938 period. Previous studies typically focused on the post–World War II era due to a lack of systematic trade data prior to 1945. Barbieri collected new data on trade, a compilation that is now part of the Correlates of War Trade data set. Data on trade are difficult to obtain, and we are often lacking information for many dyad-year cases in our data sets. This is a general problem in scientific research that is called the **missing data** problem. Many statistical programs use a procedure called **listwise case deletion** that involves the elimination of cases that are missing values for one or more variables on a given observation.

Suppose we survey ten students in class and ask them questions about their party identification, their age, and their income. Suppose that all ten students provide information about party identification and age, but four students fill nothing in for the income question. If we analyzed these data, the computer program would throw out the four cases missing income values and give us results for only six students' responses. Whether this omission is problematic depends on the process by which the data became missing. Suppose there were four students who just forgot to fill this question out and they have a mean income and standard deviation fairly similar to the six students who completed the question. We could treat these data as **missing at random (MAR)** (King et al. 2001; Gleditsch 2002b). Analysis of the data with the missing observations would not be too problematic because the remaining cases are representative of the larger group.

Suppose, however, that the four students who failed to report their income all come from wealthy families with trust funds. In this case, the missing data are not missing at random because the value of another variable (high income) predicts whether the observation is missing. Scholars can use various strategies to help fill in missing data, such as multiple imputation, which uses values of other variables to help guess the value of the missing variable (King et al. 2001). If there was a correlation between Republican Party identification, older age, and higher income, for example, we might be able to guess the missing value of income by predicting it based on the other observed factors.

Barbieri (1996) points out these missing data problems in her article. She notes that her sample contains only 20 percent (14,341 dyad-years) of the total population of dyad-years from 1870–1938 (70,293). Thus, we have lost 80 percent of cases simply by adding three trade variables to our analysis! This would be okay if we believed the data were missing at random, but when we are dealing with international trade data, the chances for this are pretty small. First, trade data are typically compiled and reported by governments, and thus there must be a certain minimum level of state capacity in order for this function to be carried out. This means that many of the countries for which we are lacking trade data tend to have certain features, such as low income levels or autocratic governments. The countries that we have trade data for, especially as we move back further in time, are likely to be powerful and wealthier states. Second, trade can be disrupted by the very things we are interested in studying, such as MIDs and wars. During war, trade often drops significantly because investors fear the risks of putting money into a conflict zone. Governments also become less capable of collecting and reporting day-to-day statistics when they are fighting interstate wars.

Several strategies have been developed by international relations scholars to address these serious missing data problems for trade (Gleditsch 2002b; Barbieri, Keshk, and Pollins 2009) and other economic data such as foreign direct investment (Li and Vashchilko 2010). It is common to have trade flow data in one direction only. For example, we might know the value of U.S. exports to Mexico in 1950, but we may lack data from the Mexican government on imports from the United States in that year. As Gleditsch (2002b, 715) notes, we could have data on four possible trade flows for a hypothetical dyad, AB: (1) exports from A to B, (2) exports from B to A, (3) imports by A from B, and (4) imports by B from A. The values for (1) should be equal to the values for (4); likewise, values (2) and (3) should be equal. The U.S.-Mexico example shows that we might have data for (1) but lack data for (4). Things get tricky when coding trade flows because these values are not always the same because they are reported by government agencies that can make mistakes, and we often get one-sided reporting. Gleditsch (2002b) suggests filling in these missing values by estimating one of the values (e.g., exports from A to B) that is missing with a corresponding value that we have data for and that should be equivalent (e.g., imports by B from A). Another strategy is **interpolation**, which involves filling in missing values for trade across time. If we knew the value for U.S. exports to Mexico in 1950 and 1952 but were missing the value in 1951, we could guess the 1951 data point by taking the average of exports in 1950 and 1952. An additional decision rule, which can be more controversial, is to code any dyads with missing trade statistics as having no trade (i.e., we fill in these scores as zero).[1]

We can get an idea about how nonrandom the missing data problem is by examining the descriptive statistics for the variables in the full sample relative to the more restricted data set (due to missing observations). We can also examine the relationships between the control variables and militarized disputes in the restricted sample. In

Barbieri's (1996) article, she reports that the mean probability of a MID in a given year from 1870–1938 in her data set is 0.019, a value almost three times as large as the probability for all dyad-years (0.007). The probability of war (0.0009) is also higher in the restricted (trade) sample compared with the probability of war for all dyad-years (0.0005). This reflects in part the fact that the dyads in the sample with trade data are much more likely to be contiguous states with large populations. Many economists use a **gravity model** for trade that predicts the total level of dyadic trade in a given year as a function of distance between two states, the population size of each state, and the overall wealth (or gross domestic product) level of each state (Hegre 2009). While Barbieri finds her particular sample to have a higher likelihood of conflict, her results for the control variables are fairly similar to other dyad-year dispute studies (e.g., Bremer 1992b, Chapter 2, this volume). She shows in Table 1 that contiguity increases the risks for MIDs while joint democracy and power preponderance lower the chances for disputes; alliances have no significant effect. The consistency of these patterns for the control variables in comparison with other conflict studies gives us more confidence in interpreting the findings for her economic interdependence measures.

Barbieri (1996) begins her analysis with what she calls the **null model**. This involves analyzing the onset of MIDs with no independent variables in the model, just a Y-intercept (or constant). She then adds her variables in the various estimated models in Tables 1 and 2 and then calculates a **likelihood ratio (LR) test** comparing the null model to each larger model with multiple variables added. In Table 1, we see two asterisks by each of the LR statistics, showing us that the variables we have added (e.g., Salience, Contiguity, Joint democracy, Alliance, and Relative capabilities in Model 1) improve our ability to account for the variance in the dependent variable (MID onset). We see a similar pattern in Table 2, where the LR statistics are all statistically significant at the 95 percent level. Given that the economic interdependence measures are not significant individually in Table 2, we would infer that other factors in the model probably do the work in explaining variation in dyadic war onset (e.g., Contiguity, Relative capabilities).

Note

1. See also the discussion of missing data in Barbieri et al. (2009).

Questions

1. How is *Salience* different conceptually from *Symmetry* in Barbieri's theory? Which of these factors do you think would have the strongest *independent* effect on MIDs or wars?

2. Consider two hypothetical dyads, AB and CD. Suppose the values of each side's dyadic trade share are as follows: TradeShare$_A$ = 0.8, TradeShare$_B$ = 0.3, TradeShare$_C$ = 0.1, and TradeShare$_D$ = 0.3. Which dyad do you think would have the highest likelihood of experiencing a militarized dispute? Why? Use Figure 2 to help generate your expectations.

3. If leaders in the dyads AB and CD were seeking to ensure peaceful interactions in the future of these dyads, what kinds of strategies could they take with respect to their trading partnerships?

Further Reading

Barbieri, K. 2002. *The liberal illusion: Does trade promote peace?* Ann Arbor: University of Michigan Press.

Gleditsch, K. S. 2002b. Expanded trade and GDP data. *Journal of Conflict Resolution* 46 (5): 712–24.

Hegre, H. 2004. Size asymmetry, trade, and militarized conflict. *Journal of Conflict Resolution* 48 (3): 403–29.

Levy, J. S., and K. Barbieri. 2004. Trading with the enemy during wartime. *Security Studies* 13 (3): 1–47.

Russett, B., and J. R. Oneal. 2001. *Triangulating peace: Democracy, interdependence, and international organizations.* New York: W. W. Norton.

Chapter 11

A Unified Statistical Model of Conflict Onset and Escalation

William Reed

Many scholars have sought to isolate the causes of escalation, but discrepancies between the theoretical expectations and the empirical results persist. I attribute these discrepancies to a *selection effect*. Pairs of states do not become entangled in hostilities randomly. They instead select or are selected into disputes by a strategic process. Following previous empirical research focusing on selection effects (Achen 1986; Smith 1996a, 1996b, 1998, 1999; Gartner and Siverson 1996; Leeds and Davis 1997; Signorino 1999), I employ a statistical model to control for the interdependent relationship between the onset of disputes and escalation to war over the time period of 1950–1985. The results suggest that controlling for the selection effect statistically stipulates a link between the formal and empirical studies of escalation.

The scholarly literature on what causes escalation is mixed. Although some suggest that joint democracy inhibits escalation (Rousseau et al. 1996), others find that joint democracy actually makes dyads more escalatory (Senese 1997). There is also some disagreement about the effect of military capabilities on conflict onset compared to escalation (Morgan 1984, 1990, 1994; Morrow 1989; Fearon 1994b; Bueno de Mesquita, Morrow, and Zorick 1997). It seems reasonable to suspect that the factors that influence conflict onset may also affect escalation directly and/or indirectly. If this is the case, it is important to consider how the factors that influence

onset and escalation may be related to each other. Constructing a unified statistical model offers a first cut at modeling the process of conflict. Similar to the formal literature (Morrow 1989; Bueno de Mesquita and Lalman 1992; Fearon 1994a, 1994b; Smith 1998, 1999) that describes explicitly the selection process by which states get into and escalate disputes, I address the same issue from an empirical perspective (Smith 1996b, 1998, 1999; Signorino 1999). Modeling such selection empirically manages sources of bias and allows one to make truer inferences about the conflict generating process.

To summarize what follows, the first section of the paper discusses briefly the theoretical literature on escalation. Next I develop a strategy for modeling conflict onset and escalation simultaneously. In the third section I describe the data and variables I use in this study. I present and review the results from my empirical evaluations in the fourth section. I conclude with a brief summary of the results and their implications for international relations research.

Theories of Escalation

One weakness of the standard explanations of conflict is that few differentiate between onset and escalation. They instead theorize about how the probability of war changes, dependent upon some set of relevant variables. Morrow (1989) attributes much of the gap between theoretical expectations

Source: William Reed, "A Unified Statistical Model of Conflict Onset and Escalation," *American Journal of Political Science* 44, no. 1 (January 2000): 84–93. © 2000 by the Midwest Political Science Association. Reproduced with permission of Blackwell Publishing Ltd.

and empirical results to selection bias and model misspecification.[1] Some formal models of escalation anticipate that although some of the same factors influence conflict onset and escalation, their effects are not consistent across onset and escalation. Recent research focuses especially on the relationship between the distribution of capabilities, satisfaction with the status quo, and regime type and escalation (Rousseau et al 1996; Senese 1997; Bueno de Mesquita, Morrow, and Zorick 1997). I use two established explanations of interstate conflict to develop some hypotheses that relate these variables to conflict escalation: power parity and the democratic peace.

Power Parity

There are strong theoretical reasons to believe that the ratio of capabilities between states should influence the likelihood of conflict onset (Kugler and Lemke 1996).[2] Power parity theory argues that states become entangled in hostilities when they are dissatisfied with the status quo and have the ability to modify the status quo. When states have relatively equal amounts of power, they have the opportunity to change the status quo. If states are satisfied with the status quo, they have no incentive to initiate conflict regardless of their relative power (Lemke and Werner 1996). Likewise, dissatisfied states only initiate conflict when they are powerful enough to have a chance to win. Dissatisfaction with the status quo and power parity are thus expected to be related positively to the onset of hostilities. Once states are in a dispute, however, the effect of parity on escalation may differ. Within a dispute, when states have equal amounts of power, they may recognize that the costs of war are likely to be quite high and the outcome uncertain. Dyads characterized by parity within a dispute may be less prone to escalate to war.

There is strong empirical support for this proposition (Kugler and Lemke 1996). Rough equality of power seems to increase the probability of conflict onset, and uneven power relations seem to decrease it. A few studies find a similar relationship between parity and escalation (Siverson and Tennefoss 1984;

Moul 1988). Yet, some formal literature suggests that parity may have the opposite effect on escalation. Bueno de Mesquita, Morrow, and Zorick (1997) argue that although standard theories of world politics such as the balance of power and power parity suggest that the distribution of capabilities between states has a monotonic effect on the likelihood of war, their formal model predicts a nonmonotonic effect for power parity. Morgan (1990) argues specifically that, within a crisis, the greater the disparity of capabilities between the actors, the more likely the crisis will end in war.

The theoretical relationship between power parity and conflict onset goes along with the effect of status quo evaluations (Kugler and Lemke 1996; Lemke and Reed 1996). Within this framework, the international status quo is a recognized order of international interactions. The dominant power constructs the status quo so that it benefits from it. Following the Second World War, the United States established a status quo that encouraged political and economic liberalism through organizations such as the General Agreement on Tariffs and Trade (GATT), the International Monetary Fund (IMF), and so on. States dissatisfied with the status quo have incentives to initiate hostilities with the hope of modifying the international order.[3] Dissatisfaction with the status quo should increase the likelihood of conflict onset, and satisfaction with it should be pacifying. States satisfied with the status quo have nothing to fight over. Since few satisfied states should become involved in disputes, there should be little if any relationship between status quo evaluations and escalation.

The Democratic Peace

There are two general explanations for the observed peace between democratic states. Those who focus on domestic institutional structures argue that democratic leaders are confronted with political costs. Others argue democratic norms are at the root of the observed peace between pairs of democracies. Democracies socialize their leaders to manage political hostility through compromise and negotiation.

This "live and let live" domestic norm is externalized to the realm of international interactions. Bueno de Mesquita and Lalman (1992) argue that joint democracy should decrease the incentives to engage in preemptive behavior, and Fearon (1994a) maintains that jointly democratic dyads should be able to signal their resolve more clearly. The formal models combined with the wealth of empirical evidence suggest that joint democracy may prevent war.

All of the explanations for the democratic peace suggest that jointly democratic dyads should be less prone to become involved in militarized disputes. The theoretical expectations for the effect of joint democracy on escalation, however, are somewhat mixed. The normative explanation arguably implies that jointly democratic dyads should be less likely to escalate their disputes to war. Yet, Fearon's (1994a) model suggests that democratic dyads should be less likely to initiate disputes; once they have committed to militarized action, those disputes may be more prone to escalate to war. Perhaps joint democracy may have little effect on escalation. Since few democratic dyads become involved in disputes, joint democracy may have a statistically insignificant effect on escalation.

Previous empirical results on this topic are mixed. Senese (1997) finds that jointly democratic dyads are more likely to escalate their disputes under some conditions, but Rousseau et al. (1996) find that joint democracy has a weak pacifying effect on escalation.[4] Most agree that joint democracy decreases the probability of conflict onset, but its effect on escalation is not as clear.

Unobserved Variables

Much of the formal literature on escalation argues that selection into a dispute and subsequent escalation are influenced by unobservable variables such as resolve and the willingness to take risks (Morrow 1989). States frequently enter a dispute with limited information about their opponent's expected payoffs. They are unsure about their opponent's willingness to take risks or about their opponent's levels of resolve. Once this information is disclosed, it is likely to influence escalation. Since these unobserved variables are excluded from most empirical studies, model misspecification is a potentially severe problem. A unified statistical model of onset and escalation should recognize the influence that these unobserved variables may have on escalation.

One way to get a feel for how the unobserved variables that cause dyads to become involved in a dispute influence their escalation is to model onset and escalation jointly. If one models onset and escalation separately, one necessarily omits the potentially important but unobserved variables like risk propensity and resolve. Resolve, for instance, is relegated to the error term of both equations. There may be a statistical link then between the error terms that should closely mirror the theoretical link scholars posit when they refer to a continuous process of conflict moving from low stages like onset through higher stages like escalation. If one estimates this statistical link between the two error terms, it should hint at the strength of the actual link between the two phases of the conflict process. The full information maximum likelihood (FIML) statistical procedure employed in this article (and discussed at length below) explicitly estimates the statistical link (p) and thus allows me to make inferences about how interconnected onset and escalation are. Moreover, by estimating this statistical link, FIML allows me to correct for the influence of onset on escalation (which exists if the error terms are linked). I can thus manage the associated threat to statistical inference that should occur if I assume onset and escalation are independent when they are linked.

Perhaps the sign on p should be negative (Fearon 1994b). A negative sign on p suggests that the unobserved variables such as resolve, propensity to take risks, and prior beliefs that cause dyads to become involved in disputes have the opposite influence on subsequent escalation. Fearon argues: "If crises are characterized by private information and costly signaling, then states will 'select themselves' into or out of crises according to prior beliefs, and this fact will have implications for subsequent inferences and choices. One consequence is that the rationalist hypotheses that are true for general deterrence may be exactly reversed for immediate deterrence" (1994b, 245).

These theoretical expectations suggest the following directional hypotheses.

Hypothesis 1 *Pairs of states characterized by power parity are more likely to experience conflict onset, but they may be less likely to escalate their disputes to war.*

Hypothesis 2 *Pairs of states characterized by joint democracy are less likely to experience conflict onset, but once a dispute begins, the effect on escalation may be minimal.*

Hypothesis 3 *Pairs of states characterized by joint satisfaction with the status quo are less likely to experience conflict onset, but once a dispute begins, the effect on escalation may be minimal.*

Hypothesis 4 *Unobserved factors that cause states to become involved in a dispute may inhibit escalation.*

Unifying Onset and Escalation

Case selection plays an important role in studies of conflict escalation (Morrow 1989; Most and Starr 1989). Studies of escalation frequently treat cases in which there was no onset as omitted observations. Researchers typically identify a group of onset cases (crises or disputes) and then attempt to differentiate empirically between crises/disputes that did escalate and those that did not. If the variables that cause conflict onset and those that cause conflict escalation are unrelated, this approach creates no bias. If the covariates of onset and escalation are related, it is necessary to consider the nonevents where onset did not occur. To the degree that common variables determine both the onset of hostilities and the escalation of conflict, selecting cases based on conflict onset introduces potential selection bias.

Since studies that rely on a set of disputes produce a sample that has been nonrandomly selected, none of the usual statistical techniques including cross-tabulation or regression analysis produce reliable estimates (Achen 1986, 97). One way to manage the threat of selection bias is to estimate jointly the likelihood of dyads becoming involved in a dispute and escalating the dispute to war.

Since the outputs of the onset and escalation processes are observed discretely, maximum likelihood estimation provides a useful framework for just such a model (Fisher 1922; King 1989). In the analysis that follows, I code onset as occurring when $dyad_i$ is involved in a dispute at $time_t$, and I code escalation as occurring if the dispute becomes a war. There are thus two realizations of the dependent variable that both take on the value of 0 or 1. Three outcomes are possible: (1) $dyad_i$ does not experience conflict onset; (2) $dyad_i$ experiences onset, but the dispute does not escalate to war; (3) $dyad_i$ experiences conflict onset and the dispute escalates to war.[5]

I utilize a censored probit that accounts for selection to model this process statistically (Greene 1996a). Let y_1^* be a latent variable that measures conflict onset, and let y_2^* be a latent variable that measures escalation. I assume that y_i^* is influenced by a vector of observed explanatory variables X_i and a disturbance term u_i. The latent variables y_1^* and y_2^* are not observed. Instead, we observe the dichotomous realizations of y_1 and y_2, (disputes and wars). The following model structure is proposed.

$$y_1^* = X_1\beta_1 + \mu_1$$
$$y_2^* = X_2\beta_2 + \mu_2$$

We can only observe escalation, y_2, if there is a dispute, $y_{1i}^* > 0$. That is,

$$Conflict - Onset = \begin{cases} 1, \ if \ y_1^* > 0 \\ 0, \ if \ y_1^* \leq 0 \end{cases}$$

$$Escalation = \begin{cases} observed, \quad if \ y_1 = 1 \\ unobserved, \ if \ y_1 = 0 \end{cases}$$

The disturbance terms u_1 and u_2 are assumed to follow a joint normal distribution with $E[u_1] = E[u_2] = 0$, $Var[u_1] = Var[u_2] = 1$ and $Cov[u_1, u_2] = p$. With these assumptions, the log-likelihood function reads[6]

$$\ln L = \sum_{y_1=0} \ln\left(1 - \phi(\beta_1' X_1)\right)$$
$$+ \sum_{y_1=1, y_2=0} \ln \phi_2\left(\beta_1' X_1, -\beta_2' X_2, \rho\right)$$
$$+ \sum_{y_1=1, y_2=1} \ln \phi_2\left(\beta_1' X_1, -\beta_2' X_2, \rho\right)$$

where ϕ is the distribution function of the univariate normal and ϕ_2 is the bivariate normal distribution function. The first term on the right-hand side relates to the censored observations for dyads that never become involved in a militarized dispute. The second and third terms relate to the dyads that are in a dispute that does not escalate to war and those disputing dyads that do escalate to war, respectively.

There are at least three alternatives to the bivariate probit specification. The standard approach adopted in the empirical literature is to model dispute onset and escalation separately using either two logits or probits (i.e., one equation for onset and a separate one for escalation). The weakness of this strategy is that it explicitly assumes that onset and escalation are independent. Technically, these studies constrain ρ to 0. If this assumption of independence turns out to be wrong, the estimates of the models will be inconsistent. If some of the same variables influence both onset and escalation, then the indirect effect that onset has on escalation must be modeled.

An alternative modeling strategy uses an ordered probit or logit. This technique includes the information about onset and escalation in the same model, but it assumes that the directional effects of the independent variables are constant across onset and escalation. If this assumption of monotonicity is violated, results are also inconsistent. Finally, it is possible to utilize a two-stage model based on the work of Heckman (1979) and utilized by Huth (1996). In this technique two logits or probits are estimated. The predicted probabilities from the first model (onset) are saved and transformed into Mill's inverse ratio. This new variable is included in the second model (escalation). Including Mill's inverse ratio as an independent variable in the escalation model accounts for the probability of any dyad being selected into an analysis of dispute escalation. The weakness of this approach is that the model is heteroskedastic and thus inefficient. In spite of the limitations, this technique was employed to check for the robustness of the results reported below. The substantive and statistical results are similar to those reported in the third column of Table 1. This suggests that my main conclusions about onset influencing escalation and about the nonmonotonic effects of the variables are not a function of the FIML technique. Since the censored probit is efficient among all estimators and allows for the explanatory variables to have nonmonotonic effects, it seems most appropriate for the task here.

Data and Variables

I use a sample of cases from Oneal and Russett (1997). The unit of observation is the relevant dyad year. I observe dyads over the time period of 1950–1985,[7] using the Militarized Interstate Dispute (MID) data to operationalize both conflict onset and escalation (Jones, Bremer, and Singer 1996). A MID is an international interaction that involves threats, displays, or actual uses of force that are explicit, overt, and government sanctioned. I code a dyad as being involved in a dispute, as having experienced conflict onset, when a MID occurs. I code dyads as escalating if the MID advanced to war as defined by the Correlates of War (COW) project. These are both dichotomous variables that I assign a value of 1 when a dispute or war occurs and 0 otherwise.[8]

Explanatory Variables

Three variables are of special theoretical interest in this study: power parity, status quo evaluations, and joint democracy. To control for other variables that may influence the conflict generating process, I include three additional variables: alliance ties, economic interdependence, and changes in economic development.

Table 1   A Unified Model of Onset and Escalation

Variable	$\hat{\beta}$ (S.E.)	$\hat{\beta}$ (S.E.)	$\hat{\beta}$ (S.E.)	ΔPr
Onset α	−0.486 (0.033)‡		−0.484 (0.032)‡	—
Power Parity	0.353 (0.083)‡		0.356 (0.090)‡	+0.13
Joint Democracy	−0.611 (0.066)‡		−0.611 (0.066)‡	−0.18
Joint Satisfaction	−0.166 (0.065)‡		−0.165 (0.066)‡	−0.06
Alliance	0.040 (0.052)		0.042 (0.054)	—
Development	−0.010 (0.005)†		−0.010 (0.005)†	−0.15
Interdependence	−1.472 (3.420)		−1.432 (4.368)	—
Escalation α		−0.543 (0.056)‡	0.648 (0.096)‡	—
Power Parity		−0.086 (0.218)	−0.333 (0.189)†	−0.05
Joint Democracy		−1.279 (0.440)‡	−0.305 (0.342)	—
Joint Satisfaction		−0.582 (0.316)‡	−0.051 (0.303)	—
Alliance		−0.864 (0.166)‡	−0.637 (0.153)‡	−0.08
Development		0.057 (0.012)‡	0.048 (0.009)‡	+0.21
Interdependence		−34.504 (28.944)	−3.887 (14.829)	—
ρ Selection Effect			−0.772 (0.053)‡	
Log-Likelihood	−2810.693	−436.185	−3194.134	
Sample Size	20990	947	20990	

Note: Statistically significant parameter estimates are denoted by † ($p \leq .05$) and ‡ ($p \leq .01$).

Power Parity. To indicate dyads characterized by parity, I divide the relative power of the weaker state by the relative power of the stronger state. I represent both states' power with the Correlates of War Project's Composite Capabilities Index. This index ranges between 0 and 1. I code dyads at parity if the ratio of capabilities is greater than or equal to 0.80; 0 otherwise. Many other studies operationalize the ratio of capabilities as the power of the stronger state in the dyad divided by that of the weaker state. I employ the dichotomous indicator because it allows the model to converge more efficiently.

Status Quo Evaluations. I operationalize status quo evaluations in terms of alliance similarity to the dominant power (Bueno de Mesquita 1975; Kim 1991). Following Lemke and Reed (1996, 1998), I compare the alliance portfolios of all the states in the system to that of the United States after World War II, because the U.S. was what power parity theory calls the dominant power. This measure gauges each state's satisfaction with the systemic status quo. I calculate τ_B for each state in the system. The statistic ranges from −1 to +1, with a score of + 1 indicating perfect similarity between the state's alliance portfolio and that of the dominant power. As the score becomes less positive, approaching −1, the dissimilarity of the alliance portfolios is greater. Again, following Lemke and Reed (1996), I code states as satisfied with the status quo if τ_B is positive and dissatisfied otherwise. In this data set there are 5450 jointly satisfied dyads.

Joint Democracy. I use Polity III's index of democracy to operationalize joint democracy (Jaggers and Gurr 1995). I code states as democratic if they score 6 or above on the eleven-point scale of democracy and jointly democratic if both states score a 6 or above on the Polity III eleven-point scale.[9]

Alliance. COW alliance data indicates the presence of an alliance in the dyad (or if the states in the dyad are indirectly allied by both sharing an alliance with the United States). I code the alliance variable as 1 if the members of the dyad have a defense pact in common; otherwise, 0. Allied dyads are often argued to be less conflict prone. As might be expected, there is a relatively high correlation between the alliance and status quo evaluations variables.

Economic Interdependence. Oneal and Russett (1997) argue that economic interdependence decreases the likelihood of a dyad becoming involved in militarized disputes (Polachek 1980; Gasiorowski 1986a). A high level of economic interdependence within a dyad is assumed to increase the level of constraints, and thus the costs of conflict are expected to be greater. This measure of the degree of economic interdependence within a dyad is calculated relative to national income (Oneal and Russett 1997). The lower dependence score between the two states in the dyad is included in the model.

Economic Development. Economic development is also a dyadic indicator. It is the rate of economic growth of the less developed member of the dyad. Oneal and Russett (1997) calculate the average annual change in real GDP per capita for the states in the dyad over the previous three-year period. They argue that states experiencing an economic decline may have an incentive to become involved in foreign conflict in order to divert attention away

from domestic concerns (Ostrom and Job 1986; James 1988; Russett 1990).

Peace Years. To test and correct for temporal dependence, I estimate the onset phase of the model with consideration of potential time-related problems (Beck, Katz, and Tucker 1998). I control for temporal dependence by including in the onset phase of the model dummy variables representing the years of peace a dyad has experienced since its last militarized interstate dispute. I construct a variable that counts the number of years since a dyad was last in a dispute. This variable ranges from 0 to 34 years. From this variable I create thirty-five temporal dummy variables. I include thirty-four temporal dummy variables in the onset phase of the model.[10]

Empirical Evaluations

The first column of Table 1 reports results from the statistical model of conflict onset. As anticipated by much of the empirical literature, power parity has the expected positive effect on conflict onset. Dyads characterized by joint democracy and/or joint satisfaction with the status quo are less likely to be involved in disputes. Economic development is also found to have a pacifying effect on conflict onset.

I continue by estimating the escalation phase of the equation without statistically controlling the effect of conflict onset. I present the coefficients from this model in the second column of Table 1 for comparison with estimates from the unified model. Without statistically controlling the effect of conflict onset, joint democracy, joint satisfaction with the status quo, and alliance have the expected pacifying effect on escalation. Power parity is found to be unrelated to escalation, and developing dyads appear more prone to escalate their disputes.

I estimate the unified model and present the results in the third column of Table 1. One can compare the results from the unified model with the separate models of onset and escalation presented in first and second columns.[11] Comparing the estimates of the unified model to those of the independent probits illustrates the bias introduced by nonrandom selection.

The estimates of the unified model demonstrate that onset and escalation are related. The likelihood ratio test demonstrates that the unified model provides a much better approximation of the conflict generating process than the independent probits.[12] The coefficient on ρ, the correlation between the disturbances in the two phases of the model, indicates how the processes of onset and escalation relate to each other. Since onset and escalation are assumed to be independent in the first two columns, ρ is constrained to zero. In the unified model, however, ρ is statistically significant and negative. The coefficient on ρ is over sixteen times the size of its standard error, suggesting that the null hypothesis that onset and escalation are independent ($\rho = 0$) can be confidently rejected. Substantively, the negative sign on ρ suggests that the unmeasured variables that get dyads into a dispute actually inhibit the escalation of those disputes to war.

Many formal models focus on the effect of uncertainty on escalation. States are uncertain about important variables such as risk propensity, resolve, and prior beliefs. These variables likely affect the probability of conflict onset. Unfortunately, such characteristics are un-observable at worst or difficult to measure at best. Virtually all empirical studies of onset and escalation fail to include them as explanatory variables. Thus, these variables almost certainly appear in the disturbance term of the first phase of the model. The sign on ρ provides an estimate of the effect of these variables on the escalation process. If joint resolve is one of the unmeasured variables, the estimate of ρ suggests that jointly resolved dyads are unlikely to become involved in a dispute. If a dispute occurs between two states with a high degree of resolve, however, that dispute should be more prone to escalate to war. Perhaps leaders get into disputes to gather private information about the other side with the expectation of being able to stop short of war.

The estimates from the unified model are almost identical to those of the independent probits for conflict onset. This is as expected since the escalation behavior of dyads should not influence the prior likelihood of onset.

The differences between the unified model and the independent probits are striking. The unified model suggests that although both joint democracy and joint satisfaction with the status quo have a powerful pacifying effect on conflict onset, *they do not influence escalation*. When ρ is constrained to 0 (as in the second column) however, they both appear to have a pacifying effect on escalation. This result is somewhat surprising given the strong priors relating joint democracy to peaceful interactions. Perhaps the result is related to the joint democracy index. The joint democracy index, based on the Polity III data, suggests that there is only one jointly democratic dyad that escalates a dispute to war (Turkey and Cyprus 1974). Since the coding of this case is questioned by some scholars (Ray 1995a), it is useful to explore the result further. To test for the robustness of the results, the models were re-estimated using an alternative index of joint democracy.[13] The results are robust against this departure from the original index of joint democracy. Since the result does not appear to be driven by the measurement of joint democracy, it is useful to consider why joint democracy does not appear to influence escalation once onset is considered.

The difference between the unified model and the independent probits is that the unified model corrects for selection. That is, the unified model controls for the indirect effect of joint democracy on conflict escalation through its direct effect on conflict onset. When onset is excluded from models of escalation, the impact of joint democracy on escalation is inflated. Because the effects of joint democracy on onset and on escalation are positively correlated, the joint democracy coefficient in the escalation phase picks up some of the effect of joint democracy through conflict onset. Once I control for onset, the escalation effect disappears. This result does not refute the democratic peace proposition. It suggests instead that jointly democratic dyads avoid war because they rarely become involved in militarized disputes.

The sample of disputes analyzed here is not characterized by the majority of jointly democratic dyads. Only 6 percent of the dyads in the subsample of disputes are jointly democratic, compared to 23 percent of the dyads in the full data set. Few jointly satisfied dyads are involved in disputes as well. Prior to onset, 26 percent of the dyads are jointly satisfied. Within the subsample of disputes, only 14 percent are jointly satisfied. Jointly democratic or jointly satisfied dyads are more peaceful. They rarely become involved in disputes and thus have little opportunity to wage wars.

Studies that begin with dyads that are already in disputes assume that the mean propensity to escalate for jointly democratic and jointly satisfied dyads in disputes is the same as the mean propensity to escalate for jointly democratic and jointly satisfied states in the full sample of dyads involved and uninvolved in disputes. The unified model suggests that this is a tenuous assumption. The case is made clear with respect to the nonmonotonic effect of parity. Power parity appears to influence the behavior of dyads differently depending on whether they are in disputes or not. Balance of power theorists suggest that as one side in a dispute becomes more powerful, the probability of war increases monotonically. Power parity theorists, however, assert that as states approach an equal distribution of power, the probability of war increases monotonically. The unified model shows that there is no simple monotonic relationship between power distributions and war. The effect of parity is instead nonmonotonic as anticipated by Bueno de Mesquita, Morrow, and Zorick (1997). Dyads characterized by parity are more likely to experience militarized conflict, but less prone to escalate their disputes to war.

The unified model suggests that power parity has a pacifying effect on escalation, but when ρ is constrained to 0 there appears to be no relationship between power parity and escalation. Again, once the indirect effect of parity is controlled for, its direct effect on escalation is clearer. Economic development, like power parity, has a nonmonotonic influence on conflict. Although developing dyads are less likely to be involved in disputes, they are more prone to escalate their disputes to war.

The fifth column of Table 1 presents changes in the probability of onset and escalation when the variable of interest moves from its minimum to its maximum value. These probabilities are calculated by holding the dichotomous variables at their modes and the continuous variables are their means.[14] Joint democracy has the largest substantive effect on conflict onset. Moving from not jointly democratic to jointly democratic decreases the probability of conflict onset by 18 percent. Developing dyads are also less prone to experience onset. The probability of onset is decreased by 15 percent if the dyad is developing. Joint satisfaction with the status quo is modestly pacifying on conflict onset, decreasing the probability of onset by 5 percent. Power parity significantly increases the likelihood of onset. Dyads characterized by power parity are 13 percent more likely to become involved in disputes than dyads characterized by a disparate distribution of power.

Only power parity, alliance, and development have statistically significant effects on escalation. Dyads characterized by power parity are less prone to escalate disputes to war. Power parity decreases the probability of escalation by 5 percent (statistically controlling its positive effect on onset). Dyads that share an alliance are also less escalatory. Sharing an alliance dampens the probability of escalation to war by 8 percent. Developing dyads are found to be more escalatory, increasing the probability of escalation by 21 percent. Consider for example an especially dangerous dyad characterized by an uneven distribution of capabilities that does not share an alliance tie. If this dyad's rate of development is declining, the probability that it will escalate to war is .006. If this dyad's rate of development is increasing, however, the probability of escalation increases to .22. Consider likewise a dyad characterized by an average level of development and with no alliance tie. When this dyad is at parity the probability of escalation is .07. With an uneven distribution of capabilities, however, the probability of the same dyad escalating is .12.

Conclusion

The central result of this research is that conflict onset and escalation are related processes. The unified model of onset and escalation demonstrates this empirically and also suggests that the determinants of conflict influence escalation differently than they do onset. This result can be interpreted in at least two ways. Perhaps once a dispute starts, the process that generates escalation is different from that of onset. Contextual or background variables may play a larger role in onset, and the interdependent relationship between states in a dispute may be more important for escalation. Theories such as power transition, the democratic peace, and other models that rely on contextual variables may *set the stage* for interstate conflict onset. Once onset occurs, game theory, spatial models of conflict, and other formal approaches that focus on strategic interaction may provide a much richer explanation of escalation. It may be, however, that since almost all established theories do not distinguish between conflict onset and escalation, there may be little they can tell us about violence short of war. Perhaps future research might code onset at a higher level of conflict and then evaluate its impact on the process of escalation. If a large negative correlation still exists between the onset and escalation processes, there may be some need to revise current theories of world politics to account for the differences between onset and escalation. Although some formal models specify explicitly the relationship between variables that influence both conflict onset and escalation, a more rigorous theoretical framework is needed. This framework might link the traditional contextual theories of conflict onset with the more formal theories of escalatory strategic interactions between states once a dispute is underway.

In conclusion, the unified model of onset and escalation demonstrates that it is essential for researchers interested in escalation to consider first how states become involved in disputes. The onset of disputes and the escalation of disputes are interconnected but distinct phases of an integrated conflict process. It is crucial that studies of conflict onset and escalation should reflect both their relationship to each other and the possibly different effects that various variables have on each.

Notes

Author's Note: This research is funded by a grant from the National Science Foundation (SBR-9730407). Replication materials are available from the author. I wish to thank Douglas Lemke, Chris Achen, Dave Clark, Paul Huth, Ashley Leeds, Will Moore, Cliff Morgan, Jim Morrow, Karoline Mortensen, Charles Ostrom, Jim Ray, Evan Ringquist, Randolph Siverson, Alastair Smith, and Suzanne Werner for comments and suggestions. I thank John Oneal and Bruce Russett for making their data publicly available.

1. Some of the formal literature (Morrow 1989; Morgan 1990; Fearon 1994b; Bueno de Mesquita, Morrow, and Zorick 1997) goes so far as to suggest that the selection bias and misspecification in the empirical literature result in estimates with reversed signs. Morgan (1990), specifically, argues that although power parity is found to increase the likelihood of escalation in many studies, his formal model anticipates the opposite effect. Fearon (1994b) asserts that researchers should make a distinction between the effect of relative capabilities before and after a threat has been made, and he predicts that the sign on this variable may change after the initial threat.

2. Parity is used in the context of dyads in this paper. A number of other studies examine the relationship between the distribution of power in the international system and the likelihood of interstate war. For a discussion of this literature see Powell (1996).

3. There are also some formal expectations about status quo evaluations and interstate conflict. Powell (1996) argues that the probability of war is directly related to the level of dissatisfaction with the status quo. Powell's model suggests that dissatisfied states are unlikely to make counter-offers in a crisis situation. Rather, they tend to either accept the initial offer or to fight.

4. Hart and Reed (forthcoming) also find a weak pacifying relationship between joint democracy and escalation.

5. It is impossible (given the coding rules on the two dependent variables) for there to be a war without first having a dispute. Thus, the model operates as though the dependent variables are outputs of a sequential process rather than being determined simultaneously.

6. This likelihood function is based on the work of Meng and Schmidt (1985) and has been used by Dubin and Rivers (1989). It is a simple modification of a bivariate probit model that accounts for selection. The likelihood function is maximized in full-information maximum likelihood (FIML). FIML treats all equations and parameters jointly and is efficient among all estimators with normally distributed disturbances (Greene 1996a). To check for the robustness of the results the models were also estimated in limited information maximum likelihood (LIML). Even though LIML is less efficient than FIML, the results are robust. These models can be estimated in Limdep 7.0 and are discussed in chapter 22 of the Limdep 7.0 manual.

7. Since the results are limited to the Cold War period, it should be noted that these results are tentative and may not generalize to other time periods or to other designations of dyads within the 1950–85 time frame.

8. The data I use contain 20990 cases. Dispute onset occurs in 947 cases, and 213 of these 947 disputes are coded as escalating to war.

9. Oneal and Russett (1997) utilize an alternate indicator of dyadic democracy that ranges from –10 to +10. To check for the robustness of the results, I re-estimated the models with this alternative index of democracy. Both specifications of joint democracy yield similar results.

10. Two of these dummy variables are dropped from the analysis because of collinearity.

11. I include temporal dummy variables in the models but they do not appear in Table 1.

12. The equation for the likelihood ratio test in this case is $Llratio = -2(LL_{independent\text{-}onset} + LL_{independent\text{-}escalation} - LL_{unified\text{-}model})$.

13. The weak link index of democracy utilized by Oneal and Russett (1997) was employed as an alternate operational definition of joint democracy. Even with this alternate index, joint democracy does not appear to have a statistically significant effect on escalation.

14. The probabilities for the escalation phase of the model are calculated by holding ρ at –0.77. For a discussion of calculating the marginal effects in a bivariate probit see Greene (1996b).

EDITORS' COMMENTARY

Major Contributions: Power Preponderance

Reed's (2000) study is noted for making two very important contributions to the study of IR, both related to the effect of the onset of conflict for the escalation of conflict to war. First, he brings the idea of selection bias to the field and provide a statistical method for analyzing it. In many ways, this is the purpose of his study—to define selection bias and show how it can be important. He does this by looking at joint democracy and power variables. Second, he produces a very important finding on the democratic peace, although he does not emphasize this finding. He is among the first to eliminate the significance of the joint democracy variable as a predictor of war. He does this by controlling for the factors that bring about a militarized interstate dispute (MID) in the first place. It turns out that it is these variables (in the first stage) that account for why democracies do not fight each other. Put in more everyday language—democracies do not fight each other because they get into very few disputes (MIDs) in the first place. This finding is also consistent with a later finding by Huth and Allee (2002, 267) that one of the reasons democratic states do not fight each other over territorial issues is that they rarely threaten or use force over these issues. In other words, they handle the few territorial disagreements they have in a way that they do not become MIDs (see also Allee and Huth 2006). In addition, they have very few territorial issues (Mitchell and Prins 1999). Thus, joint democracies have two things going for them—they have few territorial issues, and these rarely give rise to territorial MIDs. It is the avoidance of conflict at the first stage that is the key for understanding why democracies do not fight each other. What goes on at the second stage (escalation to war) is not as significant.

As noted by Bremer (1992b, Chapter 2, this volume), many of the early studies of war analyzed only those cases that reached a high violence threshold, such as 1,000 or more battle deaths. This was problematic because it did not allow scholars to understand the dynamic conflict process (Diehl 2006). War is the end result of a process that begins with some challenge to the status quo and is characterized by a series of reciprocal diplomatic and violent exchanges. In some instances, states might be deterred from initiating a militarized dispute. Several studies in this volume focus on all dyad years (Bremer 1992b) or politically relevant dyad-years (Oneal and Russett 1999c, Chapter 9) to create a set of cases where conflict might occur but in most instances does not. Other studies look at escalation processes, considering the possibility that states might engage in brinkmanship at a lower level of violence and not escalate the situation to a higher level of force. For example, Asal and Beardsley (2007, Chapter 13, this volume) analyze the severity of violence in interstate crises, seeking to determine if crises with a larger number of nuclear armed states are less violent. Most conflict scholars focus on one process or the other, considering the onset of militarized disputes or crises, or the escalation of disputes or crises to war, but do not consider how these processes are related theoretically and empirically.

Reed (2000) shows that this is problematic because many of the standard covariates included in interstate conflict models can have different effects on conflict onset and conflict escalation. He gives an example with respect to **power parity** where two states have roughly even military and economic capabilities. Several theories predict that conflict is more likely to occur in dyads characterized by power parity, including power transition theory and the bargaining model of war. Both states in a power parity dyad think that they have a decent chance of winning a conflict when facing an equal adversary, and thus they might be willing to engage in brinkmanship over an important issue, such as ownership of a piece of territory. However, once a dispute has begun, the same power parity variable could have deterrent effects on the chances for escalation to war. The two sides might realize that by escalating the dispute to war, they are very likely to face high costs on the battlefield.

Reed (2000) makes a similar argument about the effect of joint democracy on conflict onset and escalation. Most democratic peace theories, such as the structural and informational theories, predict that jointly democratic dyads should be less likely to become involved in militarized disputes. Democracies are more likely to use peaceful negotiation tactics to resolve contentious issues in world politics. These theories would expect the strongest relationship between democracy and peace to occur at the conflict onset stage. Other theories, such as the normative model, predict that democracies will be less likely to escalate a dispute to war once it emerges because their norms of compromise and nonviolence will allow them to reach a settlement without resorting to war (on these two models, see Maoz and Russett 1993). Empirical analyses of the conflict onset process show a strong negative relationship between joint democracy and militarized conflict (e.g., Oneal and Russett 1999c). Analyses relating joint democracy and escalation of disputes to war produce more mixed findings, with some studies showing a positive effect of joint democracy on MID escalation to war (Senese 1997) and others showing a negative relationship between these factors (Rousseau et al. 1996). Most of the studies in the democratic peace literature, though, analyze conflict onset and escalation separately and fail to control for the ways in which foreign policy decision making for both stages is part of a broader, integrated process.

Reed (2000) relates this discussion to some of the research on conflict that employs **game theory** models. These models capture strategic interaction between two or more states and consider how actions further down the decision-making tree (e.g., war) influence decisions earlier in the process (e.g., MID initiation). Countries begin disputes with limited information about their opponents' capabilities and resolve. This lack of complete information is one of the key components of the bargaining model of war (Fearon 1995), explaining why states might fight a war even though it is costly. Once a dispute is under way, states have an opportunity to signal their resolve in the crisis situation. Consider a situation of extended deterrence where one state (e.g., China) threatens another state (e.g., Taiwan), which has ties to a third state (e.g., United States). Ex ante ties between the protégé and defender (e.g., the military alliance between Taiwan and the United States) provide information to the potential attacker about the chances for the third party to step into the conflict. Thus, factors such as alliance or trade ties between the defender and protégé might increase the chances for successful general, extended deterrence. In this case, the potential attacker is deterred from initiating a conflict against the protégé. However, if general deterrence fails and the attacker initiates a militarized dispute, it could probe the defender's resolve by threatening or displaying force against the target. Many of the factors that we think influence conflict onset or conflict escalation can be modeled directly by including these variables in our statistical models.

Yet Reed (2000) notes that unobserved factors are also important for strategic game theory models, and we are not able to capture these processes directly. For example, we have a hard time capturing the level of resolve for the potential attacker, protégé, or defender. How important is Taiwan's independence to the United States, and how many costs would it be willing to pay to defend this foreign policy issue? If China were to invade Taiwan, how resolved would the Taiwanese government and people be in resisting this attack? We have a hard time empirically determining the value that states place on particular objectives, measuring their propensity to take risks, or the willingness they have to suffer costs for their goals (Rosen 1972). The factors that cannot be measured directly get captured in the **error term** or **residual** of the statistical model. In Reed's study, we have two equations: one for conflict onset and one for conflict escalation. Each of these equations has a corresponding error term. He estimates a **censored probit** or **selection model** to capture the correlation between the unobservable factors that influence the selection stage (conflict onset) and the factors that affect the outcome stage (conflict escalation).

Reed's (2000) empirical results show that variables such as power parity and joint democracy can have different effects on MID onset and escalation to war. Dyads in which the weaker state has 80 percent or more of the dominant state's capabilities (parity) are more likely to experience MID onset compared with dyads in which one side has a preponderance of power. However, power parity has a negative effect on MID escalation to war; thus, states might be willing to engage in lower level violence to probe their equal adversaries, but they are less willing to take the risks in these cases to escalate the situation to a higher severity level. Reed shows that joint democracy has differential effects on the two stages of conflict as well. Jointly democratic dyads are significantly less likely to experience MIDs in comparison with nondemocratic or mixed dyads. What is key is that joint democracy has no effect on the chances for escalation to war once we take into account the processes linking the stages of onset and escalation. Other factors have varying effects as well; dyads experiencing positive economic growth are less likely to experience MID onset but more likely to escalate MIDs to war once they are under way. Reed's study resulted in a much broader set of conflict scholars using selection models to understand conflict processes more fully. For example, Senese (2005) showed that contiguous states are more likely to have any MID (i.e., in the first MID onset stage) but that contiguity has no effect at the second stage, MID escalation to war. At the second stage, the presence of a territorial MID is the major factor that is related to war. Senese's (2005) use of a two-stage selection model makes Bremer's (1992b) study of contiguity more precise and places the importance of contiguity at the first stage rather than the second.

Methodological Notes: Selection (Censored Probit) Models

As noted above, Reed (2000) uses a **selection model** to capture the correlation between the unobservable factors that influence the selection stage (conflict onset) and the factors that affect the outcome stage (conflict escalation). These unobservable factors appear in the error terms of the model. To understand the concept of a residual, consider a simple **regression** model of a student's grade (Y) as a function of the percentage of total classes she attends in a semester (X).

$$Y = \alpha + \beta X + \mu.$$

We could estimate the parameters in this linear model with an estimation procedure called ordinary least squares (OLS). We could get a rough estimate of how each unit increase in attendance relates to a student's course grade (presumably the effect is positive!). A regression model finds the line that minimizes the sum of the squared distances between each data point (e.g., each student's grade and attendance) and the regression line. However, not all of the data points fall exactly on the line. Some students' grades will be lower than expected based on their attendance, while other students who did not come to class very often might have performed better than expected. The distance between the data point and the point on the estimated regression line is called the error term or the residual (μ). This error term exists because other factors that influence students' grades are not included. Some of these could be omitted variables that could be measured but were excluded from the model for some reason (e.g., overall grade point average, gender, year in school). Leaving out important variables is problematic because this can bias the effect that we estimate for the included variables. We might overestimate the effect of attendance on grade, for example, if we do not take into account the student's overall collegiate record.

Other factors that are unobservable could influence the overall grade, too, such as a student's work ethic or interest level in the material. A student who attended all classes may have done worse than predicted by the regression model because he or she did not spend any time outside of class reading the course material or studying for exams. Reed (2000) applies this same idea to his article to see how unobservable factors such as resolve or states' willingness to take risks influence the onset of MIDs and escalation of MIDs to war.

In a censored probit model, we have two equations, one for conflict onset and one for conflict escalation. In this particular model, both equations have dummy dependent variables (1/0), although it is possible to have the selection equation model a dichotomous variable (e.g., go to college or not) and the outcome equation model a continuous variable (e.g., post-college salary). Heckman (1979) developed these kinds of models to look at the effects of gender on the salary gap. Reed starts with a general version of the model where he assumes that conflict onset and escalation could be captured with some kind of latent, continuous variables (y_1^* , y_2^*). We do not observe these underlying latent variables; rather, we capture them through a dichotomous representation (dispute or no dispute, escalation to war or not).

$$\text{Selection equation: } y_1^* = X_1\beta_1 + \mu_1$$

$$\text{Outcome equation: } y_2^* = X_2\beta_2 + \mu_2$$

We only get to the outcome equation (stage two) if we observe a dispute in the selection equation—for example, $y_1^* > 0$ for case i. We can calculate the correlation between the error terms in the two equations, what Reed (2000) calls ρ (rho). In other words, $\rho = \text{Correlation}[\mu_1, \mu_2]$. If $\rho = 0$ (the null hypothesis), then the two stages of onset and escalation would be independent from each other. If ρ is positive, this tells us that the unobservable factors that influence conflict onset are positively related to the unobservable factors that affect escalation to war. This might occur if a high level of resolve increases the chances for dispute onset and makes a state more likely to follow through, even if it means fighting a costly war. If ρ is negative, then unobservable factors would be positively related to one decision but negatively related to the other. Imagine that a state was willing to suffer great costs for its goals, a factor that could increase its propensity for escalation to war. Yet high willingness to suffer could make a state reluctant to start a conflict in the first place. In Table 1, we see in the third column that the estimated value of ρ equals −0.772, which is significantly different from zero, allowing us to reject the null hypothesis that conflict onset and escalation are independent. The negative sign tells us that unobservable factors that get countries into militarized disputes inhibit their willingness to escalate the situation to war. It could be that jointly resolved states typically avoid militarized conflicts with each other, but when a dispute occurs, they are willing to escalate the dispute to war. The negative correlation is created by joint resolve depressing the chances for MID onset but increasing the chances for MID escalation.

In Table 1, Reed (2000) first estimates the models for onset and escalation separately, as has been done in much of the conflict literature using data on politically relevant dyad-years from 1950–1985. He then estimates the censored probit model, which captures the relationship between onset and escalation. We can see that the variables in the MID onset model have similar effects no matter whether we model onset separately (column 1) or in the selection model (column 3). Dyadic MIDs are less likely between pairs of states that are jointly democratic, jointly satisfied, experiencing economic growth, and power preponderant. In the second column, Reed estimates an escalation model (alone). He finds that escalation to war is less likely in dyads that are characterized by power parity, those that are jointly democratic and satisfied, and those that are allied; war is more likely in dyads that are experiencing positive economic growth. We can see, though, that several of these findings are altered when we consider selection effects (column 3). Now joint democracy and joint satisfaction with the status quo are no longer significant predictors of escalation to war. The effects of these two variables are overestimated when we consider escalation as a distinct process. Selection models are useful tools for testing theories that involve strategic interactions over dynamic conflict processes.

Questions

1. When we say there is a possible selection bias going on, what do we mean? For example, if we say there is a selection effect between MID onset and MID escalation to war, what do we mean?

2. What is Reed's major finding regarding the democratic peace? According to his findings, why do democratic states not fight each other?

3. Go to Table 1. In column 3, what is the significance of joint democracy (in the first stage)? In column 4, what is the significance of joint democracy (in the second stage)? What are the implications of these significance levels for the democratic peace?

4. In Table 1, column 4 what is the significance of rho (ρ Selection Effect)? What does this tell us about the presence of selection effects and the correlation of error terms?

5. In Table 1, look at the changes in predicted probabilities for the selection model in column 5. Which variable(s) has the largest substantive influence on MID onset and escalation to war?

Further Reading

Allee, T., and P. K. Huth. 2006. Legitimizing dispute settlement: International legal rulings as domestic political cover. *American Political Science Review* 100 (2): 219–34.

Huth, P. K., and T. Allee. 2002. *The democratic peace and territorial conflict in the twentieth century.* Cambridge, UK: Cambridge University Press.

Ray, J. L. 2003a. A Lakatosian view of the democratic peace research program. In *Progress in international relations theory: Appraising the field,* ed. C. Elman and M. F. Elman. Cambridge: MIT Press.

_____. 2003b. Explaining interstate conflict and war: What should be controlled for? *Conflict Management and Peace Science* 20 (2): 1–31.

Senese, P. D. 2005. Territory, contiguity, and international conflict: Assessing a new joint explanation. *American Journal of Political Science* 49 (4): 769–79.

Chapter 12

Bordering on Peace

Democracy, Territorial Issues, and Conflict

Douglas M. Gibler

M ost democratic peace scholarship takes regime type as given and then estimates its effect on the likelihood of conflict. This paper deviates from that formula by endogenizing regime type to test whether joint democracy is actually an instrumental variable that represents an absence of territorial issues in particular dyads, especially neighbors. If states are most likely to have issues with their neighbors, but some neighbors remove these issues from contention, peaceful relationships should exist among these states outside of regime type. I argue that democracy and peace might both be symptoms—not causes—of the removal of territorial issues between neighbors, and in this sense the "empirical law" of democratic peace might be spurious (Levy 1988).

In the sections that follow, I examine literature on the steps to war explanation of conflict and the democratic peace, noting potentially useful points of accommodation between their findings. Next, I outline a theory that understands both peace and regime type—in particular, democracy— to be the product of specific patterns of border relationships. I then test this theory against a model of conflict that controls for the effects of border relationships and find that joint democracy does not exercise a pacifying effect on dispute initiation.

Territorial Issues and the Steps to War

Contiguity enjoys wide empirical support as one of the key factors influencing the likelihood of war in dyads (Richardson 1960b; Garnham 1976; Wallensteen 1981; Gochman and Leng 1983; Diehl 1985b; Vasquez 1987, 1993, 1995, 1996b, 2001; Holsti 1991; Kocs 1995; Gibler 1996, 1997; Hensel 1996; Huth 1996; Senese 1996, 1997; Vasquez and Henehan 2001; Bennett and Stam 2003). Bremer (1992b) provides some of the most compelling evidence, demonstrating that contiguity is the single most important independent variable in predicting the war-proneness of a dyad. In his analysis of "dangerous dyads" between 1815 and 1965, contiguous states are 35 times more likely to experience war than noncontiguous states. In short, states are far more likely *ceteris paribus* to fight their neighbors than any other states. But contiguity, as a constant for neighboring states, does not cause war on its own; rather, it serves as the primary locus of territorial issues, which are a fundamental underlying cause of war (Holsti 1991; Goertz and Diehl 1992a; Vasquez 1995, 1996).

The steps-to-war explanation of conflict begins with the assumption that issues are the underlying causes of war and notes that territorial issues are the most war-prone of all issue types (Vasquez 1987, 1993, 1995, 1996b, 1997, 2001; Gibler 1996, 1997;

Source: Douglas M. Gibler, "Bordering on Peace: Democracy, Territorial Issues, and Conflict," *International Studies Quarterly* 51 (2007): 509–32. © International Studies Association. Reproduced with permission of Blackwell Publishing Ltd.

Vasquez and Gibler 2001; Vasquez and Henehan 2001; Senese and Vasquez 2003; Colaresi and Thompson 2005; Senese 2005). To the extent that they give rise to disputes about which states make decisions that ultimately lead to either peaceful resolution or war, issues represent underlying causes of conflict. The steps-to-war theory distinguishes those issue types most likely to be handled peacefully, through compromise and negotiation, from those most likely to be handled aggressively, through traditional, power politics behaviors like military build-ups, alliance making, and demonstrations of resolve in crisis bargaining. These power politics behaviors represent proximate causes of—or steps along the path to—war, aggravating the conflict process once issues are defined.

Vasquez (1993) argues that leaders have learned through a kind of realist folklore to address territorial issues with power politics behaviors, as territory is a critical factor in identity, security, and prosperity for the modern state. Of all issue types, those involving territory prove to be the most war-prone (Huth 1996; Vasquez 2001; Huth and Allee 2002), and pairs of states lacking territorial issues should be highly unlikely to experience conflict—especially when they are neighbors, because the issues over which they fight are simply less contentious.

The Democratic Peace and the Steps to War

The democratic peace literature centers on the finding that no two democracies have gone to war with one another in the modern era (Small and Singer 1976), and a sizeable body of literature has emerged that verifies the pacifying effects of democracy, especially in dyads (Rummel 1983; Chan 1984; Weede 1984, 1992; Levy 1988; Bremer 1992b, 1993; Ray 1993, 1995b; Russett 1993; Oneal and Russett 1997, 1999c). For all its empirical strength, however, consensus on the causes of the democratic peace remains elusive. While monadic arguments about the general peacefulness of democracies have performed poorly in tests (Ray 1995b), the dyadic nature of the democratic peace has enjoyed far

greater support and has been the subject of a great deal of inductive theory-building. In this section, I examine the democratic peace in terms of its three dominant theoretical models and several important findings that have emerged from both proponents and critics. I then offer a way to reconceptualize these findings and lay the groundwork for an alternative theory of democratic peace.

Theoretical Models

Three models dominate the democratic peace literature: normative, structural, and institutional. Each model looks to domestic regime type as the independent variable responsible for peace, though they disagree over the theory necessary to explain it and the specific expectations about state behavior that should constitute the peace.

Norms. Following Immanuel Kant's (1991 [1795]) assertion that states with republican constitutions should transcend the anarchy and relative gains considerations of the international system and achieve a kind of cooperative peace, the normative model assumes that states externalize the methods of conflict resolution that define their regime types. These democratic norms are externalized when doing so is not a threat to basic security, such as when dealing with fellow democracies or substantially weaker states (Doyle 1986; Maoz and Russett 1993; Dixon 1994; Oneal and Russett 1997, 1999c).

Domestic Structures. The structural model focuses on the difficulties democracies face in mobilizing for war (Small and Singer 1976; Rummel 1983; Bueno de Mesquita and Lalman 1992; Lake 1992; Fearon 1994b). The need in democratic systems to generate broad public support and to win legitimacy from a variety of decentralized sources of authority represent structural constraints that make the process of mobilizing for war more difficult than in autocratic regimes. Only in rare cases, such as clear security emergencies, can democracies win the support of enough competing domestic interests to go to war. The process is slow and transparent, and in cases of joint-democratic disputes, diplomatic solutions can usually be found before either state wins enough domestic support for a war. Less-constrained autocratic regimes should be able to mobilize for war much faster, presenting the kind of immediate threat against which democratic polities are more likely to win support for violent action. Democracies are thus unlikely to fight one another, although they are more likely to aggressively engage less democratic states.

Institutions. The institutional model derives democratic peace from two factors: the hesitancy of leaders in democratic states to risk unwinnable wars and the fact that democracies, once committed to war, "try harder" than autocracies and tend to win most of their wars, thus becoming unattractive targets for aggression (Reiter and Stam 1998a,b, 2000; Bueno de Mesquita, Morrow, Siverson, and Smith 1999; Bueno de Mesquita, Smith, Siverson, and Morrow 2003). Democratic leaders must distribute public goods such as prosperity and security to stay in power, while autocratic leaders are loyal to a smaller winning coalition who can be more easily placated with private goods, such as the spoils of conquest. Autocrats, able to divert the costs of war to a populace to whom they are not accountable, are thus more likely to resort to war but, because defeat is less a threat to regime survival, do not try hard to win. Democracies, in contrast, fight only those wars they can win, and when committed, they fight hard.

Findings

Several important findings emerge from the democratic peace literature beyond the simple dyadic peace, but as yet they have not been subsumed under a single theory. As noted above, the absence of war between democratic states forms the core of the democratic peace. However, democracies are no less war-prone in general than other states; they simply do not fight each other (Russett 1993). Second, democracies are more likely than other states to submit their disputes to negotiation and arbitration instead of resorting to force (Dixon 1994; Raymond 1994; Brecher and Wilkenfeld 1997; Mousseau

1998; Huth and Allee 2002). Both findings suggest that, given the opportunity, democracies will act peacefully and will not resort to unprovoked attack. Studies also suggest that democracies are uniquely able to refrain from escalating territorial disputes to war (Bueno de Mesquita et al. 1999; Mitchell and Prins 1999; Huth and Allee 2002). Gleditsch (2002a), who recasts the democratic peace as a regional phenomenon, notes two other critical regularities: democracies rarely if ever fight wars on or near their home territory, and democracies tend to cluster together in space and time, creating regional zones of peace.

Alternatives

Each of the above findings is consistent with the assertion that democracies have avoided war with one another because of a lack of territorial issues. First, if neighboring states do not have territorial issues they should be highly unlikely to fight *a priori*. To the extent that states with stable borders fight wars at all, they are unlikely to do so on or near their home territory. Should these states enter into disputes with distant states, they are less likely to involve threats to their territorial integrity; as such, they should be less likely to follow the power politics path to war identified in the steps-to-war model and more likely to seek peaceful negotiation and arbitration. To the extent that democracies experience territorial disputes, they are likely to be distant.[1]

Second, if states are more likely to become democratic in the absence of territorial issues, then democracies should cluster around stable interstate borders. As a result of settling their borders, neighbors should experience greater chances of both having a peaceful relationship and becoming democratic. In short, if democracies do not fight each other, it is because the borders between them had to be settled before democracy could take root. Precisely because democracies *share* stable borders, peace between them is likely.

This argument also makes sense in light of several important challenges to the democratic peace, notably in Reed's (2000) finding that joint democracy exerts a pacifying effect only on dispute onset and not on escalation to war. Joint democracies are simply less likely to experience disputes than other dyads; if these joint democracies tend to interact across shared stable borders, then this result is clearly expected.

Especially among newly independent or transitioning states, both of whom are likely to experience territorial disputes (Vasquez 1993, 1995), new democratic institutions might actually increase the likelihood of disputes escalating to war (Mansfield and Snyder 1995; Thompson and Tucker 1997; Snyder 2000). Territorial issues might then represent clear obstacles to democratic consolidation in transitioning states. While democratic peace scholars generally account for this by holding that the pacific benefits of democracy work chiefly in "mature" democracies (Maoz and Russett 1993), it is probably more plausible that the incidence of territorial issues, which are most likely during and after transition periods, might be the cause. That the difference between young and old democracies is explained away in this fashion is unsatisfactory, as the distinction underlying it—the propensity for territorial issues—is a key omitted variable.

Fearon and Laitin (2003) note that democracies, especially young ones, are no less likely than nondemocracies to experience insurgencies and civil wars, despite expectations that the protection of civil rights and broad participation should pacify rival ethnic groups. Many of the conditions that favor civil war—and, by extension, democratic breakdown—tend to be those that also destabilize borders: recent independence, favorable terrain, foreign support for guerillas, and past colonial legacies. The eruption of civil war poses a threat to the territorial status quo in much the same way that transitions do; neighbors are uncertain whether, first, violence will spread or, second, whether the victors will respect the established division of territory in the region. The result should be a clearly heightened sense of territorial threat. From this perspective, the conditions that favor insurgencies and civil wars also indicate the presence of an unstable or ill-defined border; thus many of the indicators of border instability in the next section are drawn from the insurgency literature.

The confluence of these findings suggests that, if stable borders have something to do not only with peace but also with prospects for democracy, there is reason to believe that the relationship between democracy and peace is spurious. The next step in this argument, then, is to establish the connection between stable borders and the development of democracy.

Borders, Conflict, and Democracy

In this section I outline a theory that links regime type to the international environment through the process of participating in and responding to threats of territorial conflict. I draw on the links between domestic and international politics implicit in Boix's (2003) model of regime choice, as well as an updated variant of Hintze's (1975 [1906]) analysis of "insular" states, to construct a simple argument about the role of interstate borders, conflict, the costs of repression, and the consequences for domestic organization. I argue that democracy is most likely to take root when the threat of fighting wars on or near a state's home territory is low—that is, when the territorial status quo of a state's borders is settled.

The Politics of Democratic Transitions in a Militarized State

Boix (2003) develops a formal model that captures the relationships between wealthy and poor in a society and bases the wealthy's decision over whether to maintain an autocratic regime or establish a democracy on the distribution and mobility of economic assets. When inequality is low, the poor make few redistributive demands on the wealthy and the costs of transitioning to a power-sharing agreement—a democratic constitution—are low. Additionally, when capital is highly mobile, the high taxation and extraction of an autocratic elite are more tenuous, as assets can flee to less repressive regimes. The costs of repression also figure prominently in the analysis, and when the elite can easily suppress redistributive pressures from below, autocratic outcomes are most likely. Democracy becomes a stable equilibrium when no single actor—whether the wealthy in power or the potentially victorious poor—has an incentive to play an exclusionary strategy; that is, relative to the costs of accepting a democratic outcome, the cost of imposing the preferred distributive regime are prohibitively high.

Repression by the elite is often easier in militarized societies, suggesting a simple path from potential conflict to regime type. States that experience consistent external threats to their home territory are more likely to construct large militaries and to experience slower economic development, resulting in a relatively low cost of repression for the elite, as well as more intense redistributive pressures from the poor. The elites then have an incentive to pursue an exclusionary strategy in the maintenance of the autocratic order, and autocracies should be quite skilled at maintaining this level of domination. When borders are stable and peaceful, however, economic growth becomes possible, reducing the differences between rich and poor, raising the costs of repression, and increasing the mobility of capital, rendering strategies of high taxation increasingly difficult. The relative size and power of the military diminishes, and democracy emerges as a possible equilibrium. Finally, because borders are interstate institutions, stability on one side frequently translates into stability on the other, and democracy spreads across peaceful interstate borders, emerging in zones of stable peace where the regional territorial status quo is accepted.

That the level of external threat should play a role in shaping forms of military and domestic organization is hardly a new idea, emerging at least a century ago in the work of German historian Hintze (1975 [1906]). Hintze argued that continental states facing persistent threats to their security build highly centralized state apparatuses to support the large standing armies needed for security, whereas states protected by geography, like islands, tend to build more decentralized militias and democratic regimes. The problem for Hintze's original theory, though, is that many of the Central European autocracies

followed the path of Britain and Switzerland and have since democratized, even clustering together in regional zones of democracy (Gleditsch 2002a). Further, most large-n examinations of democratization find little or no association between external threat and state centralization; only direct participation in war seems to matter (see Reiter 2001, for example).

The Effects of Territorial Threat on Militarization, Taxation, Centralization, and Growth

I argue that this absence of strong findings is probably due to a focus on all types of international conflict rather than isolating specific, more salient threats such as territorial issues.[2] Matters involving territory are some of the most war-prone issues in international relations (Holsti 1991; Vasquez 1993, 1995, 1996b, 2001; Kocs 1995; Senese and Vasquez 2003; Colaresi and Thompson, 2005; Senese 2005), and more so than questions of policy or ideological difference, the defense or pursuit of territory prompts states to engage in provocative and violent behavior, especially when that territory is within the formal borders of the state. Threats to the homeland by revisionist neighbors are thus more likely than other threats to result in the construction of large standing armies that sit at home and provide a readily available tool for repression.

Standing armies require high levels of taxation as well as a broad centralization of authority—to acquire, arm, equip, feed, and otherwise maintain the troops, which is consistent with the findings that autocracies have more highly centralized state structures than democracies (Alesina and Spolaore 2003; Boix 2003). High taxation and centralization both contribute to a widened gap between the elite's fortunes in a democracy as compared to the *status quo*. Because high levels of military spending and frequent conflict also depress domestic consumption and economic growth, the costs of adopting democracy and conceding to the poor's redistributive demands then become far higher than the costs of using the army to pursue a strategy of exclusion and suppress competing social groups.

Settled Borders and Democratic Transitions

When threat is lower and less consistent economic growth becomes possible. Boix (2003:228) notes that sustained economic growth on the European continent, which produced the redistributive environment necessary for democracy, came only after the settling of "key territorial claims" in the seventeenth and eighteenth centuries and the attendant reduction in the frequency and threat of war. In times of lowered threat, the difference between rich and poor decreases, rendering the autocratic elite less fearful of the redistributive consequences of democracy, and assets become increasingly mobile with the emergence of diversified industries and human capital, lowering the sustainable tax rate. The military also becomes a less effective and thus more costly instrument of repression as demands upon it grow. This, combined with the narrowing gap between wealthy and poor, reduces dramatically the incentives for any group, including the autocratic elite, to pursue an exclusionary strategy. At this point, even the elite's ship is better raised by accepting democracy than continuing a policy of repression.[3]

The emergence of England as a democracy provides a nice example of how the absence of direct territorial threats reduces the likelihood of continued autocracy. As Moore (1966:32) describes, "the repressive apparatus of the English state was relatively weak, a consequence of the Civil War, the previous evolution of the monarchy, and of reliance on a navy rather than on the army. In turn the absence of a strong monarchy resting on an army and a bureaucracy, as in Prussia, made easier the development of parliamentary democracy." Conflicts for England were often but also foreign, requiring navies and militia abroad, not the standing militaries required to suppress direct threats to the homeland. Thus, as the prerequisites for institutional change— increasing per capita income, strong middle class interests, weakened central authority, etc—initiated a bargaining process between Parliament and Crown, the absence of a standing militia assured that no group could use the army to dominate other

actors and control the state. If conflicts had been local, necessitating a standing army, the Crown could have used that force to dominate Parliament (North and Weingast 1989).[4]

The Democratic Equilibrium and Democratic State Behavior

Once a democratic equilibrium emerges, breaking it becomes difficult, barring any serious external shocks (Boix 2003). Even in the face of growing or significant external threats, democracies can build large militaries without worrying that they might provide incentives for any social groups to pursue exclusionary policies. Rent seeking and exclusion will likely be punished at the polls before any would-be autocrats can alter institutions through vertical conflict. This might explain why, despite a large arms buildup in the Cold War, the United States avoided developing into an autocratic "garrison state" (Friedberg 2000) or why Israel maintains democracy despite consistent and intense threats to its homeland. The democratic equilibrium also explains why one of the most prominent examinations of the peace-democracy link finds that only direct participation in wars—not lower-level disputes—significantly affects regime survival (Reiter 2001).

The clear conclusion of the theory outlined above is that mature democracies are unlikely to have direct threats to their homeland or serious conflicts with other democracies; nevertheless, democracies may engage in conflicts with other states in the system. Stated in terms of the developmental path of the state, peace, properly specified as a reduction in territorial threat, can lead to democracy because the international environment can affect directly (1) the incentives for and costs of repression and (2) the prospects for economic development and diversification. When elites in unequal or fixed-asset states can, they will pursue exclusionary strategies, and they often use conflict—because in controlling the military they control the biggest gun in the state—to maintain the current order. However, when stable expectations about peace contribute to economic growth and the decentralization of economic power, the strategies of exclusion become both less feasible and less attractive, and democracy emerges as a stable political equilibrium. Finally, because borders generally are stable or unstable for states on either side, democracy spreads across peaceful borders in regions where the territorial status quo is more or less settled, while autocracy prevails in regions where the territorial status quo remains unsettled.

Hypotheses

The theory outlined above suggests that the stabilization of borders in a region should contribute to democratization in that region, establishing what Thompson (1996) and Gleditsch (2002a) label as zones or clusters of peaceful democratic states. As neighbors experience fewer and fewer territorial issues, they are more likely to, first, have a peaceful relationship and, second, become more democratic. The democratic peace, as we know it, is simply the outgrowth of a peace between neighbors. In a purely international context, then, democracy is what can happen when neighbors no longer fear for the safety of their territory.

If democracies cluster spatially because their emergence requires the settling of territorial issues, democratic neighbors should be significantly less likely to enter into disputes than any other dyads. By extension, stable borders between autocracies, to the extent they exist, should also be peaceful. Additionally, given theoretical expectations that young states should be more prone to territorial issues and that, once in disputes, democracies may be less likely to back down, newly independent states with democratic institutions may actually be uniquely conflict-prone. These states should also be likely to experience democratic breakdown, as democracy should be less likely to survive in the presence of territorial threat.

Operationalizing Border Stability

I consider a state's border relations as either stable or unstable based on two factors. First is the extent to which some part of its territory is at risk of capture or occupation by one or more of its neighbors. Second is the degree to which the state possesses the ability to defend against territorial challenges and to pose similar threats of capture or occupation to its neighbors. Land borders and standing armies are thus crucial elements for my concept of border relations: land borders are the prime sources of threats to territoriality, and standing armies are the instrument by which states both defend their territory and threaten the territory of others. Standing armies also require highly centralized forms of state organization that may inhibit the development of democracy, and a state's border relations largely determine the need for this type of military organization.

Border relations are stable, then, when states perceive little or no threat to their sense of territoriality and when they have no designs on altering the territorial status quo. Defining stable borders without being tautological is difficult, but several characteristics of stable borders should be evident *prima facie*. Insular states, such as Great Britain, are clear examples of states with stable borders. They need not develop large standing armies to defend against threats on the frontier, because the frontier does not exist. As in Britain's case, these states may develop considerable military power in the form of navies and expeditionary armies, but these forces are distinct from standing land armies in continental states since their principal deployment is abroad. They thus pose a less serious threat to democracy than do standing armies on the home territory. States with natural borders, notably mountainous Switzerland, would likely have similar border relations.

If stable borders are difficult to define without doing so in terms of the phenomena I expect them to explain—particularly democracy and peace—unstable borders are an even greater challenge. Much of the argument about border relations depends necessarily on the perception of threat, which is often difficult to capture empirically. There is, however, some reliable empirical ground on which I can build a definition. First, only land borders can be considered unstable, as only they can provide the necessary type of threat to territoriality.

Second, I avoid defining border instability in terms of war or dispute participation to prevent problems of circularity; rather, I focus on the geographic conditions that should promote unstable borders. Third, I control for the overall capability distribution in the dyad because this often will determine the likelihood of border renegotiation, and I identify political events in neighboring countries that might affect border legitimacy.

Geography and Borders

Vasquez (1995:288) argues that, "natural frontiers that have clear salients—like rivers, mountains, deserts, lakes, and oceans—are more likely to lead to a mutually acceptable demarcation of boundaries, especially if people are not living in these areas." The logic is straightforward: geographic salients permit easier coordination. Geographic landmarks are observable to all parties, are stationary, and are thus less prone to misperception and error. Geographic landmarks therefore provide some of the easiest tools for making agreements that require coordination among two or more actors. Schelling (1960:54–58) describes the logic of this phenomenon with several examples.

First is the somewhat daunting hypothetical of meeting someone in another city without agreeing ahead of time on either the time or place for this meeting or even being able to coordinate with them through any type of communication. Where is the best place to meet? Were you to arrive in New York City, you might go to the Empire State building, at sunset or midnight, expecting the other person to be more likely to coordinate on this particular landmark at this particular time. Or for Schelling's (1960:56) colleagues at Yale University, coordination was probably easiest at Grand Central Station at noon, as most would be familiar with the train line coming into town from nearby New Haven. Of course, in either case, few would expect their coordinating counterparts to meet them on some nondescript street at some unremarkable time—there would be no focal points upon which both parties could coordinate.

Territorial maps are often replete with focal points for coordination. Imagine parachuting from a plane and needing to coordinate with another jumper already on the ground. Bridges, buildings, rivers and intersections—any prominent landmarks—would provide the best possibilities for coordination, as only a dogged search finds the person who sits waiting in an empty field. Further, even if one jumper had a strong personal preference to meet in the middle of the open field, the lay of the map would have prevented such an unrealistic outcome, just as the person in New York City would likely eat alone at their favorite local restaurant. Though strong interests might be attached to the restaurant or the open field, both places would "lose" as potential meeting places because both lack inherent clarity as focal points for coordination (Schelling 1960: 67–74).

The logic of focal points for coordination on international borders follows. Open plains, featureless desert, and even consistently rugged, mountain terrain all lack the geographically defining features upon which the leaders of two bordering states could easily coordinate. Conversely, if a river divides two states across a border, absent other defining characteristics, that geographic feature would so completely define negotiations over boundaries that any border agreement not based on the river would be inferior, even if the river substantially decreased the land available to one of the states.

Consider a hypothetical division of territory between two countries, one to the north and one to the south. In this hypothetical, a river divides the two countries and competes with a border line proposed by the southern country. The proposed border demarcation is a more equitable division of territory than the river boundary as both countries would control roughly 50% of the total land occupied by both countries while the river divides the land so that the northern country controls 70% of the territory. Nevertheless, if Schelling's analysis of coordination is correct, the river, though inequitable, would dominate debate on the international border because it provides a clear focal point upon which both countries can agree. The demarcation line proposed by the southern country is equivalent to the parachutist waiting in the open field because the river provides the more tangible focal point for coordination.

Of course, there are no guarantees that geography will always determine the focal points for international border coordination. Relative dyadic capabilities also tend to be critically important. Returning again to the hypothetical outlined above, imagine the same divisions of territory, but this time the southern country is clearly more powerful than the northern country. If this were the case, the southern country could press its claim and dictate the boundary line. Absent clear preponderance, though, the southern country would have to militarize the region north of the river, and possibly its homeland, to defend the claimed territory.

Military strategy often reinforces coordination on focal points as many types of geography carry strategic advantage as an international border. Rivers themselves, for example, are more easily defensible than the flat lands found in river basins. To defend an entire basin, the supply lines of a defender would have to stretch across a river, and the personnel defending the basin would be open to unimpeded attack. Alternately, a defender who uses a river as a border can dramatically increase the costs of attack by requiring an amphibious crossing; the supply lines that cross the river then become a disadvantage for the attacker.

France provides one of the best examples of the effects of natural frontiers on the history of international boundary lines and state development, as contemporary France traces its borders to the Atlantic, the Pyrenees, the Alps, and the Rhine—an overall border that Cardinal Richelieu claimed to be "marked out by nature" Sahlins (1990). Indeed, according to Sahlins (1990:1424), "the idea of natural frontiers sometimes provided the justification, sometimes the organizing principle, of French foreign policy," as a "bounded, delimited territory" competed with a common language and history as constitutive elements defining the French people

(see also Goemans 2006). France's border also exemplifies how relative dyadic capabilities can often trump geographic focal points like the Rhine River, as the sovereignty of Alsace and Lorraine shifted with the military capabilities of Germany.

Of course, natural landmarks and power differentials are not the only determinants of coordination on boundaries; border history, ethnicity, and possibly other factors all may play a part in border definition. For example, and again returning to the hypothetical discussed above, if previous border lines had included the region north of the river—an earlier, colonial border for example—or if an ethnic group close in kinship to the southern country had settled in the region, the claims of the southern country, evinced by the proposed border line, would be more easily made. Both the colonial border and the ethnic border provide alternate foci for coordination, and the negotiation strategy of the southern country would thus center on making those alternate focal points, rather than geography, the determinants of demarcation.

Predictors of Focal Points

To determine when focal points are likely to define an international border, I first concentrate on border topography and expect more geographic salients when international borders follow sharp differences in natural terrain. Absent a clear distinction between land types across a border, borders become ad hoc and often arbitrary. Contiguous mountainous terrain (or contiguous plains) provides few geographic salients for states to coordinate on border definition, as can be seen in the mountainous border regions between Saudi Arabia and Yemen, India and Pakistan, and the Nagorno-Karabakh between Azerbaijan and Armenia, all of which hold various insurgent groups, crossing heavily contested borders. Conversely, sharp geographic differences across the dyad add legitimacy to border demarcations, becoming the mechanism for compromise and territorial identity. Of course, geographic differences are not always stark, and therefore, employing a continuous measure of mountainous territory allows flexibility in capturing overall terrain differences between the two states of the dyad.

Another indicator of border definition that I use rests with the division of ethnic groups across international borders. Cohesive ethnic groups often coordinated on geographically dividing salients well before the development of the state system. Thus, contemporary political boundaries that divide ethnic groups are also those borders least likely to be built upon coordinating focal points. As an example, consider the divisions of the Middle East that followed the Peace at Versailles (1919). Cohesive ethnic groups were both divided and grouped not according to their pattern of settlement, but rather by the interests and capabilities of the major colonizing states (Fromberg 2001). Of course, transnational ethnic groups might also be related to Fearon and Laitin's (2003) identification of transnational insurgency support as the divided group might sympathize with plans—legislative or revolutionary—to redraw territorial boundaries to better support their ethnic brethren.

Finally, I identify differences in types of colonial heritage. I assume that land-contiguous dyads that shared the same colonial masters are also likely to have poorly defined borders. As imperial states had little need to differentiate among their colonial holdings, contiguous states gaining their independence from the same country often suffer from poor border definition. For example, French West Africa eventually became the independent states of Benin, Guinea, Mali, Côte d'Ivoire, Mauritania, Niger, Senegal, and Burkina Faso, but only after comprising administrative units within the French federation of West African states. Benin and Niger also shared a border with Nigeria, a former British colony, and the need to demarcate territories between France and Britain probably necessitated clearer border definition between these states than between the former French colonies. Unfortunately, this measure may be overwhelmed by the strong correlation between former colonial status and poverty—a strong predictor of nondemocracy. I therefore control for the effects of wealth in the analyses by also

adding the natural logarithm of the smaller per capita gross domestic product (GDP) in the dyad.

To operationalize the predictors of border salients, I identify internationally divided ethnic groups using the Minorities at Risk data set, coding a dummy variable for dyads with minority groups that believe an imagined homeland includes both states in that particular dyad. Dyads of contiguous states that share the same colonial heritage are coded as 1 and 0 otherwise. And finally, I compute the ratio of percent mountainous terrain for each dyad, using the lowest percentage mountainous state as the numerator, to measure differences in terrain across the border. These last two border variables and the control measure for GDP utilize the replication data available from Fearon and Laitin (2003).[5]

Predictors of Border Strength

I have thus far identified three geographic indicators of unstable borders—similar terrain, ethnic groups that straddle the border, and similar colonial heritages. Each of these indicators has little chance to vary substantially over time, absent a major reorganization of the dyadic boundary. However, borders are often flexible, and their perceived stability or legitimacy does change over time. I therefore include several indicators of conditions likely to affect the legitimacy of previously drawn borders.

First, I control for the capability ratio within the dyad. The power parity literature (Kugler and Lemke 1996; and especially Geller 2000) has demonstrated that conflict is likely when dyads are at or near parity, and I agree with Wayman (1996) and Vasquez (1996b) that territorial renegotiations are a likely mechanism connecting power differentials and conflict. Large differences in power would suggest that a border is unlikely to undergo renegotiation regardless of how the border was previously defined. When a dyad approaches parity, latent territorial claims can be forwarded, upsetting the stability of the dyadic border; this makes transitions in power dangerous when they become linked to ill-defined borders. I therefore include in the analyses the capability ratio of the weaker state to the stronger state, using the latest version of the Composite Index of National Capabilities from the Correlates of War Project (Singer, Bremer, and Stuckey 1972; Singer 1988).

Second, I believe that the length of peace across the border and its overall age are both good indicators of border legitimacy. While I should include spells of peace to properly estimate coefficients in binary, cross-sectional time-series studies like this one (Beck, Katz, and Tucker 1998), I also believe that the length of peace constitutes a theoretically interesting variable.[6] Stable borders are a function of age generally: old states whose borders have long been settled and whose neighbors accept the legitimacy of their borders should also perceive a lower territorial threat. Old states should also be less aggressive in desiring the capture of territory as well, as their border relations are an accepted norm. I define the age of the border using a count variable for the number of years since the last system entry date in the dyad (Stinnett, Tir, Schafer, Diehl, and Gochman 2002), and I define the spell of peace as the time since last Militarized Interstate Dispute (Ghosn, Palmer, and Bremer 2004).

Third, as I argue above, political events in neighboring states often put in question the legitimacy of international borders (Vasquez 1995). The outbreak of civil war may lead regional leaders to fear that violence will spread or that victorious regimes might wish to redraw previous territorial divisions. I use Fearon and Laitin's (2003) dependent variable of civil war onset as an indicator of states likely to experience border instability, and I code this variable as present in the dyad if one of the states is experiencing a civil war.

Dependent Variables

The dependent variable in the first set of analyses is joint democracy; I code dyads as jointly democratic if both states have combined Polity IV scores (autocracy-democracy) equal to or greater than 6 (Marshall and Jaggers 2004). The dependent variable in the second set of analyses is the presence of a Militarized Interstate Dispute (MID), using Correlates of War definitions. I include any dyadic dispute, but only for its first year, and I exclude dyads joining an ongoing MID.

My general expectations for these variables are summarized in Figure 1. Consistent with the argument outlined above, I believe that stable borders should increase the likelihood of joint democracy while also decreasing the likelihood of conflict. Moreover, failing to include controls for the likelihood of territorial issues will introduce bias into estimates of the effects of joint democracy on conflict, possibly resulting in the observation of a spurious relationship.

Sample Selection

My sample includes all dyads from 1946 to 1999. By including observations as recent as 1999, I can compare the effects of the Cold War with other periods; this is important since Farber and Gowa (1997), among others, have argued that the democratic peace may be a function of interest similarity during that period of intense bipolarity. More important for purposes of testing the argument I sketched above is the inclusion of the 8 post–Cold War years when the norms of self-determination biased states toward entering the international system as democracies. Indeed, as Gleditsch (2002a) demonstrates, a higher percentage of states entered the system as democracies during this period than during any other decade. Also important, the 1990s witnessed the relaxation of norms against self-determination—Yugoslavia for

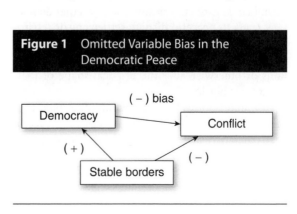

Figure 1   Omitted Variable Bias in the Democratic Peace

example—and the breakup of territorial status quos guaranteed by superpowers (Germany and the former Soviet Republics), each of which I equate with border instability.

A Note on Borders and Territorial Issues— with a Validity Test

I emulate the methodology of Starr and Thomas (2002) by concentrating on the geographic conditions likely to affect border conditions. While their data set is drawn from the 1992 Geographic Information Systems (GIS) survey and is therefore limited to the geographical distribution of states during that year (and with modifications, the years since then), my data set allows testing over a much larger temporal domain, drawing from indicators that vary with the composition of states in the system since 1946.

A focus on geography adds two important benefits for conclusions regarding tests of my overall argument. First, using geographic indicators will effectively insulate my argument from questions of reverse causality. This is important because many studies link joint democracy with peaceful dispute settlement generally (Dixon 1994) and territorial dispute settlement in particular. Bueno de Mesquita et al. (2003), for example, argue that democratic leaders would find little political leverage in the private goods of territorial claims and will therefore quickly resolve these issues, especially with other democracies. By focusing on geographic conditions, then, I am able to empirically assess whether democracy leads to peaceful dispute settlement or territorial peace leads to democracy. After all, few would contend that democracies can literally move mountains or otherwise alter the physical shape of their geographic borders.

Also importantly, by focusing on geographic conditions rather than directly measuring peaceful environments using territorial claims and disputes, the tests that follow are removed from possible strategic biases inherent in claims over territory. For example, the Issues Correlates of War (ICoW) Project identifies all international territorial claims,

largely independent of the occurrence of armed conflict (Hensel and Mitchell 2006). But unfortunately for my purposes, juridical claims may be most likely between states that have resolved *not* to go to war with each other and that instead use international institutions or other supranational legal authority for the redress of these issues. This acceptance, then, selects the dyad out of the sample likely to experience territorial threat, and given the strategic nature of juridical claims, a data set based on speeches, treaties, demonstrations, and the like would all be inappropriate indicators of peaceful territorial environments, at least for my purposes here.

Of course, the decision to launch a claim or a dispute will still find more purchase when border specification is poor, so my indicators of border stability should also be correlated with the data identifying territorial claims and disputes. To prove that this is the case, I conduct what is essentially a validity check of my measures of border salients and strength by estimating a series of logit models aimed at predicting the likelihood of territorial claims in a dyad. Again, though claims are behavioral and open to strategic bias, territorial claims should be, *ceteris paribus*, more prevalent across poorly defined borders. I code territorial claims using Huth and Allee's (2002) territorial dispute data set (from 1946 to 1995),[7] and these results are presented in Table 1.

The first model provides a base for comparing the effects of the border salient variables on the likelihood of territorial disputes. Consistent with most theoretical expectations regarding territory and conflict, dyads at parity and contiguous dyads are likely to experience territorial disputes. The internal and external conflict variables are also consistent with expectations. A civil war in one state is correlated with the initiation of a territorial dispute, and an increase in the number of years since the last MID decreases the likelihood of territorial dispute initiation. The only variable generating unexpected results is the age of the border. Older borders are more likely to experience territorial dispute initiation, but the substantive effect of this variable is quite small (results available from author).

Table 1 Predicting Territorial Disputes with the Border Variables, 1946–1995 (Logit Regression Models with Standard Errors in Parentheses)

Dependent Variable: Temporal Domain: Spatial Domain:	Huth and Allee Dispute 1946–1995 All Dyads (Nondirected)	Huth and Allee Dispute 1946–1989 All Dyads (Nondirected)	Huth and Allee Dispute 1990–1995 All Dyads (Nondirected)	Huth and Allee Dispute 1946–1995 All Dyads (Nondirected)
Contiguous Dyad	4.178** (0.048)	4.300*** (0.075)	3.894*** (0.147)	4.178*** (0.066)
Border Salient Variables				
Same colonial master before independence		0.410** (0.077)	0.722*** (0.146)	0.535** (0.068)
Ethnic border (border separates ethnic group from its brethren across the border)		−0.394* (0.069)	−0.429*** (0.129)	−0.410* (0.061)
Terrain differences [logged ratio of % mountainous (less mountainous/more mountainous)]		0.126** (0.031)	−0.047 (0.059)	0.081** (0.027)
Border Strength Variables				
Capability ratio within dyad (weaker/stronger)	0.180*** (0.069)	−0.185** (0.090)	0.415** (0.166)	−0.023 (0.078)
Years since last MID outbreak	−0.050** (0.002)	−0.058*** (0.003)	−0.039*** (0.003)	−0.052*** (0.002)
Civil war onset in at least one state of dyad	0.240*** (0.126)	0.182 (0.158)	0.530** (0.243)	0.245* (0.132)
Duration of dyad (years since youngest state's entry into state system)	0.006*** (0.001)	0.004*** (0.001)	0.011*** (0.001)	0.006*** (0.001)
Constant	−5.463*** (0.040)	−4.927*** (0.048)	−5.752*** (0.096)	−5.132*** (0.043)
Number of Contiguous Dyads	537,653	255,275	116,124	371,399
LR chi-square	12,579.30***	8,440.45***	2400.38***	10,877.39***
Pseudo R-square	0.335	0.344	0.349	0.344

***p < .01, **p < .05, *p < .10.

289

Models 2 through 4 add the border salient predictors to the estimation while also varying the temporal domain to assess possible Cold War effects. The predictors of border salients are generally consistent with the theoretical expectations outlined above. Territorial disputes are most likely when dyads share the same colonial master and when terrain differences are slight, though the effects for this latter variable are concentrated in the Cold War years. Surprisingly, however, the presence of an ethnic border is *negatively* related to territorial disputes in each time period. Thus, if ethnic groups do have a large effect on conflict escalation, as Huth and Allee (2002) suspect, this finding suggests there may be a slight selection bias: dyads dividing ethnic groups are unlikely to have territorial disputes, but when territorial disputes do erupt across ethnic borders, the likelihood of conflict is much greater.

Comparing models 2 through 4 to the baseline model, only peace years and dyad duration remain unaltered (sign and statistical significance) across the additional three models; length of peace is negatively associated with territorial disputes while territorial disputes are more likely found in older borders (though again the results are substantively small for border age). The remaining two border strength variables present variegated results across models 2 through 4, but only parity seems affected by the addition of the border salient variables. The presence of a civil war is still positive and statistically significant ($p < .10$) for the full time period even with the addition of the border salient predictors, though the effects for civil wars are concentrated in the 6 post–Cold War years. Parity is different. While changes in temporal domain alter the direction of the relationship, with parity predicting fewer territorial disputes during the Cold War, a comparison of the baseline model to the fully specified model for the entire time period suggests that the addition of border salients renders parity statistically insignificant.

Overall, these results support the validity of the border variables outlined above. As a set, the border strength and border salient variables are strongly

associated with the conditions likely to give rise to territorial disputes. Again, this is important because geography is, by nature, removed from both strategic bias and problems of endogeneity, and therefore, the border strength and border salient variables allow a test of the effects of peaceful territorial environments with independent variables that are, for the most part, exogenous to both peace and democracy. With the validity of these measures established, I turn now to an analysis of the effects of border stability on the likelihood of joint democracy and peace.

International Borders and Joint Democracy

I begin by using the stable border proxies to predict the observance of joint democracy in a dyad. As the dependent variable is dichotomous, jointly democratic or not, I again employ logistic regression. I also again split the sample into Cold War and post–Cold War time periods but also include tests of the entire temporal domain, and the results for these three periods are presented in Table 2.

My sole control variable for predicting joint democracy—the lowest level of GDP in the dyad—is positive and significant across all models. As expected, the likelihood of joint democracy increases with overall wealth. The capability ratio within the dyad is also consistently related to the observance of joint democracy. Dyads in which one state is preponderant have a greater chance of experiencing joint democracy, and I argue that this results from either (or both) a settled border that favors the claims of the stronger state and the inability of the weaker state to seek redress. Parity adds territorial threat to the dyad because revisionist states at parity with their rivals are more likely to press their latent territorial claims militarily (see Wayman 1996).

The temporal controls are consistent and positive across each model. The age of the dyad and the length of time since the last conflict increase the probability that joint democracy will be observed. Again, I argue that the duration of the dyad functions as a proxy for border age and, as such, gives an

Table 2 The Effect of Borders on the Likelihood of Joint Democracy (Logit Regression Models with Standard Errors in Parentheses)

Dependent Variable: Temporal Domain: Spatial Domain:	Joint Democracy in Dyad 1946–1989 All Dyads (Nondirected)	Joint Democracy in Dyad 1946–1989 All Dyads (Nondirected)	Joint Democracy in Dyad 1990–1999 All Dyads (Nondirected)	Joint Democracy in Dyad 1946–1999 All Dyads (Nondirected)
Smallest GDP of dyad (logged)	0.688*** (0.005)	1.009*** (0.010)	0.321*** (0.009)	0.899*** (0.007)
Border Strength Variables				
Capability ratio within dyad (weaker/stronger)	0.265*** (0.018)	0.305*** (0.033)	0.502*** (0.033)	0.346*** (0.023)
Years since last MID outbreak	0.016*** (0.000)	0.011*** (0.002)	0.026*** (0.000)	0.017*** (0.000)
Civil war onset in at least one state of dyad	−1.287*** (0.289)	−0.233 (0.327)	−3.640*** (1.013)	−1.110*** (0.305)
Duration of dyad (years since youngest state's entry into state system)	0.007*** (0.001)	0.010*** (0.001)	0.009*** (0.001)	0.008*** (0.001)
Contiguous Dyad	−0.099** (0.046)	−0.689*** (0.118)	0.533*** (0.109)	−0.133* (0.077)
Border Salient Variables				
Same colonial master before independence		0.367** (0.151)	−1.226*** (0.199)	−0.222* (0.117)
Ethnic border (border separates ethnic group from its brethren across the border)		−0.263* (0.109)	−0.504*** (0.124)	−0.270*** (0.078)
Terrain differences (logged ratio of % mountainous less mountainous/more mountainous)		−0.384*** (0.037)	−0.274*** (0.054)	−0.293*** (0.029)
Constant	−3.132*** (0.009)	−3.745*** (0.017)	−2.936*** (0.103)	−3.388*** (0.012)
Number of Contiguous Dyads	504,376	255,186	109,583	364,769
LR chi-square	31,880.63***	14,309.30***	9568.79***	23342.09***
Pseudo R-square	0.097	0.125	0.103	0.109

***$p < .01$, **$p < .05$, *$p < .10$.

indication of the likelihood that border issues have been resolved. The length of peace also estimates the overall legitimacy of the border since, after controlling for capability differences, territorial disputes increase the likelihood of conflict.

The civil war onset variable predicts (negatively) the observation of joint democracy, but this effect is only for the post–Cold War model, with a relationship strong enough to drive a statistically significant result for the entire sample. As the number of civil wars have not increased since 1991 (Fearon and Laitin 2003), the strong post–Cold War relationship is most likely due to the dampening effects of bipolarity on the ability of civil wars to destabilize territorial boundaries in neighboring regimes. The divisions in the international system were such that civil wars in neighboring states found transnational support so long as the issues of contention paralleled the fault lines of the east-west split. In other words, the proxy wars that targeted regime stability did not also possess the same revolutionary dynamic capable of threatening the territories of neighboring states. With the added legitimacy of major state support, civil wars did not also threaten system-wide political divisions that supported international border stability.

The ethnic border variable is statistically significant and exhibits a negative relationship in each sample—having an ethnic group divided by an international border decreases the likelihood of observing joint democracy in that dyad. Having the same colonial master prior to independence inhibits joint democracy in the 1990s, and this effect is strong enough to generate statistically significant results for the entire time period. The positive association between democracy and same colonial master during the Cold War is the only result inconsistent with the theoretical expectations outlined above.

The final border variable captures terrain differences between the states of the dyad, and it is statistically significant and in the expected direction for both the smaller samples and the full sample. This finding provides an important clue supporting the contention that geography matters in the development of democracy. Borders are easily demarcated when differences in terrain persist, and these results suggest that this type of border is associated with the occurrence of joint democracy.

Also interesting are the results for contiguity. The results at first suggest that contiguity increases the likelihood of joint democracy only during the post–Cold War years, and this would contradict some well established findings that democracies cluster together (see Gleditsch 2002a, for example). But it must be remembered that the border variables serve essentially as interaction terms in these models. Thus, the contiguity coefficient estimates the baseline effects of borders absent controls for terrain, colonial differences, and ethnic groups. That contiguity exhibits a strong negative relationship during the Cold War—a time period when democracies were clustered together in Western Europe and North America—therefore lends even stronger support to the argument that border type matters. Democracies are clustering, but only across well defined borders with clear geographic salients. The next step is to determine whether border type also helps explain international conflict better than regime type.

International Borders, Joint Democracy and Conflict

I estimate the effects of joint democracy and border stability on conflict using four separate logit models, covering the samples for years 1946 to 1989, 1990 to 1999, and 1946 to 1999. In all cases, the dependent variable is MID onset, and the independent variables include democracy, the minimum wealth in the dyad and the proxies for border stability.

I measure democracy using a "weak link" specification based on the lowest Polity IV score in the dyad (Dixon 1994; Oneal and Russett 1997, 1999c). I do this because the results in the last section demonstrate well that the border variables accurately predict the observance of joint democracy in the dyad; therefore, the inclusion of the border variables in the same model with joint democracy as an independent variable would introduce multicollinearity into the models. While not a large problem given the sample sizes in the analyses, the multicollinearity is unnecessary because my theory predicts only that joint democracy is likely, not the level of democracy in each state of the dyad. In other words, strong borders constitute a near necessary condition for the observance of joint democracy in the dyad, but variations in border strength do not predict variations in regime type.[8] Thus, while the border variables are highly correlated with joint democracy, the weak link specification has a more modest relationship with geography.

An even better reason for using the weak link specification is that recent research suggests it is superior to the dichotomous, joint democracy indicator for measuring the conflict effects of dyadic democracy. Developed by Dixon (1994), and used interchangeably with joint democracy by Oneal and Russett (1997, 1999c), among others, Dixon and Goertz (2005) demonstrate through a series of empirical tests that, "dyadic relations depend primarily on the behavioral constraints of the less democratic state no matter how tightly constrained its more democratic partner."

Table 3 presents the results for the models predicting international conflict. The first model again provides a baseline and demonstrates that democracy reduces the likelihood of conflict, even after controlling for wealth, parity and contiguity. Somewhat surprisingly, parity is not statistically significant in this model, though the sign is in the expected direction (positive).

Models 2 through 4 add the border control variables and vary the sample size again to assess the effects of the Cold War. Now, with the border controls added, the parity variable is statistically significant ($p < .05$) and in the expected direction in each model, while wealth and contiguity remain unchanged.

The border variables are again consistent with my theoretical expectations. Contiguity, peace years and civil war in at least one state of the dyad all increase the likelihood of MID initiation. Similarly, an international border that divides an ethnic group also has a higher chance of experiencing conflict. The dyadic duration and colonial master variables are not statistically significant in any of the three models, and while the terrain differences measure is significant in only one model (for the post–Cold War years), the sign is in an unexpected direction (negative). But these results do not necessarily refute an empirical connection between these measures and conflict. As terrain differences, same colonial master, and dyadic duration were strong predictors of joint democracy in Table 2, I conducted separate analyses (available from the author) to determine whether democracy was serving as an instrument for the effects of these border measures. As I expected, all three border variables were statistically significant and in the predicted direction for all models of international conflict that did not include the measure of democracy as an independent variable. Thus, the weak link specification of democracy—though statistically superior to the dichotomous, joint democracy variable—still captures a portion of the underlying relationship between borders and regime type, and the estimates for the border variables measure the effects of each indicator not already accounted for by the processes predicting regime type.

Finally, the key variable for these analyses is the democracy indicator, which is, as expected, not statistically significant in any of the models of conflict that include the border controls. Of course, even if level of democracy was significant, the sign demonstrates a *positive* relationship between level of democracy and conflict in each fully specified model. This finding obviously supports the proposition that democracy has little or no effect on conflict once controls are included for stable borders, especially considering the inclusiveness of these models, each with over 100,000 dyadic cases.

Restating the Democratic Peace Findings

By endogenizing the emergence of jointly democratic dyads to a series of factors that affect democracy and conflict behavior, my results suggest that what scholars know as the democratic peace is, in

Table 3 The Effect of Borders on Joint Democracy and Conflict (Logit Regression Models with Standard Errors in Parentheses)

Dependent Variable: Temporal Domain: Spatial Domain:	MID Onset 1946–1999 All Dyads (Nondirected)	MID Onset 1946–1989 All Dyads (Nondirected)	MID Onset 1990–1999 All Dyads (Nondirected)	MID Onset 1946–1999 All Dyads (Nondirected)
Lowest Democracy Score in Dyad	−0.005** (0.002)	0.003 (0.004)	0.007 (0.006)	0.004 (0.003)
Smallest GDP of dyad (logged)	0.087** (0.028)	0.320*** (0.039)	0.339*** (0.071)	0.252*** (0.033)
Border Strength Variables				
Capability ratio within dyad (weaker/stronger)	0.105 (0.101)	0.484*** (0.121)	0.660** (0.240)	0.511*** (0.108)
Years since last MID outbreak		−0.060*** (0.004)	−0.033*** (0.004)	−0.052*** (0.003)
Civil war onset in at least one state of dyad		0.804*** (0.193)	1.009*** (0.298)	0.829*** (0.161)
Duration of dyad (years since youngest state's entry into state system)		−0.001 (0.001)	0.002 (0.002)	0.001 (0.001)
Contiguous Dyad	3.988*** (0.057)	3.386*** (0.113)	3.398*** (0.218)	3.360*** (0.099)
Border Salient Variables				
Same colonial master before independence		0.128 (0.118)	−0.159 (0.267)	0.110 (0.107)
Ethnic border (border separates ethnic group from its brethren across the border)		0.278** (0.101)	0.638*** (0.184)	0.326*** (0.088)
Terrain differences (logged ratio of % mountainous less mountainous/ more mountainous)		−0.019 (0.044)	−0.173* (0.084)	−0.031 (0.039)
Constant	−6.785*** (0.053)	−5.656*** (0.075)	−6.698*** (0.166)	−5.863*** (0.067)
Number of Contiguous Dyads	504,376	255,196	109,583	364,779
LR chi-square	3,631.25***	2,793.52***	923.84***	3,696.08***
Pseudo R-square	0.199	0.227	0.272	0.234

***$p < .01$, **$p < .05$, *$p < .10$.

fact, a stable border peace. This is the first step toward looking at international conflict a little bit differently. Of course, even though the relationship between joint democracy and peace remains the core of the democratic peace literature, there still remain a host of empirical regularities generally considered supportive of democratic peace theory (see for example a partial list in Bueno de Mesquita et al. 2003: 218–219). So, while space does not permit a full discussion of all these secondary relationships, I use this brief conclusion to reinterpret, in the context of a stable border peace, several of the more important, second-order democratic peace findings.

A stable border peace implies that democratic states are more peaceful, but this is not due to any quality inherent in democratic government; rather, the development path necessary for democratization selects democracies into a group of states that have settled borders, few territorial issues, and thus, little reason for war against neighbors. With only minor, nonterritorial issues remaining for these states, mediation and arbitration become both easier and more likely for democracies, while the need for defensive alliances, military buildups, and aggressive crisis bargaining also decreases.

Because borders are international institutions, they affect the development paths of both states in the dyad, and stabilized borders that decrease the need for militarization and centralization in one state also tend to demilitarize and decentralize the neighboring state. "Zones of peace" can thus be understood as the contagion effect of stabilized borders, as democracies cluster in time and space following the removal of territorial issues. This clustering of peaceful states should also affect the economic development of the states involved. With less money needed for guns, spending for butter increases, and trade across settled borders is always preferred to the risk of crossing militarized frontiers.

A stable border peace does not necessarily imply that democracies will always be peaceful; the implication is only that democracies will have fewer conflicts relative to other types of governments. Should war occur, though, the war will likely be fought over far-flung territories since local borders have already been settled. This selection effect explains why the disagreements that democracies escalate are a matter of choice. The threat of conflict never directly affects the territorial homeland, so democratic leaders have the relative luxury of choosing their fights, or intervening when winning is easy. This renders democratic victories the product of peaceful local environments, not the result of domestic institutions that constrain leader choice or otherwise advantage democratic systems.

Many of the above reinterpretations are obviously speculative, but each is consistent with the concept of a stable border peace. When both peace and democracy are symptoms of the stabilization of the territorial status quo, the world should look differently than standard treatments of the democratic peace often see it, and this model holds promise for pointing inquiry in that direction.

Notes

Author's Note: Thanks to Mike Desch, Rich Fording, Matt Gabel, Marc Hutchison, Toby Rider, and Scott Wolford for comments on earlier drafts and especially to Kirk Randazzo for numerous discussions on methodology. Thanks also to Paul Huth and Todd Allee for sharing their data and to Paul Hensel, Adam Przeworski, and Bruce Russett and John Oneal for making their data publicly available. Unfortunately, I cannot hold anyone else responsible for the errors that remain. Replication data for the analyses in this article can be found at: http://bama.ua.eduz/~dmgibler/replication and at http://isanet.org/data_archive.html.

1. This holds true even for disputes over distant territory. For example, Huth and Allee's (2002) compilations of disputes by region include great powers—often democracies like the United States, Great Britain, and France—from outside the region, whose interests in dispute resolution should be far different from disputes with contiguous neighbors. The 1919 British and French dispute over territory along the border between French Equatorial Africa and Sudan is an important case in point, as the dispute was settled peacefully by negotiation (*ibid.* 379), yet the defense of far-flung lands likely raised few alarms about the

territorial integrity of the British and French home-lands. The same kind of noncontiguous disputes that do not threaten home territory can be found in Mitchell and Prins' data as well (see Mitchell and Prins 1999, Table 2).

2. Indeed, the few times that tests have matched processes well, the external threat literature has generated strong findings. For example, Thies (2005) is able to demonstrate that correct specification of Tilly's (1990) models confirms that grave external conflict—prolonged rivalry in this case—leads to economic centralization of the state.

3. External threats and the cheapness of defense also play an important role in Alesina and Spolaore's (2003) formal model of the size of states, as a reduced threat of war favors the survival of smaller jurisdictions that spend relatively less on defense and can more easily sustain a democratic voting rule in the determination of public policy. Their study does not provide a story for the choice of voting rule—that is, it has no theory of transitions—but it does link democracy to groups of small, more or less homogeneous states with decentralized state apparatuses. (Conversely, recent work by Acemoglu and Robinson (2006) provides a dynamic model of democratic transition but still leaves exogenous the factors influencing the costs of repression.) One of the prime linkages in the story of small states is the cheapness of defense, which emerges as a direct consequence of expectations over current and future threats to the territory of the state. Democracy flourishes best in the absence of a threat of conflict—which, in their model, favors larger, more heterogeneous, extractive, and repressive

states. Without some stable expectations of peace, then, democracy becomes difficult to manage. When democracy does emerge, it is likely to be in the context of states smaller, *ceteris paribus,* than the average autocracy, and it should happen in clusters of states whose fear of each other has ebbed. Alesina and Spolaore (2003) link democratization explicitly to the breakup of larger, more autocratic states like the Soviet Union, whose security behavior led them to choose size in the interest of defense despite greater costs, democratically speaking, of homogeneity.

4. "Had a standing army existed in England, it would have been under the control of the Crown, and the political and economic future of England would likely have been different." (North and Weingast 1989:828)

5. The Fearon and Laitin (2003) data set defines the temporal domain for the tests that follow.

6. Measuring time since last territorial dispute best captures this argument. However, I measure time since last dispute (of any kind) to correct for temporal dependence in estimating the dependent variable of any dispute onset.

7. Specifically, I code the *onset* of a territorial dispute and not the years following the initial dispute year. Note that Huth and Allee (2002) use the term "dispute," but their conceptualization is much closer to what Hensel (2001) and others label as territorial claims.

8. Joint democracy and the weak link specification are empirically distinct measures of democracy in my data set. For example, joint democracy is correlated with the weak link specification at a relatively low 0.43 in the sample that includes all years, 1946–1999.

EDITORS' COMMENTARY

Major Contributions: Territorial Peace

The democratic peace (see Oneal and Russett 1999c, Chapter 9, this volume) has been widely researched in the past thirty years. Literally hundreds of studies have been conducted related to it, and among quantitative scholars, it has been the dominant research program (Ray 2003a). Nonetheless, the democratic peace research program has its critics. One of the major criticisms of the democratic peace is that the relationship is **spurious**, which is to say that some other variable produces both peace *and* democracy. Gibler (2007) is one of the major proponents of such a criticism. He argues it is a territorial peace that accounts for peaceful dyads and for peaceful democratic neighborhoods. In the study reprinted here, he presents his basic argument and tests it.

On the basis of empirical research that shows that territorial disputes are highly war prone and are associated with many of the interstate wars in history (Vasquez 1993; Hensel 1996a; Senese 1996), Gibler (2007) argues that stable borders between neighbors will be associated with peace. In other words, remove one of the major causes of war—territorial disputes—and you should have peace. Settling borders is a key to peace. Gibler goes one step further and this makes his work different from much of the work on territory and war. He argues that stabilizing borders in a region will contribute to the democratization of the region. The causal process, as he outlines in Figure 1, is that stable borders will make territorial claims and disputes over those claims less likely. This, in turn, will make for peace between neighbors. As more neighbors in a region have stable borders, the entire region becomes a "benign environment" for the emergence of democracy. This does not mean that the absence of territorial threat will produce democracy but merely that the absence of territorial threat and war is apt to create conditions in which other variables that produce democratization—such as wealth, a middle class, and literacy—have a better opportunity to work.

The logic behind this hypothesized link between the absence of territorial disputes, peace, and democracy goes to the notion first raised by Hintze (1906/1975) and later by Tilly (1975) that war makes for strong centralized states. States faced with a hostile and threatening external environment will need a strong military, strong leadership, and high taxes (Thies 2004), all of which are most likely under a more centralized state apparatus. Gibler (2007) argues that it follows from this logic that less centralized and more democratic states are more apt to emerge and flourish in an environment where war is not prevalent.

To test this explanation, two things are necessary. First, it must be shown that stable borders reduce territorial claims and disputes. Second, it must be shown that stable borders have a positive effect on joint democracy. Gibler (2007) does both of these things. Then it must be shown that stable borders wipe out the effect of joint democracy on conflict. Before looking at the results in more detail, a couple of things about the research design need to be made clear. A close reading makes it obvious that

Gibler does not look specifically at whether borders are settled. He avoids this for fears of tautology and endogeneity (see the Methodological Notes). Instead, he assumes that if a border is stable, it will not give rise to a territorial claim to change the border and therefore there will be no conflict over territory. This can be seen as an indirect test since whether the border is settled legally or through mutual recognition is never tested by the stable border measures. At the same time, it is an interesting test that expands our knowledge about conflict because Gibler, in effect, is saying that borders with certain characteristics are intrinsically stable and will not give rise to territorial claims. This hypothesis he does test.

He begins by assuming that if borders are poorly defined because of certain geographic characteristics, then they should have more territorial claims associated with them. The difficult part of this test is to somehow measure stable borders. He argues that a stable border must have some *focal point* or unambiguous physical salient over which bargainers can agree. A river, for example, is a clear focal point, even though in the future it might move. Conversely, continuous desert, mountains, or plains provides no distinctive salient feature on which a borderline can be drawn and thus is more apt to give rise to a disagreement.

Gibler (2007) has three geographic indicators. The first indicator of stable borders that he selects is the percentage of mountainous terrain. The second indicator of a stable border is whether it separates the same ethnic group. If it does, it is considered unstable. In an age of nationalism, this would surely give rise to disagreements and territorial claims, and since Gibler is dealing with the post-World War II period (specifically 1946 on), this is a valid indicator. The final geographic indicator of a stable border is whether two bordering former colonial states had the same colonial master. Gibler argues that if they did, little attention was probably paid to the border and it will be subject to contention, but if they had different colonizers, then the borders were probably negotiated under the colonial period, and this settlement forms a precedent that serves as a focal point.

To these three geographic indicators, Gibler (2007) adds three others: the capability ratio within the dyad, the age of the border, and whether a neighbor is involved in a civil war. He argues that large differences in power make it unlikely that a border would be renegotiated. He assumes the older the border, the more stable it will be. Last, he thinks civil war involvement will have a negative impact on the stability of the boundary.

The results of these predictions are presented in Table 1. It can be seen that, overall, the indicators of unstable borders are associated with territorial disputes. For example, when two states have had the same colonial master, they subsequently make more territorial claims. When the sides are relatively equal or at parity, they make more claims. Likewise, if one is in a civil war, more territorial claims are made. The major exception to his predictions is if a border divides an ethnic group. He had expected this to be unstable, but in fact it is not. This may be due to the fact that sub-Saharan Africa is where most of these cases occur, and there the norm that colonial borders will not be challenged has been widely supported (Lemke 2002). A second exception is the age of the border; the older the border, the more territorial claims to which it gives rise.

Generally, Table 1 provides evidence that certain indicators of stable/unstable borders successfully predict whether a dyad will have territorial claims. Where an indicator does not, we can assume that it is just not a valid predictor of stable borders. Note, however, that for certain periods, especially the five-year post–Cold War 1990–1995, the signs flip (go from + to – or vice versa) or a variable becomes insignificant.

Table 2 examines whether these same variables predict joint democracy. Again, although there are exceptions and differences for the post–Cold War period, Gibler's (2007) general theoretical expectations are consistent with the evidence. The most consistent results show that preponderance is associated with joint democracy; civil war is negatively associated, as is having an ethnic group divided by the border; and terrain differences are negatively associated, as expected. It should also be pointed out that Gibler includes a conventional internal predictor of democracy—gross domestic product—and it is consistently positive. Despite some complexity and exceptions, Tables 1 and 2 provide some support for the claim that certain indicators of unstable borders are associated with territorial claims and that stable borders are associated with joint democracy. If this is true, one would also expect that joint democracies would have few territorial issues, and from Mitchell and Prins (1999), we know this is the case.

Table 3 provides the crucial test to see if stable borders will wipe out the relationship between joint democracy and peace (in terms of the absence of conflict). Model 1 (in column 2) shows that the democracy variable (row 1) is negatively and significantly related to militarized interstate dispute (MID) onset. In Models 2 to 4, the border variables are added, and they wipe out the significance of the democracy variable in each of the three periods. This means that the border variables better predict MID conflict and that joint democracy, in terms of the weakest link measure, is not significantly and negatively related to MID conflict as the democratic peace theory predicts. This is one of the few studies to wipe out the statistical significance of joint democracy. Reed's (2000) article in the previous chapter is another (with respect to escalation to war).

Gibler followed up on his 2007 article with a number of other studies that reinforced the conclusions reached here. He finds that having an external territorial threat has a negative impact on certain key democratic values and a positive impact on state centralization. Hutchison and Gibler (2007) find that external territorial threat predicts the absence of tolerance. In addition, they find that the conventional internal predictors of democracy (e.g., free speech) and individual predictors (e.g., education) do not eliminate the significance of territorial threat (MID) as a predictor. This means that key domestic democratic values are a function of not only internal variables but external ones as well. Another study (Gibler 2012, 102–4) found that sustained territorial threat (in the form of territorial rivalry) reduces the number of veto players and hence institutional constraints on a state. The same study also finds that states targeted by their neighbors in a territorial dispute have less party polarization, where more party polarization means more choice and ideological competition (Gibler 2012, 98–99). The above analyses provide evidence that territorial threat is associated with centralization and its absence with certain core democratic values, such as tolerance. Gibler and Tir (2010) look at whether settling a border will encourage democratic development. To see if a border has been settled, they look at peaceful transfers of territory that are mutually agreed upon. They find that such territorial transfers produce increases in the rate of transition to democracy (Gibler 2012, 132).

Even this last study, although it moves closer to looking at settled borders, is still like the other studies in that it uses indirect measures of border settlement. As noted, Gibler (2007) does this for certain methodological reasons (see below). However, it still would be useful to know whether legal settlements of the border reduce territorial conflict. The earliest study to suggest this is Kocs (1995), who finds (for 1945–1987) that neighbors who have legally recognized their borders are less likely to have wars. Owsiak (2012) extends this analysis by looking at the entire 1816–2001 period. He systematically measures legal border settlements and finds that such neighbors are significantly less likely to have wars or MIDs. What remains to be done is to see if this reduction is associated with subsequent democratization. Owsiak (forthcoming) does that and finds that a state that settles all its border disputes will democratize, but if any are unsettled, it will not.

Methodological Notes: Spurious Relationships

Gibler's (2007) study is centered on trying to show that the relationship between joint democracy and peace is **spurious**. A spurious relationship means that the existing statistical significance between two variables is not real but a function of some third variable that is the cause of the two variables in question. In this case, Gibler argues that territorial disputes bring about peace, and **controlling** for that will eliminate the significance of joint democracy in conflict onset models. We have seen something like this before in Susan Sample's (2002, Chapter 6, this volume) analysis in which controlling for nuclear weapons eliminates the relationship between arms races and war. Gibler does more than just control for a variable, however. He wants to argue that territorial disputes are negatively associated with joint democracy, meaning that their absence plays a role in bringing about jointly democratic states. In this way, the resolution of territorial disputes is associated not only with peace but also with democratization, especially of a neighborhood.

Gibler (2007), however, does not directly measure border settlement. He worries that critics will think that a hypothesis that maintains that settling territorial disputes will reduce the likelihood of territorial conflict will be seen as circular. He also worries about *endogeneity* issues in that it is unclear what comes first—democracy or border settlement. He therefore opts to express his theoretical analysis in terms of border stability. He says that when borders are stable, peace and democracy are both likely to occur. Stable borders, especially when measured geographically as he does, are pretty much fixed and will not be seen as a function of regime type. Therefore, they have this advantage in terms of dealing with criticism that the relationship between territorial disputes, democracy, and peace might be endogenous.

Gibler (2007) tests his claims in three tables. Each of the tables employs logistic regression (see the commentary on Bremer 1992b, Chapter 2, this volume) because the dependent variable in each is a dichotomous variable. He describes Table 1 as a **validity** check on his measures of border salience. A measure is considered **valid** if it measures what it is supposed to measure. In this case, Gibler is trying to show that looking at stable borders could serve as a proxy for the absence of territorial conflict. He does this by showing that dyads with stable borders do not have territorial claims. In Table 1, the dependent variable, which is listed in the title, is territorial claims (note he uses Huth's [1996a] language of "disputes" but explains in a footnote that these are not MIDs but diplomatic territorial claims). It can be seen in Table 1 that many of the border salient independent variables and the border strength independent variables (listed in the rows at the left) are statistically significant, and this evidence is generally consistent with the arguments presented in the article, even though there are exceptions.

Table 2 takes joint democracy as the dependent variable. Here again with some exceptions, we see that most of the independent variables are statistically significant. This means that stable borders are associated with joint democracy. This table, along with Table 1, shows that stable borders are significantly related to both the absence of territorial claims and the presence of joint democracy. In Table 3, Gibler wants to show that it is stable borders and *not* joint democracy that accounts for militarized conflict. The dependent variable here is MID onset. It can be seen in the first model (in column 2) that democracy (Lowest Democracy Score in a Dyad) is significantly and negatively related to MID onset (Oneal and Russett 1999c). In the next three columns, this variable is no longer significant as can be seen by the absence of asterisks.

Joint democracy has lost significance because in each model (in columns 3–5), the stable border variables have been introduced, and controlling for the impact of these factors eliminates the significance between democracy and MID onset. In other words, it is the effect of stable borders within joint democracies that accounts for the lack of MIDs. Put another way, stable borders will tend to have fewer MIDs, regardless of regime type (i.e., whether a dyad is democratic or nondemocratic).

If we return to each of the tables, one final useful statistic can be studied—**pseudo R-square**. Pseudo R-square reports how much of the variance in the dependent variables can be accounted for by the independent variables. This runs from zero when everything is random to 1 when there is perfect prediction. The higher the pseudo R-square, the better the model fits or technically the more variance of the dependent variable that it accounts for. The "best" model would account for 100 percent of the variance, but that almost never happens in practice. In Table 1, you can see that the pseudo R-square ranges from 0.335 to 0.349. In Table 2, the pseudo R-square ranges from 0.097 to 0.125. In Table 3, the pseudo R-square is higher, ranging from 0.199 to 0.272. This means that on the whole, the models in Table 3 are a better fit and account for more of the variance than the models in Table 2. The independent variables in his models do a better job of explaining the variance in MID onset than accounting for the variance in joint democracy.

Questions

1. In Table 3, "Lowest Democracy Score" is negatively related to conflict. What does this mean?

2. Comparing the pseudo R-square in each of the three tables, which dependent variable has the most variance accounted for? What does this tell us about Gibler's success in explaining the relationship between democracy, territorial disputes, and war?

3. According to Gibler, what is the main factor that makes for centralized states?

Further Reading

Gibler, D. 2012. *The territorial peace: Borders, state development and international conflict.* Cambridge, UK: Cambridge University Press.

Gleditsch, K. S. 2002a. *All international politics is local.* Ann Arbor: University of Michigan Press.

Owsiak, A. P. 2012. Signing up for peace: International boundary agreements, democracy, and militarized interstate conflict. *International Studies Quarterly* 56 (1): 51–66.

Rosecrance, R. N. 1986. *The rise of the trading state: Commerce and conquest in the modern world.* New York: Basic Books.

Chapter 13

Proliferation and International Crisis Behavior

Victor Asal and Kyle Beardsley

Introduction

The primary justification for the US invasion of Iraq in 2003 was the fear that the Iraqi government was developing weapons of mass destruction (WMD), which included the possibility that Saddam Hussein was continuing in his efforts to build nuclear weapons. Preventing the proliferation of nuclear weapons has been a driving force behind US policy towards North Korea and Iran as well. Much of the literature about nuclear weapons since the 1950s has been about how to control or eliminate them, and enormous diplomatic effort has been invested in constraining their proliferation. Is the effort to stop proliferation—which can be measured in lost lives, diplomatic effort, and billions of dollars—worthwhile? Are there possible advantages to proliferation that might justify a different attitude towards the spread of nuclear weapons? This article attempts to provide empirical insight for part of this broad question. Proliferation may lead to a host of problems, ranging from nuclear terror to nuclear accidents to war (Sagan & Waltz, 2003). This article has a narrower focus and examines only the issue of war.

Specifically, we seek to answer the question posed by Waltz (Sagan & Waltz, 2003: 6): 'Do nuclear weapons increase or decrease the chances of war?' One side of this discussion contends that proliferation will lead to a decrease in the level of interstate violence

because 'Nuclear weapons, then and now, deter threat or retaliation posing unacceptable damage' (Cimbala, 1998: 213). The opposing argument questions the very logic of deterrence as suggested above when it comes to nuclear weapons. Aron (1965), for example, argues that new proliferators may not be as rational as the original nuclear states. Thus, as nuclear weapons spread, the deterrence that operated between the Soviet Union and the United States of America during the Cold War might not apply.

Much of the literature on the impact of nuclear weapons does not empirically test the arguments made (Geller, 2003: 37; Huth & Russett, 1988: 34). Here, we strive to move beyond speculation to observe the impact of nuclear proliferation on the level of violence used in crises. We examine the relationship between the severity of the violence in crises in the International Crisis Behavior (ICB) dataset and the number of involved states with nuclear weapons, controlling for other factors that increase the likelihood of severe violence.[1] We find that crises involving nuclear actors are more likely to end without violence. Also, as the number of nuclear actors involved in a crisis increases, the likelihood of war continues to drop. Drawing from Waltz (Sagan & Waltz, 2003) and the rational deterrence literature, we argue that states facing the possibility of a nuclear attack will be more willing to concede or back down from violent conflict.

Source: Victor Asal and Kyle Beardsley, "Proliferation and International Crisis Behavior," *Journal of Peace Research* 44, no. 2 (2007): 139–55.

Proliferation: Good or Bad; for What and Whom?

Not surprisingly, much of the current literature examines the nature of nuclear proliferation from the perspectives or interests of the United States of America (Clark, 1997; Powell, 2003). For the USA, non-proliferation means fewer enemies with the ability to threaten the American heartland. But proliferation may damage more than the USA's ability to defend itself. Proliferation may severely constrain the projection of US or Western force abroad in regions of strategic importance (Payne, 1997).

The negative impact of proliferation on the security environment, however, may be seen in a very different light if the security and political interests of the USA do not drive the analysis. Indeed, several non-US perspectives reject non-proliferation arguments, as 'dividing states into "responsible" ones who can set and change the rules of the game and those "irresponsible" nations who have to accept the rules leads to discriminatory ideas of non-proliferation' (Mashhadi, 1994: 107; see also Goheen, 1983).[2] Or, as Singh (1998) bluntly states, arguments for non-proliferation may be dismissed as 'Nuclear Apartheid'.

For some states, proliferation has such important strategic value that they will make any effort to go nuclear, as in the case of Iraq in the 1980s and 1990s (Kokoski, 1995). The justification for proliferation in countries like India, Iraq, and Pakistan is often security (Sagan, 1996/97). Mearsheimer (1990: 20) argues, 'states that possess nuclear deterrents can stand up to one another, even if their nuclear arsenals vary greatly in size'. Gallois (1961) was one of the first to make this argument for the value of proliferation for smaller states based on the deterrent value that even a small number of nuclear weapons can provide. During the Cold War, and despite superpower nuclear umbrellas, this logic was persuasive for the French as well as for the British and the Chinese (Goldstein, 2000: 360).

Clearly, the direction the missile is pointing may have serious implications for a country's views on proliferation. As Waltz suggests, 'weapons and strategies

change the situation of states in ways that make them more or less secure' (Sagan & Waltz, 2003: 6). We suggest judging proliferation by the impact it has on international crises and the probability that a war will result. Does the participation of a nuclear state in a crisis increase or decrease the likelihood that the crisis will devolve into war? And, since proliferation implies the wider spread of nuclear weapons, we also ask if there is a difference in impact when a crisis involves more than one participant that has nuclear capabilities. While there have been few empirical tests of whether the presence of nuclear actors increases or decreases a crisis's proclivity for war, we are unaware of any studies that consider the impact of additional nuclear actors.

Nuclear Weapons and Instability

The anti-proliferation argument about the possible contribution of nuclear weapons to the outbreak of war rests on the fear that these weapons, given their destructive capabilities, are inherently dangerous and their spread to a variety of places is counterproductive.

> What dangers does proliferation pose? In the short term, the great dangers are a regional nuclear war, which could obliterate cities, kill millions and devastate downwind areas; and nuclear terrorism. . . . Over the longer term, there will be new nuclear threats as more and more nations acquire more sophisticated delivery systems. (Forsberg et al., 1995: 2)

Given the magnitude of the risk that nuclear weapons pose, those who argue against proliferation do not see a payoff that matches the risks. Nuclear weapons are 'obstacles to, rather than facilitators of, international security' (Hanson, 2002: 361). Anti-proliferators (1) question whether nuclear weapons prevent war (a question of the very utility of deterrence); (2) wonder about its applicability to new proliferators and their rationality, even though it may have worked between the USA and the Soviet Union during the Cold War; (3) fear a war during a transition period to nuclear status of a member of an existing rivalry; and (4) fear the dangers of nuclear weapons being controlled by countries where the military is the deciding voice. In this article, we focus on the first of these questions and test if participation of one or more nuclear states in a crisis increases or decreases the likelihood that the crisis will devolve into war.[3]

McGwire (1994: 215) rejects the claim that nuclear weapons prevent major wars, except within a very narrow context. He gives examples of Vietnam, the Iran–Iraq War, and the Korean War. Based on his analysis of international crises, Geller supports this conclusion, stating that 'nuclear weapons cannot be relied upon to impede escalatory behavior by either nuclear or non-nuclear antagonists. . . .

Nuclear disputes, however, show a pronounced tendency to escalate (short of war) and to engage coercive tactics that include the limited use of force' (Geller, 1990: 307). Payne (1997) and Hanson (2002) go even further by raising the possibility that nuclear weapons were not even important to keeping peace between the superpowers.

Nuclear Weapons and Restraint

Other, more optimistic, scholars see benefits to nuclear proliferation or, perhaps not actively advocating the development of more nuclear weapons and nuclear-weapon states, see that the presence of nuclear weapons has at least been stabilizing in the past. For example, some scholars are confident of the promise of the 'nuclear peace'.[4] While those who oppose proliferation present a number of arguments, those who contend that nuclear weapons would reduce interstate wars are fairly consistent in focusing on one key argument: nuclear weapons make the risk of war unacceptable for states. As Waltz argues,

the higher the stakes and the closer a country moves toward winning them, the more surely that country invites retaliation and risks its own destruction. States are not likely to run major risks for minor gains. War between nuclear states may escalate as the loser uses larger and larger warheads. Fearing that, states will want to draw back.

Not escalation but deescalation becomes likely. War remains possible, but victory in war is too dangerous to fight for. (Sagan & Waltz, 2003: 6–7)

'Nuclear war simply makes the risks of war much higher and shrinks the chance that a country will go to war' (Snyder & Diesing, 1977: 450). Using similar logic, Bueno de Mesquita & Riker (1982) demonstrate formally that a world with almost universal membership in the nuclear club will be much less likely to experience nuclear war than a world with only a few members.

Supporters of proliferation do not see leaders of new nuclear states as being fundamentally different from those of the old nuclear states in terms of their levels of responsibility (Arquilla, 1997), nor do they see them facing unique challenges in managing and securing these weapons (Feaver, 1992/93: 162–163). The response to the argument that small powers, non-Western powers, and military powers will behave less responsibly than the USA and other 'responsible' powers is that the evidence does not support the view that new nuclear powers are 'different' in the worst sense of the word (Lavoy, 1995; Hagerty, 1998; Arquilla, 1997; Feldman, 1995; Karl, 1996/97). Van Creveld (1993: 124) sums up this viewpoint when he points out that 'where these weapons have been introduced, large-scale interstate warfare has disappeared'.

Dismissing the fear that deterrence will not work if the arsenal is not big enough or under enough control, Chellaney (1995) contends that the Cold War is evidence that even minimum deterrence is sufficient. In support, Feaver (1992/93: 186) argues that 'even a modest nuclear arsenal should have some existential deterrent effect on regional enemies, precisely because decapitation is so difficult'. There are those who argue that security is increased at a systemic level when the number of nuclear states increases because of the level of uncertainty created when more than one or two players are playing with a nuclear deck. When this happens, 'the probability of deliberate nuclear attack falls to near zero with three, four, or more nuclear nations' (Brito &

Intriligator, 1983: 137). Cimbala (1993: 194) agrees, arguing that 'it is only necessary to threaten the plausible loss of social value commensurate with the potential gains of an attacker'.

Assessing Proliferation Using Deterrence Theory

The causal mechanism in a proliferation optimist argument like that of Waltz (Sagan & Waltz, 2003), which expects war to be less likely as the number of nuclear actors increases, is connected to a rationalist view of nuclear deterrence (see Zagare & Kilgour, 2000; Huth, 1999). Proliferation optimists implicitly contend that, as the number of nuclear actors in the system increases, the proportion of disputes involving nuclear actors should increase as well.[5] That is, all else being equal, the more of any type of actor you add to the playing field of international politics, the more likely that that type of actor will be involved in a crisis. If nuclear weapons increase the prospects of deterrence, then proliferation should result in more crises with restrained actors that are prone to back down instead of escalate.

Rational deterrence advances the notion that actors are effectively able to deter other states from aggression if they can credibly posture themselves as resolute and strong states. States with nuclear weapons should be especially effective at deterrence if they can convince their adversary that there is some possibility nuclear weapons would be used. Nuclear states may resort to brinkmanship or costly signals to overcome the credibility problem (Schelling, 1960, 1962, 1966; Powell, 1988, 1989, 1990; Fearon, 1994a). As long as there is some probability that a state would use a nuclear weapon against an opponent, the enormity of the costs of that event should be enough to deter opponents from escalating in a conflict even if the probability of that event is low.

While Zagare & Kilgour (2000) point to a number of inconsistencies in 'classical deterrence theory', as advocated by such scholars as Waltz, the general argument that nuclear weapons can decrease the willingness of actors to engage in violent conflict is consistent with Zagare & Kilgour's 'Perfect Deterrence Theory'. In their view, deterrence is a function of both capabilities and credibility. The capability to inflict great damage is the only necessary condition for deterrence, and the strength of deterrence will generally be improved as the credibility of nuclear use increases. Relevant to Perfect Deterrence Theory, this article does not advance the notion that deterrence will never fail, just as Zagare & Kilgour (2000) formally demonstrate that deterrence can fail in many instances. Our logic is probabilistic in that nuclear weapons should decrease the likelihood of violent conflict, not eliminate it.

The formal models of Zagare & Kilgour (1993, 2000) and Kilgour & Zagare (1991) suggest that as an actor increasingly values the status quo more than fighting, the ability for deterrence to succeed increases. Applied to nuclear weapons, if a state making a demand faces higher expected costs of war because of the threat of nuclear retaliation, then that actor is more likely to prefer backing down to fighting. Kilgour & Zagare (1991: 321) state, 'by increasing the costs of warfare, deterrence becomes more likely as the credibility requirements of a deterrent threat become less onerous'.

This leaves one to wonder why the state with nuclear weapons does not then try to exploit the willingness of the other side to shy away from conflict and simply make large demands of its own. Under this logic, the nuclear actor might raise its demands until the other actor has a reasonable relative valuation of fighting and the probability of war is roughly the same as if there were no nuclear deterrent. But if demands are made according to a risk-return-tradeoff, under similar assumptions modeled by Powell (1999: 101), then increases in the expected costs of war of an opponent should be greater than any increases in the demands of exploitive actors.

So, the probability of war should decrease as the costs of war increase, even if the demands also increase in response.

Rational deterrence theory is by no means undisputed (see Morgan, 2003). Sagan (Sagan & Waltz, 2003: 50) argues, 'the assumption that states behave in a basically rational manner is of course an assumption, not an empirically tested insight'. This article addresses Sagan's point directly, as we hypothesize what would follow if Waltz's view of deterrence generally worked and then use empirical tests to see if the observed world looks as predicted. If Waltz is wrong, then we should not see a pacifying effect of nuclear weapons in international crises.

Data and Methods

International Crisis Behavior Data

To study the impact of nuclear weapons on international crisis behavior, we employ the International Crisis Behavior (ICB) dataset (Brecher & Wilkenfeld, 1997). The database includes 434 international crises from 1918 to 2001. Following Huth & Russett (1990), the set of crises should be an appropriate set of cases because these are all instances in which some challenge or threat is made, and there is some possibility of deterrence success or failure. In this way, the mechanisms specific to immediate deterrence are tested, which Morgan (2003) notes are generally understudied in the deterrence literature. An actor is defined as being in crisis when some value is threatened, there is a finite time to react to the threat, and there is an increase in the perception of military hostilities.

Hypotheses and Variables

Arguments that see a positive link between nuclear weapons and crisis stability suggest that we should see less violence in crises involving nuclear states and that the severity of violence should decrease as the number of states that possess nuclear weapons increases.

Anti-proliferation arguments often contend that we should see more violence induced by either accidental war due to miscalculations of power or a desire for pre-emptive war. At the very least, anti-proliferation work, such as Sagan's (Sagan & Waltz, 2003), disputes the claim that nuclear weapons will lead to greater constraint in the foreign policies of possessing actors. In this article, we test the optimists'

view. That is, does the involvement of nuclear actors in a crisis lessen the likelihood that violence will be used? Thus, our dependent variable is intensity of violence, an ordinal variable that ranges from 'no violence' to 'full-scale war'. Table 2 below describes this variable and others more closely. We test the following hypotheses:

H0: The probability that a crisis will have higher levels of violence will not be affected by the number of nuclear actors.

H1: The more nuclear crisis states involved in an international crisis, the higher the probability that the crisis will have lower levels of violence.

The independent variable that is relevant to the hypotheses is a count of the number of nuclear actors involved in each crisis. Note that we do not distinguish between status quo and revisionist actors because such a distinction does not necessarily follow from the theoretical framework. Morgan (2003) argues that there should not be much of a difference between an understanding of deterrence—where the status quo state has nuclear weapons—and an understanding of compellence—where the revisionist state has nuclear weapons. Like Morgan, our expectations are based on an assumption that nuclear weapons will affect all aspects of coercive diplomacy. That is, nuclear actors should be better able to make other states back down short of war, whether they are defending the status quo or not. In addition, the information about which states are status quo or defender states is not readily available in the ICB data. Indeed, it is difficult to make such decisions as an outside observer, especially when a pre-emptive attack on a state that will likely threaten the status quo in the future might appear from the outside as a revisionist attack.

One of the models used in the analysis uses a different primary explanatory variable. This is a variable that identifies whether the crises involve any 'nuclear dyads' in which actors on both sides of a conflict have nuclear weapons. The included variable can help identify whether the mere addition of nuclear actors to a crisis breeds restraint, or whether it is just a dyadic phenomenon where both sides feel the deterrent effect.

The first challenge is determining who has nuclear weapons. While the first and second generation of nuclear powers (China, France, United Kingdom, USA, and Russia/USSR) went public when they achieved 'nuclear power status', this is not true for any of the third-generation nuclear powers. There are also three nuclear inheritor countries (Belarus, Kazakhstan, and Ukraine) where the issue of who has command and control (Russian forces or the militaries of the new countries) was often unclear to the outside observer. This latter group is not problematic for this analysis because none of them were involved in an international crisis. This still leaves the problem of determining when India, Israel, North Korea, Pakistan, and South Africa became nuclear powers. To make this assessment, we have largely relied on data from the following organizations: the Federation of American Scientists, the Nuclear Threat Initiative, the Council for a Livable World, the *Bulletin of the Atomic Scientists*, the Center for Defense Information, and the Center for Nonproliferation Studies. In addition, we have turned to the academic literature for a closer look at those countries whose move into the nuclear club has been more opaque. Where there is a disagreement, we have coded the transition to being a nuclear power based on what appears to be a plurality of opinion. Table 1 presents the dates that we use and the key sources of information we relied on for each. Given the fact that the lack of a nuclear test does not mean a country does not have nuclear capability and the additional hazy nature of some of the information, we dated the nuclear status of each country from the beginning of the year that it was reported to have nuclear capability. Thirteen countries are listed as becoming nuclear powers at some time over the last fifty years. Of those, four have given up on being nuclear powers: South Africa, Belarus, Kazakhstan, and Ukraine. Of these four, only South Africa has been involved in an international crisis.

We control for a number of factors in the analysis. First, we control for the number of actors in a crisis, to avoid a confounding relationship in which our key explanatory variable is actually just picking up the diffusion potential of crises and not the actual effect of nuclear weapons. The gravity of the threat in a crisis is also controlled for to account for a potential selection effect, best characterized by Fearon (2002), who comments on the debate between Lebow & Stein (1990) and Huth & Russett (1990). The set of cases in which there are serious threats may appear different with regard to various outcome variables, because these are the cases in which general deterrence has failed, and there is at least one very resolved actor. While there may be additional similar, unobservable selection processes that we do not account for, including threat gravity is one cut at trying to control for the differences that might be expected in crises with serious threats versus crises with lesser threats. The discussion section expands on this issue.

The third control variable is whether the crises are protracted or not. Nuclear actors may develop nuclear weapons for security purposes related to the presence of protracted conflicts (Sagan, 1996/97), and protracted conflicts tend to be associated with higher levels of violence (Caprioli & Boyer, 2001; Brecher & Wilkenfeld, 1997; Brecher, 1999; Bremer, 1992b; Brecher & James, 1988). We also control for the difference in capabilities, as the possession of nuclear weapons parallels the possession of other military capabilities that might be related to levels of crisis violence in ways unrelated to nuclear weapons. Zagare & Kilgour (2000) argue that the capability level necessary for deterrence to work can be achieved with conventional weapons, so controlling for capability allows us to test for the relevance of nuclear weapons. This variable is constructed using the CINC score index from the National Military Capabilities (NMC) data, which allows an analyst to compare the potential military capacities of countries. The value used for each observation is the mean difference in CINC score between opposing actors listed in the

Table 1 Nuclear Capabilities

Country	Year Achieved Nuclear Capabilities	Year End	Citations†
Belarus*	1991	1996	
China•	1964	Ongoing	
France•	1960	Ongoing	
India•	1974	Ongoing	http://www.nti.org/e_research/profiles/India/index.html http://www.fas.org/nuke/guide/india/nuke/index.html
			Hagerty (1998: 73)
Israel•	1967	Ongoing	http://www.fas.org/nuke/guide/israel/nuke: 1966/67
			Cohen (1998: 232, 274): late 1966/67
Kazakhstan*	1991	1995	
North Korea**•	1992	Ongoing	http://www.nti.org/e_research/profiles/NK/Nuclear/index.html: 1991 http://www.fas.org/nuke/guide/dprk/nuke/cia111902.html: 1992
			Cirincione, Wolfsthal & Rajkumar (2002: 244): capability possibly since before 1994
Pakistan•	1987	Ongoing	http://www.nti.org/e_research/profiles/Pakistan/index.html: 1989–90 http://www.fas.org/nuke/guide/pakistan/nuke/index.html: 1987
			Hagerty (1998: 82, 99–95): possibly 1983, most probably by 1986/87
South Africa•	1978	1993	Horton (1999): 1977 or 1979
			Liberman (2001: 54): 1978
			Albright (1994): 1979
			http://www.fas.org/nuke/guide/rsa/nuke/stumpf.htm: 1979 http://cns.miis.edu/research/safrica/chron.htm: 1978
Ukraine*	1991	1996	
United Kingdom•	1952	Ongoing	
USA•	1945	Ongoing	
Russia/USSR•	1949	Ongoing	

•Involved in a crisis as nuclear power.

†For countries that have had opaque nuclear policies; we include the different dates when there are discrepancies.

*Belarus, Kazakhstan, and Ukraine had possession of nuclear weapons on their territories, but it appears that they did not have operational control of these weapons. All nuclear warheads were reported removed from their territories by 1996 or 1995. In any case, none of the countries have been involved in an international crisis since their independence.

**The start of North Korea's status as a nuclear power is still very unclear. Of all the countries listed, the determination of North Korean status is the least certain.

dyadic ICB data (Hewitt, 2003). The presence of jointly democratic dyads is controlled for in order to avoid any potentially confounding relationships between the democratic peace and the role of nuclear weapons.

Two additional control variables are included in separate models to demonstrate robustness across potentially mitigating phenomena. First, a variable that indicates whether any of the actors involved in a crisis are 'new' nuclear actors is used to take another look at some of the proliferation-pessimist views. If it is the case that the five nuclear-weapon members of the NPT are inherently more responsible than the actors that developed nuclear weapons later, then there should be different propensities toward violence in crises with the newer nuclear actors. Second, one of the models includes a dummy variable that indicates if one of the superpowers was a crisis actor. This variable is used to account for the fact that the USA and Soviet Union/Russia were involved in 75 crises since 1945 and may behave differently than other nuclear actors because of their superpower status. This variable also captures some of the variation in the number of nuclear

Table 2   Variables Used in Analysis

Variables	Mode	Mean	Standard Deviation
(DV) Intensity of violence (sev)	2	2.349	1.049
1) No violence			
2) Minor clashes			
3) Serious clashes			
4) Full-scale war			
(IV1) Number of nuclear powers involved in crisis (nuke): from 0 to 5	0	.655	.889
(IV2) Number of crisis actors (cractr)	2	2.187	1.173
1) One actor			
2) Two actors			
3) Three actors			
4) Four actors			
5) Five actors			
6) Six actors			
7) More than six actors			
(IV3) Gravity of crisis threat* (gravcr)	0	.206	.405
0) Non-grave threat			
1) Threat of grave damage or to existence			
(IV4) Protracted conflict* (protract)	1	.633	.483
0) Non-protracted conflict			
1) protracted conflict			
(IV5) Difference in capabilities (cincdif)	—	.0380	.0527

Variables	Mode	Mean	Standard Deviation
(IV6) Jointly democratic opponents (jointdem)	0	.0534	.225
0) No dyads jointly democratic			
1) Jointly democratic dyad			
(IV7) Jointly nuclear dyad (nukedyad)	0	.0749	.264
0) No dyads jointly nuclear			
1) Jointly nuclear dyad			
(IV8) New nuclear actor (newnuke)	0	.137	.344
0) No involvement of actors that developed nuclear weapons after 1964			
1) Involvement of 'new' nuclear actors			
(IV9) Superpower crisis actor	0	.170	.376
0) The USA and USSR/Russia are not crisis actors			
1) The USA or USSR/Russia are crisis actors			

Note: Observations: 281.

Explanations for IV2, IV3, and IV4 are taken from http://www.icbnet.org/Data/icb1v4-1codebook.pdf and Brecher & Wilkenfeld (1997). IV1 counts the number of actors that have nuclear weapons in a crisis, based on the actors in the dyadic ICB data (Hewitt, 2003). IV5 is the absolute mean difference in CINC scores of any dyad in the conflict, where the CINC scores are from the National Material Capabilities 3.0 1 data (Singer, Bremer & Stuckey, 1972), and the dyads are determined by Hewitt's (2003) ICB dyadic data. IV6 considers a crisis as having jointly democratic opponents when the Polity IV (Marshall & Jaggers, 2002) composite index is at least six for each of the actors in at least one of the dyads in a crisis.

*Originally, these variables had more categories, but they are used as binary variables here to ensure that they are ordinal.

weapons that crisis actors possess and may have some implications for the debate over whether just a few nuclear weapons are sufficient for deterrence to work.

When analyzing the impact of nuclear weapons using the ICB dataset, one can decide either to analyze only the period when nuclear weapons were available, 1945 to the present, or to use both the periods before and after the presence of nuclear weapons in the analysis. The post-WWII period is most appropriate, as the set of observations prior to this time period had no potential to have variation in the independent variable. Of the 285 crises that the dyadic ICB dataset lists from 1945 to 2001, a little less than 45% (131) involved at least one nuclear power. Table 3 illustrates how many nuclear crises involved more than one nuclear actor.

Table 3 Number of Nuclear Actors Involved in Crisis in Crises with Nuclear Actors, 1945–2001

Number of Nuclear Actors Involved in Crisis	Number of Crises of This Type*	Relative Frequency
1	97	74.05
2	21	16.03
3	8	6.11
4	4	3.05
5	1	0.76

*Total = 131.

Analysis

Given the ordinal nature of the dependent variable, we use maximum-likelihood ordered-logit estimation (ologit) to analyze the data. To interpret the coefficients from the logistic regression, we use the Clarify simulation program (King, Tomz & Wittenberg, 2000; Tomz, Wittenberg & King, 2003) to generate probabilities that allow us to see how our independent variables affect the dependent variable. We do this with the control variables set at their mode or mean. In this way, we assess the impact of the number of nuclear actors involved in a crisis in the most common circumstances (with the other variables set at their mode).

As Model 1 in Table 4 illustrates, all of our variables are statistically significant except for the protracted conflict variable. Our primary independent variable, the number of nuclear actors involved in the crisis, has a negative relationship with the severity of violence and is significant. This lends preliminary support to the argument that nuclear weapons have a restraining affect on crisis behavior, as stated in *H1*.

It should be noted that, of the crises that involved four nuclear actors—Suez Nationalization War (1956), Berlin Wall (1961), October Yom Kippur War (1973), and Iraq No-Fly Zone (1992)—and five nuclear actors—Gulf War (1990)—only two are not full-scale wars. While this demonstrates that the pacifying effect of more nuclear actors is not strong enough to prevent war in all situations, it does not necessarily weaken the argument that there is actually a pacifying effect. The positive and statistically significant coefficient on the variable that counts the number of crisis actors has a magnitude greater than that on the variable that counts the number of nuclear actors. Since increases in the number of overall actors in a crisis are strongly associated with higher levels of violence, it should be no surprise that many of the conflicts with many nuclear actors—by extension, many general actors as well—experienced war. Therefore, the results can only suggest that, keeping the number of crisis actors fixed, increasing the proportion of nuclear actors has a pacifying effect. They do not suggest that adding nuclear actors to a crisis will decrease the risk of high levels violence; but rather, adding more actors of any type to a crisis can have a destabilizing effect.

Also in Table 4, Model 2 demonstrates that the effect of a nuclear dyad is only approaching statistical significance, but does have a sign that indicates higher levels of violence are less likely in crises with opponents that have nuclear weapons than other crises. This lukewarm result suggests that it might not be necessary for nuclear actors to face each other in order to get the effect of decreased propensity for violence. All actors should tend to be more cautious in escalation when there is a nuclear opponent, regardless of their own capabilities. While this might weaken support for focusing on specifically a 'balance of terror' as a source of stability (see Gaddis, 1986; Waltz, 1990; Sagan & Waltz, 2003; Mearsheimer, 1990), it supports the logic in this article that nuclear weapons can serve as a deterrent of aggression from both nuclear and non-nuclear opponents.[6]

Model 3 transforms the violence variable to a binary indicator of war and demonstrates that the principal relationship between the number of nuclear actors and violence holds for the most crucial outcome of full-scale war. Model 4 demonstrates that accounting for the presence of new nuclear actors does not greatly change the results. The coefficient on the *new nuclear actor* variable is statistically insignificant, which lends credence to the optimists' view that new nuclear-weapon states should not be presupposed to behave less responsibly than the USA, USSR, UK, France, and China did during the Cold War. Finally, Model 5 similarly illustrates that crises involving superpowers are not more or less prone to violence than others. Superpower activity appears to not be driving the observed relationships between the number of nuclear-crisis actors and restraint toward violence.

It is important to establish more specifically what the change in the probability of full-scale war is when nuclear actors are involved. Table 5 presents

Table 4 Multivariate Models of Violence Levels, 1945–2001

	Ordered Logit		Logit	Ordered Logit	
	1	2	3	4	5
Number of nuclear powers	−0.372	—	−0.560	−0.412	−0.355
	(2.18)**		(2.03)**	(1.95)**	(2.06)**
Nuclear dyad	—	−0.699	—	—	—
		(1.51)			
Number of crisis actors	0.657	0.599	0.936	0.675	0.696
	(5.07)***	(4.80)***	(4.98)***	(4.80)***	(4.92)***
Gravity of crisis threat	1.100	0.989	1.218	1.089	1.140
	(3.52)***	(3.23)***	(2.94)***	(3.46)***	(3.58)***
Protracted conflict	0.348	0.337	0.897	0.335	0.350
	(1.44)	(1.40)	(1.90)*	(1.37)	(1.44)
Difference in capabilities	−4.526	−6.253	−7.666	−4.137	−3.023
	(1.92)*	(2.90)***	(1.50)	(1.57)	(0.96)
Jointly democratic opponents	−1.055	−0.936	−1.293	−1.058	−1.072
	(2.04)**	(1.82)*	(1.16)	(2.05)**	(2.08)**
New nuclear actor	—	—	—	0.131	—
Superpower involvement	—	—	—	(0.33)	−0.320
					(0.70)
Constant	—	—	−4.194	—	—
			(7.50)***		
Cut 1	0.103	0.084	—	0.139	0.188
	(0.281)	(0.283)		(0.301)	(0.306)
Cut 2	1.604	1.577	—	1.640	1.689
	(0.289)	(0.291)		(0.310)	(0.315)
Cut 3	3.201	3.161	—	3.236	3.290
	(0.346)	(0.346)		(0.362)	(0.370)
Observations	281	281	281	281	281
Pseudo R-squared	0.088	0.085	0.245	0.088	0.088

Absolute value of z statistics in parentheses.

*significant at 10% in a two-tailed t-test; **significant at 5%; ***significant at 1%.

the probability of different levels of violence as the number of nuclear actors increases in the Clarify simulations. The control variables are held at their modes or means, with the exception of the variable that counts the number of crisis actors. Because it would be impossible to have, say, five nuclear-crisis actors and only two crisis actors, the number of crisis actors is held constant at five.

As we can see, the impact of an increase in the number of nuclear actors is substantial. Starting from a crisis situation without any nuclear actors, including one nuclear actor (out of five) reduces the likelihood of full-scale war by nine percentage points. As we continue to add nuclear actors, the likelihood of full-scale war declines sharply, so that the probability of a war with the maximum number of nuclear actors is about three times less than the probability with no nuclear actors. In addition, the probabilities of no violence and only minor clashes increase substantially as the number of nuclear actors increases. The probability of serious clashes is relatively constant.

Overall, the analysis lends significant support to the more optimistic proliferation argument related to the expectation of violent conflict when nuclear actors are involved. While the presence of nuclear powers does not prevent war, it significantly reduces the probability of full-scale war, with more reduction as the number of nuclear powers involved in the conflict increases.

As mentioned, concerns about selection effects in deterrence models, as raised by Fearon (2002), should be taken seriously. While we control for the strategic selection of serious threats within crises, we are unable to control for the non-random initial initiation of a crisis in which the actors may choose to enter a crisis based on some ex ante assessment of the outcomes. To account for possible selection bias caused by the use of a truncated sample that does not include any non-crisis cases, one would need to use another dataset in which the crisis cases are a subset and then run Heckmantype selection models (see Lemke & Reed, 2001b). It would, however, be difficult to think of a different unit of analysis that might be employed, such that the set of crises is a subset of a larger category of interaction. While dyad-year datasets have often been employed to similar ends, the key independent variable here, which is specific to crises as the unit of analysis, does not lend itself to a dyadic setup. Moreover, selection bias concerns are likely not valid in disputing the claims of this analysis. If selection bias were present, it would tend to bias the effect of nuclear weapons downward, because the set of observed crises with

Table 5   Probability of Different Levels of Severity of Violence Based on Number of Nuclear Powers Involved*

Severity of Violence	Number of Nuclear Powers					
	0	1	2	3	4	5
(1) No violence	0.04	0.05	0.07	0.11	0.15	0.21
(2) Minor clashes	0.11	0.14	0.18	0.23	0.27	0.30
(3) Serious clashes	0.30	0.34	0.36	0.36	0.34	0.31
(4) Full-scale war	0.56	0.47	0.38	0.30	0.24	0.19

*cractr = 5, gravcr = 0, protrac = 1, cincdif = .0481, jointdem = 0.

nuclear actors likely has a disproportionate share of resolved actors that have chosen to take their chances against a nuclear opponent. Despite this potential mitigating bias, the results are statistically significant, which strengthens the case for the explanations provided in this study.

Conclusion

The presence of nuclear weapons has an important and pacific impact, a finding that lends support for an optimistic view of the stabilizing effect of nuclear weapons. Waltz's (Sagan & Waltz, 2003: 7) contention that 'the presence of nuclear weapons makes states exceedingly cautious' seems to be borne out. Simply put, when nuclear actors are present, states—both nuclear and non-nuclear—resort to violence less often, because they do not want to risk the exceptional costs of a nuclear strike. Given the fact that much of the examination of this issue has been impressionistic (Geller, 2003), this finding is important for our continuing effort to better understand the advantages and disadvantages of nuclear proliferation, as well as its effects.

We should also note that this was a 'hard' test for the pro-proliferation argument—we are not asking if nuclear dyads are less likely to go to war. Our analysis indicates that the presence of nuclear-weapons states as crisis actors, regardless of which side they are on, decreases the likely level of violence. This fits with the theoretical arguments of proliferation optimists and rational-deterrence theorists. Despite the support for the optimists, the evidence is not as overwhelming as one might wish, given the costs involved if there is a mistake in the calculations of leaders armed with nuclear weapons during a crisis. A 37% change in the probability of full-scale war is a large amount, but as Waltz (Sagan & Waltz, 2003: 6) points out, the costs of a mistake can be nothing short of 'destruction'. Is a change of 37% in probability worth taking the risk that proliferation may reach a ruler who is truly irrational? In either case, the findings suggest avenues for future research using the ICB dataset to explore various impacts that nuclear weapons have on crisis behavior.

Our findings shed light only on the general impact that increasing the number of nuclear participants in a crisis has on the outcome of that crisis. We do not address other potential perils that proliferation might bring, such as greater risks of accident or the higher risks of use by terrorist networks. The pacification effect of nuclear states in crises is only one of many important factors to consider when states adopt their proliferation stances. And it should not be lost that the pacification effect is only so strong, as some serious violent conflicts have occurred between nuclear-weapon states. Zagare & Kilgour (2000) demonstrate that deterrence can fail in any number of situations. The costs of failed deterrence are so great when there are nuclear weapons involved that policymakers must seriously weigh the benefits of decreasing the likelihood of deterrence failure with increasing the costs of each failure instance.

Finally, the motivations, behaviors, and outcomes for the various actors beyond the level of violence experienced remain beyond the scope of our present analysis. Given our findings, a closer look at the different outcomes for nuclear actors and non-nuclear actors in crises suggests itself as a useful next step in our understanding of the impact of nuclear proliferation.

Notes

Authors' Note: The replication data are available for download at www.prio.no/jpr/datasets. Please see http://cidcm.umd.edu/icb for a complete description of the International Crisis Behavior data and an interactive database of the crises. Please direct all correspondence to VAsal@email.albany.edu.

1. We should note that our unit of analysis is the crisis. Our findings do not get at the behavior of specific states and the different outcomes of crises for different states. We should also note that we do not test the question of how the number of nuclear weapons each actor possesses impacts crisis behavior. The question of minimal deterrence is important, but it lies beyond the scope of the current study, which seeks to examine the impact of the very presence of nuclear actors.

2. Mason (1992: 149) argues that this attitude is also part of what motivated French resistance to an anti-proliferation attitude prior to their membership to the Non-Proliferation Treaty. 'France disagrees with the underlying logic of the Non-Proliferation Treaty, which is seen as an additional manifestation of "patronizing Anglo-Saxon Puritanism" which finds it normal to divide the world into civilized countries (i.e., countries which would have a responsible attitude toward their nuclear weapons) and uncivilized countries (i.e., the rest of the world).'

3. The scope of this article precludes us from addressing other key aspects about the merits of proliferation. The first of these aspects is the increased chance of nuclear accidents. Sagan argues that the danger of accidents in countries that do not have the resources and technical know-how of the USA makes non-proliferation an important goal (Sagan & Waltz, 2003). Interestingly, the same concerns lead Feaver & Niou (1996: 229) to advocate assisted proliferation to prevent 'unsafe nuclear arsenals—ones prone to accidental or unauthorized use'. The second major issue not addressed in this article is the possibility that proliferation increases the chance that nuclear weapons will fall into the hands of terrorists. For the argument against proliferation that this possibility suggests, see Allison et al. (1996). Finally, we do not fully address the question of whether the new proliferators behave differently than the old proliferators or whether there would be an increased risk of accidents. For an explication of the arguments dealing with nuclear accidents and the different nature of the new proliferators, see Brito & Intriligator (1996), Feaver (1992/93), Kaiser (1989), and Sagan (1994).

4. Gaddis (1986) discusses how the presence of nuclear weapons contributed to restraint between the USA and the USSR. Kahn (2001: 61) similarly argues, 'given that all-out wars have almost become a thing of the past due to the prevailing nuclear deterrent relationship between the adversaries in these volatile regions, it seems that scholarly focus should now shift from nuclear war dynamics to the more crucial aspect—the protracted conflict itself.'

5. It is not clear how strong this effect may be, since the possession of nuclear weapons may affect an actor's probability of being in a serious dispute. The authors leave a complete examination of how proliferation might affect crisis onset to future research. The point is that proliferation increases the opportunity for nuclear actors to participate in disputes.

6. Geller (1990), building from Snyder & Diesing (1977) and Osgood & Tucker (1967), actually finds that nuclear dyads are more likely to escalate (short of war) in conflict situations because there is a higher 'threshold' for competitive risk-taking when both sides know that all-out war should be avoided at all costs. With a negative but insignificant coefficient on the nuclear dyad variable, our results suggest that there might be competing effects in a nuclear dyad. Both sides will be restrained from high levels of violence but more comfortable at lower levels of escalation. We leave further explanation of the specific dynamics within a nuclear dyad to future research.

EDITORS' COMMENTARY

Major Contributions: Nuclear Weapons

Asal and Beardsley (2007) ask whether nuclear weapons increase or decrease the chances for war, an idea that is central to many theories of international relations, including neorealism (Waltz 1979) and deterrence theory (Schelling 1960), as well as modern policy debates about the dangers of nuclear proliferation (Forsberg et al. 1995). Theorists who do not see nuclear proliferation as a major threat argue that nuclear weapons raise the costs of war to unacceptable levels, making it unlikely that nuclear powers will fight a war against each other (Waltz 1981; Mearsheimer 1993). This logic has been used to explain the lack of major warfare between the United States and Soviet Union during the Cold War. Skeptics point to many problems that could arise with new countries acquiring nuclear weapons, including the chances for nuclear accidents, the dangers of having these weapons in regional disputes involving territorial borders (e.g., India-Pakistan or North Korea–South Korea), and the emergence of nuclear weapons in states with more military control over foreign policy, which could increase the chances of aggressive foreign policies and nuclear war (Sagan 1994). Asal and Beardsley provide one of the first systematic empirical tests of the competing arguments in the literature. Their evidence is consistent with the viewpoint that sees the benefits of nuclear proliferation, as crises involving more states with nuclear weapons are *less likely* to escalate to high levels of violence. On the other hand, the probability of war is still as high as one in five in interstate crises involving many nuclear states, a likelihood that may be too large for the skeptics to accept. In addition, the presence of nuclear weapons is often associated with an increase in the number of militarized interstate disputes (Geller 2012).

The benefits of nuclear weapons are often linked to the theoretical model of **deterrence** as described by Thomas Schelling (1960, see also Kahn 1960). In this model, there is one state, the **defender**, which is the state seeking to maintain the status quo on some issue (e.g., British ownership of the Falkland Islands), and another state, the potential **attacker**, which is seeking to alter the status quo (e.g., Argentina's claim to own the Falkland Islands). The defender seeks to prevent something undesirable happening, such as war, by threatening to retaliate with nuclear or other weapons against a potential attacker and cause unacceptable damage to the other side if it goes through with its attack plan. The ability to inflict punishment is greater if a country has weapons that can cause a lot of damage, such as nuclear weapons, which create physical damage similar to conventional explosives but at a much higher energy rate (e.g., temperatures in the tens of millions of degrees).[1] Thus, nuclear war is seen as a much greater deterrent than conventional weapons because the damage can be so extensive that the revision being sought is not worth the cost of nuclear war.

This kind of situation is often described as **direct deterrence** because it involves a defender protecting itself against outside attacks. Another common situation involves threats and actions to protect the interests of other states, or **protégés**, a situation labeled **extended deterrence**. The United States' efforts to prevent nuclear strikes by the Soviet Union on the American homeland during the Cold War provide an example of direct deterrence, while the United States' efforts to prevent Soviet attacks on Western Europe offer an example of extended deterrence. It was said that in this situation, the United States "extended" its nuclear umbrella over Western Europe to protect it. Deterrence theory also distinguishes between **general deterrence**, or situations where the possibility of attack exists but the threat of attack is not imminent or just implicit, and **immediate deterrence**, where both sides believe the chances for an attack are high or an explicit threat has been made. An example of general deterrence is U.S. defense of its homeland during the Cold War, while an example of immediate deterrence is the 1960 Berlin Crisis when Kennedy threatened to go to nuclear war if the U.S.S.R. or East Germany took over West Berlin.

The literature on deterrence identifies several factors that improve the chances for successful deterrence. One important factor relates to the **credibility** of the defender's threats against the potential attacker. Deterrence is said to be **credible** when a challenger believes that the defender will resort to war, including the use of nuclear weapons, to resist demands. Since most observers believe that states will go to war to defend their homeland, credibility is much more of an issue in extended deterrence, where a defender in effect is risking war and the possible damage or destruction of its own homeland to protect the territory of a third party (i.e., the protégé). Enhanced capabilities improve a defender's chances for deterring attacks by signaling the ability to achieve a battlefield victory should war break out and by indicating a willingness to employ costly measures to punish attacks (Zagare and Kilgour 2000). By virtue of the significant physical damages that nuclear weapons can cause, they decrease the likelihood of attack by another state.[2] Schelling (1960) focused on two mechanisms for achieving credibility: tying hands and brinkmanship. In a crisis situation, states can signal their resolve to remain firm and defend themselves or one of their protégés by engaging in provocative actions that push the two sides to the "brink" of war. In the 1962 Cuban Missile Crisis, for example, President Kennedy ordered a naval blockade of Cuba to prevent the Soviet Union from delivering materials for nuclear weapons to the island state. This act pushed the two sides very close to war but created a credible signal to the Soviet Union that the United States would not back down, a signal reinforced by a personal communication from President Kennedy's brother, Attorney General Robert Kennedy, to Soviet Ambassador Dobrynin in Washington (Kennedy 1969).

States can also enhance the credibility of deterrent threats by tying their hands in some way. Consider the desire to prevent an attack on a protégé, such as U.S. defense of Western Europe during the Cold War. By placing troops and missiles on the territories of its allies, the U.S. government signaled its willingness to defend the targets against Soviet attack. American troops in Berlin were called a "trip wire"—they had no chance to turn back a military attack, but their defeat would ensure an American resort to war. Another strategy for tying hands is to sign a military alliance. The United States' defense pact with Taiwan (since 1954), for example, can strengthen the deterrent threat against potential invasion by mainland China. The actions of tying hands and brinkmanship serve as signals to potential attackers that any belligerent acts will be met with some kind of response.[3] Asal and Beardsley (2007) test the deterrence hypothesis in two ways. First, they hypothesize that the more nuclear states that are involved in an international crisis, the lower the levels of violence in the crisis. This is designed to capture the increasing potential costs for war that could occur if crisis escalation unfolds. Second, they also include a measure for nuclear dyads, which equals 1 if any states on opposing sides of an interstate crisis have nuclear weapons.

As noted by Asal and Beardsley (2007), the linkage between nuclear weapons and successful deterrence has been questioned by a variety of scholars and pundits. One argument suggests that nuclear weapons might be dangerous in regional settings, especially if the states involved have ongoing border disputes (e.g., India-Pakistan in Kashmir). Another argument sees the potential for nuclear terrorism; while nuclear weapons could deter future interstate wars, having a larger supply of nuclear weapons globally increases the risks for nonstate actors to acquire and use such weapons. This also relates to the potential dangers of nuclear accidents. Many new nuclear proliferators do not have the same level of bureaucracy and oversight mechanisms that the original nuclear states such as the United States and U.S.S.R. had (Sagan 1994). There is also a heightened risk of preventive war during the development phase of a state's nuclear program (Fuhrmann and Kreps 2010).[4] Others argue that nuclear weapons could be employed by states with military leaders, such as generals, because military officers are more inclined to adopt offensive tactics and see war as inevitable in a situation of rivalry (Sagan 1994). The anti-proliferators would expect the presence of more states with nuclear weapons in a crisis situation to increase the chances for accidents or escalation or, at a minimum, have no effect on the likelihood of crisis escalation.

Asal and Beardsley's (2007) empirical analysis is somewhat consistent with deterrence theory. They find that as the number of nuclear actors in a crisis increases, the severity of violence in the crisis decreases. For example, the probability of full-scale war in a crisis drops from 0.56 if there are no states with nuclear weapons involved to 0.19 if there are five countries with nuclear weapons in the crisis.[5] As noted earlier, this does leave a roughly one in five chance for war in these situations, which is still quite high, but the lower levels of crisis severity are consistent with Schelling's (1960) ideas about brinkmanship. States with nuclear weapons might use threats and military action in a crisis situation, but the possibility of escalating the situation to a very costly nuclear war more often results in one side backing down. The authors note that crises with a higher number of actors face greater risks for escalation overall but that the probability of war is three times less likely if a large number of nuclear states are present. Yet there are situations, such as the Gulf War and the Yom Kippur War, where high levels of violence occurred even in the face of four or five nuclear actors in the crisis, and thus nuclear weapons did not deter conventional warfare. Of course, it should be noted that in these cases, there was no real chance of nuclear weapons being used.

Methodological Notes: Ordered Logit Models

Asal and Beardsley (2007) identify thirteen countries that have been nuclear powers since 1945 (Table 1). They analyze data on 281 crises from 1945 to 2001 that are coded by the International Crisis Behavior (ICB) project (Brecher and Wilkenfeld 1997). They use the crisis as the unit of analysis, where the key dependent variable is an **ordinal** scale representing the highest level of violence that occurred in the crisis: (1) no violence, (2) minor clashes, (3) serious clashes, or (4) full-scale war. The authors use an **ordered logit model** (Table 4, Models 1–2, 4–5), which is designed to capture the relationship between an ordinal dependent variable and several independent variables. They also collapse this variable into a dichotomous measure that equals 1 if the crisis experienced full-scale war and zero otherwise; they use this variable in the **logit model** (Table 4, Model 3). The ordered logit model assumes that some underlying continuous variable represents the dependent variable of interest (Long 1997). The categories of the ordered variable are separated by theoretical thresholds or **cut points**. Consider the following example (adapted from Long 1997, 116):

$$1 \text{ (no violence)} \quad \text{if } \tau_0 = -\infty \leq y_i^* < \tau_1$$
$$y_i = 2 \text{ (minor clashes)} \quad \text{if } \tau_1 \leq y_i^* < \tau_2$$
$$3 \text{ (serious clashes)} \quad \text{if } \tau_2 \leq y_i^* < \tau_3$$
$$4 \text{ (war)} \quad \text{if } \tau_3 \leq y_i^* < \tau_4 = \infty$$

We can see that there are three basic cut points for this variable: τ_1 is the cut point between no violence and minor clashes, τ_2 is the cut point between minor and serious clashes, and τ_3 is the cut point between serious clashes and war. In Asal and Beardsley's Table 4, these are estimated at the bottom of the table as "Cut 1," "Cut 2," and "Cut 3." This has the effect of forcing the predicted values into one of the four levels on the ordinal scale for violence levels.

We can still estimate the effects of the independent variables in a way similar to the logit model, where a positive coefficient indicates that an increase in that independent variable (e.g., the 0.657 estimate for number of crisis actors in Model 1) increases the chances of observing a higher value on the ordinal scale for crisis violence. We also determine the statistical significance of each variable in the same way we have described previously, by dividing the estimate (β) by the standard error (ε) and then seeing if the calculated Z statistic is approximately greater than 2 (for a two-tailed hypothesis test). Asal and Beardsley (2007) report the Z statistics in parentheses. We can see for number of crisis actors in Model 1, for example, that the estimated Z score is 5.07, a value much larger than 2, implying that we can reject the null hypothesis that β equals zero (or that the number of crisis actors has no effect on the violence level in a crisis). The authors use a series of asterisks to indicate the significance level for each estimated parameter, ranging from 90 percent (*) to 95 percent (**) to 99 percent (***). Their key theoretical variable, number of nuclear powers, has a negative sign and is statistically significant at the 95 percent level in each of the estimated models. This supports their main hypothesis that crises are less likely to escalate as the number of states with nuclear capabilities in the crisis increases.

However, the nuclear dyad variable is not statistically significant, which means that it is not necessary for nuclear states to be on opposite sides of the crisis for a deterrent effect to operate. This is not surprising given that 74 percent of the crises involving nuclear states involve only a single nuclear power (Table 3). But it does raise some questions about whether they are actually testing a theory of mutual nuclear deterrence. They merely show that the presence of a (single) nuclear state decreases violence levels, but such an effect could occur with conventional strength, too. They try to test this alternative hypothesis in Table 4, Model 5 by coding whether one of the two superpowers (United States or U.S.S.R.) was an actor in the crisis. This would capture the presence of a powerful state with both significant conventional and nuclear forces. They find that this variable is not statistically significant, while the number of nuclear powers remains an important predictor of crisis severity. They also compare newer nuclear actors with older ones in Model 4 and find no support for the anti-proliferators' claim that these newer actors are more likely to escalate crises to war.

In Table 5, they present the predicted probabilities from their ordered logit model, setting the control variables at their mean or mode and then varying the number of nuclear powers. The calculation of these probabilities depends on the cut points described above. Thus, we calculate the probability that the dependent variable takes on a specific value (e.g., minor clashes) given that the independent variable takes on a specific value (e.g., number of nuclear actors equal to zero). We then calculate these conditional probabilities by increasing the value of the independent variable (e.g., the number of nuclear actors increases from zero to five). We can then compare the probabilities by looking across any given row. We can see, for example, that the probability of no violence in an ICB crisis increases from 0.04 if there are no actors with nuclear capabilities to 0.11 if there are three nuclear powers.

Asal and Beardsley (2007) note a potential problem of **selection bias** in their sample (see Reed 2000, Chapter 11, this volume). They are looking at crises or situations where general deterrence failed to some degree. If deterrent threats worked perfectly, then we would not observe any crisis situations. Thus, the situations we observe must be cases where the potential attacker is quite resolved because it is willing to incur potential retaliation by one or more nuclear states. In this case, the bias would tend to underestimate the effect of nuclear weapons on successful deterrence because we are looking at situations where actors challenged defenders despite facing a nuclear retaliation. It is difficult to test theories such as deterrence because the set of cases we observe (e.g., crises or militarized interstate disputes) are not randomly drawn from the set of possible crises but exhibit particular characteristics. This implies that some factors that might deter the onset of a crisis, such as a strong conventional forces advantage, may have no effect on escalation to war once a crisis begins (Fearon 1994a). There are different strategies that one can use to deal with this selection effect, including Heckman selection models and matching models (see Reed 2000).

Notes

1. Nuclear weapons are explosive devices that get their energy from the splitting (fission) or the combining (fusion) of atomic nuclei.
2. Conventional weapons also improve the defender's chances for successful deterrence if the balance of local military capabilities favors the defender (Huth and Russett 1993).

3. There is disagreement about whether military alliances are successful in deterring attacks; see Leeds (2003a; 2005, Chapter 4, this volume) and Senese and Vasquez (2005, Chapter 7, this volume).
4. Fuhrmann and Kreps (2010, 844) find that states are willing to initiative preventive attacks against states developing nuclear weapons programs if they have a history of militarized disputes with the target state, if the proliferating government is more autocratic, and if the two sides' foreign policy preferences are dissimilar.
5. This value for five nuclear actors is taken from the ICB data set and indicates the highest number of nuclear states that ever participated in any single crisis (e.g., 1990 Gulf War).

Questions

1. Do you think the risks of war from proliferation of nuclear weapons to additional states are greater than the benefits that such weapons might have in deterring future interstate wars? Why or why not?

2. In Table 5, it appears that the number of nuclear actors in a crisis has different effects depending on the level of violence in the crisis. Compare how the probability of serious confrontations changes as the number of nuclear powers increases from zero to five to how the probability of full-scale war changes. Why do you think these effects are stronger for full-scale war?

3. If we wanted to test (general) deterrence theory, we would need to identify situations where potential attackers might attack but are deterred from doing so. How could we identify these kinds of situations empirically and differentiate them from situations where nothing happens because the potential attackers have no incentives to attack?

Further Reading

Huth, P., and B. Russett. 1993. General deterrence between enduring rivals: Testing three competing models. *American Political Science Review* 87 (1): 61–75.

Kahn, H. 1960. *On Thermonuclear War*. Princeton, NJ: Princeton University Press.

Kugler, J. 1984. Terror without deterrence: Reassessing the role of nuclear weapons. *Journal of Conflict Resolution* 28 (2): 470–506.

Mueller, J. 1988. The essential irrelevance of nuclear weapons. *International Security* 13 (2): 55–79.

Sagan, S. 1994. The perils of proliferation: Organization theory, deterrence theory, and the spread of nuclear weapons. *International Security* 18 (4): 66–107.

Schelling, T. C. 1960. *The strategy of conflict*. Cambridge, MA: Harvard University Press.

Chapter 14

The Precarious Nature of Peace

Resolving the Issues, Enforcing the Settlement, and Renegotiating the Terms

Suzanne Werner

1. Introduction

Although wars are often fought to prevent further aggression and to establish a lasting peace, reality often differs significantly from these hopes. While the end of a war can inaugurate a durable peace and cooperative relationship between former adversaries, the termination of one conflict often introduces only a short breathing spell until the beginning of the next violent encounter. I seek to understand the conditions conducive to a lasting peace.

For a conflict to recur, at least one of the adversaries must reverse a prior decision; a belligerent must challenge an agreement it had previously accepted as preferable to continued fighting. Explanations for the duration of peace must then consider not only that the adversaries are fighting again, but that they previously had agreed to stop fighting. Three explanations account for this reversal and the resumption of conflict, with varying degrees of success. The first explanation identifies the belligerents' failure to obtain *resolution* of the underlying issues as the source of the problem. The second explanation suggests that the absence of *enforcement* provisions in the original settlement accounts for the recurrence of conflict. The final explanation considers the former belligerents' incentives to *renegotiate* the terms of the settlement.

I first develop in greater detail these three explanations for the duration of peace and derive several testable propositions from each perspective. Next, I explain my research design and measurement choices and then evaluate the hypotheses with a hazard model. The evidence indicates that incentives to renegotiate the settlement are a key source of recurrent conflict. While some evidence exists that the absence of enforcement provisions increases the risk of recurrent conflict, there is little evidence to support the contention that the existence of unresolved issues adversely affects the duration of peace. I conclude by discussing these findings and noting some possible limitations of my research design and data.

2. Three Explanations for the End of Peace

The resurgent interest in the durability of peace and the danger of recurrent conflict can be traced in large part to the empirical discovery of enduring rivalries (Diehl 1998). Most conflict in the international system takes place among a small number of states that fight over and over again. Since a pair of states can fight again only if they had agreed previously to stop fighting, a decision to resume a conflict is also a decision to reverse a prior decision. Whereas the belligerent previously preferred to

Source: Suzanne Werner, "The Precarious Nature of Peace: Resolving the Issues, Enforcing the Settlement, and Renegotiating the Terms" *American Journal of Political Science* 43, no. 3 (July 1999): 912–34. © 1999 by the Midwest Political Science Association. Reproduced with permission of Blackwell Publishing Ltd.

accept a particular settlement rather than continue the conflict, the belligerent now prefers to continue the conflict rather than to maintain the settlement.[1] Since conflicts recur when a belligerent challenges a prior settlement, I approach the question of recurrent conflict by asking why some settlements last longer than others. From existing literature on recurrent conflict, I explore three distinct, but not necessarily antithetical, explanations for the duration of peace. These three explanations highlight in turn the importance of issue resolution, the problem of enforcement, and the possible dangers of renegotiations.

2.1 Resolution of the Issues

The first explanation for the resumption of conflict focuses on the failure of the original peace settlement to resolve the underlying issues. While all conflict settlements require the mutual agreement of both sides, in some instances that agreement arises out of duress or is compelled on one side by the other. As a result, either the settlement does not directly address the political issues in dispute or the settlement decides these issues at the expense of the weaker side. While such agreements may settle the conflict, they are unlikely to resolve it as they have not eliminated, and in fact may have exacerbated, the underlying issues in dispute (Miall 1992; Hensel 1994). Since grievances remain, such exploitative or incomplete agreements provide a permissive condition for the resumption of hostilities. An agreement, in contrast, that actually resolves the dispute not only ends the violence but also eliminates the source of conflict by providing a win-win solution for both sides.

This argument suggests several hypotheses. Most obviously, agreements imposed on one side by the other are unlikely to last. Randle, for instance, argues that "achieving truly peaceful relations requires positive and eventually successful efforts to resolve active issues, voluntarily and consensually on the part of the parties; and this can be accomplished only by negotiations" (1974, 310). Negotiated settlements may also be more likely to last because they represent a compromise between the desires of both sides and thus have greater claims to fairness (Oren 1982). In contrast, punitive settlements like those dictated to the French in 1870 or to the Germans in 1918 contain the seeds of their own destruction by creating a desire for vengeance (Randle 1973; Holsti 1991; Hampson 1996). This argument thus suggests that the risks of recurrent conflict are higher if the peace settlement was imposed rather than negotiated.

Conditions that either encourage or enable the belligerents to focus on the issues in dispute and to craft agreements that address the grievances of both sides are also likely to encourage a durable peace. The involvement of mediators in the termination of conflict is often cited as one such factor (Miall 1992; Zartman 1995). The purpose of mediation is to help the belligerents come to a mutually acceptable settlement. Mediators do so by "persuading the parties to change their perceptions of the value of current situations and future outcomes" (Zartman 1995, 21) and by building trust and restoring confidence between the disputants (Hampson 1996, 8–9). Since mediators are involved in conflict termination only at the behest of the disputants, they cannot force a decision on either side. Even when a mediator goes beyond merely providing information and transmitting messages to actively proposing solutions and setting the agenda, her purpose ultimately is to facilitate, not to dictate, a compromise (Dixon 1996). Although mediators are not always successful, settlements that do arise out of mediation are likely to have directly addressed the issues in dispute and incorporated the needs of both sides. As a consequence, the risks of recurrent conflict are likely lower if a mediator intervened than if no such intervention occurred.

If the dispute concerns issues that are not fundamental to the belligerents' identity or existence, it may also be easier for them to formulate an agreement with which both parties are content. Disputes over highly salient issues, in contrast, are unlikely to be resolved since domestic or ideological constraints often prevent either party from permanently eschewing their desired objective, even if they are willing to accept temporary compromises when necessity dictates. Many argue that territorial issues are like this (Diehl and Goertz 1988; Vasquez 1993; Huth 1996). Territory is not only a valuable resource but is also frequently a symbol of the nation-state. Settlements over territory may only exacerbate existing grievances by creating displaced persons that serve as prominent reminders of past losses. This argument thus suggests that the risks of recurrent conflict are likely higher for territorial conflicts than for conflicts fought over other types of issues.

The ability to realize a decisive military victory is the final condition frequently posited to influence the belligerents' propensity to address the underlying issues. Zartman (1995), for instance, argues that the development of a "hurting stalemate" on the battlefield is a necessary, and perhaps sufficient, condition for conflict resolution. A hurting stalemate leads both sides to recognize not only the high cost but also the futility of a military solution to the conflict. Since neither side can attain its objectives on the battlefield, a political compromise becomes the only option. Hensel (1994), however, has made the exact opposite argument. He argues that the belligerents rarely address the underlying issues in the absence of a decisive military victory for one of the belligerents. Instead, if a military stalemate occurs, the fighting stops simply because the belligerents are exhausted, not because they have satisfactorily resolved the issues in dispute. This literature thus proposes two competing hypotheses about the likely effects of military stalemates on the risks of recurrent conflict. While Zartman's argument implies that the risks of recurrent conflict are likely lower in the presence of military stalemate, Hensel's reasoning suggests that military stalemates increase the risks of recurrent conflict.

Despite the plausibility of the issue resolution argument, two important theoretical weaknesses exist. First, issue resolution is logically a more complete explanation for the survival of peace than for its death. Although resolution of the issues may ensure the continuation of peace, failure to resolve

the issues clearly does not ensure the occurrence of conflict. The belligerents' successful termination of the first conflict indicates clearly that peace can be obtained even if a belligerent is dissatisfied with the settlement. Second, the argument rests on the somewhat idealist assumption that the belligerents can craft a settlement that permanently resolves the issues in dispute. If issues that were once resolved can become unresolved over time, then the distinction drawn between a settlement that merely terminates the conflict and one that actually resolves the issues in dispute is ephemeral at best.

2.2 Enforcement of the Settlement

A second explanation for the resumption of conflict highlights the well-known problem of enforcement under anarchy (Fearon 1998). The peace may fail and hostilities may resume if the original peace settlement failed to protect adequately against defection by one or both of the belligerents.

While both parties may agree that a particular settlement is preferred to the continuation of war, one or both belligerents may anticipate gains by failing to observe its terms or implement its conditions. While such unilateral defections may seem irrational since such defections can result in the resumption of the war, they may make sense if the belligerent thinks that his opponent may not detect or punish noncompliance. This perspective suggests that peace settlements are extremely fragile since they often resemble a prisoners' dilemma where a cooperative outcome is difficult, if not impossible, to maintain (Fortna 1998).

The potential vulnerability of peace agreements to unilateral defection suggests several testable hypotheses. First, agreements will be particularly vulnerable during implementation of the settlement terms. Once a settlement is reached, one or both sides must take actions to honor their side of the bargain. Such actions may include withdrawal or demobilization of forces, alteration of policies, exchange of territory, and payment of reparations. Temptation to defect is high during this stage because actually honoring the agreement requires substantial and costly action.

Once the belligerents have crossed the hurdle of implementation, however, honoring the agreement requires only the maintenance of the status quo. As time passes, the new status quo garners staying power as norms are created around it. As such norms develop, barriers to a renewal of the conflict are erected as the new status quo acts as both a focal point and constraint (Gelpi 1997a). Thus, as time passes, *ceteris paribus*, the risks of recurrent conflict decline.

Second, in contrast to the expectations derived from the issue resolution argument, this argument suggests that imposed settlements are likely to last longer than negotiated settlements (Maoz 1984; Licklider 1995). Since only one side makes promises of future behavior, imposed settlements are generally easier to enforce. While an imposed settlement may specify numerous conditions to which the losing side must conform, few if any provisions are demanded of the winner. In addition, the terms of an imposed settlement also frequently reduce the loser's ability to unilaterally defect by requiring that the loser disarm upon surrender (Calahan 1944; Ikle 1991). If the victor imposes a new regime on the defeated state, the opportunity for the loser to defect from the terms is virtually eliminated. Not only is the loser occupied by the victor, but the victor also has the opportunity to choose a government it considers "trustworthy" (Thomson, Meyer, and Briggs 1945). This argument thus suggests that the risks of recurrent conflict are less if the war ended in an imposed settlement, especially one that deposed the loser's government, rather than in a negotiated settlement.

Third, settlements are also more likely to endure if third parties provide explicit security guarantees (Randle 1974; Fortna 1998). Third parties can reduce the belligerents' incentives to break the agreement by increasing the chances that a violation will be detected and by increasing the expected costs of any violation. United Nations forces, for instance, are now often dispatched with the stated purpose of keeping the peace. Although the mandate of such forces is often limited, such peacekeeping forces can help to enforce an agreement by creating space between the two sides and by assisting the belligerents monitor the other side's compliance with the settlement terms (Bailey 1982; Hillen 1998). This argument thus suggests that the risks of recurrent conflict are likely lower if a third party provides security guarantees than if no such provisions are made.

A final factor that may increase the enforceability of an agreement and thus increase the probability that it will last is the existence of an explicit contract summarizing the conditions under which future relations will take place (Holsti 1991; Hampson 1996). Although a cease-fire or armistice can end the fighting, a peace treaty provides answers for such important questions as the disposition of territory, the handling of prisoners of war and displaced persons, and the resumption of future economic and legal relations between the belligerents. Some peace settlements also include provisions for the management of future disputes and explicit mechanisms to secure compliance. In the absence of a formal agreement, remaining ambiguities may encourage the belligerents to test the boundaries of the settlement (Randle 1973; Bailey 1982; Hampson 1996). This argument suggests that the risks of recurrent conflict are likely lower if a peace treaty exists to clarify the settlement than if no such comprehensive agreement is signed.

Although these hypotheses appear reasonable, it is important to note that each rests on the problematic assumption that some settlements are fatally flawed because they do not ensure compliance. If either belligerent expected that the other would not honor the agreement, it is improbable that they would accept the agreement in the first place (Walter 1997; Fearon 1998; Leeds 1998). Ironically, this implies that while the possibility of defection may undermine the belligerents' ability to reach an agreement in the first place, such problems provide a much weaker explanation for the resumption of conflict. Since the least enforceable agreements are never formed, the settlements that do arise are a biased sample of all possible agreements. Given this selection process, we should not expect that the relationship between the conditions of the original settlement and the risks of recurrent conflict should be as strong as often presumed.[2]

2.3 Incentives to Renegotiate

While the last argument highlighted the familiar problem of enforcement, this argument considers the bargaining problem (Morrow 1994; Fearon 1995, 1998). Conflict may recur as a consequence of a belligerent's attempt to renegotiate the distributional terms of the agreement. This argument assumes that the initial conflict terminated when the belligerents reached a mutually acceptable compromise regarding an appropriate distribution of the prize in dispute. When bargaining occurs in the shadow of force, the actual terms agreed to reflect the belligerents' mutual expectations about the consequences of continued fighting (Kecskemeti 1958; Wittman 1979; Pillar 1983; Goemans 1996; Werner 1998). This implies that as long as those expectations remain the same, the bargain struck between the belligerents should persist since neither side expects that a resumption of conflict would result in a better deal. This bargain becomes untenable, however, if those expectations change (Blainey 1988; Wagner 1993). If either belligerent anticipates that a new conflict would have a better outcome than the last, then an incentive to renegotiate the settlement exists. If the belligerents are unable to strike a new bargain, conflict may resume.

This argument suggests several testable hypotheses. First, a change in the distribution of power between the belligerents likely undermines the durability of peace by creating incentives to renegotiate the settlement. Such a change may convince one belligerent that a previous loss could be rectified or that a moderate victory could be improved (Randle 1974; Lieberman 1994, 1995). The bigger the change, the more likely the belligerents will expect that a new war would have a different outcome than the last. Since such changes in power are not always transparent and since there exist good reasons to conceal or misrepresent such changes, attempts to renegotiate the settlement without recourse to violence may frequently fail. This argument suggests that the risks of recurrent conflict increase if the belligerents' relative power changes.

Second, a change in the government of either belligerent also likely undermines the durability of peace by creating incentives to renegotiate a settlement and by impeding the belligerents' ability to do so peacefully (Randle 1974). On the one hand, such changes can bring to power a government far more adventuresome or bellicose than the last. A new, hawkish government may believe that it could obtain a better deal than did the last government either because it is more willing to accept risks or because it enjoys greater political support. Even a change that brings to power a more dovish regime may make a settlement untenable by convincing the other side that additional gains might now be realized. Rapid, unexpected political changes are likely the most problematic. Such changes may not only create incentives to renegotiate, but they may also reduce the chances of doing so peacefully by promoting enough uncertainty that the belligerents are unable to reach a new bargain. This argument thus suggests that the risks of recurrent conflict increase if either belligerent experiences a change in leadership, especially if that change is rapid or unexpected.

Finally, this argument suggests that conditions that facilitate the belligerents' ability to peacefully renegotiate any changes to the settlement will promote the durability of peace by relieving the need to make such changes violently. The expected costs of conflict are one such factor since they enlarge the range of agreements that each belligerent considers preferable to a state of war. Since the expectation of a costly conflict increases the parties' willingness to make concessions, negotiations of potentially costly disputes are more likely to be successful than are negotiations for which the costs of failing to reach agreement are expected to be low (Morrow 1986, 1989; Fearon 1995). As a consequence, if the belligerents expect that the costs of resuming a conflict are high, they will not only be more likely to maintain the original settlement but also to accept revisions to that settlement rather than resume the war. The expectation of high costs thereby mitigates the risks associated with renegotiations by facilitating their success. This argument thus suggests that the risks of recurrent conflict decrease as the expected costs of failing to reach a new bargain increase.

Like the first two arguments, this final explanation has limitations. Most important, while this argument explains well why a former belligerent may attempt to renegotiate a settlement, it does not explain fully why such attempts sometimes result in violence. The renegotiation argument, however, does avoid a significant problem that afflicts the first two explanations. It does not assume as the others do that the problem rests in flaws in the original settlement. Rather, it implies that an agreement that was originally acceptable became untenable as a consequence of changes subsequent to the settlement. As a result, it avoids the necessity of drawing the problematic conclusion that the belligerents initially accepted a flawed agreement. Despite this significant difference, it is important to note that these three arguments are not antithetical explanations for the recurrence of conflict. Problems associated with each may in fact all afflict a settlement at the same time. In the worst case scenario, the source of conflict may remain unresolved, unilateral incentives to cheat may exist, and incentives to renegotiate the bargain may arise.

3. Data Analysis Methods

I use a hazard model to evaluate the hypotheses derived from the issue resolution, enforcement, and renegotiation explanations of the duration of peace. Hazard analysis estimates a hazard rate which is defined as the instantaneous rate at which a subject experiences an event after duration t, given that the subject was at risk at time t. I use the Weibull specification of the hazard function to account for the effects of time on the duration of peace.[3] The Weibull specification estimates the relationship between the likelihood that an event will end at time t and the duration of the event at t, or the event's duration dependence, through a shape parameter p. The parameter p may be greater than, less than, or equal to 1 indicating positive, negative, or no duration

dependence. If the passage of time decreases the risk of recurrent conflict, then negative duration dependence exists and p will be less than 1. I incorporate time-varying covariates in this model by dividing each peace-dyad into one-year intervals. A division of one year is chosen because data are collected annually on capabilities and regime changes. This results in one record per peace-dyad per one-year period. Of course, only those variables that vary across time differ between records within a peace-dyad. Each one-year interval of peace contributes to the log-likelihood function calculated for the entire duration of peace of the dyad. I omit any year in which one member of a peace-dyad is not independent, since lack of independence precludes the dyad from experiencing a recurrent conflict. This most often affects states occupied by the victors after a decisive defeat in war.

4. Operationalization

4.1 Spatial and Temporal Domain

I am interested in the duration of peace between dyads formerly at war with each other. I identify dyads previously at war between 1816 and 1992 by the Correlates of War data set reported in Small and Singer (1982).[4] A dyad previously at war becomes a peace-dyad in my data set if the states were on opposing sides and if they actually engaged each other militarily in the war. This second criterion is most relevant for the two world wars where many states entered and exited a war before other states had joined the conflict and where some states were on opposing sides but never fought each other. States that did not participate in the war at the same time or never engaged each other are not included.

4.2 Duration of Peace and Censored Cases

I identify the duration of peace for a dyad previously at war in three ways. In the first instance, I adopt a stringent definition for peace: peace terminates if one of the belligerents either threatens or uses force against the other. This criterion defines peace as far more than the absence of war, since the continuation of peace requires the absence of any *threat* of war. In order to identify interstate disputes involving the threat or use of force, I utilize the updated Correlates of War Militarized Interstate Dispute (MID) data set (Jones, Bremer, and Singer 1996). This data set identifies each instance a state is involved in an interstate dispute involving the threat or use of force. The second definition of peace is less stringent: peace terminates only if one of the belligerents actually uses force against the other. I identify such high-intensity disputes with the hostility level indicator in the MID data set. This variable ranges from 1 to 5, where scores greater than 3 indicate the use of force. The final definition of peace is the least stringent of the three, since it requires not merely the use of force but the occurrence of another war between the belligerents. Disputes escalate to a condition of war if force is used that results in at least 1,000 battle deaths. Such disputes have a score of 5 on the hostility level variable in the MID data set.

Many dyads never experience a recurrent conflict, by any definition, during the period of observation. If a dyad did not experience a dispute prior to the end of 1992, the case is censored because the true duration of peace for the dyad is unobserved. In my data sets, censoring occurs in 51 percent of the cases where peace ends with the threat of force, 55 percent of the cases where peace ends with the use of force, and 80 percent of the cases where peace ends with a war. A hazard model incorporates information from such right-censored data in the overall likelihood function via the survivor function. The survivor function indicates the probability that the duration of some event is *at least* of length *t*. The overall likelihood function is then a combination of the survivor function for censored data and the cumulative probability distribution function that indicates the probability that an event will end by time *t* for uncensored data. Where the true duration of peace is observable, the duration of peace varies considerably. Duration varies between 1 day and 84 years where peace ends with the threat of force, between 1 day and 127 years where peace ends with the use of force, and between 1 month and 85 years where peace ends with war.

Given the very different thresholds of violence required to terminate peace in these three data sets, I anticipate that the results may differ between them. The onset of another war requires not only that the belligerents were dissatisfied with the prior settlement but also that they were willing to resort to force to effectuate a change that they could not achieve through negotiations. The threat or use of force, in contrast, indicates a much lower level of escalation. The threat or use of force often indicates only that at least one belligerent was dissatisfied with the settlement and not that either belligerent intended to fundamentally challenge it. As a result, I anticipate that the results will generally be stronger when a lower threshold of violence is used since each explanation focuses primarily on the belligerents' dissatisfaction with the settlement or on their incentives to renegotiate the agreement. With the possible exception of the renegotiation argument, each argument is less able to anticipate when dissatisfaction will actually result in a resumption of war.

4.3 Independent Variables

Issue Resolution. I create four dummy variables to indicate whether an *imposed settlement,* a *mediation attempt,* a *territorial issue,* and a *military stalemate* existed during the war or at its termination.[5] I code each dummy variable 1 if the condition obtained and 0 if it did not. The issue resolution argument anticipates that the risk of recurrent conflict is higher after an imposed settlement and a territorial war, lower if mediation occurred, and uncertain if the war ended in a military stalemate. With the exception of the variable for mediator involvement, data are drawn from the recently updated Correlates of War MID data set. Since information on mediation is not readily available, I relied on a variety of sources including Ralston (1929), Touval and Zartman (1985), Clodfelter (1992), and Dupuy and Dupuy (1996) as well as on case histories of particular wars. I define mediation as nonbinding intervention by a third party to assist two or more contending parties manage a conflict (Kleiboer 1996).

Enforcement. The shape parameter, p, in the hazard model indicates the impact of *time* on the risk of recurrent conflict. I use the imposed settlement variable discussed above to evaluate whether *imposed settlements* decrease the risk of recurrent conflict by securing the agreement. I also create a dummy variable that equals 1 only in the special case that the imposed settlement involved an *imposed regime change* on the defeated state and 0 if it did not. I create a dummy variable that equals 1 if a *third party guarantee* existed and 0 if it did not. A third party, either a nonbelligerent state or an international organization, provides a guarantee if it either places troops on the territory of one of the belligerents or threatens to intervene if war resumes.[6] This variable can vary within a peace-dyad since a third party can remove its troops or renounce its promise after a period of time. Finally, I create a dummy variable that equals 1 in the years that a *Peace Treaty* existed and 0 in the years that a cease-fire or armistice existed. The enforcement argument anticipates that the passage of time, the imposition of a settlement by the victor on the vanquished (especially the imposition of a new regime), the existence of a third-party guarantee, and the formation of a peace treaty will decrease the risk of recurrent conflict. For information on war endings and the intervention of third parties I relied on a variety of sources including Conwell-Evans (1929), Israel (1967), Parry (1969), Dupuy and Dupuy (1996), Clodfelter (1992), and Neack (1995).

Renegotiations. I measure *change in the relative power* of the belligerents as the difference in their growth rates in each year of observation.[7] I utilize the Correlates of War power index that includes a composite of the demographic, industrial, and military power of each state. To indicate *leadership changes*, I create two dummy variables. The first dummy variable equals 1 if either belligerent experienced a constitutional change in its executive in that year and 0 if neither did. The regular transfer of power after an election in a democracy is included as a constitutional leadership change. The second dummy variable equals 1 if either belligerent experienced an extra-constitutional change in the top government elite and/or in its effective control of the nation's power structure in that year and 0 if neither did. This data is available from Banks (1997) and is supplemented with information from Bueno de Mesquita and Siverson's leadership change data set, Lentz (1994), and Mackie and Rose (1991) as well as historical accounts of specific countries.

To measure the belligerents' *expected military costs* of recurrent conflict, I create two cost variables. I assume for both variables that experiences in the prior war drive expectations about the likely costs of any subsequent conflict. For the first variable, I measure the sum of the battle deaths as a proportion of its population suffered by each belligerent in the prior war. I take the natural log of this variable because the distribution of the data is very skewed. The second costs variable indicates the possibility that a recurrent conflict will diffuse to include other states. I create a dummy variable that equals 1 if the prior war was multilateral and 0 if it was bilateral. Data for expected costs are obtained from Small and Singer (1982). The renegotiation argument anticipates that changes in relative power and in leadership (especially political changes that are large and unexpected) increase the risk of recurrent conflict. Expectations of high costs, in contrast, reduce the risks by increasing the likelihood of successful renegotiation.

5. Results

Columns 1–3 of Table 1 display the results for each definition of peace termination. The coefficients estimate the impact of each variable on the hazard rate for peace. As a result, positive coefficients suggest that a one-unit increase in the variable of interest increases the hazard rate so that the peace ends more quickly. Conversely, negative coefficients imply that the hazard rate decreases as the variable of interest increases so that the peace endures for a longer time. Columns 4–7 of Table 1 present the substantive effects of the variables on the duration of peace. Columns 5–7 report the ratio between the hazard rate with one variable increased or decreased from its mean or mode value (as indicated in column 4) and the "base" hazard rate for which all the variables are held at their mean (continuous variables) or mode (dichotomous) values. If the variable has no substantive effect, the ratio will equal 1.0 because the "revised" hazard rate and the "base" hazard rate are the same. The deviation of the ratio from 1.0 thus indicates the variable's substantive effect.

5.1 Issue Resolution

The evidence provides only weak support for the variables derived from the issue resolution argument. Territory is the only variable that significantly affects the risk of recurrent conflict. The positive hazard coefficient of the territorial variable in all three data sets indicates that settlements of territorial issues are more likely to fail than are settlements of other issues. The variable is statistically significant, however, only when peace terminates with the threat or use of force. In these cases, the substantive effect of territory on the risk of recurrent conflict is relatively high, increasing the hazard rate by approximately 35 percent. When peace terminates with the onset of another war, territory is not statistically significant and its effect is much less, increasing the hazard rate by only 17 percent. These differences make sense given that the issue resolution argument provides only a permissive condition for the end of peace and does not provide a direct explanation for the decision to resume a conflict.

The remaining hypotheses of the issue resolution argument receive little empirical support. The imposed settlement variable is never statistically significant, and the coefficients in columns 2 and 3

Table 1 Estimates of Effects on Hazard Rate, Log Relative Hazard Form

	Threat	Force	War		Threat	Force	War
Peace Ends with:	1	2	3	4	5	6	7
Variable		β Z Scores		Change		Revised Hazard Rate/ Base Hazard Rate	
Imposed Settlement	0.002 (0.007)	−0.168 (−0.564)	−0.559 (−1.249)	1 to 0	0.99	1.09	1.49
Mediator	0.152 (0.643)	0.236 (1.014)	0.215 (0.639)	0 to 1	1.08	1.13	1.17
Territorial Issue	0.584** (2.959)	0.520** (2.491)	0.220 (0.715)	0 to 1	1.35	1.32	1.17
Stalemate	0.039 (0.119)	−0.074 (−0.224)	−0.980 (−1.584)	0 to 1	1.02	0.96	0.50
P	0.505** (−10.139)	0.535** (−8.388)	0.711** (−3.004)	—	—	—	—

(Continued)

Table 1 (Continued)

Peace Ends with:	Threat	Force	War	4	Threat	Force	War
	1	2	3		5	6	7
Variable	β Z Scores			Change	Revised Hazard Rate/ Base Hazard Rate		
Victor-Imposed Regime Change	−0.643* (−2.256)	−0.634* (−2.218)	−2.464** (−2.327)	0 to 1	0.72	0.72	0.17
Guarantor	1.028 (3.656)	0.859 (2.841)	0.764 (1.806)	0 to 1	1.69	1.57	1.72
Peace Treaty	0.148 (0.752)	−0.126 (−0.612)	0.374 (1.114)	0 to 1	1.08	0.94	1.30
Change in Relative Power	1.049** (3.223)	1.286** (4.251)	1.565** (4.429)	+ 1sd + 3sd to Max	1.08 1.25 2.48	1.10 1.34 3.67	1.17 1.60 8.29
Constitutional Leadership Chg.	−0.011 (−0.060)	−0.151 (−0.788)	−0.241 (−0.855)	0 to 1	1.00	0.92	0.84
Non-Constitutional Leadership Chg.	0.519* (1.662)	0.768** (2.595)	0.127 (0.263)	0 to 1	1.30	1.50	1.09
Military Costs	−0.090** (−3.174)	−0.088** (−3.112)	−0.109** (−4.082)	to Min −2sd to Max	1.86 1.25 0.83	1.86 1.27 0.82	2.75 1.55 0.71
Multilateral War	−0.573** (−3.220)	−0.497** (−2.482)	−0.285 (−0.795)	1 to 0	1.34	1.30	1.22
Constant	−2.926** (−7.955)	−3.101** (−7.275)	−5.158** (−7.534)	—	—	—	—
LL_0	−422.50	−391.65 −	−202.69				
LL_1	−388.06	−355.72 −	−170.18				
Chi 2	90.92**	69.69**	69.89**				
N Peace-Dyads	278	278	279				
N Peace-Failures	135	123	55				

**p < .01, *p < .05; one-tailed tests for all variables except Imposed Settlements and Stalemates are in the opposite direction than anticipated. The available evidence suggests that despite the alleged claims of greater fairness and inclusiveness, negotiated settlements are not superior to imposed settlements and may in fact be an inferior means of ensuring peace.[8]

The mediator variable is also never statistically significant and the coefficients are in the opposite direction than anticipated by the argument. Despite suggestions that mediators promote the resolution of conflicts and evidence that mediation can help to end ongoing disputes (Dixon 1996), mediation seems to have little effect on the likelihood that settlements last.[9]

Finally, the stalemate variable is never statistically significant, which suggests that stalemates do not consistently increase or decrease the prospects for resolution and a durable peace, contrary to both arguments presented. Although the results indicate that the military outcome of a war is unrelated to the duration of a subsequent peace settlement, it is possible that a military stalemate encourages conflict resolution under some conditions but discourages resolution under others. Failure to specify those conditions may mask the true relationship. Interestingly, the stalemate variable does approach statistical significance when peace terminates with the onset of another war. In this case, a military stalemate also appears to have a considerable impact on the hazard rate, reducing it by almost one-half. Since the military outcome does not consistently affect the risks of less-intense forms of recurrent conflict, however, it is unlikely that this result implies that military stalemates promote the resolution of the underlying issues as argued by Zartman (1995). More likely, the anticipation of another stalemate may occasionally deter the belligerents from escalating a subsequent crisis to the point of war.

5.2 Enforcement

The results in Table 1 also provide only mixed support for the variables emphasized by the enforcement argument. As anticipated by the argument, the shape parameter, p, is less than 1.0 and is statistically significant in all three data sets, suggesting the presence of negative duration dependence. All else being equal, the implementation stage of a settlement does seem to be a particularly dangerous time. Once the terms of the agreement are implemented, peace seems to become institutionalized and less likely to fail. This result, however, should be interpreted with some caution, at least for the first two data sets. When peace ends with the threat or the use of force, peace-dyads with high hazard rates likely experience a recurrent conflict fairly soon after the war and then leave the risk set. As Allison explains, "As time goes on, this selection process yields risk sets that contain individuals with predominantly low risks" (1984, 32). As a result, the hazard rate may only *appear* to decline over time as a result of differences across peace-dyads that are not incorporated in the model. This selection process, however, does not affect the third data set where peace terminates with the onset of another war because dyads that experience another war do re-enter the data set as soon as the war is over. Significantly, the 0.71 p value in column 3 indicates that peace-dyads do not merely appear to have a lower risk of failure over time, but that the risk of failure does in fact decline as time passes, albeit at a slower rate than suggested by the 0.505 and 0.535 p values in columns 1 and 2.

As discussed above, the imposed settlement variable is not statistically significant in any of the three data sets.[10] It is negative, however, in two of the three data sets as would be anticipated if imposed settlements are easier to enforce than are negotiated settlements. These results thus provide some support for earlier work that finds that imposed settlements consistently last longer than do negotiated settlements (Maoz 1984; Licklider 1995). The evidence strongly indicates, however, that an imposed settlement that deposes the loser's government does enhance the durability of peace. The variable is negative and statistically significant in each of the three data sets. Its substantive effect is also considerable. A victor-imposed regime change cuts the hazard of a threat or use of force to approximately two-thirds of its value without an imposed regime change and, even more substantively, cuts the hazard of another war to less than one-fifth of its original value. While merely imposing a settlement does not guarantee a secure peace, imposing a new regime does seem to contribute to a more stable postwar environment.

The remaining two hypotheses suggested by the enforcement argument, however, receive no support. In contrast to expectations, the evidence indicates that third-party guarantees increase, rather than decrease, the risk that a peace settlement fails. In all three data sets, the hazard coefficient is positive and statistically significant. This result supports recent work by Diehl, Reifschneider, and Hensel (1996) and Dixon (1996) that shows that third-party peace-keeping efforts do not consistently promote conflict management and prevention. This positive effect on the risks of recurrent conflict is quite substantial, increasing the hazard rate by as much as 72 percent when peace ends with the onset of war. On the one hand, this result may be spurious. Third parties may only offer guarantees in the cases where they perceive that the risk of recurrent conflict is very high. That they occasionally fail to preserve the peace between these dangerous dyads should not then indicate that guarantors actually contribute to postwar instability. On the other hand, intervention by third parties may in fact increase the risk of failure if their intervention frequently results in settlements that are vulnerable to renegotiations. Bailey (1982, 2), for instance, notes that the UN's initial response to any conflict is to demand that the belligerents stop fighting and frequently that they withdraw their forces back to their original positions. If fighting stops as a result of pressure from a third party, cease-fire lines may not reflect the belligerents' perceptions of what would have occurred if fighting had continued. If pressure from a third party encourages a political settlement based on precedent rather than perceptions of military advantage, the belligerents may anticipate that a better settlement could be obtained if fighting were to resume. Under such conditions, the bargain becomes untenable as soon as the attention of the third-party wavers.

Finally, there is no evidence that peace treaties reduce the risks of recurrent conflict. The peace treaty variable is not statistically significant and is in fact positive in two of the three data sets. Some caution in interpreting this result, however, is advisable. These results may not indicate the true impact of formal agreements if treaties are more likely to be signed under certain conditions. Goertz and Diehl (1992b), for instance, actually use the existence of a treaty as an indicator of illegitimacy, arguing that legitimate settlements do not require formal agreements. The positive correlation between peace treaties and imposed settlements suggests that such arguments likely have merit. If treaties are often signed when postwar relations are particularly hostile, then such conditions may mask any positive effects of explicitness. Since many such situational variables are included in the analysis, however, it is unlikely that subsequent inquiries will find that formal agreements are clearly superior to less explicit settlements.

5.3 Renegotiations

Although the evidence provides only mixed support for the issue resolution and enforcement arguments, the evidence indicates that conditions encouraging renegotiations are a key source of recurrent conflict. The results reveal that changes in relative power significantly increase postwar instability. The coefficient is statistically significant and positive in each of the three data sets. Changes in relative power have the greatest substantive effect in the third data set where peace ends with the onset of war. When the value of the power variable is set to one standard deviation above its mean value, the hazard rate increases by 17 percent. When the value of the power variable is raised to three standard deviations above its mean value, the hazard of another war increases by approximately 60 percent. Massive changes in relative power, admittedly rare events, can increase the hazard of another war by more than 800 percent. This sizeable effect on the recurrence of war suggests that changes in power not only encourage the belligerents to challenge the settlement, but may also hamper efforts to renegotiate that settlement peacefully, especially when the changes are dramatic.

The evidence also suggests that unexpected, fundamental changes in the government of either belligerent tend to increase the risks of recurrent conflict. The coefficient of the non-constitutional leadership change variable is positive in all three data sets, although it is statistically significant only when peace terminates with the threat or the use of force. In these cases, a nonconstitutional leadership change can increase the hazard of another conflict by as much as 50 percent. Its effect on the hazard rate is minimal when peace terminates with another war. The evidence does not indicate, however, that anticipated, marginal governmental changes increase the risks of recurrent conflict. The constitutional leadership change variable never approaches statistical significance and is in fact negative in all three data sets. These results suggest that political change likely affects the possibility of conflict through its effects on expectations and uncertainty. Small changes in government do not fundamentally alter expectations about the likely consequences of another conflict. Small governmental changes also do not significantly increase levels of uncertainty. As a result, only when a fundamental, unexpected leadership change occurs do belligerents become more likely to challenge a settlement and less likely to be able to do so without resorting to violence.

Finally, the evidence indicates that expected costs have a significant effect on the risks of recurrent conflict. The coefficients of both expected cost variables are consistently negative across all three data sets, suggesting that as the costs of the last war increase the risks of recurrent conflict decline. Both cost variables are also statistically significant in all instances except one; the variable indicating whether the prior war was multilateral or bilateral is not statistically significant when peace ends with the onset of another war. The substantive effect of expected costs on the risks of recurrent conflict is also considerable. Peace settlements of bilateral wars, for instance, are approximately 30 percent more likely to be challenged by the use of force than are settlements of multilateral wars. Settlements of wars with relatively low military costs are also particularly vulnerable. Decreasing the value of the military cost variable by two standard deviations below its mean value, for instance, increases the hazard of another war by 55 percent. These results support the findings of Fortna (1998) and differ from those presented by Hensel (1996b). The evidence thus indicates that high expected costs do seem to reduce the chances of recurrent conflict by facilitating successful renegotiations.

6. Discussion

The empirical results provide much more consistent support for the hypotheses generated from the renegotiation argument than for either the issue resolution or the enforcement arguments. On the one hand, it is possible that the weak or mixed results for the first two arguments are a consequence of limitations of my data and research design. As I note in my discussion of the results, the circumstances under which several variables obtain may mask their direct effects. Mediation, guarantors, and formal agreements do not occur in a vacuum but arise as a consequence of a series of decisions by the actors involved. The results may reflect, at least in part, the circumstances under which these conditions occur, rather than the direct effect of the variables. In addition, possible biases created by my case selection may affect the results. A case enters into the data set only when historical consensus concurs that a war did in fact end. If fighting stopped and then began again shortly thereafter, it is likely that history would not judge this as the end of the war. As a result, the war endings that are in my data set are those that endured at least some minimum length of time. This selection bias may explain in part the mixed support for the enforcement argument. Since this argument focuses primarily on the failure to implement agreements, many of the aborted endings that are not included in the data set may be explained by this argument.[11] A final problem is created by the possibility that some of the variables may have multiple effects. A peace treaty, for instance, may not only affect contract enforcement but may also indicate issue resolution. While I present the arguments made most frequently in the literature, additional research may suggest alternative interpretations.

Although the data and research design may provide a partial explanation, the pattern of results is not surprising given that of the three explanations the renegotiation argument provides the most direct explanation for why the belligerents might reverse a prior decision to settle a conflict by threatening or using force. The decision is reconsidered and renegotiations begun because the conditions that obtained at the time of the settlement have changed. The weak results, particularly for the issue resolution argument, are not surprising given that this argument provides only a weak permissive condition for recurrent conflict. In addition, any advantages a "good" settlement may have are only temporary if subsequent changes can alter the belligerents' perspective of that settlement.

7. Conclusions

The literature on enduring rivalries has demonstrated that a large proportion of conflict in the international system occurs between a fairly small number of states. This suggests that the maintenance of peace agreements between former belligerents and the successful renegotiation of those agreements is fundamental to the prevention of violent conflict in the international system. Initial evidence presented in this article provides interesting clues about the stability of peace agreements and the dangers of recurrent conflict.

I find little evidence that some settlements are prone to failure because they fail to resolve the issues in dispute. Negotiated settlements, mediated settlements, and settlements of stalemated wars are not more durable than other types of settlements. Settlements of territorial conflicts are also not more likely than other types of conflicts to be followed by another war. Territorial conflicts, however, do seem more vulnerable to a recurrence of low-intensity conflict than settlements of other types of issues.

I also find only mixed support for the enforcement argument. Consistent with this argument, peace does seem to be at greater risk soon after the conflict concludes than years later when the peace has become institutionalized. The imposition of a new regime on the defeated state also significantly reduces the risk of a subsequent conflict, although imposed settlements generally do not. However, in contrast to expectations, neither a treaty nor a guarantor makes settlements more durable. In fact, the evidence indicates that guarantors actually increase the risk of failure. Whether this result is spurious or authentic is unclear.

Finally, I find much stronger evidence for the renegotiation argument. As predicted by this argument, changes in the distribution of power consistently increase the risk that the peace settlement breaks down. Also violent leadership changes, if not constitutional leadership changes, increase the risk that peace fails. This effect, however, holds only for recurrent conflicts short of war. Finally, as the renegotiation argument suggests, settlements of costly wars are more likely to endure than settlements of less costly conflicts. If, as suggested by the evidence, settlements can become vulnerable as a consequence of political or military changes, then efforts to establish peace cannot end when the fighting stops but must instead continue as attempts to renegotiate the settlement occur.

Notes

Author's Note: This research was supported in part by the Emory University Research Committee and a grant from the National Science Foundation, SBR-9727888. I would like to thank Page Fortna, Ashley Leeds, Doug Lemke, Robin Moriarity, Eric Reinhardt, Dani Reiter, Chris Zorn, three anonymous reviewers, and the editor of *AJPS* for their helpful comments. I would also like to thank Robin Moriarity, Brian Lai, and Aimee Lipschutz for their valuable research assistance.

1. I use the term, "settlement," to refer to the agreement reached between the belligerents at the end of the war. The agreement may be explicitly stated in a peace treaty or implicitly understood by the parties to reflect cease-fire lines or the post-bellum status quo.

2. This critique, of course, does not imply that the enforcement problem is irrelevant to recurrent conflict. Rather, I argue only that the emphasis typically placed on features of the *original* settlement is likely misplaced. To the extent enforcement of the settlement becomes a problem, it is likely due to events that occurred *subsequent* to the settlement and that were not foreseen by the negotiators. Future work thus should focus on such events like technological shifts that can create incentives to defect that did not previously exist.

3. I utilize STATA 5.0 (command: stweib) to estimate the model.

4. My data differs from the Correlates of War data on two important cases. First, rather than code China and Japan as being involved in two wars consecutively, the Sino-Japanese War and World War II, I code this as one war ending on August 14, 1945. Second, rather than code North Vietnam and Cambodia as being involved in two wars consecutively, the Vietnam War and the Vietnamese-Cambodian War, I code this as one war ending on January 1, 1979. Historical evidence suggests that the belligerents did not perceive these as two different wars. See Chandler (1992) and Nguyen-vo (1992) on the Vietnam-Cambodian conflict and Lattimore (1990) and Ch'i (1982) on the Chinese-Japanese conflict.

5. The reference category for imposed settlements not only includes negotiated settlements but also wars ending without a settlement. Likewise, the reference category for military stalemates not only includes decisive outcomes but also wars ending in compromise outcomes. However, there are only four cases where the war ends without a settlement and only one case where the war ends in a compromise outcome. In order to ensure that these cases were not producing misleading results regarding the virtues of negotiated versus imposed settlements and stalemated versus decisive outcomes, I reversed the reference categories in both cases and re-estimated the model. These changes did not affect the results.

6. Note that this is an imperfect measure of third party guarantees. The measure indicates only the *attempt* to guarantee a contract via the deployment of troops or the issuance of a threat. The measure does not indicate whether such attempts were either credible or effectual. UN troops, for instance, may often be unable to significantly raise the costs of defection because of their limited mandate and resources.

7. The formula is $|((P_{i,t} - P_{i,t-1})/P_{i,t-1}) - ((P_{j,t} - P_{j,t-1})/P_{j,t-1})|$, where P represents the Power of the subscripted state, i or j, at time t or t−1. I also measured change in relative power as the percentage change in the belligerent's relative power: $|(P_{i,t}/P_{j,t}) - (P_{i,t-1}/P_{j,t-1})|/(P_{i,t-1}/P_{j,t-1})$. The correlation between this variable and the difference in the belligerents' growth rates is 0.74. The final results are consistent regardless of the measure of changes in power used.

8. How a war ends politically and how it ends militarily are highly correlated. The correlation between imposed settlements and military stalemates is between −0.76 and −0.83 depending on the data set. In order to ensure that the standard errors were not inflated by multicollinearity, I re-estimated the model omitting first the stalemate variable and then the imposed settlement variable. Neither variable became statistically significant when the other variable was omitted.

9. It is possible that the positive coefficient is spurious. If mediators are more likely to become involved in conflicts that are difficult to resolve, then it may appear that mediation enhances the risk that a settlement will fail. However, the opposite argument could also be made. It may be that mediators become involved in the "easy" cases since mediators require the consent of the belligerents. Mediators may also avoid the cases that they feel are hopeless.

10. There is obviously a high correlation between imposed settlements and an imposed regime change. In order to ensure that multicollinearity did not inflate the standard errors of the imposed settlement variable, I omitted the imposed regime change variable and re-estimated the model. The results do not change.

11. I do not mean to suggest that every cease-fire in a war should ultimately be included in the data set. Many if not most cease-fires are signed with the intent of using the period of calm to negotiate an agreement. The cease-fire breaks down when and if the belligerents do not reach a settlement. Ideally, one would include in the data set any stoppage in the fighting where the belligerents actually reached some kind of implicit or explicit settlement.

EDITORS' COMMENTARY

Major Contributions: Enforcing Settlements

Werner (1999) seeks to understand why some pairs of states maintain peaceful relations after fighting an interstate war (e.g., Iran-Iraq War of 1980–1988), while other dyads experience additional wars after their first war (e.g., India-Pakistan First Kashmir War of 1948–1949 followed by the Second Kashmir War of 1965).[1] This pattern of repeated conflicts is often called **recurrent conflict** and relates to the literature on **enduring rivalries** (Klein et al. 2006, Chapter 5, this volume), which seeks to explain why certain pairs of states experience repeated conflicts over time. Theoretically, Werner focuses on three factors that influence the durability of postwar peace: (1) resolution of the issues, (2) enforcement of the settlement, and (3) incentives to renegotiate. She finds the strongest empirical support for the third mechanism, incentives to renegotiate, showing that conditions that have changed since the termination of the previous war can give one or both parties incentives to return to the battlefield. Rapid changes in states' regimes or military capabilities can create conditions ripe for future conflicts.

The first theoretical factor, resolution of issues, considers what was being contested in the previous war. In the case of the First Kashmir War, for example, what was at stake was a disagreement between India and Pakistan about whether Kashmir would become part of one state or the other. In 1947, the ruler of Kashmir, Maharaja Hari Singh, advocated for the neutrality of Kashmir, a position that Pakistan did not accept; India stepped in militarily after Pakistan sent troops to the area. The Second Kashmir War was a continuation of the first war in the sense that the same unresolved issue was at the heart of the conflict. While Kashmir had come under Indian rule, Pakistan felt that many Kashmiri citizens were unhappy with this outcome. As we saw in the discussion of enduring rivalry, many dyads with repeated conflicts have ongoing territorial disputes such as Kashmir. Territorial issues are often highly salient to both sides (Hensel et al. 2008, Chapter 3, this volume), and the use of realpolitik tactics further increases the chances for future conflicts (Senese and Vasquez 2005, Chapter 7, this volume). Werner (1999) has a similar prediction that recurrent conflict is more likely following a war if the conflict involves a territorial dispute.

Werner (1999) also examines the way in which the previous war ended, which relates to her second mechanism, enforcement of the settlement. One possibility is for the winner of a war to force an **imposed settlement** on the losing state(s) after victory in war. In the Iraq War, for example, the United States forced Saddam Hussein from power, won the war, and installed a more democratic regime. On the other hand, war may end with a more balanced outcome in terms of a **military stalemate** or a **negotiated settlement**. The Second Kashmir War ended with a military stalemate that was negotiated between India and Pakistan. Werner discusses the theoretical debate in the literature regarding the expected effects of imposed settlements or decisive victories on the durability of peace. One side of the debate sees imposed settlements as problematic because they can fuel grievances in the losing state(s). Consider the punitive reparations that were imposed on Germany following World War I and the role that these costs may have played in the rise of Hitler's power and territorial ambitions leading to World War II. On the other side of the debate is a view that sees one-sided victories and imposed settlements as enhancing the durability of peace. One idea is that wars are often fought because two sides have disagreements about who would win a war should it occur and thus that a very decisive victory by one side makes the postwar relative capability distribution clear (Blainey 1988). A second idea is that the victor can impose its will on the losing side by replacing its leaders, moving the state closer to the victor's preferred foreign policy positions. In either case, the losing side is less likely to challenge the victor in the future because it projects a low chance for victory should war reemerge.

Werner (1999) also discusses the costs of the previous war in her third causal mechanism, incentives to renegotiate. If two states fight a very costly war, such as the Iran-Iraq War (more than one million casualties), they are unlikely to return to the battlefield quickly due to the effects of **war weariness**. Having just paid high costs for the previous war, the belligerents are unlikely to fight again quickly. Situations where there are both high costs and stalemates in terms of fighting are often called **hurting stalemates** (Zartman 1995), and they are believed to produce the impetus for durable peaceful agreements. In the Iran-Iraq War, both sides suffered many costs and the stalemate that continued during the fighting of the war resulted in both sides eventually accepting a United Nations brokered ceasefire agreement. In essence, both governments in the war suffered enough costs to view termination of the fighting as preferable to continuing the war effort. Werner notes that there are disagreements in the literature about the effects of stalemates on peace durability. This disagreement stems partly from combining the outcomes and the costs of war into a single concept. The idea of a hurting stalemate, for example, considers a situation of stalemate in the war alongside really high battlefield costs. Other scholars (Hensel 1994, 1999) separate these concepts by coding the outcome of a war (e.g., stalemate) as distinct from the costs of the war (e.g., battle deaths).

Quackenbush and Venteicher (2008) point to another issue in this literature (see also Senese and Quackenbush 2003). Werner's (1999) variable for imposed settlement focuses on the way in which the outcome of a war was obtained. This is distinct from the nature of the settlement on the ground in terms of whether it was one-sided (e.g., decisive) or more balanced (e.g., compromise or stalemate). Quackenbush and Venteicher find that the way in which the settlement is reached has a larger effect on the durability of peace than whether the military outcome is one-sided or more of a stalemate. When comparing all wars with decisive military outcomes, for example, they find that those settlements that were imposed have more durable peace following the war than those that were created through negotiated processes. In this regard, the manner in which the outcomes are achieved at the end of war may be more essential than whether there was a military stalemate or decisive victory on the battlefield.

Werner (1999) argues that imposed settlements lead to more durable periods of peace because they are easier to enforce, especially if third parties or mediators can help to provide security guarantees to the belligerents. Highly institutionalized peace treaties that contain provisions for monitoring, demilitarized zones, troop withdrawals, and peacekeeping are more successful at maintaining peace in the aftermath of interstate wars (Fortna 2004). Agreements that focus on mechanisms for reducing bargaining uncertainty, such as hotlines and third-party enforcement, are well positioned to maintain postwar peace (Mattes 2008). Dyads with more democratic members are also in a better position for enforcing the terms of a war settlement should conflict occur due to their ability to make more credible commitments to peace (Senese and Quackenbush 2003). While Werner does not find imposed settlements to have a statistically significant effect on peace durability in her analyses, she does show that imposed settlements preserve peace if they depose the loser's government. The postwar peace settlement between the United States and Iraq, for example, would be expected to be durable given the way in which the United States deposed the Iraqi leader.

Werner (1999) finds two factors to be extremely significant for predicting the durability of peace, both of which relate to the third theoretical mechanism for incentives to renegotiate peace agreements. The first factor is a change in the distribution of relative power between the belligerents that occurs sometime after the end of the previous war. Following the Iran-Iraq War, the two governments maintained fairly similar military capabilities in the late 1980s and 1990s. If one side's military capabilities were to change quickly, such as Iran acquiring nuclear weapons, this dynamic could alter the calculations of the Iranian government and increase its willingness to bargain more aggressively over diplomatic issues. The second factor is a change in the government of either belligerent state, especially if the change is quick and unexpected. If the new leader that comes to power is more hawkish than the previous government, this could increase the chances for renewed conflict. Empirically, Werner finds support for both of these mechanisms. The chances for renewed war can be as high as 60 to 800 times more likely when there are rapid shifts in dyadic relative military capabilities. Furthermore, nonconstitutional leadership changes can increase the likelihood of additional conflicts by 50 percent. She finds, though, that leadership changes that occur regularly in democratic regimes do not have an effect on the risks for renewed conflict; only those regime or leadership changes that are unexpected alter the long-run situation preserving dyadic peace. This is consistent with the broader view in the literature that democracies are able to make more credible long-term commitments in international relations (Lipson 2003).

While Werner's (1999) study focuses on the durability of peace following interstate wars, her ideas have influenced other scholarly work on conflict. Studies that expand the set of conflicts to include militarized interstate disputes (MIDs) also find that rapid changes in relative capabilities increase the likelihood of recurrent MIDs (Senese and Quackenbush 2003; Quackenbush and Venteicher 2008; Quackenbush 2010). Leeds (2003b) applies the logic of Werner's theory to her study of alliance reliability. She analyzes why states do not live up to the terms of their military alliance treaties (see also Leeds et al. 2000). Similar to Werner, she finds that allies are more likely to renege on their promises in wartime if they experienced rapid changes in power or if they experienced major regime changes since the time the alliance treaty was signed. Likewise Werner, Lo, Hashimoto, and Reiter (2008) find strong evidence that foreign-imposed regime changes have a strong, positive effect on the durability of postwar peace in a longer temporal sample (1914–2001). In short, all of these studies show that the key to preserving interstate peace is to minimize the forces that encourage belligerents to negotiate for a better deal in the future.

Methodological Notes: Duration Models

Werner (1999) is interested in analyzing the durability of postwar peace. She uses a **duration model** to identify factors that increase or decrease the chances for peace to continue or fail (e.g., a situation where states experience renewed warfare). Duration models are used by insurance companies to determine the risk factors that influence how long a person lives to help the companies set a fair price for insurance policies. For example, do people have shorter lives if they smoke a lot, fail to exercise, or eat too much? In these studies, we are seeking to determine the chances for a particular event (e.g., death), taking into account those individuals who are both alive and dead in our sample. Individuals who are alive are treated as **censored** observations because they have a chance of experiencing the event (death), but they have not yet experienced it. In Werner's study, the data are made up of all dyads that have experienced at least one interstate war. She requires the dyads to have engaged each other in the war directly and to have been participants in the war at the same time. This helps avoid cases in large multilateral wars where conflicts in one arena (e.g., the Western front in World War II) can be distinct from conflicts in other arenas (e.g., the Pacific front in World War II) both spatially and temporally. She then codes each dyad-year following a war to see if another war or MID event occurs. The dyad is censored in this context if it has not experienced another war (e.g., Iran-Iraq). She finds that 51 to 80 percent of her total dyads are right censored in this way, not experiencing an additional MID or war as of the end of the data set in 1992. Other dyads experience "failure" if they have another MID or war (e.g., India-Pakistan, Second Kashmir War). Werner considers peace failure at lower levels of hostility, including the threat or use of military force. She codes this information from the MID data set's hostility level scale, which ranges from low-level threats to full-scale war (1,000 or more battle deaths).

In a duration model, the **hazard rate** "gives the rate at which units fail (or durations end) by t given that the unit has survived until t. . . . This rate may be increasing such that the likelihood of failure increases as time passes, or the rate may be decreasing, such that the likelihood of failure decreases as time passes" (Box-Steffensmeier and Jones 2004, 14). Imagine that the chances for renewed war are really high in the first couple of years following a war but that the chances for war drop over time as peace endures. In this case, the **shape parameter** (p) would take on a value less than 1, indicating that the risk of failure would decline over time. In Werner's Table 1, we can see that her estimates of p range from 0.505 to 0.711, showing that the chances for renewed conflict are highest in the period just following an interstate war. Werner uses a particular duration model called the **Weibull** model, which accounts for the changing probability of event failure over time. The hazard rate for the Weibull model can be represented as follows (Box-Steffensmeier and Jones 2004, 25):

$$h(t) = \lambda p(\lambda t)^{p-1} \qquad t > 0, \lambda > 0, p > 0$$

Thus, when $p < 1$, the hazard rate is monotonically decreasing with time, implying that the chances for renewed conflict are dropping.

The estimated coefficients in the Weibull model tell us how each independent variable influences the hazard rate for peace. If a coefficient is positive (e.g., Territorial Issue, 0.584 in Model 1, Table 1), then the factor increases the hazard rate and makes it more likely that peace will fail (or more likely that the event of war or MID will occur). If a coefficient is negative (e.g., Victor-Imposed Regime Change, −0.643 in Model 1, Table 1), then as this variable increases, the chances for peace improve and the failure event is less likely to occur. Scholars often plot the hazard rates to show how the chances for failure change across different values of the variables (e.g., Territorial Issues vs. Non-territorial Issues).

The first set of variables (Imposed Settlement, Mediator, Territorial Issue, and Stalemate) is designed to capture the first causal mechanism of resolving the issues. We can see that only one factor in this group is statistically significant, Territorial Issue, and that a war over territory increases the chances for another MID (but not another war, Model 3). The second group of variables (Victor-Imposed Regime Change, Guarantor, and Peace Treaty) examines the enforcement factors, and Werner (1999) finds that Victor-Imposed Regime Change is the only factor that increases the durability of peace (in addition to time itself). The final group of variables (Change in Relative Power, Constitutional and Non-constitutional Leadership Change, Military Costs, and Multilateral War) captures the various incentives states may have to renegotiate the terms of the peace settlement of the previous war. She finds that all of these factors have significant effects on the durability of peace except constitutional leadership changes. Rapid regime changes and shifts in power threaten the durability of peace and increase the chances for recurrent conflicts. She finds, however, that these forces can be mitigated by high costs in the previous war; thus, states are less likely to engage in renewed violence if the previous war involved a lot of battle deaths or many states (e.g., a multilateral war).

The substantive effects of the variables are shown on the right-hand side of Table 1. She illustrates how the hazard rate changes as each independent variable is altered while holding the other variables at their mean or mode. If a variable has no effect on peace durability, it would have a hazard rate equal to 1. If the factor makes war more likely to occur, this will produce a hazard rate greater than 1. For example, territorial issues increase the hazard rate of a threat of force to 1.35, showing a 35 percent increase over the baseline hazard. If the factor makes conflict less likely to recur, then the hazard rate would be less than 1. For example, a Victor-Imposed Regime Change reduces the hazard rate to 0.17 for war, showing a 83 percent drop in the chances for war in these cases. The imposition of a new government following the Iraq War, for example, should have reduced the chances for future war between the United States and Iraq. Werner (1999) reports that the risk of war is more than 800 percent higher with the maximum change in relative capabilities. She gets this number in the row labeled "to Max" under the column labeled "War," where she shows the hazard rate to be equal to 8.29. This is an 800 percent higher rate than the baseline hazard (1).

Werner (1999) notes the possibility of **selection effects** in her analysis (Reed 2000, Chapter 11, this volume). For example, by selecting only pairs of states that have experienced at least one war, we are already analyzing a set of dangerous dyads. They might have certain characteristics that make the group different from the larger set of possible dyads. She finds that mediators have no effect on the chances for durable peace, but it could be that this particular sample is biased against mediators appearing effective if they choose to mediate in the "hard" cases where conflict is most likely to fail. One possible solution to this nonrandom selection process would be to use a duration-selection (DURSEL) model, which accounts for the processes that influence whether dyads experience war in the first place and then models the durability of peace in the second stage (Boehmke, Morey, and Shannon 2006).

Note

1. These examples are taken from version 4.0 of the Correlates of War Interstate War data set (http://www.correlatesofwar.org/COW2%20Data/WarData_NEW/WarList_NEW.html#New COW War List).

Questions

1. Werner finds that peace is quite durable when the victor of a war imposes a regime change, as the United States did in the Iraq War. What are some of the potential costs or problems that can arise with this general strategy?

2. In Table 1, what is the substantive effect of "Military Costs" and "Multilateral War" on the chances for a threat of force or the use of force? Hint: compare the revised hazard rates with the baseline hazard rate (1).

3. Why do you think territorial issues often increase the risks for threats or uses of military force but have no effect on the chances for another interstate war? Is this consistent with other studies we have examined?

Further Reading

Blainey, G. 1988. *The causes of war*. 3rd ed. New York: Free Press.

Box-Steffensmeier, J., and B. S. Jones. *Event history modeling: A guide for social scientists*. New York: Cambridge University Press.

Fortna, V. P. 2004. *Peace time: Cease-fire agreements and the durability of peace*. Princeton, NJ: Princeton University Press.

_____. 2008. *Does peacekeeping work? Shaping belligerents' choices after civil war.* Princeton, NJ: Princeton University Press.

Hensel, P. R. 1994. One thing leads to another: Recurrent militarized disputes in Latin America, 1816–1990. *Journal of Peace Research* 31 (3): 281–98.

_____. 1999. An evolutionary approach to the study of interstate rivalry. *Conflict Management and Peace Science* 17:175–206.

Quackenbush, S. L., and J. F. Venteicher. 2008. Settlements, outcomes, and the recurrence of conflict. *Journal of Peace Research* 45 (6): 723–42.

Senese, P. D., and S. L. Quackenbush. 2003. Sowing the seeds of conflict: The effect of dispute settlements on durations of peace. *Journal of Politics* 65 (3): 696–717.

Chapter 15

War and the Survival of Political Leaders

A Comparative Study of Regime Types and Political Accountability

Bruce Bueno de Mesquita and Randolph M. Siverson

O n 6 April 1982, six days after the Argentine invasion of the Falkland Islands, the New York Times correspondent in Buenos Aires gave this evaluation of the position of Argentine president Leopoldo Galtieri: "Political leaders here . . . agree he has greatly enhanced his political power and stature" by invading the Falkland Islands. At the same time Galtieri's political fortunes were in ascent, British prime minister Margaret Thatcher was being attacked by the British press for what was perceived as tardy reaction to the situation. In those few days, her political fortunes fell almost as much as those of Galtieri had risen. However, less than four months after Galtieri's stature had been ascendent he was out of office, while slightly more than a year after successfully repelling the Argentine forces, Thatcher and her party were returned to parliamentary power by a large majority.[1]

Of course, the Falkland's War was not a major conflict on the scale of, say, World War II or the Crimean War, and its value as a case from which we may generalize about the effects of war is limited. Nonetheless, it does serve as a striking example of the relationship investigated here—the effects of war on the tenure of political leaders and on their regimes among nations involved in war.

We first discuss the relationship between war performance and the subsequent fate of national political leaders. We then offer a model and seven related hypotheses accounting for what happens to leaders because of their war policies and describe our data and research design before reporting the results of our tests of four of the hypotheses. Because of presently existing data limitations, tests of three of the hypotheses must be postponed.

The research presented here represents an extension of our previous work on the political consequences of war in which we examined the effects of a state's initial position in a war (i.e., initiator or target), its outcome, and the costs of the war on the probability of the nonconstitutional overthrow of the state's political regime (Bueno de Mesquita, Siverson, and Woller 1992). Although the research reported here shares a broad set of interests in linkage politics with the earlier work (Rosenau 1969), it differs significantly in that the model used here is both more rigorous and more extensively specified than that used in the previous work. Moreover, because our present focus is on the survival time of the individual political leaders who were responsible for government policy at the point the state entered the war, our empirical tests are both more sensitive

Source: Bruce Bueno de Mesquita and Randolph M. Siverson, "War and the Survival of Political Leaders: A Comparative Study of Regime Types and Political Accountability," *American Political Science Review* 89, no. 4 (December 1995): 841–55. Copyright © 1995 American Political Science Association. Reprinted with the permission of Cambridge University Press.

than those in the previous paper and speak more clearly to neorealist explanations of international politics and war. As we shall show, our results obtain even when we control for the dependent variable in the previous study, nonconstitutional regime overthrow. Consequently, the results here capture the strong additional effects on leadership survival that follow from our model, above and beyond the effects shown in our earlier analysis.[2]

War Performance and the Fate of Leaders

Norpoth has observed that "war and economics have few rivals when it comes to making or breaking governments" (1987, 949). Our attention is directed at the "war" part of this assertion. Although many probably agree with the idea, the evidentiary base on which this assertion rests is both fairly narrow in terms of the range of time periods and governmental types studied and also, in some respects, ambiguous.[3] Data for the United States and the United Kingdom indicate that international crises and war can have an effect on the public's evaluation of political leaders. In the context of the United States, various studies (but most notably Brody 1992; Brody and Page 1975; Kernell 1978; Mueller 1973) have attempted to connect variations in presidential popularity to foreign policy events and participation in international crises. Although Mueller and Kernell portray presidents as generally benefiting from the short-run "rally" effects of foreign policy events, Brody's analysis draws out a more complex process in which a president may or may not enjoy a gain in popularity, depending upon a variety of factors, the most notable being the articulation of criticism by opinion leaders from either the media or the political opposition. However, there is little direct evidence bearing on the effect of war itself, although it is obviously worth pointing out that neither Truman nor Johnson was willing to hazard a try at reelection while engaged in wars that had divided the American public.

More broadly, with respect to the United Kingdom, Norpoth, using time-series methods, examined the impact of economic performance and the course of the Falkland's War on citizen ratings of Thatcher and the Conservative party between June 1979 and July 1985. He concluded that the independent effect of the Falkland's victory was worth between five and six additional percentage points to the vote for the Conservatives in the 1983 general election victory.[4]

All of these results are intriguing, but their domain is limited to the United States and Great Britain in the second half of the twentieth century. Absent is any broadly based theory or research on the general question of the effects of war involvement and war outcome on the political fortunes of the leaders who were responsible for them, even when those leaders presided over nondemocratic governments. This lacuna represents a major gap in our understanding of political accountability and the implications of such accountability for the selection of foreign policies.

Are political leaders and their regimes at greater hazard if they involve their nation in a war than if they do not? Is their political fortune affected by the outcome of the war? Does the effect, if any, fall equally across different types of political systems? Is the anticipation of domestic political punishment for failed policies an important element in shaping how nations relate to each other or, as suggested by neorealists, are these domestic factors minor features in the arena of international politics?

We contend that there are strong reasons to believe that a close connection exists between war and the domestic fate of governments and that the consequences of that connection can be and are anticipated by political leaders. Defeat in war almost always alters the loser's freedom of action by some measure, reducing the nation's autonomy over its own foreign policy or depriving the vanquished state of sovereignty over some portion of its citizens, territory, or national product (Morrow 1987). Compared to the often ambiguous outcomes of international conflicts and crises (see, e.g., Kernell 1978; Mueller 1973; Brody 1992) or even economic policy, evidence of loss from a war is much clearer to populations. Moreover, in nations without functional electoral systems, such evidence is far clearer to members of the elite, who themselves may have both the opportunity and motive for replacing leaders.

How can we assess the effects of war involvement and outcome on political leaders? One straightforward factor that would seem to be intimately tied to the welfare of any national leader is whether, given war participation, that leader's tenure in office is shortened or lengthened as a consequence of the state's performance in the war. Continuation in office may reasonably be seen as a reward, while removal from office (as opposed to natural death) in one way or another may be seen as punishment. We propose that leaders care about maintaining themselves in power—that they seek to maximize their reselection and, through the opportunities offered by continuing in power, to promote their own policy objectives. To achieve their objectives they must anticipate the effects their policies will have on the politically relevant domestic audience (Fearon 1994b). Consequently, we expect that they will ex ante try to avoid policies that they believe will ex post foreshorten their hold over the perquisites of political leadership.

The Problem of Political Survival

We begin with several assumptions. First, all politics is competitive. The issues over which—like the rules in which—the competition takes place differ across political units, and both the issues and the rules are subject to change. This portrait of politics is, of course, not remarkable.

Second, we assume that political leaders are intent on maintaining themselves in power and use the available tools of power and rules to accomplish this end. In like manner, we assume that all political leaders have opponents, most of whom are members of the leader's own political system, with their own ambitions for office. At the same time, leaders will often pursue policies that place them in opposition to those outside their own political system. Broadly speaking (and leaving natural causes aside), leaders then are subject to removal by their internal and external opposition or, quite possibly, some combination of the two. To be sure, we cannot dismiss instances in which a leader is removed by his or her "friends," who fear the costs to themselves of the leader remaining in power, but in this case, the friends have become opponents. Finally, given the opportunity, each opponent will be willing to pay a certain price to remove a leader.

Leaders, of course, recognize the existence of opposition and the designs of others on the office they hold. They consequently select policies to minimize the opportunities available to those seeking to remove them from power.

The ambition to remain in power, then, encourages political leaders to behave more responsibly than if they viewed the holding of office as a burden rather than as a prize (Fearon 1994; Morgan and Bickers 1992). Enhancing the welfare of relevant constituents (to the extent that it is successful) removes from the opposition the most salient issues that can be used against a leader.

Several studies have tried to express a generic theory of the domestic politics relevant to foreign policy decision making (G. Allison 1971; Bueno de Mesquita, Newman, and Rabushka 1985; Bueno de Mesquita and Stokman 1994; Putnam 1988; Richards et al. 1993; Tsebelis 1990). We share with several of these approaches an interest in building on Black's (1958) median voter theorem and incorporating the notion that leaders want to be reselected. We also share the notion that voting is just a special case of the articulation of power or political influence and control, so that Black's theorem, suitably adapted, is relevant to policy formation in authoritarian as well as democratic regimes (Bueno de Mesquita, Newman, and Rabushka 1985; Bueno de Mesquita and Stokman 1994). It is just that in authoritarian regimes the median voter or pivotal power is drawn from a much smaller set of constituents than is true in democracies. In authoritarian regimes, then, as in democratic governments, the clique of leaders who can count on support from a majority of the relevant resources—whether they be guns, dollars, or votes— can expect to win office and retain it. With this in mind, we suggest the following model of governmental accountability for decisions about war.

Suppose that each nation consists of a set of stakeholders interested in influencing foreign policy decisions. In a democracy, this set may include everyone or nearly everyone in the society. In more authoritarian regimes, the set probably includes a more limited array of organized or unorganized interests. The military, politically active religious groups, business interests, government bureaucrats, and the population at large are a small sampling of such possible stakeholders. Each of these various groups engages in strategic maneuvers to promote their particular foreign policy agenda at the expense of alternative approaches to international politics.

At the end of the process of bargaining and possible logrolling, competing and allied internal interests come to a decision. We assume that the decision is equivalent to the policy stance of the median "voter," in other words, the policy preference of the median powerholder at the end of the bargaining process. Of course, since voting per se often does not take place or is not meaningful (especially in authoritarian societies), this median position is that policy supported by the individual or group that can count on the ability to mobilize more than half of the sum of all stakeholders' utilized power on behalf of its agenda against any possible challenge. The median stakeholder is the pivot around whom a winning coalition forms.

For the purposes of the present analysis, we do not elaborate a complete theory of domestic political decision making and its relationship to foreign policy. Instead, we describe a simplified model of implications that follow from such theories of domestic interest group competition. By keeping the model simple we naturally raise the prospects of having fairly robust results, and focus on broad generalizations as opposed to detailed nuances of the role of foreign policy and the retention of the leader in power. Additionally, because our model is rather general it cannot rule out some alternative explanations of the phenomena we discuss. That said, it is

important to consider these caveats in the context of a model that is an integrated whole and generates a number of significant, testable hypotheses.

In describing these implications we begin by assuming that preferences across policy issues are single-peaked. This means that for each stakeholder the utility for any given resolution of an issue declines monotonically with the Euclidean distance from that decision maker's most preferred choice (i.e., the stakeholder's ideal point). We further assume that all utility functions are quadratic, reflecting the notion of declining marginal utility. This latter assumption is for ease of computation and does not materially affect our results.

Although many problems in international affairs and foreign policy are quite complex, involving the possibility of trade-offs and linkages across policy issues, we assume that this is not true of the most fundamental questions. For problems involving the risk of war, we assume that issues collapse to a single policy dimension having to do with the overall contribution of the putative policy to the welfare of the leadership's backers and opponents. This is broadly consistent with the realist notion that treats the state as a unitary actor.

Our view, however, differs from the realist approach in that the selection of policy options and the accompanying demands and actions taken in the international arena are not dictated by external, structural considerations. Rather, the choice of goals and actions is given shape by the domestic agenda of the leadership, as well as by the feasibility constraints of the external environment. Prudent leaders make choices that they think will help them retain power: they choose in such a way that they do not precipitate an internal overthrow of their authority. Consequently, their foreign policy goals may be seen as endogenous to their domestic political concerns rather than just to the international system's structure.

Because we have assumed single-peaked preferences and unidimensional issues on questions related to the threats of warfare, and because we propose that the coalition controlling a majority of political influence within a nation is expected to get its way, Black's (1958) median voter theorem can be applied. This means that the policy objective of the interested party located at the median of the distribution of power on the policy in question is the objective expected to prevail internally. The median power occupies the position that can, in head-to-head competition with any other proposed policy, muster a majority coalition. As such, it is the policy stance that maximizes internal political security, the position least susceptible to internal defeat.

With the median voter theorem in mind, we assume that on questions that involve the risk of war all nations can be summarized by examining the characteristics of three critical stakeholders:

1. the stakeholder or interested party, denoted as V, who controls the median power position;

2. the incumbent leader, called I; and

3. a challenger, called C, who wishes to gain control over the government's foreign policy.

So, with the state denoted as S we can say $\{V, I, C\} \in S$. V, of course, is itself an element in the preference distribution of all the stakeholders or interested parties in S. We assume further that policy objectives over which war is waged fall along a single policy continuum, denoted as R, with $\{X_C^*, X_C, X_V^*, X_I, X_I^*\} \in$ R. (Terms with a superscript $*$ are ideal points and belong to the actor named by the subscript. Terms without superscripts are the publicly taken policy positions of the subscripted actor.) The term X_C^* represents the ideal point, or most preferred foreign policy, of the challenger for power, and X_C expresses the actual policy position openly supported by the challenger in its attempt to woo the median stakeholder V away from supporting I. The other terms have analogous interpretations.

Incumbents can have an advantage over challengers in our model because they can earn political credit for their past performance or demonstration of reliability if they pursue foreign policies that satisfy V. This means that V can gain utility from the past performance of the incumbent, which is broadly consistent with the idea of retrospective voting (Fiorina 1981). Incumbents with bad records are more likely to be turned out; incumbents with good records from V's perspective have an edge in the ongoing campaign to remain in power. But incumbents also have a disadvantage because V bears the costs associated with the foreign policies pursued by the incumbent and V is not reluctant to pass judgment on I in response to these costs. I can accumulate negative credits as well as positive ones. Costs occur as a result of actions in wartime whether the war ultimately proves to be successful or not, as well as potentially arising as a consequence of policies by I that alienate V.

Let R denote the accumulated costs or benefits associated with the past performance of political leaders. We assume that the more constituents who have to be satisfied by a political leader, the smaller R is—and indeed that as the number of constituents rises so does the likelihood that $R < 0$. This is consistent with the notion of the coalition of minorities effect identified by Mueller (1973). The longer a leader has been in power, the greater the opportunity the leader has to alienate part of his or her coalition of supporters, gradually eroding the chances of holding onto support from the median voter (Powell and Whitten 1993; Rose and Mackie 1983). In authoritarian regimes, where fewer constituencies have to be satisfied, leaders are better able to fulfill the wants of their crucial backers. Consequently, $R > 0$ is probably true for authoritarian leaders, while $R < 0$ is more likely to be true for leaders in democratic states. In any event, whether positive or negative, it is likely that R for democratic leaders is smaller than R for authoritarian leaders. R_t, is the benefits or costs from the leader's performance on the job at a specific time in the past (denoted by the index t), with $t = 0$ being the present.

If a current wartime policy is implemented and succeeds (i.e., the nation in question wins the war), we assume that the reliability benefits R are increased by $R_0 > 0$ but that if the policy fails, then $R_0 \leq 0$. R_0 is, then, one of the critical elements at stake for an incumbent engaged in a war. R_t decays over time so that recent demonstrations of reliability are more valuable to V (and therefore to I) than are demonstrations in the more remote past. Similarly, recent policy failures are more costly than old ones that have been survived. We denote this decay effect by discounting earlier demonstrations of competence or incompetence by d_t, with $0 < d < 1$, so that

$$R = R_0 + \sum_{t=n}^{1} d^t R_t.$$

The benefits of competence ($R > 0$) or the costs of incompetence ($R < 0$) are realized by I only so long as he or she remains in power. Consequently, when an incumbent is replaced, R returns to zero for the former incumbent. Since the challenger has not yet had an opportunity to demonstrate competence or incompetence, V expects $R = 0$ when the challenger first comes to power.

Incumbents, of course, serve only for a finite (though usually indeterminate) time. We denote this by specifying that R accumulates over the interval from the time when the leader first comes to power, $t = n$, to the present moment, $t = 0$. The leader's tenure in office, then, at the time a war starts, is the interval from $t = n$ to $t = 0$ (i.e., the moment the war starts). Assuming that R_t is a constant that decays in value at the rate d^t, then R is a logarithmic function of tenure in office that reflects the marginally declining impact of past successes or past failures on the current evaluation of I's job performance.

In addition to the costs or benefits associated with the leader's overall performance, we assume that there are direct transaction costs associated specifically with waging war. Let L denote the transaction costs or losses borne by the society (i.e., summarized by V) as a result of the implementation of wartime actions by I. These costs represent a burden of war that leaders must overcome if they are to be kept in office.

The fundamental dynamic in our conceptualization of domestic politics revolves around the expectation that incumbents wish to retain power and challengers wish to replace incumbents. This means that actor I wishes to remain more appealing to V than is C. However, I and C not only want power, they also have policy objectives of their own. That is why we have defined their ideal points as well as their public stance on the policy questions of the day. Thus our candidates for leadership may be pulled in two directions: to do what V wants and to do what they

Table 1   Utilities for the Incumbent (I), Challenger (C) and Median Voter (V) under Alternative War and Outcome Scenarios

Outcome Scenarios	Utilities		
	Incumbent	**Challenger**	**Median "Voter"**
Wins & retained	$-(XI - XI^*)2$ $+ R$	$-(Xc^* - XI)2$	$-(Xv^* - XI)2$ $+R - L$
Wins & replaced	$-(Xc - XI^*)2$	$-(Xc^* - Xc)2$	$-(Xv^* - Xc)2$
Lost & retained	$-(XI - XI^*)2$	$-(Xc^* - XI)2$	$-\left(X_v^* - X_I\right)^2$ $+\sum_{t=n}^{1} d^t R_t - L$
Lost & replaced	$-(Xc - XI^*)2$	$-(Xc^* - Xc)2$	$-(Xv^* - Xc)2$

themselves want on foreign policy questions. They are not merely motivated by a desire for power and may be quite principled in terms of their policy interests. But when torn between personal preferences and constituent expectations, the successful political leader is likely to be someone who recognizes that politics is the art of the possible.

The political costs and benefits of alternative choices that are reflected by these assumptions are summarized as a set of utility values. Table 1 displays the utilities for I, C, and V under the four scenarios of interest to us:

1. I is expected to win the war it wages and I is retained in power;

2. I is expected to win but is removed from power anyway, being replaced by C;

3. I is expected to lose the war and is retained nevertheless; and

4. I is expected to lose and is replaced.

The incumbent, I, can be sure of retaining power only so long as V believes it is better off with I than with C. I remains the incumbent if V's utility for retaining I is greater than V's utility for replacing I with C. With P defined as V's subjective probability estimate that I will win the war it is involved in, V will retain I in power if

$$P[-\left(X_V^* - X_I\right)^2 + R - L] + (1-P)[-\left(X_V^* - X_I\right)^2$$
$$+ \sum_{t=n}^{1} d^t R_t - L] > -\left(X_V^* - X_C\right)^2 \tag{1}$$

Several inferences can be drawn from expression 1. Solving for PR_0, which reflects the expected political stakes for both I and V from the war, we see that retention in office requires that

$$PR_0 > \left(X_I + X_C - 2X_V^*\right)\left(X_I - X_C\right) - \sum_{t=n}^{1} d^t R_t + L \tag{2}$$

The incumbent has control over several factors in expression 2. These include selecting events for

which the probability of success is believed to be high and picking policies that are not so objectionable to V that the policies become an encumbrance to I's retention of power. I naturally tries to pick X_I to ensure that the inequality in expression 2 is satisfied, while C, of course, picks its policy position to try and thwart I. Yet C and I are also constrained in selecting a policy because neither I nor C will wander so far from their respective ideal points that gaining or holding power is a pyrrhic victory.

It is evident from expression 2 that C has little incentive to locate itself at the same policy position as I. Being Tweedledum to I's Tweedledee (Downs 1957) simply means that I will be retained if

$$PR_0 > L - \sum_{t=n}^{1} d^t R_t \tag{3}$$

It is evident from expression 3 that if $R > 0$, then, barring costs expected to be large enough to offset all of I's reliability credits, C has no chance of removing I no matter how poor I's chances of bringing the country to a victorious outcome in the war. Even if $P = 0$ (i.e., defeat is expected to be a sure thing), the expected costs must outweigh the credit for past performance accumulated by V in order for C to be chosen over I. Of course, if R_t is negative, C has an easier time removing I. Even in that case, however, rather than be Tweedledum, C's best hope of gaining power is to support a position sufficiently close to X_v^*. Even in the worst case for I, when C adopts X_v^*, I can retain power provided that

$$PR_0 + \sum_{t=n}^{1} d^t R_t - L > \left(X_I - X_V^*\right)^2 \tag{4}$$

Clearly we see in expression 4 that I is constrained to stay relatively close to V's ideal point if C adopts that position. I can drift away only to the extent that its past reliability and the expected reliability gains from the present war are large enough to offset its policy difference and the expected transaction costs from the war. If its past performance has accumulated costs rather than benefits, then, of course, I

will have a more difficult time holding on to power, having to rely exclusively on the benefits derived from the current war.

Is it possible for I to prefer that C gain power rather than choose a policy stance X_I that is more distasteful to I than losing power to C? In order for I to prefer a government led by C over a government led by I, it must be true that

$$-\left(X_I - X_I^*\right)^2 + R < -\left(X_C - X_I^*\right)^2 \qquad (5)$$

if I expects to win the war, or

$$-\left(X_I - X_I^*\right)^2 < -\left(X_C - X_I^*\right)^2 \qquad (6)$$

if I expects to lose the war.

Expressions 5 and 6 suggest some consequential differences between democracies and authoritarian states, given our assumption that R for democracies is smaller than R for authoritarian states (including the prospect that $R < 0$ is more likely for democratic leaders than authoritarian leaders). Expression 5 implies that democratic leaders are more likely to leave office voluntarily than are authoritarian rulers. If $R > 0$, then it should be obvious that I would never pick X_I such that X_C is preferred by I to its own position. Consequently, I cannot prefer a government led by C to a government led by itself so long as $R > 0$ in our model, which presumably includes all authoritarian leaders and some democratic leaders. Authoritarian leaders can be expected to seek to hold office for life, never stepping aside on principled grounds. Some democratic leaders can be expected to behave quite differently, even choosing to lose office rather than pursue objectionable policies.

I can, of course, choose a different policy position than C, but the choice will be in favor of a policy closer to I's ideal point and never farther away. Then, the range of policy choices that I can make is constrained. C will do best, in terms of maximizing its chances of being selected to replace I, by picking V's ideal point as its own policy position (even

though that is not C's ideal point), as we have already mentioned. I, then, can drift away from the median stakeholder's policy preference up to the limit of the value of the reliability benefits that I generates for V, less whatever costs are associated with I's war policy. If I's accumulated R values are negative, then I cannot drift away from V's ideal point, presuming that it is known to I. Avoiding war must thus be inherently better for I than waging war unless $R_0 > L.$[5]

It is evident, then, that X_I is endogenous, being chosen strategically (as is X_C) to facilitate I's retention of power and to maximize I's expected utility. X_C, naturally, is chosen by C to try to reverse the above inequalities in an attempt to induce V to prefer C to I. The threat of being replaced by C constrains I not to wander too far from X_v^*, while I's own policy concerns constrain the incumbent not to drift too far from its own ideal point. Leaders who want to retain power can rarely afford to hold an uncompromising commitment to the pursuit of the policies represented by their ideal point. Such "true believers" are unlikely to survive politically unless they happen to have the good fortune that their ideal point is the same as X_v^*.

In the scheme we have proposed, I can have a distinct advantage over C and can also suffer a distinct disadvantage from its actions. The advantage stems from its reputation for reliability if that is positive. In expression 2, the authoritarian incumbent's past record of performance decreases the size of the righthand side of the inequality, making it easier to stay in power even if the war is lost. The opposite is true for democratic leaders for whom $R < 0$. And the bigger the prospective stakes in the war (R_0) for I, the more likely it is that the incumbent will fight even with a small chance of success. These implications of our simple model give us the following initial hypotheses:

Hypothesis 1. *The odds in favor of political survival increase as a function of the logarithm of the time that the leader has already been in office for* *authoritarian leaders, while the odds of survival increase less—or even decrease—for democratic leaders.*

Hypothesis 2. *The greater the prospective benefits of the war (PR_0), the more likely the incumbent will wage the war rather than resolve its differences through other means. Conversely, the smaller those prospective benefits, the less likely the retention threshold will be passed and, therefore, the less likely the incumbent will risk its position by fighting and the more likely the incumbent will be deposed if it does take the risk of fighting.*

Both of these hypotheses are testable. However, only the first one is central to the concerns addressed here. Consequently, we test hypothesis 1 and defer a test of hypothesis 2 to a future study focused on war behavior rather than leadership retention.

The incumbent must bear the burden for the failure of diplomacy and for the lost lives and property that are bound to result from war (L). This term, of course, makes it harder to keep power. The gains of reputation, if any, may be offset by the expected losses in the war. This suggests that the selection of wars to fight is itself endogenous. We have already seen that PR_0 influences the likelihood that a leader will be retained in office. The size of this term is within the control of political leaders to the extent that leaders can choose to resolve disputes short of war if the value of PR_0 is expected to be too small to lead to retention. Thus we have already seen one way in which war selection is endogenous to domestic political circumstances. Now we see that the endogeneity also extends to the impact that war costs are expected to have on domestic politics.

A leader can reduce the size of L by offering concessions to a foreign adversary in the hope of precluding a war so costly that it threatens to drive one from power. Likewise, one can eschew initiating a war expected to culminate in such high costs. Consequently, the wars we observe in nature are

presumably a biased sample of the prospective wars that were considered and rejected. It follows then that the observed wars are those expected to have low enough costs that they would not jeopardize the leader's retention of power. This suggests two additional hypotheses:

Hypothesis 3. *All else being equal, the greater the expected costs in war (L), the more likely the incumbent will be replaced by the domestic political process.*

Hypothesis 4. *All else being equal, the greater the expected costs from a prospective war, the higher the probability that the leader will not engage in war but rather resolve international differences through other means, such as negotiations.*

Hypotheses 3 and 4, like 1 and 2, are testable. Hypothesis 3, like hypothesis 1, is focused on our central concern with the accountability of political leaders. Consequently, it will be tested here. Hypothesis 4, like hypothesis 2, is more oriented toward an investigation of dispute escalation than toward an evaluation of the survival of political leaders. We defer to a later study any tests of hypothesis 4.

The reliability variable in our model reveals several important features of incumbency. The longer a leader has been in power prior to the onset of a war, the greater the opportunity the leader has had to amass credit for reliability or to lose supporters as part of the coalition-of-minorities effect. The latter effect is more likely to arise the more dependent the leader is on multiple constituencies, while the former effect is more likely to be realized by authoritarian leaders who must satisfy more limited constituencies. Thus, all else being equal, the longer an authoritarian incumbent has been in power, the more likely it should be that the incumbent will be retained in office once a war begins, even if the war is lost. The beneficial effects of a long prewar incumbency should be significantly muted (and can even be reversed) in democracies relative to authoritarian leaders. This can be seen more clearly from expressions 7 and 8:

$$R - L > \left(X_I - X_C \right) \left(X_I + X_C - 2X_V \right) \quad (7)$$

$$\sum_{t=n}^{1} d^t R_t - L > \left(X_I - X_C \right) \left(X_I + X_C - 2X_V \right) \quad (8)$$

Expression 7 denotes the conditions under which V prefers to retain I if I wins the war while expression 8 denotes the conditions for retaining I when I loses the war. Of course the left side of expression 7 is strictly larger than the left side of expression 8, because $R_0 > 0$ in a victorious war, so that the incumbency advantage is, not surprisingly, greater if one is victorious. This suggests a fifth hypothesis:

Hypothesis 5. *Tenure in office has a greater beneficial impact on the political survival of incumbents expected to win their wars than on incumbents expected to lose.*

From expression 2, it is evident that the longer an authoritarian I (or a democratic I not suffering from the coalition of minorities effect) has been in power (and therefore the greater the accumulated reliability benefits) the smaller P can be and still satisfy the requirements for retention in office. In a comparative static sense this means that the longer the tenure of an authoritarian leader, the easier it is for that leader to believe that he or she can survive the political consequences of losing a war. Consequently, authoritarian "old-timers" in office can more readily afford to pursue foreign policies that represent a gamble, with a high risk of failure. Newcomers to power, conversely, cannot afford such boldness and are thus more likely to avoid high-risk gambles in foreign policy. All else being equal, then, long-surviving nondemocratic leaders should be more likely to wage losing wars (or wars in general) than incumbents who are newer to their positions. We state this as our sixth hypothesis:

Hypothesis 6. *The longer an authoritarian leader has been in power, the higher the probability that the leader will risk waging a war, including waging a war that ultimately is lost.*

Hypothesis 6 suggests that long-standing authoritarian leaders engage in riskier wars not because of any inherent flaw in their character but because of an inherent feature of the political conditions that keep them in power. Their country's political institutions facilitate their dangerous behavior. It is also evident that as the authoritarian incumbent's tenure in office grows longer, I can afford to drift away from policies preferred by V because of the cushion provided by its reputation for reliability among its limited constituency. Paradoxically, those who have been reliable to their key followers in the past can afford to be less reliable to them in the future. Recall that in our model V is prepared to retain I in power even if C's policies are closer to those desired by V than are I's, provided $R > 0$. V selects its leaders in terms of an evaluation of overall welfare not just on the basis of current policy stances. This provides I with the opportunity to shift its policies closer to its own ideal point and away from V's preferences as I's reputation for reliability grows with its tenure in office. This suggests our final hypothesis:

Hypothesis 7. *The longer an authoritarian leader has been in power, the more likely he or she is to pursue personal policy preferences rather than the policies of V.*

This final hypothesis, though interesting and a clear implication of our model, is, like hypotheses 2 and 4, reserved for a future study because it is not central to our concern with leadership survival.

Hypotheses 1, 3, 5, and 6 form the core of our present investigation. Each of these four hypotheses refers to a feature of leadership retention that links war behavior and regime type to domestic political considerations rather than to the high politics of a realist or structuralist view of international affairs. These hypotheses represent summary statements of more detailed implications of the basic model of war choices we have delineated. Some are intuitive, but some are surprising.

In particular, we believe it is surprising that longevity in office makes leaders, particularly authoritarian leaders, more prone to wage wars, especially wars they can expect to lose. We also think it is surprising that longevity facilitates political survival for authoritarian leaders more than for democratic elites, especially in light of the proposition that it also facilitates the waging of losing wars. But even the intuitively more apparent hypotheses are important to test. We should always bear in mind that intuition can be fickle or wrong. Simply because something *seems* to make sense does not mean that it reflects how the world actually works. Also, we should feel greater confidence in counter-intuitive propositions if they are part of a theoretical structure that yields many intuitively anticipated results. Finally, even when ideas seem intuitive, it is useful to pin them down within a logical structure so that we can see more clearly how they relate to other concepts and exactly how they relate to each other.

The Data

Hypotheses 1, 3, and 5 link the survival of political leaders after the onset of war to their prior tenure in office, expected costs, regime type, and the expected outcome respectively. To test these hypotheses, we require data that permit us to relate the length of time a policymaker is able to remain in power after war onset, the outcome of the war, the costs of the war, the prewar tenure of the leader, the openness of the political regime, and the expectations that those around the leader had with respect to that leader's continued ability to rule. Most of the data are fairly straightforward, and some of them are widely available.

The states participating in war between 1816 and 1980 are given in the well-known collection of the Correlates of War Project reported in Small and Singer's (1982) *Resort to Arms*. The data set not only reports on national involvement in all international wars between 1816 and 1980 with at least a

thousand battle-related fatalities but also identifies the states that were the eventual winners and losers. From this list we exclude several groups of states. First, we exclude states that participated in wars beginning after 1975 because of uncertainty with respect to the casualty data (the need for which we shall explain). Second, because we are interested in the domestic political aspects of war involvement, we also exclude those cases in which the relevant political leader is deposed by the direct use of force by an external party.[6] For example, the cases of the Netherlands and Belgium in 1940 are excluded from the data, as is the case of Germany in 1945. However, the case of Premier Tojo, who led Japan into war in 1941, is included in the data set because he was driven from office well before the end of the war and the United States occupation. Finally, although we originally intended to include cases where the outcome was sufficiently unclear that it could be called a tie, all of these were associated with the Korean War. Rather than rest our analysis of this effect on only one war, we do not consider these cases. Our final data set consists of 191 cases of state war participation between 1823 and 1974.

Data measuring the duration in office of the political leaders who were the heads of the governments at the time the war began were derived from several sources. Our basic source of data was Spuler, Allen, and Saunders' (1977) *Rulers and Governments of the World*. These data were checked against the historical chronology given in Langer's (1972) *Encyclopedia of World History*, Bienen and van de Walle's (1991) *Of Time and Power*, and the *Cambridge Encyclopedia* (Crystal 1990, RR 42–67). Post-1965 data were also checked against *Facts on File*.

In selecting the relevant leader whose longevity in office is of interest, we identify the individual who was the *head of government* (as distinguished from the head of state, if relevant) at the time the war began. In the large majority of cases the head of government was the individual most responsible for formulating and implementing policy regarding war decisions. In democratic countries the identification was straightforward, with the prime minister, chancellor, or president (as appropriate) being the designated head of government. For nondemocratic governments more judgment was required. We tried to ascertain whether there existed a cabinet or council of ministers or a comparable entity serving under the head of state or whether there existed a legislative body concurrent with the head of state. In either case, we identified the leader of this cabinet or council of ministers or the leader of the legislative body as the relevant decision maker. If such a council, cabinet, or legislative body existed concurrent with a head of state, Spuler and his colleagues identified the relevant ministers and generally provided enough information to determine which individual was the chief minister or leader and thus, by assumption, was responsible for policy. Of course, in some instances there is nothing to substitute for historical knowledge, because the apparent constitutional form of the government had little to do with the actual exercise of political power. For example, we consider Stalin to have been the responsible political leader for the Soviet Union between 1928 and 1953, and Mao for China between 1949 and 1976, rather than anyone listed as being the leader of a council of ministers. Beyond this, in some instances the histories of the individual states were examined, and in a few cases these histories were particularly useful in determining who actually held political power.

From these data, the central items of information we ascertained were four: (1) the date the leader entered office; (2) the date the war began; (3) the date the leader left office; and (4) if the leader left before the end of the war, whether that exit was the result of death or a political removal.[7]

We are interested in ascertaining the effect of several variables on the survival of the political leader who takes a state into war. One of these is the outcome of the war. Here we focus our attention on wars in which there is a fairly clear winner and loser. We have taken the win/lose designations from the Correlates of War data set.

We are also concerned with the costs and benefits to a leader's political fortunes that result from longevity in office. We share with others the claim that democratic institutions impose political constraints (e.g., the coalition-of-minorities effect) on leaders to a greater degree than is true in authoritarian settings. Therefore, we assume that democratic leaders are constrained in their foreign policy choices by the acquisition either of reliability costs or smaller reliability benefits than is true for authoritarians over time, while authoritarian leaders are liberated in their actions by reliability credits that redound to them from the actions they take to satisfy their much more limited constituencies (Bueno de Mesquita and Lalman 1992; Maoz and Russett 1993; Morgan and Campbell 1991). Consequently, we are interested in the interactive effect of regime type with tenure in office as factors influencing political survival. The interaction of regime type and tenure is taken as our general indicator of R, the reliability cost or benefit in our model.

To calculate the impact of R from our model, we must specify whether each leader operated in a democratic or authoritarian setting. Gurr (1990) has undertaken an extensive survey of political systems in the nineteenth and twentieth centuries, reporting, among other things, a relatively rigorous measure of the extent to which various states were democratic. The scale runs from 0 (no democracy) to 10 (high democracy). All the states we cover are surveyed at the time of interest, so we have an estimate of the extent to which any state is democratic at, as nearly as possible, the time of the war onset. We measure the democraticness or authoritarianism of the institutions in each state by treating all cases that Gurr coded as 6 or above as democratic and those below 6 as authoritarian, coded as 1 and 0, respectively.[8] With this dummy variable, DEMO, in place, we create TENURE * DEMO. TENUREL is the logarithm of a leader's total time in office prior to the war (plus 1), while TENURE * DEMO is simply the product of DEMO and TENUREL. In accord with our hypotheses, we anticipate that TENUREL * DEMO increases the hazard of being removed from office relative to that experienced by authoritarian leaders while TENUREL alone decreases the risk of removal.

In other words, democratic leaders of states at war are expected to survive for a shorter time than their nondemocratic counterparts.

The transaction costs of war include losses in life and property and the attendant forgone opportunities that the destruction of lives and property entails. Although Organski and Kugler (1980) have been able to estimate some important dimensions of war cost for a few nations, we know of no data set that provides a usable measure of these costs for the number of nations with which we will deal. However, one reasonable alternative measure is available in the war lethality data contained in the Small and Singer data (1982, table 4.2). Small and Singer list for each nation's war participation the number of battle deaths per 10,000 population. This measure is particularly attractive because it is consistent across time and controls for population size. We expect this transaction cost measure to decrease the likelihood that a political leader will be retained in office.

At this point, it may be useful to lay out briefly the relationship between the hypotheses and the data. Hypothesis 1 indicates that the odds of political survival increase as a function of the logarithm of the time the leader has already been in office for authoritarian leaders (TENUREL) while the odds of survival increase less or even decrease for democratic leaders TENUREL * DEMO. The sources used to provide estimates of the postonset survival of leaders also provide the necessary data on the prewar tenure in office of each leader. Hypothesis 3 is testable against the reported battle deaths per 10,000 population, the form of which used here is the log because (1) the data are highly skewed and (2) increasing battle deaths probably have a decreasing marginal impact that would otherwise be exaggerated (Jackman 1993). In accordance with hypothesis 5, we expect that winning the war increases survival rates. The measure of war outcome is, of course, post hoc for leaders removed from office before the end of the war. It contains information that might not have been known to V at the time that the relevant constituents had to decide whether to retain or remove I. Here we treat the actual outcome as a post

hoc indicator of probable expectations while the war was going on in those cases in which the leader was not retained to the end of the conflict.

Hypothesis 6 addresses expected changes in the conditions under which a leader would choose to wage a war. In particular, it indicates that the longer an authoritarian leader has been in power, the more likely the leader will choose to wage war, including high-risk wars that are lost. The likelihood of choosing high-risk wars (i.e., wars, on average, lost more often) is expected to be negatively associated with tenure in office for democratic leaders. To test this proposition, we examine the relationship between the logarithm of tenure in office (as suggested by the time discounting of past performance) and the outcome of the wars fought, taking into account whether the leader headed a democratic or authoritarian regime. If the hypothesis is correct, then the logarithm of tenure in office will be negatively associated with the likelihood of winning the war for authoritarian leaders and will be positive for democratic leaders. A second test examines the prewar tenure of authoritarian leaders whose nations engaged in war, comparing that tenure to the average total seniority of leaders in states that did not engage in warfare. If our hypothesis is correct, leaders of warring states should, on average, have already been in office before the war started for a longer time than is true for the total tenure in office of their counterparts in states that did not wage war. Authoritarian old-timers, recall, are hypothesized to pursue riskier foreign policies than their less senior counterparts.

To summarize, from hypotheses 1, 3, and 5 we have the following empirical expectations:

Leader's Post-War-Onset Political Survival

$$= a + b_1 \text{ TENUREL} - b_2 \text{ TENUREL * DEMO}$$

$$- b_3 \text{ (BATTLE DEATHS/10K)L} + b_4 \text{ WIN} + \epsilon;$$

and from hypothesis 6 we expect

$$\text{WIN} = c - b_5 \text{ TENUREL} + b_6 \text{ TENUREL *}$$
$$\text{DEMO} + \epsilon;$$

and

Average prewar tenure in warring states

> average total tenure for authoritarian leaders of nonwarring states.[9]

We add one additional test in which we control for nonconstitutional changes in the regime. In an earlier study (Bueno de Mesquita, Siverson, and Woller 1992) we reported a strong association between war performance and the survival of political regimes. Naturally, if a regime falls to domestic opposition, this may increase the likelihood that the individual key leader also falls from power. We are interested, therefore, in ascertaining the impact of our hypotheses on the survivability of leaders when we control for the effects of a nonconstitutional turnover in regime. The test adds the variable NONCON as follows:

Leader's Post-War-Onset Political Survival

$= a + b_1$ TENUREL $- b_2$ TENURE * DEMO

$- b_3$ (BATTLE DEATHS/10K)L

$+ b_4$ WIN $- b_5$ NONCON $+ \in$.

Event History and Survival Analysis

Our approach to testing the specification of the model involves the application of survival analysis, often referred to as event history (by sociologists) or duration analysis (by economists). The dependent variable in the present case, the length of time a leader remains in power after the onset of the war, is exactly the kind of problem for which survival analysis was designed. The fundamental element of survival analysis is the estimation of the hazard rate, which may be thought of as the natural rate for the ending of some event or process. Here we are interested in the hazard rate faced by political leaders from the time their state enters into a war.

The hazard rate has two elements. The first is the underlying baseline rate of termination as if the event whose duration we are measuring is unaffected by anything. The second is the effect of the various covariates—specified as independent variables—that are seen as affecting the survival, in log-linear form, of the units of interest. In this case those units are the leaders.

There are two key advantages to event history methods over others. The first of these is that they allow us to include within the analysis cases that otherwise would be excluded or treated improperly. In the present instance, some of the leaders in our data set died in office through natural causes. The use of regression methods makes these cases problematic because their inclusion would inappropriately treat them as the political "deaths" that are of interest, while their exclusion removes from the estimate the information that they survived in office at least until their death. Event history analysis, however, allows us to include such information because these cases are treated as "censored"—that is, they are identified as lasting at least as long as the time until biological death. The contribution of such censored cases to the likelihood is then produced through the survivor function rather than the density function that is used on the noncensored cases.[10]

Second, it permits the hazard rate to change with the passage of time. The exact nature of this variation is, in fact, a critical element in distinguishing among survival models. While there are several such models, a graph of the hazard for our data shows it to be monotonically decreasing. Many survival models do not apply to a monotonically increasing or decreasing hazard, but the Weibull model accommodates such a pattern (P. Allison 1984). A plausible alternative to the Weibull is the exponential model in which the hazard is constant. A graphic method of distinguishing between the appropriateness of these models is to plot $\log(-\log(S(t))$ against $\log(t)$, where $S(t)$ is the survivor function defined by the Kaplan-Meier product-limit estimate and (t) is survival time (Kalbfleisch and Prentice 1980, 24). If the result is a straight line, the data may be judged to come from a Weibull distribution; but if the line has a slope of 1, the distribution is exponential. In the present case the scatter is on a straight line, but with a slope of less than 1, supporting the judgment of a Weibull with a decreasing hazard.[11]

Data Analysis

We turn now to an examination of the effects of the variables which compose our model.[12] The main question is, Does prior tenure in office, in combination with the authoritarianism or democraticness of the political system, the battle deaths per 10,000 population, and war outcome have the anticipated effect on the length of time that a political leader survives in office after the onset of the war? Table 2 reports the results of the maximum likelihood estimates based on censored Weibull regression for both the initial model and the one incorporating nonconstitutional overthrow of the regime. The coefficients are the estimated effect of the variable on the hazard rate of leaders; thus, negative values indicate a decreased hazard, or longer survival. The results reported in Table 2, column 1, reveal that all of the variables in the model have the predicted effect on political survival. Longer prewar tenure for authoritarian leaders and victory for all leaders extend time in office, while high overall battle deaths reduce subsequent time in office.[13] Our theory predicts that prewar tenure in office will be less advantageous to democratic leaders relative to their nondemocratic counterparts. Since the coefficient for the effect of the length of prewar tenure for democratic leaders is estimated through the interaction TENUREL * DEMO, we obtain the estimate of the coefficient for just the democratic leaders by summing the coefficients for the interaction and the prewar tenure of all leaders (i.e., .33 − .48 = −.15). The coefficient of −.15 is greater than −.48, demonstrating that prewar tenure contributes less to the survival of the democratic leaders than of the authoritarian leaders, but is it, as we predict in the model, a significantly different effect? This can be shown by two F-tests. First, a test of the difference between this coefficient and the TENURE coefficient (−.48) yields an F of 13.17 ($p < .001$). Second, we test the difference between −.15 and 0, and obtain an F of .76 ($p = .38$). As our model predicts, the leaders of democratic states derive less

advantage from prewar office holding than do the authoritarians; in fact, it is indistinguishable from no advantage whatever.[14]

The results are perhaps best understood as relative risks (or risk ratios), which are shown in Table 2, column 2.[15] In these expressions values above 1.00 (the baseline) indicate an increased risk that the leader would not survive in office, while hazards below 1.00 indicate that the survival rate has risen as the hazard has fallen. More precisely, the hazard's deviation from 1.00 is interpreted as the percentage increase or decrease in the likelihood of political survival resulting from the marginal impact of the independent variable, so that the relative effects of the variables can be discerned by the magnitudes of the hazards.[16]

Exponentiating the coefficient given for authoritarian leaders (−.48) produces a hazard of .62, which means that a one-unit increase in the length of their prewar tenure (an order of magnitude, since we are using the log of tenure) reduces the risk of postwar removal by 38%. In contrast, similar tenure for democratic leaders produces no significant benefit in survival (exp. [−.48 + .33] = .86, which, as we have seen, is statistically indistinguishable from zero). Thus regime type evidently makes an appreciable difference in the prospects of surviving a war politically, with democratic leaders placed at considerably higher risk than their authoritarian counterparts. Even victory does not enhance survivability as much as prewar tenure for authoritarians; nor does victory fully offset the increased hazard for democratic leaders. Victory reduces the overall risk of removal by 25%. Finally, all else being equal, it is easier for political leaders to survive low-cost wars than higher-cost ones. The risk of being turned out of office increases by 8% with each order-of-magnitude increase in the log of battle deaths per 10,000 population.[17]

Hypotheses 1, 3 and 5 are well supported by the evidence. What about hypothesis 6, which contains one of our more surprising expectations? Recall that this hypothesis indicates that authoritarian leaders who have been around a long time are better able to engage in risky foreign policies, even gambling on

Table 2 The Effect of War on Political Survival Time of Leaders: Censored Weibull Regression Test of Hypothesis 1, 3 and 5

Independent Variables	Coefficient (1)	Hazard Rate[a] (2)	Coefficient (3)	Hazard Rate[a] (4)
TENUREL	−.48**	.62	−.47**	.62
	(.09)		(.08)	
TENUREL * DEMOCRACY	.33*	1.38	.36*	1.44
	(.16)		(.16)	
(BATTLE DEATHS/10K) L	.08*	1.08	.07*	1.07
	(.04)		(.04)	
WIN	−.28*	.75	−.26*	.77
	(.16)		(.15)	
NONCONSTITUTIONAL OVERTHROW	—	—	.51*	1.67
			(.19)	
Constant	−.53**	—	−.62**	—
	(.19)		(.20)	
Sigma[b]	1.44	—	1.43	—
	(.08)		(.08)	
χ^2	34.2	—	39.8	—
Probability	<.01	—	<.01	—

Note: Entries in columns 1 and 3 are unstandardized regression coefficients with standard errors in parentheses. $N = 191$.

[a]On the hazard rate, see n. 15.

[b]On sigma, see n. 16.

*p < .05, one-tailed.

**p < .01, one-tailed.

wars that have a relatively high probability of ending in defeat. Newer leaders and democratic leaders, by contrast, are not expected to take such large risks, and so pick and choose their fights more carefully, engaging in wars with a higher probability of leading to victory. The results of the logit analysis bear out the hypothesis. The actual result is

$$WIN = .49 - .35 \text{ TENUREL} + .77 \text{ TENUREL} * DEMO,$$

with $N = 191$ and one-tailed probability $= .002$. The individual variables are also highly significant. The probability that the effect of TENUREL arose by chance is only .017. For TENUREL * DEMO, the probability that its effect is due to chance is only .007.

Hypothesis 6 implies a second, equally surprising result. Relatively short term authoritarian leaders have not had the opportunity to build up the reservoir of good will (R) among their few essential constituents that facilitates taking the risks of war. Democratic leaders are less likely than authoritarian leaders to have built up such a reservoir of good will after they have been in power for a long time. If democratic leaders are going to wage war, they are better off doing it early, before they have lost support as a result of the cumulative impact of the coalition of minorities effect. Consequently, on average we expect authoritarian leaders who engaged in war to have a longer prewar period in office than (1) the total tenure of all leaders who do not wage war and (2) democratic leaders who do wage war.

By moving slightly outside our data set, we can test these two expectations. Of our 191 cases, 106 are also to be found in the Bienen and van de Walle data set describing the political survival of 2,258 leaders around the world in the period since 1820. In this data set, the average total tenure of the non-warring leaders is 3.32 years ($N = 2{,}152$), while the average total tenure of those leaders who ultimately engaged in war is 8.52 years ($N = 106$). The difference is highly significant, with $t = 6.9$. The average prewar tenure of all of the authoritarian leaders in our data set is 5.66 years, which is significantly longer than the total tenure of all the nonwarring leaders in the Bienen and van de Walle data set. The average prewar tenure of democratic leaders is only 2.57 years, which is significantly shorter than the prewar longevity or leadership experience of authoritarian leaders. The result is surprising, but consistent with our expectations. Long-serving authoritarian leaders are more likely to wage war than are relative newcomer democratic leaders. Democratic leaders are more likely to wage war

early in their years in office, while their support is still high (Gaubatz 1991).

Hypothesis 6—like hypotheses 1, 3, and 5—seems to run directly counter to neorealist expectations and also to our general intuition. As such, it provides an additional basis from which to question the fundamental basis of neorealism and to suggest greater attention to the interplay between domestic politics and international affairs.

Before concluding, we examine the robustness of our results regarding hypotheses 1, 3, and 5 by controlling for the impact of nonconstitutional regime change produced by internal opposition. This test will help clarify the extent to which our model accounts for variations in leadership survival after controlling for regime change, a factor for which we have previously suggested an explanation (Bueno de Mesquita, Siverson, and Woller 1992). Table 2, column 3, contains the results of adding to our original model a dummy variable coded 1 for all the regimes that were overthrown by internal opposition either during the war or within three years of the war's end. As can be seen, even after controlling for nonconstitutional regime changes, the evidence in support of our hypotheses is quite robust. Nonconstitutional regime changes increase the risk of political removal by 67%, a very hefty effect. Still, the effects shown in the original model continue to obtain. The hazards, reported in column 4, show that authoritarian leaders continue to derive the same political benefits from their apparent ability to avoid problems such as the coalition of minorities. Similarly, winning and battle-related costs both continue to have significant effects of about the same magnitude as reported in the test that did not control for nonconstitutional regime change. In sum, our model's predicted effects are independent of our own earlier reported results for nonconstitutional regime change.

Conclusion

Our investigation has found that those leaders who engage their nation in war subject themselves to a domestic political hazard that threatens the very essence of the office-holding *homo politicus*—the retention of political power. The hazard is mitigated by longstanding experience for authoritarian elites, an effect that is muted for democratic leaders, while the hazard is militated by defeat and high costs from war for all types of leaders. Additionally, we find that authoritarian leaders are inclined to fight wars longer after they come to power than are democratic leaders. Further, democratic leaders select wars to participate in that have a lower risk of defeat than is true for their authoritarian counterparts. These results, which are implied directly by the specification of our model, obtain across a time span of over 150 years and encompass a broad spectrum of political systems and types of leadership removal. The evidence is consistent with the claim that decisions to go to war are endogenous to the domestic political setting of the leaders.

Such a result runs counter to expectations from neorealist theory. In that theory, war policies are endogenous to the international system and not to the domestic political situation. This is seen most clearly in Waltz's proposition that

> the elements of *Realpolitik*, exhaustively listed, are these: the ruler's, and later the state's, interest provides the spring of action; *the necessities of policy arise from the unregulated competition of states; calculation based on these necessities can discover the policies that will best serve a state's interests;* success is the ultimate test of policy, and success is defined as preserving and strengthening the state. (1979, 117, emphasis added)

We agree that policymakers care about the security of their state (though perhaps not necessarily as their paramount concern), and it is almost impossible to believe that the problem of maintaining or enhancing security does not enter into the calculations they make with respect to the policies that should be pursued. How does one square those facts with our assertion that internal political considerations are fundamental to external policy selection? The answer to this question depends upon what one takes to be the central assumption of neorealist theory.

If one proceeds from the basic neorealist assumption that states maximize their power to maximize their security and does not go further, then the theory is almost certainly false. However, if one extends the theory (in a way not previously done) by (1) assuming that policymakers want to stay in power for the rents, as well as for the policy opportunities thus afforded (Lake 1992) and (2) observing that declining security (as indicated here by war loss and costs) shortens time in power, then the linkage between internal politics and external policies is established. Thus the leader—whether president, prime minister, or president-for-life—who adopts policies that reduce the security of the state does so at the risk of affording his or her political opponents the opportunity of weakening the leader's grasp on power. Put differently, a leader's search for the security of the state intertwines with the search for policies that will maintain the leader in power against domestic opposition. The desire to remain in power thus provides the linchpin between the threats and uncertainties of the international system and the inevitable imperatives of fending off the domestic opposition.

Writing almost 25 years ago, James Rosenau (1969) lamented the fact that students of international relations did not have a well-developed framework— much less a well-developed theory— for linking political processes internal to the state with those that were external. In particular, he called attention to the absence of any theory that could account for the effect of foreign policy events on the tenures of political leaders:

> Consider the processes whereby the top political leadership of a society acquires and maintains its position of authority. To what extent are these processes dependent on events that unfold abroad? Under what conditions will the stability of cabinets and the tenure of presidents be reduced or otherwise affected by trends in the external environment? Are certain leadership structures more

vulnerable to developments in the international system than others? Political theory presently offers no guidance as to how questions such as these might be researched and answered. (p. 5)

More recently, Putnam (1988) called attention to the linkages between international and domestic politics.

Putnam's conceptualization of the logic of two-level games is certainly an advance over much of the past work on linkage politics, but although his concluding sentence is an admonition for empirical research, he fails to specify a model. The present research both specifies a model and offers data that are highly consistent with that model. With this knowledge in hand, we can no longer afford to treat domestic politics as ending at the water's edge, as neorealism is inclined to do. Foreign policy, instead, is better seen as intimately connected to the desire of leaders to maintain themselves in power.

Notes

Authors' Note: The authors acknowledge with gratitude the helpful advice of Timothy Amato, Colin Cameron, Kurt Taylor Gaubatz, Robert Hanneman, Dale Heien, Robert W. Jackman, David Rocke, Alastair Smith, Richard Tucker, and Paul Warwick. We also benefitted from the able research assistance of Monica Barczak, Letitia Lawson, Ross Miller, Steve Nicholson, and Eric Siegal. We thank the Berkeley Young Women's Christian Association and Raymond Wolfinger, both of whose assistance facilitated the completion of this work. Siverson's work was supported by the University of California's Institute on Global Conflict and Cooperation; additional support was received from the National Science Foundation under grant SBR-9409225. An earlier version of this paper was presented at the annual meeting of the American Political Science Association, Washington, 1993.

1. We are indebted to Gary Woller for calling this particular example to our attention.

2. There is a different way of putting this: all the political leaders used in this study left office, but only 36 of the regimes were overthrown by nonconstitutional means, and in 20 of these the responsible leader at the time of the entry into war had been removed from office *before* the overthrow of the regime.

3. The literature on the effects of economic performance on regimes and political leaders is quite large. Good summaries of the research are to be found in Lewis-Beck and Eulau 1985 and Norpoth, Lewis-Beck, and Lafay 1991. Although almost all of this work is within the domain of democratic political systems, research by Londregan and Poole (1990) demonstrates that military coups are more likely when economic performance has been poor.

4. However, Sanders, Ward, and Marsh (1991) argue that the Falkland's effect is exaggerated and that Thatcher's rise in the polls can be traced more clearly to economic policies and conditions.

5. It should be noted that we assume a game of complete and perfect information here. In later investigations we intend to examine the implications of uncertainty on the general effects suggested here.

6. To be sure, from a risk assessment point of view, policymakers cannot be indifferent to the possibility that a failed conflict policy may result in their removal by a foreign power. Indeed, it happens. In the present instance, however, we note that in the cases that would otherwise constitute our data base, removal by a foreign power took place only 19 times. However, our data probably understate the extent to which removal through this means occurs, because in many such cases the initiator is so "successful" that the casualties are not sufficiently numerous to qualify the event for inclusion in the war data set (e.g., the United States intervention in Grenada).

7. Not all deaths are neatly managed, because some are not natural. While Franklin Roosevelt died a nonpolitical death, Anwar Sadat did not. However, Sadat's assassins did not succeed in capturing power and replacing him with someone who would bring Egypt's policies closer to their own. All political leaders are potentially subject to assassination, but the success of such attempts in the absence of a group able to seize power may be random. Consequently, in cases where assassins were not able to seize the state, we coded their departure as a "natural death." However, if a leader died as the direct result of a successful coup or revolution, the death was treated as a political removal.

8. One potential difficulty with this is that warfare sometimes changes governments. Few of such changes, however, are large enough to alter the state's score on the democracy index. For example, while the United Kingdom suspended elections during most of World War II, the democracy score remained unchanged at 10.

9. The two equations specified here are not intended to suggest a system of simultaneous equations but, rather, tests of hypotheses that follow directly from our model. Still, the dependent variable of one is an independent variable in the other so that it might be possible to conceptualize the argument as implying simultaneity. However, it should be noted that the factors hypothesized to explain the variable Win are also independent variables in the first equation and so cannot be used as instruments for Win. Having said that, we did test the argument as if there were a set of simultaneous equations. To do so, we calculated the predicted values of WIN from a logit analysis and substituted those predicted values into the first equation. Not surprisingly, the predicted values of WIN did not have a significant effect on the dependent variable, given that the predicted values were necessarily collinear with the effects of the remaining independent variables in the first equation. This had to be so because the remaining variables were exactly the same as the ones used to generate predicted values of WIN. As our results show, however, WIN itself is significantly related to the survival of political leaders even when the other independent variables are taken into account. This is the expectation derived from our model and suggests that additional factors explain war outcomes beyond those hypothesized here.

10. For a general introduction to survival methods, see P. Allison 1984. Applications in political analysis are growing. Some noteworthy examples of its use are to be found in the various papers of Warwick (1992a, 1992b, 1993). Also see King et al. 1990 and Hanneman and Steinback 1990.

11. Copies of the graph of the hazard and the plot of the integrated hazard against the log of survival time are available from Siverson.

12. The means, standard deviations, and ranges on the four main independent variables are

Variable	Mean	SD	Min.	Max.
TENUREL	1.34	.91	0[a]	3.45
(BATTLE DEATHS/10K)L	1.93	1.65	0[a]	6.32
DEMOCRACY	.24	.43	0	1
WIN	.54	.49	0	1

[a]These values simply report numbers too small to register. For example, in the 1956 Suez War, the United Kingdom suffered 40 battle deaths, which, as a proportion of that state's population, is recorded in the data set at the value given above.

13. In keeping with the fact that our model leads to expectations about the direction of each relationship, one-tailed tests of significance are reported in the table.

14. The model we have tested does not include the main effect of democracy even though the interaction of democracy and tenure is present. We do this because we have no theoretical reason for including democracy. Nonetheless, we now report the same model including democracy as a main effect, and from the very small changes in the coefficients that attend this and the absence of a fit for democracy itself, we conclude that there is no empirical reason for including it either.

Variable	Coefficient (SE)
TENUREL	−.51
	(.10)
TENUREL * DEMOCRACY	.44
	(.25)
(BATTLE DEATHS/10k)L	.08
	(.04)
WIN	−.26
	(.15)
DEMOCRACY	−.17
	(.31)
Constant	−.48
	(.21)

Variable	Coefficient (SE)
Sigma	1.44
	(.08)

15. Hazards are found by exponentiating the coefficients from the regression (P. Allison 1984, 28).
16. In Weibull regression, a shape parameter sigma describes whether the hazard is increasing or decreasing with time. When the hazard is decreasing, sigma has a value greater than 1.00. The value of sigma for our model is 1.44 (with a standard error of .08), so the hazard is decreasing, a result that is similar in character to that reported by Bienen and van de Walle (1991). In some statistics programs and in Greene 1993, the shape parameter is 1/sigma, in which case the effect of the shape parameter as increasing or decreasing the hazard relative to the baseline of 1.00 is the opposite of that given here.
17. Selecting the appropriate model for the overall hazard (in this case the Weibull) does not mean that other problems of misspecification are avoided. In ordinary least squares, diagnostics would be approached with the analysis of residuals. However, as Greene explains, "There is no direct counterpart to the set of regression residuals with which to assess the validity of the specification of the duration [i.e., survival] model" (1993, 722). Greene, nonetheless, does offer a test for specification, based on the use of "generalized residuals" (ε^2), to test the second moment restriction that $E(\varepsilon^2) = 2$ (Greene 1993, 722–23; Lancaster and Chesher 1985b, 37). Since some of our observations are censored, the residuals are appropriately adjusted as:

$$\hat{e}(t) = \begin{bmatrix} \varepsilon(t) \text{ if uncensored} \\ \varepsilon(t) + 1 \text{ if censored.} \end{bmatrix}$$

With the adjusted residuals, the second moment restriction is $s_e^2 = \sum(C_i / N)$, where s_e^2 is the sample variance of $\hat{e}(t)$ and $\sum(C_i / N)$ is the proportion of censored cases in the sample. The test statistic for the second moment restriction is implemented by running an ordinary least squares in which unity is regressed on $(\hat{e}_i - 1)^2 - C_i$, and all $\partial \mathcal{L}_i / \partial \theta_j$ where θ_j $(j = 1, \ldots k)$ represent parameters of the model. The test statistic is computed as N, the sample size, multiplied by the uncentered R^2 and under the null hypothesis has an asymptotic $\chi^2(1)$ distribution (Lancaster and Chesher 1985b). In the present instance, the value of the test statistic is .974, which is well below the 3.84 level necessary to reject the hypothesis at the 5% level. Additionally, we plotted the integrated hazard against the generalized residuals, the result of which was a 45-degree line characteristic of the Weibull (Lancaster and Chesher 1985a).

EDITORS' COMMENTARY

Major Contributions: Leader Survival

The democratic peace literature (Oneal and Russett 1999c, Chapter 9, this volume) looks at the relationship between states' regime characteristics and the likelihood of militarized conflict. As we discussed previously, the structural theory of the democratic peace expects democratic leaders to be more cautious when initiating conflicts because these leaders know that their jobs can be on the line should the war go poorly. Empirical analyses show that democracies are much more successful in war than nondemocracies (Lake 1992). This raises a question, though, about whether war outcomes actually influence a leader's tenure. In other words, are leaders who win wars more likely to stay in office for a longer period of time? Do democratic leaders get punished by their domestic audience after wars more strongly than their autocratic counterparts, especially if they lose the war? Does it matter how long a leader was in office prior to initiating a war? Bueno de Mesquita and Siverson (1995) address these questions in their article. They consider the influence of war outcomes, war costs, and differences across regime types on the length of time that leaders survive in office.

This article is one piece of a broader research agenda by the authors that focuses on how domestic institutions influence conflict (and vice versa). In *The Logic of Political Survival,* they develop a theory called the **selectorate** model (Bueno de Mesquita et al. 2005), which relates the size of the selectorate (S or who can choose a leader) and the size of the winning coalition (W or how many members of the selectorate are needed to keep the leader in office) to a variety of outcomes such as war. In authoritarian systems, the selectorate is small, often a group of military officers that protects a dictator or an exclusive political party such as the Communist Party in China. In democracies, the selectorate typically involves all citizens eligible to vote, while the winning coalition is the 50.1+ percent of the vote required to win office. In their theory, Bueno de Mesquita and his coauthors focus on the ratio of these two factors (W/S) when making predictions about war and other domestic factors such as economic growth rates and the level of corruption. They develop a **game theory** or mathematical model to understand the strategic interaction between leaders, other actors in domestic politics, and leaders and actors in other countries. The basic logic of the model is that if a leader depends on a large selectorate and a large winning coalition (e.g., President Barack Obama), then the leader is more likely to provide public goods to the citizens. Public goods are things that can benefit a wide group of people such as national security or education. In countries where the selectorate and winning coalition are small (e.g., Saudi Arabia), the leaders can sustain themselves in power by providing private goods to an elite group. Private goods could include special tax policies or protective tariffs for particular groups that support the regime.

In Chapter 6 of *The Logic of Political Survival,* the authors explain how the size of the selectorate and the winning coalition influence states' decisions for war and their chances for victory (Bueno de Mesquita et al. 2005, 213–72). They show that democracies select wars carefully, picking ones where they have an advantage, and that democracies try harder to win wars once they are under way. If democracies anticipate that they will lose, they are more likely to negotiate a peaceful settlement to the contested issue and avoid war altogether. Autocratic leaders can afford to be riskier in waging wars, although they view democracies as less attractive targets. Democracies are willing to target weaker adversaries to increase the chances for success, fighting colonial and imperial wars frequently. Weaker democracies, however, are likely to seek negotiated settlements when experiencing conflicts with stronger democratic states.

The 1995 article in this volume focuses on the relationship between war outcomes and the survival of leaders in office. Leaders can lose office either through regular means, such as the loss of an election, or through irregular means, such as coups or a regime created through foreign imposition. Bueno de Mesquita and Siverson assume that all politics is competitive (even in small *W/S* states), that all leaders wish to stay in office, and that there is some opponent or challenger who would be willing to replace the leader. To win office, the leader must pay attention to the **median voter** or the person around which the winning coalition forms. In democracies, you can think about the median voter as a person in the center of the left-right ideological spectrum. In autocracies, the median voter might be a key general or political figure in a one-party system. All leaders have a certain level of support at any given moment in time, although this typically erodes over the course of their leadership cycle. Wars can help leaders improve their support levels, especially if the state wins the conflict and the voters perceive the leader to be more competent.

On the basis of their model, Bueno de Mesquita and Siverson (1995) derive several hypotheses. First, they predict that authoritarian leaders are more likely to stay in power the longer they have been in office. Leaders with long tenure, such as Fidel Castro, are able to sustain office longer than leaders in democratic systems, such as Margaret Thatcher or Ronald Reagan. Second, they predict that leaders select themselves into conflicts that they think they can win. Third, they argue that leaders are more likely to lose office if the wars they wage generate high costs, such as many battle deaths or economic costs. Fourth, they expect leaders to negotiate resolutions to situations if they anticipate high costs in war. This is similar to the hypotheses in their 2005 book, in which they argue that weaker democracies negotiate against strong democratic adversaries. Fifth, they predict that wars can be waged more readily by leaders who have longer prewar tenure because they can afford to gamble on high-risk foreign policies. Sixth, they link the previous hypothesis to regime characteristics, expecting autocratic leaders to wage war later in their tenure and democratic leaders to wage war earlier in their leadership terms. The final hypothesis anticipates that authoritarian leaders will pursue policies that the median voter might not prefer; their longevity insulates them from potential punishment by the domestic audience, making leaders more likely to pursue their personally preferred policies.

Bueno de Mesquita and Siverson (1995) find support for their hypotheses in the empirical tests. First, they show that authoritarian leaders get a stronger benefit from being in office for longer periods of time in comparison to democratic leaders, consistent with hypothesis 1. Second, they find that battle deaths increases the hazard rate, so leaders are more likely to be removed following costly wars, supporting hypothesis 3. Victory in war lowers the chance that a leader will be removed by office by 25 percent. Consistent with hypothesis 6, they find an interactive effect between prewar tenure and regime type, with authoritarian leaders waging war later in their leadership terms. Democratic leaders are more likely to initiate wars early in their leadership.

This article was a path-breaking study in a much larger literature that examines the factors that influence leaders' survival in office, including regime characteristics, economic growth, economic sanctions, and time in office. Some of the findings in this article have been questioned. For example, Chiozza and Goemans (2004) compare the effects of lower level crises and wars on leaders' tenure, finding surprisingly that the effects of crises and wars are similar on leader survival despite their significant cost differences. This is similar to some studies in the diversionary literature that find small rally effects for leaders who initiate conflicts for political gain (e.g., Lian and Oneal 1993). Thus, while the findings linking democratic regimes and success in war are consistent with the logic of the selectorate model, the relationships between war costs, outcomes, and leader survival are more unclear.

Methodological Notes: Game Theory Models

Bueno de Mesquita and Siverson (1995) develop a game-theoretic model to understand the relationship between war and leaders' survival in office. There are two broad types of **game theory models**: (1) decision-theoretic models that focus on the actions of a single actor and (2) strategic interaction models that examine the interactions between two or more actors. Bueno de Mesquita's (1981) first book, *The War Trap*, develops an expected utility model that focuses on unilateral decisions for war by states. He determines if the expected benefits from fighting a war exceed the expected costs of war and then predicts that positive expected utility (greater than zero) is a necessary condition for war. A second book by Bueno de Mesquita and Lalman (1992) develops a strategic choice model to understand how domestic politics influence states' decisions for war, providing a theoretical framework for understanding the democratic peace phenomenon. The third book, *The Logic of Political Survival* (Bueno de Mesquita et al. 2005), creates a more generalizable theory that can explain variation in foreign policy behavior and strategic interactions across all types of regimes.

Game theory models involve a specification of the players of the game (actors), the strategies the actors can employ, and the information actors have about their own preferences, other actors' preferences, and the bargaining environment. In Bueno de Mesquita and Siverson's (1995) model, they identify three key actors: (1) a **Stakeholder** who controls the median power position, V; (2) an **Incumbent** leader, I; and (3) a **Challenger** who wishes to gain control over the government, C. The voter can gain utility from the past performance of the incumbent and that utility can be positive or negative. The authors use the term R to denote this accumulated set of benefits and costs from the incumbents' previous performance. When a new leader comes to power, $R = 0$. They also assume that R decays over time, such that the voters pay attention to more recent actions by the leader. They speculate that R is probably positive for authoritarian leaders due to their ability to pay off supporters through private goods provisions, while R is typically negative for democratic leaders. Many U.S. presidents, for example, start with a high approval rating when they first take office and then experience a general decline in public support over time. Leaders can try to use war as a tool for demonstrating competence, but because war is costly, the state must pay some kind of transaction costs for waging it. This is similar to the idea in the bargaining model of war that war is costly (Fearon 1995).

Each actor in the game receives a utility for each potential outcome of the strategic interaction game (Table 1). For example, if an incumbent wins a war and is retained in office, the incumbent receives $-(X_I - X_I^*)^2 + R$, while the median voter receives $-(X_V^* - X_I)^2 + R - L$. The game is solved using backward induction, where the players consider the outcomes of the game and then maximize their utilities by moving upward through the game (tree). In essence, the incumbent would consider what might happen if she initiates a war and then tries to anticipate the actions of the voters and the challenger depending on whether she wins or loses the war. This produces a set of **equilibrium** solutions that identify strategies players would select and have no incentives to deviate from. There are a variety of equilibrium solution concepts in game theory, but scholars often report the **Nash equilibrium,** named after the game theorist, John Nash. A Nash equilibrium involves a situation where no player can benefit from switching to a different strategy if the other players retain their current strategy. In the famous Prisoner's Dilemma game, for example, mutual defection is a Nash equilibrium because neither player has an incentive to cooperate if they know the other player will defect.

The hypotheses that are presented in the article are based on comparative statics given the equilibrium solutions in equations (1) and (2). For example, you could change the value of R to determine the conditions under which the challenger might successfully remove the incumbent from power. Comparisons between democratic and authoritarian leaders are made by changing the value of R from negative to positive. The effects of the costs of war are evaluated by changing the value of L in the model. These kinds of models are advantageous because they make the assumptions underlying the theory transparent, and they provide a rigorous methodology for deriving hypotheses logically from the model.

Bueno de Mesquita and Siverson's empirical tests are designed to evaluate four of the total hypotheses (1, 3, 5, and 6). They collect data on 191 cases of war participation between 1823 and 1974. They then code the length of postwar tenure (TENUREL) for each of the 191 cases, focusing on the leader who was in power at the start of the war. They interact this variable with a dummy variable for democracy (DEMO), which equals 1 if the country scores 6 or higher on the Polity democracy scale (0–10). They also capture the costs of the war in terms of the logged total battle deaths [(Battle Deaths/10K)L] and the outcome of the war (WIN), coding whether the specific leader in question won the war. To test hypothesis 6, they treat the win/lose variable as the dependent variable.

Like Werner (1999, Chapter 14, this volume), they use a **Weibull duration model** when testing hypotheses about leader tenure. Failure in this particular model represents a leader being removed from office. In Table 2, column 3, they also include a variable for nonconstitutional overthrow to distinguish the regular leadership transition cases from the irregular ones. The (right) censored cases in the data represent those leaders who were still in power as of the last year of the data set (1974). Recall that the **shape parameter** (p) in a Weibull model tells us how the chances for failure (e.g., a leader losing office) change over time. Bueno de Mesquita and Siverson (1995) report a value called **sigma**. The shape parameter, p, is equal to 1/sigma. In the Werner study, a value of $p < 1$ tells us that the hazard rate is monotonically decreasing with time, or that the chances for renewed conflict are dropping. Given that sigma is the inverse value of p, if we observe values of sigma greater than 1, this also implies a declining hazard rate. The authors estimate the value to be 1.44 for their first model, showing that the chances that leaders lose office decline as the number of years they have been in power increases.

The authors generate an **interaction term**, multiplying the variable for TENUREL by the variable for regime type, DEMO. They call this variable, TENUREL * DEMOCRACY. They include the interaction to capture the differences between authoritarian and democratic leaders. The theory predicts that authoritarian leaders are more insulated from losing office. We see support for this proposition in Table 2 by setting the value of democracy to zero. The interaction term then drops out of the model and we are left with the estimate for TENUREL, which is equal to −0.48 and statistically different from zero (**). Negative values in the duration model imply that the likelihood of failure or leader removal is lower; authoritarian leaders are less likely to lose office than their democratic counterparts as the number of years in office increases. To determine the effect of tenure in office on future survival for democratic leaders, we must add together the two coefficients (−0.48 + 0.33 = −0.15). As reported by the authors, they cannot say that this value is different from zero, and thus democratic leaders who begin a war with a longer prewar tenure period have no advantage at holding office after the war compared with their newer, democratic leader counterparts. More recent studies examining leader survival have used a very comprehensive data set on leaders from 1875–2004 called the Achigos Dataset (Goemans, Gleditsch, and Chiozza 2009).

Questions

1. Based on the game theory model and empirical findings, under what conditions are leaders most likely to lose office following a war?

2. In Table 2, what is the substantive effect of logged battle deaths/10K on leader survival time? Hint: examine the effect on the hazard rate in column (3).

3. In Table 2, which variable seems to have the largest substantive effect on whether a leader stays in office or is removed?

Further Reading

Bueno de Mesquita, B., A. Smith, R. M. Siverson, and J. D. Morrow. 2005. *The logic of political survival*. Cambridge: MIT Press.

Chiozza, G., and H. E. Goemans. 2004. International conflict and the tenure of leaders: Is war still *ex post* inefficient? *American Journal of Political Science* 48 (3): 604–19.

_____. 2011. *Leaders and international conflict*. Cambridge, UK: Cambridge University Press.

Goemans, H. E., K. S. Gleditsch, and G. Chiozza. 2009. Introducing Archigos: A dataset of political leaders. *Journal of Peace Research* 46 (2): 269–83.

REFERENCES

Abel, C. F., and M. A. Tetreault, eds. 1986. *Dependency theory and the return of high politics.* New York: Greenwood.

Acemoglu, D., and J. A. Robinson. 2006. *Economic origins of dictatorship and democracy.* New York: Cambridge University Press.

Achen, C. H. 1986. *The statistical analysis of quasi experiments.* Berkeley: University of California Press.

Adler, E., and M. Barnett. 1998. Security communities in theoretical perspective. In *Security communities,* ed. E. Adler and M. Barnett. New York: Cambridge University Press.

Aitken, N. D. 1973. The effect of the EEC and EFTA on European trade: A temporal cross-sectional analysis. *American Economic Review* 63 (5): 881–92.

Albright, D. 1994. South Africa and the affordable bomb. *Bulletin of the Atomic Scientists* 50 (4): 37–47.

Aldrich, J. H., and F. D. Nelson. 1984. *Linear probability, logit and probit models.* Sage University Paper series on Quantitative Applications in the Social Sciences. Beverly Hills, CA: Sage.

Alesina, A., and E. Spolaore. 2003. *The size of nations.* Cambridge: MIT Press.

Allee, T., and P. K. Huth. 2006. Legitimizing dispute settlement: International legal rulings as domestic political cover. *American Political Science Review* 100 (2): 219–34.

Allison, G. 1971. *The essence of decision: Explaining the Cuban missile crisis.* Boston: Little, Brown.

Allison, G., O. Cote, R. A. Falkenrath, and S. E. Miller. 1996. *Avoiding nuclear anarchy: Containing the threat of loose Russian nuclear weapons and fissile material.* Cambridge: MIT Press.

Allison, P. D. 1984. *Event history analysis.* Number 07–046. Beverly Hills, CA: Sage.

Altfeld, M. E. 1983. Arms races?—And escalation? A comment on Wallace. *International Studies Quarterly* 27 (2): 225–31.

Andersen, P., J. Baumgardner, J. M. Greig, and P. F. Diehl. 2001. Turning down the heat: Influences on conflict management in enduring rivalries. *International Interactions* 27 (3): 239–74.

Arad, R. W., and S. Hirsch. 1981. Peacemaking and vested interests: International economic transactions. *International Studies Quarterly* 25 (3): 439–68.

Aron, R. 1965. *The great debate: Theories of nuclear strategy.* Trans. E. Pawel. Garden City, NJ: Doubleday.

Arquilla, J. 1997. Nuclear weapons in South Asia: More may be manageable. *Comparative Strategy* 16 (1): 13–32.

Asal, V., and K. Beardsley. 2007. Proliferaction and international crisis behavior. *Journal of Peace Research* 44 (2): 139–55.

Azar, E. 1972. Conflict escalation and conflict reduction in an international crisis: Suez, 1956. *Journal of Conflict Studies* 16 (2): 183–201.

Babst, D. V. 1964. Elective governments—A force for peace. *The Wisconsin Sociologists* 3 (1): 9–14.

———. 1972. A force for peace. *Industrial Research* 14 (4): 55–58.

Bailey, S. D. 1982. *How wars end: The United Nations and the termination of armed conflict, 1946–1964.* Oxford, UK: Clarendon.

Balogh, T. 1963. *Unequal partners, volume one: The theoretical framework.* Oxford, UK: Blackwell.

Banks, A. S. 1997. *Cross-national time series archive.* New York: Computer Solutions Unlimited.

Barbieri, K. 1992. Economic interdependence and dyadic dispute proneness, 1873–1939. Paper presented at the annual meeting of the Peace Science Society (International), Pittsburgh, PA.

———. 1994a. Does economic interdependence reduce dyadic conflict? Paper presented at the annual meeting of the International Studies Association, Washington, D.C.

———. 1994b. Economic interdependence: A path toward peace or source of interstate conflict? Paper presented at the annual meeting of the American Political Science Association, New York.

———. 1995. Economic interdependence and militarized conflict, 1870–1990. PhD diss., Binghamton University.

———. 1996. Economic interdependence: A path to peace or a source of interstate conflict? *Journal of Peace Research* 33 (1): 29–49.

———. 1998. International trade and conflict: The debatable relationship. Paper presented at the annual meeting of the International Studies Association, Minneapolis, MN.

———. 2002. *The liberal illusion: Does trade promote peace?* Ann Arbor: University of Michigan Press.

Barbieri, K., O. M. G. Keshk, and B. M. Pollins. 2009. Trading data: Evaluating our assumptions and coding rules. *Conflict Management and Peace Science* 26 (5): 471–91.

Beck, N. 1999. Trade and conflict in the Cold War era: An empirical analysis. Paper presented at the annual meeting of the American Political Science Association, Atlanta, GA.

Beck, N., J. N. Katz, and R. Tucker. 1998. Taking time seriously: Time-series–cross-section analysis with a binary dependent variable. *American Journal of Political Science* 42 (4): 1260–88.

Ben-Yehuda, H. 2001. Territoriality, crisis and war in the Arab–Israel Conflict, 1947–94. *Journal of Conflict Studies* 21 (2): 78–108.

Bennett, D. S. 1993. *Security, economy, and the end of interstate rivalry.* PhD diss., University of Michigan.

———. 1996. Security, bargaining, and the end of interstate rivalry. *International Studies Quarterly* 40 (2): 157–83.

———. 1997. Measuring rivalry termination, 1816–1992. *Journal of Conflict Resolution* 41 (2): 227–54.

———. 1999. Parametric methods, duration dependence, and time-varying data revisited. *American Journal of Political Science* 43 (1): 256–70.

Bennett, D. S., and T. Nordstrom. 2000. Foreign policy substitutability and internal economic problems in enduring rivalries. *Journal of Conflict Resolution* 44 (1): 33–61.

Bennett, D. S., and A. C. Stam III. 2000. EUGene: A conceptual manual. *International Interactions* 26 (2): 179–204.

———. 2002. EUGene: Expected utility generation and data management program, version 2.40 documentation. http://www.eugenesoftware.org

———. 2004. *The behavioral origins of war.* Princeton, NJ: Princeton University Press.

Bercovitch, J., and P. F. Diehl. 1997. Conflict management of enduring rivalries: The frequency, timing, and short-term impact of mediation. *International Interactions* 22 (4): 299–320.

Bidwell, R. L. 1970. *Currency conversion tables: A hundred years of change.* London: Rex Collings.

Bienen, H. S., and N. van de Walle. 1991. *Of time and power: Leadership duration in the modern world.* Stanford, CA: Stanford University Press.

Black, D. 1958. *The theory of committees and elections.* Cambridge, UK: Cambridge University Press.

Blainey, G. 1973. *The causes of war.* New York: Free Press.

———. 1988. *The causes of war.* 3rd ed. New York: Free Press.

Blalock, H. M. 1972. *Social statistics.* New York: McGraw-Hill.

Blanchard, J.-M. F., and N. M. Ripsman. 1994. Peace through economic interdependence? Appeasement in 1936. Paper presented at the annual meeting of the American Political Science Association, New York.

Blomström, M., and B. Hettne. 1984. *Development theory in transition.* London: Zed Books.

Bliss, H., and B. Russett. 1998. Democratic trading partners: The liberal connection. *Journal of Politics* 58 (4): 1126–47.

Boehmer, C. R. 2008. A reassessment of democratic pacifism at the monadic level of analysis. *Conflict Management and Peace Science* 25 (1): 81–94.

Boehmke, F. J., D. S. Morey, and M. Shannon. 2006. Selection bias and continuous-time duration models: Consequences and a proposed solution. *American Journal of Political Science* 50 (1): 192–207.

Bohman, J., and M. Lutz-Bachmann, eds. 1997. *Perpetual peace: Essays on Kant's cosmopolitan ideal.* Cambridge: MIT Press.

Boix, C. 2003. *Democracy and redistribution.* New York: Cambridge University Press.

Bolks, S., and R. J. Stoll. 2000. The arms acquisition process: The effect of internal and external constraints on arms race dynamics. *Journal of Conflict Resolution* 44 (5): 580–603.

Boulding, K. E. 1962. *Conflict and defense: A general theory.* New York: Harper & Row.

Box-Steffensmeier, J., and B. S. Jones. 2004. *Event history modeling: A guide for social scientists.* New York: Cambridge University Press.

Braithwaite, A., and G. Palmer. 2003. The escalation, geography, and evolution of militarized disputes. Paper presented at the annual meeting of the Peace Science Society (International), Ann Arbor, MI.

Braumoeller, B., and A. Sartori. 2004. The promise and perils of statistics in international relations. In *Models, numbers, and cases: Methods for studying international relations,* ed. D. Sprinz and Y. Wolinsky-Nahmias. Ann Arbor: University of Michigan Press.

Brecher, M. 1993. *Crises in world politics: Theory and reality.* New York: Pergamon.

———. 1999. International studies in the twentieth century and beyond: Flawed dichotomies, synthesis, cumulation. *International Studies Quarterly* 43 (2): 213–64.

Brecher, M., and P. James. 1988. Patterns of crisis management. *Journal of Conflict Resolution* 32 (3): 426–56.

Brecher, M., and J. Wilkenfeld. 1991. International crises and global instability: The myth of the "long peace." In *The long postwar peace: Contending explanations and projections,* ed. C. W. Kegley Jr., 85–104. New York: HarperCollins.

———. 1997. *A study of crisis.* Ann Arbor: University of Michigan Press.

Bremer, S. A. 1980a. National capabilities and war proneness. In *The correlates of war: II. Testing some realpolitik models,* ed. J. D. Singer, 57–82. New York: Free Press.

———. 1980b. The trials of nations. In *The correlates of war: II. Testing some realpolitik models,* ed. J. D. Singer. New York: Free Press.

———. 1991. Some observations on advancing the scientific study of war. Paper presented at the workshop on Advancing the Scientific Study of War, Washington, D.C.

———. 1992a. Are democracies less likely to join wars? Paper presented at the annual meeting of the American Political Science Association, Chicago, IL.

———. 1992b. Dangerous dyads: Conditions affecting the likelihood of interstate war, 1816–1965. *Journal of Conflict Resolution* 36 (2): 309–41.

———. 1993. Democracy and militarized interstate conflict, 1816–1965. *International Interactions* 17 (3): 231–49.

———. 2000. Who fights whom, when, where, and why? In *What do we know about war?* ed. J. A. Vasquez, 23–36. Lanham, MD: Rowman & Littlefield.

Bremer, S., and T. R. Cusack, eds. 1993. Advancing the scientific study of war [Special issue]. *International Interactions* 19 (1–2).

———. 1995. *The process of war.* Amsterdam: Gordon and Breach.

Brito, D. L., and M. D. Intriligator. 1983. Proliferation and the probability of war: Global and regional issues. In *Strategies for managing nuclear proliferation,* ed. D. L. Brito, M. D. Intriligator, and A. D. Wick. Lexington, MA: Lexington Books.

———. 1996. Proliferation and the probability of war: A cardinality theorem. *Journal of Conflict Resolution* 40 (1): 206–14.

Brodie, B. 1946. *The absolute weapon.* New York: Harcourt Brace.

Brody, R. A. 1992. *Assessing the president: The media, elite opinion, and public support.* Stanford, CA: Stanford University Press.

Brody, R. A., and B. Page. 1975. The impact of events on presidential popularity. In *Perspectives on the presidency,* ed. A. Wildavsky. Boston: Little, Brown.

Brooks, S. G. Forthcoming. The globalization of production and international security. PhD diss., Yale University.

Bueno de Mesquita, B. 1975. Measuring systemic polarity. *Journal of Conflict Resolution* 19 (2): 187–216.

———. 1981. *The war trap.* New Haven, CT: Yale University Press.

———. 1982. Where war is likely in the next year or two. *U.S. News and World Report,* May 3.

Bueno de Mesquita, B., and D. Lalman. 1992. *War and reason: Domestic and international imperatives.* New Haven, CT: Yale University Press.

Bueno de Mesquita, B., J. D. Morrow, R. M. Siverson, and A. Smith. 1999. An institutional explanation of the democratic peace. *American Political Science Review* 93 (4): 791–807.

———. 2003. *The logic of political survival*. Cambridge: MIT Press.

Bueno de Mesquita, B., J. Morrow, and E. Zorick. 1997. Capabilities, perception, and escalation. *American Political Science Review* 91 (1): 15–27.

Bueno de Mesquita, B., D. Newman, and A. Rabushka. 1985. *Forecasting political events*. New Haven, CT: Yale University Press.

Bueno de Mesquita, B., and W. H. Riker. 1982. An assessment of the merits of selective nuclear proliferation. *Journal of Conflict Resolution* 25 (2): 283–306.

Bueno de Mesquita, B., and R. M. Siverson. 1995. War and the survival of political leaders: A comparative study of regime types and political accountability. *American Political Science Review* 89 (4): 841–55.

Bueno de Mesquita, B., R. Siverson, and G. Woller. 1992. War and the fate of regimes: A comparative analysis. *American Political Science Review* 86 (3): 638–46.

Bueno de Mesquita, B., A. Smith, R. M. Siverson, and J. D. Morrow. 2005. *The logic of political survival*. Cambridge: MIT Press.

Bueno de Mesquita, B., and F. Stokman. 1994. *European community decision making*. New Haven, CT: Yale University Press.

Buzan, B. 1984. Economic structure and international security: The limits of the liberal case. *International Organization* 38 (4): 597–624.

Calahan, H. A. 1944. *What makes a war end?* New York: Vanguard.

Caprioli, M., and M. A. Boyer. 2001. Gender, violence, and international crisis. *Journal of Conflict Resolution* 45 (4): 503–18.

Carter, D. B., and C. S. Signorino. 2010. Back to the future: Modeling time dependence in binary data. *Political Analysis* 18 (3): 271–92.

Cederman, L.-E. 1998. Back to Kant: Reinterpreting the democratic peace as a collective learning process. Unpublished manuscript, Political Science Department, University of California at Los Angeles.

Ch'i, H.-S. 1982. *Nationalist China at war*. Ann Arbor: University of Michigan Press.

Chan, S. 1984. Mirror, mirror on the wall . . . Are the freer countries more pacific? *Journal of Conflict Resolution* 28 (4): 617–48.

———. 1997. In search of democratic peace: Problems and promise. *Myerson International Studies Review* 41 (1): 59–91.

Chandler, D. 1992. *A history of Cambodia*. Boulder, CO: Westview.

Chaney, C. K., R. M. Alvarez, and J. Nagler. 1998. Explaining the gender gap in U.S. presidential elections. *Political Research Quarterly* 51 (2): 311–39.

Chellaney, B. 1995. Naiveté and hypocrisy: Why antiproliferation zealotry does not make sense. *Security Studies* 4 (4): 779–86.

Chiozza, G., and H. E. Goemans. 2004. International conflict and the tenure of leaders: Is war still *ex post* inefficient? *American Journal of Political Science* 48 (3): 604–19.

———. 2011. *Leaders and international conflict*. Cambridge, UK: Cambridge University Press.

Choucri, N., and R. C. North. 1975. *Nations in conflict*. San Francisco: Freeman.

———. 1989. Lateral pressure in international relations: Concept and theory. In *Handbook of War Studies*, ed. M. I. Midlarsky. Boston: Unwin Hyman.

Cimbala, S. 1993. Nuclear weapons in the new world order. *Journal of Strategic Studies* 16 (2): 173–99.

———. 1998. *The past and future of nuclear deterrence*. Westport, CT: Praeger.

Cioffi-Revilla, C. 1998. *Politics and uncertainty: Theory, models and applications.* Cambridge, UK: Cambridge University Press.

Cirincione, J., J. B. Wolfsthal, and M. Rajkumar. 2002. *Deadly arsenals: Tracking weapons of mass destruction.* New York: Carnegie Endowment for International Peace.

Clark, D. H. 2003. Can strategic interaction divert diversionary behavior? A model of U.S. conflict propensity. *Journal of Politics* 65 (4): 1013–39.

Clark, M. T. 1997. Proliferation in the second nuclear age. *Orbis* 41(1): 130–9.

Claude, I. L., Jr. 1962. *Power and international relations.* New York: Random House.

Clodfelter, M. 1992. *Warfare and armed conflicts.* Jefferson, NC: McFarland and Company.

Cohen, A. 1998. *Israel and the bomb.* New York: Columbia University Press.

Cohen, B. J. 1973. *The question of imperialism.* New York: Basic Books.

Colaresi, M. P., K. D. Rasler, and W. R. Thompson. 2007. *Strategic rivalries in world politics: Position, space, and conflict escalation.* Cambridge, UK: Cambridge University Press.

Colaresi, M. P., and W. R. Thompson. 2002. Hot spots or hot hands? Serial crisis behavior, escalating risks, and rivalry. *Journal of Politics* 64 (4): 1175–98.

———. 2005. Alliances, arms buildups and recurrent conflict: Testing a steps-to-war model. *Journal of Politics* 67 (2): 345–64.

Conwell-Evans, T. P. 1929. *International arbitration from Athens to Locarno.* Stanford, CA: Stanford University Press.

Cooper, R. N. 1968. *The economics of interdependence: Economic policy in the Atlantic community.* New York: McGraw-Hill.

Coser, L. A. 1956. *The function of social conflict.* New York: Free Press.

Crescenzi, M. J. C., and A. J. Enterline. 2001. Time remembered: A dynamic model of interstate interaction. *International Studies Quarterly* 45 (3): 409–31.

Crystal, D. 1990. *The Cambridge encyclopedia.* Cambridge, UK: Cambridge University Press.

Cusack, T. R., and M. D. Ward. 1981. Military spending in the United States, Soviet Union, and the People's Republic of China. *Journal of Conflict Resolution* 25 (3): 429–69.

Dassel, K., and E. Reinhardt. 1999. Domestic strife and the initiation of violence at home and abroad. *American Journal of Political Science* 43 (1): 56–85.

de Vries, M. S. 1990. Interdependence, cooperation and conflict: An empirical analysis. *Journal of Peace Research* 27 (4): 429–44.

de Wilde, J. 1991. *Saved from oblivion: Interdependence theory in the first half of the 20th century. A study of the causality between war and complex interdependence.* Aldershot, UK: Dartmouth.

DeRouen, K. R., Jr. 1995. The indirect link: Politics, the economy, and the use of force. *Journal of Conflict Resolution* 39 (4): 671–95.

Diehl, P. F. 1983. Arms races and escalation: A closer look. *Journal of Peace Research* 20 (3): 205–12.

———. 1985a. Arms races to war: Testing some empirical linkages. *Sociological Quarterly* 26 (3): 331–49.

———. 1985b. Contiguity and military escalation in major power rivalries, 1816–1980. *Journal of Peace Research* 29 (3): 333–44.

———. 1991. Geography and war: A review and assessment of the empirical literature. *International Interactions* 17:11–27.

———. 1992. What are they fighting for? The importance of issues in international conflict research. *Journal of Peace Research* 29 (3): 333–44.

———, ed. 1998. *The dynamics of enduring rivalries.* Urbana: University of Illinois Press.

———. 2006. Just a phase? Integrating conflict dynamics over time. *Conflict Management and Peace Science* 23 (3): 199–210.

Diehl, P. F., and M. J. C. Crescenzi. 1998. Reconfiguring the arms race–war debate. *Journal of Peace Research* 35 (1): 111–18.

Diehl, P. F., and G. Goertz. 1988. Territorial changes and militarized conflict. *Journal of Conflict Resolution* 32 (1): 103–22.

———. 2000. *War and peace in international rivalry.* Ann Arbor: University of Michigan Press.

———. 2012. The rivalry process: How rivalries are sustained and terminated. In *What do we know about war?* ed. J. A. Vasquez, 83–109. Lanham, MD: Rowman & Littlefield.

Diehl, P. F., J. Reifschneider, and P. R. Hensel. 1996. UN intervention and recurring conflict. *International Organization* 50 (4): 683–700.

Diggle, P. J., K.-Y. Liang, and S. L. Zeger. 1994. *Analysis of longitudinal data.* Oxford, UK: Clarendon.

Dixon, W. J. 1989. Political democracy and war: A new look at an old problem. Paper presented at the annual meeting of the International Studies Association, London, England.

———. 1993. Democracy and the management of international conflict. *Journal of Conflict Resolution* 37 (1): 42–68.

———. 1994. Democracy and the peaceful settlement of international conflict. *American Political Science Review* 88 (1): 14–32.

———. 1996. Third-party conflict management techniques. *International Organization* 50 (4): 653–82.

Dixon, W., and S. Gaarder. 1992. Presidential succession and the Cold War: An analysis of Soviet-American relations, 1948–1992. *Journal of Politics* 54 (1): 156–75.

Dixon, W., and G. Goertz. 2005. Weakest links, compensability and the liberal peace: A note on measurement validity. In *Social science concepts: A user's guide,* ed. G. Goertz. Princeton, NJ: Princeton University Press.

Dixon, W. J., and B. Moon. 1993. Political similarity and American foreign trade patterns. *Political Research Quarterly* 46 (1): 5–25.

Dixon, W. J., and P. D. Senese. 2002. Democracy, disputes, and negotiated settlements. *Journal of Conflict Resolution* 46 (4): 547–71.

Domke, W. K. 1988. *War and the changing global system.* New Haven, CT: Yale University Press.

Dougherty, J. E., and R. Pfaltzgraff Jr. 1990. *Contending theories of international relations.* 3rd ed. New York: HarperCollins.

Downs, A. 1957. *An economic theory of democracy.* New York, NY: Harper & Row.

Downs, G. W., and D. M. Rocke. 1995. *Optimal imperfection: domestic uncertainty and institutions in international relations.* Princeton, NJ: Princeton University Press.

Doyle, M. W. 1986. Liberalism and world politics. *American Political Science Review* 80 (4): 1151–69.

Dreyer, D. R. 2010. Issue conflict accumulation and the dynamics of strategic rivalry. *International Studies Quarterly* 54 (3): 779–95.

———. 1997. *Ways of war and peace.* New York: W. W. Norton.

Dubin, J., and D. Rivers. 1989. Selection bias in linear regression, logit, and probit models. *Sociological Methods and Research* 18 (2–3): 360–390.

Dupuy, R. E., and T. N. Dupuy. 1996. *The encyclopedia of military history.* New York: Harper & Row.

Duvall, R. 1976. An appraisal of the methodological and statistical procedures of the correlates of war project. In *Quantitative international politics: An appraisal,* ed. F. W. Hoole and D. A. Zinnes, 67–98. New York: Praeger.

Emmanuel, A. 1972. *Unequal exchange: A study of the imperialism of trade.* New York: Monthly Review Press.

Enterline, A. J., and K. S. Gleditsch. 2000. Threats, opportunity, and force: Repression and diversion of domestic pressure, 1948–1982. *International Interactions* 26 (1): 21–53.

Epstein, M., ed. 1913. *The statesman's yearbook, 1913.* London: Macmillan.

Farber, H., and J. Gowa. 1995. Polities and peace. *International Security* 20 (2): 123–46.

———. 1997. Common interests or common polities? *Journal of Politics* 57 (2): 393–417.

Fearon, J. D. 1994a. Signaling versus the balance of power and interests. *Journal of Conflict Resolution* 38 (2): 236–69.

———. 1994b. Domestic political audiences and the escalation of international disputes. *American Political Science Review* 88 (3): 577–92.

———. 1995. Rationalist explanations for war. *International Organization* 49 (3): 379–414.

———. 1997. Signaling foreign policy interests: Tying hands versus sinking costs. *Journal of Conflict Resolution* 41 (1): 68–90.

———. 1998. Bargaining, enforcement, and international cooperation. *International Organization* 52 (2): 269–305.

———. 2002. Selection effects and deterrence. *International Interactions* 28 (1): 5–29.

Fearon, J. D., and D. D. Laitin. 2003. Ethnicity, insurgency, and civil war. *American Political Science Review* 97 (1): 75–90.

Feaver, P. 1992–1993. Command and control in emerging nuclear nations. *International Security* 17 (3): 160–87.

Feaver, P., and E. M. S. Niou. 1996. Managing nuclear proliferation: Condemn, strike, or assist. *International Studies Quarterly* 40 (2): 209–34.

Feldman, S. 1995. Middle East nuclear stability: The state of the region and the state of the debate. *Journal of International Affairs* 49 (1): 205–30.

Filson, D., and S. Werner. 2002. A bargaining model of war and peace: Anticipating the onset, duration, and outcome of war. *American Journal of Political Science* 46 (4): 819–37.

Fiorina, M. P. 1981. *Retrospective voting in American national elections.* New Haven, CT: Yale University Press.

Fisher, R. A. 1922. On the mathematical foundations of theoretical statistics. *Philosophical Transactions of the Royal Statistical Society of London Series A* 222:309–60.

Fordham, B. O. 1998. The politics of threat perception and the use of force: A political economy model of U.S. uses of force, 1949–1994. *International Studies Quarterly* 42 (3): 567–90.

Fordham, B. O., and C. C. Sarver. 2001. Militarized interstate disputes and United States uses of force. *International Studies Quarterly* 45 (3): 455–66.

Forsberg, R., W. Driscoll, G. Webb, and J. Dean. 1995. *Nonproliferation primer: Preventing the spread of nuclear, chemical, and biological weapons.* Cambridge: MIT Press.

Fortna, V. P. 1998. A peace that lasts: Agreements and the durability of peace. PhD diss., Harvard University.

———. 2004. *Peace time: Cease-fire agreements and the durability of peace*. Princeton, NJ: Princeton University Press.

———. 2008. *Does peacekeeping work? Shaping belligerents' choices after civil war*. Princeton, NJ: Princeton University Press.

Foster, D. M. 2006. State power, linkage mechanisms, and diversion against nonrivals. *Conflict Management and Peace Science* 23 (1): 1-21.

Friedberg, A. 2000. *In the shadow of the garrison state: America's anti-statism and its Cold War grand strategy*. Princeton, NJ: Princeton University Press.

Friedman, T. L. 1999. *The lexus and the olive tree*. New York: Farrar, Straus, and Giroux.

Friedrich, R. J. 1982. In defense of multiplicative terms in multiple regression equations. *American Journal of Political Science* 26 (4): 797–833.

Fromberg, D. 2001. *A peace to end all peace: The fall of the Ottoman empire and the creation of the modern Middle East*. New York: Holt.

Fuhrmann, F., and S. E. Kreps. 2010. Targeting nuclear programs in war and peace: A quantitative empirical analysis, 1941–2000. *Journal of Conflict Resolution* 54 (6): 831–59.

Gaddis, J. L. 1986. The long peace: Elements of stability in the postwar international system. *International Security* 10 (4): 99–142.

———. 1987. The long peace: Elements of stability in the postwar international system. In *The long peace: Inquiries into the history of the Cold War*, ed. J. L. Gaddis. Oxford, UK: Oxford University Press.

Gallois, P. 1961. *The balance of terror: Strategy for the nuclear age*. Trans. R. Howard. Boston: Houghton Mifflin.

Garnham, D. 1976. Dyadic international war, 1816–1965: The role of power parity and geographical proximity. *Western Political Quarterly* 29 (2): 231–42.

Gartner, S. S., and R. M. Siverson. 1996. War expansion and war outcome. *Journal of Conflict Resolution* 40 (1): 4–15.

Gartzke, E. 1998. Kant we all just get along? Opportunity, willingness and the origins of the democratic peace. *American Journal of Political Science* 42 (1): 1–27.

———. 2007. The capitalist peace. *American Journal of Political Science* 51 (1): 166–91.

Gartzke, E., and M. W. Simon. 1999. "Hot hand": A critical analysis of enduring rivalries. *Journal of Politics* 61 (3): 777–98.

Gasiorowski, M. 1986a. Economic interdependence and international conflict: Some cross-national evidence. *International Studies Quarterly* 30 (1): 23–28.

———. 1986b. Structure and dynamics in international interdependence. In *Dependency theory and the return of high politics*, ed. M. A. Tetreault and C. F. Abel. New York: Greenwood.

Gasiorowski, M., and S. Polachek. 1982. Conflict and interdependence: East-West trade linkages in the era of detente. *Journal of Conflict Resolution* 26 (4): 709–29.

Gaubatz, K. T. 1991. Election cycle and war. *Journal of Conflict Resolution* 35 (2): 212–43.

Geller, D. S. 1990. Nuclear weapons, deterrence, and crisis escalation. *Journal of Conflict Resolution* 34 (2): 291–310.

———. 1993. Power differentials and war in rival dyads. *International Studies Quarterly* 37 (2): 173–94.

———. 2000. Status Quo orientation, capabilities, and patterns of war initiation in dyadic rivalries. *Conflict Management and Peace Science* 18 (1): 73–96.

———. 2003. Nuclear weapons and the Indo-Pakistani conflict: Global implications of a regional power cycle. *International Political Science Review* 24 (1): 137–50.

———. 2012. Nuclear weapons and war. In *What do we know about war?* ed. J. A. Vasquez. Lanham, MD: Rowman & Littlefield.

Gelpi, C. 1997a. Crime and punishment: The role of norms in crisis bargaining. *American Political Science Review* 91 (2): 339–60.

———. 1997b. Domestic diversions: Governmental structure and the externalization of domestic conflict. *Journal of Conflict Resolution* 41 (2): 255–82.

———. 1999. Alliances as instruments of intra-allied control. In *Imperfect unions: Security institutions over time and space,* ed. H. Haftendorn, R. O. Keohane, and C. A. Wallander. New York: Oxford University Press.

Ghosn, F., and G. Palmer. 2003. Codebook for the militarized interstate dispute data, version 3.0. http://cow2.la.psu.edu

Ghosn, F., G. Palmer, and S. Bremer. 2004. The MID 3 data set, 1993–2001: Procedures, coding rules, and description. *Conflict Management and Peace Science* 21 (2): 133–54.

Gibler, D. 1996. Alliances that never balance: The territorial settlement treaty. *Conflict Management and Peace Science* 16 (1): 75–97.

———. 1997. Control the issues, control the conflict: The effects of alliances that settle territorial issues on interstate rivalries. *International Interactions* 22 (4): 341–68.

———. 2000. Alliances: Why some cause war and why others cause peace. In *What do we know about war?* ed. J. A. Vasquez, 145–64. Lanham, MD: Rowman & Littlefield.

———. 2007. Bordering on peace: Democracy, territorial issues, and conflict. *International Studies Quarterly* 51 (3): 509–32.

———. 2009. *International military alliances, 1648–2008.* Washington, D.C.: Congressional Quarterly Press.

———. 2012. *The territorial peace: Borders, state development and international conflict.* Cambridge, UK: Cambridge University Press.

Gibler, D. M., T. J. Rider, and M. L. Hutchison. 2005. Taking arms against a sea of troubles: Conventional arms races during periods of rivalry. *Journal of Peace Research* 42 (2): 131–47.

Gibler, D., and M. Sarkees. 2004. Measuring alliances: The correlates of war formal interstate alliance data set, 1816–2000. *Journal of Peace Research* 41 (2): 211–22.

Gibler, D., and J. Tir. 2010. Settled borders and regime type: Democratic transitions as consequences of peaceful territorial transfers. *American Journal of Political Science* 54 (4): 951–68.

Gilpin, R. 1981. *War and change in world politics.* New York: Cambridge University Press.

Gleditsch, K., and M. Ward. 1997. Double take: A re-examination of democracy and autocracy in modern polities. *Journal of Conflict Resolution* 41 (3): 361–83.

Gleditsch, K. S. 2002a. *All international politics is local.* Ann Arbor: University of Michigan Press.

———. 2002b. Expanded trade and GDP data. *Journal of Conflict Resolution* 46 (5): 712–24.

Gleditsch, N. P., and H. Hegre. 1997. Peace and democracy: Three levels of analysis. *Journal of Conflict Resolution* 41 (2): 283–310.

Gleditsch, N. P., and J. D. Singer. 1975. Distance and international war, 1816–1965. In *Proceedings of the International Peace Research Association, Fifth General Conference*, ed. M. R. Khan, 481–506. Oslo, Norway: International Peace Research Association.

Gochman, C. S. 1990a. The geography of conflict: Militarized interstate disputes since 1816. Paper presented at the annual meeting of the International Studies Association, Washington, D.C.

———. 1990b. Capability-driven disputes. In *Prisoners of war: Nation-states in the modern era*, ed. C. S. Gochman and A. N. Sabrosky, 141–59. Lexington, MA: Lexington Books.

———. 1991. Interstate metrics: Conceptualizing, operationalizing, and measuring the geographic proximity of states since the Congress of Vienna. *International Interactions* 17 (1): 93–112.

Gochman, C., and R. Leng. 1983. Realpolitik and the road to war: An analysis of attributes and behavior. *International Studies Quarterly* 27 (1): 97–120.

Gochman, C. S., and Z. Maoz. 1984. Militarized interstate disputes, 1816–1976: Procedures, patterns, and insights. *Journal of Conflict Resolution* 28 (4): 586–616.

Goemans, H. E. 1996. Domestic politics and the causes of war termination. PhD diss., University of Chicago.

———. 2000. *War and punishment: The causes of war termination and the First World War*. Princeton, NJ: Princeton University Press.

———. 2006. Territory, territorial attachment and conflict. In *Territoriality and conflict in an era of globalization*, ed. M. Kahler and B. Walter. New York: Cambridge University Press.

Goemans, H. E., K. S. Gleditsch, and G. Chiozza. 2009. Introducing Archigos: A dataset of political leaders. *Journal of Peace Research* 46 (2): 269–83.

Goergiou, G. M., P. T. Kapopoulos, and So Lazaretou. 1996. Modelling Greek-Turkish rivalry: An empirical investigation of defense spending dynamics. *Journal of Peace Research* 33 (2): 229–39.

Goertz, G. 1994. *Contexts of international politics*. Cambridge, UK: Cambridge University Press.

———. 2005. *Social science concepts: A user's guide*. Princeton, NJ: Princeton University Press.

Goertz, G., and P. F. Diehl. 1990. Territorial changes and recurring conflict. In *Prisoners of war: Nation-states in the modern era*, ed. C. S. Gochman and A. N. Sabrosky, 57–72. Lexington, MA: Lexington Books.

———. 1992a. *Territorial changes and international conflict*. New York: Routledge.

———. 1992b. The empirical importance of enduring rivalries. *International Interactions* 18 (2): 151–63.

———. 1993. Enduring rivalries: Theoretical constructs and empirical patterns. *International Studies Quarterly* 37 (1): 147–71.

———. 2000. (Enduring) rivalries. In *Handbook of war studies II*, ed. M. Midlarsky. Ann Arbor: University of Michigan Press.

Goertz, G., B. Jones, and P. F. Diehl. 2005. Maintenance processes in international rivalries. *Journal of Conflict Resolution* 49 (5): 742–69.

Goheen, R. F. 1983. Problems of proliferation: U.S. policy and the third world. *World Politics* 35 (2): 194–215.

Goldstein, A. 2000. *Deterrence and security in the 21st century*. Stanford, CA: Stanford University Press.

Goldstein, J. 2011. *Winning the war on war: The decline of armed conflict worldwide.* New York: Plume/Penguin Group.

Gowa, J. 1994. *Allies, adversaries, and international trade.* Princeton, NJ: Princeton University Press.

———. 1999. *Ballots and bullets: The elusive democratic peace.* Princeton, NJ: Princeton University Press.

Greene, W. H. 1990. *Econometric analysis.* New York: Macmillan.

———. 1993. *Econometric analysis.* 2nd ed. New York: Macmillan.

———. 1996a. *Econometric analysis.* New York: Macmillan.

———. 1996b. Marginal effects in the bivariate probit model. Working paper EC-96-11, Stern School of Business, New York University.

Greig, J. M. 2001. Moments of opportunity: Recognizing conditions of ripeness for international mediation between enduring rivals. *Journal of Conflict Resolution* 45 (6): 691–718.

Grieco, J. M. 1988. Realist theory and the problem of international cooperation: Analysis with an amended prisoner's dilemma model. *Journal of Politics* 50 (3): 600–24.

Gurr, T. R. 1990. Polity II: Political structures and regime change, 1800–1986 [data set]. Ann Arbor: Inter-University Consortium for Political and Social Research, University of Michigan.

Gurr, T. R., K. Jaggers, and W. H. Moore. 1989. *Polity II handbook* [Mimeo]. Boulder: University of Colorado.

Haas, E. B. 1958. *The uniting of Europe.* Stanford, CA: Stanford University Press.

———. 1964. *Beyond the nation-state.* Stanford, CA: Stanford University Press.

Hagerty, D. T. 1998. *Lessons from South Asia.* London: MIT Press.

Hampson, F. O. 1996. *Nurturing peace: Why peace settlements succeed or fail.* Washington, D.C.: U.S. Institution of Peace Press.

Hanneman, R. A., and R. L. Steinback. 1990. Military involvement and political instability: An event history analysis, 1940–1980. *Journal of Military and Political Sociology* 18 (1): 1–23.

Hansen, H., S. M. Mitchell, and S. C. Nemeth. 2008. Mediating interstate conflicts: Regional vs. global international organizations. *Journal of Conflict Resolution* 52 (2): 295–325.

Hanson, M. 2002. Nuclear weapons as obstacles to international security. *International Relations* 16 (3): 361–80.

Harrison, E. 2004. State socialization, international norm dynamics and the liberal peace. *International Politics* 41 (4): 521–42.

Hart, R., and W. Reed. 1999. Selection effects and dispute escalation. *International Interactions* 25 (3): 243–63.

Hayslett, H. T., Jr. 1968. *Statistics made simple.* New York: Doubleday.

Heckman, J. D. 1979. Sample selection bias as a specification error. *Econometrica* 47 (1): 153–62.

Hegre, H. 2004. Size asymmetry, trade, and militarized conflict. *Journal of Conflict Resolution* 48 (3): 403–29.

———. 2009. Trade dependence or size dependence? The gravity model of trade and the liberal peace. *Conflict Management and Peace Science* 26 (1): 26–45.

Heidt, B. 1998. Inherency, contingency, and theories of conflict and peace. Unpublished manuscript, Yale University.

Henderson, E. A. 2002. *Democracy and war: The end of an illusion.* Bolder, CO: Lynne Rienner.

Henehan, M. 2001. The effect of territory on dispute escalation among initiators: A research note. Paper presented at the annual meeting of the International Studies Association, Hong Kong.

Hensel, P. R. 1994. One thing leads to another: Recurrent militarized disputes in Latin America, 1816–1990. *Journal of Peace Research* 31 (3): 281–98.

———. 1996a. Charting a course to conflict: Territorial issues and militarized interstate disputes, 1816–1992. *Conflict Management and Peace Science* 15 (1): 43–73.

———. 1996b. The evolution of interstate rivalry. PhD diss., University of Michigan.

———. 1998. Interstate rivalry and the study of militarized conflict. In *Conflict in world politics: Advances in the study of crisis, war, and peace*, ed. F. P. Harvey and B. D. Mor, 162–204. New York: St. Martin's.

———. 1999. An evolutionary approach to the study of interstate rivalry. *Conflict Management and Peace Science* 17:175–206.

———. 2000. Territory: Theory and evidence on geography and conflict. In *What do we know about war?* ed. J. A. Vasquez, 57–84. Lanham, MD: Rowman & Littlefield.

———. 2001. Contentious issues and world politics: The management of territorial claims in the Americas, 1816–1992. *International Studies Quarterly* 45 (1): 81–109.

Hensel, P. R., and S. M. Mitchell. 2005. Issue indivisibility and territorial claims. *Geo Journal* 64 (4): 275–85.

———. 2006. Issues Correlates of War (ICoW) project. http://www.icow.org

Hensel, P. R., S. M. Mitchell, and T. E. Sowers II. 2006. Conflict management of riparian disputes: A regional comparison of dispute resolution. *Political Geography* 25 (4): 383–411.

Hensel, P. R., S. M. Mitchell, T. E. Sowers II, and C. L. Thyne. 2008. Bones of contention: Comparing territorial, maritime, and river issues. *Journal of Conflict Resolution* 52 (1): 117–43.

Herz, J. 1950. Idealist internationalism and the security dilemma. *World Politics* 2 (2): 157–80.

Hess, G. D., and A. Orphanides. 1995. War politics: An economic, rational-voter framework. *American Economic Review* 85 (4): 828–47.

Hewitt, J. J. 2003. Dyadic processes and international crises. *Journal of Conflict Resolution* 47(5): 669–92.

———. 2005. A crisis-density formulation for identifying rivalries. *Journal of Peace Research* 42 (2): 183–200.

Hillen, J. 1998. *The blue helmets: The strategy of UN military operations*. Washington, D.C.: Brassey's.

Hintze, O. [1906] 1975. Military Organization and State Organization. In *The Historical Essays of Otto Hintze*, ed. F. Gilbert. Reprint, New York: Oxford University Press.

Hirsch, L. P. 1986. Incorporation into the world economy: Empirical tests of dependency theory. In *Dependency Theory and the Return of High Politics*, ed. M. A. Tetreault and C. F. Abel. New York: Greenwood.

Hirschman, A. O. [1945] 1980. *National power and the structure of foreign trade*. Reprint. Berkeley: University of California Press.

Holsti, K. J. 1991. *Peace and war: Armed conflicts and international order, 1648–1989*. Cambridge, UK: Cambridge University Press.

Holsti, O. R., P. T. Hopmann, and J. D. Sullivan. 1985. *Unity and disintegration in international alliances*. Lanham, MD: University Press of America.

Horn, M. D. 1987. Arms races and the international system. PhD diss., University of Rochester.

Horton, R. E. 1999. *Out of (South) Africa: Pretoria's nuclear weapons experience.* Occasional paper. Colorado Springs, CO: USAF Institute for National Security Studies.

Hughes, B. 1971. Transaction analysis: The impact of operationalization. *International Organization* 25 (1): 132–9.

Huntington, S. P. 1958. Arms races: Prerequisites and results. *Public Policy* 8 (1): 41–86.

———. 1991. *The third wave: Democratization in the late twentieth century.* Norman: University of Oklahoma Press.

Huntley, W. 1996. Kant's third image: Systemic sources of the liberal peace. *International Studies Quarterly* 40 (4): 45–76.

Hutchison, M. L., and D. M. Gibler. 2007. Political tolerance and territorial threat: A cross-national study. *Journal of Politics* 69 (1): 128–42.

Huth, P. K. 1988. *Extended deterrence and the prevention of war.* New Haven, CT: Yale University Press.

———. 1990. The extended deterrence value of nuclear weapons. *Journal of Conflict Resolution* 34 (2): 270–90.

———. 1996. *Standing your ground: Territorial disputes and international conflict.* Ann Arbor: University of Michigan Press.

———. 1998. Major power intervention in international crises, 1918–1988. *Journal of Conflict Resolution* 42 (6): 744–70.

———. 1999. Deterrence and international conflict: Empirical findings and theoretical debates. *Annual Review of Political Science* 2 (1): 25–48.

Huth, P. K., and T. Allee. 2002. *The democratic peace and territorial conflict in the twentieth century.* Cambridge, UK: Cambridge University Press.

Huth, P. K., and B. Russett. 1984. What makes deterrence work? Cases from 1900 to 1980. *World Politics* 36 (4): 496–526.

———. 1988. Deterrence failure and crisis escalation. *International Studies Quarterly* 32 (1): 29–45.

———. 1990. Testing deterrence theory: Rigor makes a difference. *World Politics* 42 (4): 466–501.

———. 1993. General deterrence between enduring rivals: Testing three competing models. *American Political Science Review* 87 (1): 61–75.

Ikenberry, G. J. 2001. *After victory: Institutions, strategic restraint, and the rebuilding of order after major wars.* Princeton, NJ: Princeton University Press.

Ikle, F. C. 1991. *Every war must end.* New York: Columbia University Press.

International Monetary Fund (IMF). 1993. *Direction of trade (ICPSR 7623).* Washington, D.C.: IMF.

Israel, F. L. 1967. *Major peace treaties of modern history, 1648–1967.* New York: Chelsea House.

Jackman, R. W. 1993. *Power without force.* Ann Arbor: University of Michigan Press.

Jaggers, K., and T. R. Gurr. 1995. Tracking democracy's third wave with the Polity III data. *Journal of Peace Research* 32 (4): 469–82.

———. 1996. Polity III: Regime change and political authority, 1800–1994. 2nd release. T. R. Gurr, producer. Ann Arbor, MI: Inter-University Consortium for Political and Social Research, distributor.

James, P. 1988. *Crisis and war.* Montreal: McGill-Queen's University Press.

James, P., and A. Hristoulas. 1994. Domestic politics and foreign policy: Evaluating a model of crisis activity for the United States. *Journal of Politics* 56 (2): 327–48.

James, P., and J. Oneal. 1991. Influences on the president's use of force. *Journal of Conflict Resolution* 35 (2): 307–32.

Jervis, R. 1976. *Perception and misperception in international politics.* Princeton, NJ: Princeton University Press.

———. 1978. Co-operation under the security dilemma. *World Politics* 30 (2): 167–214.

Johnson, J. C., and B. A. Leeds. 2011. Defense pacts: A prescription for peace? *Foreign Policy Analysis* 7 (1): 45–65.

Jones, D. M., S. A. Bremer, and J. D. Singer. 1996. Militarized interstate disputes, 1816–1992: Rationale, coding rules, and empirical patterns. *Conflict Management and Peace Science* 15 (2): 163–213.

Kahn, H. 1960. *On thermonuclear war.* Princeton, NJ: Princeton University Press.

Kahn, S. 2001. A nuclear South Asia: Resolving or protracting the protracted conflict? *International Relations* 15 (4): 61–78.

Kaiser, K. 1989. Nonproliferation and nuclear deterrence. *Survival* 31 (2): 123–36.

Kalbfleisch, J. D., and R. Prentice. 1980. *The statistical analysis of failure time data.* New York: John Wiley.

Kant, I. 1970. *Perpetual peace: A philosophical sketch.* In *Kant's political writings,* ed. H. Reiss. Cambridge, UK: Cambridge University Press.

Kant, I. 1991. *Perpetual peace.* In *Kant's political writings 1795,* ed. H. Reiss. Cambridge, UK: Cambridge University Press.

Karl, D. J. 1996/1997. Proliferation pessimism and emerging nuclear powers. *International Security* 21 (3): 87–119.

Kecskemeti, P. 1958. *Strategic surrender: The politics of victory and defeat.* Stanford, CA: Stanford University Press.

Kegley, C., and N. Richardson. 1980. Trade dependence and foreign policy compliance: A longitudinal analysis. *International Studies Quarterly* 24 (2): 191–222.

Kennedy, R. F. 1969. *Thirteen days.* New York: Norton.

Keohane, R., and J. Nye. 1977, 1997. *Power and interdependence: World politics in transition.* Boston: Little, Brown.

Keohane, R. O., and L. Martin. 1995. The promise of institutionalist theory. *International Security* 20 (1): 39–51.

Kernell, S. H. 1978. Explaining presidential popularity. *American Political Science Review* 72 (2): 506–22.

Kilgour, D. M., and F. C. Zagare. 1991. Credibility, uncertainty and deterrence. *American Journal of Political Science* 35 (2): 305–34.

Kim, S. Y. 1998. Ties that bind: The role of trade in international conflict processes. PhD diss., Yale University.

Kim, W. 1991. Alliance transitions and great power war. *American Journal of Political Science* 35 (4): 833–50.

King, G. 1987. Presidential appointments to the Supreme Court. *American Politics Quarterly* 15 (3): 373–86.

———. 1989. *Unifying political methodology.* New York: Cambridge University Press.

———. 1997. *Solution to the ecological inference problem.* Princeton, NJ: Princeton University Press.

King, G., J. Alt, N. Burns, and M. Laver. 1990. A unified model of cabinet dissolution in parliamentary democracies. *American Journal of Political Science* 34 (3): 846–71.

King, G., J. Honaker, A. Joseph, and K. Scheve. 2001. Analyzing incomplete political science data: An alternative algorithm for multiple imputation. *American Political Science Review* 95 (1): 49–69.

King, G., M. Tomz, and J. Wittenberg. 2000. Making the most of statistical analyses: Improving interpretation and presentation. *American Journal of Political Science* 44 (2): 347–61.

Kleiboer, M. 1996. Understanding success and failure of international mediation. *Journal of Conflict Resolution* 40 (2): 360–89.

Klein, J. P., G. Goertz, and P. F. Diehl. 2006. The new rivalry dataset: Procedures and patterns. *Journal of Peace Research* 43 (3): 331–48.

Kocs, S. 1995. Territorial disputes and interstate war. *Journal of Politics* 57 (1): 159–75.

Kohn, G. C. 1986. *Dictionary of wars.* New York: Doubleday.

Kokoski, R. 1995. *Technology and the proliferation of nuclear weapons.* New York: Oxford University Press, in conjunction with SIPRI.

Kroll, J. A. 1993. The complexity of interdependence. *International Studies Quarterly* 37 (3): 321–47.

Kugler, J. 1984. Terror without deterrence: Reassessing the role of nuclear weapons. *Journal of Conflict Resolution* 28 (2): 470–506.

Kugler, J., and D. Lemke, eds. 1996. *Parity and war: Evaluations and extensions of "The War Ledger."* Ann Arbor: University of Michigan Press.

Lakatos, I. 1970. Falsification and the methodology of scientific research programmes. In *Criticism and the growth of knowledge,* ed. I. Lakatos and A. Musgrave, 91–196. Cambridge, UK: Cambridge University Press.

Lake, D. 1992. Powerful pacifists: Democratic states and war. *American Political Science Review* 86 (1): 24–37.

Lancaster, T., and A. Chesher. 1985a. Residual analysis for censored duration data. *Economics Letters* 18 (1): 35–38.

———. 1985b. Residuals, tests, and plots with a job matching illustration. *Annales de l'Insee* 59–60: 47–70.

Langer, W. 1972. *Encyclopedia of world history.* Boston: Houghton Mifflin.

———. 1980. *An encyclopedia of world history.* 5th ed. Boston: Houghton Mifflin.

Lasswell, H. J., and A. Kaplan. 1950. *Power and society.* New Haven, CT: Yale University Press.

Lattimore, O. 1990. *China memoirs: Chiang Kai-shek and the war against Japan.* Tokyo: University of Tokyo Press.

Lavoy, P. R. 1995. The strategic consequences of nuclear proliferation. *Security Studies* 4 (4): 695–753.

League of Nations. Annual Volumes. *International trade statistics.* Geneva, Switzerland: League of Nations.

———. 1910–1940. *Memorandum on international trade and balance of payments statistics.* Geneva, Switzerland: League of Nations.

Lebow, R. N. 1981. *Between peace and war.* Baltimore: Johns Hopkins University Press.

Lebow, R. N., and J. G. Stein. 1990. Deterrence: The elusive dependent variable. *World Politics* 42 (3): 208–24.

Leeds, B. A. 1998. Comprehending cooperation: Credible commitments and international relations. PhD diss., Emory University.

———. 1999. Domestic political institutions, credible commitments, and international cooperation. *American Journal of Political Science* 43 (4): 979–1002.

—————. 2003a. Do alliances deter aggression? The influence of military alliances on the initiation of militarized interstate disputes. *American Journal of Political Science* 47 (3): 427–39.

—————. 2003b. Alliance reliability in times of war: Explaining state decisions to violate treaties. *International Organization* 57 (4): 801–27.

—————. 2005. Alliances and the expansion and escalation of militarized interstate disputes. In *New directions for international relations,* ed. A. Mintz and B. Russett, 117–34. Lanham, MD: Lexington Books.

Leeds, B. A., and D. R. Davis. 1997. Domestic political vulnerability and international disputes. *Journal of Conflict Resolution* 41 (6): 814–34.

Leeds, B. A., A. G. Long, and S. M. Mitchell. 2000. Re-evaluating alliance reliability: Specific threats, specific promises. *Journal of Conflict Resolution* 44 (5): 686–9.

Leeds, B. A., J. M. Ritter, S. M. Mitchell, and A. G. Long. 2002. Alliance treaty obligations and provisions, 1815–1944. *International Interactions* 28 (3): 261–84.

Lemke, D. 1993. Multiple hierarchies in world politics. PhD diss., Vanderbilt University.

—————. 1996. Small states and war: An expansion of power transition theory. In *Parity and war: Evaluations and extensions of The War Ledger,* ed. J. Kugler and D. Lemke. Ann Arbor: University of Michigan Press.

—————. 2002. *Regions of war and peace.* Cambridge, UK: Cambridge University Press.

Lemke, D., and W. Reed. 1996. Regime types and status quo evaluations. *International Interactions* 22 (2): 143–64.

—————. 1998. Power is not satisfaction. *Journal of Conflict Resolution* 42 (4): 511–16.

—————. 2001a. The relevance of politically relevant dyads. *Journal of Conflict Resolution* 45 (1): 126–44.

—————. 2001b. War and rivalry among great powers. *American Journal of Political Science* 45 (2): 457–69.

Lemke, D., and S. Werner. 1996. Power parity, commitment to change, and war. *International Studies Quarterly* 40 (2): 235–60.

Leng, R. 1983. When will they ever learn? Coercive bargaining in recurrent crises. *Journal of Conflict Resolution* 27 (3): 379–419.

Lenin, V. I. [1939] 1990. *Imperialism, the highest stage of capitalism.* Reprint. New York: International Publishers.

Lentz, H. M. 1994. *Heads of states and governments: A worldwide encyclopedia of over 2,300 leaders, 1945 through 1992.* Jefferson, NC: McFarland & Company.

Lerner, D. 1956. French business leaders look at EDC. *Public Opinion Quarterly* 24 (1): 212–21.

Levy, J. 1981. Alliance formation and war behavior: An analysis of the great powers, 1495–1975. *Journal of Conflict Resolution* 25 (4): 581–613.

—————. 1988. Domestic politics and war. *Journal of Interdisciplinary History* 18 (4): 653–73.

—————. 1989a. The diversionary theory of war: A critique. In *Handbook of war studies,* ed. M. I. Midlarsky, 259–88. Ann Arbor: University of Michigan Press.

—————. 1989b. The causes of war: A review of theories and evidence. In *Behavior, society, and nuclear war,* ed. P. E. Tetlock, J. L. Husbands, R. Jervis, and P. C. Stern, 209–333. New York: Oxford University Press.

Levy, J. S., and K. Barbieri. 2004. Trading with the enemy during wartime. *Security Studies* 13 (3): 1–47.

Levy, J. S., and W. R. Thompson. 2005. Hegemonic threats and great power balancing in Europe, 1495–2000. *Security Studies* 14 (1): 1–33.

Lewis-Beck, M., and H. Eulau. 1985. Economic conditions and electoral outcomes in trans-national perspective. In *Economic conditions and electoral outcomes,* ed. H. Eulau and M. Lewis-Beck. New York: Agathon.

Lewis-Beck, M. S. 1990. *Economics and elections: The major Western democracies.* Ann Arbor: University of Michigan Press.

Li, Q., and T. Vashchilko. 2010. Dyadic military conflict, security alliances, and bilateral FDI flows. *Journal of International Business Studies* 41 (5): 765–82.

Lian, B., and J. R. Oneal. 1993. Presidents, the use of military force and public opinion. *Journal of Conflict Resolution* 37 (2): 277–300.

Liao, T. F. 1994. *Interpreting probability models: Logit, probit, and other generalized linear models.* Thousand Oaks, CA: Sage.

Liberman, P. 2001. The rise and fall of the South African bomb. *International Security* 26 (2): 45–86.

Licklider, R. 1995. The consequences of negotiated settlements in civil wars, 1945–1993. *American Political Science Review* 89 (3): 681–90.

Lieberman, E. 1994. The rational deterrence theory debate: Is the dependent variable elusive? *Security Studies* 3 (3): 384–427.

———. 1995. What makes deterrence work? Lessons from the Egyptian-Israeli enduring rivalry. *Security Studies* 4 (4): 851–910.

LIMDEP version 5.1. 1988. New York: Economic Software.

Lindsey, J. K. 2004. *Statistical analysis of stochastic processes in time.* Cambridge, UK: Cambridge University Press.

Lipson, C. 2003. *Reliable partners: How democracies have made a separate peace.* Princeton, NJ: Princeton University Press.

Lo, N., B. Hashimoto, and D. Reiter. 2008. Ensuring peace: Foreign-imposed regime change and postwar peace duration, 1914–2001. *International Organization* 62 (4): 717–36.

Londregan, J. B., and K. Poole. 1990. Poverty, the coup trap, and the seizure of executive power. *World Politics* 42 (2): 151–83.

Long, J. S. 1997. *Regression models for categorical and limited dependent variables.* Thousand Oaks, CA: Sage.

Luard, E. 1986. *War in international society.* New Haven, CT: Yale University Press.

MacKenzie, K. 1980. *The English parliament.* Harmondsworth, UK: Penguin.

Mackie, T. T., and R. Rose. 1991. *The international almanac of electoral history.* 3rd ed. London: Macmillan.

Maddala, G. S. 1983. *Limited-dependent and qualitative variables in econometrics.* Cambridge, UK: Cambridge University Press.

Maddison, A. 1991. *A long run perspective on saving.* Groningen, the Netherlands: Institute of Economic Research, University of Groningen.

———. 1995. *Monitoring the world economy, 1820–1992.* Paris: Organization for Economic Cooperation and Development.

Majeski, S. J. 1983. Mathematical models of the United States military expenditure decision-making process. *American Journal of Political Science* 27 (3): 485–514.

Mansbach, R., and J. Vasquez. 1981. *In search of theory: A new paradigm for global politics.* New York: Columbia University Press.

Mansfield, E. D. 1994. *Power, trade, and war.* Princeton, NJ: Princeton University Press.

Mansfield, E. D., and J. Snyder. 1995. Democratization and the danger of war. *International Security* 20 (1): 5–38.

Manski, C. 1989. Anatomy of the selection problem. *Journal of Human Resources* 24 (3): 343–60.

———. 1995. *Identification problems in econometrics.* Cambridge, MA: Harvard University Press.

Maoz, Z. 1984. Peace by empire? Conflict outcomes and international stability, 1816–1976. *Journal of Peace Research* 21 (3): 227–41.

———. 1996. *Domestic sources of global change.* Ann Arbor: University of Michigan Press.

———. 2005. Dyadic MID dataset. Version 2.0. http://psfaculty.ucdavis.edu/zmaoz/dyadmid.html

Maoz, Z., and N. Abdolali. 1989. Regime types and international conflict, 1816–1976. *Journal of Conflict Resolution* 33:3–36.

Maoz, Z., and B. D. Mor. 2002. *Bound by struggle: The strategic evolution of enduring international rivalries.* Ann Arbor: University of Michigan Press.

Maoz, Z., and B. Russett. 1993. Normative and structural causes of democratic peace, 1946–1986. *American Political Science Review* 87 (3): 624–38.

Marshall, M. G. 1999. *Third world war.* Lanham, MD: Rowman and Littlefield.

Marshall, M. G., and K. Jaggers. 2002. *Polity IV project: Dataset user's manual.* http://www.cidcm.umd.edu/inscr/polity

———. 2004. *Polity IV project: Political regime characteristics and transitions, 1800–1999.* http://www.cidcm.umd.edu/inscr/polity/

Martin, L., and B. Simmons. 1998. Theories and empirical studies of international institutions. *International Organization* 52 (4): 729–57.

Mashhadi, H. 1994. Multilateral agreements. In *Disarmament and arms limitation obligations: Problems of compliance and enforcement,* ed. S. Sur. Brookfield, VT: Dartmouth.

Maslow, A. H. 1970. *Motivation and personality.* 3rd ed. New York: HarperCollins.

Mason, R. 1992. Nuclear weapons and arms control in Europe. In *Nuclear deterrence and global security in transition,* ed. D. Goldfischer and T. W. Graham. Oxford, UK: Westview.

Mastanduno, M. 1993. Do relative gains matter? In *Neo-realism and neoliberalism: The contemporary debate,* ed. D. Baldwin. New York: Columbia University Press.

Mattes, M. 2008. The effect of changing conditions and agreement provisions on conflict and renegotiation between states with competing claims. *International Studies Quarterly* 52 (2): 315–34.

McGwire, M. 1994. Is there a future for nuclear weapons? *International Affairs* 70 (2): 211–28.

McMillan, S. 1997. Interdependence and conflict. *Mershon International Studies Review* 41 (1): 33–58.

Mearsheimer, J. 1989. Assessing the conventional balance: The 3:1 rule and its critics. *International Security* 13 (4): 54–89.

———. 1990. Back to the future: Instability in Europe after the Cold War. *International Security* 15 (1): 5–56.

———. 1993. The case for a Ukrainian nuclear deterrent. *Foreign Affairs* 72 (3): 50–66.

———. 1994–1995. The false promise of international institutions. *International Security* 19 (3): 5–49.

Meernik, J. 1994. Presidential decision making and the political use of force. *International Studies Quarterly* 38 (1): 121–38.

Meernik, J., and P. Waterman. 1996. The myth of the diversionary use of force by American presidents. *Political Research Quarterly* 49 (3): 573–90.

Meng, C.-L., and P. Schmidt. 1985. On the costs of partial observability in the bivariate probit model. *International Economic Review* 26 (1): 71–86.

Miall, H. 1992. *The peacemakers: Peaceful settlement of disputes since 1945*. London: Macmillan.

Midlarsky, M. 1984. Preventing systemic war. *Journal of Conflict Resolution* 28 (4): 563–84.

Miers, A. C., and T. C. Morgan. 2002. Multilateral sanctions and foreign policy success: Can too many cooks spoil the broth? *International Interactions* 28 (2): 117–36.

Miller, R. A. 1995. Domestic structures and the diversionary use of force. *American Journal of Political Science* 39 (3): 760–85.

Mitchell, B. R. 1982. *International historical statistics for Africa and Asia*. New York: New York University Press.

———. 1983. *International historical statistics for the Americas and Australasia*. Detroit, MI: Gale.

———. Various years. *International historical statistics*. Cambridge, UK: Cambridge University Press.

Mitchell, S. M. 2002. A Kantian system? Democracy and third party conflict resolution. *American Journal of Political Science* 46 (4): 749–59.

Mitchell, S. M., S. Gates, and H. Hegre. 1999. Evolution in democracy-war dynamics. *Journal of Conflict Resolution* 43 (6): 771–92.

Mitchell, S. M., and W. H. Moore. 2002. Presidential uses of force during the Cold War: Aggregation, truncation, and temporal dynamics. *American Journal of Political Science* 46 (2): 438–52.

Mitchell, S. M., and B. C. Prins. 1999. Beyond territorial contiguity: Issues at stake in democratic militarized interstate disputes. *International Studies Quarterly* 43 (1): 169–83.

———. 2004. Rivalry and diversionary uses of force. *Journal of Conflict Resolution* 48 (6): 937–61.

Mitchell, S. M., and C. G. Thies. 2011. Issue rivalries. *Conflict Management and Peace Science* 28 (3): 230–60.

Mitchell, S. M., and C. L. Thyne. 2010. Contentious issues as opportunities for diversionary behavior. *Conflict Management and Peace Science* 27 (5): 461–85.

Mitrany, D. 1964. *A working peace system*. Chicago, IL: Quadrangle.

Modelski, G., ed. 1987. *Exploring long cycles*. Boulder, CO: Lynne Rienner.

Moore, B. 1966. *Social origins of dictatorship and democracy*. Boston: Beacon.

Morgan, P. M. 2003. *Deterrence now*. Cambridge, UK: Cambridge University Press.

Morgan, T. C. 1984. A spatial model of crisis bargaining. *International Studies Quarterly* 28 (4): 407–26.

———. 1990. Power, resolve and bargaining in international crises: A spatial model. *International Interactions* 15 (3–4): 279–302.

———. 1994. *Untying the knot of war*. Ann Arbor: Michigan University Press.

Morgan, T. C., and C. J. Anderson. 1999. Domestic support and diversionary external conflict in Great Britain, 1950–1992. *Journal of Politics* 61 (3): 799–814.

Morgan, T. C., and K. N. Bickers. 1992. Domestic discontent and the external use of force. *Journal of Conflict Resolution* 36 (1): 25–52.

Morgan, T. C., and S. H. Campbell. 1991. Domestic structure, decisional constraints and war behavior: So why Kant democracies fight? *Journal of Conflict Resolution* 35 (2): 187–211.

Morgan, T. C., and G. Palmer. 2002. A model of foreign policy substitutability: Selecting the right tools for the job(s). *Journal of Conflict Resolution* 44 (1): 11–32.

Morgan, T. C., and V. L. Schwebach. 1991. Domestic structure and war. Paper presented at the annual meeting of the International Studies Association, Vancouver, Canada.

————. 1992. Take two democracies and call me in the morning: A prescription for peace? *International Interactions* 17 (4): 305–20.

Morgenstern, K. K., and K. P. Heiss. 1973. *Long term projections of power: Political, economic, and military forecasting.* Cambridge, MA: Ballinger.

Morgenthau, H. J. 1964. *Politics among nations.* 3rd ed. New York: Knopf.

Morrow, J., R. Siverson, and T. Tabares. 1998. The political determinants of international trade: The major powers, 1907–90. *American Political Science Review* 92 (3): 649–61.

Morrow, J. D. 1986. A spatial model of international conflict. *American Political Science Review* 80 (4): 1131–49.

————. 1987. On the theoretical basis of risk attitudes. *International Studies Quarterly* 31 (4): 423–38.

————. 1989. Capabilities, uncertainty, and resolve: A limited information model of crisis bargaining. *American Journal of Political Science* 33 (4): 941–72.

————. 1994. Alliances, credibility, and peacetime costs. *Journal of Conflict Resolution* 38 (2): 270–97.

Most, B. A., and H. Starr. 1989. *Inquiry, logic and international politics.* Columbia: University of South Carolina Press.

Moul, W. B. 1988. Great power nondefense alliances and the escalation to war of conflicts between unequals, 1815–1939. *International Interactions* 15 (1): 25–43.

Mousseau, M. 1998. Democracy and compromise in interstate conflicts, 1816–1992. *Journal of Conflict Resolution* 42 (2): 210–30.

————. 2002. An economic limitation to the zone of democratic peace and cooperation. *International Interactions* 28 (2): 137–64.

————. 2003. The nexus of market society, liberal preferences, and democratic peace: Interdisciplinary theory and evidence. *International Studies Quarterly* 47 (4): 483–510.

————. 2012. Capitalist development and civil war. *International Studies Quarterly* 56 (3): 470–83.

Mueller, J. 1973. *War, presidents, and public opinion.* New York: John Wiley.

————. 1988. The essential irrelevance of nuclear weapons. *International Security* 13 (2): 55–79.

————. 1989. *Retreat from doomsday.* New York: Basic Books.

Neack, L. 1995. UN peace-keeping: In the interest of community or self? *Journal of Peace Research* 32 (2): 181–96.

Nemeth, S. C., S. M. Mitchell, E. A. Nyman, and P. R. Hensel. 2007. UNCLOS, EEZs, and the management of maritime claims. Working paper, University of Iowa.

Nguyen-vo, T.-H. 1992. *Khmer-Viet relations and the third Indochina conflict.* Jefferson, NC: McFarland & Company.

Norpoth, H. 1987. Guns and butter and governmental popularity in Britain. *American Political Science Review* 81 (3): 949–59.

Norpoth, H., M. Lewis-Beck, and J.-D. Lafay. 1991. *Economics and politics: The calculus of support.* Ann Arbor: University of Michigan Press.

North, D. C., and B. R. Weingast. 1989. Constitutions and commitment: The evolution of institutions governing public choice in seventeenth-century England. *Journal of Economic History* 49 (4): 803–32.

O'Leary, M. 1976. The role of issues. In *In search of global patterns,* ed. J. Rosenau, 318–25. New York: Free Press.

Oneal, J. R. 1989. Measuring the material base of the contemporary East-West balance of power. *International Interactions* 15 (2): 177–96.

Oneal, J. R., F. Oneal, Z. Maoz, and B. Russett. 1996. The liberal peace: Interdependence, democracy and international conflict, 1950–1986. *Journal of Peace Research* 33 (1): 11–28.

Oneal, J. R., and J. L. Ray. 1997. New tests of the democratic peace controlling for economic interdependence, 1950–1985. *Political Research Quarterly* 50 (4): 751–75.

Oneal, J. R., and B. Russett. 1997. The classical liberals were right: Democracy, interdependence, and conflict, 1950–1985. *International Studies Quarterly* 40 (2): 267–94.

———. 1999a. Assessing the liberal peace with alternative specifications: Trade still reduces conflict. *Journal of Peace Research* 36 (4): 423–42.

———. 1999b. Is the liberal peace just an artifact of Cold War interests? Assessing recent critiques. *International Interactions* 25 (3): 213–41.

———. 1999c. The Kantian peace: The pacific benefits of democracy, interdependence, and international organizations, 1885–1992. *World Politics* 52 (1): 1–37.

———. 2000. Why an identified systemic model of the democratic peace nexus' does not persuade. *Defence and Peace Economics* 11 (1): 197–214.

———. 2005. Rule of three, let it be? When more really is better. *Conflict Management and Peace Science* 22 (4): 292–310.

Oneal, J., and H. C. Whadey. 1996. The effect of alliance membership on national defense burdens, 1953–88. *International Interactions* 22 (2): 105–22.

Oren, N. 1982. Prudence in victory. In *The termination of wars,* ed. N. Oren. Jerusalem: The Magness Press.

Organski, A. F. K. 1958. *World politics.* New York: Knopf.

———. 1968. *World politics.* 2nd ed. New York: Knopf.

Organski, A. F. K., and J. Kugler. 1980. *The war ledger.* Chicago: University of Chicago Press.

Osgood, R. E., and R. W. Tucker. 1967. *Force, order, and justice.* Baltimore: Johns Hopkins University Press.

Ostrom, C. W., and B. Job. 1986. The president and the political use of force. *American Political Science Review* 80 (2): 541–66.

Owsiak, A. P. 2012. Signing up for peace: International boundary agreements, democracy, and militarized interstate conflict. *International Studies Quarterly* 56 (1): 51–66.

———. 2013. Democratization and international border agreements. *Journal of Politics* 75 (3).

Palmer, G., and T. C. Morgan. 2006. *A theory of foreign policy.* Princeton, NJ: Princeton University Press.

Parry, C. 1969. *The consolidated treaty series.* New York: Oceana.

Payne, K. B. 1997. *Deterrence in the second nuclear age.* Lexington: University Press of Kentucky.

Peceny, M. 1997. A constructivist interpretation of the liberal peace: The ambiguous case of the Spanish-American War. *Journal of Peace Research* 34 (4): 415–30.

Petersen, K., J. Vasquez, and Y. Wang. 2004. Multiparty disputes and the probability of war, 1816–1992. *Conflict Management and Peace Science* 21 (1): 1–16.

Pillar, P. R. 1983. *Negotiating peace: War termination as a bargaining process.* Princeton, NJ: Princeton University Press.

Polachek, S. W. 1980. Conflict and trade. *Journal of Conflict Resolution* 24 (1): 57–78.

———. 1992. Conflict and trade: An economics approach to political international interactions. In *Economics of arms reduction and the peace process,* ed. W. Isard & C. H. Anderton. Amsterdam: North-Holland.

Polachek, S. W., and J. McDonald. 1992. Strategic trade and the incentive for cooperation. In *Disarmament, economic conversion and peace management,* ed. M. Chatterji and L. Forcey. New York: Praeger.

Pollins, B. 1989a. Does trade still follow the flag? *American Political Science Review* 83 (2): 465–80.

———. 1989b. Conflict, cooperation and commerce: The effect of international political interactions. *American Journal of Political Science* 33 (3): 737–61.

Popper, K. 1959. *The logic of scientific discovery.* London: Hutchinson.

———. 1962. *Conjectures and refutations.* New York: Basic Books.

Potter, W. C. 1980. Issue area and foreign policy analysis. *International Organization* 34 (3): 405–27.

Powell, G. B., and G. D. Whitten. 1993. A cross-national analysis of economic voting: Taking account of the political context. *American Journal of Political Science* 37 (2): 391–414.

Powell, R. 1988. Nuclear brinkmanship with two-sided incomplete information. *American Political Science Review* 82 (1): 155–78.

———. 1989. Nuclear deterrence and the strategy of limited retaliation. *American Political Science Review* 83 (2): 503–19.

———. 1990. *Nuclear deterrence theory: The search for credibility.* New York: Cambridge University Press.

———. 1996. Stability and the distribution of power. *World Politics* 48 (2): 239–67.

———. 1999. *In the shadow of power.* Princeton, NJ: Princeton University Press.

———. 2003. Nuclear deterrence theory, nuclear proliferation, and national missile defense. *International Security* 27 (4): 86–118.

———. 2006. War as a commitment problem. *International Organization* 60 (1): 169–203.

Prescott, J. R. V. 1987. *Political frontiers and boundaries.* London: Unwin Hyman.

Putnam, R. 1988. Diplomacy and domestic politics: The logic of two-level games. *International Organization* 42 (3): 427–60.

Quackenbush, S. L., and M. Rudy. 2009. Evaluating the monadic democratic peace. *Conflict Management and Peace Science* 26 (3): 268–85.

Quackenbush, S. L., and J. F. Venteicher. 2008. Settlements, outcomes, and the recurrence of conflict. *Journal of Peace Research* 45 (6): 723–42.

Raiffa, H. 1982. *The art and science of negotiation.* Cambridge, MA: Harvard University Press.

Raknerud, A., and H. Hegre. 1997. The hazard of war: Reassessing the evidence for the democratic peace. *Journal of Peace Research* 34 (4): 385–404.

Ralston, J. H. 1929. *The League Council in action.* Oxford, UK: Oxford University Press.

Randle, R. F. 1973. *The origins of peace.* New York: Free Press.

———. 1974. "Comments." In *From war to peace: Essays in peacemaking and war termination,* ed. D. S. Smith. New York: Columbia University Press.

———. 1987. *Issues in the history of international relations.* New York: Praeger.

Rasler, K. A., and W. R. Thompson. 1989. *War and state making: The shaping of the global powers.* Boston: Unwin Hyman.

———. 2003. Territorial disputes and strategic rivalry. Paper presented at the annual meeting of the American Political Science Association, Philadelphia.

Ray, J. L. 1990. Friends as foes: International conflict and wars between formal allies. In *Prisoners of war: Nation-states in the modern era,* ed. C. S. Gochman and A. N. Sabrosky, 73–91. Lexington, MA: Lexington Books.

———. 1993. Wars between democracies: Rare or nonexistent? *International Interactions* 18 (3): 251–76.

———. 1995a. *Democracy and international conflict.* Columbia: University of South Carolina Press.

———. 1995b. Global trends, state-specific factors and regime transitions, 1825–1993. *Journal of Peace Research* 32 (1): 49–63.

———. 1997. Does democracy cause peace? *Annual Review of Political Science* 1 (1): 27–46.

———. 2000. On the level(s): Does democracy correlate with peace? In *What do we know about war?* ed. J. A. Vasquez, 299–316. Lanham, MD: Rowman & Littlefield.

———. 2001. Integrating levels of analysis in world politics. *Journal of Theoretical Politics* 13 (4): 355–88.

———. 2003a. A Lakatosian view of the democratic peace research program. In *Progress in international relations theory: Appraising the field,* ed. C. Elman and M. F. Elman, 205–44. Cambridge: MIT Press.

———. 2003b. Explaining interstate conflict and war: What should be controlled for? *Conflict Management and Peace Science* 20 (2): 1–31.

Raymond, G. A. 1994. Democracies, disputes, and third party intermediaries. *Journal of Conflict Resolution* 38 (1): 24–42.

Reed, W. 1998. The relevance of politically relevant dyads. Paper presented at the annual meeting of the Peace Science Society (International), New Brunswick, NJ.

———. 2000. A unified statistical model of conflict onset and escalation. *American Journal of Political Science* 44 (1): 84–93.

Reinhardt, E. 2001. Adjudication without enforcement in GATT disputes. *Journal of Conflict Resolution* 45 (2): 174–95.

Reiter, D. 2001. Does peace nurture democracy? *Journal of Politics* 63 (3): 935–48.

Reiter, D., and A. C. Stam III. 1998a. Democracy and battlefield military effectiveness. *Journal of Conflict Resolution* 42 (3): 259–77.

———. 1998b. Democracy, war initiation, and victory. *American Political Science Review* 92 (2): 377–89.

———. 2000. *Democracies at war.* Princeton, NJ: Princeton University Press.

Rengger, N. J., with J. Campbell. 1995. *Treaties and alliances of the world.* 6th ed. New York: Stockton.

Richards, D., T. C. Morgan, R. K. Wilson, V. Schwebach, and G. D. Young. 1993. Good times, bad times, and the diversionary use of force. *Journal of Conflict Resolution* 37 (3): 504–35.

Richardson, L. F. 1960a. *Arms and insecurity.* Pacific Grove, CA: Boxwood.

———. 1960b. *Statistics of deadly quarrels.* Pittsburgh, PA: Boxwood.

Robinson, W. S. 1950. Ecological correlations and the behavior of individuals. *American Sociological Review* 15 (3): 351–57.

Rose, R., and T. T. Mackie. 1983. Incumbency in government: Asset or liability? In *Western European party systems,* ed. H. Daalder and P. Mair. Beverly Hills, CA: Sage.

Rosecrance, R. N. 1963. *Action and reaction in world politics: International systems in perspective.* Boston: Little, Brown.

———. 1986. *The rise of the trading state: Commerce and conquest in the modern world.* New York: Basic Books.

Rosen, S. 1972. War power and the willingness to suffer. In *Peace, war and numbers,* ed. B. Russett, 167–84. Beverly Hills, CA: Sage.

Rosenau, J. N. 1966. Pre-theories and theories of foreign policy. In *Approaches to comparative and international policies,* ed. R. B. Farrell. Evanston, IL: Northwestern University Press.

———, ed. 1969. *Linkage politics.* New York: Free Press.

———. 1971. Pre-theories and theories of foreign policy. In *The scientific study of foreign policy,* ed. J. N. Rosenau, 27–93. New York: Free Press.

Rousseau, D. L., C. Gelpi, D. Reiter, and P. K. Huth. 1996. Assessing the dyadic nature of the democratic peace, 1918–1988. *American Political Science Review* 90 (3): 512–33.

Roy, B. A. 1997. Intervention across bisecting borders. *Journal of Peace Research* 34 (1): 3–14.

Rummel, R. J. 1963. Dimension of conflict behavior within and between nations. *General Systems* 8 (1): 1–50.

———. 1968. The relationship between national attributes and foreign conflict behavior. In *Quantitative international politics: Insights and evidence,* ed. J. D. Singer, 187–214. New York: Free Press.

———. 1972. *The dimensions of nations.* Beverly Hills, CA: Sage.

———. 1983. Libertarianism and international violence. *Journal of Conflict Resolution* 27 (1): 27–72.

———. 1985. Libertarian propositions on violence within and between nations: A test against published results. *Journal of Conflict Resolution* 29 (3): 419–55.

———. 1997. Is collective violence correlated with social pluralism? *Journal of Peace Research* 34 (2): 163–75.

Russett, B. 1963. *Community and contention: Britain and America in the twentieth century.* Cambridge: MIT Press.

———. 1967. *International regions and the international system: A study in political ecology.* Chicago: Rand McNally.

———. 1985. The mysterious decline of American hegemony, or, is Mark Twain really dead? *International Organization* 32 (2): 207–31.

———. 1989. Economic decline, electoral pressure and the initiation of interstate conflict. In *Prisoners of war?* ed. C. S. Gochman and A. N. Sabrosky, 123–40. New York: Lexington Books.

———. 1990. *Controlling the sword: The democratic governance of national security.* Cambridge, MA: Harvard University Press.

———. 1993. *Grasping the democratic peace: Principles for a post–Cold War world.* Princeton, NJ: Princeton University Press.

———. 1998. A neo-Kantian perspective: Democracy, interdependence, and international organizations in building security communities. In *Security communities in comparative perspective,* ed. E. Adler and M. Barnett. New York: Cambridge University Press.

Russett, B., and R. J. Monsen. 1975. Bureaucracy and polyarchy as predictors of performance: A cross-national examination. *Comparative Political Studies* 8 (1): 5–31.

Russett, B., and J. R. Oneal. 2001. *Triangulating peace: Democracy, interdependence, and international organizations.* New York: W. W. Norton.

Russett, B., J. R. Oneal, and D. R. Davis. 1998. The third leg of the Kantian tripod: International organizations and militarized disputes, 1950–85. *International Organization* 52 (3): 441–67.

Russett, B., J. D. Singer, and M. Small. 1968. National political units in the twentieth century: A standardized list. *American Political Science Review* 62 (3): 932–51.

Russett, B., and H. Starr. 2000. From democratic peace to Kantian peace: Democracy and conflict in the international system. In *Handbook of war studies,* ed. M. Midlarsky. 2nd ed. Ann Arbor: University of Michigan Press.

Sabrosky, A. N. 1980. Interstate alliances: Their reliability and the expansion of war. In *The Correlates of War, II,* ed. J. D. Singer, 161–98. New York: Free Press.

Sacko, D. 1998. Measures of hegemony. Paper presented at the annual meeting of the Peace Science Society (International), New Brunswick, NJ.

Sagan, S. 1994. The perils of proliferation: Organization theory, deterrence theory, and the spread of nuclear weapons. *International Security* 18 (4): 66–107.

———. 1996–1997. Why do states build nuclear weapons? *International Security* 21 (3): 54–86.

Sagan, S., and K. Waltz. 2003. *The spread of nuclear weapons: A debate renewed.* New York: W. W. Norton.

Sahlins, P. 1990. Natural frontiers revisited: France's boundaries since the seventeenth century. *American Historical Review* 95 (5) : 1423–51.

Sample, S. G. 1996. Arms races and the escalation of disputes to war. PhD diss., Vanderbilt University.

———. 1997. Arms races and dispute escalation: Resolving the debate. *Journal of Peace Research* 34 (1): 7–22.

———. 1998a. Military buildups, war, and realpolitik: A multivariate model. *Journal of Conflict Resolution* 42 (2): 156–75.

———. 1998b. Furthering the investigation into the effects of arms buildups. *Journal of Peace Research* 35 (1): 119–23.

———. 2000. Military buildups: Arming and war. In *What do we know about war?* ed. J. A. Vasquez, 165–95. Lanham, MD: Rowman & Littlefield.

———. 2002. The outcomes of military buildups: Minor states vs. major powers. *Journal of Peace Research* 39 (6): 669–92.

Sanders, D., H. Ward, and D. Marsh. 1991. Macroeconomics, the Falklands War, and the popularity of the Thatcher government: A contrary view. In *Economics and politics,* ed. H. Norpoth, M. Lewis-Beck, and J.-D. Lafay. Ann Arbor: University of Michigan Press.

Sarkees, M. R. 2000. The Correlates of War data on war: An update to 1997. *Conflict Management and Peace Science* 18 (1): 123–44.

Sayrs, L. W. 1989. *Pooled time series analysis.* Newbury Park, CA: Sage.

———. 1990. Expected utility and peace science: An assessment of trade and conflict. *Conflict Management and Peace Science* 11 (1): 17–44.

Schelling, T. C. 1960. *The strategy of conflict.* Cambridge, MA: Harvard University Press.

———. 1962. Nuclear strategy in Europe. *World Politics* 14 (3): 421–33.

———. 1966. *Arms and influence.* New Haven, CT: Yale University Press.

Schroeder, P. W. 1999. A pointless enduring rivalry: France and the Hapsburg monarchy, 1715–1918. In *Great power rivalries,* ed. W. R. Thompson. Columbia: University of South Carolina Press.

Schultz, K. A. 1999. Do democratic institutions constrain or inform? Contrasting two institutional perspectives on democracy and war. *International Organization* 53 (2): 233–66.

Schumpeter, J. A. 1939. *Business cycles.* New York: McGraw-Hill.

Senese, P. D. 1996. Geographic proximity and issue salience: Their effects on the escalation of militarized interstate conflict. *Conflict Management and Peace Science* 15 (2) 133–61.

———. 1997. Between dispute and war: The effect of joint democracy on interstate conflict escalation. *Journal of Politics* 59 (1): 1–27.

———. 2005. Territory, contiguity, and international conflict: Assessing a new joint explanation. *American Journal of Political Science* 49 (4): 769–79.

Senese, P. D., and S. L. Quackenbush. 2003. Sowing the seeds of conflict: The effect of dispute settlements on durations of peace. *Journal of Politics* 65 (3): 696–717.

Senese, P. D., and J. Vasquez. 2003. A unified explanation of territorial conflict: Testing the impact of sampling bias, 1919–1992. *International Studies Quarterly* 47 (2): 275–98.

———. 2004. Alliances, territorial disputes, and the probability of war: Testing for interactions. In *The scourge of war,* ed. P. F. Diehl, 189–221. Ann Arbor: University of Michigan Press.

———. 2005. Assessing the steps to war. *British Journal of Political Science* 35:607–33.

———. 2008. *The steps-to-war: An empirical study.* Princeton, NJ: Princeton University Press.

Signorino, C. 1999. Strategic interaction and the statistical analysis of international conflict. *American Political Science Review* 93 (2): 279–98.

Simmons, B. A. 1999. See you in court? The appeal to quasi-judicial legal processes in the settlement of territorial disputes. In *A road map to war: Territorial dimensions of international conflict,* ed. P. Diehl, 205–37. Nashville, TN: Vanderbilt University Press.

———. 2002. Capacity, commitment, and compliance: International institutions and territorial disputes. *Journal of Conflict Resolution* 46 (6): 829–56.

Singer, J. D. 1958. Threat-perception and the armament-tension dilemma. *Journal of Conflict Resolution* 2 (1): 91–123.

———. 1969. The incomplete theorist: Insights without evidence. In *Contending approaches to international politics,* ed. K. Knorr and J. N. Rosenau, 62–86. Princeton, NJ: Princeton University Press.

———. 1979. *The Correlates of War I.* New York: Free Press.

———. 1988. Reconstructing the Correlates of War dataset on material capabilities of states, 1816–1985. *International Interactions* 14 (2): 115–32.

———. 1991. Peace in the global system: Displacement, interregnum, or transformation? In *The long postwar peace: Contending explanations and projections,* ed. C. W. Kegley Jr., 56–84. New York: HarperCollins.

Singer, J. D., S. Bremer, and J. Stuckey, 1972. Capability distribution, uncertainty, and major power war, 1820–1965. In *Peace, war, and numbers,* ed. B. Russett, 19–48. Beverly Hills, CA: Sage.

Singer, J. D., and M. Small. 1966a. National alliance commitments and war involvement, 1815–1945. *Peace Research Society (International) Papers* 5:109–40.

———. 1966b. Formal alliances, 1815–1939: A quantitative description. *Journal of Peace Research* 3 (1): 1–31.

———. 1968. Alliance aggregation and the onset of war, 1815–1945. In *Quantitative international politics: Insights and evidence,* ed. C. F. Alger and J. D. Singer, 247–86. New York: Free Press.

———. 1995. *National military capabilities data.* Ann Arbor: University of Michigan.

Singh, J. 1998. Against nuclear apartheid. *Foreign Affairs* 77 (5): 41–52.

Siverson, R. M., and P. F. Diehl. 1989. Arms races, the conflict spiral, and the onset of war. In *Handbook of war studies,* ed. M. I. Midlarsky, 195–218. Boston: Unwin Hyman.

Siverson, R. M., and J. King. 1979. Alliances and the expansion of war. In *To auger well: Early warning indicators in world politics,* ed. J. D. Singer and M. D. Wallace, 37–49. Beverly Hills, CA: Sage.

Siverson, R. M., and H. Starr. 1990. Opportunity, willingness, and the diffusion of war. *American Political Science Review* 84 (1): 47–67.

———. 1991. *The diffusion of war: A study of opportunity and willingness.* Ann Arbor: University of Michigan Press.

Siverson, R. M., and M. Tennefoss. 1984. Power, alliance, and the escalation of international crises, 1816–1965. *American Political Science Review* 78 (4): 1057–69.

Small, M., and J. D. Singer. 1969. Formal alliances, 1816–1965: An extension of the basic data. *Journal of Peace Research* 6 (3): 257–82.

———. 1976. The war-proneness of democratic regimes, 1816–1965. *Jerusalem Journal of International Relations* 1 (1): 50–68.

———. 1982. *Resort to arms: International and civil wars, 1816–1980.* Beverly Hills, CA: Sage.

Smith, A. 1995. Alliance formation and war. *International Studies Quarterly* 39 (4): 405–25.

———. 1996a. Diversionary foreign policy in democratic systems. *International Studies Quarterly* 40 (2): 133–53.

———. 1996b. To intervene or not to intervene: A biased decision. *Journal of Conflict Resolution* 40 (1): 16–40.

———. 1998. Extended deterrence and alliance formation. *International Interactions* 24 (4): 315–43.

———. 1999. Testing theories of strategic choice: The example of crisis escalation. *American Journal of Political Science* 43 (4): 1254–83.

Snidal, D. 1993. Relative gains and the pattern of international cooperation. In *Neorealism and neoliberalism: The contemporary debate,* ed. D. Baldwin. New York: Columbia University Press.

Snyder, G., and P. Diesing. 1977. *Conflict among nations.* Princeton, NJ: Princeton University Press.

Snyder, G. H. 1994. Crisis bargaining. In *Classic readings of international relations,* ed. P. Williams, D. M. Goldstein, and J. M. Shafritz. Belmont, CA: Wadsworth.

———. 2000. *From voting to violence: Democratization and nationalist conflict.* New York: W. W. Norton.

Soroos, M. 1977. Behavior between nations. *Peace Research Reviews* 7 (2): 1–107.

Spanier, J. W. 1980. *American foreign policy since World War II.* 8th ed. New York: Holt, Rinehart and Winston.

Spiegel, H. W. 1991. *The growth of economic thought.* 3rd ed. Durham, NC: Duke University Press.

Spiezio, K. E. 1990. British hegemony and major power war, 1815–1939: An empirical test of Gilpin's model of hegemonic governance. *International Studies Quarterly* 34 (2): 165–81.

Sprecher, C., and K. DeRouen Jr. 2002. Israeli military actions and internalization-externalization processes. *Journal of Conflict Resolution* 46 (2): 244–59.

Sprout, H., and M. Sprout. 1965. *The ecological perspective on human affairs.* Princeton, NJ: Princeton University Press.

Spuler, B., C. G. Allen, and N. Saunders. 1977. *Rulers and governments of the world.* Vol. 3. London: Bowker.

Stam, A. C., III. 1996. *Win, lose or draw.* Ann Arbor: University of Michigan Press.

Starr, H., and B. A. Most. 1976. The substance and study of borders in international relations research. *International Studies Quarterly* 20 (4): 581–620.

———. 1978. A return journey: Richardson, "frontiers," and wars in the 1946–1965 era. *Journal of Conflict Resolution* 22 (3): 441–67.

Starr, H., and G. D. Thomas. 2002. The nature of contiguous borders: Ease of interaction, salience, and the analysis of crisis. *International Interactions* 28(2): 213–35.

StataCorp. 1997. *Stata Statistical Software.* Release 5.0. College Station, TX: Stata Corporation.

The statesman's yearbook. Annual volumes, 1864–1940. London: Macmillan.

Stevenson, D. 1996. *Armaments and the coming of war: Europe 1904–1914.* Oxford, UK: Clarendon.

Stinnett, D., and P. F. Diehl, 2001. The path(s) to rivalry: Behavioral and structural explanations of rivalry development. *Journal of Politics* 63 (3): 717–40.

Stinnett, D., J. Tir, P. Schafer, P. F. Diehl, and C. Gochman. 2002. The Correlates of War project direct contiguity data, version 3. *Conflict Management and Peace Science* 19 (2): 58–66.

Stoll, R. 1984. The guns of November: Presidential re-elections and the use of force. *Journal of Conflict Resolution* 28 (2): 231–46.

Suganami, H. 1996. *On the causes of war.* Oxford, UK: Clarendon.

———. 2002. Explaining war: Some critical observations. *International Relations* 16 (3): 307–36.

Sullivan, M. P. 1990. *Power in contemporary international politics.* Columbia: University of South Carolina Press.

Summers, H., A. Heston, D. Nuxoll, and B. Aten. 1995. *The Penn World Table (Mark 5.6a).* Cambridge, MA: National Bureau of Economic Research.

Terrell, L. M. 1977. Attribute differences among neighboring states and their levels of foreign conflict behavior. *International Journal of Group Tensions* 7 (1): 89–108.

Thies, C. G. 2004. State building, interstate and intrastate rivalry: A study of post-colonial developing country extractive efforts, 1975–2000. *International Studies Quarterly* 48 (1): 53–72.

———. 2005. War, rivalry, and state building in Latin America. *American Journal of Political Science* 49 (3): 451–65.

Thompson, W., and R. Tucker. 1997. A tale of two democratic peace critiques. *Journal of Conflict Resolution* 41 (3): 428–54.

Thompson, W. R. 1988. *On global war.* Columbia: University of South Carolina Press.

———. 1995. Principal rivalries. *Journal of Conflict Resolution* 39 (2): 195–223.

———. 1996. Democracy and peace: Putting the cart before the horse? *International Organization* 50 (1): 141–74.

———. 1999. *Great power rivalries.* Columbia: University of South Carolina Press.

———. 2001. Identifying rivals and rivalries in world polities. *International Studies Quarterly* 45 (4): 557–86.

Thompson, W. R., and D. R. Dreyer. 2011. *Handbook of international rivalries, 1494–2010*. Washington, D.C.: CQ Press.

Thomson, D., E. Meyer, and A. Briggs. 1945. *Patterns of peacemaking*. London: Kegan Paul, Trench, Tribner, and Company, Ltd.

Tilly, C. 1975. Reflections on the history of european state-making. In *Formation of national states in Western Europe,* ed. C. Tilly, 3–83. Princeton, NJ: Princeton University Press.

———. 1990. *Coercion, capital, and European states, A.D. 990–1990*. Cambridge, UK: Blackwell.

Tir, J., and P. F. Diehl. 2002. Geographic dimensions of enduring rivalries. *Political Geography* 21 (2): 263–86.

Toft, M. D. 2003. *The geography of ethnic violence*. Princeton, NJ: Princeton University Press.

Tomz, M., J. Wittenberg, and G. King. 2003. *CLARIFY: Software for interpreting and presenting statistical results, version 2.1.* Cambridge, MA: Harvard University. http://GKing.Harvard.Edu

Touval, S., and W. Zartman, eds. 1985. *International mediation in theory and practice*. Boulder, CO: Westview.

Tsebelis, G. 1990. *Nested games*. Berkeley: University of California Press.

Tufte, E. B. 1978. *Political control of the economy*. Princeton, NJ: Princeton University Press.

U.S. Department of Commerce. 1976. *Historical statistics of the United States: Colonial times to 1970*. New York: Basic Books.

van Creveld, M. 1993. *Nuclear proliferation and the future of conflict*. New York: Free Press.

Van Evera, S. 1999. *The causes of war*. Ithaca, NY: Cornell University Press.

Vasquez, J. A. 1987. The steps to war: Toward a scientific explanation of Correlates of War findings. *World Politics* 40:108–45.

———. 1993. *The war puzzle*. New York: Cambridge University Press.

———. 1995. Why do neighbors fight? Proximity, interaction, or territoriality? *Journal of Peace Research* 32 (3): 277–93.

———. 1996a. Distinguishing rivals that go to war from those that do not: A quantitative comparative case study of the two paths to war. *International Studies Quarterly* 40 (4): 531–58.

———. 1996b. When are power transitions dangerous? The contribution of the power transition thesis to international relations theory. In *Parity and war: A critical reevaluation of the war ledger,* ed. J. Kugler and D. Lemke, 35–56. Ann Arbor: University of Michigan Press.

———. 1997. The realist paradigm and degenerative versus progressive research programs: An appraisal of neotraditional research on Waltz's balancing proposition. *American Political Science Review* 91 (4): 899–912.

———. 2001. Mapping the probability of war and analyzing the possibility of peace: The role of territorial disputes. *Conflict Management and Peace Science* 18 (2): 145–73.

———. 2004. The probability of war, 1816–1992. Presidential address to the International Studies Association. *International Studies Quarterly* 48 (1): 1–27.

———. 2009. *The war puzzle revisited*. New York: Cambridge University Press.

Vasquez, J. A., and D. M. Gibler. 2001. The steps to war in Asia, 1931–1945. *Security Studies* 10 (3): 1–45.

Vasquez, J. A., and M. T. Henehan, eds. 1992. *The scientific study of peace and war.* Lexington, MA: Lexington Books.

———. 2001. Territorial disputes and the probability of war, 1816–1992. *Journal of Peace Research* 38 (2): 123–38.

———. 2011. *Territory, war, and peace.* New York: Rutledge.

Vasquez, J. A., and C.-N. Kang. 2013. How and why the Cold War became a long peace: Some statistical insights. *Cooperation and Conflict* 48 (1): 28–50.

Vasquez, J. A., and C. S. Leskiw. 2001. The origins and war-proneness of international rivalries. *Annual Review of Political Science* 4 (1): 295–316.

Vasquez, J. A., and B. Valeriano. 2010. Classification of interstate wars. *Journal of Politics* 72 (2): 292–309.

Wagner, R. H. 1993. The causes of peace. In *Stopping the killing: How civil wars end,* ed. R. Licklider. New York: New York University Press.

———. 2000. Bargaining and war. *American Journal of Political Science* 44 (3): 469–84.

Wallace, M. D. 1979. Arms races and escalation: Some new evidence. *Journal of Conflict Resolution* 23 (1): 3–16.

———. 1980. Some persisting findings: A reply to Professor Weede. *Journal of Conflict Resolution* 24 (2): 289–92.

———. 1981. Old nails in new coffins: The *para bellum* hypothesis revisited. *Journal of Peace Research* 18 (1): 91–95.

———. 1982. Armaments and escalation: Two competing hypotheses. *International Studies Quarterly* 26 (1): 37–56.

———. 1990. Racing redux: The arms race–escalation debate revisited. In *Prisoners of war: Nation-states in the modern era,* ed. C. S. Gochman and A. N. Sabrosky, 115–22. Lexington, MA: Lexington Books.

Wallersteen, P. 1973. *Structure and war: On international relations 1920–1968.* Stockholm: Raben and Sjogren.

———. 1981. Incompatibility, confrontation, and war: Four models and three historical systems, 1816–1976. *Journal of Peace Research* 18 (1): 57–90.

Wallerstein, I. 1974. The rise and future demise of the world capitalist system. *Comparative Studies in Society and History* 16 (4): 387–415.

Walt, S. M. 1987. *The origins of alliances.* Ithaca, NY: Cornell University Press.

Walter, B. 1997. The critical barriers to civil war settlement. *International Organization* 51 (3): 335–64.

———. 2003. Explaining the intractability of territorial conflict. *International Studies Review* 5 (4): 137–53.

Waltz, K. N. 1959. *Man, the state and war.* New York: Columbia University Press.

———. 1979. *Theory of international politics.* Reading, MA: Addison-Wesley.

———. 1981. *The spread of nuclear weapons: More may be better.* Adelphi Papers, No. 171. London: International Institute for Strategic Studies.

———. 1990. Nuclear myths and political realities. *American Political Science Review* 84 (3): 731–45.

Ward, M. D., and U. Widmaier. 1982. The domestic-international conflict nexus: New evidence and old hypotheses. *International Interactions* 9 (1): 75–101.

Warwick, P. 1992a. Ideological diversity and government survival in Western European parliamentary democracies. *Comparative Political Studies* 25 (3): 332–61.

———. 1992b. Rising hazards: An underlying dynamic of parliamentary government. *American Journal of Political Science* 36 (4): 857–76.

———. 1993. Economic trends and government survival in Western European parliamentary democracies. *American Political Science Review* 86 (4): 875–87.

Way, C. 1997. Manchester revisited: A theoretical and empirical evaluation of commercial liberalism. PhD diss., Stanford University.

Wayman, F. W. 1990. Alliances and war: A time-series analysis. In *Prisoners of war?* ed. C. Gochman and A. Sabrosky, 93–113. Lexington, MA: Lexington Books.

———. 1996. Power shifts and the onset of war. In *Parity and war: Evaluations and extensions of The War Ledger,* ed. J. Kugler and D. Lemke, 145–62. Ann Arbor: University of Michigan Press.

———. 2000. Rivalries: Recurrent disputes and explaining war. In *What do we know about war?* ed. J. A. Vasquez, 219–34. Lanham, MD: Rowman & Littlefield.

Wayman, F. W., and D. M. Jones. 1991. Evolution of conflict in enduring rivalries. Paper presented at the annual meeting of the International Studies Association, Vancouver, Canada.

Weede, E. 1976. Overwhelming preponderance as a pacifying condition among contiguous Asian dyads, 1950–1969. *Journal of Conflict Resolution* 20 (3): 395–412.

———. 1980. Arms races and escalation: Some persisting doubts. *Journal of Conflict Resolution* 24 (2): 285–87.

———. 1984. Democracy and war involvement. *Journal of Conflict Resolution* 28 (4): 649–64.

———. 1992. Some simple calculations on democracy and war involvement. *Journal of Peace Research* 29 (4): 377–83.

Wendt, A. 1999. *Social theory of international politics.* New York: Cambridge University Press.

Werner, S. 1998. Negotiating the terms of settlement: War aims and bargaining leverage. *Journal of Conflict Resolution* 42 (3): 321–43.

———. 1999. The precarious nature of peace: Resolving the issues, enforcing the settlement, and renegotiating the terms. *American Journal of Political Science* 43 (3): 912–34.

———. 2000. Deterring intervention: The stakes of war and third-party involvement. *American Journal of Political Science* 44 (4): 720–32.

Werner, S., and D. Lemke. 1997. Opposites do not attract: The impact of domestic institutions, power, and prior commitments on alignment choices. *International Studies Quarterly* 41 (3): 529–46.

Wilkenfeld, J., and M. Brecher. 1984. International crises, 1945–1975: The UN dimension. *International Studies Quarterly* 28 (1):45–67.

Wilson, T. 1986. *The myriad faces of war: Britain and the Great War, 1914–1918.* Cambridge, England: Polity.

Wittman, D. 1979. How a war ends: A rational model approach. *Journal of Conflict Resolution* 23 (4): 743–63.

Woodbury, A. C. 1991. *Counting Eskimo words for snow: A citizen's guide.* Accessed February 6, 2013, from http://www.princeton.edu/~browning/snow.html

World Bank. 1997. *World development indicators* [CD-ROM]. London: World Bank.

Wright, Q. 1965. *A study of war.* Chicago: University of Chicago Press.

Yamamoto, Y., and S. A. Bremer. 1980. Wider wars and restless nights: Major power intervention in ongoing war. In *The Correlates of War,* vol. 2, ed. J. D. Singer, 199–229. New York: Free Press.

Zacher, M. W. 2001. The territorial integrity norm: International boundaries and the use of force. *International Organization* 55 (2): 215–50.

Zagare, F. C., and D. M. Kilgour. 1993. Asymmetric deterrence. *International Studies Quarterly* 37 (1): 1–27.

———. 2000. *Perfect deterrence.* Cambridge, UK: Cambridge University Press.

Zartman, W. 1989. *Ripe for resolution.* New York: Oxford University Press.

———. 1995. *Elusive peace: Negotiating an end to civil wars.* Washington, D.C.: The Brookings Institution.

Zorn, C. J. 2001. General estimating equation models for correlated data: A review with applications. *American Journal of Political Science* 45 (2): 470–90.

INDEX

accidents, 28, 59–60, 146, 315–16, 319
  nuclear, 303, 316–17, 319
actors, 24, 36, 43, 66, 84, 124,
    129–30, 134, 137, 139, 150, 153,
    173, 186, 234–5, 247, 260, 282,
    284, 306–8, 310–12, 314–15, 319,
    321, 335, 349–50, 366, 368–9
adversaries, 41, 43, 45, 53, 65, 68, 137,
    172, 174, 197, 203, 306, 316, 323
agreements, 25, 45, 56, 64, 68, 71, 73,
    76, 83, 136, 323–30, 333–7, 340
alliances, 3–4, 8, 13, 15–24, 27–8, 56,
    63–81, 86, 110, 133–40, 142–53,
    155–63, 165–7, 187, 196, 202,
    204–6, 208, 210–11, 214–15, 218,
    220–1, 240, 248–9, 256, 264–5,
    267, 271–2, 278, 318, 322,
    399–400, 403–4
  agreements, 63, 75
  commitments, 67–8, 73–7, 136, 203,
    232, 240, 243
  configurations, 136, 147, 151–2
  counter, 133–4
  defensive, 64, 66–75, 77–80, 295
  effects of, 65, 68, 78, 143, 207, 250
  ententes, 13, 15–17, 76, 202, 240
  formal, 13, 76, 136, 141, 240
  formation, 75, 81, 133–4, 153,
    389, 400
  influence, of 64, 67, 73
  interstate, 76, 81
  membership, 76, 220
  neutrality pacts, 66–8, 70, 72–3, 76,
    78, 80, 202, 215
  offensive, 64, 66, 68–70, 72–5,
    77–80

  partners, 77, 80, 136, 140
  portfolios, 67, 69, 72, 79, 216, 220,
    264–5
  relevant, 135–6, 139–42, 144, 147,
    151–2, 154, 158
  reliability, 340
  systems, 151–2, 195, 218
  ties, 239, 245, 250, 263, 267
  treaties, 75–7, 341
  types, 250
allies, 8, 19–22, 63–6, 68–71, 73–4,
    76–80, 125, 134, 136, 140,
    143–8, 150–2, 160, 163, 172,
    188, 195, 202, 204, 209,
    211–13, 215, 318, 340
Allison, Graham, 316, 333, 347, 358,
    364–5
armed conflict, 35, 40–2, 44–5, 47, 51,
    207, 288
arms
  buildups, 106–10, 122, 127, 131,
    160, 167
  races, 4, 10–11, 76, 101, 106,
    124, 126–8, 130–1, 133–4,
    137, 139, 141–5, 147–53,
    157–8, 160–2, 167, 174,
    191, 300
Asal, Victor, 77, 270, 303–4, 306, 308,
    310, 312, 314, 316–22
ATOP (Alliance Treaty Obligations
    and Provisions), 67, 75
attack, 10, 64, 73–4, 169,
    177, 185, 229, 272, 285,
    317–18, 322
attackers, 10, 271–2, 317–18, 321–2
Austria, 24, 38, 52

autocracies, 199–200, 208, 215,
218–19, 225, 279, 281–3, 347,
354, 356, 359, 367, 370
leaders, 349, 352–9, 361–2, 367,
369–70

Barbieri, Katherine, vii, 219, 221–2,
226, 231–2, 234, 236, 238–40,
242, 244–6, 248–57
bargaining, 8, 56, 63–4, 66, 72, 325,
327–8, 334, 340, 380
battle deaths, 4, 11, 216, 270, 329–30,
339, 341–2, 357–60, 364, 367–9
battlefield, 271, 325, 338–9
Beardsley, Kyle, viii, 303–4, 306, 308,
310, 312, 314, 316, 318, 320, 322
Beck, Nathaniel, 177–8, 193, 205, 221,
265, 287
belligerents, 170, 323–30, 333–7,
339–41
benefits, 39, 64–5, 196, 204, 208–9,
213–14, 225, 229, 231, 233–5,
243, 245, 251, 260, 305, 315,
317, 322, 349–52, 356, 366,
368–9
of democracy, 196, 207, 221, 223
distribution of, 64–5, 204
Bennett, D. Scott, 33, 61, 74, 83,
89–90, 100, 171, 177, 186–7, 277
bivariate analyses, 6, 18, 20, 22, 28,
32, 129, 263
borders, 7, 28, 57, 102, 111, 178,
279–81, 283–95, 298–300, 302
colonial, 25, 285, 298
definition, 285–6
disputes, 4, 55, 88, 99, 158, 192,
292, 300, 319
ethnic, 285, 289–91, 294
international, 284–7, 292–3
relations, 283, 287
salients, 286, 288, 290, 301
settled, 290, 295, 300
stable, 226, 279–80, 283, 287–8,
290, 292–3, 295, 297–301
strength, 286, 289–91, 293–4, 301
unstable, 283–4, 286, 299
variables, 286, 289–90, 292–3,
299, 301

Bremer, Stuart, A., 5–6, 8, 10, 12, 14,
16, 18, 20, 22, 24, 26–33, 43,
56–7, 59, 67, 76–8, 98, 112, 128,
165, 176–7, 187, 190–1, 193,
218, 220, 226–8, 239–40, 243,
249–50, 256, 263, 270, 273,
277–8, 287, 301, 308, 329
brinkmanship, 270–1, 306, 318–19
Bueno de Mesquita, Bruce, 8, 23, 154,
158, 217–18, 220, 224, 234,
259–61, 264, 267–8, 278–9, 288,
295, 305, 330, 345–8, 350, 352,
354, 356, 358, 360–2, 364, 366–71

capabilities, 8, 27, 56, 71, 76, 92,
140, 153, 177–8, 197, 199,
202–4, 208, 213, 216, 228,
260, 264, 271, 286, 306, 308–10,
312–13, 328
balance of, 107–10
CINC scores, 12, 25, 68, 240, 248,
308, 311
imbalance, 47–9, 61
nuclear, 105, 112, 304, 308–9,
320–1
ratio, 12, 202, 205–6, 209–11, 215,
228, 286, 289–91, 294, 298
relative, 23, 42, 45, 50, 130, 153,
157, 177–82, 184, 232, 239–40,
242, 244–5, 256, 268, 340, 343
challengers, 38, 64–9, 71, 73, 77, 108,
131, 180, 318, 349–50, 367–9
potential, 64, 66–7, 69, 72–3, 78–9
China, 55, 125, 127, 136, 141, 271–2,
308–9, 312, 356
civil wars, 105, 135, 170, 280, 282,
287–8, 290, 292–3, 298–9, 344
claims, 39–40, 42–3, 47, 50–2, 288
territorial, 38, 40, 42–4, 47, 49, 52,
58, 285, 288, 290, 297–9, 301
Cold War, 55, 57, 99, 106, 108, 110,
116, 126, 128–9, 136, 139, 141,
147, 149–52, 161–3, 182, 188,
195–6, 199–200, 207–8, 213–15,
218, 222, 226, 282, 287, 290,
292–3, 303–5, 312, 317–18
Colonial, 44, 217
master, 286, 289–94, 298

ABOUT THE EDITORS

Sara McLaughlin Mitchell is Professor of Political Science and recipient of the Faculty Scholar Award (2007–2010) and Collegiate Scholar Award (2011) at the University of Iowa. She is Co-Director of the Issue Correlates of War Project and an Associate Editor of *Foreign Policy Analysis*. She received her PhD in Political Science from Michigan State University in 1997. She is coauthor of *Domestic Law Goes Global: Legal Traditions and International Courts,* has edited three special journal issues, and has published over two dozen journal articles and book chapters in leading outlets, including the *American Journal of Political Science, Journal of Politics, International Studies Quarterly,* and *Journal of Conflict Resolution*. She is the recipient of five major research awards from the National Science Foundation and the U.S. Agency for International Development, as well as numerous research grants from the University of Iowa and Florida State University. Her areas of expertise include international conflict, democratic peace, international organizations, diversionary theory, international courts, conflict management, and territorial, maritime, and river issues.

John A. Vasquez is the Thomas B. Mackie Scholar and Professor of Political Science at the University of Illinois at Urbana-Champaign. He is the author of several books, including *The War Puzzle Revisited, The Steps to War* (with Paul Senese), and *The Power of Power Politics*. He has also published articles in the *American Political Science Review, Journal of Politics, International Organization, International Studies Quarterly, World Politics,* and *Journal of Peace Research,* among others. He served as President of the International Studies Association (2002–2003) and the Peace Science Society (1999–2000). His areas of expertise include territory, rivalry, and interstate conflict.

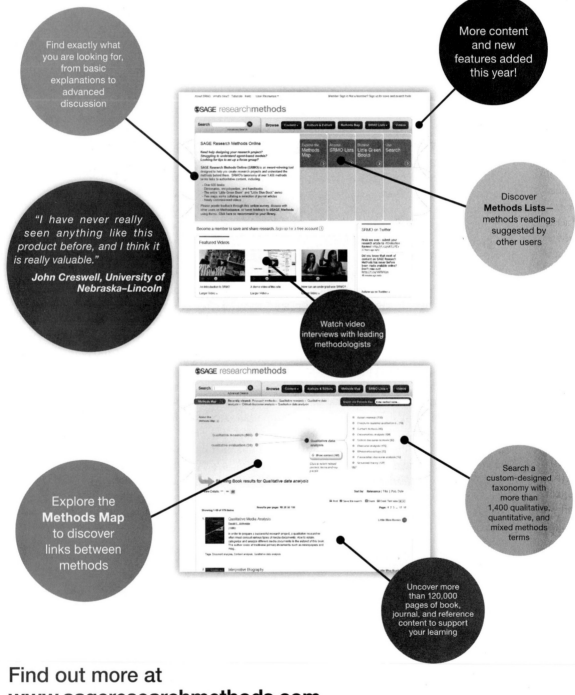

⑤SAGE research**methods**

The essential online tool for researchers from the world's leading methods publisher

Find exactly what you are looking for, from basic explanations to advanced discussion

More content and new features added this year!

Discover **Methods Lists**— methods readings suggested by other users

"*I have never really seen anything like this product before, and I think it is really valuable.*"

John Creswell, University of Nebraska–Lincoln

Watch video interviews with leading methodologists

Explore the **Methods Map** to discover links between methods

Search a custom-designed taxonomy with more than 1,400 qualitative, quantitative, and mixed methods terms

Uncover more than 120,000 pages of book, journal, and reference content to support your learning

Find out more at
www.sageresearchmethods.com